FISHING IN OREGON

FISHING IN OREGON

Eighth Edition

Madelynne Diness Sheehan
and Dan Casali

Photography by Steve Terrill

FLYING PENCIL PUBLICATIONS
Portland, Oregon

Published by Flying Pencil Publications. Address all inquiries to:
Flying Pencil Publications
33126 SW Callahan Road
Scappoose, Oregon 97056
(503) 543-7171

Book and cover design by Mary Stupp-Greer

Printed in the United States of America
by Network Graphics, Portland, Oregon

10 9 8 7 6 5 4 3 2

Library of Congress Catalog Card Number: 94-061995

ISBN: 09164673-10-4

Publisher's Notice:
Water-related sports, and travel associated with them, are by their very nature hazardous. Risks include, but are not limited to, those related to terrain, weather, equipment, wild animals, errors in judgment, and physical limitations (not the least of which is the inability of humans to breathe while underwater). This book does not describe every hazard associated with fishing in Oregon. Furthermore, despite diligent efforts, it may contain errors of typography, cartography, or content. This book's maps are for planning reference only, not for navigation. Flying Pencil Publications and the authors shall have no liability or responsibility with respect to physical harm, property damage, or any other loss or damage asserted to be caused directly or indirectly by the information in this book. We sigh and regret that our society has reached such a litigious state that it is necessary to include a paragraph like this in a book about goin' fishin'.

CONTENTS

MAPS

ACKNOWLEDGEMENTS

Sincere thanks to the men and women of the Oregon Department of Fish and Wildlife, whose good work on behalf of Oregon fishing has made this book possible. In providing information for this edition, they have, as in the past, given generously of their time and knowledge.

In particular, I would like to acknowledge the assistance of the following ODF&W biologists: Gary Anderson, Will Beidler, Reese Bender, Keith Braun, Bob Buckman, Jerry Buttler, Mike Evenson, Ted Fies, John Fortune, Jon Germond, Mike Gray, David Haight, John Haxton, Wayne Hunt, John Johnson, Bill Knox, Dave Liscia, Dave Loomis, Steve Mamoyac, Jay Massey, Curt Melcher, Jim Newton, Ray Perkins, Amy Stewart, Steve Thiesfeld, Walt Weber, George Westfall, Tim Unterwegner, Mark Wade, Duane West, Jeff Zakle, and Jeff Ziller. Thanks also to Jim Griggs of the Confederated Tribes of the Warm Springs Reservation, and to Don Ratliff of PGE at Round Butte Dam.

Individual anglers throughout the state were generous in providing information about their home waters. Special thanks to Al Burnnell for his insight into fly-fishing the Rogue, Patty Burres of the Women's Angling Society for sharing her understanding of walleye fishing in Lake Umatilla, Mac Huff and Jeff Moore for their insights into fishing the waters of Northeast Oregon, Mark Henry for his understanding of the middle Willamette and Siltcoos Lake, and Scott Richmond for his careful reading and helpful comments on my write-ups of the Deschutes River and Cascade Lakes. Ron Blogett's maps of Nestucca, Trask, and Wilson rivers add a touch of nostalgia (and a lot of good information).

Thanks to Steve Terrill, who pursued photographs for this edition with dedication and an artist's eye; and to the team of talented and good-hearted artist/designers who assisted in the cartography, design, graphics, and layout of this edition: Mary Stupp-Greer, Lynn Kertell, Myra Clark, and Peggy Hindahl.

Thanks also to proofreader and indexer Dorothy Robertson for her contribution to the coherency of this book, and to reader and enthusiastic supporter Carol Moon. Special appreciation to my husband Mike Sheehan, for his continuing inspiration and encouragement to do good work.

I also wish to acknowledge the contribution of the late Henning Helstrom, whose *Henning's Guide* provided the original data base and concept for this book.

REFERENCES

Atlas of Oregon Lakes; Daniel M. Johnson; Portland State University; Portland, OR.

Coos County Bass & Panfish Guide; Pete Heley; Reedsport, OR

Depth Contour Map & Recreational Guide of Brownlee Reservoir; Northwest Hydrographic Survey; Jerome, ID

Fishing In Oregon's Deschutes River; Scott Richmond; Flying Pencil Publications, Scappoose, OR.

Fishing In Oregon's Cascade Lakes; Scott Richmond; Flying Pencil Publications, Scappoose, OR.

Fishing Holes A Short Cast from Portland; Jack Webster; The Oregonian, Portland, OR.

Oregon Atlas & Gazeteer; DeLorme Mapping; Freeport, Maine

Oregon Coast Bass & Panfish Guide; Pete Heley; Reedsport, OR.

Oregon Geographic Names; Lewis A. MacArthur; Oregon Historical Society; Portland, OR.

Oregon State Parks; Jan Bannan; The Mountaineers; Seattle, WA

River Collections: Rogue, Applegate, Illinois Access maps; Middle Rogue Steelhead Chapter of Trout Unlimited; Grants Pass, OR

INTRODUCTION

Fishing In Oregon is based on the premise articulated by Lee Wulf that a lake or stream without anglers is also without friends. Oregon's waters and fisheries need friends today as never before.

This edition is both an introduction (and welcome) for new Oregon anglers, and an update for old friends. Friends need to keep in touch. Much has changed in the five years since the previous edition went to press.

I thought of those changes throughout the summer as I worked on maps for the new edition and, in the early mornings, as I drove my daughter to her job at a Columbia County ranch. As we crossed an arm of Scappoose Bay, inevitably a blue heron would be poised on the mud flat, as still as a dry fly angler waiting for a trout to take. Sometimes I imagined I saw a rod and the twitch of a mended line.

The bay was mostly mud flat this summer, as were many other Oregon waters. As summer drew to a close and I began the job of assembling and assimilating all the information I'd been gathering for the new book, I wondered what I would find. Was Oregon fishing as bleak as it appeared to be in the daily coverage of the coho crisis? the mercury alerts on Owyhee and Brownlee reservoirs? the threatened listing of bull trout as an endangered species? And would it ever rain again?

In October, as the rains came and the Eighth Edition of *Fishing In Oregon* took shape, I saw that—for all the changes, for all the losses, there is still much to celebrate, appreciate, and enjoy in Oregon angling.

There is also much to do. The coincidence of lingering drought and unfavorable ocean conditions have alerted us to the need for action. Fortunately, unlike most other natural resources, our waters and the fisheries they support are renewable. And there are many ways, both large and small, that we can help reclaim fishing in Oregon from its present down-turn.

At the simplest level, we can abide by, and support, regulations and legislation aimed at protecting and nurturing our fish populations. We can introduce youngsters and Oregon newcomers to fishing in order to insure the perpetuation of sport fishing's friendship base. And we can teach them angling ethics (obey the rules, take only what you need, do no damage, leave the environment better than you found it).

We can also keep our eyes open and ears tuned for threats to fishery habitat in our daily lives. Report damaging mining, logging, agricultural, grazing, industrial, and construction activity. Hold others accountable to the laws that protect fisheries.

And finally, we can take an active role in fishery rehabilitation by volunteering our time. The Oregon Department of Fish and Wildlife offers many opportunities for volunteer effort, as do organizations such as Oregon Trout and Northwest Steelheaders.

Fishing In Oregon, Eighth Edition has been lovingly assembled as a guide to Oregon's fisheries as they are today. I offer it to you to use as an escape from life's dramas. Those of you who are just getting to know us—explore, enjoy, and become a friend. Old friends—keep alive the vision of what has been and can be.

Good fishing forever.

—Maddy Sheehan

HOW TO USE THIS BOOK

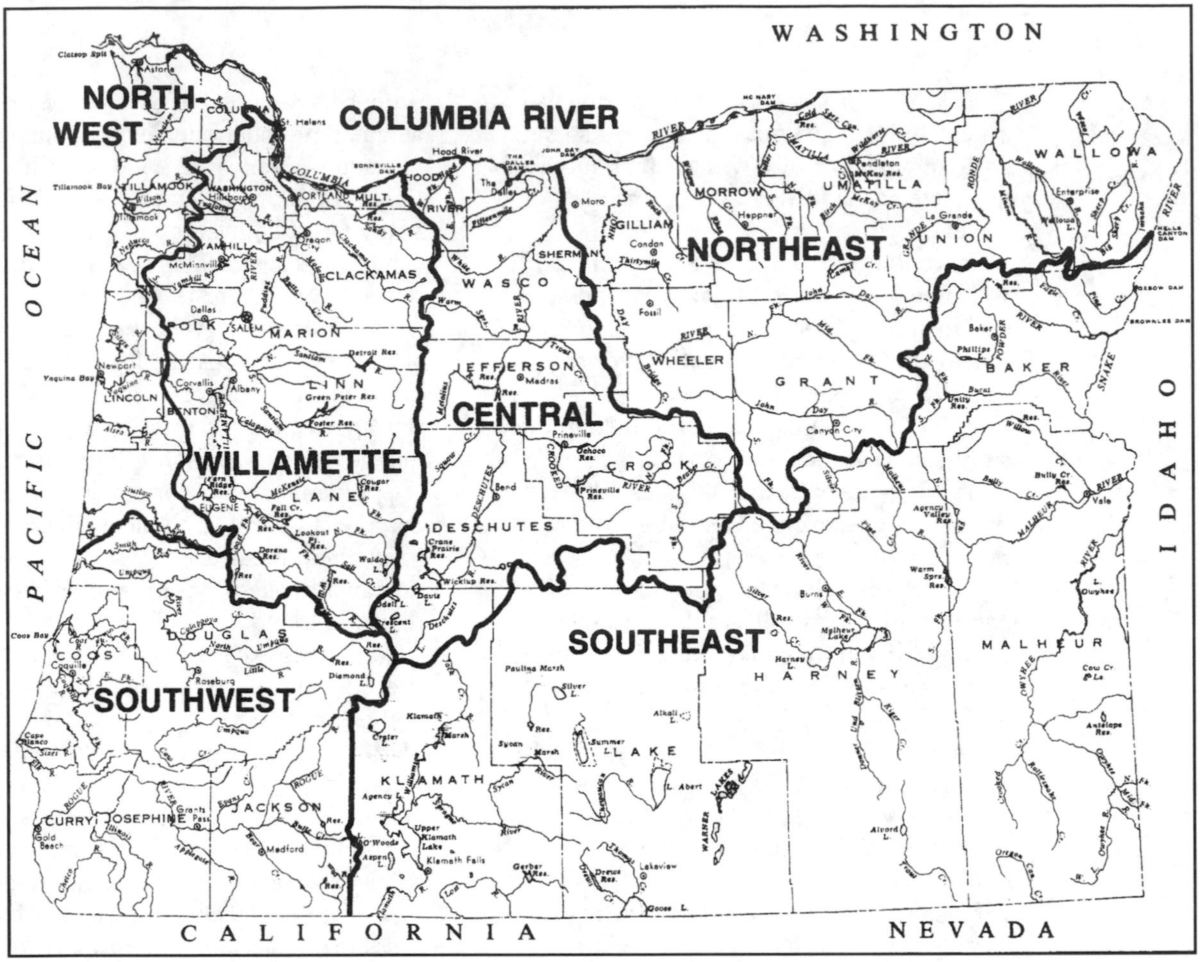

Fishing In Oregon is presented in seven chapters corresponding to the seven angling zones of the *Oregon Sport Fishing Regulations* synopsis. Use the map above to determine the zone of waters that interest you. Waters within each chapter are listed alphabetically. A complete Index at the end of the book provides a statewide alphabetical listing of waters, with page references.

The Appendices include zone-by zone listings of warmwater fisheries, waters restricted to artificial flies and lures, wheelchair accessible fisheries, and fisheries suitable for youngsters. A salmon and steelhead "return chart" indicates when these fish are generally in the rivers, and should be used in conjunction with the current regulation synopsis.

The introduction to each chapter includes a zone map and a brief description of the zone's outstanding characteristics, fisheries, climate, road and trail conditions, and visitor facilities. For further information about a specific fishery, call the Oregon Department of Fish and Wildlife district office nearest that water. All ODF&W office phone numbers are listed in the Appendix.

Road and trail directions to each water listed in *Fishing In Oregon* are generally given in the opening paragraphs. Angler services and facilities are listed near the end of each write-up. For additional information about National Forest roads and campgrounds, call the relevant ranger district office, listed in the Appendix.

While *Fishing In Oregon* often mentions specific angling and boating restrictions in effect at the time of publication, anglers and boaters should refer to the current angling and boating regulations for the final word.

Map symbols used throughout *Fishing In Oregon* are listed here.

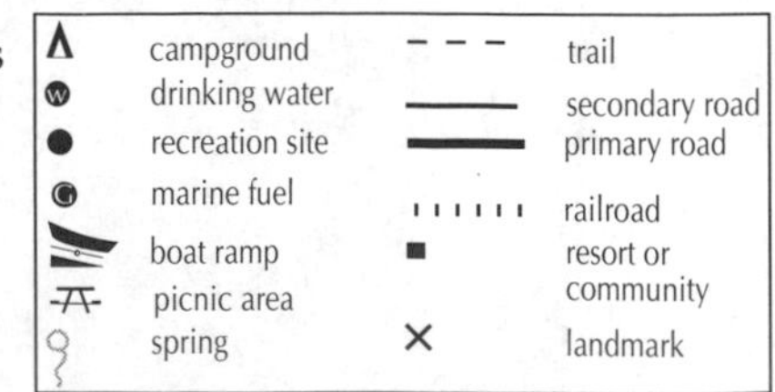

NORTHWEST ZONE

The Northwest Zone is all waters draining directly to the Pacific Ocean north of, but not including, the Umpqua River drainage; and those portions of Columbia River tributaries upstream from the railroad bridges near their mouths, northwest from the city of St. Helens.

The Northwest Zone is defined by the Pacific Ocean, which alternately laps and roars against its west flank at beach, bay, and rocky cape. The ocean fills valley cauldrons with morning fog, and launches flotillas of clouds that condense over the Coast Range and replenish the region's dozens of rivers and streams. The ocean cools the summer breeze, moderates the winter chill, and is a constant presence in the tang of air, the dripping green of moss-draped trees, and the ubiquitous company of seagulls.

A dozen great rivers pour out of the Coast Range and into the Pacific off the Oregon coast. Spring and fall chinook, chum, and coho salmon rear and return here, as do steelhead, both wild and hatchery produced. Cutthroat trout are resident in most tributary streams. Some go to sea and return pounds heavier and silvery blue. Clams, crabs, redtail perch and rock fish inhabit the lower tidewaters, and redtails ride the surf along most beaches. Halibut, cabezon, and cod lurk among the submerged rocks of offshore reefs.

Small lakes tucked into the sand dunes offer a mix of trout and warmwater fishing, as does big, productive Siltcoos Lake. Bass, yellow perch, crappie, bluegill, and catfish are also plentiful in the many sloughs along the lower Columbia River, which forms this zone's northern boundary.

Within this zone are many of the state's premier salmon and steelhead rivers. They bear the names of the native Americans who lived off their bounty. Nestucca. Alsea, Siuslaw. Siletz. Nehalem. Others carry the names of the first white settlers. Wilson, named for a founder of the dairy industry that still dominates the tidewater valleys. Trask, for a pioneer trapper and logger.

These waters share many common characteristics, such as traditionally strong runs of winter steelhead. But each has its own character and offers unique angling opportunities. The Nestucca and Siletz, for example, also host runs of summer steelhead. Coho runs on the Alsea and Klaskanine are entirely hatchery-generated and may remain open to angling despite closures elsewhere. Fall chinook, beleaguered in some systems, continue to return in good numbers to Yaquina, Alsea, and Nehalem bays. Sea-run cutthroat, while diminished everywhere, are holding their own in the big Nestucca.

The Northwest zone has its share of angling gems. There's Siltcoos Lake, which floats in the mist like a Scottish loch at the edge of Siuslaw National Forest, luring anglers with the region's best lake fishing for wild cutthroat and the opportunity to land a trophy bass. High quality stream trout fishing can be found in the South Fork Alsea and in Lake Creek. And the essence of "pristine" is available to hearty anglers in the zone's two exquisite Drift Creeks.

The Northwest Zone is accessed north to south by scenic Hwy. 101, which hugs the coast except for a brief inland detour around the Three Capes (Meares, Lookout, and Kiwanda). Roads inland follow the major rivers as they breach the forested slopes of the Coast Range. Just beyond the heads of these river valleys, within view of the mountain range, are the state's largest cities: Portland, Salem, Albany, Corvallis, and Eugene.

The major east-west roads are all paved, though primarily two-lane and poorly lighted for night driving. Passing lanes are provided in areas of steepest grade, and slow-vehicle turn-outs help ease congestion. A network of logging roads connects watersheds and main roads, accessing tributaries and upper reaches. Though open to public use, most are unpaved, with portions less than two-lane. When traveling them during weekdays, keep an eye out, and an ear tuned, for logging trucks.

The highest point in the Coast Range (Saddle Mt.) is only 3,282 ft., but snow and ice can make driving hazardous from November to May, and severe rainstorms and fog are possible year-round. The northwest zone

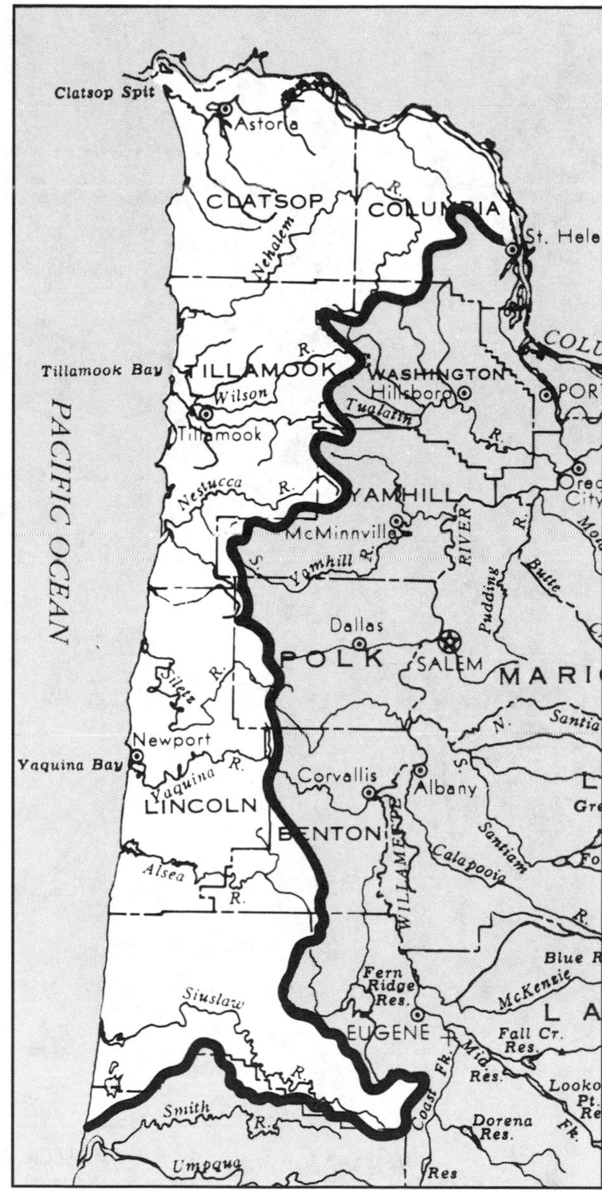

averages over 180 days with measurable rainfall each year. A pleasant side effect of this deluge is moderate temperatures. Averages vary from about 40 degrees in winter to 60 degrees in summer. Summer warming (such as it is) is delayed at the coast, with seasonal highs occurring in late August.

Settlements in the mountains are limited to the lower elevations at either end. Campgrounds are sparse along the rivers, but state parks with camping areas dot the coast, and private RV parks and reasonably priced motels are plentiful all along Hwy. 101.

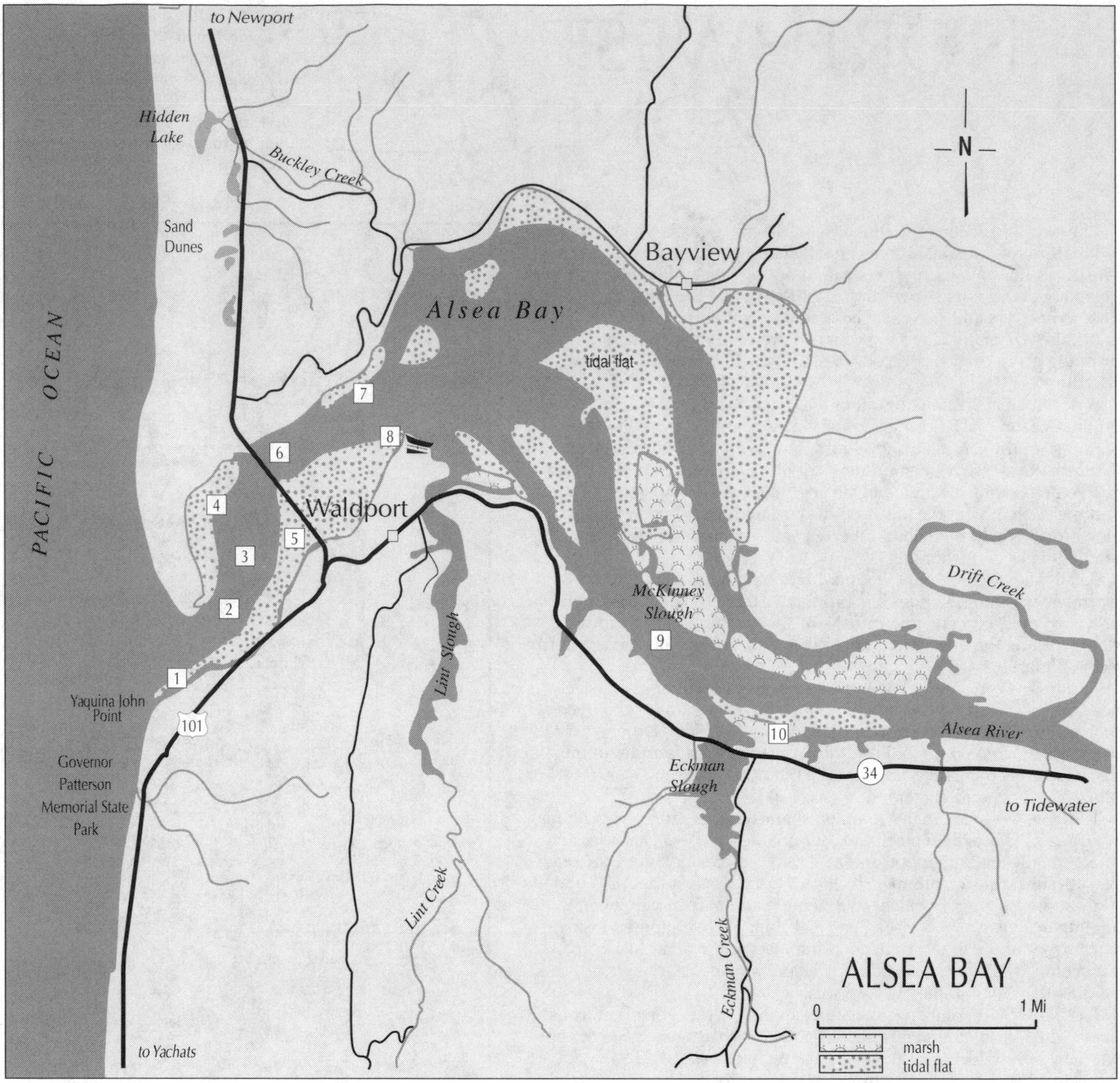
to Newport
Hidden Lake
Buckley Creek
Sand Dunes
PACIFIC OCEAN
Alsea Bay
Bayview
N
tidal flat
7
8
6
4
Waldport
5
3
2
1
Yaquina John Point
101
Governor Patterson Memorial State Park
to Yachats
Lint Slough
Lint Creek
McKinney Slough
9
Drift Creek
10
Alsea River
Eckman Slough
34
to Tidewater
Eckman Creek
ALSEA BAY
0
1 Mi
marsh
tidal flat

1 **SECONDARY CHANNEL** - Bank fish for salmon in fall.

2 **SAND BAR**

3 **LOWER MAIN CHANNEL** - Fish for fall salmon, crab.

4 **LOWER BAY FLATS NORTH** - Dig for clams, cockles.

5 **LOWER BAY FLATS SOUTH** - Firm sand, not mud; walk out at low tide and fish for coho and chinook in late Aug., perch all summer; dig cockles.

6 **MID-CHANNEL** - Hwy. 101 bridge to Waldport docks best area for perch; salmon and crab available.

7 **OLD BRIDGE FLATS**- Park below old bridge and walkout for cockles at low tide, perch at high and low.

8 **PUBLIC DOCKS**

9 **MOUTH OF THE ALSEA** - Troll for salmon July-Sept., jacks Sept.-Oct., Sea-runs June-Oct.; no perch above Eckman Slough.

10 **SOFTSHEL CLAMS** - Park off road across Eckman causeway.

ALDER LAKE One of the Oregon dune lakes, a 3-acre trout lake in Siuslaw National Forest, 7 1/2 miles north of Florence. Alder is just west of Hwy. 101, about 1/2 mile north of Sutton Lake. Look for a sign on the highway.

The lake is stocked with legal rainbow twice yearly. Buck Lake is 1/4 mile south and Dune Lake is 1/4 mile further. Both are similar to Alder in size and fishing. There is a campground at the north end of Alder Lake. Recommended for small fry.

ALSEA BAY Lightly fished in early season, offering calm and productive waters close to its boat ramps. Alsea Bay is a good place to introduce family and friends to salmon fishing, especially during fine fall weather when the salmon and lively jacks are in. Six miles long, with tidewater extending about 12 miles upriver, it can be reached in just over an hour from Corvallis by way of Hwy. 34. Hwy. 101 approaches it from north and south.

There are 8 moorages along the bay, from Waldport up to Tidewater, and almost all have launching facilities or rental boats. Most angling takes place right in front of the moorages, convenient to hot coffee.

A good run of fall chinook supports an increasing bay fishery in September and October. Salmon are caught in the lower main channel and at the mouth of the Alsea. Bank anglers work the lower south side bay flats below Hwy. 101.

The Alsea has a small run of wild spring chinook which enter the bay May through July, however fishing for them is discouraged and may be restricted in the future.

Coho are present September through November, but are being carefully monitored for run strength. Fishing for them is subject to mid-season closures, so check with the district ODF&W office for a last-minute update. Jack salmon, traditionally a popular fall fishery here, are less present than in past years.

Trolled herring, feathered spinners, Kwikfish, and Hot Shot lures are effective for adult salmon. Cluster eggs drifted under a bobber seem to attract the jacks.

Perch fishing is good in the bay from spring through fall. Perch are caught from the Hwy. 101 Bridge to the public docks at Waldport, and from the Old Bridge flats at high and low tide. There are no perch above Eckman Slough. Shrimp, clam necks, kelp worms, and sand crabs are all available locally for bait.

Sea-run cutthroat, once a popular fishery at the mouth of the Alsea, are in decline here as elsewhere on the Oregon coast. Fishing for them traditionally took place from June through September.

Crabbing continues to be very good here. The most popular area is the main channel below Lint Slough. Cockles are dug on the Lower Bay Flats (south shore), which have comfortably firm sand rather than mud, and on the Old Bridge Flats above the 101 Bridge. Both cockles and gapers are dug on the smaller Lower Bay Flats north shore. Softshell clams are available in the flats above Eckman Slough.

Flounder are no longer plentiful in Alsea Bay or in any other bay on the Oregon coast, however they are occasionally caught.

Services and supplies are abundant along the bay, with motels and restaurants in Waldport. There is a Forest Service campground 5 miles south at Tillicum Beach.

ALSEA RIVER A highly regarded winter steelhead and coho salmon stream, about 55 miles long, heading in the coast range west of Corvallis and entering the Pacific Ocean at Waldport. The main river provides excellent winter steelhead catches, as do its two main tributaries, Five Rivers and Drift Creek. The Alsea is closely followed by Hwy. 34 from its mouth to above the confluence of the North Fork. Good secondary roads follow all the major tributaries. The mouth is reached by Hwy. 101.

The Alsea continues to maintain a strong run of hatchery-reared winter steelhead, though its numbers have been severely depressed since 1986. At this time, about 2,000 fish are caught annually.

Steelhead appear here in late November, and the run peaks in December and January. Fish are often available through the end of March. There's a lot of good water, with a fair share of snags and tackle-grabbing boulders. Popular steelhead spots are at the head of tide, the Hatchery Hole, Barclay Drift, The Maples (at Lake Creek), and the Strawberry Patch. Non-finclipped steelhead must be released unharmed, so anglers must use barbless hooks December 1-March 31.

There is a coho hatchery on the Alsea, and at times there is a fishery here for fin-clipped coho. Contact the district ODF&W at Newport for last-minute update. Coho and fall Chinook are generally in the river September through November. The fall chinook run peaks in late September, and the coho in October. Most salmon are taken by trolling in the bay at Waldport and above, but casting produces fish up to the forks. Small flies and lures are commonly used.

Sea-run cutthroat are present in May and again in fall, but their population is severely depressed here as elsewhere along the Oregon coast.

Flood level on the Alsea is 18 ft. Boat angling is allowed up to Mill Creek, just below the town of Alsea. There are a number of spots where boats can be launched, some of which have small user fees. Rental boats, supplies and accommodations are available at Waldport, in the Alsea Bay area, and at several points upriver. There is a Forest Service camp 17 miles upstream from Waldport.

ALSEA RIVER, NORTH FORK A beautiful stream, well suited to fly angling, entering the main Alsea at the town of Alsea. It is easily accessed from county

The Alsea's lower bay flats offer firm sand from which to fish for perch and salmon.

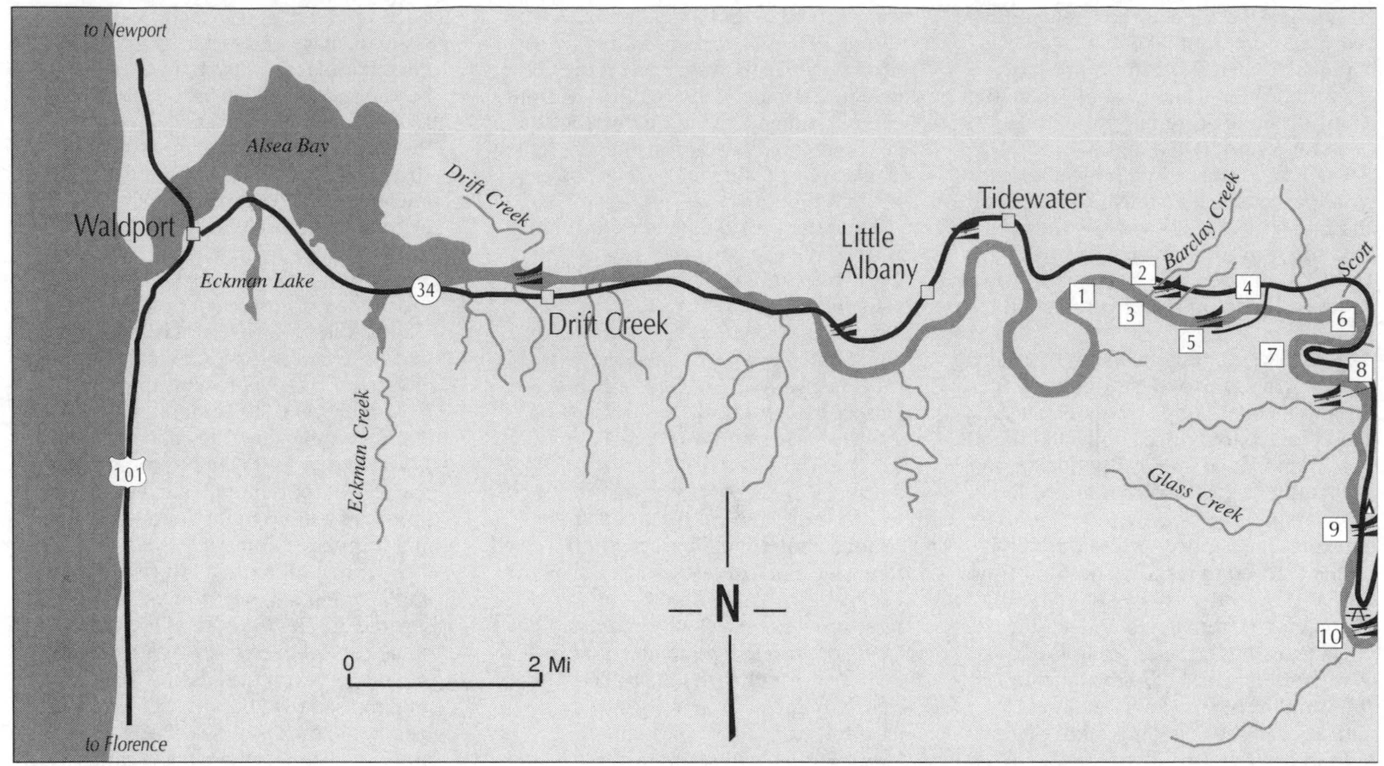

1 **SAND HOLE** - Head of tide; private property; boat-fishing only.
2 **BARCLAY HOLE** - First good hole above tidewater; good low water hole for salmon or steelhead.
3 **SOUTH BANK BARCLAY**- Ask permission to access good private bank fishing; cross river on Boundary Rd. then turn rt. on So. Bank.
4 **SCOTT CREEK HOLE** - Ledges and channels; fish just below creek; bring lots of tackle.
5 **HELLION RAPIDS** - Deep hole just below rapids.
6 **HOOTENANY TRAIL** - Forest Service access trail up to Rock Crusher Hole; trail runs under edge of highway.
7 **ROCK CRUSHER HOLE** - Rocks, ledge, channels.
8 **MIKE BAUER WAYSIDE** - Public boat ramp; popular for plunking; wheelchair accessible.
9 **BLACKBERRY CAMPGROUND** - Public boat ramp; deep holes; overnight camping with RV spaces; nice forest trail.
10 **MAPLES HOLE** - Deep plunking water; boat ramp, parking, picnic area.
11 **FIVE RIVERS BRIDGE** - Productive fishing from bridge to Maples hole; channels, ledges, rocks, holes. good bank access with productive slots close to shore.
12 **FIVE RIVERS BOAT RAMP**
13 **OLD PUT-IN HOLE** - Plunking hole just above Five Rivers Put-In at bend of road.
14 **LOW WATER BRIDGE PUT-IN** - Good bank angling.
15 **STONY POINT BOAT RAMP** - Good gravel put-in with parking at Transformer Hole; good bank fishing upstream.
16 **FOREST SERVICE CAMPGROUN**D
17 **SWINGER BRIDGE** - Put-in just below bridge.
18 **BEAR CREEK LODGE** - Bank fishing just above lodge.
19 **DIGGER MT. MILL BRIDGE** - Good fishing above & below, across stream from highway; private property; ask permission to fish.
20 **PRIVATE PARK** - Access fee.
21 **FALL CREEK BOAT LAUNCH** - Popular boat slide into Fall Cr. 1/4 mile above Alsea; drift into Alsea.
22 **MISSOURI BEND PARK** - Log skid; picnic facilities; lots of parking.
23 **SALMONBERRY BRIDG**E - Boat launch; good drifting and plunking.
24 **CAMPBELL PARK PUT-IN** - Fish just below.
25 **MILL CREEK BOAT RAMPS** - Upper limit for boats; fish the stretch from boat ramps up to Mill Cr.; accessible good drifts throughout.
26 **ALSEA RANGER STATION** - bank access with permission; ask at farm houses.

A good run of fall chinook enters the Alsea in September and October.

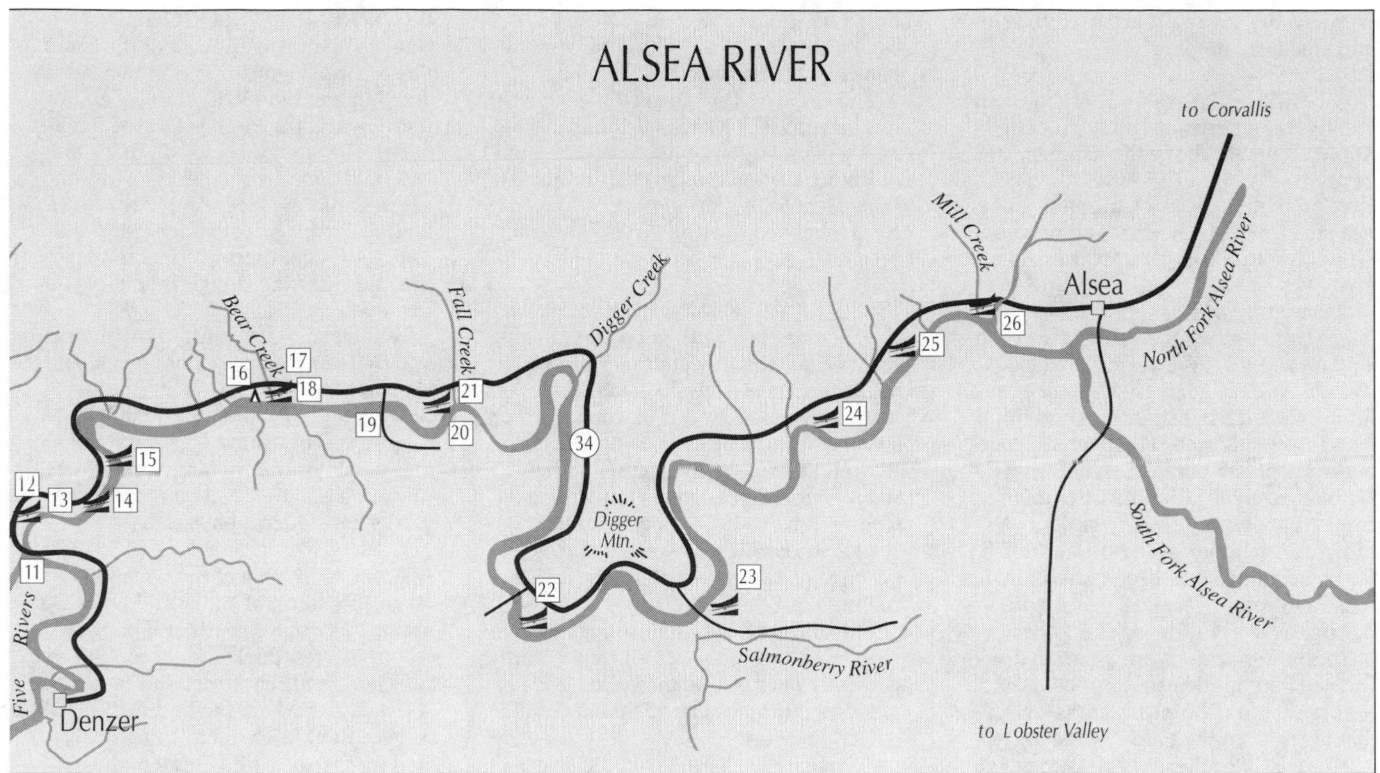

and logging roads running north and west from Hwy. 34.

Fishing for wild cutthroat trout is generally good when the season opens, and holds up for several months. Good numbers of winter steelhead are usually taken each year in the lower water, as well as a small number of spring and fall chinook and coho. There is a trout and steelhead hatchery about one mile above Hwy. 34. Angling from a floating device is prohibited throughout the North Fork.

ALSEA RIVER, SOUTH FORK Excellent for wild cutthroat trout both above and below its falls. This fair size fork of the Alsea (average width 40 feet) flows into the main river from the SW at the town of Alsea. County roads access it and many of its tributaries, with BLM land bordering much of its run.

The South Fork offers good cover for trout, but limited food sources. If the water is clear, light leader fly fishing, single eggs, caddis worms, or small bits of crawfish tail are your best bet. Only small numbers of steelhead and salmon are caught here. The nearest campground is 7 miles SE of Alsea.

ARCH CAPE CREEK A fair stream for sea-run cutthroat in spring and late fall. Only 4 miles long, it flows 6 miles south of Cannon Beach, off Hwy. 101. Arch Cape has some good pools and brush, but is surrounded by mostly residential property, so be sure to ask permission. There is a campground at Oswald West State Park.

BARK SHANTY CREEK Tributary of the Trask River. Closed to all angling to protect spawning grounds..

BEAR CREEK (Clatsop Co.) Tributary of the Columbia, managed for wild cutthroat and steelhead. The stream flows into the river east of Astoria near Swensen. Access to the stream across Cavenham timber property has been curtailed due to poor angler behavior.

BEAVER CREEK (Columbia Co.) A good bass stream at its lower end, where it is known as Beaver Slough. Best fishing is in late summer. The stream flows about 25 miles west from near Rainier to the town of Clatskanie. It is crossed many times by Hwy. 30 and approached by secondary roads.

A sparse population of resident cutthroat may be found in the upper stream. It is not stocked. Beaver Creek is open to salmon and steelhead to 200 ft downstream of the lower falls, but only a few are taken here each year.

BEAVER CREEK (Lincoln Co.) A short coastal stream, good for cutthroat trout, located about 6 miles south of Newport. A county road follows the creek to Hwy. 101.

Beaver Creek has a catch and release steelhead fishery up to the county bridge at Ona, about 3 miles upstream of Hwy. 101.

Sea-run cutthroat were traditionally present in late summer and fall, but are now scarce. Coho salmon enter in October and November. There is a boat ramp just off Hwy. 101. A state park at the mouth provides picnic facilities.

BEAVER CREEK (Tillamook Co.) A good cutthroat stream with lots of cover and many deep pools, traditionally fished for sea-run. This stream enters the main Nestucca River at the town of Beaver, about 15 miles south of Tillamook on Hwy. 101. It has an East fork and a West fork, for a total of about 15 miles of stream. A fair road follows each fork. A few salmon and steelhead are taken up to the West Beaver Creek deadline. It is closed to coho fishing.

BEAVER SLOUGH COMPLEX, (Columbia Co.) An extensive slough area in the lower Columbia River offering good fishing for bass and panfish. NE of the town of Clatskanie, boat access is available from the Columbia by Wallace Slough or from the Clatskanie River, with some bank access at road crossings. The entire slough offers good fishing for about 15 species, with crappie and perch most abundant. April and May are the best months for these fish, which can run to 5 pounds. Very small wobblers or weighted streamers can be used to catch them, or an abundance of rough fish here can be used for crappie bait.

BENEKE CREEK A good early season trout stream with some sea-run showing in early fall if the water rises. This creek enters the Nehalem River at Jewell and is about 14 miles long if you include its tributary, Walker Creek. A good road parallels the stream. It is closed to salmon and steelhead angling.

BIG CREEK (Clatsop Co.) A good winter steelhead stream, with a wild cutthroat available above the hatchery in early season. About 15 miles long, Big Creek enters the lower Columbia sloughs near the town of Knappa. Followed by Hwy. 30 south from Knappa Junction, it is easily reached from the road for most of its length.

A good number of steelhead and coho salmon ascend this stream. The peak months for steelhead are December and January, with fish caught in good numbers through March. The catch averages about 2,000 fish per year. Coho show in October, and fall chinook are present from August through November. However, salmon fishing on Columbia River tributaries has been closed midseason in recent years, so check with the district ODF&W office for an update.

Special restrictions are associated with the hatchery on this stream, so check current regulations carefully, and stay 200 feet away from the hatchery fishways.

There is 1/2 mile of public access on the east bank, between the old highway bridge and the new one, but about half the property along the stream is in private hands. Be sure to get permission.

BIG CREEK RESERVOIRS Two 20-acre reservoirs on the north edge of Newport, owned by the city and open for year around angling. Located just north of Yaquina Bay, the reservoirs are accessible from Hwy. 101 by way of Big Creek Rd. just north of Hotel Newport and south of Agate Beach. Motors are prohibited, and only rafts, float tubes and car-top boats can be launched from shore. Most anglers fish from the bank beside the road.

The reservoirs are stocked heavily with rainbow trout in March, April, and May, and contain largemouth bass and brown bullhead. Bait or spinner/bait combinations seem to work best here. Recommended for small fry. Wheelchair accessible.

Tidewater is a good place to start the season.

BIG ELK CREEK A major tributary of the Yaquina river with good bank fishing for wild fall chinook and hatchery reared winter steelhead. Big Elk enters the Yaquina at Elk City. It is reached from the coast by driving east on Hwy. 20 from Newport to Toledo, then crossing the main river and following it upstream on County Rd. 533 to Elk City. A county road at Eddyville follows Bear Creek down to its confluence with Big Elk, then follows Big Elk to Elk City.

The steelhead run is at its peak here in December and January. Fall chinook are generally most abundant in October. Resident cutthroat provide good fishing in May and June.

BLIND SLOUGH Offers opportunities to catch bass to 5 pounds, and large yellow perch on their spawning migration in March and April. Crappie and catfish are also available, with some fall fishing for chinook and coho. Covering 194 acres, it is reached by county roads heading north from Knappa Junction or Brownsmead Junction on Hwy. 30.

The slough can be fished from the north bank, which has a road paralleling it. In late fall, coho and chinook move through the slough, and a few are taken by trolling. Chinook show in September, and coho and jacks in October and November. There's a lot of private property here, so ask permission before you cross questionable land. Blind Slough connects to many other smaller sloughs, most of which are productive for bass and panfish.

BLUE LAKE (Tillamook Co.) Once a 3-acre cutthroat lake on the south side of the divide, Blue lost its fishery when the dam blew out. It's hardly even a pond now, with roads very deteriorated. No reconstruction is planned at this time.

BRADBURY SLOUGH All the Columbia river bass and panfish species can be found in this good size slough, just west of Quincy, about 3 miles NE of Clatskanie on Hwy. 30. Two other sloughs, Johns and Deadend, are connected to it. Small boats can be launched, and there is some access from bridges and the county road. It is only lightly fished.

BROWNSMEAD SLOUGH Offers good bass and panfish, just east of the community of Brownsmead. The Brownsmead junction on Hwy. 30 is 20 miles east of Astoria, and the town is located 5 miles north. The slough is over 10 miles long and holds good water levels with tide gates. Banks are steep, and bank access is limited except from county roads and bridges. One unimproved boat ramp near the middle of the slough is suitable for car-tops.

White and black crappie are abundant, and there are lots of yellow perch, and yellow, black, and brown bullhead. Bluegill and bass are occasionally taken. Bottom worm fishing is best for catfish and perch. Bobber fishing with white meat or a spinner/bait combination works best for crappie and bass.

BUCK LAKE One of the Oregon Dune lakes, just south of Alder and Dune lakes, about 7 1/2 miles north of Florence. About 5 acres, Buck is stocked with rainbow and cutthroat trout, and may have some bass. Park on the highway shoulder just south of Buck Lake Trailer Park. A trail on the west side of the highway leads a few hundred feet to the lake. Fish from the sand dune on the west side. Best fishing is in April, May, and June, before the water warms. There is a Forest Service campground at Alder Lake.

BURKES LAKE Just off Ridge Rd., one mile west of Warrenton, a 6.3-acre pond containing largemouth bass.

BUSTER CREEK A small early-season cutthroat stream flowing west into the Nehalem River near Tidesport, about halfway between Elsie and Jewell. The middle stream can be reached by the Grand Rapids Road and by Wage Road, which cross both forks of the creek SE of Jewell. In early season this is a good cutthroat stream, but it is hard to fish because of the brush. A single egg or a small double spinner with worm might work. Another trick that has produced here is to dribble a dark fly pattern off the brush.

CAPE MEARES LAKE An unusual lake, containing trout and bass, created several years ago by diking on the Cape Meares side of Tillamook Bay. It is about 10 miles from Tillamook off the Bay Ocean Rd. The lake covers about 90 acres with maximum depth of 10 ft. Aquatic vegetation is quite thick in places along the edges, and gets worse throughout the summer.

The lake is stocked fairly heavily with legal rainbow several times each spring, and there are usually some nice holdovers from the previous season. If you feel like you've hooked an aquatic cheetah, chances are you're into one of the adult hatchery-reared steelhead that ODF&W plants here when they have a few returns in excess of their hatchery stocking needs. You can count these twenty-inchers as trout in your daily take, and you don't need a steelhead tag.

Largemouth bass are well established here, but because reproduction is low, you might consider releasing bass unharmed in order to help maintain the fishery. A few bluegill are also present.

A slightly unstable pier is available for the sure-footed. Nearby bay and beach offer alternative saltwater fishing opportunities. There is a campground 10 miles south at Cape Lookout State Park.

CARCUS CREEK Tributary to the Clatskanie River, flowing from the south and meeting the Clatskanie about 8 miles SE of the town of Clatskanie near the Firwood School. This is a cutthroat stream, but it takes a good brush beater to make it pay. It's lightly fished, but the beaver ponds have been known to make the trip worthwhile.

CARNAHAN LAKE A private 9-acre lake just west of Hwy. 101 about 5 miles north of Gearhart, and just north of Cullaby Lake. Maximum depth is 15 ft., and the lake is very weedy. It is closed to public access at this time.

CARTER LAKE A typical dune lake with good trout fishing, one mile long and 200 feet wide. It is reached by Hwy. 101 about 9 miles south of Florence and about 12 miles north of Reedsport. The lake is on the west side of the highway. A very brushy shoreline makes it difficult to fish from shore, though there has been better bank access in recent low water years.

Carter is stocked with legal rainbow and occasional brood fish to 5 pounds, a well as surplus adult hatchery steelhead. These may be counted as trout in the daily catch, and you don't need a steelhead tag.

There is a public campground at the east end of the lake, with a concrete boat ramp, parking, and picnic facilities.

CEMETERY LAKE A 10-acre Clatsop County fishery for black crappie, warmouth, bluegill, largemouth bass, and yellow perch, connected by pipe to Smith Lake. Access is through the Astoria cemetery.

CHAMBERLAIN LAKE Quite prominent on most maps, this 11-acre lake is located at the Scout camp just south of Cape Lookout State Park. It is not open to public angling.

CLATSKANIE RIVER Flows through the town of Clatskanie and enters the Columbia River about mid-way between St. Helens and Astoria. Do not confuse this with the Klaskanine River, which is near Astoria. This is a good all around stream offering many types of fishing. About 26 miles long, it features cutthroat trout as well as a good steelhead run and a few coho salmon.

Roads parallel and cross the river in many spots and it has several good tributaries. The headwaters can be reached from the St. Helens-Vernonia Rd. by taking the gravel road north to Apiary. The lower stream is best reached from Clatskanie. Gravel and boulders make it an ideal fly stream, but there are brushy areas where bait or spinner will work best.

There's a lot of private land along the lower Clatskanie.

Resident cutthroat are available throughout the season. Sea-run linger in tidewater from July until September, then begin moving upstream.

The Clatskanie has a nice winter steelhead run, but fishing is restricted to catch and release of non-finclipped steelhead.

There's lots of private land along the lower river, but landowners continue to be generous about allowing access. Be a courteous visitor. Supplies are available in Clatskanie.

CLATSKANIE SLOUGH A very good bass and panfish water connected to the lower Clatskanie River accessed by coun-

Depoe Bay offers quick access to excellent offshore fishing.

ty roads just north of Clatskanie on Hwy. 30. The slough is controlled by tide gates. There are no boat ramps, and access is limited to a few auto and foot bridges. Good size yellow and black crappie and brown bullhead are plentiful. Perch, bluegill, and bass are present but not numerous. It is pretty much a still-fishing setup. Recommended for small fry.

CLEAR LAKE (Clatsop Co.) An 8-acre largemouth bass fishery on private property, one mile north of Warrenton.

CLEAR LAKE (Lane Co.) About 160 acres, offering largemouth bass, yellow perch, and trout. Located about 3 miles north of Florence on Hwy. 101, just north of Munsel Lake, Clear Lake is quite prominent on maps. There is no public road to the lake, but there is some public access on the west shore, about a mile hike in.

CLEAR LAKE (Tillamook Co.) Not to be confused with Spring Lake, about a mile down the road. A small, poor cutthroat lake, about 3 acres and very shallow, it is located just south of Rockaway on the east side of Hwy. 101. It contains cutthroat trout, but isn't very productive. It is now surrounded by private land, and public access is doubtful.

CLEAWOX LAKE Popular because of its location within Honeyman State Park a few miles south of Florence. Stocked with rainbow trout and an occasional brood trout, the lake has also been a sleeper for largemouth bass and crappie, with yellow perch, brown bullhead, and bluegill available. It's a good bet in early season before the campers get too numerous. The lake covers about 82 acres, and boats with motors are allowed.

COFFENBURY LAKE A 50-acre trout lake within Fort Stevens State Park, about 2 miles west of Warrenton. The lake is long and narrow, in a deep depression between sand dunes. Maximum depth is 9 feet near the north end. The north end of the lake is easily reached by a good road.

Coffenbury is stocked annually with legal trout, and a few adult steelhead. Best fishing is earlier in the season. It also contains yellow perch and brown bullhead, but is a poor producer of warm water species.

There is a trail all the way around the lake, and several fishing floats.

Ft. Stevens is one of Oregon's most extensive state parks, including a full service campground, bike and hiking trails through coastal forest, as well as access to some of the state's finest razor clam digging and surf fishing. Recommended for small fry. Wheelchair accessible, but floats lack safety edges.

COLLARD LAKE A private 32-acre lake located about 3 miles north of Florence and one mile east of Hwy. 101. The lake contains yellow perch, bluegill, brown bullhead, and largemouth bass, but at present has no public access.

COOK CREEK A fair cutthroat and steelhead stream flowing SE into the lower Nehalem, about 7 miles from the town of Nehalem. The creek is about 18 miles long, including tributaries, and enters the Nehalem at a point shown as Batterson on most maps. A gravel road parallels the creek. Starting in 1994, the creek will be managed for wild trout and steelhead.

A good fly stream, with lots of boulders and gravel and not too brushy, it has quite a few cutthroat in early season. Open for winter steelhead up to the south fork, there are about 5 miles of good angling. The steelhead stocking program is scheduled to end in 1994. Clipped hatchery steelhead should still be present through the 1995-96 season. All non-finclipped steelhead must be released unharmed.

Cook Creek is a spawning stream for coho and fall chinook. When salmon are present, take care not to disturb them.

The closest supply point is Wheeler.

CRABAPPLE LAKE A swampy 22-acre lake in Ft. Stevens State Park. Fish it early in the season for largemouth bass and yellow perch before the weeds choke out access. You'll need a boat or float tube to get beyond the weeds.

CREEP AND CRAWL LAKE A swampy 5-acre pond in Ft. Stevens State Park, offering bluegill fishing in early season. By mid-summer the lake is usually weedbound. You'll need a boat or float tube to get beyond the weeds.

CRESCENT LAKE (Tillamook Co.) An 11-acre lake 5 miles north of Tillamook Bay on Hwy. 101 near Manhattan Beach. Just north of Lytle Lake (and connected to it), Crescent covers 11 acres, but has grown increasingly shallow due to siltation.

Recent activity by resident beavers has restricted boat access, but this is a great place to observe a good looking beaver dam, and maybe even a few of the engineers at work.

Largemouth bass are available, and trout fishing holds up as long as the stocked rainbow and cutthroat last. Recommended for small fry who like beavers.

CRIMM'S ISLAND SLOUGH A Columbia River slough 6 miles NE of Clatskanie, with known populations of white and black crappie.

CRONIN CREEK A wild cutthroat stream that enters the Nehalem from the east, about 10 miles south of Elsie, on the lower Nehalem Rd. The fish usually leave right after the first of the season, but show again in late fall. The stream can also be reached by coming up the Nehalem from Mohler. The lower mile provides most of the fishing.

CULLABY LAKE A good panfish lake and family fishing spot. It is just east of Hwy. 101 about 4 miles north of Gearhart and about 12 miles south of Astoria. The lake is a long and narrow 220 acres, about 1 1/2 miles from north to south and usually less than 1/4 mile wide. Its depth ranges 6-12 feet.

Cullaby usually provides excellent angling from spring through late fall for crappie, bluegill, perch, brown bullheads and largemouth bass. Cullaby is not stocked with trout.

Bullhead fishing is excellent at the south end of the lake, especially in March. For nice bass, try working the snags on the east bank of the lake where the weeds aren't so thick. A boat is essential to reach the fish later in summer when the lake chokes up with aquatic weeds. A county park with boat ramp and picnic areas extends half-way around the west side of the lake. There are docks at the north end and mid-way around the lake.

DEADWOOD CREEK A wild cutthroat trout stream, with a few steelhead and chinook, tributary to Lake Creek in the Siuslaw system. It joins Lake Creek from the north about 30 miles upstream from Florence, accessed from Hwy. 36 (Florence to Junction City) by a paved road that parallels its length.

Best fishing is in the early season.

The creek is closed to all angling October 1 to November 30 to protect spawning chinook.

The closest campground is at Knowles, 4 miles east of Mapleton on Hwy. 126.

DEER ISLAND SLOUGH A large bass and panfish slough on the lower Columbia about 35 miles west of Portland. Access is from the town of Deer Island on Hwy. 30. Goat Island Slough connects to it. Boat access is from the county road. About 15 species of fish are present, with crappie, perch, and brown bullhead most numerous. Some good size bass are taken on plugs and spinners. It is bordered by a lot of private property, but access permission is usually granted. The slough can also be reached from Shell Beach.

DEPOE BAY An excellent portal to the open sea. This is a very unusual salt water bay, located south of Siletz Bay and crossed by Hwy. 101 about 10 miles south of Taft. It is about 100 miles from Portland by way of highways 18 and 101. The bay itself is very small, fed by two small streams, but it's a popular spot to take off for outside halibut, salmon, and bottom angling. The entry into the ocean is through a narrow channel, and boats coming in and out usually have quite an audience on the highway bridge and at the State Park rest area on the bluff.

A fleet of commercial fishing boats makes daily trips from June through October in pursuit of bottom fish, halibut, and salmon. There's no angling to speak of in the small bay, except for occasional catches of bottom fish and a few coho picked up late in the fall. For a quick way to get offshore, the bay is perfect. A large public boat ramp and parking area is located on the south side of the bay.

Although its access to the open sea is considered one of the least hazardous on the coast, normal safe boating procedures should be followed. If in doubt, check with the Coast Guard crew based on the bay. In any event, make sure your boat is safely equipped, with a spare motor available, as on any ocean trip.

Salmon start showing well outside the bay in late June, with both coho and chinook taken on trolled wobblers, spinners, or on herring. At times the fish are right on top, but anglers often have to go deep for them. Most fishing takes place within a few miles of the buoys marking the channel entrance. There are about 40-50,000 angler trips out of Depoe Bay each year, and the average catch per trip is usually the highest on the coast. Private anglers out of Depoe fish the reefs as far south as Yaquina Head Lighthouse (a few miles). Reefs north of Depoe extend to the mouth of the Siletz. Fish 8-30 fathoms for lingcod, rockfish, greenling, and cabezon. Halibut are caught as well, especially to the north. Following the commercial boats is also an acceptable tactic for locating good fishing grounds.

Charter boats make trips of two hours, four hours, and all-day. They can't guarantee your limit, but they have the equipment and know-how to locate fish, and you'll be in safe hands. Charter boats supply tackle and bait. Bring warm clothes and rain gear.

If salmon or halibut aren't available, you can concentrate on bottom fish, using herring or jigs of several kinds. Coastal tackle shops provide gear and information. Rockfish, snapper, perch, lingcod, and the rare flounder can all be taken in this area. One of the best bottom fishing spots out of Depoe Bay is Government Reef to the north.

DEVILS LAKE (Lincoln Co.) A large coastal lake with bass, panfish, and a fair trout fishery. Covering almost 700 acres, it is located on Hwy. 101 a few miles south of Lincoln City. Hwy. 18 through McMinnville offers the best route from the valley. The lake has a serious aquatic weed problem which has been addressed by the introduction of grass carp. It is illegal to fish for the carp.

Legal rainbow are stocked from spring into early summer, providing the bulk of the trout fishing here, with the average fish measuring 11 inches. Carry-over rainbow reach 18-20 inches.

The lake's brown bullhead population is doing well. Channel catfish were planted here but are dwindling. Black crappie to 13 inches are present in good numbers. Yellow perch to 14 inches and largemouth bass to 5 pounds are also present.

Devils Lake State Park at the SE corner of the lake has a campground, boat ramp, and picnic area.

DIBBLEES SLOUGH A Columbia River slough west of Rainier. It is SW of the popular salmon beach known as Dibblees Beach, accessed by county roads and by boat from the Columbia at Rainier. It can also be reached by the river road under the Longview Bridge. Crappie and brown bullhead are the main catch here, with bottom bait and bobbed the best technique. The slough is used for log storage, and fishing under the log rafts often produces crappie.

DRIFT CREEK (Alsea watershed) A good size stream with native runs of salmon, steelhead, and cutthroat trout, opening into Alsea Bay about 3 miles east of Waldport. About 30 miles long and 30-60 ft. wide, it carves a narrow canyon through thick woods, including stands of old growth timber. Its lower waters can be approached from the north side of Alsea Bay by a road running east, and by boat from the bay itself. Logging roads bisect the upper stream, and several marked trails make the steep descent into the canyon. It's a 1,200 ft. drop over 2 miles on the Horse Creek Trail, 1,000 feet on the newer Harris Ranch Trail. This is a roadless area of old growth timber.

The creek offers good fishing for resident cutthroat trout from late May throughout the season.

This creek also hosts important runs of coho, winter steelhead, and sea-run cutthroat, and is considered a key watershed in the effort to restore the coast's anadromous fish populations. The creek is being monitored carefully by the US Forest Service. All steelhead in Drift Creek are wild and must be released unharmed. And while restrictions are not in place at this time, anglers are urged *not* to fish Drift Creek for salmon of any species.

Boat moorages and public ramps are available on Alsea Bay for explorations of the lower creek, which is heavily posted against bank fishing.

DRIFT CREEK (Siletz watershed) A good coastal cutthroat stream with an important run of wild winter steelhead. Drift Creek enters Siletz Bay at Cutler City, one mile north of the Siletz River Rd. 229. It flows about 18 miles with average width 35 feet. About one mile north of Kernville, a road heads west from Hwy. 101 and follows Drift Creek more than 10 miles. Access within the first 8 miles requires a hike south to the stream. The upper water is reached by the Drift Creek Trail and by logging roads.

Drift Creek offers high quality angling for catch and release wild winter steelhead January through March, and for cutthroat trout in summer. The fall chinook run is currently strong, with fish available in October and November.

Like Drift Creek in the Alsea drainage, this Drift Creek is considered to be a key watershed in the effort to restore anadromous fish runs.

Stocking of hatchery steelhead has been discontinued, and all non-finclipped steelhead must be released unharmed.

Road access is limited, and best angling is available by hiking through roadless areas above and below Drift Creek Camp.

The camp is at about stream mile 12. Another camp is located about 5 miles up on Schooner Creek. Devils Lake State Park, north of Taft on Hwy. 101, also provides camping facilities. Supplies and accommodations are available in the Siletz Bay area.

DUNE LAKE A stocked trout lake north of Sutton lake. See Alder and Dune lakes for directions.

ECKMAN LAKE A 45-acre lake adjacent to the lower Alsea River beside Hwy. 34, about 2 miles east of Waldport.

There's fair fishing here early in the season for rainbow and cutthroat. A few largemouth bass are lurking in these waters, remnants of a less than successful stocking program. Brown bullhead are also present. There is a boat ramp here, but no campground

ECOLA CREEK (a.k.a. Elk Cr.) A good cutthroat and steelhead stream, just 10 miles long including both forks, flowing directly into the ocean at Cannon Beach.

Though the creek is managed for wild fish, it attracts a lot of stray hatchery steelhead. Best steelhead fishing is in January and February. The stream is open for steelhead up to the forks, about 1 mile above Hwy. 101. Non-finclipped steelhead must be released unharmed.

The stream's sea-run and coho populations are dangerously low.

ELBOW LAKE A 13-acre lake south of Tahkenitch Lake, on the west side of Hwy. 101. The lake is visible from the highway. Pull off the highway and park at the south end of the lake, where cartop boats can be launched. Fish for rainbow and yellow perch. Best bank access is along the highway, as the west side is too brushy. Recommended for small fry.

ERHART LAKE A good, small, very scenic rainbow lake on the west side of Hwy. 101, about 8 miles south of Florence near Siltcoos Lake. This is a beautiful little lake, reminiscent of those in the high Cascades. Stocked quite heavily with rainbow, it holds up well into summer. Fly anglers will lose less gear than hardware fishermen.

Erhart is heavily fished through spring, mostly from shore. A trail leads down to the lake from the highway. There is a little gravel road that goes around to the far shore where you can bank fish or launch a car-top boat. There are good campgrounds nearby.

EUCHRE CREEK (Siletz area) A fair cutthroat stream entering the Siletz River about 24 river miles above the bay, 4 miles downstream from the town of Siletz. Hwy. 229 crosses it just above its mouth.

Not heavily fished, it affords good cover for trout, rich food sources, and fair cutthroat fishing in early season. It's easy on tackle, too. Only about 10 miles long and about 25 feet wide, it has a good population of wild cutthroat trout.

FIVE RIVERS A major tributary of the Alsea River, about 18 miles long with average width 75 ft. Five Rivers enters the Alsea from the south about 20 miles upstream from Waldport, 23 miles west of the town of Alsea off Hwy. 34. A good road follows the stream to its headwaters.

Five Rivers has many nice pools and bedrock ledges, and offers good cutthroat angling well into the season. Crayfish tails, wet flies, or sand shrimp drifted under the ledges can produce nice size trout.

Winter steelhead are not stocked, so fishing for them from January through March is catch and release, and barbless hooks are required.

Five Rivers has an important run of wild coho salmon, generally present in late October and November. Angling may well be restricted to protect them, so check with the district ODF&W office for an update.

Camping along the river is limited to some sites among the blackberries. There is a developed campground on the Alsea toward Waldport.

FLOETERS POND A hike-in cutthroat lake, one of a group of small lakes originally built by Crown Zellerbach in their tree farm areas, now owned by Cavenham Forest Industries (CFI). Covering only about 3 acres and difficult to reach, it provides wild cutthroat angling in spring and early summer. The lake is dominated by snags and fallen logs, and at times beavers have dammed the outlet.

The pond is about 5 miles SE of Vernonia and 3 miles north of the Columbia County line. To get there, take the trail south from the Vernonia - Scappoose Hwy., starting 1.5 miles east of the BLM picnic area on the East Fork Nehalem. It's a 1 1/2 mile hike south to the lake.

Continued access to the pond is dependent on our good manners.

FOGARTY CREEK A small stream flowing into the ocean through Fogarty State Park, about 4 miles south of Siletz Bay. A few cutthroat are taken in the upper section, but its too small for much angling. Some perch and kelp fish are taken off the rocks at the outlet. There is a nice picnic area on the creek, but overnight camping is prohibited.

GNAT CREEK A fair cutthroat stream, with good runs of hatchery-reared steelhead. It enters the lower Columbia by way of Blind Slough, crossing Hwy. 30 a few miles east of Knappa. About 9 miles long, it heads near Nicolai Mt. and has a lot of beaver ponds in its headwaters.

Steelhead in the stream from November or December to March. Fall chinook enter Gnat already ripe for spawning and should be left undisturbed.

GOAT ISLAND SLOUGH A 55-acre slough on the Columbia River NE of Columbia City at Reichold Chemical Plant. Look for white crappie, brown bullhead, largemouth bass, bluegill, and yellow perch. There is public access at the south end only.

GUNNERS LAKES Two small cutthroat lakes on tree farm land belonging to Cavenham Forest Industries. The lakes are 1/2 and 3 acres in size. To get to them, turn south off the county road at Chapman, then take the first left off Columbia Rd. About 3 miles west, you will cross the lower and largest lake at the dam. Keep track of the power line on your way in here, as it crosses the second lake.

The lakes are no longer stocked, by the owner's request, to discourage angler use. Wild cutthroat are still available.

This is an example of a nice little fishery that has been limited by the bad manners of a few thoughtless anglers.

HEBO LAKE A 2-acre cutthroat lake 3.5 miles east of the Hebo Ranger Station on the Hebo Mt. Rd. The lake is shallow throughout and contains good feed. It is stocked with cutthroat through the spring. Still-fishing is the preferred method, although fishermen also troll. Fly fishing with streamers produces well in early season. Small boats can be launched,

There is a campground here, and several wheelchair accessible fishing opportunities.

HULT RESERVOIR A wild cutthroat fishery with some panfish opportunities, located about 4 miles north of Horton, 10 miles from Triangle Lake. It provides fair angling for largemouth bass in spring. There is a good bluegill and brown bullhead population (average size 9 inches), with a few cutthroat also taken. The reservoir has a small boat ramp. Additional recreational facilities are scheduled for construction by BLM.

HUMBUG CREEK A fine cutthroat stream, about 9 miles long, entering the Nehalem just south of Elsie. Hwy. 26 parallels the creek and crosses both the east and west forks. It has some boulders and gravel, but is primarily a bedrock stream.

Try working a spinner and worm hookup along the ledges, though the best bait is probably the caddis larva found along stream bottom. Break open the pebbly case and thread the critter on a single egg hook or hook it on the ugliest sparse no. 12 fly you have. Cast to the riffles and slicks. This is a good bet even late in the season.

INDIAN CREEK A large tributary of Lake Creek, with rainbow, cutthroat, and a small run of salmon and steelhead. It joins Lake Creek about 2 miles above that creek's confluence with the Siuslaw, about 2 miles north of Swisshome. The creek is about 20 miles long and averages 30-40 feet wide. A county road follows the stream north from Hwy. 36, about 40 miles west of Junction City. There is a lot of private land along the stream, but some access through public forest land.

Indian Creek offers good trout cover, with deep pools, bedrock ledges, and overhanging brush. It's a good bait stream for a month or so in early season. The creek is closed to all angling October 1 to November 30 to protect spawning chinook.

KAUPPI LAKE A 5-acre lake owned by Longview Fiber. No longer stocked due to weed problems, it does have a few wild cutthroat and stunted crappie available. The lake is pretty hard to find. Leave Vernonia, and go to the tree farm office, then turn left. Take the Crooked Creek Rd. for 6 miles to Kauppi Rd., turn right, and continue 3.9 miles. The lake can be seen from that point. Keep your window open and a sharp eye out for oncoming log trucks. Weeds seal the lake in late summer, and there are lots of logs and snags. Deepest water (10 feet) is on the eastern edge.

KILCHIS RIVER A good winter steelhead and chinook salmon stream, with limited opportunities for chum salmon. The Kilchis enters Tillamook Bay just north of the Wilson River and the town of Tillamook. It's only about 20 miles long but offers a lot of fishing.

One of the first coast rivers to clear, the Kilchis heads in the Tillamook State Forest.

The upper stream is gravelly with scant cover, but the lower river has very good trout habitat. Cutthroat angling is good here, though the river's fine searun population, which shows up in August, has been severely depressed in recent years.

Fall chinook, often late to arrive in the Kilchis, are holding their own here. Best catches are often in November. The chum salmon run is very low, and the fishery is currently regulated for a limited catch and release season. Check the regulations for dates. The river is closed to coho angling.

Winter steelhead are the river's strongest run, with fish available November through March. A small summer steelhead hatchery program here will probably be phased out due to budget concerns. At this time, summer steelhead are still present all summer, entering the river in May.

There's good access to the Kilchis. An improved public boat ramp, Park's Landing, is about 200 yds. above Hwy. 101 on Alderbrook Rd. The county maintains a picnic and recreational area about 5 miles from the mouth. Below the park, most land is private, but the owner allows access for a modest fee. Note the coin box at Curl Road Bridge. Above the park, the river flows through Tillamook State Forest. There is a landing at Mapes Creek, with the lowest take-out at Park's Landing. Supplies and accommodations are available in Tillamook.

Flood level on the Kilchis is 11 ft., with optimum fishing at 6 ft., and acceptable levels between 5.3 and 7 ft. The Kilchis runs approximately the same as the Wilson River. For a Wilson River gauge reading, call (503) 261-9246.

KLASKANINE RIVER A good cutthroat and winter steelhead stream, with a run of hatchery coho. Heading in the coast range west of Jewell, the Klaskanine flows about 20 miles into Young's Bay near Astoria. A paved road, Hwy. 202, follows the North Fork, and a gravel road follows the South Fork closely for several miles.

The Klaskanine provides good trout habitat with quite a few boulders and gravel bars, and some good but brushy holes that are best fished with bait. Cutthroat stocking program was discontinued after the 1993 season. Sea-run cutthroat return to the river in late August or early September, depending on the rainfall.

Steelhead begin showing in the mainstem in early December, and the fishing holds up through February. Good numbers are caught in the mainstem, with even better fishing in the north fork, and considerably smaller numbers caught in the south fork.

Salmon hatcheries on both north and south forks of the Klaskanine provide stock for the Young's Bay gillnet fishery. Jacks returning to the hatcheries have offered a lively sport fishery in the river, arriving in September and remaining through the winter. In 1993-94, however, all Columbia River tributaries were closed to salmon fishing, but since all coho in the Klaskanine are hatchery reared, there is a good chance that the fishery may be reopened.

A boat ramp at head of tide allows anglers to motor up about a half mile to access salmon when regulations allow. There is a 3/4 mile public access which begins at the first cement bridge above tidewater and continues (with the exception of two small private holdings) to the hatchery deadline. The North Fork is open for steelhead up to 200 feet below the salmon hatchery.

A road parallels the South Fork, but access to the stream is primarily owned by Cavenham Forest Industries, which has posted the land against public use due to abuse of the privilege in past years.

KLICKITAT LAKE A small lake in the headwaters of the North Fork of the Alsea River near the divide between Yaquina and Alsea. It has small wild cutthroat in abundance. It's shown on most maps as a landmark.

LAKE CREEK (Lane Co.) A very good winter steelhead stream. Lake Creek is a major tributary of the Siuslaw River, joining the Siuslaw at Swisshome. The Siuslaw River Rd. from the upper river joins Hwy. 36 about 42 miles west of Junction City. Lake Creek is followed by Hwy. 36 from just above Triangle Lake downstream to its mouth. It is an extremely clear stream, since Triangle Lake serves as a sediment trap. It really has to rain to muddy it up. A ladder at the falls just below Triangle Lake allows salmon to access an additional 100 miles of spawning ground.

A favorite of Eugene-Springfield drift fishermen, the creek has traditionally had a good winter steelhead run which picks up in December and holds steady into March. A couple hundred coho and chinook salmon are taken each fall.

Lake Creek also offers excellent trout fishing in its upper stretch. Heavily fished, it is stocked with cutthroat for the first few months of the season. The creek

Lake Lytle is lightly fished and may contain some surprises for bass and trout anglers.

above Triangle Lake near Blachly also offers good trout angling in early season.

There are drift boat put-ins at Green Creek, the mouth of Indian Creek, and near the mouth of Deadwood Creek. About 1/2 mile below the mouth of Green Creek is an area called The Horn that is extremely dangerous and should not be run by drift boats. Take out 1/4 mile above this area at the highway gravel pile site. Konnie Fishing Access below the Horn can be used for a good drift down to the take-out at Tide (about 4 miles).

The creek flows through a lot of private land, so beware of trespassing.

LEWIS AND CLARK RIVER A wild steelhead and cutthroat stream emptying into Young's Bay. It is reached from Astoria by way of Warrenton on the Miles crossing. A road follows the stream to its headwaters near Saddle Mt. From 50 to 75 feet wide in many places, the stream has some nice fly water.

A good winter steelhead run hits the river in December and remains through March. The river has a very weak coho run, and a modest number of chinook which enter the river near their spawning time and should not be disturbed. All non-finclipped steelhead must be released unharmed.

LILY LAKE (Lane Co.) A nice opportunity to fish for native cutthroat in a pretty meadow setting near the ocean. This small lake is located on the west side of Hwy. 101, about 10 miles north of Florence. Take Baker Beach Rd. to the trailhead (unsigned). A 1/4-mile trail leads to the lake.

Lily is lightly fished for its 14-inch cutthroat. This is the perfect place for a float tube, since the lake has a thick border of reeds that prohibits launching a boat. Managed by the US Forest Service, the lake is not stocked, and is restricted to catch and release angling with barbless hooks and artificial flies or lures.

LITTLE ELK RIVER A fair wild cutthroat stream, tributary of the Yaquina River, joining the Yaquina near Eddyville on Hwy. 20, the Newport-Corvallis Hwy. Only 11 miles long and fairly small, it is followed by Hwy. 20 upstream from Eddyville.

LOBSTER CREEK A good early-season trout stream, major tributary of Five Rivers, which it joins about 3 miles above the junction of Five Rivers with the Alsea at Hwy. 34. Lobster Creek is about 20 miles long. A good road follows the creek upstream from its mouth. It has a healthy wild cutthroat population and is a good bait fishing stream. It hosts a small run of wild steelhead and offers limited opportunities for fall chinook. Some coho may be present. The stream is open up to Little Lobster Creek.

LOST LAKE (Columbia County) Formerly a small beaver pond with native cutthroat in the headwaters of the Clatskanie River, it was truly lost when its beaver dams were destroyed by persons unknown. Too bad.

LOST LAKE (Elsie area) A 15-acre rainbow lake east of Spruce Run Park on the Nehalem River. There is a steep logging road running east up Spruce Run Creek to the lake's north end, about 4-5 miles. It has been somewhat improved in recent years and is car accessible.

The lake is on private land and is sometimes blocked in spring by windfalls. The water is 20 feet deep at the deepest spot in the center of the north end. Rainbow fingerlings are stocked periodically, and some reach good size. Some-carry over fish of decent size are also available.

It's a fairly popular lake, but angling success tapers off after the first months of spring. It's difficult to get a boat in the water, but quite a few anglers troll, with spinner and worms favored. A few people fish it late in summer and get sizable fish on flies and bait. Small live crayfish fished near the bottom have produced some big ones. It's pretty snaggy, so bring plenty of tackle.

LOST LAKE (Lane Co.) An early season trout lake, covering 6 acres, just east of Hwy. 101 about mid-way between Tahkenitch and Siltcoos lakes. The dirt access road off Hwy. 101 just south of

Carter Lake is now closed to cars, but anglers can park off the highway and walk in.

A good early season lake, it is stocked with rainbow in spring and has some resident cutthroat. Fishing slacks off when the water warms. Boats can be slipped in (no ramp) but are not necessary to fish this narrow water. There are campgrounds north and south on Hwy. 101.

LOST LAKE (Westport Area) A small private lake with some bass, about 2 miles SW of Westport. A gravel road leads from Westport to the lake. It provides some early fishing for local anglers with permission from the owners.

LYTLE LAKE A 65-acre coast lake with both bass and trout. Lytle is located just north of Rockaway on the east side of Hwy. 101. It is connected to Crescent Lake. Lytle is shallow and prone to heavy weed growth. Since it is lightly fished, it might contain some surprises.

It contains both rainbow and cutthroat and is stocked in early spring. The largemouth bass fishery is catch and release only. Crappie are present in small numbers. Trout fishing is best in spring and early summer, bass in summer and fall.

Facilities include a public boat ramp off 12th St. on the NE shore with ample parking, and a public dock and along the highway shoulder. Supplies, facilities, and services are available in Rockaway.

MAGRUDER SLOUGH A good warmwater fishery on the lower Columbia River. Magruder is located on Hwy. 30 about 3 miles east of Westport and is about 5 miles long. Most surrounding land is private, but bank fishing permission is usually given. County roads and bridges also provide access. Car-top boats can be launched in a few spots.

This is primarily a still-fishing show due to heavy vegetation. Crappie and bullhead are numerous. Bluegill, perch, and a few bass are also present.

MAPLE CREEK A fair wild cutthroat stream about 10 miles long, flowing into Siltcoos Lake from the NE. A county road parallels the stream to near its source. It can be reached from Hwy. 101 by several county roads in the vicinity of Siltcoos Lake. The creek provides fair native cutthroat in early season, and has a some largemouth bass near the mouth. It flows through private property, so ask permission before you approach the stream.

MARIE LAKE (Tillamook Co.) A little pothole just .6 acre at Twin Rocks, east of Hwy. 101. It contains largemouth bass.

MAYGER SLOUGH A Columbia River slough 3 miles NW of Downing, east of Crimm's Island. It contains white crappie and bluegill.

MERCER LAKE A good trout lake with lots of big, wily bass. Mercer covers over 340 acres east of Hwy. 101, about 5 miles north of Florence. A county road leads from the highway around the south shore.

Though plentiful, Mercer's largemouth are reputed to be very difficult to catch. The local bass clubs like to fish the lake at night, but their success rate has been less than exceptional. The areas around the Mercer Creek outlet and the inlet creeks in the upper arms are worth a try.

There are several species of panfish in the lake, with yellow perch and small bluegills predominant. Perch to 14 inches are caught from bank and boat. Try fishing around the docks.

The lake is stocked with good numbers of rainbow each spring. Not heavily fished, it provides some good trout fishing from early spring well into the summer. Larger carry-over trout are available in fall.

Mercer has a brushy shore that makes bank angling difficult. There is a resort on the lake where supplies and rental boats are available. The resort boat ramp is closed to general public use, but there is a public ramp about 2 1/2 miles around the lake. There are no campgrounds on Mercer.

MIAMI RIVER A good coastal river offering a variety of fishing. Only about 14 miles long, entering Tillamook Bay just east of Garibaldi, it has a good native cutthroat population, as well as fall chinook, winter steelhead, chum salmon, and coho. The river can be reached from Foley Creek Rd. upstream, and from Hwy. 101 near the lower end. A good road parallels the stream. The most popular stretch flows through agricultural land.

A fair steelhead run peaks early in January, and a run of larger steelhead (12-18 pounds) comes in late February and early March.

The forest stretch above the old mill, about 5 miles above Hwy. 101, is particularly good for early steelheading.

There is a fair fall chinook run, and coho are present in late October, though the fishery for them is closed. The Miami and nearby Kilchis River share the distinction of having the largest chum salmon runs on the Oregon coast. However, these populations are now greatly diminished, and fishing for chum is currently limited to a brief catch and release season from mid-September to mid-November. Check current regulations for exact dates. Chum are caught using normal drift fishing techniques with eggs, corkies, and small spinners (green lures are preferred by most anglers). Fly fishing for these big fish in the less congested areas is a real kick.

Much of the lower river is posted. Flood level on the Miami is similar to that of the Wilson River, 11 ft. Optimum fishing is at 6 ft., and acceptable levels are between 5.3 and 7 ft. Use the Wilson River as a gauge to determine the status of the Miami. For a gauge reading, call (503) 261-9246.

MIDDLE LAKE (Clatsop Co.) Prominent on maps, this lake is located in the headwaters of Bear Creek in the Astoria watershed and is not open to the public.

MILES LAKE A small lake just west of the road between Woods, on the lower Nestucca, and Sand Lake, several miles north of Woods. Under private ownership at present, it contains rainbow trout and catfish.

MUNSEL LAKE A good trout and bass lake of about 93 acres, quite deep, and lightly fished. It is located about 2 1/2 miles north of Florence and about one mile east of Hwy. 101. A paved road leads to the lake.

Don't be fooled by the clarity of the water. There are plenty of fish here. Trout fishing is good in the spring and holds up well into summer. Munsel is stocked with legal rainbow and brook trout each season and has a good native cutthroat population, with an occasional stocking of brood trout to 5 pounds. Most anglers troll. A brushy shoreline limits bank fishing.

Big largemouth bass (to 7 pounds) have been taken on plugs and lures. Try the creek inlet to the north, and around the docks. There's also a good population of yellow perch. There is a county boat ramp at the lake, and campgrounds about 4 miles north on Hwy. 101.

NEACOXIE LAKE (a.k.a. Sunset Lake) See Sunset Lake.

NECANICUM RIVER A very pretty stream, about 22 miles long, flowing into the Pacific at Seaside. Heading near Saddle Mt. west of Elsie, it is paralleled by paved roads through Coast Range forest for most of its length. It can be reached from the south by Hwy. 53 in the Nehalem area, and from the north by Hwy. 101.

There's a lot of private land in the lower end, but it's fairly easy to fish at many points above. It can get very low in summer but is a good drift river in winter.

A hatchery run of winter steelhead begins appearing in November, depending on water levels, and peaks in December or January. There is also a pretty good fishery for wild steelhead (catch and release) in February and March.

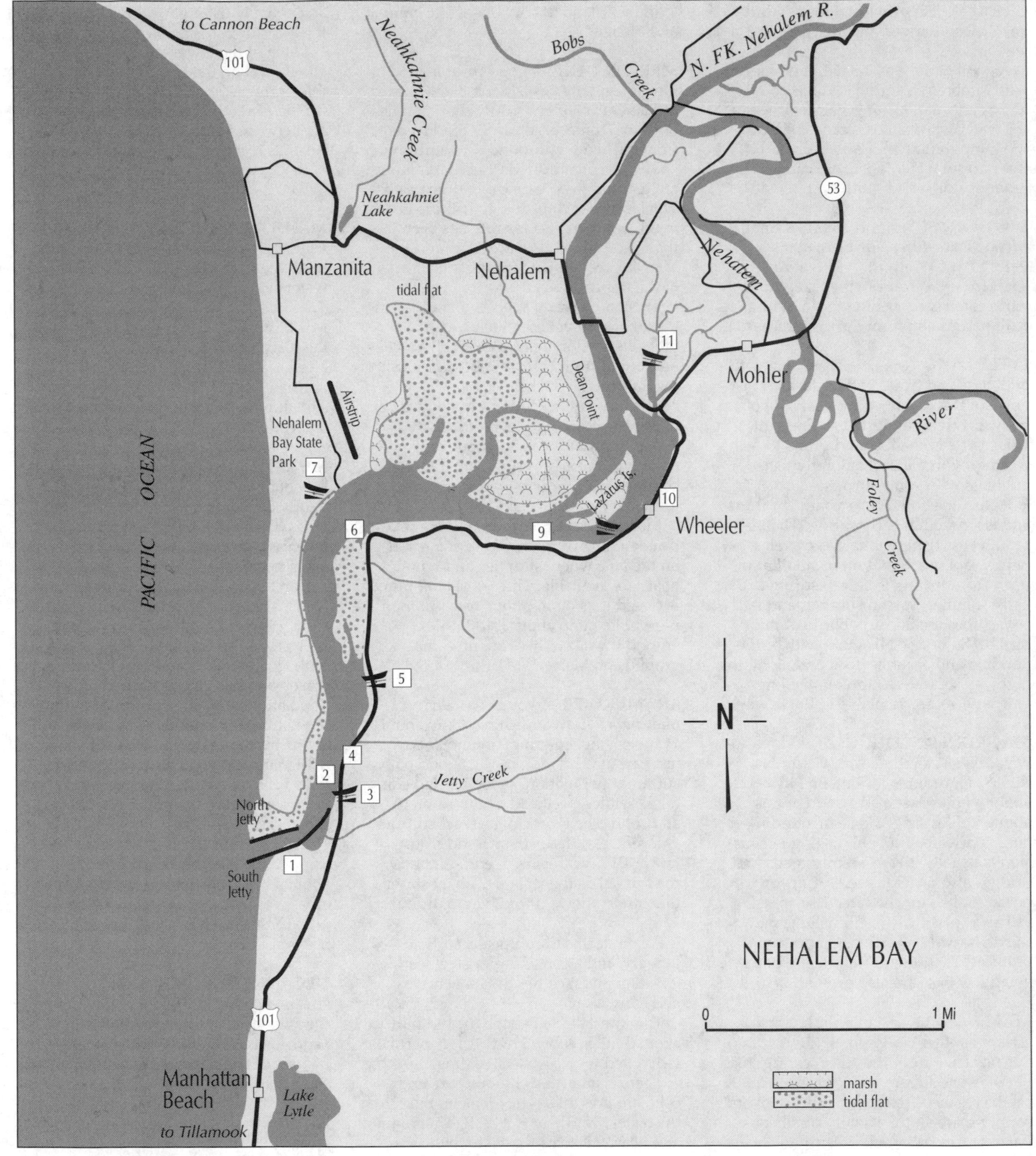

1 SOUTH JETTY - Popular fishery for perch, rockfish, greenling, salmon in fall; access from beach or at Jetty Fishery.

2 LOWER CHANNEL - Anchor and fish for perch, rockfish, greenling; troll for salmon; crab year-round

3 JETTY FISHERY - Public boat ramp; jetty access.

4 HWY. 101 ROCKS - Frequent pull-offs access rocks for pile perch.

5 BRIGHTON MOORAGE - Public boat ramp.

6 FISHERY PT. - Downstream boundary for coho; fish up to forks.

7 NEHALEM BAY STATE PARK - Boat ramp, picnic area, camping.

8 MUD FLATS - Good softshell clam bed; short walk from end of Bayside Gardens Rd. to flats.

9 UPPER BAY - Troll for salmon, sea-run cutthroat.

10 WHEELER MARINA - Public boat ramp.

11 COUNTY BOAT RAMP

The Necanicum has a fair native cutthroat population, augmented by hatchery stocking. The hatchery fish are stocked before trout season opens to give them a head start on getting out to sea. A fair number return, plump and feisty, in late August. There is some good fly water in the lower stream above tidewater, and fly fishing for sea-run cutthroat in late summer can be terrific. Bait and spinner seem to work best on the hatchery trout.

A fall chinook fishery is being nursed along by local anglers, who rear the chinook in private ponds, then release them after 4-5 months. A fall chinook fishery in tidewater is open at this time.

Summer steelhead and coho are also present in small numbers.

There is very little public opportunity for bank fishing. Some anglers fly fish for steelhead from the 12th Avenue Bridge. Most streamside land is privately owned, so be sure to ask permission before you approach the stream.

Most anglers drift the river. Boats can be put in at Clootchie Creek County Park (home of the big Sitka Spruce off Hwy. 26), Johnson's Rock Pit near the Hwy. 101 Bridge, an ODF&W access above the golf course just south of Seaside off Hwy. 101, in Seaside next to the School District Administration Office, and just north of Broadway in Seaside.

Rental boats are available at a number of Nehalem Bay moorages.

NEHALEM BAY The first bay south of Cape Falcon, fourth largest on the Oregon coast, with fair fishing both in the bay and offshore. To reach Nehalem Bay from Portland, drive west on Hwy. 26, then turn south on Hwy. 101. Or take Hwy. 6 to Tillamook, then Hwy. 101 north about 23 miles. It takes about 1 1/2 hrs. to reach the bay from Portland. Tidewater extends up to Eck Creek on the main Nehalem.

Angling activity in spring and early summer focuses on bottom and surf fish. Good size perch, rockfish, and greenling, and an infrequent flounder, are taken on shrimp, clam necks, and kelp worms. Good catches are made from the south jetty and from the rocks off Hwy. 101. Best fishing is on the incoming tide. Anglers also anchor and fish for these species in the lower channel, but be wary of frequently rough conditions in the lower bay. Fishing the surf for perch from beaches north and south of the bar can be excellent.

In early summer salmon appear at the Nehalem bar. The Nehalem bar can be very dangerous, especially in high winds. Check with local moorage operators or the Coast Guard for a condition update.

Salmon stay outside the bay until late summer.

Jack salmon are the first to enter after the early fall rains. They are taken on cluster eggs, small lures, and spinners. Adult chinook enter sometimes as early as August, followed by a small run of coho. In 1993, the bay experienced one of its best ever chinook seasons.

In 1994, ocean salmon sport regulations permitted fishing for chinook salmon off the Nehalem Bar, though the coho fishery was closed here as elsewhere on the Oregon coast. Emergency closures in the bay itself included a complete closure on coho fishing throughout the bay, and on chinook fishing in the lower bay (below Fishery Point) from June 20 through August 15. Salmon are caught in the bay until November. Early season catches are near the mouth, then the run moves upstream. Bay anglers generally troll with spinners, herring, or Kwikfish-type lures.

Crabbing is generally good in summer and fall. Most seem to leave with the freshets in winter and spring, but some good catches are made even in late winter if you don't mind the cold. Best crabbing is in the lower channel. Rings and bait are available at most moorages. Softshell clams are easily dug in the flats about 3 miles up from the mouth. Follow Bayside Gardens Rd. to the dead end. There are about 400 acres of digging flats here. There are other small flats along both sides of the river, but the best spot is the large cove across from Wheeler. There is also a small local fishery in the bay for sturgeon.

Several moorages offer boat rentals, tackle, bait, and other supplies from Brighton upstream to Wheeler. Nehalem Bay State Park, just south of Manzanita, has pleasant sites for trailers and tents, picnic area, boat ramp, bike trails, and ocean access. There is also an airstrip within the park.

NEHALEM RIVER A good steelhead, salmon, and cutthroat stream, third longest river on the Oregon coast. It flows over 100 miles, entering Nehalem Bay at the town of Nehalem, easily reached from any direction. Now managed for wild fish, the river was last stocked with hatchery-reared cutthroat in 1993, and with hatchery-reared steelhead in 1994. The hatchery fish apparently never made up much of the total catch despite the effort and expense devoted to getting them into the river.

The Lower Nehalem River Rd. follows the river from Nehalem Bay to Elsie. County Rd. 202 follows the upper river through Jewell, Birkenfeld, Mist, Pittsburg, and Vernonia. It is crossed twice by Hwy. 26.

A large stream, heavily fished and accessible, it is close to both the coast and to the Portland area. Popular with steelheaders and salmon anglers, it's also an excellent cutthroat stream. Large cutthroat are taken in the lower river throughout the season.

Although most Nehalem salmon catches are made in the bay, there is a small summer chinook run that is lightly fished here in June and July. Coho are present from late September on, but the river is closed to coho fishing. Chinook jacks show up in August and are fished from Nehalem Falls down.

Steelheading on the Nehalem takes place from December through March, with best fishing often in March. The best steelhead water is in the lower 13-14 miles, and most is accessible only by boat. There is some plunking water at Roy Creek Park, and some good bank access at Falls County Park. The east bank of the productive Salmonberry Riffle has been closed to access by the

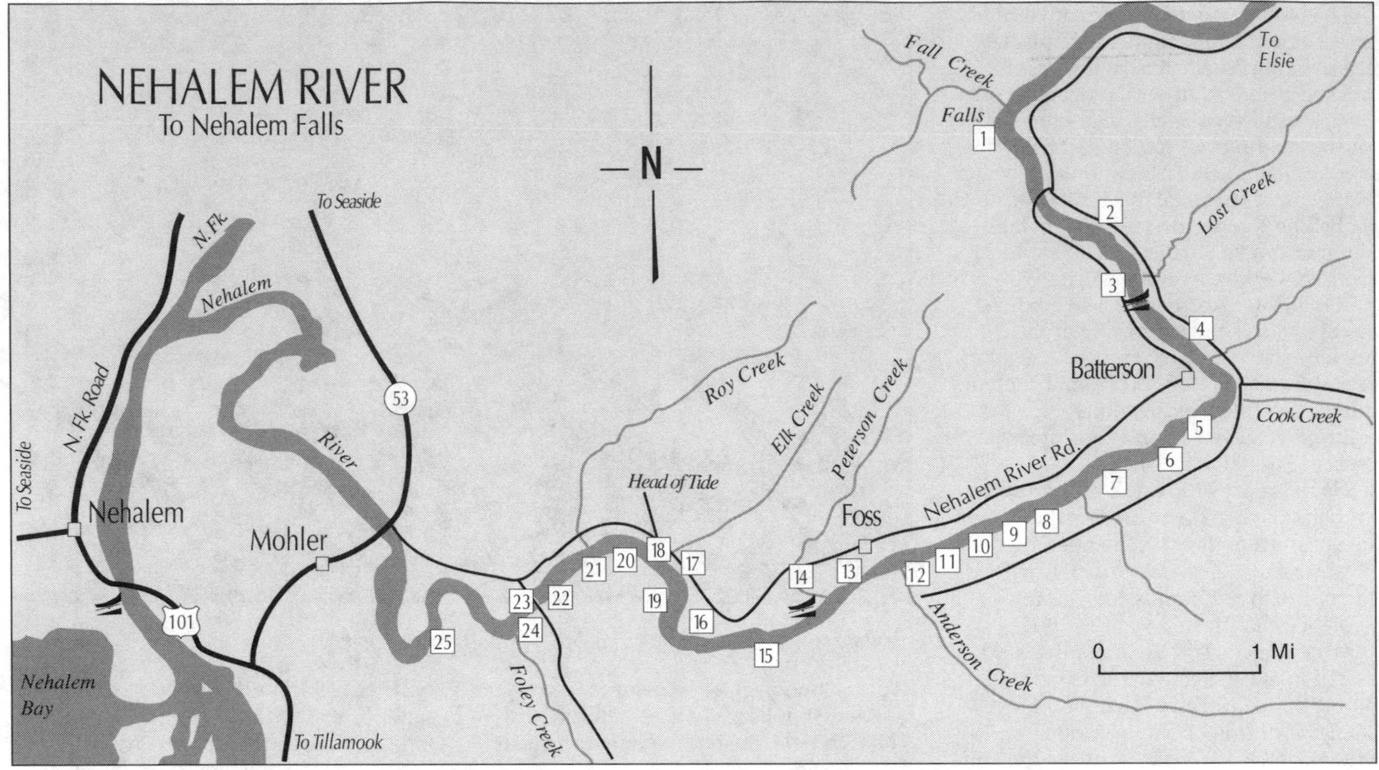

1 **NEHALEM FALLS** -Good bank access at County Park; good holes & drifts upstream are often far apart; limited boating above this point; don't boat the falls.

2 **LOST CREEK HOLE** - Nothing between here and the next one except for pros; big boulders, some fish in pockets.

3 **BEAVER SLIDE** - Put-in only; slide drift boats down bank; park adjacent to county road.

4 **SACRIFICE HOLE** - A real tackle snatcher but a good producer.

5 **BATTERSON RIFFLES** - Overhead pipeline about 2/3 way down.

6 **ROCK HOLE** - Strictly for plunking.

7 **CATTLE GUARD HOLE** - Plunker's paradise, both banks; drifters down the middle.

8 **STONE HILL HOLE** - Good drifting; brushy banks.

9 **CLOVER PATCH HOLE** - Excellent for plunking during high water; good drifting in low water; good drift water between here and Lindsay.

10 **LINDSAY RIFFLE** - Best for plunkers; still eddy on north side holds fish; drift upper end at low water.

11 **ANDERSON CREEK HOLE** - Fish lie along south bank; boat drift only.

12 **FOSS DRIFT** - Fish below at piling close to brush.

13 **FREEZEOUT HOLE** - Sun never shines here, plunkers; pretty water, drifters.

14 **MOHLER SAND & GRAVEL** - Gravel bar put-in or take-out; park along county road.

15 **UPPER WINSLOW DRIFT** - Long straight gravel bar drift; better slow down going through here.

16 **WINSLOW DRIFT** - Doesn't look as good as it is, though holding fewer fish than in days gone by.

17 **ROCK CRUSHER DRIFT**

18 **TWILIGHT HOLE** - Watch for jacks right after first fall rains, Sept. through Oct.

19 **MIDDLE EASOM DRIFT** - Slow water from here on down.

20 **EASOM DRIFT** - Just below big rock.

21 **WALKER HOLE** - Right across from Roy Creek.

22 **FENCE HOLE** - Good August, September fly-fishing for cutthroat.

23 **STUMP HOLE** - Another good cutthroat spot early and late in day.

24 **FOLEY CREEK DRIFT** - Drift boats fish NW side; plunkers access from south bank.

25 **LIVERPOOL** - Plunking in tidewater.

landowner, but anglers can still fish it from the west bank. There is also bank access at Foley Creek and Batterson Riffles.

Drift boats are popular on the lower river, where there are two boat ramps. One is at Roy Creek, a rough ramp about 3 miles upstream from Nehalem. The other is the Beaver Slide below Lost Creek on the county road about 100 yards downstream from the State Forest Guard Station. Best boating is below Beaver Slide. There are additional ramps in tidewater at Wheeler and at Nehalem below the bridge. Flood level on the Nehalem is 13 ft. Best drift fishing is at 4.5 ft, with acceptable levels between 4 ft. and 5.2 ft. Plunkers do well with the river as high as 9 ft. A river gauge reading for the Nehalem is available by calling the National Weather Service Forecast Office in Portland at (503) 261-9246.

Accommodations and supplies are available in the Nehalem Bay area. Watch for well-marked closure regulations at Nehalem Falls about 2 miles above Cook Creek.

NEHALEM RIVER, EAST FORK A small stream about 12 miles long. It is only a fair bait stream for wild cutthroat. It flows into the Nehalem at Pittsburg, 2 miles north of Vernonia. A good road parallels the stream, and very little is private posted land. It can also be reached from Scappoose by the county road to Pittsburg.

NEHALEM RIVER, NORTH FORK A good salmon and steelhead stream. It is followed for about 7 miles NW by Hwy. 53. From that point a gravel road parallels the stream to the east. This private road is not open to cars, but anglers are welcome to walk in. The upper stream can be reached by road from Hamlet.

The North Fork is about 24 miles long and carries a good flow. The upper stream has good spawning gravel, and the lower stretch is a productive mix of boulder and gravel with rich feeder streams such as Coal Creek and Soapstone Creek.

Cutthroat offer good fishing in early spring, late summer, and fall. Sea-run are in tidewater from July until the rains come. A healthy wild fall chinook run appears in August and is present through November. Jack salmon are available in September and October. A good run of hatchery-reared coho usually appears in early November, followed by steelhead in December. The hatchery coho fishery was still open in 1994, but may be closed in the future. Check current regulations and watch for seasonal updates, or call the district ODF&W office for an update. A hatchery on the North Fork produces steelhead and coho for the river. A wheelchair facility at the hatchery offers excellent opportunities to catch steelhead in an area that is closed to the general public. Two ladders at the falls allow fish to access the upper river. Fish at least 200 feet away from the ladders.

There are two boat accesses on the North Fork. A private ramp located just below the county line at river mile 6 allows a drift to the second ramp at head of tide. To make arrangements for a car shuttle, call the operator of the private ramp at (503) 368-5365. Experienced boaters who have scouted the river and

1 **UPPER TIDEWATER** - Troll for fall chinook, sea-run Aug.-Oct.; bank fishing at county park.

2 **NESTUCCA RAMP** - Small gravel public ramp beside sporting goods store 2 mi. from Hwy. 101 on pacific City Loop; limited parking; drift down or motor up for fall chinook, sea-run.

3 **PACIFIC CITY RAMP** - Improved public ramp 2 mi. north of town; accesses lower bay; traditional Airport Hole has shifted to ramp side of river; good fishery for fall chinook; small early spring chinook fishery.

4 **TROLL** mid-bay for fall chinook.

5 **FISHER LANDING** - Unimproved public ramp; bank angling from parking area slightly down bay for fall chinook (Guardrail Hole) Aug.-Oct.; limited parking.

6 **CANNERY HILL** - lower deadline for coho fishing during emergency closure.

7 **MOUTH OF LITTLE NESTUCCA** - Fish for perch, sea-run, greenling in channel off rocky point; accessible by boat only.

8 **LITTLE NESTUCCA FLATS** - Softshell flats; marker on road indicates access trail; limited parking.

9 **SOFTSHELL FLATS** - Best digging on the bay for softshell clams; mostly boat access.

10 **LITTLE NESTUCCA CHANNEL** - Troll for fall chinook, sea-run, occasional perch in lower reach.

11 **MOUTH OF BAY** - Can be productive but dangerous boat fishery for fall chinook, perch, greenling, crab; bank fishery accessed by hiking through park.

12 **LITTLE NESTUCCA/101 RAMP**- Improved ramp; bank access from bridge upstream; fish for fall chinook Aug.-Oct., sea-run July-Sept.

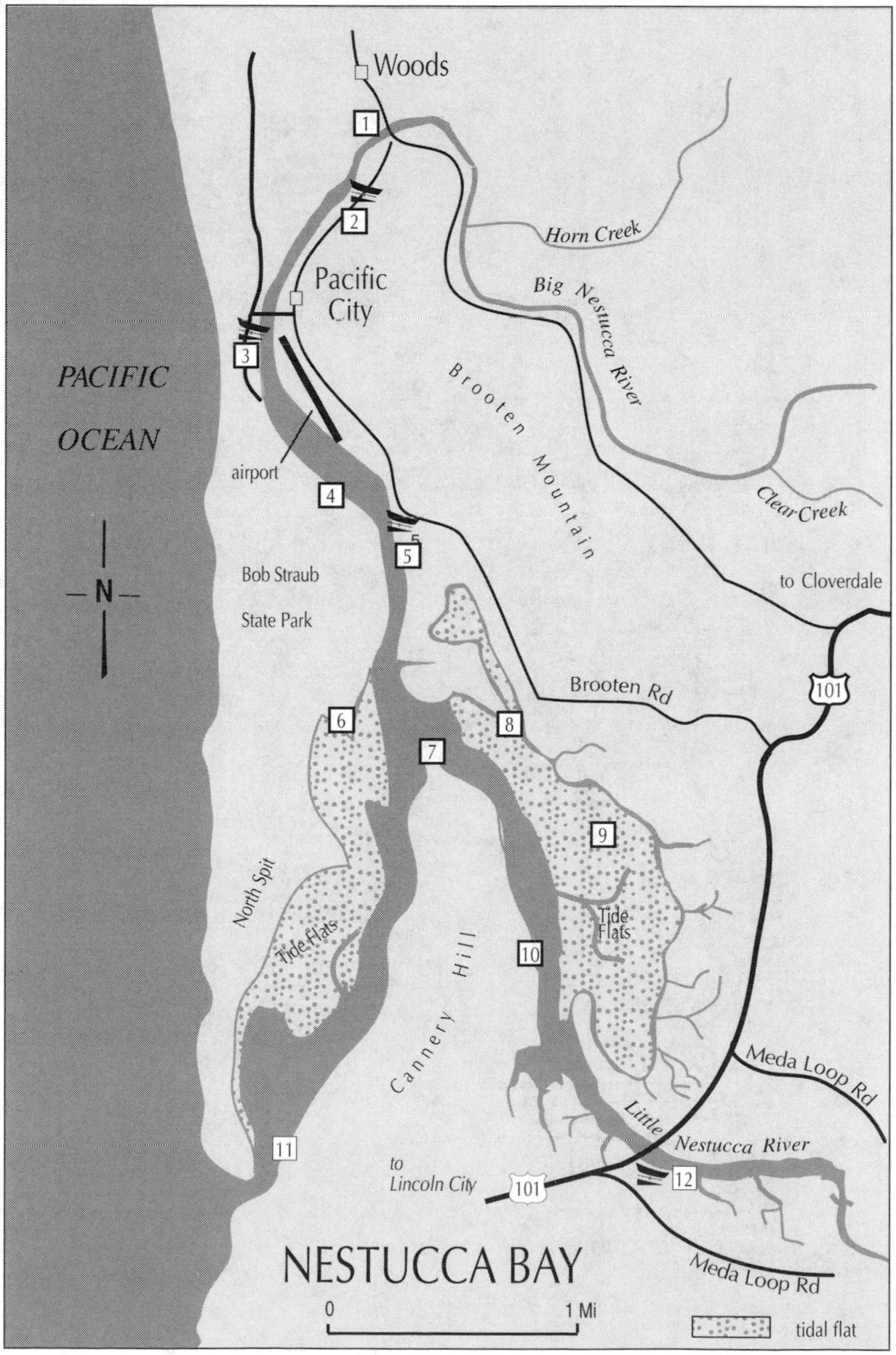

NESTUCCA BAY

Woods
Pacific City
PACIFIC OCEAN
airport
Horn Creek
Big Nestucca River
Brooten Mountain
Clear Creek
to Cloverdale
Bob Straub State Park
Brooten Rd
101
North Spit
Tide Flats
Cannery Hill
Meda Loop Rd
Little Nestucca River
to Lincoln City
0 1 Mi
tidal flat

Nestucca River

©Ron Blogett

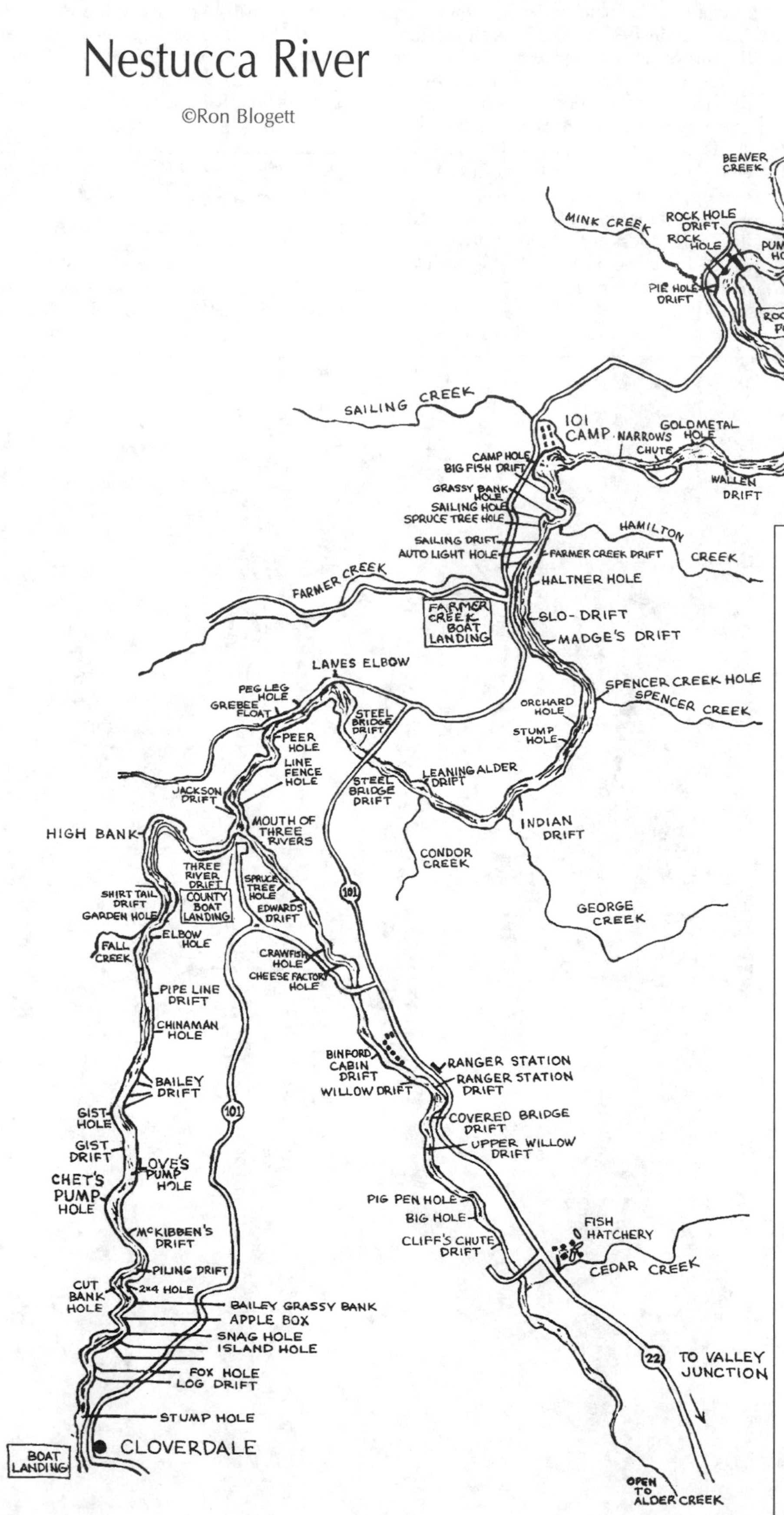

are prepared for some significant whitewater may also put in at the hatchery.

NESKOWIN CREEK (a.k.a. Slab Creek) A fair coastal cutthroat stream about 7 miles long, entering the ocean at Neskowin, about 4 miles south of Nestucca Bay. Hwy. 101 follows most of the stream up from Neskowin.

A closure on salmon and steelhead fishing in the creek has recently been lifted to allow catch and release angling with barbless hooks. Check the current regulations for complete information.

There is a Forest Service campground about 5 miles south of Neskowin. Supplies and accommodations are available in town.

NESTUCCA BAY Created by the Big Nestucca coming in from the NW and the Little Nestucca from the SW, forming a wishbone shaped tidal area that offers a variety of bay fisheries. Just 20 miles south of Tillamook by way of Hwy. 101, it's a quick trip here from the Willamette Valley. Because it's a very shallow bay, boaters must be alert to depth and tide, or find themselves high and dry on the flats at ebb. The water deepens above Pacific City.

Fall chinook are the primary salmon fishery here. The coho fishery (always small in Nestucca Bay) has been closed, and spring chinook seem to high-tail it once they turn in from the Pacific and are best fished in the rivers in June and July. Fall chinook are present in August and September. Anglers drift and float eggs, and use herring or trolled spinners. Bobber fishing with eggs is also productive. The Airport Hole, across from the

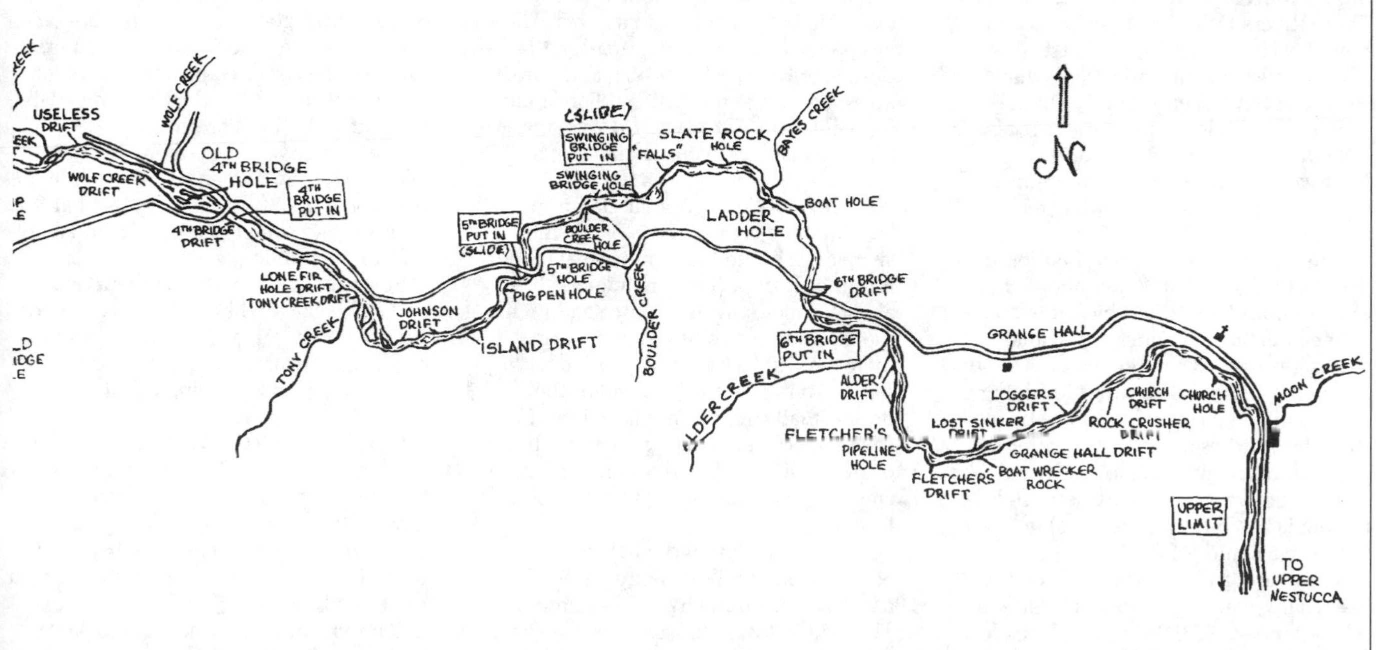

airport below the Pacific City boat ramp, is a popular spot in the upper bay. There's also good trolling mid-bay. Lower bay trollers need to be wary of tide conditions and rough water. Bank anglers can fish for chinook at the Guardrail Hole at Fisher Landing, an unimproved public ramp south of Pacific City off Brooten Rd. It is also possible to bank fish the mouth of the bay by hiking the north spit through Bob Straub State Park.

In 1994, salmon fishing in the lower bay (below Cannery Hill) was limited by an emergency closure. All salmon fishing was prohibited seaward from Cannery Hill from June 20 through August 15. After August 15, the entire bay re-opened for chinook.

Perch are available in the shallows of the lower bay and in the Little Nestucca Channel, and surf fishing for perch is good anytime off the beach at Bob Straub State Park. For perch, time your fishing to the tide. Off the beaches, fish the incoming tide. Inside the bay, fish the last two hours of high tide. Greenling are also available near the mouth and at the mouth of the Little Nestucca.

Sea-run cutthroat make an appearance in late summer, and there is a small fishery for them in the upper tidewater. Large spinner and bait combinations seem to work best. Trolled Kwikfish-type lures also produce. Crab can be taken in the lower deep areas of the bay. Steelhead pass through the bay but are primarily caught in the rivers.

The best softshell clamming in the bay is on the Little Nestucca Flats just off Brooten Rd., about 2 miles south of Pacific City. Almost any minus tide exposes the beds, and since you can't get out to fish the bay then anyway, you might as well dig in.

There is a novel summer fishery off Cape Kiwanda just north of Pacific City. A fleet of dories launches from the beach and fishes 6-7 miles off shore. The skill of the dory operators is legendary, and their catch rate is very high for chinook, lingcod, snapper, and halibut. Even if you don't go out yourself, it's interesting to watch the dories break through the surf. A good road leads to the dory launching area. It should be noted that launching through the surf should not be attempted by novices. Charter dory rides may be available.

Supplies, facilities, and good advice are available in Pacific City. There's a gravel boat ramp beside the sporting goods store in town, and another public ramp a couple of miles south of town. You can also launch at Fisher Landing off Brooten Rd. and at the Little Nestucca Ramp off Meda Loop Rd.

If you are a flyer, the airport is less than 100 yards from the estuary, with marinas within walking distance. Its only an 1,800 ft. strip, so be sharp. Best approach is from the south.

NESTUCCA RIVER (a.k.a. Big Nestucca) A real gem of an all-around stream. This big river flows 55 miles and runs 50-100 ft. wide in the lower stretch. Easily accessed, it is crossed and followed by Hwy. 101 from Pacific City to Beaver. County Rd. 858 follows the river upstream from Beaver into the Siuslaw National Forest. From inland, the Nestucca can be reached by a direct road west from Carlton.

Though the sea-run cutthroat population is down in all coastal streams, the Netucca's run is holding its own. Hatchery cutthroat are no longer stocked, but there is still a small fishery for sea-run in August as high up as river mile 25. The Nestucca is rich in natural feed, so rigged bait must appear natural to tempt the fish here.

A nice run of spring chinook starts in late May with the peak in June and July. The bigger fall chinook and coho runs begin in late August. The salmon remain in tidewater until the fall rains and reach the upper river in October. Even after the rains, the majority of anglers fish the river below Hebo, since the salmon population thins out above Three Rivers and Beaver Creek. In 1994, the river was subject to an emergency closure on all coho fishing.

Steelhead are in the river year-round. Scrappy 4-7 pound hatchery-reared summer steelhead appear in tidewater in April, and by August they seemed almost nose to tail in some years throughout a 20-mile section of the river. The return of summer steelhead continues to be excellent, and the winter run is even larger. Anglers tempt them with all types of lures, flies, and bait. Crayfish tails and sand shrimp were traditional favorites, but with current regulations requiring release of all non-finclipped steelhead, bait (though legal) is not advised during the winter season. Barbless hooks are required December 1 through March 31. Fish the deep holes and stay out of sight if fishing from the bank. Morning and evening, when the sun is not on the water, are the best times.

Bank anglers pick fish out of even murky water here. There's bank access to the Cottonwood Hole, Pipeline Hole, Three Rivers Drift, Orchard Hole, and Lone Fir Hole. There are at least 40 well known holes, drifts, and riffles where steelhead have been known to linger.

The river is closed to all angling above Elk Creek. Most tributaries of the Nestucca are closed to all angling. At this time, only Beaver Creek and Three Rivers are open.

The Nestucca offers good boating from the 4th bridge down. Water above the bridge should be drifted by knowledgeable boaters only. Guides are available. Boating is ideal when the water is about 3 feet above normal summer level. For best results, the river should not be too clear. It muddies quite rapidly after a good hard rain and doesn't clear quickly. Flood level on the Nestucca is 18 ft. Best fishing is at 4.5 ft, with acceptable levels between 3.6 and 5.4 ft. A river gauge reading can be obtained by calling the National Weather Service Forecast Office in Portland at (503) 261-9246. Check local tackle shops for an update on the progress of the runs.

Tillamook County, the Dept. of Fish and Wildlife, the Highway Dept., and local sportsmen have all pitched in to make launching places available. There are public boat ramps at Pacific City, Cloverdale, Three Rivers, and Farmer Creek and put-ins (more and less developed) upriver.

There's a campground at Castle Rock on Three Rivers, and two camps 14 and 17 miles upstream from Beaver. Several boat rentals and moorages are available in tidewater. Accommodations and supplies are plentiful from Beaver to the mouth.

NESTUCCA RIVER, LITTLE A fair winter steelhead stream. The Little Nestucca enters the Big Nestucca one mile above the ocean near Oretown, about 3 miles south of Pacific City. It heads in Yamhill County and flows past the community of Dolph on Hwy. 22, from which point a road follows the stream closely down to its mouth. No longer stocked, this is a good native cutthroat stream.

The Little Nestucca has a fall chinook run which usually returns in October with the rains. Some coho also show in October. Steelhead peak in December and January and are taken in good but reduced numbers since the stocking program is being phased out. All non-finclipped steelhead must be released unharmed. Use barbless hooks December 1 through March 31.

Formerly open for steelhead to its headwaters, the river is now closed above the Forest Service bridge at Dolph. All tributaries of the Little Nestucca are closed to all angling.

Supplies and accommodations are available in the Nestucca Bay area. There is a public access area with parking facilities at the Hwy. 101 crossing, and bank access continues on National Forest land for 3 miles up. The Hwy. 101 crossing is a popular place for bank casting.

NETARTS BAY A popular clamming and crabbing area. Netarts Bay is the sixth largest in the state in total area, but it is of little importance to anglers. It is about 7 miles long and quite shallow for the most part, with few channel areas more than 10 feet deep at high tide. No major rivers feed the bay, and of the dozen small streams that flow into it from the east, none harbor many salmon or steelhead. The bay does offer good crabbing and clamming opportunities, however.

It's a quick hour and a half run to Netarts from the Willamette Valley. The bay is about 4 miles SW of Tillamook. The road follows the bay's eastern shore.

Netarts is one of five major crabbing bays on the Oregon coast. As in all bays, the winter rush of fresh water draws crab out into the open sea. They usually return in September, October, and November. In low-water years, good catches of crab are taken in the bay year around. Both dungeness and red rock crab are found in Netarts. Crab rings and bait are available for rent, but you'll need a boat, as there are no piers here.

Clamming is really the main attraction at Netarts, with many good flats. The big flat off the spit at Cape Lookout State Park and the little flat on the north bayshore near the mouth yield tremendous numbers of cockle, butter, gaper, and littleneck clams and a few razors. Whiskey Creek Flats and Wilson Beach are less productive but worthwhile. Moorage operators make trips to these flats when the tides are favorable and will help you get started. Check current regulations for catch limits.

Kelp greenling and tomcod are caught in the bay from time to time. The north end and the area known as the Boiler Hole, just south of the county boat launch, are good for perch at times.

For these and other bottomfish, sand shrimp, clam necks, or kelp worms are good bait and can be purchased locally. Wind a few turns of pink thread or strands of fluorescent yarn around your baited hook to better secure it.

In summer and fall there are always a few bottom fish caught, but nothing exceptional. In October and November a few coho and chum salmon enter the bay, but Netarts is closed to angling for either species.

Netarts is a safe bay for family fun, as the water is so shallow that boat accidents are rare. Stay away from the Netarts bar, though, which is shallow and rough, a good spot to flip a boat if you are inexperienced. Veteran boaters do cross the bar in calm weather to fish the reef beyond Arch Rocks for rockfish, halibut, and other bottom fish.

A word of warning—there are a number of privately owned oyster beds in the bay. These are off-limits to public harvest. There are no oyster beds in Oregon available to the public.

Several outlets on the bay rent boats and sell tackle and bait. There is a good county boat ramp and motel accommodations in Netarts. Lookout State Park, just south, offers camping facilities.

OLALLA RESERVOIR A 120-acre reservoir on Olalla Creek, tributary to the Yaquina, a few miles east of Toledo. Owned by Georgia Pacific, it is open to public fishing for its bass, panfish, and trout. It can be accessed from Toledo by a road off Hwy. 20

Rainbow and cutthroat are stocked, with average catch 10 inches and some to 14 inches. Largemouth bass, brown bullhead, and bluegill are also in residence. The largemouth bass are in the mid-size range, but they are plentiful and a popular local fishery. Sportsmen have added submerged timber to the reservoir to provide additional bass habitat. There's a boat ramp on the lake, but motors are prohibited.

PEBBLE CREEK A small tributary of the upper Nehalem, entering the river from the south at Vernonia. About 13 miles long, it is followed closely by roads. It is a fair early-season cutthroat stream but doesn't hold up long and is not stocked.

PERKINS LAKE A 5-acre coastal lake stocked with rainbow, about 10 miles south of Florence. the lake is just west of Hwy. 101 and a few miles north of Tahkenitch Lake. Park on the old Hwy. 101 shoulder. You can bank fish or launch a small boat from the old road along the north shore of the lake. It's very brushy around the shoreline, so a boat or float tube is helpful.

Some good catches are made fishing bait early in the season. Fly angling can pay off later when angling pressure drops. Large trout are sometimes taken. There's a campground at Carter Lake about one mile north.

PLYMPTON CREEK A small creek with native cutthroat, tributary to the Columbia in the vicinity of Puget Island. Its mouth is near Westport on Hwy. 30. About 8 miles long, it heads near Nicolai Mt. and offers fair trout fishing in early season in stretches away from the road. The creek is closed to angling for salmon and steelhead, which enter the creek dark and ready to spawn. Do not disturb them.

PRESCOTT SLOUGH A 9-acre Columbia River slough off Hwy. 30 west of the decommissioned Trojan Nuclear Power Plant, featuring a smorgasbord of bass and panfish. West of Trojan and the entrance to Prescott Beach, the slough first appears as a narrow ditch paralleling the highway, then heads toward a grove of trees. You can slip a canoe or car-top boat into the water, or fish from the tall grass on the banks. Each tide brings new recruits of largemouth bass, with best fishing near the Columbia River outlet and along the base of the adjoining bluff. White crappie and brown bullhead are available in the channel, as well as yellow perch, bluegill, and warmouth bass.

QUARTZ LAKE A small but fairly deep cutthroat lake. It is located just south of Hwy. 26, about 2 miles east of the Jewell junction, some 50 miles west of Portland. Follow Quartz Creek Rd. south of Hwy. 26, 2.5 miles west of the big Sunset Rest Area. It is also possible to get to the lake from Elsie.

The land surrounding the lake has all been cut over, and the lake is brushy and hard to fish. There are lots of snags. About 4 acres, Quartz has produced some nice cutthroat.

RECREATION LAKE A 27-acre lake adjacent to the decommissioned Trojan Nuclear Power Plant on Hwy. 30 and open to public use by permission of PGE. The lake is stocked with legal trout and contains panfish. Its wetlands setting is alluring but eerie, with cooling tower and concrete reactor bunker as a back-drop. A friend once took a photo there that came out pink. Personally, I wouldn't linger there, or eat anything that came out of the lake.

RILEA SLOUGH At National Guard Camp Rilea, about 3 1/2 miles SW of Warrenton. The public is allowed access to fish for yellow perch, white crappie, largemouth bass, and bluegill, except during Guard maneuvers. Check in at the guard station entrance or armory office, or call (503) 861-4000.

RINEARSON SLOUGH A Columbia River slough, lightly fished but offering fair bass and panfish opportunities. The slough is NW of Rainier, some 45 miles from Portland. It can be accessed from the Columbia downstream from Longview Bridge. A number of side roads to the south cross or meet the slough. All the Columbia species are present, with crappie, perch, bluegill, and bass predominant. The only boat access is from the Columbia River. The banks are all privately owned, but permission to fish is usually granted.

ROCK CREEK (Columbia Co.) A very clear trout and steelhead stream, about 20 miles long, flowing into the upper Nehalem at Vernonia. It is a very popular stream, heavily fished in early season. A county road follows the creek from the NW side of Vernonia to Keasey. Private logging roads continue upstream and are accessible to the public when the gate is open (which it usually is). You can also reach the stream from the Sunset Rest Area at about milepost 30. Keep your ears open for log truck traffic at the upper end.

Rock Creek has a good native cutthroat population. It is not stocked. After October 31 it is open for winter steelhead up to the former Keasey Dam site, which is about 15 miles up from the mouth. All non-finclipped steelhead must be released unharmed. Best steelhead action is in December and January. This is a good fly stream, very resistant to muddying. It does flow through a lot of private land, so ask for permission when you feel you might be intruding.

SALMON RIVER (Lincoln Co.) A fairly short coastal stream but a real producer of fall chinook. It heads in the coast range in northern Lincoln County and flows 24 miles to the ocean just north of Lincoln City. Followed by Hwy. 18 from McMinnville for most of its length, it is crossed by Hwy. 101 a few miles above its mouth.

One of the better small streams on the coast, it reliably produces good catches of fall chinook, though its winter steelhead, coho, and sea-run cutthroat populations are down. A salmon and steelhead hatchery above Otis, at about river mile 4, releases thousands of smolts into the river annually, and attracts almost equal numbers of anglers during the return migration. The Salmon River is primarily a bank fishery, as most of the riffles are shallow gravel bars. Unfortunately, bank access is limited, with most salmon angling taking place just below the hatch-

Steelhead are fished in the Nestucca River year-round.

Large perch are caught in Siletz Bay in spring and summer.

ery and at the Hwy. 101 Bridge downstream. The Dept. of Fish and Wildlife hatchery is on the North Bank Rd. at Otis. Anglers fish a 1/4-mile stretch down from the hatchery on both north and south banks. Park at the hatchery or pull off Hwy. 18 to fish the opposite bank.

At the Hwy. 101 Bridge, anglers park and fish from the bank both upstream and down. The land downstream from the bridge is public land, part of the Cascade Head National Scenic Research Area. Boat anglers launch at the ramp on Three Rocks Rd. below the bridge and motor up to popular holes. Few anglers boat higher than 3/4 mile. When the river is high enough to allow boating up to the hatchery, fishing is usually off.

Sea-run cutthroat are the first migrants to appear in the river, entering in late July. They are fished till September, when attention turns to Chinook. The coho run follows, but is closed to angling. Peak fishing for fall chinook is in September and October. Steelhead are in the stream from December through March. All non-finclipped steelhead must be released unharmed.

In the Rose Lodge area off North Bank Rd. Anglers fish for steelhead from the bridge at Rose Lodge and from roadside pull-offs.

Above Rose Lodge, the river passes through a corridor of state land (the Van Duzer Corridor) and offers high quality opportunities for cutthroat in summer, and for catch and release wild steelhead in winter.

The Salmon River is most productive for both chinook and winter steelhead after a muddy spell. The river usually clears quickly. The stream is currently being stocked with hatchery trout in the spring, but this program may be discontinued to protect the wild strain.

The riverbank between Otis and Hwy. 101 is all privately owned, but some landowners do grant permission to fish. Be sure to ask before you wet your line. There are two privately owned RV encampments on the river. The one near Hwy. 101 is operated by an RV membership organization without general public access. The camp near Rose Lodge is available for public use, though space is limited. Supplies are available at several service stations along the upper river. There are tackle stores on the lower river, and supplies and accommodations in the Lincoln City area.

SALMONBERRY RIVER A very important nursery for the Nehalem's wild steelhead population. About 18 miles long, the Salmonberry enters the Nehalem about 11 miles south of Elsie on the Lower Nehalem River Road. Anglers can walk up from the mouth along the railroad tracks, but be aware that trains do make the run several times a day. Be especially wary of the tunnels in the upper river. The upper river can be reached by way of the Camp 10 Rd. off Hwy. 26 east of the big Sunset Wayside.

The Salmonberry's steelhead run peaks in February and March. All steelhead in the river are wild and must be released unharmed. Anglers must use single barbless hooks all year, and are restricted to using artificial flies and lures during trout season, May 28 to October 31. This is a fair cutthroat stream in the spring, and sea-run appear after the fourth of July.

SAND CREEK A short stream flowing into Sand Lake about 20 miles south of Tillamook. A nursery stream for salmon and steelhead, the creek is closed to all fishing.

Sand Creek has a fair run of sea-run cutthroat which starts up in July and August. They remain in the river until late spring, when they run back to sea. Crayfish tails and spinner and worms will produce some nice fish. There are rumors of a wild coho salmon run in late October (but no reported catches), and there may be some steelhead in February and March. Camping facilities are available at Sand Lake, Island Park, and at Cape Lookout State Park.

SAND LAKE Not really a lake, but a tidal basin at the mouth of Sand Creek, south of Tillamook. A popular recreation spot, it is reached by the county road leaving Hwy. 101 at Hemlock, or by going north from Woods on the Lower Nestucca Rd.

Sea-run cutthroat enter Sand Lake in July and August. Chum salmon come in November and December, but the fishery for them is closed. Steelhead enter in February and March, but few are taken here. Most angling is from boats or by bank casting on the east side of the island. A bridge crosses to the island from the county road, and boats can be easily launched.

Flounder fishing has fallen on hard times here as elsewhere on the Oregon coast, but a few are still taken. Fishing for them is concentrated mostly between the south side of the island and the outlet. Blue prawns, which can be purchased locally, make good bait for flounder as do mud shrimp and nightcrawlers. Surf perch fishing is possible on either side of the ocean outlet. Crabbing takes place just inside the inlet.

The county maintains a park on an island in the center of Sand Lake, and there is a campground on the NW shore near the ocean.

SANDY ISLAND SLOUGH A Columbia River slough north of Goble, with a known population of black crappie.

SCHOONER CREEK A small wild cutthroat stream with chinook and wild winter steelhead runs. It empties into the north end of Siletz Bay just east of Taft and is crossed by Hwy. 101 at its mouth. A county road follows the stream for most of its 10 mile flow. The stream varies in width from 25 to 50 feet and has a lot of deep pools and brushy banks. It's pretty snaggy. Winter fishing is restricted to the lower 4 miles.

Some chinook are taken in September and October, but most salmon angling in the Siletz system takes place in Siletz Bay. The creek is closed to coho angling.

Steelhead are in the creek from December through February. Best cutthroat fishing is in early season, though some larger fish are taken in the lower end in August and September.

Barbless hooks are required for all angling throughout the year. The upper deadline during the winter season is Erickson Creek. There's overnight camping at Devils Lake, about 4 miles south.

SEARS LAKE A small lake near Tierra Del Mar beach, between Sand Lake and Woods, located just east of the county road. This lake is privately owned at present and is not open to the public. It contains a few cutthroat trout.

SHAG LAKE (a.k.a. Burk's Lake) A small lake, less than 5 acres, located near Fort Stevens State Park, best in early season before heavy weed growth. Very difficult to find, it is about 1/2 mile north of the gravel road from Warrenton to Fort Stevens Park, east of the paved road to Hammond. Shag is lightly fished for bass and panfish.

SILETZ BAY A moderately fished bay about 5 miles long from the jaws at Taft up to Kernville Bridge, used primarily by non-anglers, including a growing fleet of windsurfers. The Siletz River enters the bay at Kernville, while Drift Creek and Schooner Creek enter to the north. The bay has silted up considerably as a result of logging practices in the '30s and '40s. Not a good destination bay for anglers, but a pleasant place to clam or crab if you're vacationing at Lincoln City.

From early spring to summer the chief angling here is for bottom fish, primarily perch. Favorite baits are ghost or sand shrimp, kelp worms, and clam pieces. Perch to 3 pounds have been caught up to the Kernville Bridge starting in May. They leave well before the fall rains. In general, the best catches are made from boats anchored in the bay, but casting from shore near the bay mouth can be good. Flood tide is the preferred time.

Crabbing is excellent during the early part of the year. Rings and bait are available locally, and can be fished from public docks on the bay.

In late summer and fall, sea-run cutthroat arrive and are taken on trolled spinners and worms from Kernville upstream. Some anglers do well using shrimp as bait.

Salmon angling outside the bay starts as early as July with the arrival of chinook at the jaws. The coho fishery is closed here as elsewhere on the Oregon coast, both in the ocean and bay. In late September and October chinook are available throughout the bay, though most catches are made in the Siletz River itself. The total catch for river and bay in 1986 was about 1,300. A good number of big jacks also appear regularly with the run.

Chinook are usually caught in the upper bay. Coho were traditionally taken with herring near the jaws. Many anglers cast from the banks between Taft and the jaws. Be prepared to lose lots of terminal gear, as the bottom is rocky. Salmon anglers use spinners with feathered hooks or Kwikfish-type lures. Steelhead pass through the bay, but are primarily taken in the river.

Bait can be purchased locally, but gathering your own is not difficult. Shrimp bait are easily found at low water in the flats all along the bay. Herring for bait (or eating) are taken intermittently through the summer months.

Surf casters can do well on the ocean side of the jaws. The beach drops off rapidly, and at low water there's easy casting for redtail.

The tide flats between Cutler City and Kernville have good numbers of softshell clams. Any zero tide makes the flats accessible.

A number of reasonably priced moorages with rental boats and ramps are available along the bay and upriver. On weekends, it's a good idea to make reservations. A large state park is located at Devils Lake just north of the Bay, and there are other campgrounds further south on Hwy. 101. Siletz Bay State Park in the Taft area of Lincoln City offers fine opportunities for viewing seals and aquatic birds, including brown pelicans in summer. Tackle shops, grocery stores, and motels are plentiful in the area. The Siletz bar is dangerous. There are no jetties, and a number of lives have been lost in crossing. The lower bay is also dangerous.

SILETZ RIVER A fine all around stream flowing about 70 miles, offering good angling for trout, fall chinook and both summer and winter steelhead. The river enters the bay at Kernville, at the junction of Hwy. 101 with Hwy. 229, which follows the lower part of the river. It's accessible from the Corvallis area by way of Hwy. 20 and county roads to the Logsden area, and from the Newport-Toledo area by Hwy. 229.

The river is very fishable, with few snags. The main boating area is from the town of Siletz down through tidewater, although a lot of drifters put in upstream at Moonshine Park. The town of Siletz has a good ramp with parking and picnic facilities at the Hwy. 229 Bridge. The Siletz muddies easily, and eggs work best when the water's turbid.

Salmon start moving through the bay in late July or August, and fishing holds up well until late fall. Over a thousand fish are taken annually.

Steelhead are taken every month of the year in the Siletz. The river is stocked with both summer and winter run fish, and there are wild runs of both. An estimated 80% of the current steelhead population is hatchery reared. All non-finclipped steelhead must be released unharmed. Summer steelhead have two peaks, in June, and again in October. The winter run peaks in December/January.

The upper river is heavily stocked with hatchery cutthroat, some of which go to sea and return to tidewater in July. The sea-run returns, however, are diminished here as elsewhere in Oregon.

The lower river and bay have many moorages where boats, bait, and tackle are available. Flood level on the Siletz is 16 ft. Optimum level for boating is 6.6, with acceptable levels from 4-6 ft. To learn the current gauge reading, call the

Fishing dories launch from the beach near Cape Kiwanda, north of Pacific City.

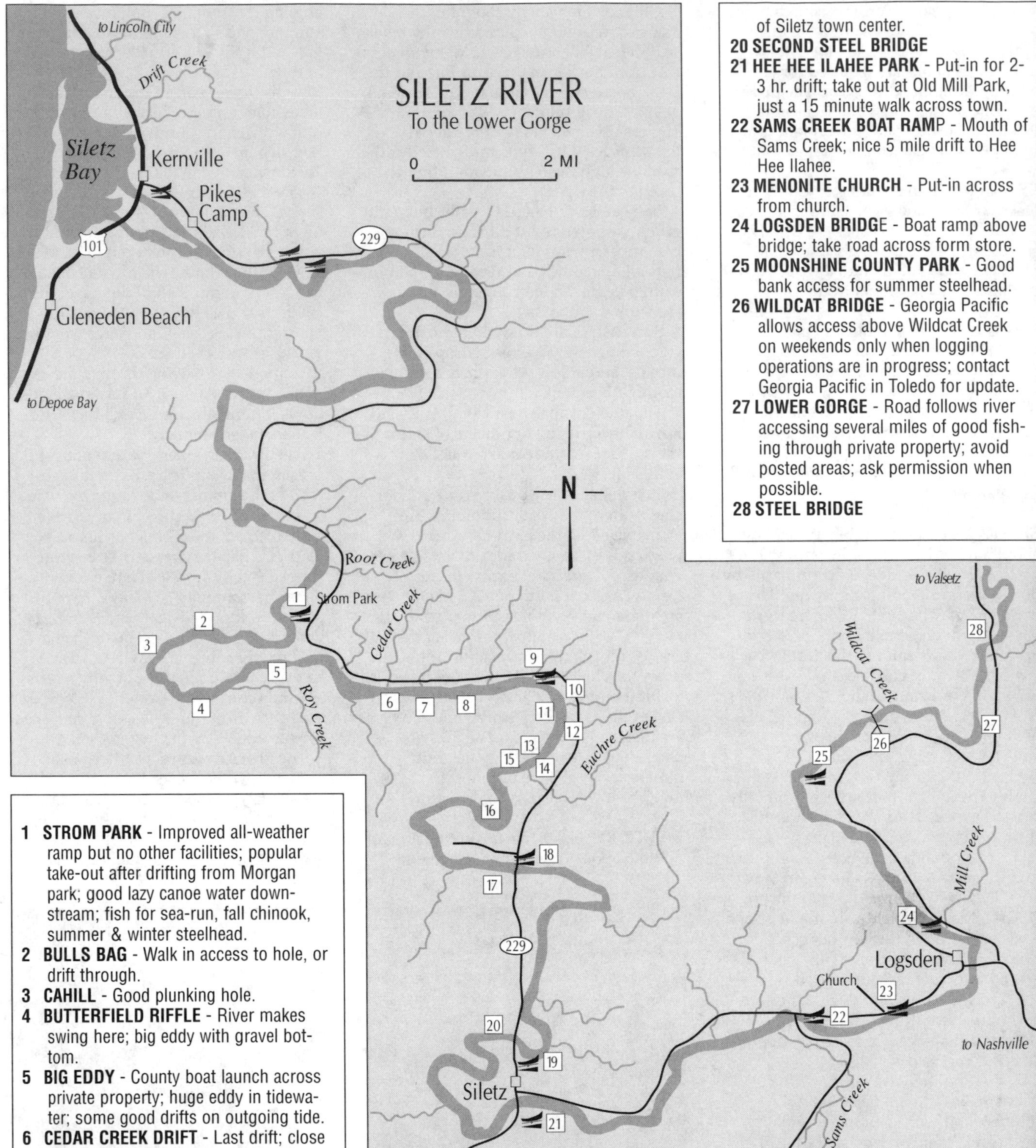

1 **STROM PARK** - Improved all-weather ramp but no other facilities; popular take-out after drifting from Morgan park; good lazy canoe water downstream; fish for sea-run, fall chinook, summer & winter steelhead.
2 **BULLS BAG** - Walk in access to hole, or drift through.
3 **CAHILL** - Good plunking hole.
4 **BUTTERFIELD RIFFLE** - River makes swing here; big eddy with gravel bottom.
5 **BIG EDDY** - County boat launch across private property; huge eddy in tidewater; some good drifts on outgoing tide.
6 **CEDAR CREEK DRIFT** - Last drift; close to highway.
7 **BLACKBERRY HOLE** - Plunking; good drift at lower end.
8 **GRAVEL HOLE** - Private; good drift from boat.
9 **MORGAN PARK** - County boat ramp.
10 **BLUFF HOLE** - Fish the head of this one; solid rock, but gets snaggy further down; about 300 yds. below Swinging Bridge.
11 **SWINGING BRIDGE** - A few fishing shacks here.
12 **HOLE JUST ABOVE SWINGING BRIDGE** - Good boat hole; plunking at low water.
13 **MITCHELL HOLE** - Beautiful drift, best for boats.
14 **FRENCH HOLE** - Nice fishing for drifters and plunkers; walk down from road 150 ft.
15 **EUCHRE CREEK HOLE** - Mouth of Euchre Cr.
16 **KUSYDOR DRIFT** - Nice spot; calm edges with swift center.
17 **SHOCK (OJOLLA) HOLE** - Just below bridge; good drift, fairly slow; fish both sides of river.
18 **FIRST STEEL BRIDGE** - Put-in just above bridge; you need a very long rope or cable to lower boat.
19 **OLD MILL PARK BOAT RAMP** - Just north of Siletz town center.
20 **SECOND STEEL BRIDGE**
21 **HEE HEE ILAHEE PARK** - Put-in for 2-3 hr. drift; take out at Old Mill Park, just a 15 minute walk across town.
22 **SAMS CREEK BOAT RAMP** - Mouth of Sams Creek; nice 5 mile drift to Hee Hee Ilahee.
23 **MENONITE CHURCH** - Put-in across from church.
24 **LOGSDEN BRIDGE** - Boat ramp above bridge; take road across form store.
25 **MOONSHINE COUNTY PARK** - Good bank access for summer steelhead.
26 **WILDCAT BRIDGE** - Georgia Pacific allows access above Wildcat Creek on weekends only when logging operations are in progress; contact Georgia Pacific in Toledo for update.
27 **LOWER GORGE** - Road follows river accessing several miles of good fishing through private property; avoid posted areas; ask permission when possible.
28 **STEEL BRIDGE**

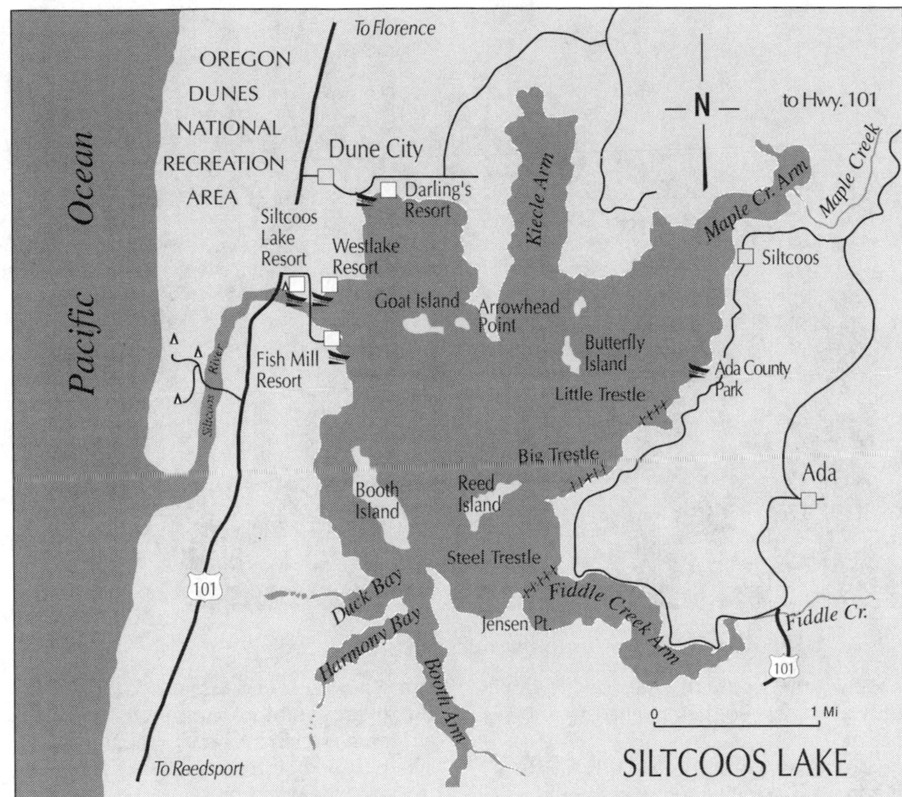

National Weather Service at (503) 261-9246.

SILTCOOS LAKE One Oregon's premier warmwater fisheries, tucked well off Hwy. 101 in a beautiful wooded setting about 6 miles south of Florence. Canary Rd. about 3 miles south of Florence across from Honeyman State Park accesses the lake's east shore and returns to the highway south of the lake. The lake is connected to the ocean by the Siltcoos River outlet, which flows 2 miles to the sea.

Fishermen who have tasted the fabulous fishing offered by Siltcoos have a singular dream—to orchestrate one great evening rise (participation mandatory) of what must be millions of brown bullhead, yellow perch, crappie, bass, bluegill, trout, steelhead, and salmon.

The 3,000-acre lake is considered to be one of the top warm water fisheries in the Northwest, cherished by dedicated bass anglers as well as generations of Oregon small fry who learned about fish by hooking into the lake's abundant big yellow perch.

Largemouth bass fishing varies with the weather and the month, but can be very good here the year around. A number of bass tournaments take place on the lake. Five pounders are common, and bass to 8 pounds have been taken, particularly in late winter and early spring. Bass fishing is fine throughout the summer, though the size will not come up to early spring fishing. Bass angling is particularly good in the Booth Arm, Fiddle Creek Arm, Maple Creek Arm, and Harmony Bay. Bass are also taken in good numbers along the west shore opposite Booth Island, and near the east shore of Booth Island. Plugs and plastic worms are effective year-round. Live bait is prohibited.

Perch, brown bullhead, crappie, and bluegill are best in summer when other species are hard to catch. The brown bullhead fishery is often very good. Although catfish are generally fished at night, this popular cat can be caught in large numbers in the early morning. Most bullhead anglers fish the bottom with worms. Some good areas are near the east shore just south of the little trestle, south of goat Island, near the north shore at the west side of the Kiechle Arm opposite Butterfly and Grass islands, and in uppermost Fiddle Creek Arm. Perch can be caught throughout the lake. Try the area between Grass and Butterfly Islands, just west of Goat Island, and just offshore from Ada.

Siltcoos is the best lake for wild cutthroat in the area. In addition, it is heavily stocked with legal rainbow each spring. Six or 7 pound holdovers aren't uncommon, and at least one 9 pounder has been taken in recent years. Good catches are made in the Kiechle Arm, near the mouth of the Maple Creek Arm by Siltcoos, and northeast of Booth Island, among other places The big

Siltcoos Catfish

Siltcoos Lake is one of the state's top warmwater fisheries.

wooden trestle on the east shore is a good place for crappie.

The lake is closed to coho fishing. Small runs of steelhead and sea-run cutthroat move through the lake heading for spawning grounds in the Siltcoos River. All steelhead in Siltcoos are wild and must be released unharmed.

There is a public boat ramp at Westlake with a wheelchair accessible fishing pier, and another ramp in the county park just north of Ada. Camping is available nearby at Ada County Park, at Honeyman State Park, and at several forest service campgrounds on the Siltcoos River. There are a number of resorts on the lake, including Darling's, Fish Mill Lodges, and Westlake Resort, which offer cottage lodging, boat and motor rentals, tackle, supplies, and fishing tips. Fish Mill and Darling's also have trailer parks with hook-ups. Supplies, good restaurants, and additional accommodations are available in Florence.

SILTCOOS RIVER The outlet stream of Siltcoos Lake, traditionally fished for sea-run cutthroat, coho, and steelhead. It is about 7 miles south of Florence and flows only about 2 miles before entering the ocean.

The Siltcoos offers good cutthroat fishing in early spring and again in fall. It's closed to coho fishing, but open for catch and release wild winter steelhead. Fish don't enter the stream until the water is high enough to breach the bar, usually around October. It's possible to fish by boat, but most anglers bank cast.

There is a public boat ramp just north of Westlake. Westlake Resort and Fish Mill Lodges are situated on either side of the river's juncture with the lake. A large Forest Service campground complex is located along the river, with four separate campgrounds. The road into the campgrounds is a little over one mile south of the Westlake turnoff. These campgrounds generally support the dune buggy crowd. More camping is available at Honeyman State Park to the north. There's good largemouth bass fishing in the river in late summer.

SIUSLAW BAY A good variety bay west of Eugene, offering fine clamming, crabbing, and fishing from late spring through fall. Hwy. 126 provides direct access from the Willamette Valley.

A lot of salmon are just outside the bar from mid-June to October. The Siuslaw bar used to be a tough one, and even the current jetties don't guarantee easy passage. When the bar is closed, some anglers troll the lower channel near the Coast Guard lookout, but only the rare salmon is taken there.

In July the bay and tidewater welcome sea-run cutthroat and jack salmon. These fish run to 18 inches, and the fishery for them holds up through August or September. Spinners and worms take most of the fish, but eggs drifted under bobbers work well, too. Flies are effective as the fish start moving up tributary streams.

The bay is closed to coho fishing, but the fall chinook run is strong and growing more so, with best fishing in August, September and October from Cushman to Mapleton. Trolling with spinners and lures is the most popular method.

A run of shad enters in May and June. These are fished in the extreme upper tidewater area between Mapleton and Brickerville. Jigging with small darts is popular, but shad are a lot of fun on a fly rod, and a tasty treat despite the bones.

This bay is the northernmost limit for striped bass. A few show up in February and March, following the smelt run.

Siuslaw Bay is the northernmost limit for striped bass in Oregon.

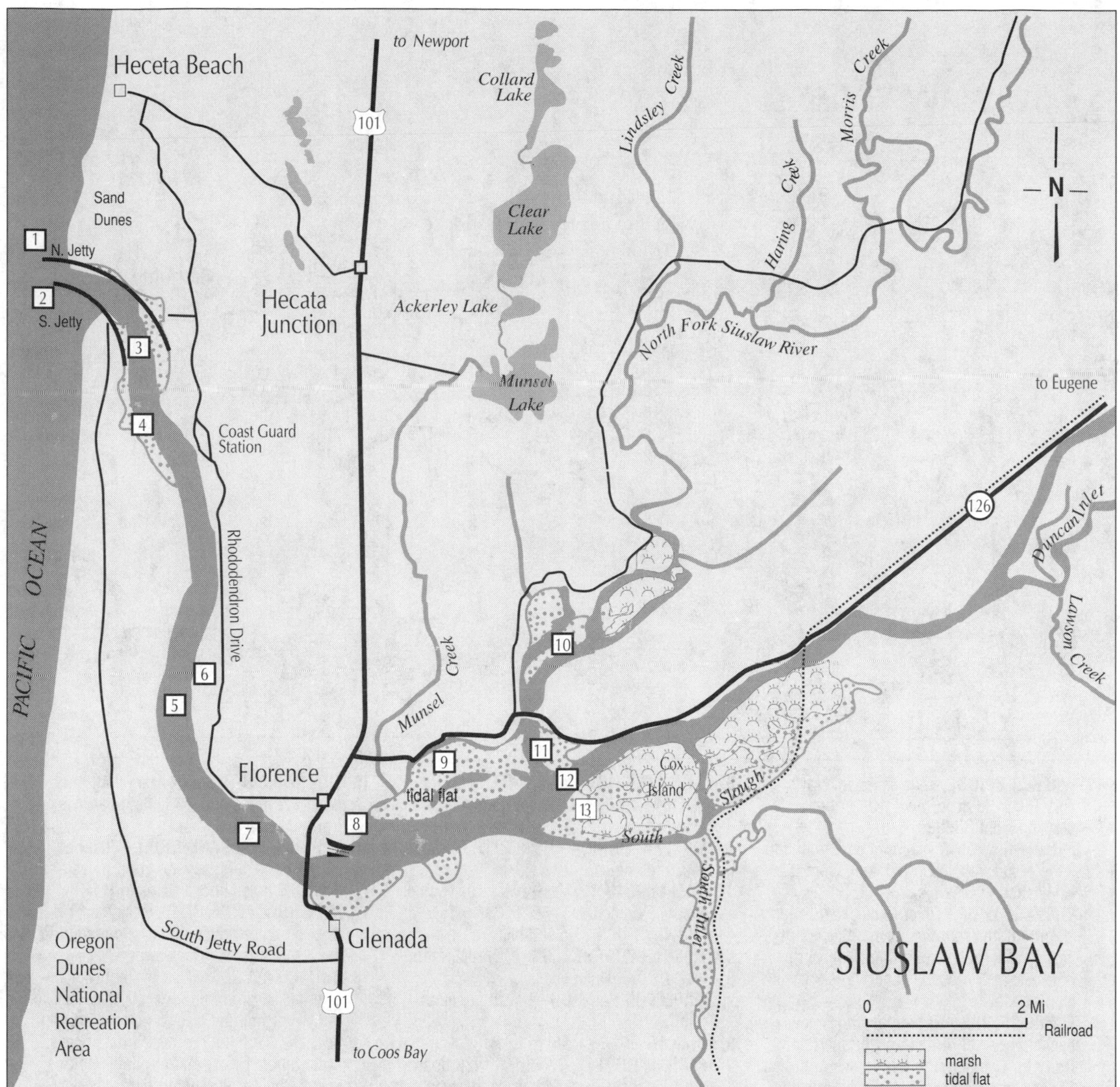

1 **NORTH JETTY** - Fish for redtail perch, greenling spring and summer; best March-May, but rough seas may limit access.

2 **SOUTH JETTY**- Fish for redtail, greenling.

3 **LOWER CHANNE**L - Best crabbing in the bay on in-coming tide; some perch fishing, rare salmon taken.

4 **THE ROCK DOCK** - Concrete pier popular for crabbing, some perch; wheelchair accessible; good soft shells below.

5 **FLOUNDER HOLE** - Few flounder these days, but still a good hole for perch; good crabbing in vicinity.

6 **BEACH** - Bank fishery for perch.

7 **UPPER CHANNEL** - Fair late summer crabbing; anchor among pilings and fish the run of redtail perch mid-May to July, striped perch and pile perch spring through fall.

8 **CITY DOCKS AND BOAT RAMP** - Crab & fish for perch; public RV park.

9 **NORTH FORK CLAM BED WEST** - Tremendous producer of softshell clams; access below bridge from gravel pull-offs.

10 **MOUTH OF NORTH FORK** - Troll or cast lures to head of tide (3 miles to Portage) for sea-run July through Sept., salmon Aug. through Nov.; access from Bender Landing on North Fork.

11 **NORTH FORK CLAM BED, EAST** - Dig for larger but less numerous softshell; access from pull-off below bridge.

12 **MOUTH OF SIUSLAW** - Troll to Mapleton for sea-run and salmon, Aug. & Sept.

13 **COX ISLAND** - Nature Conservancy marshland preserve; boat access only for good clam flats.

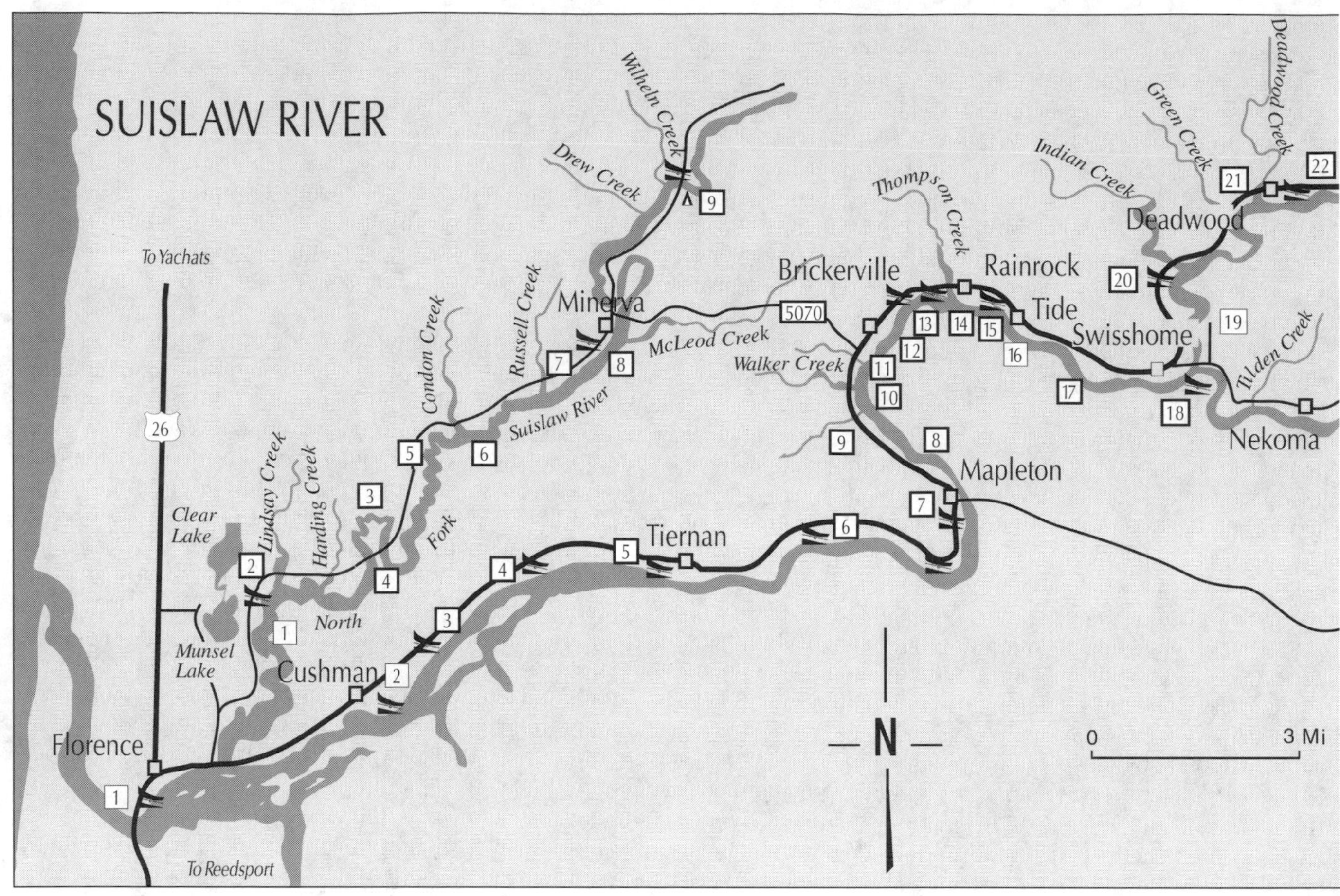

1 **WALKER BRIDGE** - Two miles up North Fork River Rd. from hwy. 126; mostly plunked from bridge.
2 **BENDER LANDING** - County park with concrete boat ramp; good plunking from bank; wheelchair accessible.
3 **PORTAGE LOOP** - River makes 2-mile loop about 5.6 miles above hwy. 126; good fishing, good walking; road follows about one mile. Respect private property. Ask permission to fish.
4 **FUNKE BRIDGE** - Good plunking hole beneath second bridge on Portage Loop; room for 8 anglers on both sides of stream. Respect private property. Ask permission to fish.
5 **DAVIDSON RANCH** - Easy fishing from bridge and for 2 miles above and below; 8 miles up N. Fork Rd. Respect private property. Ask permission to fish.
6 **HUNTINGTON BRIDGE** - Just above mouth of Condon Cr.; lots of open fishing above and below bridge. Respect private property. Ask permission to fish.
7 **CEDAR HOLE** - Large deep plunking hole by big cedar tree 9 miles up. Respect private property. Ask permission to fish.
8 **HOUGHTON LANDING** - Just down from guard rail; good plunking hole with public boat access 9.6 miles up.
9 **CAMPGROUND** - Good bank access from here on up.

SIUSLAW MAINSTEM

1 **HOLIDAY HARBOR** - Paved public boat ramp.
2 **SIUSLAW MARINA** - Hoist facility 4 miles east of Florence.
3 **CUSHMAN MARINA** - Gravel ramp 3 miles east of Florence.
4 **MIDWAY DOCK** - Hoist facility.
5 **TIERNAN BOAT ACCESS** - ODF&W ramp.
6 **C&D DOCK** - Hoist Facility.
7 **MAPLETON LANDING** - Paved public boat ramp.
8 **DOLLAR HOLE** - Head of tide.
9 **FARNAM RIFFLE** - Good drift from boat; plunking just below Farnam landing boat slide; picnic area at landing about 2 miles above Mapleton.
10 **WALKER RIFFLE** - Good drift from boat just down from guard rail, 2.5 mile above Mapleton.
11 **GAUGING STATION HOLE** - Good deep plunking hole 3 miles above Mapleton.
12 **BRICKERVILLE HOLE** - Primitive boat slide; take trail to river just above last house above Brickerville; good plunking hole; fish close to bank.
13 **THOMPSON CREEK** - Four very good holes along edge of highway; includes good boat access site; good plunking in fast water.
14 **RAINROCK HOLE** - Extremely popular and productive plunking water; watch for long wide highway shoulder just below Thompson Creek; fair boat access.
15 **TIDE WAYSIDE** - County park with boat ramp 5.9 miles above Mapleton across from Big Red's Market.
16 **RED HILL HOLE AND DRIFT** - Just before railroad crossing; several good holes and drifts 6.5 miles above Mapleton.
17 **MILL HOLE AND DRIFT** - Walk back through mill to river, about one mile of fishing 7 miles above Mapleton.
18 **CHURCH ACCESS** - Turn off highway at Evangelical Church in Swisshome, keep to right after railroad tracks; good drifts from boat and bank; unimproved boat access. Church hole below church, Sand Hole above Church. Private property. Ask permission to fish.
19 **KONNIE MEMORIAL FISHING ACCESS** - Concrete ramp with parking; bank access above mouth of Lake Cr. accesses The Horn; wheelchair accessible.
20 **INDIAN CREEK** - Hole just below creek; boat ramp.
21 **GREEN CREEK HOLE** - Good drift from boat and bank.
22 **DEADWOOD CREEK BOAT ACCESS** - Popular concrete ramp for drift boat launching; good holes for 5 miles upstream to Greenleaf Cr.
23 **SWISSHOME TO RICHARDSON BRIDGE** - 12 miles of beautiful water, easily accessible; mostly bank fished, but some boat access.

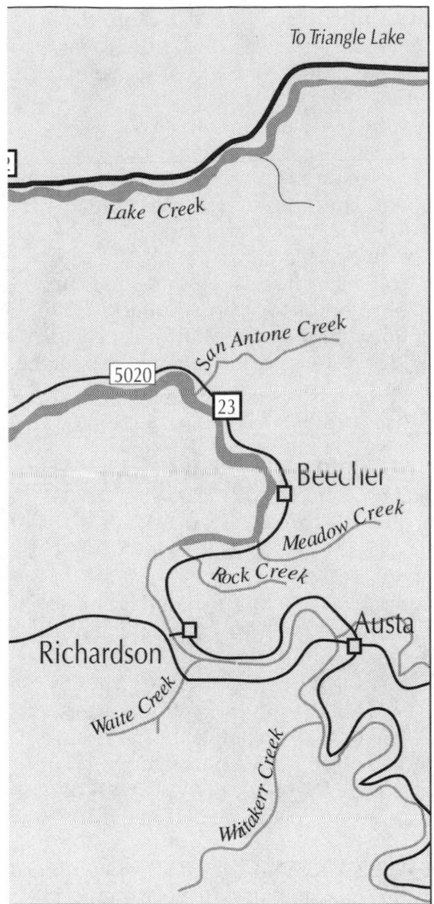

Fishing from the rocks along shore or off the jetties will produce perch and greenling on shrimp or clam necks. Jetty fishing is best March through May, but rough seas may discourage access then. Angling from the jetties remains popular throughout the summer. A concrete pier east of the south jetty, locally called the Rock Dock, offers good crabbing and perch fishing. It is wheelchair accessible.

Crabbing is best in the lower channel around the coast guard station or off the Rock Dock, and is fair just above and below the Hwy. 101 Bridge.

For clam connoisseurs, Siuslaw Bay offers some of the best softshell flats on the coast. The flats to the west of the North Fork mouth are extremely productive. The flats to the east of the mouth produce fewer, but larger softshells. Cox Island, at the mouth of the Siuslaw, is a Nature Conservancy wildlife preserve, with good clam flats accessible only by boat.

There are three public boat ramps on the bay, near the Hwy. 101 Bridge at Florence, at Tiernan, and at Mapleton. Good accommodations are available in the area, with many motels and campgrounds within a short distance. Several marinas near the bridge provide boat rentals, gas, tackle, bait, and other supplies.

In 1994, Siuslaw Bay was closed to both coho and chinook angling from June 20 through August 15.

SIUSLAW RIVER A good fall chinook and winter steelhead stream, heading in the Coast Range west of Eugene and Cottage Grove and flowing over 100 miles to the ocean near Florence. The river is not heavily fished. A fish ladder at the falls on Lake Creek (a major tributary of the Siuslaw) allows salmon access to 100 miles of spawning ground above Triangle Lake, further enhancing the growing run.

The Siuslaw is approached from the Willamette Valley by driving west from Eugene on Hwy. 126, which crosses the mainstem at Austa. From here one may turn downstream on a county road to Swisshome and the sea, upstream on a county road and a maze of logging roads that follow the river far into the hills, or continue on Hwy. 126 to its intersection with Hwy. 36 at Mapleton.

The entire stream is open for trout during the regular season. The river is planted quite heavily with cutthroat. These fish provide good angling in the spring, and a dwindling number return as sea-run in the fall. The sea-run usually return in several runs during August and September, although occasionally they hit the river all at once and scoot upriver. Angling for sea-run occurs mostly in the tidewater portion of the river (from Mapleton downstream).

The fall chinook run has been growing steadily over the last 5-6 years. Chinook are in the river from September through December, but are dark and inedible after November. They are fished up into Lake Creek, but most are caught in tidewater between Cushman and Mapleton.

The winter steelhead run has been poor lately. Hatchery steelhead have been heavily stocked in the past and are available as keepers. Non-finclipped steelhead must be released unharmed. The run enters the river in late November and holds strong through February. Drifting the lower river produces much of the catch. This stream is often murky in winter. If you get to the river and find this to be so, you might try fishing Lake Creek, which is usually clear and a good steelhead producer.

Shad run up the Siuslaw in respectable numbers in May and June. Most angling effort is concentrated between Mapleton and Brickerville, but the fish get as far up as Swisshome.

There are many boat ramps on the main river, including a public ramp at Tiernan. There is a wheelchair accessible fishing pier on Lake Creek near its confluence with the Siuslaw. The pier accesses good winter steelhead, chinook, and trout water. The Siuslaw is a wide, fast stream requiring skillful and cautious boating, especially in the upper areas. Guide service is available in Eugene, Swisshome, and Florence.

There are campgrounds at Honeyman State Park on the coast, Knowles Creek (USFS) about 3 miles east of Mapleton, Whittaker Creek (BLM) 1.5 miles south of Austa, and Clay Creek (BLM) about 10 miles upstream from Whittaker Creek. Supplies are available at Mapleton and Florence, and at several marinas on the lower river. Accommodations are available in Florence.

SIUSLAW RIVER, NORTH FORK A cutthroat trout stream with a fair run of winter steelhead. This good size tributary of the Siuslaw River enters Siuslaw Bay just east of Florence. The river is paralleled by a good paved road that runs north from Hwy. 126 about one mile east of Florence. The upper river can also be reached from Hwy. 36 at Firo on Forest Rd. 5070, which crosses the river at the Minerva logging camp.

About 25 miles long and 30-50 feet wide, it is not heavily fished. The bottom is primarily bedrock, sand, and gravel and there is little cover for fish.

The North Fork offers fair early season fishing for wild cutthroat and in past years welcomed a good number of sea-run cutthroat in the fall. Sea-run presence is considerably reduced at this time, however. The North Fork is exclusively a bank fishery, as the river is too small for boats.

Camping facilities are available at Honeyman State Park just south of Florence, or at North Fork Siuslaw Campground about 3 miles upstream from Minerva.

SKOOKUM LAKE (Tillamook Co.) A small lake about 10 miles SW of Tillamook at the head of Fawcett Creek in the Tillamook river watershed. It is a reservoir for Tillamook City Water and is closed to public fishing.

SLUSHER LAKE A 20-acre bass and panfish lake at Camp Rilea. The public is welcome to fish when the National Guard is not holding maneuvers. The lake contains largemouth bass, yellow perch, and brown bullhead. Check in at the gate or the armory office, or call ahead at (503) 861-4000.

SMITH LAKE (Clatsop Co.) A long, narrow, shallow lake at the junction of the Hammond Rd. with Hwy. 101, about 2 miles south of Warrenton. It is on the west side of Hwy. 101. It contains crappie, bluegill, brown bullhead, perch, and largemouth bass. Fish it early in the season, as it has a severe weed problem. In fact, weeds have diminished a very good bass fishery here. There is no bank access, but you may be able to put a small boat in (or launch a float tube) at the north end. This is another lake to try while

Garibaldi is home to the Tillamook Bay charter fleet.

camping at Fort Stevens State Park. See also Coffenbury.

SMITH LAKE (Tillamook Co.) A fairly small lake north of Tillamook Bay on Hwy. 101, west of the highway just north of Barview. The lake covers 35 acres, and is relatively free of aquatic weeds. The central area of the lake averages 8-12 ft. deep.

Smith is occasionally stocked with legal rainbow in spring. It's a good prospect for early season angling with bait and lures fished from the bank. It also contains brown bullhead and largemouth bass. The bass haven't done well, but bullhead are plentiful and receive little pressure.

Boat launching is a problem, although a boat is not necessarily needed. Camp Magruder, a Methodist Church camp available for group rentals, is located on the lake. The use of motors is discouraged because of children in row boats.

SOAPSTONE LAKE A small cutthroat lake in the North Fork of the Nehalem drainage whose outlet is Soapstone Creek. To reach it (good luck), drive to the Necanicum junction on Hwy. 26, SW of Cannon Beach, then turn south on Hwy. 53. After about 8 miles and just before crossing the North Fork, turn NE onto Coal Mountain Ridge Rd. At about 1.5 miles you can spot the lake to the north. It's a 20-minute walk to the lake.

Soapstone covers 10 acres and is over 20 ft. deep. Full of brush and snags, it can be fished for wild cutthroat with flies, bait, or lures from the many logs that jut into the lake. It's usually a good early season lake.

SOUTH LAKE A 5-acre trout lake just south of Hebo Lake, about ten miles from Hebo Ranger Station on the forest road west from the junction of highways 14 and 101. Check at the sport shop at Hebo for exact location. It's generally inaccessible until mid-May, as the road is usually full of mudholes.

The lake is stocked with rainbow catchables several times in spring, It has a lot of crayfish, which are a good choice for bait fishing. It's full of snags, so bring along plenty of tackle. A good lake to try when you're in the Hebo neighborhood.

SPRING LAKE (a.k.a. Ocean Lake) A fair bass fishery, with put-and-take rainbow and cutthroat trout. About 13 acres, it is 1/2 mile north of Barview to the north of Tillamook Bay. The lake is just east of Hwy. 101 near Twin Rocks. You might be able to get a raft in, but most angling is done from the bank along the highway.

SPRUCE RUN LAKE A small lake with lots of fish south of Elsie in the coast range, about 70 miles from Portland. To get there, see Lost Lake (Elsie). Spruce Run is a 1/2 mile hike SE of Lost Lake. Spruce Run heads Spruce Run Creek and has lots of small wild cutthroat trout. Only 3 acres, it is brushy and hard on tackle.

SUNSET LAKE (a.k.a. Neacoxie Lake) A very long, narrow lake, popular for bass and trout. It is just west of Hwy. 101 in the resort area about 4 miles north of Gearhart. To get there, take the road west from Hwy. 101 just north of the Cullaby Lake junction. This road crosses over the north end of Sunset Lake.

Sunset is about 2 miles long and less than 500 ft. wide. It covers about 110 acres, with lots of water over 15 feet deep, offering good early season fishing for stocked rainbow. Best trout catches are made from mid-lake to the south end, where the water is deepest.

Good size largemouth bass are also present. Best bass fishing is below the narrows, in the small pockets on the west shore. The lake also contains a small number of yellow perch, crappie, and brown bullhead, but is really not a good warm water fishery. There's good bank fishing, and boats can be launched at the county ramp on the north side of the bridge. Public parking is available on the west shore near the bridge. There's a resort near the bridge.

SUTTON LAKE Two fair size bodies of water connected by a narrow channel, with a total area of about 100 acres. It is located on the east side of Hwy. 101 about 6 miles north of Florence. Sutton has a few wild cutthroat and is stocked heavily in spring with legal rainbow. It's a good panfish lake, with strong populations of yellow perch and largemouth bass. This is a nice recreational area, and the lake is not fished hard. There is a large Forest Service campground on Sutton Creek about 1/4 mile west of the lake, and a boat ramp off Hwy. 101.

SWEET CREEK A small stream with native cutthroat and steelhead, entering the Siuslaw River about 10 miles upstream from Florence. It can be reached by Hwy. 36 and a county road which follows it south. The creek is fair for cutthroat in early season, and a few return as sea-run in the fall. It is not stocked. It has a fair steelhead run for a creek this size, with fishing from December to March. Sweet Creek does not have good public access. Ask permission before you cross private land.

TAHKENITCH LAKE A good, large coastal lake 5 miles south of Siltcoos Lake, potentially as productive as Siltcoos, but less popular. It covers more than 1,500 acres, located just east of Hwy. 101, about 13 miles south of Florence.

Everyone in the family can catch fish here, but you'll need a boat. The shore is too brushy for bank angling. Best fishing is for crappie, bluegill, and yellow perch. Largemouth are regulated as a catch and release fishery from April 1 through June 15. Crappie are very plentiful, and bluegill 5-7 inches are in good supply. Kids love to fish for them on bobbers and worms, and a fly rod with poppers can be fun. Yellow perch 10-12 inches can be found along the shore line and on the bottom in deeper water.

Largemouth bass in the 10 pound class were taken from Tahkenitch in years past, but bass fishing has fallen off in recent years. Look for largemouth in the arms, along the weedy shoreline, and near the trestles and other structures. Weedless plugs and spinners produce well.

There's a small wild cutthroat population, and legal rainbow are stocked each year. A few steelhead are taken each winter. A small run of coho enters the lake in November, but the lake is closed to coho angling.

There are public boat ramps on the Hwy. 101 right-of-way and at Tahkenitch Landing Campground. A resort at the creek mouth provides rental boats, motors, and tackle. The lake is served by two good size campgrounds, one across the highway from the lake and one at Tahkenitch Landing.

TENMILE CREEK (Lane Co.) A good little stream for wild cutthroat and winter steelhead. It is 15 miles south of Waldport, crossed at its mouth by Hwy. 101. The creek is about 11 miles long and runs from 15-30 ft. wide. There is plenty of cover for fish, but it can be hard on tackle.

The stream is not stocked, but is a good producer of wild cutthroat early in season and late in the fall. This little stream actually had a run of over a thousand winter steelhead in the early 1970s, but the run has declined sadly.

There's a lot of private land here, so ask permission before you fish. A good road follows the stream almost to its source and eventually ties in with Indian Creek Rd. heading north from the Hwy. 36. There's a campground 5 miles upstream from Hwy. 101, and a state park campground 4 miles south of the river mouth on Hwy. 101.

THREE RIVERS A good salmon, steelhead, and cutthroat stream, tributary to the Big Nestucca. Three Rivers enters the Nestucca about 1/2 mile north of Hebo. A medium size stream, only about 14 miles long, it nevertheless carries a lot of water. The mouth is near the junction of highways 101 and 14. Hwy. 14 follows it south towards Dolph.

Three Rivers is a good wild cutthroat stream in spring. Boulders, gravel, and undercut banks make it good fly water, and it is easily waded.

Fall chinook and coho come up river in October, but angling for coho is prohibited. The river is stocked with both summer and winter steelhead, and there is a wild winter run. Peak winter fishing is in late December and January, depending on water conditions. Non-finclipped steelhead must be released unharmed.

Easily fished from the bank, Three Rivers has some nice gravel drifts where yarn and eggs are effective. The mouth of Three Rivers is an ideal hole for all species and is very popular.

There is a hatchery about 1.5 miles above Hebo. The river is closed to all

Spring chinook angling in Tillamook Bay gets serious in April.

angling from the hatchery weir to the south from June 1 through October 31 to protect spring chinook and summer steelhead brood stock. There is a public landing at the mouth of Three Rivers, but much of the lower area is private property, so get permission before you fish. Supplies and accommodations are available at Hebo, and there is a campground about 5 miles south of Hebo on Hwy. 14.

THREEMILE LAKE A fair size dune lake that features good perch and cutthroat angling for the determined angler. The lake is in the Oregon Dunes National Recreation Area about one mile NW of the northernmost reach of Winchester Bay. It shows up quite well on the recreation area map available from the US Forest Service.

About 1 1/2 miles north of Gardiner on Hwy. 101, County Rd. 247 heads west along Threemile Creek (which does NOT flow from or into the lake). Follow the road to within 1/2 mile of the ocean, and hike north about .7 mile to the lake. Threemile has yellow perch which run to 14 inches and cutthroat over 14 inches, but it's a bear to fish without a boat. It's a good place for a raft or float tube.

TILLAMOOK BAY A very productive bay, Oregon's second largest, exceeded in size only by Coos Bay. Halibut and bottom fish are the featured attractions of the big off-shore charter fleet that operates out of Garibaldi. Fall chinook are fished inside and beyond the bar as regulations allow. Crab, perch, and clams are plentiful. Garibaldi is the main port town. One of the closest bays to Portland, it is approached by good roads, and almost any spot on shore can be reached by car and a short walk. Tillamook Bay is also home to one of the Northwest's largest concentrations of waterfowl.

From the Willamette Valley, the bay is about 1 1/2 hrs. drive. From Portland, follow Hwy. 26 west to Banks, then Hwy. 6 to Tillamook. Turn south on Hwy. 101, which skirts the bay on its east and north shores. Bay Ocean Rd. follows the south and west shores.

In 1993 the Garibaldi charter fleet developed a target fishery on Pacific halibut. The halibut season usually opens in early May, with season length determined by quotas set annually by an international commission. Catch rate in 1993 was one fish per angler, with average catch 30 lbs. and some to 90 lbs.

Garibaldi is also a major port for Oregon's ocean salmon fishery, especially now that ocean salmon angling has been restricted to the waters south of Cape Falcon. In 1994 The offshore spring chinook fishery was open May 1 through June 5 from Cape Falcon to Humbug Mt., and an additional 14 days from June 6 to June 19 in the immediate Tillamook area (the "Tillamook Bubble", from Twin Rocks on the north to Pyramid Rock off Cape Meares). The fall chinook offshore fishery was scheduled to be open October 1 to October 31 in the Tillamook Bubble only. All coho fishing was closed both in the bay and offshore.

The Tillamook bar can be quite dangerous to cross, so keep your eye on weather conditions, and be extremely careful. Small boats can only expect to get outside about 25 percent of the time, even in summer. The favorite salmon spot is just south of the whistler buoy about a mile beyond the bar. A good destination for rockfish and lingcod is Three Arch Rocks off Cape Meares. Fish at 8-15 fathoms. Halibut are about 20 miles offshore due

Perch and greenling are fished off the rocks at Barview Park, Tillamook Bay.

west of the bar. Most are caught in 9 fathoms and deeper. Charter boats head out regularly and are recommended for safe and successful halibut fishing.

First fishing in the bay in spring is for various surf and bottom fish, though even in January and February, casting from the rocks or jetties from the Barview area to Bay City can produce lingcod, rockfish, and perch. The north jetty is the more protected of the two for early season outings. Later, perch and greenling are also fished from boats near the rock outcrops of the lower main channel, off the rocks at Barview Park near the mouth, and at the Old Garibaldi Coast Guard Pier, which has been refurbished and is open for public angling. It extends 700 feet into the bay and is also used for crabbing and, at the end, a chance for chinook. This pier is wheelchair accessible. South jetty anglers take lingcod and chinook on bigger bait, or night fish for sea bass. Lingcod are also taken in the Barview area by boaters drifting herring. Common bottom fish baits are shrimp, clam necks, and kelp worms. Park-and-fish spots are available off Hwy. 101 from Bay City north to Hobsonville Point, an area that skirts the famous Ghost Hole, a popular salmon trolling area accessed by boats from public ramps in Bay City and downtown Garibaldi. The Bay City ramp is functional only at high tide.

Salmon angling in the bay usually gets serious in April, and for a month or two spring chinook are caught as they make their way toward the mouths of the Wilson and Trask. Five good size rivers empty into Tillamook Bay, the Wilson, Trask, Miami, Kilchis, and Tillamook. Fall chinook are available from late August till late October. Boat anglers troll the lower main channel, in front and behind the south jetty, the Ghost Hole, and the upper channel as well as the mouth of the Tillamook River. Herring, either whole or plug cut, is favored as high up as Memaloose Pt. From Memaloose up, spinners and Kwikfish type lures are used. Some anglers give the Kwickfish a herring or anchovy wrap. Spinners and lures also seem to be favored by anglers at the popularly named Sheep Corral an area in the channel opposite Kilchis Pt.

The Ghost Hole, just south of Hobsonville Point, is a favorite spot for large chinook. Some successful bay anglers claim that fishing for chinook is best on the incoming tide through high slack.

Like all coastal waters, Tillamook Bay is subject to emergency closures, dependent on estimates of anadromous runs and the state of the various fisheries. In 1994 the entire bay was closed to coho angling, and the extreme lower bay (below Kincheloe Point) was closed to chinook from June 20 through September 30. Check with the local tackle shops or the district ODF&W office for an update before planning a fishing trip that targets salmon.

An occasional steelhead is picked up by lure trollers late in the season. There's a very good bank fishery for perch just off the Hobsonville Point. Park and fish from the rocks.

Sturgeon angling is holding steady, with best catches in the Ghost Hole, off the mouth of the Trask, and off the Bay Ocean Flats. These sturgeon are presumed to be migrants from the Columbia River, though old timers say there are sturgeon in Tillamook Bay year-round. Best catches are made from mid-February to mid-April.

1 **BARVIEW PARK** - County park with camping, RV hook-ups; fish off the rock fill for perch.

2 **NORTH JETTY** - Fish for rockfish, some perch, salmon off furthest point.

3 **LOWER BAY** - Below painted rocks; troll for salmon; fish rock outcrops for greenling and perch.

4 **OLD COAST GUARD PIER** - Dig flats for clams; fish for crab from pier; all facilities upgraded.

5 **OLD MILL & GARIBALDI** - 2 public boat ramps; pay to launch

6 **MOUTH OF MIAMI** - Bank fishing below railroad bridge for fall chinook, chum salmon.

7 **HOBSONVILLE PT**. - perch in May & June

8 **GHOST HOLE** - Popular for salmon, perch, sturgeon at upper end, pile perch off Hobsonville Pt.; hole goes to 35 ft.

9 **BAY CITY RAMP** - Unimproved public ramp with poor access at low tide.

10 **PARKS LANDING** -Improved ramp is lowest take-out on Kilchis; provides bay access for car-top boats, but not at low water.

11 **HOQUARTEN SLOUGH** - Boat ramp on First St., Tillamook; accesses Hoquarten & Doughterty sloughs & lower Trask; shallow at low tides; fish sloughs for fall chinook in low water years.

12 **CARNAHAN PARK RAMP** - Improved ramp at end of 5th St., City of Tillamook; accesses lower Trask tidewater and upper bay; heavily used; fee.

13 **THE STURGEON HOLE** - fish for fall chinook & sturgeon, possible spring chinook or sea-run; limited parking.

14 **MOUTH OF TRASK** - Troll for sea-run, chinook.

15 **MEMALOOSE PT**. (Oyster House Hole) Improved county ramp accesses mouth of Tillamook salmon fishery; fee to launch.

16 **PICKET FENCE AT ROCKY Pt.** - Troll for sea-run up to Tillamook River.

17 **BAY OCEAN RD**. - Bank fish for fall chinook among pilings along main channel

18 **SHEEP CORRAL** - Salmon trolling among pilings

19 **MID-BAY** - Troll for salmon

20 **OLD CHANNEL** - Sporadic sturgeon

21 **MUD FLATS** - Hike across flats at low tide to fish for sturgeon; beware of rising tide and soft mud.

22 **CLAM FLATS** - boat access.

23 **BAY OCEAN TRAIL** - 3 mile bike or hike on gravel road to South Jetty

24 **CRAB HARBOR** - Well sheltered and popular.

25 **SOUTH JETTY** - Less angling pressure, more wind, rougher sea; fish for perch, fall chinook, rockfish; use bigger bait for lingcod; night fish for sea bass.

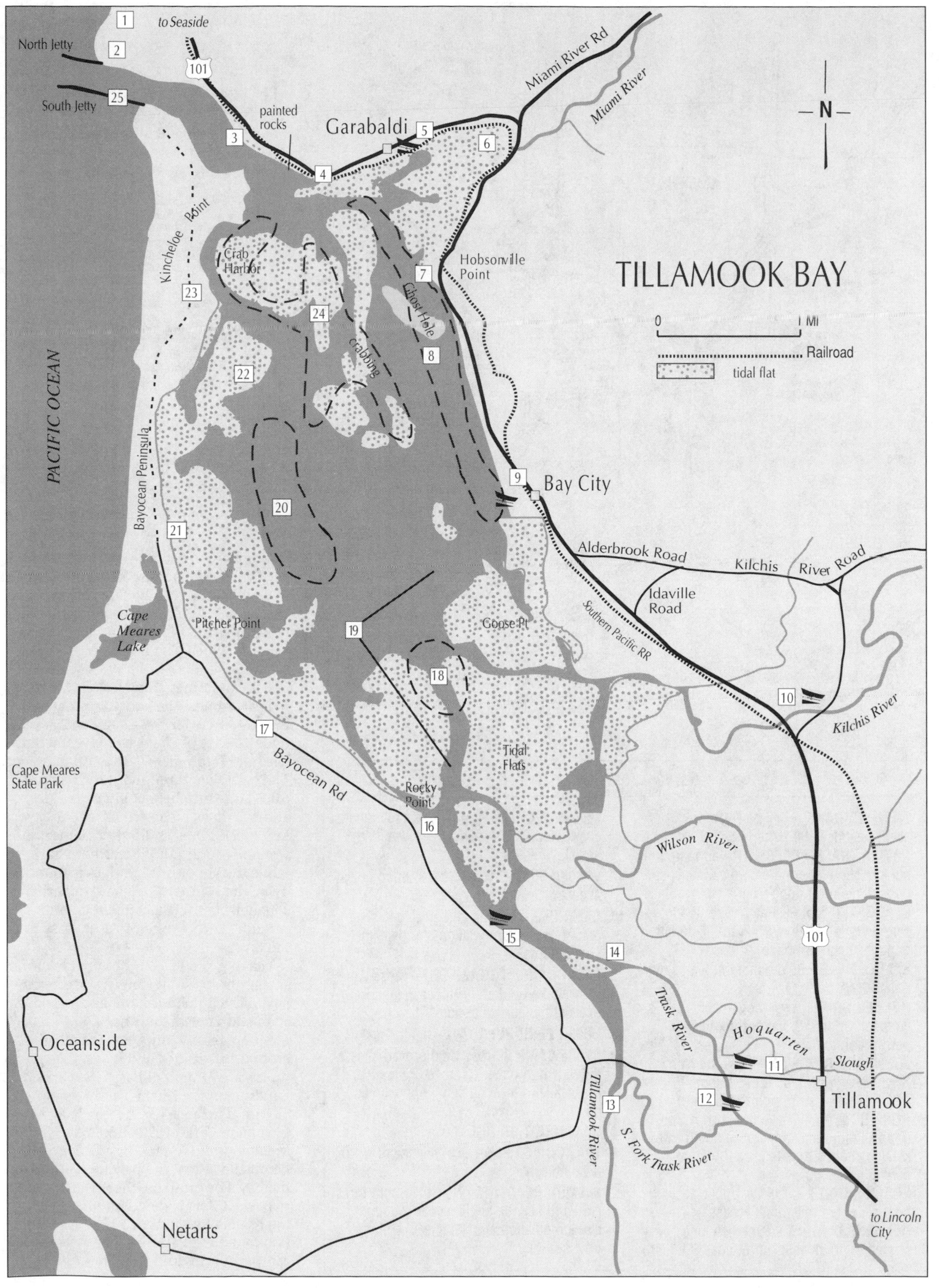
TILLAMOOK BAY
0
1 MI
Railroad
tidal flat
N
to Seaside
North Jetty
South Jetty
101
painted rocks
Garabaldi
Miami River Rd
Miami River
Kincheloe Point
Crab Harbor
Hobsonville Point
Ghost Hole
crabbing
PACIFIC OCEAN
Bayocean Peninsula
Bay City
Alderbrook Road
Kilchis River Road
Idaville Road
Southern Pacific RR
Cape Meares Lake
Pitcher Point
Goose Pt
Kilchis River
Cape Meares State Park
Bayocean Rd
Tidal Flats
Rocky Point
Wilson River
Trask River
Hoquarten Slough
Oceanside
Tillamook River
Tillamook
S. Fork Trask River
to Lincoln City
Netarts
1
2
3
4
5
6
7
8
9
10
11
12
13
14
15
16
17
18
19
20
21
22
23
24
25

Trask River

©Ron Blogett

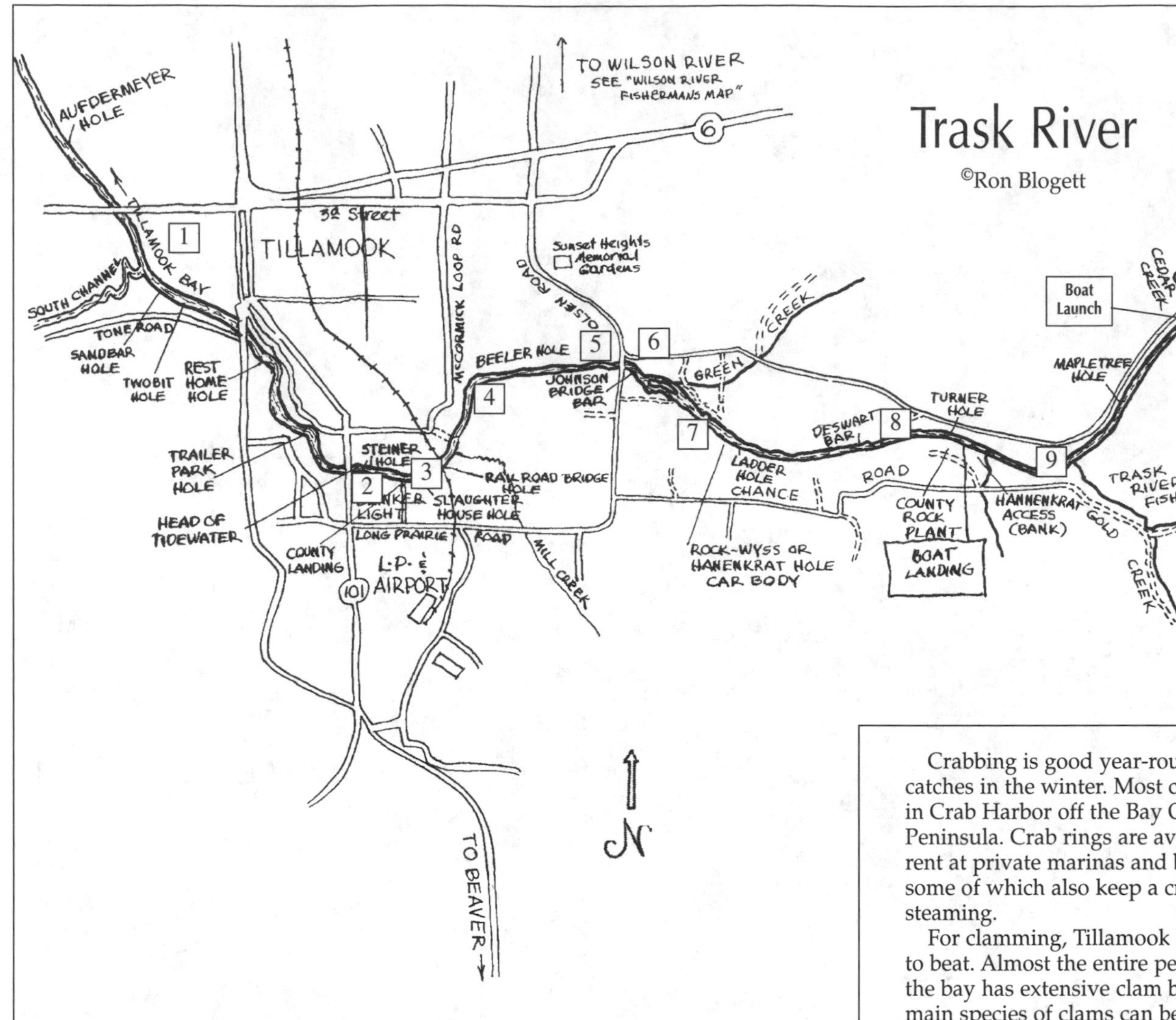

1 **FIFTH ST. RAMP** - City of Tillamook; accesses tidewater fisheries.
2 **LOWER TRASK ACCESS** - Paved ramp and bank angling at good salmon & steelhead hole; drive in off Long Prairie Rd.
3 **SLAUGHTER HOLE** - Pay to fish good salmon hole below railroad bridge in fall; park at slaughter house.
4 **BEALER HOLE** - Boat fishery at big salmon hole.
5 **HOLDEN DRIFT** - Walk down from Johnson Bridge. Private property. Ask permission to fish.
6 **JOHNSON BRIDGE DRIFT** - Good salmon & steelhead drift just above bridge. Private property. Ask permission to fish from bank.
7 **ROCK HOLE** - Bedrock chute drops into good salmon hole; anchor on south side; steelhead drift. Private property; boat fishing only.
8 **LOREN'S DRIFT** - ODF&W public access boat slide; 1/4 mile bank access.
9 **HANENKRAT DRIFT** - Bank fish long stretch of good water off Chance Rd. just below fish hatchery; modest fee to launch; check regulations for hatchery deadline and closures.
10 **WILDLIFE HOLE** - Steep bank, good holes; about 1/4 mile of bank access.
11 **DAM HOLE** - Salmon and steelhead plunking; check regulations for deadline and closures.
12 **LAST CHANCE TO TAKE-OUT** - most people take-out before Upper Peninsula to avoid big curlers at point.
13 **UPPER PENINSULA TAKE-OUT**
14 **STONE CAMP SLIDE** - Unimproved slide; drift down to upper or Lower Peninsula; road leads in through camp opposite cut-off to Wilson River.
15 **GIRL SCOUT BRIDGE**
16 **TRASK RIVER PARK** - confluence of North & South forks
17 **SALMON DEADLINE** - North & South forks closed to salmon angling year-round; check regulations for steelhead & short trout season.

Crabbing is good year-round with best catches in the winter. Most crabbers work in Crab Harbor off the Bay Ocean Peninsula. Crab rings are available for rent at private marinas and bait shops, some of which also keep a crab cooker steaming.

For clamming, Tillamook Bay is hard to beat. Almost the entire perimeter of the bay has extensive clam beds. All the main species of clams can be gathered here, although razors are getting scarce. The tidal flats throughout the bay produce large numbers of gaper, cockles, and softshells on a zero or less tide. Littleneck clams and butter clams are generally found in the northern bay, while the gaper or blue clam is found all over. The southern bay has primarily softshell clams. Check the regulations carefully before digging, as its easy to get the limit.

Herring can be caught in the bay from spring through fall. Anglers use herring jigs to catch them for bait and eating. A shad run appears in June.

Moorages and supplies are plentiful around three sides of the bay. Free public ramps are located at Bay City, Parks Landing on the Kilchis, and Hoquarten Slough. There's a fee to launch at Carnahan Park in Tillamook, at Memaloose Pt. on the Bay Ocean Peninsula and at the private marinas on the bay. For campers, there is a big county park at Barview and another just up the Kilchis River. About 12 miles south, Lookout State Park has an excellent campground with lots of space.

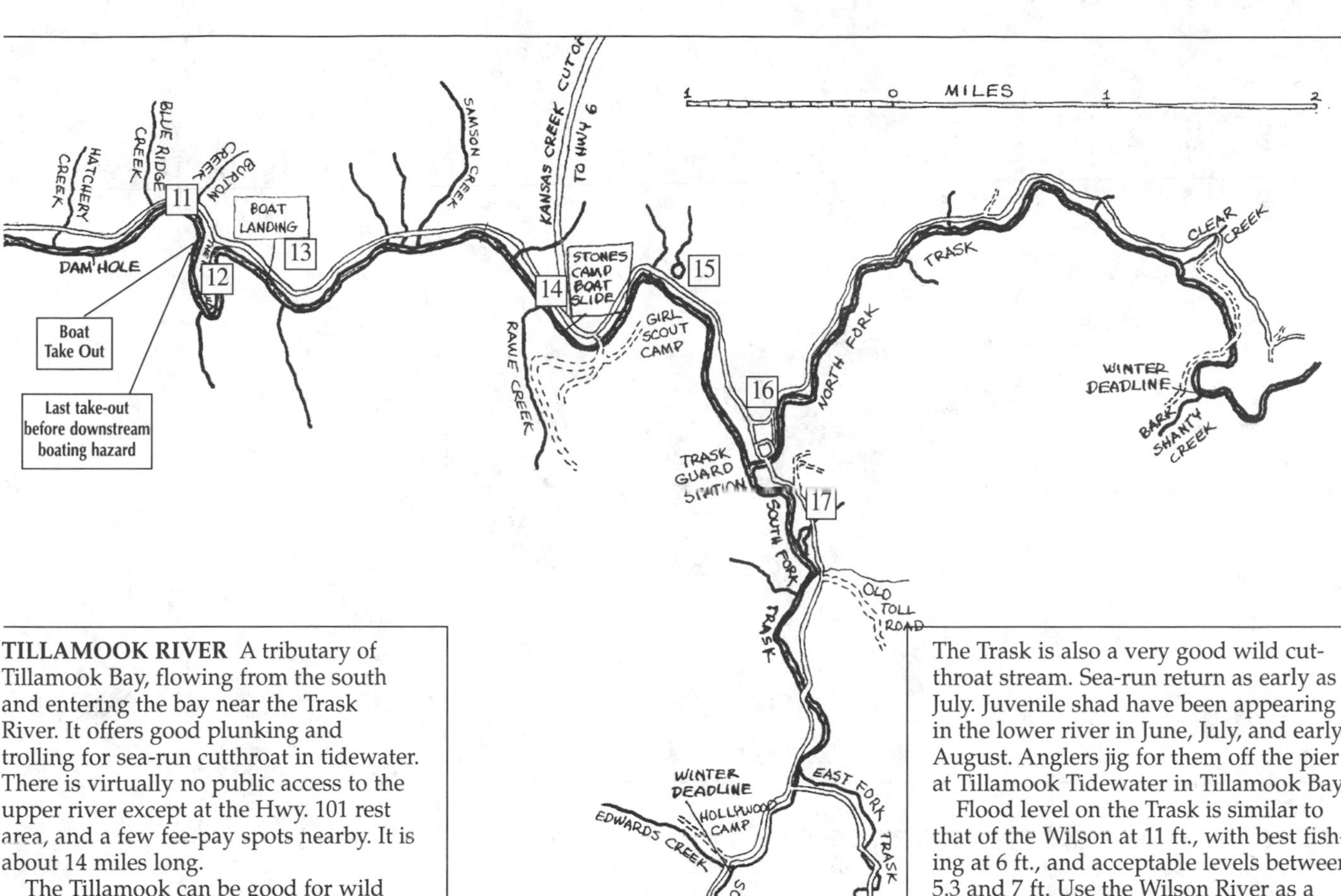

TILLAMOOK RIVER A tributary of Tillamook Bay, flowing from the south and entering the bay near the Trask River. It offers good plunking and trolling for sea-run cutthroat in tidewater. There is virtually no public access to the upper river except at the Hwy. 101 rest area, and a few fee-pay spots nearby. It is about 14 miles long.

The Tillamook can be good for wild cutthroat trout and has one of the coast's better sea-run fisheries. Sea-run are present from July through September in the tidewater reach. The river is best for plunking, as it has very few riffles or boulder areas. A few white sturgeon are taken each year, usually by surprised cutthroat plunkers. The river gets very low and warm in summer.

More salmon and steelhead are caught here than in the Miami, but less than in the Kilchis. Fall chinook show in late September and October. Coho move in about a month later, but the river is closed to coho angling. Cluster eggs work well, and there's always the chance of taking jack salmon. Steelhead fishing is best from late December to January. The hatchery steelhead program here is being phased out, but finclipped steelhead will be available for a while longer. All non-finclipped steelhead must be released unharmed.

Burton Bridge Boat Ramp on the Tillamook River Road provides access to the tidewater. Supplies and accommodations are available at Tillamook.

TRASK RIVER A very good steelhead and salmon river. The Trask is a large stream, about 50 miles long, entering Tillamook Bay at Tillamook just south of the Wilson River. It is crossed by Hwy. 101 at the head of tidewater, and both the mainstem and the north and south forks are followed by county and state forest roads.

It has lots of boulders and gravel stretches with some excellent fly water. The north fork is an exceptionally pretty fly stream. The south fork was ravaged by a forest fire in 1951 and was closed for a number of years but has now come back. In fact, the Tillamook Burn is officially healed, and the river reflects the forest's good health. Though the Trask still muddies, it clears quickly, and it no longer drops early now that the forest is holding.

The Trask is managed for wild steelhead, but a few hatchery strays do join both summer and winter runs. Steelhead are in the river year-round, but the winter run is by far the larger. The winter run begins building in December and holds through March. Sections of both forks are open for winter steelheading.

There is a major fall chinook run on the Trask, and spring chinook appear in the river in April, with the run peaking in June. The Trask is also a very good wild cutthroat stream. Sea-run return as early as July. Juvenile shad have been appearing in the lower river in June, July, and early August. Anglers jig for them off the pier at Tillamook Tidewater in Tillamook Bay.

Flood level on the Trask is similar to that of the Wilson at 11 ft., with best fishing at 6 ft., and acceptable levels between 5.3 and 7 ft. Use the Wilson River as a gauge. A random recorded listing of some Oregon river gauge readings is available by calling the National Weather Forecasting Office in Portland at (503) 261-9246. River gauge readings are printed in *The Oregonian* daily.

TRIANGLE LAKE A very good lake for bass, panfish, kokanee, and trout. This 290-acre lake is west of Blachly on Hwy. 36, about 23 miles west of Junction City. It can be reached from the coast by Hwy. 36 from Florence.

Close to the Willamette Valley, it attracts many anglers and provides good numbers of panfish and bass throughout spring and summer. Bluegill are very plentiful, and there are brown bullhead, and perch, in addition to largemouth bass. Most fish are taken on simple bait, but evening fly-fishing and plugging can produce some nice bass. Its tributaries supply a good population of wild cutthroat. Kokanee are well established. Fish deep for these landlocked sockeye salmon.

There is a fishing pier and a boat ramp with limited parking. Water skiers abound in summer, so best fishing is early and late in the day, which suits the bass just fine anyway.

VERNONIA LAKE This popular 45-acre former mill pond is located at the south end of the town of Vernonia. It has a population of bluegill, largemouth bass, and

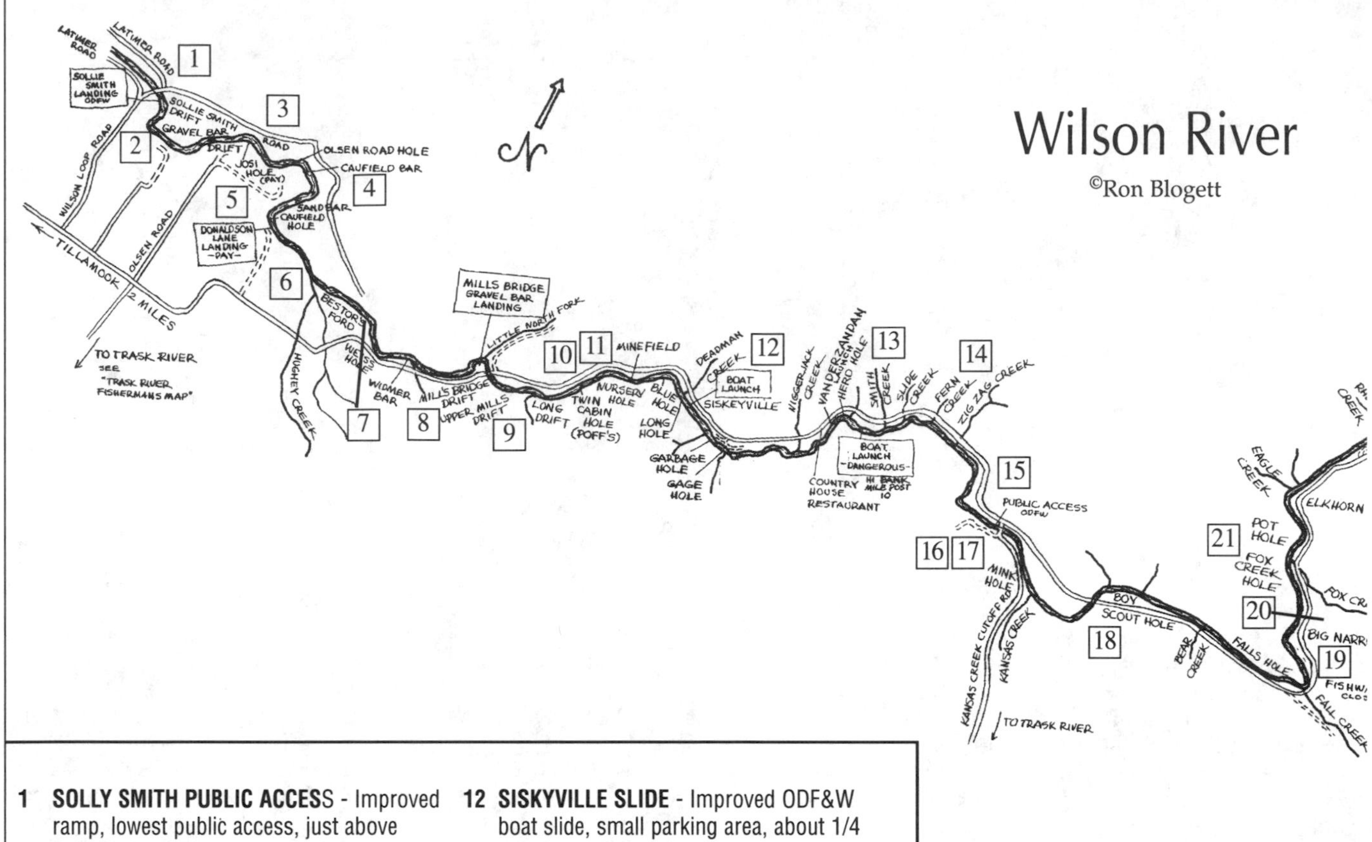

Wilson River

©Ron Blogett

1 **SOLLY SMITH PUBLIC ACCESS** - Improved ramp, lowest public access, just above Solly Smith Bridge; used as take-out; some bank fishing.

2 **TITTLE HOLE** - Chinook only, no steelhead.

3 **LOWER JOSI** - Good drift near center of Josi Farm; long drift at low end of hole; pay to bank fish.

4 **UPPER JOSI** - Salmon hole; tail-out for steelhead; pay to fish from bank.

5 **DONALDSON BAR** - Quarter mile steelhead drift; pay to put-in or take-out at gravel bar.

6 **GUARD RAIL** - Gravel bar and 1/2 mile drift; one of the popular spots on the river.

7 **TRAILER PARK HOLE** - Bank access for paying guests only.

8 **MILLS BRIDGE BAR** - County-owned access to put-in or take-out at gravel bar; good bank fishing for steelhead and salmon; handicapped anglers park on bar, others in lot.

9 **JUST ABOVE THE BRIDGE** - Public access from south bank.

10 **SLIDE AREA** - one-half mile of good steelhead drift water downstream and up to Blue Hole.

11 **MING CREEK PUBLIC ACCESS** - Public bank angling for steelhead and salmon; no boat ramp.

12 **SISKYVILLE SLIDE** - Improved ODF&W boat slide, small parking area, about 1/4 mile below Siskeyville.

13 **VANDERZANDEN SLIDE (HERD HOLE)** - Improved boat slide; quarter mile of north bank access on either side; good hole; some parking.

14 **YERGEN ACCESS** - Public access upstream about 1/4 mile; watch for small turn-out at about road mile 13.5;trail to river starts 200 ft. downstream from parking area; good steelhead water and access to salmon holding hole. Please use trail.

15 **ZIG ZAG PUBLIC ACCESS** - bank access, about 1,160 ft.

16 **KANSAS CREEK BRIDGE** - Access to 3/4 mile south bank, 1/2 mile north bank downstream; good steelhead water.

17 **KANSAS CREEK BRIDGE HOLE** - Right under bridge; good for salmon, steelhead.

18 **DEMOLAY CAMP HOLE** - County park; rough water here to swinging bridge; put-in not recommended; good salmon hole; good steelhead drift upstream.

19 **FALL CREEK PUBLIC ACCESS** - Good winter steelhead water; drift 200 ft. above Fall Creek; fish pockets behind rocks 200 ft. downstream; no angling within 200 ft. of fishway at mouth of Fall Creek.

20 **BIG NARROWS** - Walk in on trail from turn-out just upstream of mile post 14; good summer steelhead and salmon hole.

21 **FOX CREEK HOLE** - Salmon and summer steelhead hole just below mouth.

22 **OVERBANK** - Good sea-run cutthroat hole; steep bank.

23 **MUESIAL CREEK HOLE** - Good summer steelhead.

24 **KEENIG BRIDGE HOLE** - Salmon holding hole and summer steelhead right under bridge. County park on north bank has been closed but may re-open.

25 **JORDAN CREEK BRIDGE HOLE** - Good for both winter and summer steelhead; stay below bridge.

26 **HARRY SMITH HOLE** - Good for salmon.

27 **TURN-OUT HOLE** - Turn-out on north side of Hwy. 6

28 **CEDAR CREEK HOLE** - Chinook holding area just below mouth of Cedar Creek.

29 **CEDAR CREEK DRIFT** - Good for summer steelhead.

30 **COYOTE HOLE** - Good for summer steelhead.

31 **JONES CREEK BRIDGE HOLE** - Fish right under bridge for salmon, steelhead; Park has been closed but may re-open.

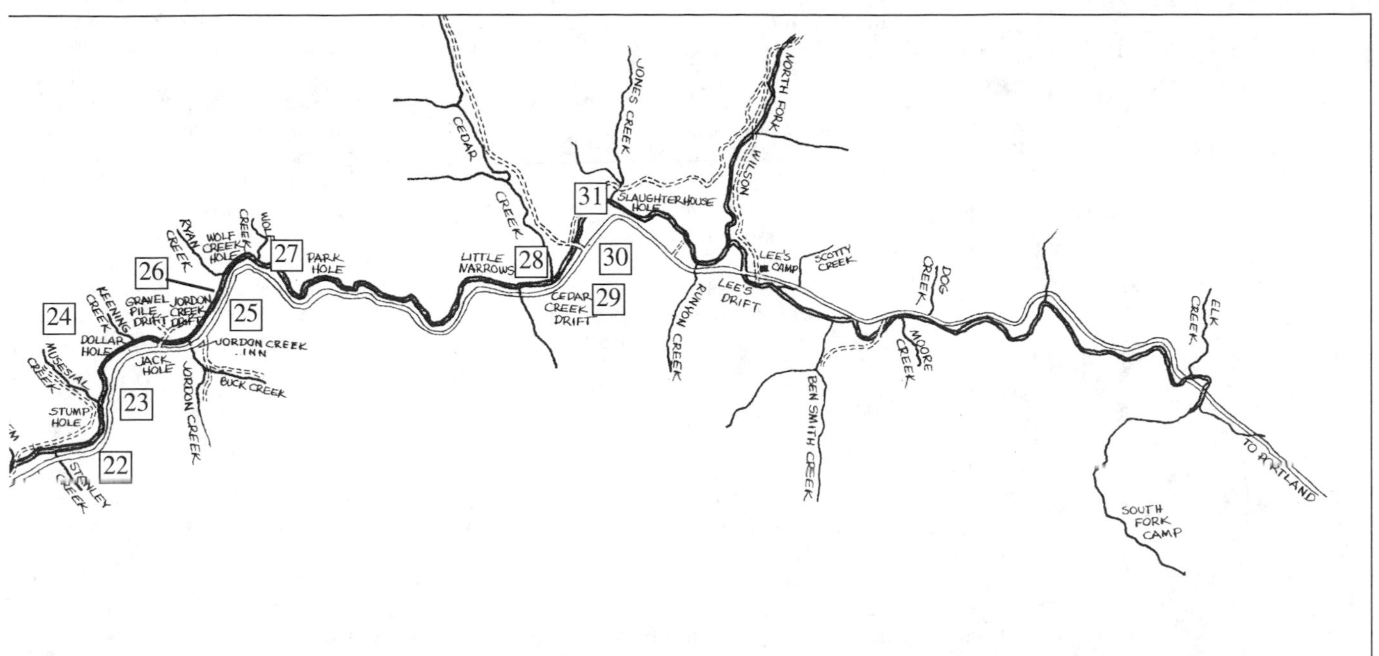

perch. The lake is stocked with legal rainbow several times a year. It has good bank access. Boats are allowed, but motors are prohibited. Wheelchair accessible.

WEST LAKE A good bass and panfish lake just 3 miles north of Gearhart, east of Hwy. 101. The highway follows its western shore, and a county road follows the western shore. About 1/2 mile long, it is similar in character and fishing to Sunset, Cullaby, and South. It contains good size perch and crappie, and fair size bluegill. Largemouth bass are available, with a few 2 pounds or better. Small boats can be launched off the road crossing. Fishing is best early in season before heavy weed growth.

WESTPORT SLOUGH An extensive slough area with over 15 species of bass and panfish, located just north and east of Westport on Hwy. 30, 10 miles west of Clatskanie on the lower Columbia. A number of bridges and county roads provide good access. The slough mouth can be reached by going north on the Columbia from Woodson Boat Ramp, or from the public ramp at Westport.

It has lots of white and black crappie, and fair numbers of bluegill, brown bullhead, and yellow perch. This is excellent largemouth bass water, with bass to 7 pounds taken on plugs and spinners.

WILSON RIVER Consistently one of the top ten producers of salmon and steelhead on the Oregon coast, a popular and accessible river that enters Tillamook Bay. It flows through Coast Range timberland then out across the bucolic Tillamook Valley, where black and white cows graze

Wilson River summer steelhead fishing picks up in May.

beside its banks. It is followed closely by Hwy. 6, also known as the Wilson River Rd., which runs west from Forest Grove west of Portland.

Steelhead are in the Wilson year-round. The winter run picks up in December and holds through March. The summer run picks up in May and carries on through August. The river is stocked with both summer and winter steelhead and has wild runs. Non-finclipped steelhead must be released unharmed.

Spring chinook generally enter the stream in April, and the run peaks in June and July. A much larger fall chinook run begins in October and peaks in November.

The Wilson has traditionally welcomed many sea-run cutthroat from about the middle of July. But sea-run returns are down here as in other Oregon coast streams.

Access to the Wilson is from pull-offs on Hwy. 6. The banks can be steep, with some bushwhacking necessary. There is excellent access to bank fishable waters below the forks at Fall Creek, Herd Hole, Kansas Creek Bridge, Lee's Bridge, Mining Creek, Siskeyville, and Zig Zag Creek. Boat drifting is popular in the lower 10 miles from the ramp at Siskeyville, about 2 miles above Mills Bridge, with take-out at Solly Smith Bridge about one mile east of Tillamook. Supplies and accommodations are available at Tillamook and at several places along the river.

The South Fork Wilson River enters the mainstream 3-4 miles above Lee's Camp (on Hwy. 6). Above the South Fork confluence, the mainstream Wilson is popularly known as the Devils Lake Fork. Both South Fork and Devils Lake Fork are currently closed to all angling, as are all other tributaries other than the Little North Fork, which is open for catch and release trout fishing with barbless hooks, and for steelhead from January 1 through March 31. Flood stage on the Wilson is 11 ft. Call National Weather Forecasting for a gauge reading, 503-261-9246.

WOAHINK LAKE A large lake with good fishing for yellow perch to 14 inches. Its shoreline forms the eastern boundary of Honeyman State Park, 3 miles south of Florence. Woahink is very popular for water sports and recreation, but the water isn't very productive for fishing. It covers 350 acres and receives plants of legal rainbow each spring. It also has wild cutthroat and a fair largemouth bass population. There are two excellent boat ramps at the north end of the lake, and campgrounds at the state park.

YACHATS RIVER (Pronounced yaw-hots) A small coastal river entering the ocean just south of the town of Yachats, and crossed by Hwy. 101 near its mouth. Only about 15 miles long, it ranges from 30-50 feet wide. A good road, County Rd. 804, follows the main stream and both forks for most of their length.

The Yachats has a fair population of wild cutthroat and has traditionally offered good sea-run angling in late summer and early fall. All its steelhead are wild, so plan on catch and release here. Steelhead are present from late November through March. Most steelhead angling takes place in the lower few miles.

The river is closed to coho angling, but a scattering of chinook enter the river. Nearby Beachside State Park, on the ocean about 4 miles north, used to host a unique surf smelt fishery in the late spring, but smelt have not been seen in recent years.

There is lot of posted land along the stream. Ask permission of landowners before you approach the stream. There are campgrounds at state parks north and south on Hwy. 101, or in the Siuslaw National Forest near the headwaters.

YAQUINA BAY Outlet for the Yaquina River system, one of the most popular and productive bays on the Oregon Coast. Newport has a large charter fleet that pursues bottom fish throughout the year, halibut and salmon as regulations allow. The bay covers 1,700 acres, and tidewater runs up about 13 miles.

The Yaquina enters the ocean just west of the community of Newport, about 110 miles from Portland, and is easily reached by Hwy. 101 from north and south. From the Albany-Corvallis area, it's only an hour's drive on Hwy. 20 down the Yaquina River. The north bay shore is easily accessed by a road east to Toledo. Access on the south shore is limited to the stretch from Hwy. 101 east to Hinton Point. About half-way up the bay, Oysterville (on the south side) can be reached by a secondary road from Toledo.

Beyond the Yaquina bar, halibut are caught from the whistler buoy to the lighthouse on Yaquina Head off Agate Beach. Halibut anglers drift herring on the bottom at around 30 fathoms. Bottom dwellers, such as greenling, lingcod, cabezon, and rockfish are pursued over a series of reefs from the bay's south jetty south to Waldport. Most of these fish can be found at 8-15 fathoms. Avoid the reef just off the end of the south jetty, and begin fishing at the airport (the beacon is visible). Whole herrings or leadhead jigs with plastic worms are favored for this fishery. Larger lingcod, red snapper, and halibut are fished at The Rockpile, about 13 miles west southwest of Newport. Fishing here is at 15 to 30 fathoms and deeper. The salmon fishery outside of Yaquina Bay has been severely limited in recent years. In 1994, offshore salmon activity was limited to a brief spring chinook fishery from May 1 to June 5. The bar is usually safe to cross, but checking with the Coast Guard is always a good idea.

These days, bottom fish are the most popular fishery within the bay. Cabezon and striped perch are taken from the south jetty, which is studded with rock breakwaters that offer prime rockfish habitat. Both rockfish and greenling are fished from the north jetty. Bank anglers catch perch from the Gas Plant dock, at the old La Paz Marina, and along the north shore around navigational marker 25. Boat anglers take perch in the lower bay and around the rocks off Coquille Pt.

Salmon activity within the bay has changed considerably in recent years. The private coho aquaculture facility that contributed significant numbers of fish to the coho sportfishery here, folded in 1991. In 1994, emergency regulations closed the bay to coho fishing, and to spring chinook from June 20 to August 15. Herring is the choice salmon bait, either mooched or trolled, and can be obtained locally or caught easily by jigging almost anywhere in the bay.

In late fall, chinook action moves further up the bay. Anglers anchor and fish, or troll from September to

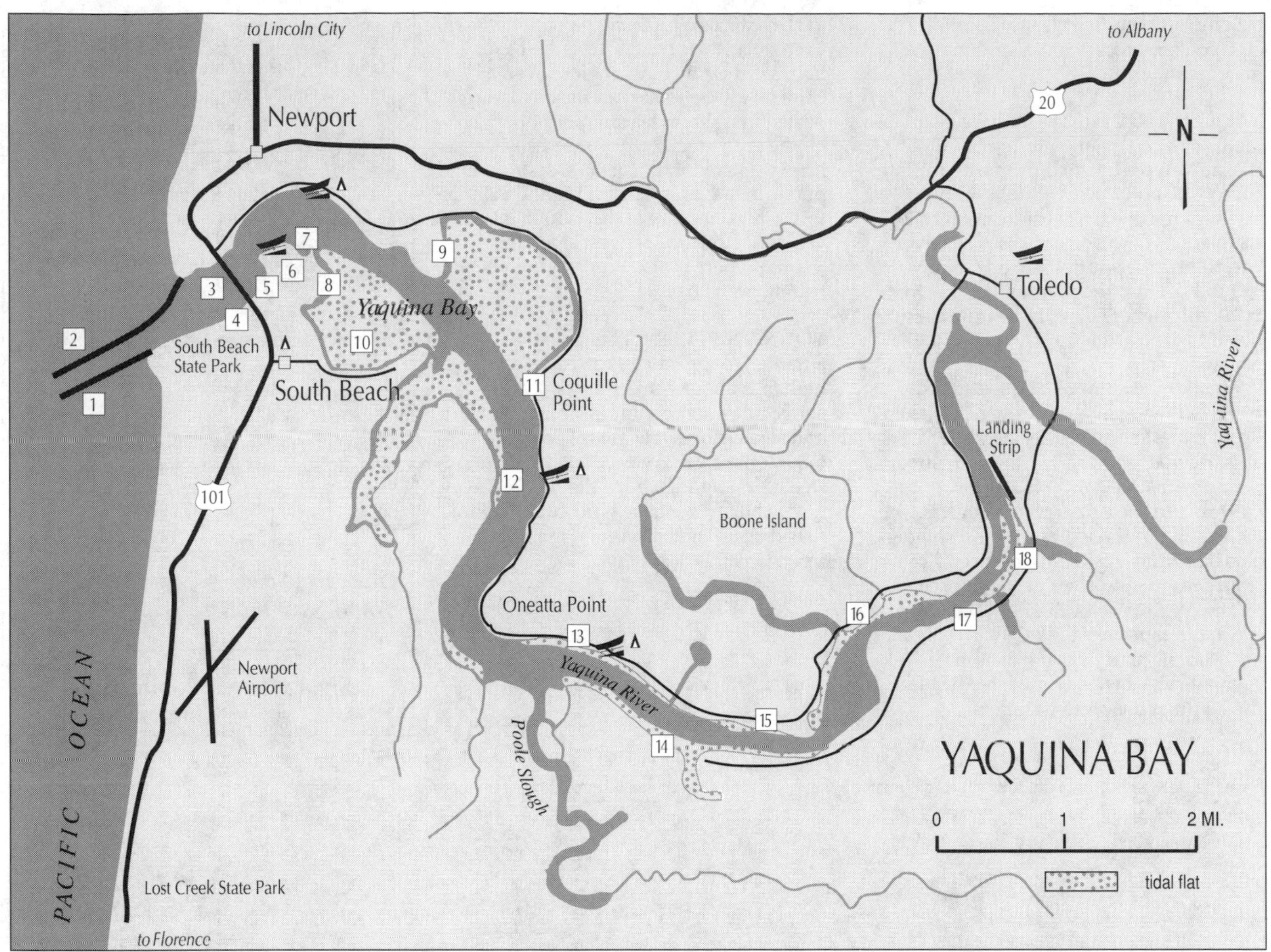

1 **SOUTH JETTY** - Fish for cabezon, greenling, striped perch; road goes directly to jetty.

2 **NORTH JETTY** - From State Park, take long stairs and rock-hop to jetty; fish for rockfish, greenling, cabezon, striped perch.

3 **LOWER BAY** - Anchor or troll for salmon Sept.-Nov.; also dungeness crab, lingcod, striped perch.

4 **BRIDGE FLATS SOUTH** - Dig for cockle and gaper clams.

5 **PUBLIC DOCK** - Dungeness crab

6 **MARINA BREAKWATERS** - Fish for perch; public access to Newport Marina at Southbeach.

7 **BREAKWATER FLAT** - Dig on south side of flat only for gapers; boat access only.

8 **AQUARIUM**

9 **GAS PLANT DOCK** - Wheelchair accessible dock; fish from dock and west bank for perch spring through fall.

10 **UP-BAY FLATS** - Dig for cockle, gaper clams; access from Science Center parking lot or Idaho Pt.

11 **COQUILLE PT.** - Fish the rocky area from the bank for perch.

12 **TROLL** - for salmon, September - November.

13 **MARKER 25** - Fish from bank for perch & sturgeon; intermittent bank access from marker upstream for perch, sturgeon; dig flats for softshell clams.

14 **SOFTSHELL FLATS NORTH**- Dig for softshells.

15 **SOFTSHELL FLATS** - Best digging for softshells.

16 **MARKER 37** - Navigational marker on road; bank fish deep water for sturgeon.

17 **MARKER 38** - Fish off South Bay Road for sturgeon winter & spring.

18 **CREITSER'S ISLAND** - Boat to island for good softshell digging; access from Toledo public boat ramp.

November. Spinners and Kwikfish-type lures are popular.

There is a small sturgeon fishery mid-bay in winter and spring. Bank anglers can fish for sturgeon off South Bay Road. Jigging for herring at South Beach Marina is a great way to introduce kids to fishing. The catch rate is very high in February and March. Use a herring jig (a small bare hook with yarn). Tackle is available locally.

Crab are taken year round. Pots are available for rent, and bait can be obtained locally. Pots are used rather than rings to discourage hungry seals. Check at the marina for current hot spots, or try casting pots about 1/2 mile above the bridge on either side of the channel.

Newport is a delightful coast town with all the flavor of a working fishing port. Just being at dockside when a big charter boat starts unloading its catch is a thrill. If you have a chance, stop by the Oregon State University Marine Science Center. This is a very fine aquarium complex, and admission is free. You'll long remember the octopus that greets you in the lobby.

Newport Marina at South Beach, operated by the Port of Newport, is near the Marine Science Center, with extensive public docks, charter boats, a full service public RV park, and other support facilities, including a fish cleaning station, crab cooker, grocery store, and marine information center.

YAQUINA RIVER The Yaquina is a medium-size stream entering Yaquina Bay at Newport, fished primarily for fall chinook. County Rd. 515 follows the stream's north bank west from Hwy. 101 to Toledo. There one can cross the river and follow the south bank on County Rd. 533 to Elk City, and County Rd. 539 to Eddyville, where County Rd. 180 cuts north to follow the upper river to the Nashville area.

Most of the chinook angling takes place in the lower bay, but fish are taken up to the salmon and steelhead deadline at Eddyville, about 2 1/2 miles upstream.

Early season angling is fair for wild cutthroat in the upper river. Anglers troll for sea-run in the lower river on spinner and bait from July through the end of trout season. The river is not stocked.

The confluence of Big Elk Creek and the Yaquina River at Elk City is a popular area for cutthroat, as well as fall chinook. A small run of wild winter steelhead in the Yaquina draws few anglers.

YOUNG'S BAY A small bay on the Columbia River near Astoria that is primarily fished by local anglers. A small chinook gillnet fishery in the bay is supported by salmon rearing pens operated by the gillnetters. In 1993, the fishery was briefly opened to the general sportfishing public in late May. For information about this fishery, inquire at the Tide Point convenience store on the west side of Astoria. There is also limited sturgeon fishing in the bay.

YOUNG'S RIVER The main stream entering Young's Bay near Astoria. A high falls about 9 miles up (1/2 mile above tidewater) is impassable to salmon and steelhead. A few are taken in tidewater, but the river is closed to salmon and steelhead angling above the first highway bridge below the falls. Wild cutthroat are fished up to the falls and in the upper river, which is accessed by logging roads.

Yaquina Bay's large charter fleet pursues bottom fish throughout the year, salmon and steelhead in season.

SOUTHWEST ZONE

The Southwest Zone is all waters draining directly to the Pacific Ocean south of, and including, the Umpqua River drainage; and those portions of the Klamath River drainage in Jackson County.

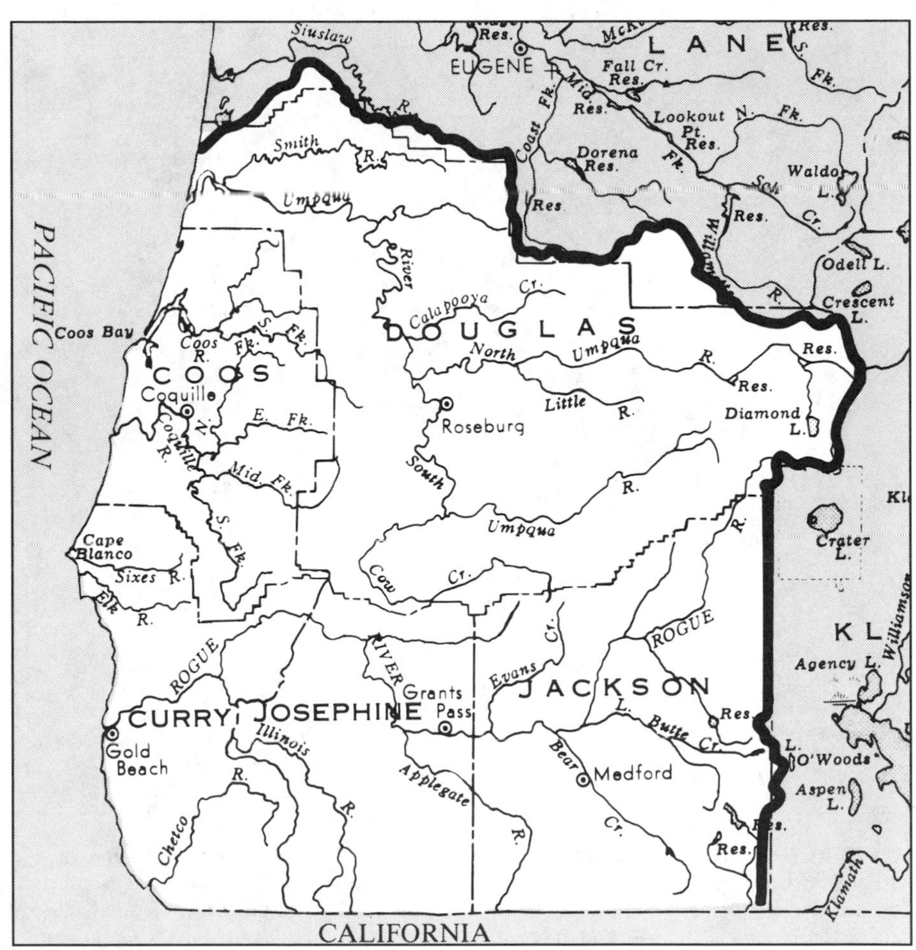

The variety of fishing and vistas offered by the Southwest Zone is exemplifed by its two biggest rivers, the Rogue and the Umpqua.

Each of these giants extends its boarding house reach over 200 miles, from the west slope Cascades to the Pacific Ocean, offering opportunities for trout, salmon, steelhead, bass, clams, crab, perch, and cod in settings as distinct as the glacial peaks of the high Cascades, a fir-rimmed reservoir, the county fairgrounds in Roseburg, a highway bridge in Grants Pass, a gravel bar in a rocky canyon, a myrtle grove on a tidewater slough, a rock jetty overlooking the Pacific surf.

It encompasses portions of three mountain ranges (the Cascades, Coast Range, and Siskiyous), three national forests (Siskiyou, Umpqua, and Winema), and four federally designated wilderness areas (Wild Rogue, Rogue-Umpqua Divide, Sky Lakes, and Kalmiopsis).

In the southwest, the coastal climate is subtly warmer than it is to the north. Inland, temperature extremes are greater, with colder winters and hotter summers. Annual rainfall varies from over 100 inches per year in the western Siskiyou Mts. to less than 20 inches at Medford.

Bass fishing is growing in popularity here as elsewhere in the state. Pro-bass tournaments take place throughout the summer at Tenmile Lakes on the coast, and smallmouth bass are the number one fishery on the lower Umpqua from May through October. Bass and other warmwater species are thriving in the region's big reservoirs: Applegate, Ben Irving, Cooper Creek, Emigrant Lake, Howard Prairie, Plat 1, Selmac, and Willow Creek.

Salmon and steelhead, though struggling in the wake of a seven year drought and unfavorable ocean currents, are far from deposed in the affection and efforts of southwestern anglers. They are the primary fisheries in the zone's major rivers: Applegate, Chetco, Coquille, Illinois, Millicoma, Smith, Rogue, and Umpqua.

Rogue River steelhead, both wild and hatchery, are faring better than their northern cousins, probably due to localized ocean conditions. Rogue River coho runs are stable, and coho are running strong in the Smith River. Isthmus Slough in south Coos Bay offers a developing fishery for hatchery-reared fall chinook and coho, as does the Coquille. The West Fork Millicoma has developed a strong run of hatchery-reared winter steelhead.

The Southwest Zone is also rich in opportunities to fish for large trout. Big browns are plentiful in Lemolo and Toketee reservoirs. Rainbow to 8 lbs. are available in Diamond and Fish lakes. And 20" rainbow are caught and released year-round in the tailrace fishery (called *The Holy Water*) below Rogue River's Lost Creek Dam.

The Southwest Zone is accessed by Hwy. 101 on the coast, and by I-5, which runs north-south from Portland into California between the Coast and Cascade mountain ranges. Routes inland from the coast are limited to Hwy. 38 (which leads from Reedsport on the lower Umpqua to Cottage Grove), Hwy. 42 (which follows the lower Coquille and emerges from the Coast Range at Roseburg), and Hwy. 199, (which heads northwest from Crescent City, CA to Grants Pass). There is no through-road along the Rogue River between I-5 and the Coast.

Two highways access the zone's Cascade Mt. fisheries. Hwy. 138 follows the North Umpqua upstream from Roseburg. Hwy. 62 follows the Rogue River upstream from Central Point. Secondary roads in all mountain areas are generally graded, but unpaved and unlighted.

Campgrounds are plentiful in the national forests , but are less so on the coast. Motels and private RV parks are plentiful on the coast, and are available inland near major communities. Many of the larger lakes and reservoirs offer "resort" facilities. Visitors should be aware that most of these resorts, while pleasant and comfortable, are somewhat rustic.

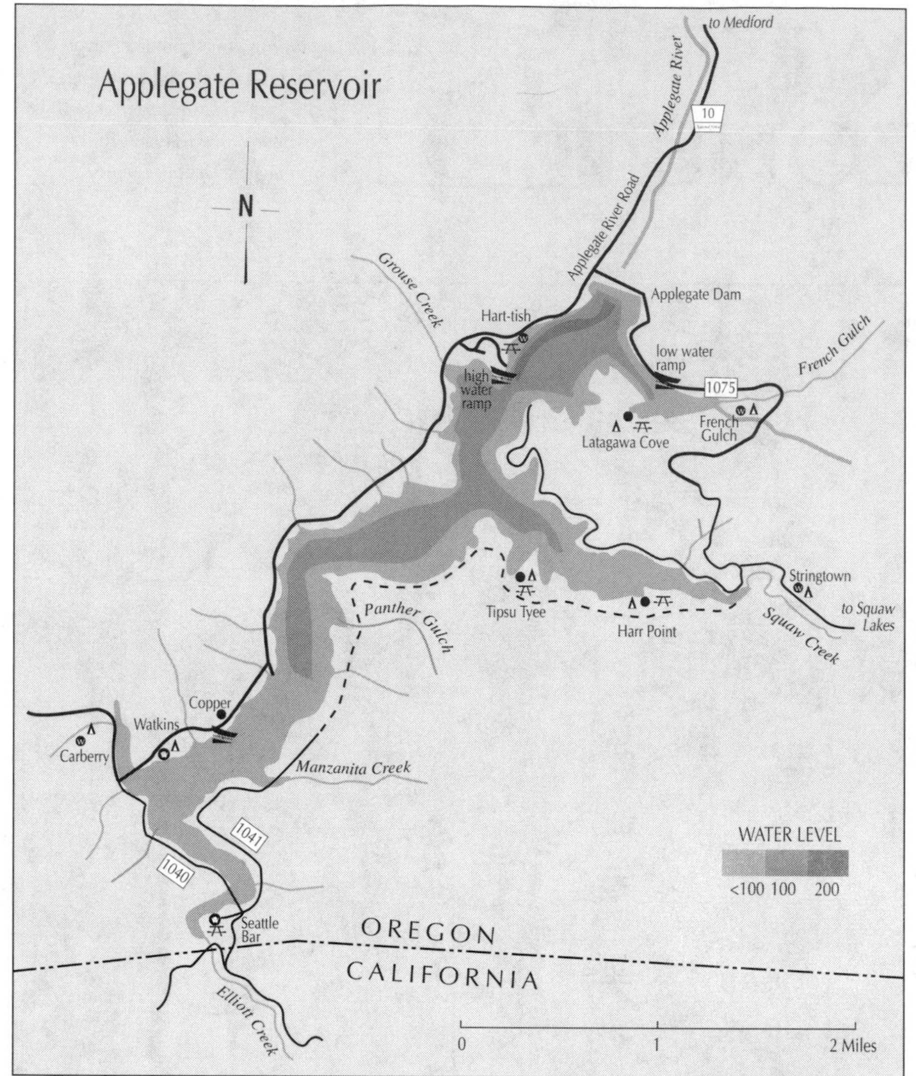

AGATE RESERVOIR A good bass and panfish lake on Upper Dry Creek, NE of Medford. From Hwy. 62 in Medford, take Lake of the Woods Hwy. 140. Watch for signs. Agate covers 216 acres and is open year around, but fishing's best in spring. Abundant yellow perch, good numbers of crappie, largemouth bass, brown bullhead, and bluegill are available. A canoe, float tube, raft, or rowboat is useful here. Motors are prohibited. There's a picnic area, but no overnight camping.

ALTA LAKE A narrow 32-acre hike-in lake in the Seven Lakes Basin of the Sky Lakes Area, Rogue River National Forest. The basin is accessed by several trails from the west with trailheads on forest roads 3780, 3785, and 3790. The trailhead on Forest Rd. 3780, leading to Trail 980 then Trail 979 is designated the Alta Lake Trail on the Sky Lakes Wilderness map.

Seven Lakes Basin is also approached by trails from the east, heading at Sevenmile Marsh. At Ft. Klamath on Hwy. 62, turn west on County Rd. 1419. At about 4 miles, when the county road bears right, continue straight then turn right onto Forest Rd. 3334 to Sevenmile Marsh Campground. Follow Trail 3703. At its junction with the Pacific Crest Trail, take the left fork. The trail west to Grass and Middle lakes is less than 3 miles from the junction. About 1/2 mile further on the PCT, a trail leads west to Cliff Lake. To reach Alta, follow the Cliff Lake Trail past Cliff and South lakes. At the next trail junction, head north to Alta.

One of the last lakes in the area to thaw, Alta offers fair fishing for stocked brook trout. There is a natural campsite at the north end, and good trail access to other fishable lakes east in the basin. See also Middle, Grass, and Cliff.

APPLEGATE RESERVOIR A popular, deep multi-purpose reservoir on the upper Applegate river within view of the picturesque Siskiyou mountains. The pool varies from 990 to 360 acres, with a maximum depth of 225 ft. near the dam and an average depth of 83 ft. It offers good opportunities for stocked trout, large and smallmouth bass, and crappie. The reservoir's relatively low elevation provides a good growing season for warm water fish. A 10-mph speed limit throughout the reservoir helps preserve the peaceful wilderness-like setting.

From Medford or Grants Pass, take Hwy. 238 south to the reservoir access road, which becomes Forest Rd. 10. At the reservoir, the left fork leads to French Gulch and Stringtown campgrounds on the upper NE arm of the reservoir. The right fork leads to Watkins and Carberry camps at the southern end. A trail from French Gulch follows the east shore all the way to Manzanita Cr., about 4 miles. The entire shoreline, about 18 miles, can be hiked.

The reservoir is stocked annually with 25,000 legal rainbow and 150,000 fingerlings, as well as an occasional batch of juvenile chinook which grow to 16 inches and resemble kokanee.

Largemouth bass to 9 pounds have been caught here. Though not as productive as shallower reservoirs, Applegate has some good bass, particularly in shallower Squaw Creek Arm, and among the submerged forest in the Carberry Arm. Both white and black crappie are available in the shallows at the heads of the arms and in the bays. Fishing is best in late spring, while the lake is still full and cool. Smallmouth bass are well established near rocky structures.

There are two year around boat ramps, at Hart-tish Campground on the northwest shore and at Copper near Watkins Campground on the southwest shore. A ramp east of the dam near French Gulch Campground is usable only at low water. Latagawa, Tipsu Tyee, and Harr Point campgrounds are hike-in or boat-in only. Additional campgrounds are located on the Applegate River Rd., including a group camp at Flumet Flat available by reservation (Call (503) 770-6806 or 899-1544). Campsites at nearby Squaw Lakes are available by reservation only. Wheelchair accessible restroom facilities are available at Carberry, Watkins, and Hart-tish campgrounds.

APPLEGATE RIVER A major tributary of the Rogue River, entering the mainstem 2 miles above Whitehorse Rapids, 5 miles west of Grants Pass.

Hwy. 199 and county roads access the lower river south of the city. A county road follows the south bank east from Wilderville, and another follows the north bank east from Jerome Prairie. There is a county park on the river about 5 miles south of Jerome. From Grants Pass, head south toward Murphy, and pick up Hwy. 238. From Medford, Hwy. 38 leads to the river road cut-off at the town of Ruch. The Applegate River Rd. follows the stream to Applegate Dam.

The Applegate produces a good run of late-arriving winter steelhead that peaks in March. Best steelheading is downstream from the mouth of the Little Applegate, about 2 1/2 miles south of Ruch. Fishing for wild rainbow trout is good from early season through late spring, especially in the upper river between the Little Applegate and the dam.

Barbless hooks are required throughout the year, and non-finclipped trout and steelhead must be released unharmed except that wild steelhead (over 24 inches) may be kept during steelhead season, January 1 through March 31. The run has been very low in recent years. Angling from a floating device is prohibited.

There are several camping and picnic areas on the upper river road before you get to the reservoir, including the Cantrall-Buckley Campground just about 6 miles east of the community of Applegate about a mile past the point where Hwy. 238 crosses the river.

BABYFOOT LAKE A popular 4-acre lake in a designated botanical area just inside the Kalmiopsis Wilderness of the Siskiyou National Forest, accessible from the east. From Cave Junction, in the valley of the Illinois River, take Hwy. 199 north about 4 miles to Forest Rd. 4201, a gravel road, which you follow for roughly 10 miles. A dirt road near the end of Forest Rd. 4201 leads to the trailhead at Onion Camp. It's just a half mile hike to the lake.

Brook trout were plentiful here until someone illegally introduced largemouth bass. Fishing's best in spring and late fall. Since Babyfoot is a wilderness lake, there is no developed campground, and wilderness camping guidelines should be observed.

BEAL LAKE A hike-in lake in the northern half of the Rogue River National Forest, northernmost of the Northern Blue Lake group east of Butte Falls Ranger Station. It's a 4-mile hike from the trailhead at the end of Forest Rd. 720, off Forest Rd. 37. A shorter trail, 982, leads into the basin from the summit of Blue Rock Mt.

Fishing is spotty, but can be good for brook trout to 12 inches. This is a good lake to try in conjunction with other lakes in the area. See also Blue, Blue Canyon, Horseshoe.

BEALE LAKE A hard to reach coastal lake with a good warm water fishery, about 7 miles north of North Bend, just west of Hwy. 101. The lake covers over 100 acres, cradled in the sand dunes of the Oregon Dunes National Recreation Area. It's about 1/2 mile from the highway by trail. Lightly fished, it has good largemouth bass, perch, and bluegill angling. It is not stocked due to its inaccessibility. There are two natural campsites near the SW end of the lake.

BEN IRVING RESERVOIR
A 100-plus acre lake west of Roseburg, created by Berry Creek Dam. From Roseburg, take Hwy. 42 west, then County Rd. 365, which joins Hwy. 42 about 2 miles south of the town of Tenmile.

It is managed primarily for bass and panfish, but legal rainbow are stocked annually in March and April. Largemouth bass and bluegill are thriving. There is a boat ramp, and varied speed limits, which are posted. Boating in the upper reservoir is limited to electric motors only.

BIG BUTTE CREEK A very nice 30-mile tributary of the upper Rogue, entering the river at McLeod near Lost Creek Lake. Big Butte is one of only a handful of Rogue tributaries that are open to fishing. Most areas are closed in an effort to protect juvenile steelhead and salmon which are too often mistaken for trout. The creek is closed below Cobleigh Road.

To reach the lower stream from Medford, take Hwy. 62 north about 27 miles. To reach the upper waters, turn east off Hwy. 62 onto the Butte Falls Rd. Crowfoot, McNeil, and Cobleigh roads cross the creek. Butte Falls Rd. reaches the creek at about mile 16 and follows the south bank for about 2 miles. A dirt road crosses the creek and follows it another 2 miles to Big Butte Spring. The upper waters are accessible by taking the Butte Falls-Prospect Rd. to the Rancheria Rd. At about one mile, turn left off Rancheria. This road accesses the North Fork at about one mile and follows it for 4 1/2 miles.

A good trout stream, Big Butte features cutthroat to over 12 inches and rainbow which are stocked from late April to mid-July. North and South Fork headwaters and some tributaries are spring fed, so fishing holds up well.

BLUE CANYON LAKE A small hike-in lake in the Blue Lake group of the Sky Lakes Wilderness Area, located about one mile south of Blue Lake. From Blue Lake, take the main Trail 982 for 1/4 mile, then turn south and west on the Blue Canyon Trail. The lake is less than 1/2 mile from the fork, to the left of (and may not be visible from) the trail. There's good fishing for brook trout here in spring and fall. September and October are the best months. Bait and spinners or lures will work anytime, but switch to flies in the evening. See Blue Lake for complete directions.

Barbless hooks are required year-round on the Applegate.

BLUE LAKE (Klamath Co. a.k.a. South Blue) A 15-acre hike-in, in the south Sky Lakes Wilderness Area of the Rogue River National Forest. From Medford, take Hwy. 62 north to the Butte Falls Rd. From Butte Falls head east into the Rogue River National Forest on Forest Rd. 30, then turn left on Forest Rd. 37. Just past the Parker Meadows cut-off on the left, turn a hard right onto Forest Rd. 3770 to Blue Rock Mt. Bear left at the fork at about 4 miles, continue toward the summit. Trailhead 982, identified as the Blue Canyon Trail on the Wilderness map, is one mile past the fork, on the right. The hike to Blue Lake is less than 2 miles.

The summit of Blue Mt., about a mile further up the road, is the site of a former fire lookout tower and offers a grand view of the southern Oregon Cascades, including the rim of Crater Lake and Mt. McLoughlin. The Blue Mt. Rd. is not recommended for trailer or RV traffic. The Blue Canyon Trail continues through the basin, connecting with other trails, including the Pacific Crest Trail.

A deep lake, with a good population of brook trout to 12 inches, Blue Lake can be fished by trolling or casting lures in the deep water on the west side. Fly fishing is excellent late in the day in the shoal areas on the east side, or by sinking wet

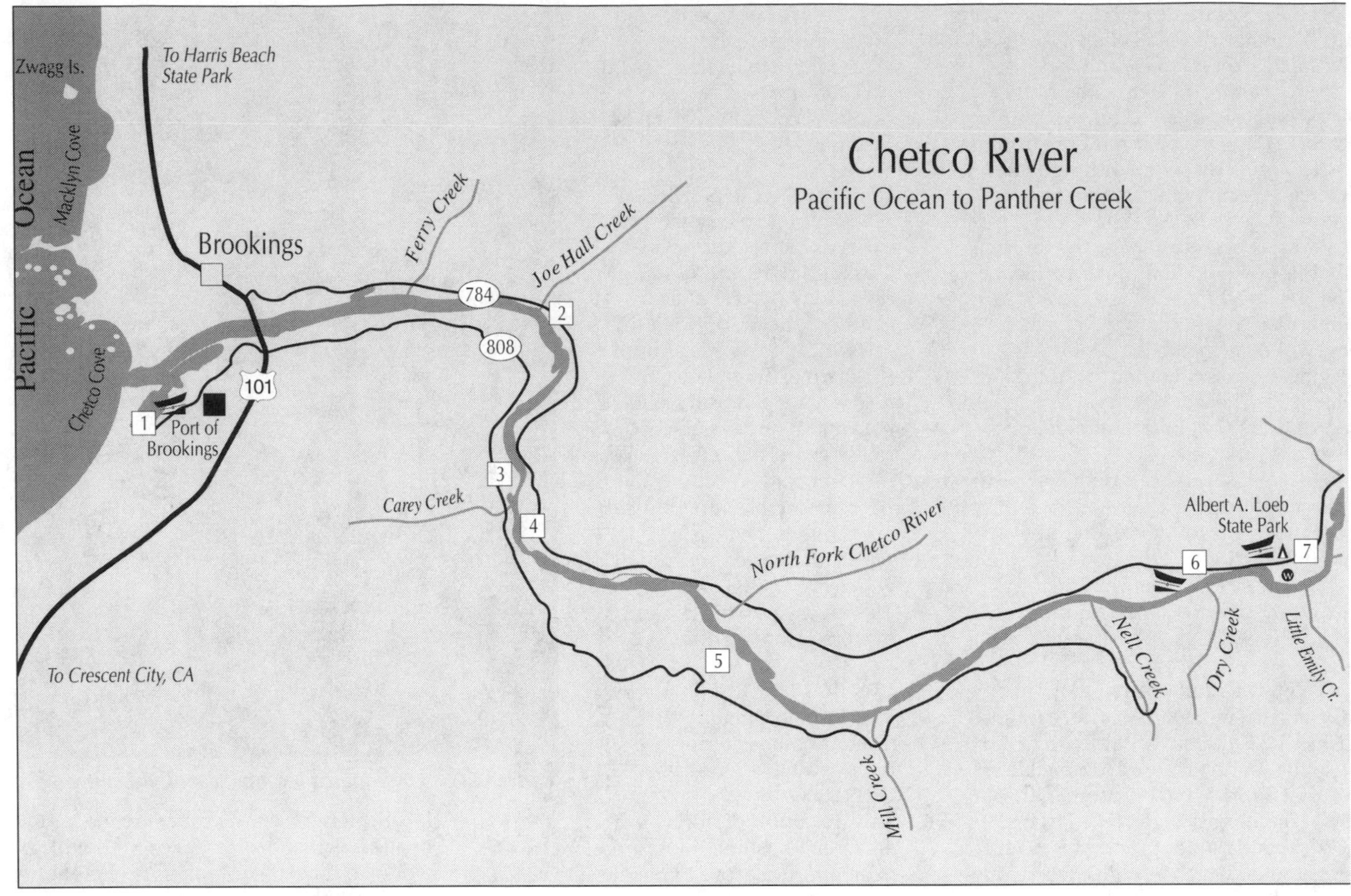

flies off the rock point on the south shore. A float tube would come in handy. There are good campsites here, as at most lakes in the area. Other fishable lakes in the basin include Horseshoe, Pear, Blue Canyon. Check for early or late season conditions at Butte Falls Ranger Station.

BOLAN LAKE A small lake near the California border in the Siskiyou Mountains. It can be reached by turning east from Hwy. 199 onto County Rd. 5560 at O'Brien, 6 miles south of Cave Junction. Continue east on this road, which north of Takilma becomes County Rd. 5828, to the border of the Siskiyou National Forest. Here the road becomes Forest Rd. 48. Follow this road for 10 twisting miles to Forest Rd. 4812, which leads 6 miles NE to the lake. The last section of road is rough and winding. It is usually snowbound until late spring.

Only about 12 acres, Bolan has brook trout to 14 inches. Fishing holds up well here throughout the season. Bait fishing is the most commonly used technique, but other methods work. There is a campground at the lake, and car-top boats can be launched.

BRADLEY LAKE A coastal lake of about 30 acres west of Hwy. 101, about 3 miles south of Bandon. It's about one mile west of the highway on the Bradley Lake Rd. China Creek flows into the lake and is crossed by Hwy. 101 just east of the lake. Fished mostly for stocked rainbow trout, Bradley provides good catches in early spring and summer. Wild cutthroat are also present, and there may be some largemouth bass.

BRUSH CREEK A classic little steelhead stream in Humbug State Park, which offers fine camping and picnic facilities in a magnificent south coast setting. The lower end of the creek is about 5 miles south of Port Orford on Hwy. 101, and it's crossed by the highway a few times near Humbug State Park. It's a rich stream with lots of gravel and boulders, and two major forks.

A steelhead run here peaks in January. Migrating cutthroat may also be taken, but the salmon that used to come into this stream have about disappeared despite efforts in the early '80s to rebuild the run. The creek is closed to coho angling.

BUCKEYE LAKE A fair, hike-in eastern brook trout lake in the Umpqua Divide Scenic Area which offers ice fishing opportunities. It is 1 1/2 miles south of Fish Lake, about 35 miles east of Tiller. Cliff Lake is just up the trail from Buckeye. For road and trail directions see Cliff Lake.

Ten-acre Buckeye has good numbers of brook trout to 18 inches. Most of the catch is 7-12 inches. Bait, spinners, and flies all work. There are improved campsites at Buckeye and nearby Cliff Lake. Supplies are available at Tiller 35 miles west, or Clearwater, 30 twisting miles north.

Anglers snowshoe in for brook trout in February and March, breaking through the ice. The road to the trailhead is often open.

BURMA POND A 5-acre pond on BLM property out of Wolf Creek. The pond is off Speaker Road. It is stocked with rainbow trout and has largemouth bass. There's easy bank access on the dike side. A float tube or light weight boat would be helpful.

BUTTERFIELD LAKE A small lake about 16 miles south of Reedsport, 1/4 mile west of Hwy. 101. Roughly 50 acres, the lake is bisected by the railroad right of way and has walk-in access only. Cutthroat trout and bass are reported, but success is unknown. It is not stocked, and there is no camping nearby.

CALAMUT LAKE A good hike-in brook trout lake 4 miles NE of Lemolo Lake just south of the Douglas/Lane County line. The road to the lake has been closed, but

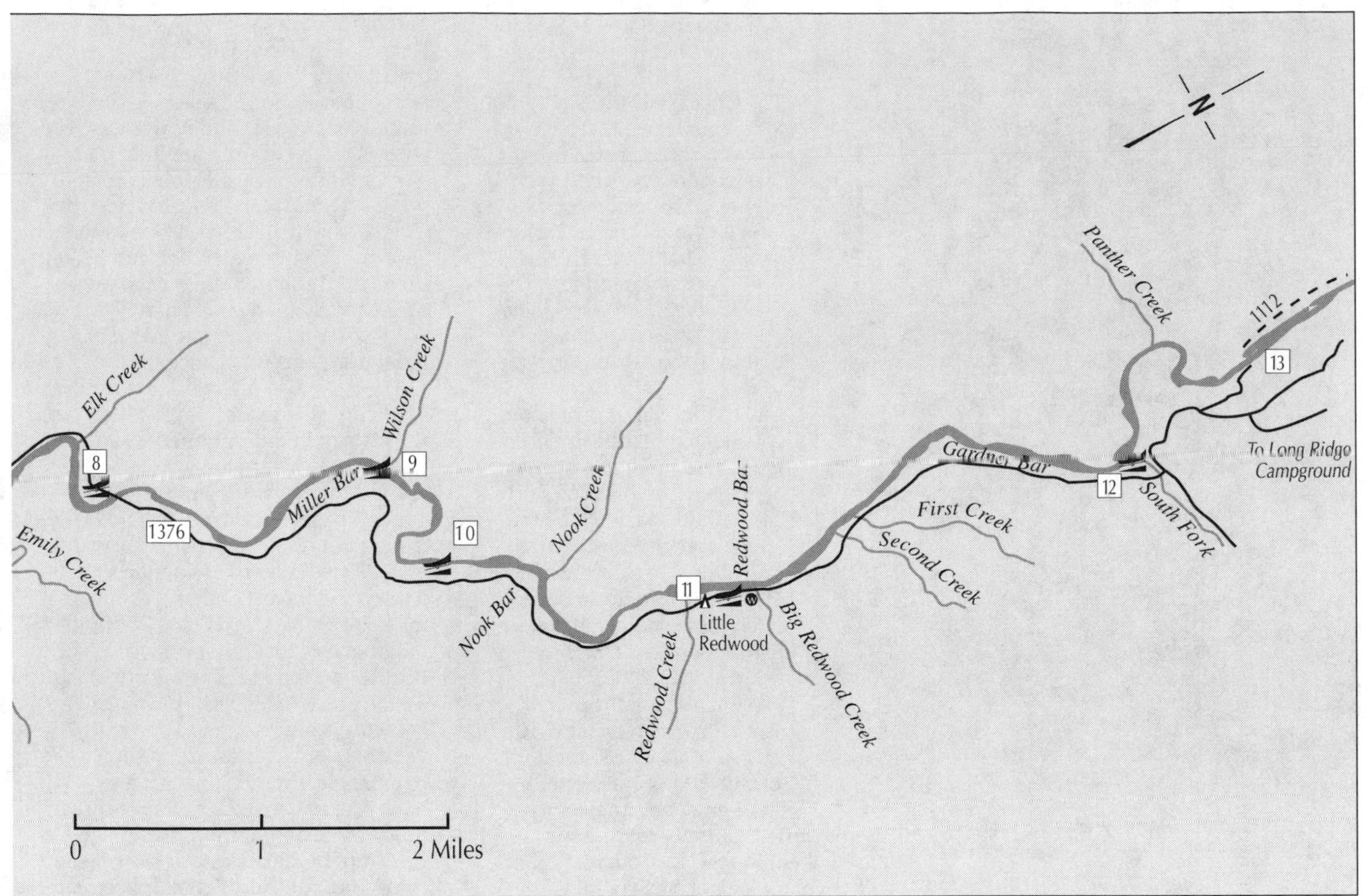

a trail leads in from Linda Lake, one mile south of Calamut.

Linda Lake is not shown on the Umpqua National Forest map. From Inlet Campground, at the east end of Lemolo Lake, take Forest Rd. 999 east 2 miles to Forest Rd. 60. Turn left on Forest Rd. 60 and at about 2 miles, turn left on Forest Rd. 700. Signs will direct you to Linda Lake. Trailhead 1494 is on the right. The hike to Calamut is just over a mile from Linda. The trail passes Lake Charlene on the way in.

Calamut covers 18 acres and offers fair fishing in spring and fall. No inlets or outlets support spawning, so it is stocked every two or three years with brook trout fingerlings. The brookies have been running 6-12 inches, with average size 10 inches. It usually can be reached in June. There are improved campsites at the lake.

1 **PORT OF BROOKINGS** - paved boat ramp accesses tidewater fishery and Oregon's safest bar crossing.

2 **MORRIS HOLE** - bank fishing for chinook October and November.

3 **TIDE ROCK** - bank fishing for chinook and steelhead October through April.

4 **SOCIAL SECURITY RAMP** - take-out and bank fishing for chinook and steelhead, October through April.

5 **PILING HOLE** - bank fishing for chinook and steelhead, October through April.

6 **MYRTLE GROVE** - drift-boat put-in & take-out from gravel bar; boat and bank access for good salmon and steelhead hole.

7 **LOEB STATE PARK** - take-out on gravel bar; bank fishing for salmon and steelhead, October through April.

8 **ICE BOX**- private; launch with permission below Second Bridge; motors prohibited above this point).

9 **MILLER BAR**- launch from gravel; bank fishing.

10 **NOOK BAR**- launch from gravel; bank fishing.

11 **REDWOOD** - launch from gravel; bank fishing.

12 **SOUTH FORK** - undeveloped launch; no bank fishing; day's drift to Loeb Park or points in between.

13 **LOW WATER BRIDGE** - abandoned road bridge still a wade even in low water; accesses miles of west bank fishing along Chetco River Trail.

CALAPOOYA CREEK (Douglas Co.) A good size tributary of the Umpqua River, about 40 miles long, entering the main river at the community of Umpqua about 10 miles downstream from the forks, 20 road miles north of Roseburg. It is crossed by Hwy. 15 just north of Sutherlin. Good roads follow the stream closely in both the lower and upper sections.

The stream has native cutthroat and rainbow trout, and receives annual plants of legal rainbow. It has a fair run of coho and steelhead along with a few fall chinook. The creek is closed to salmon and steelhead fishing during the fall salmon migration season, re-opening December 1 in time for winter steelhead. Be sure to check current regulations. There is a county park on the stream at Fair Oaks east of Sutherlin, but most property along the creek is privately owned. Be sure to ask permission to access the stream through private property.

CAMP CREEK (Douglas Co.) A fair size stream entering Mill Creek (outlet of Loon Lake) about 3 miles above its confluence with the Umpqua 4 miles west of Scottsburg. It can be reached by Hwy. 38 from Reedsport or Drain. The Loon Lake Rd. crosses Camp Creek at its lower end. A paved road follows it east for 15 miles.

It is primarily a wild cutthroat stream. Steelhead and salmon enter the creek, but angling for them is prohibited. There are

Best surf perch catches are on the incoming tide.

several picnic areas just west of Scottsburg on Hwy. 38, but no campsites.

CANTON CREEK A nice looking stream joining Steamboat Creek from the north, about a mile north of the junction of Steamboat and the North Umpqua. Canton is a sanctuary area for adult summer steelhead and is closed to all angling.

CANYONVILLE POND See Herbert Log Pond.

CARBERRY CREEK A nice trout stream, one of the inlet streams of Applegate Reservoir, entering the reservoir from the SW. Forest Rd. 10 follows the western shore of the reservoir to Carberry Campground, then follows the Carberry to its fork. Gravel roads parallel each of the forks, Sturgis and Steve.

Angling for wild cutthroat trout can be good at times.

CAREY LAKE A 12-acre rainbow lake in the Blue Lake group. For directions, see Horseshoe Lake. Hike past Horseshoe to reach Carey.

CHETCO BAY A small bay near the Oregon/California border whose good, safe bar contributes to its ranking as Oregon's top small craft port. Chetco is remote for most Oregonians, but real handy for Californians. From the Portland area it's about 340 miles on Hwy. 101, but only 24 miles from Crescent City. The section of Hwy. 101 from Gold Beach south is now one of the best stretches on the Oregon coast.

The Chetco bar leads out into a sheltered cove that is shielded from summer winds. Twelve-foot boats and even canoes go to sea on good days. Offshore anglers can fish over very productive reefs both north and south of the bar. Black rockfish are especially abundant. Charter boats offer bottom fishing trips year-round.

The traditional June offshore coho fishery has been closed in recent years. Chinook seasons are being scheduled on fairly short notice. Watch the newspaper, and check with local licensing agents or the district ODF&W office for updates. In 1994, there was a chinook-only fishery south of Humbug Mt. from August 21 through September 5, with another scheduled from October 10 through October 31 (or until 1,000 chinook are caught by sport anglers). Anglers have been required to use barbless hooks to enable them to release incidental coho.

Fall chinook enter the bay mid-September to October. Trolling, bait fishing, and fly casting are all popular methods here. There is also a popular jetty fishery for early fall chinook during the 6 weeks before the rains hit.

Bottom fishing is productive in the bay year-round. Perch fishing from the beach is excellent here most of the season, with best catches on the incoming tide. Jetty fishing for perch is only fair. The jetty is wheelchair accessible, as is a fishing pier on the south side of the bay which is good for crab and all bay species.

Accommodations are plentiful in the Brookings and Harbor areas. Charter boats, marine and fishing supplies are readily available. Harris Beach State Park 2 miles north of Brookings has a large campground. Sporthaven Trailer Park, run by the county, is just south of town. Azalea State Park at Brookings is for picnicking only.

CHETCO RIVER A very good winter steelhead and salmon stream at the extreme south end of the Oregon coast. Scenic, flanked by myrtle trees, it enters the sea at Brookings after a 50-mile run. The whole river is accessible to drift boats (no jet sleds are used here), and there is good bank access. County Rd. 784 follows the north bank of the river up to Loeb State Park. Above Loeb, Forest Rd. 1376 leads to well-known gravel bars and holes such as Ice Box, Miller, Redwood, and So. Fork.

Fall chinook are available from September through December, with peak catches in October and November. The river is closed to coho angling.

A good number of hatchery reared winter steelhead are released into the Chetco system each year. Steelhead start showing well in December, and fishing holds up through March. Peak catches are generally made in January. The Chetco is consistently among the 10 best Oregon coastal streams for winter steelhead.

The river also offers limited fishing for wild cutthroat trout in early season, and for sea-run in late summer. Sea-run are primarily fished in the lower river around the Hwy. 101 bridge.

The Oregon Dept. of Fish and Wildlife manages a number of fishing access areas. Tide Rock Access on the south bank is the lowest of these, about a half mile above the Morris Hole, a popular holding spot for salmon. Social Security Boat Ramp is about 3/4 mile upstream on the north bank. Drift boats can be launched here, though a four-wheel drive vehicle may be necessary in some years. Bank anglers can fish from a gravel bar here. The third public access is at the Piling Hole on the south bank. There is no ramp, but boats can be launched off the gravel bar. Additional opportunities for launching and take-out are at Loeb State Park and at several undeveloped gravel bars further upstream. See the accompanying map.

A 1994 District Court ruling on the Chetco's navigability at the time Oregon became a state may enable anglers to fish (without concern for landowner harassment) from side-channel and mid-stream gravel bars. The ruling concerns a popular 10-mile stretch of the river beginning one mile above the Chetco bar. The issue is scheduled for trial in February, 1995.

There are campgrounds at Harris Beach State Park 2 miles north of Brookings and at Loeb State Park 8 miles up the river road.

CLEAR LAKE (Coos Co.) Don't confuse this with the large lake of the same name just south of Reedsport in Douglas County. This Clear Lake is about 14 miles south of Reedsport on the west side of Hwy. 101, a half mile north of Saunders Lake. To reach it you have to park along the highway and cross the railroad tracks. The north end of the lake is in the Oregon Dunes National Recreation Area. It offers very good fishing for yellow perch and supports a good population of cutthroat trout. About 15 acres and quite deep, it is primarily fished by local anglers. There are no camping facilities or improvements here.

CLEAR LAKE (Douglas Co.) A large coastal lake on the east side of Hwy. 101, 7 miles south of Reedsport. It covers 290 acres and contains cutthroat trout, but is closed to angling since it provides the water supply for Reedsport.

CLIFF LAKE (Douglas Co.) A rich 7-acre hike-in brook trout lake in the south Umpqua drainage, featuring the largest brook trout in the district, successfully fished by a knowing few. Cliff is just up the trail from Buckeye Lake, about a mile south of Fish Lake in the Rogue-Umpqua Divide Wilderness just north of Grasshopper Mt., Umpqua National Forest. Hearty anglers might like to consider snowshoeing in to ice fish Cliff in February or March when the road to the trailhead is often open.

The Skimmerhorn Trail 1578 offers the most direct approach to Cliff, though other trails access the lake basin. At Tiller, on Hwy. 227, follow County Rd. 46 into the forest, where it becomes Forest Rd. 28, the South Umpqua River Rd. Continue on Forest Rd. 28 about 4 miles past South Umpqua Falls Campground where several roads branch off. Follow Forest Rd. 2823 to the right about 2 miles, then Forest Rd. 2830. Bear right at the first fork, left at the second fork. Skimmerhorn Trailhead is about one mile further at road's end. It is a designated saddle camp. The trail reaches Buckeye at about 1 1/2 miles, and Cliff 1/4 mile further.

Cliff Lake holds fish that exceed 4 pounds, but they can be cagey. Best fishing is in spring and fall. Trolling with spinners and bait produces well in spring. Ice fishing is a possibility in February and March if you're willing to snowshoe in. The road to the trailhead is often open at that time. There are improved campsites here and at Buckeye Lake.

CLIFF LAKE (Klamath Co.) A nice hike-in brook trout lake in the Seven Lakes Basin of the Sky Lakes Wilderness, at the summit between the headwaters of the Middle Fork of the Rogue and Seven Mile Creek. The basin is about 10 miles south of Crater Lake National Park.

Cliff Lake is 1/4 mile west of the Pacific Crest Trail north of Devil's Peak. It's a 5-mile hike to the lake by trails from east or west. See Alta Lake for directions.

There are nice eastern brook trout in this 10-acre lake, with plenty of shoal area for fly anglers to work over. Dark patterns, sunk and fished with slow retrieve, do well. The trout population is maintained by air stocking of fingerlings. There are natural campsites at the lake. This is a picturesque area, and if the fishing is slow here there are other lakes in the vicinity to try. See also Alta, Middle, Grass.

COOPER CREEK RESERVOIR A 140-acre multiple-use reservoir, that offers good fishing for stocked trout, largemouth bass, and panfish. The reservoir is 2 miles east of Sutherlin, about 4 miles east of the I-5 exit. From Sutherlin, take the road east to Fair Oaks, 2 miles from Hwy. 99, and turn south onto a county road which leads to the reservoir in a bit over a mile.

Douglas County maintains two nice picnic areas, each with its own concrete boat ramp. The reservoir is popular with water skiers, but there are slow-speed areas intended for fishing.

Rainbow trout are stocked each spring. Respectable numbers of good size largemouth bass are taken. Crappie angling is very good in the arms of the lake during spring and early summer. Yellow, purple, or white jigs trolled through the shallows will produce. Brown bullhead catfish are also available. There is good bank access, but anglers should be wary of steep drop-offs. An easy hiking trail goes all the way around the lake. Camping is prohibited.

Recommended for small fry. The local bass club sponsors an annual kids' derby here, providing equipment, boats, and expert guides for the youngsters. For more information contact the district ODF&W office. Wheelchair accessible fishing from dock.

COOS BAY A large productive bay with good public access, excellent crabbing, and angling opportunities year-round. Coos Bay is a 4 hour drive from the Portland area and 2 hours from Eugene. Cut through the coast range at any of the major highways and follow Hwy. 101. From I-5 at Roseburg, Hwy. 42 leads to the southern bay and popular Isthmus Slough fishery.

In these days of distressed salmon runs and intense salmon protection efforts, most angling activity beyond the Coos Bay bar is directed toward bottom fish. Anglers fishing the reefs south of the bar off Cape Arago find rockfish, cabezon, and greenling at 8-15 fathoms. The charter fleet operating out of the harbor at Charleston is available for bottom fish trips year-round, and pursues halibut and salmon as regulations allow.

Chinook and coho are outside the bay from May through September. However, emergency regulations have closed the coho fishery here and limited offshore chinook fishing to prevent incidental coho catches. In 1994, the offshore chinook fishery here was open only from May 1 through June 5. Watch the newspaper, and check with local licensing agents or the district ODF&W office for updates before planning a salmon fishing trip. Two popular spots for chinook fishing outside the bay are about one mile west and 1-2 miles north of the north jetty, and between the bar and whistle buoy. The Coos Bay bar is more easily negotiated than most, but beware of heavy wind or fog conditions.

Inside the bay, Redtail perch, greenling, and lingcod are fished from north and south jetties, and perch are caught from many docks and bridges throughout the bay, including the boat docks in Charleston, and the Charleston, Hwy. 101, and Haynes Inlet bridges. There are also good perch catches by boaters around the submerged rock jetty in the lower bay (look for the hazard markers) and by both boat and bank anglers from Fossil Pt. to Pony Pt. This area has many submerged rock structures that make good perch habitat. Best catches are on the incoming tide. Bank anglers in this area should avoid trespassing on private property, or ask permission. When on the main bay, boaters should be wary of prevailing NW winds in summer, which can turn the bay very rough when the winds meet an incoming tide. Always wear life jackets when crossing Coos Bay.

Opportunities for salmon fishing within the bay have diminished in recent years. The failure of a salmon aquaculture facility at Jordan Point in the north bay eliminated a popular sport fishery here. Fisheries in the lower bay were hard hit by emergency salmon closures. In 1994 the lower bay was closed to coho fishing during the season, and to chinook until August 15. When emergency regulations allow, anglers pursue an exciting fishery between the jetties, mooching herring on the incoming tide. Their quarry is

Bait can be gathered on the Oregon coast.

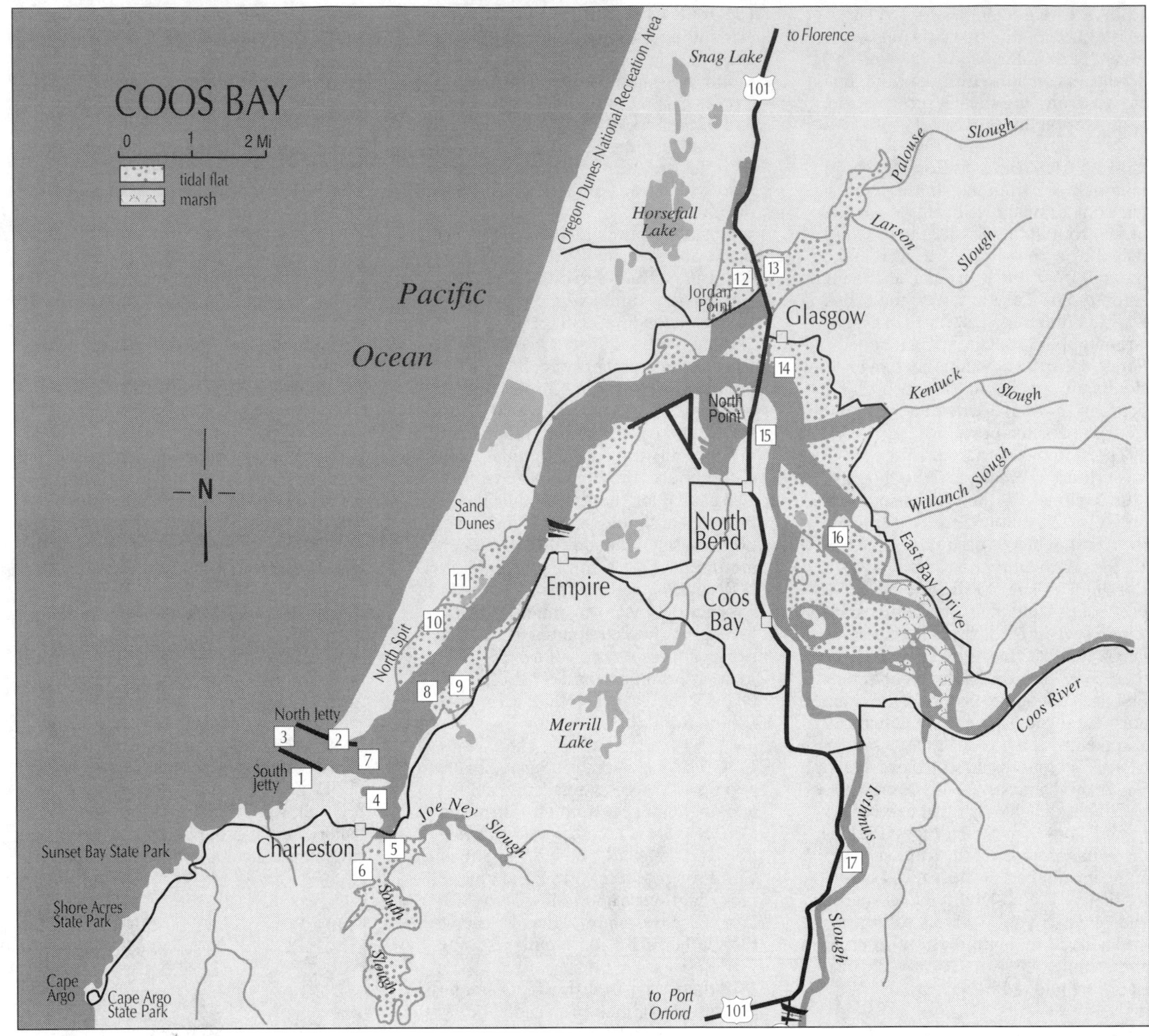

1 **SOUTH JETTY** - Park at Bastendorf County Park; fish for redtail perch, greenling, ling cod, occasional salmon.

2 **NORTH JETTY** - Fish for redtail perch, greenling, lingcod.

3 **LOWER BAY** - Troll and mooch herring for salmon.

4 **CHARLESTON WATERFRONT** - Public access to extensive boat docks for perch Feb. through summer, smelt and herring jigged June-Sept., dungeness and rock crab; gapers & cockles.

5 **CHARLESTON BRIDGE** - Park near bridge to dig Charleston Flats for cockles, gapers, some butter clams/

6 **SOUTH SLOUGH FLAT** - Fair digging for cockles, gapers, some butter clams; park along primitive Port Access Rd.. (watch for potholes).

7 **SUBMERGED ROCK JETTY** - Good fishing at high tide for perch, rockfish, greenling, occasional lingcod; identify by markers warning of hazard.

8 **FOSSIL PT.** - Natural rock structures provide good perch habitat; fish from boat and bank; beset on incoming tide; bank anglers, respect private property.

9 **PIGEON PT. FLATS** - Popular digging for gapers, butter clams; limited parking but accessible.

10 **NORTH SPIT** - Best digging on the bay for gapers, cockles, softshell; walk out at low tide along entire bay side of spit.

11 **CLAM ISLAND** - Fish for dungeness and some red rock crab off island; also gapers & cockles.

12 **MENASHA DIKE FLATS** - Closed due to toxic substance found in clams.

13 **HAYNES INLET BRIDGE** - Fish from bridge for perch.

14 **STURGEON HOLE**

15 **HWY. 101 BRIDGE** - Fish from bridge for perch.

16 **COOS CHANNEL** - Fish for shad and remnant striped bass.

17 **ISTHMUS SLOUGH** - Good bank access to coho; boat ramp upstream.

migrating salmon that move briefly into the bay in pursuit of bait fish.

A bright spot in Coos Bay salmon angling is a newly developing fishery in Isthmus Slough in the south bay. Hatchery-reared chinook and coho were first released in the Slough in 1989. An estimated 2,500 salmon returned in 1993. Fishing begins in the slough in mid-August and continues through November. Emergency regulations enacted elsewhere on behalf of wild coho have specifically excluded this fishery from closure. Anglers fish from the tide gate at the head of the slough down to the bay. Boats can be launched from a ramp at the head of the slough, off Hwy. 42. Bank anglers can park at the boat ramp and fish along the west bank. Fishing is good throughout the narrow 15-mile tongue of tidewater.

An additional salmon fishery is scheduled for development in Coos Bay beginning in 1995. Some 150,000 Rogue River spring chinook will be held for acclimation here, then released. These fish should begin returning to Coos Bay in 1998.

The striped bass fishery in Coos Bay has been in decline for 15 years. Southern Oregon is the northern extreme of this fish's successful range, with conditions for a good general spawn occurring less than once a decade. Nevertheless, there are still some stripers out there. ODF&W has been operating a limited striper enhancement program, but its impact on the fishery will be very slow due to the amount of time it takes to grow a striped bass (6-8 years to reach the 30-inch legal size). Better opportunities for striped bass can be found in Winchester Bay and the lower Smith River. Nevertheless, you may find a striper in Coos Bay's sloughs, or in the upper tidewaters from autumn through March, especially in the South Fork of the Coos River. From mid-June through mid-August a few stripers may be found in mid-bay, around the Hwy. 101 Bridge, though few have been seen here in recent years. Stripers may be tempted by a big plug or by bait and have been known to take a fly.

Fishing for sturgeon, both white and green, has been fair to good here. Anglers use big gobs of bait and fish the deep holes. A favorite spot is above the Hwy. 101 Bridge off North Point in winter and early spring.

Coos Bay has a very productive crab fishery. In fact, there are so many crabs in the bay that anglers pursuing other quarry usually prefer to use artificial bait rather than feed the crabs. Dungeness and rock crab are fished from Charleston docks and off Clam Island, among other places. Herring and smelt are jigged from the Charleston boat docks from June to September.

Best clam flats on the bay run the length of the North Spit. Walk out at low tide and dig for gapers, cockles, and softshell clams. Menasha Dike Flats also offer good digging on either side of the causeway from Hwy. 101 to Horsefall Beach. South Slough Flat offers fair digging for cockles, gapers, and some butter clams. Park along the Port Access Rd., but keep a sharp eye out for potholes.

South Slough, a natural nursery for Dungeness crab and important bait fish area just south of Charleston, has been designated a National Estuarine Reserve and is a good place to explore by canoe. Check at the interpretive center four miles south of Charleston on Seven Devils Road for important information about canoe safety in the slough.

Supplies and accommodations are available at Coos Bay, North Bend, and at Charleston, the little seaport town nearest the bar. Charleston has extensive, welcoming public docks and marinas, and is the gateway to two magnificent state parks, Shore Acres, for day use only, and Sunset Bay, which has a full service campground, including showers.

COOS RIVER The Coos River flows only a little over 4 miles from the confluence of its major tributaries, the Millicoma River and the South Coos west of Coos Bay. It is accessible from Hwy. 101. With the fading of the striped bass fishery, shad and salmon have become the main fisheries on the river.

The fall salmon run has improved significantly in recent years thanks to the efforts of local volunteers, coordinated by the Department of Fish and Wildlife's STEP program. The earliest fall chinook arrive in September. Coho follow in November, but current regulations close angling for coho on November 15.

Steelhead are usually moving through in December and January. Trolling for sea-run cutthroat is fair in late fall.

Shad angling is very popular, though primarily a boat fishery due to limited bank access. Anglers use light tackle, and the shad put up a good fight. Extremely small spinners, small wobblers, and weighted streamer flies are all successful for shad to 3 pounds. This fishery usually takes off in May and June.

Tackle, supplies, and advice are available in Coos Bay. Boats can be launched at Doras and Rooke Higgins on the Millacoma, and at the Myrtle Tree Boat Ramp on the South Coos River.

COOS RIVER, SOUTH FORK A good south coast stream with a variety of angling. It meets the Millicoma to form Coos River about 4 miles above the bay, and about 6 miles east of the city of Coos Bay. County roads parallel the stream throughout its length.

South Coos has good populations of cutthroat, fall chinook, coho, steelhead, and a large shad run, as well as a few striped bass.

Fall chinook show well in September and October. The fishery is concentrated near Myrtle Tree Boat Ramp due to large releases from an ODF&W STEP facility on Daniels Creek. In recent years coho returns to the South Fork have been substantial. However, the fishery for them has been curtailed by the general region-wide coho closure. The coho run here peaks in late November or December. In 1994, the coho fishery closed November 15.

Steelhead are available from December through February with plunking very popular. Beginning in 1994, the river will be planted with steelhead that are descended from the native Coos River strain in an effort to produce more reliable returns.

Wild cutthroat are fished early in the season and again in late fall. The river is not stocked. Occasional striped bass are caught in July.

In May and June, shad are in the South Fork, and anglers turn out in droves to cast or troll for them, using small spinners or weighted flies. Bank angling access is limited to the mouth of Daniels Creek across from the Myrtle Tree Ramp. Boaters take shad throughout the river.

COQUILLE RIVER A very good south coast stream with excellent access, entering the ocean at a small bay near Bandon after a 30-mile run down from the Siskiyous. It is crossed by Hwy. 42S at Coquille, about 20 miles up from the mouth. Hwy. 42 from Roseburg parallels the river downstream from the forks at Myrtle Point. The river hosts a small number of spring chinook, a strong population of fall chinook, a winter steelhead run that's holding its own in these dogdays, and a variety of freshwater, tidewater, and saltwater angling opportunities. The Coquille is also one of the few Oregon rivers in which there continues to be a viable coho population.

Coquille Bay is fished for salmon, various perch, Dungeness crab, and smelt. Both north and south jetties are well used by anglers, as are the Bandon City Docks, where large numbers of perch and crab are taken from April through August. Smelt are traditionally jigged from the docks in July. Softshell clams are dug primarily in the flats adjacent to the Bandon Treatment Plant.

A few spring chinook move into the river during summer, but salmon fishing begins in earnest with fall run chinook in September. Over 2,000 fall chinook were taken in 1992. Coho enter in October, and the Coquille is currently open for coho fishing until November 15. There's good

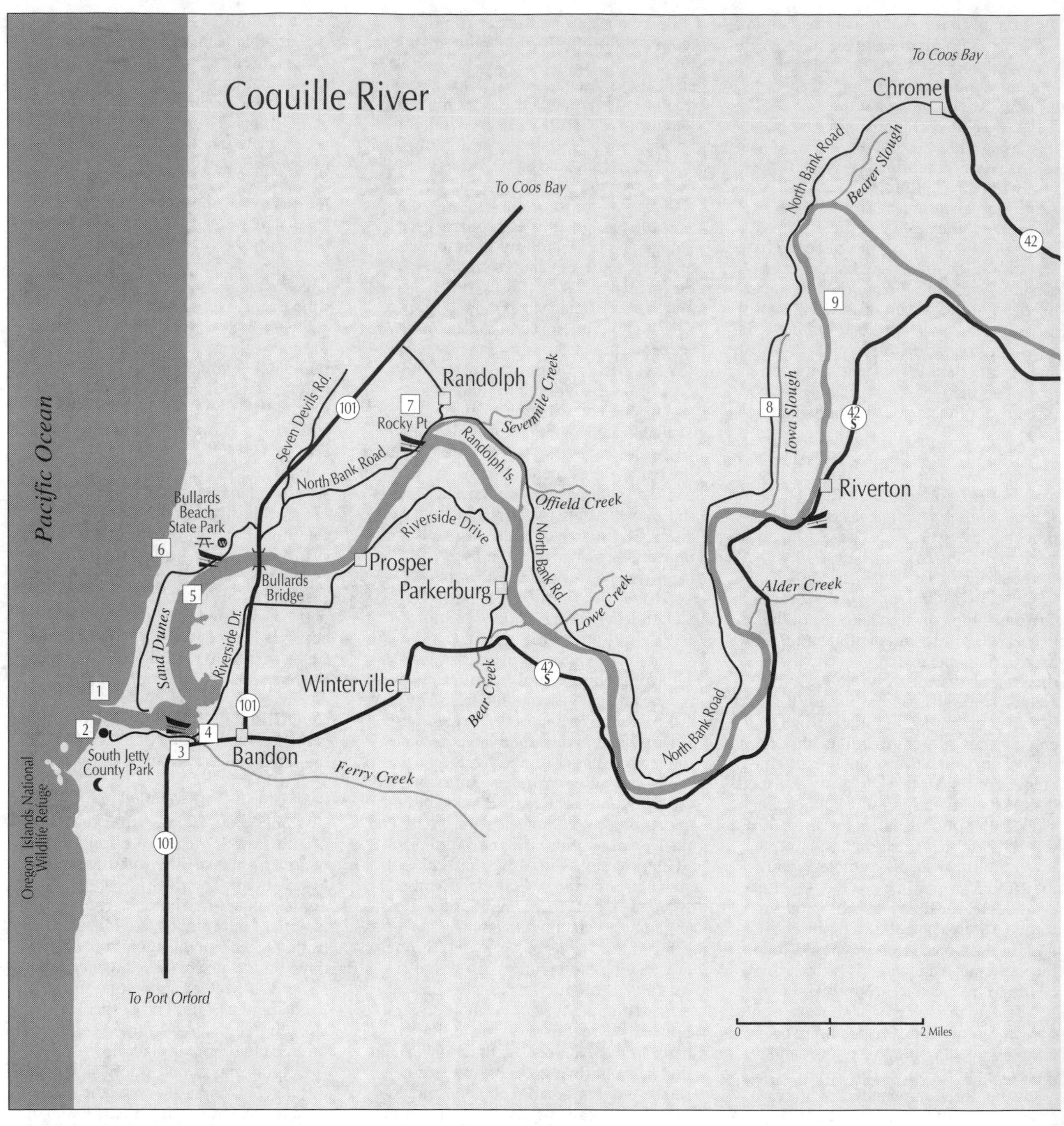

trolling in the entire lower river, with herring and lures equally popular.

Efforts to build up the Coquille salmon runs have been very successful. Activities coordinated by ODF&W's STEP program have included stream and riparian enhancement, rearing fry, and the construction and maintenance of acclimation ponds on Sevenmile Creek and Ferry Creek. There is an expanding fishery for both fall chinook and coho near Rocky Pt. Boat Ramp which may be attributed to hatchery releases in Sevenmile.

Steelhead are generally present beginning in late November, with peak returns in January and February in both tidewater and the forks. Long time anglers of the Coquille will notice that this is a later peak than in years past, due to a change in brood stock. The reported 1992 winter steelhead catch was extremely low here as elsewhere in the state, but the catch was over 1,000 two years earlier. Boat and bank plunking are popular in the upper tidewater from Arago Boat Ramp to the forks in late November into March. All non-finclipped steelhead must be released unharmed, and anglers are required to use barbless hooks from December 1 through March 31.

Trolling for sea-run cutthroat takes place in late summer and fall. Local anglers fish the lower river from Riverton to Myrtle for brown bullhead. The sloughs are home to bullhead and largemouth bass. Striped bass are rarely seen here anymore.

Salmon and steelhead fishing in the Coquille is primarily a boat show, with developed ramps at Bullards Beach State Park, Bandon Boat Basin, Rocky Point

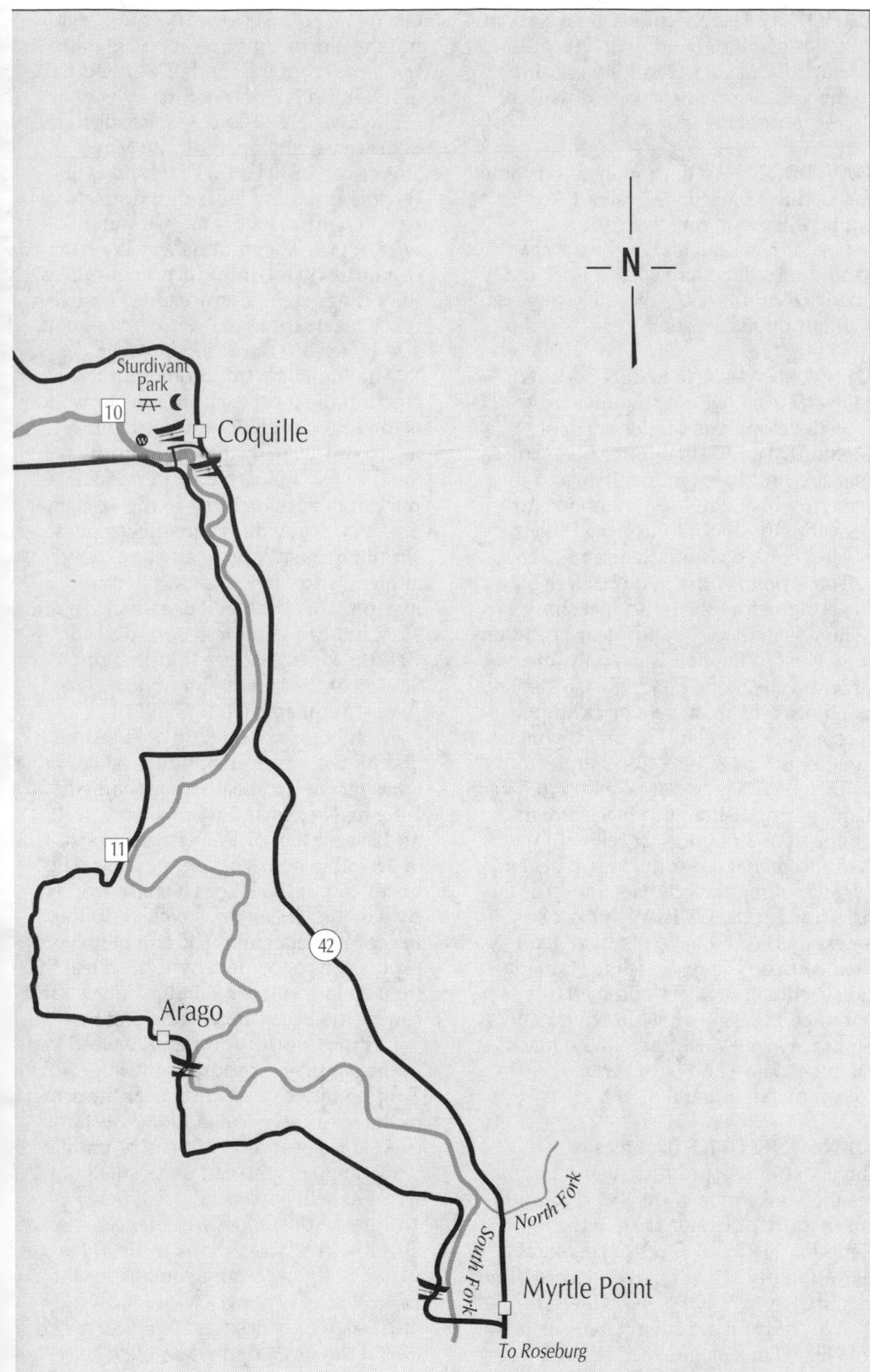

1 **NORTH JETTY** - Fish for perch, rockfish.

2 **SOUTH JETTY** - Fish for perch.

3 **BANDON BOAT BASIN** - Public ramp; fish from docks for perch & crab April through October, smelt July through September.

4 **MOUTH OF FERRY CREEK** - Returning hatchery salmon (chinook Sept.-Oct., coho Oct.-Nov.); dig flats at Bandon Treatment Plant just upstream for soft-shell clams.

5 **CRABBING** - best from Bullards downstream.

6 **BULLARDS BEACH** - prime surf fishing for perch.

7 **ROCKY PT. BOAT RAMP** - troll from here up to Sevenmile Creek for salmon.

8 **SLOUGHS** - Fish for brown bullhead, largemouth bass.

9 **RIVERTON TO MYRTLE PT.** - fish for brown bullheads in open water, July-September.

10 **STURDIVANT PARK** - fish from float for salmon, steelhead, and cutthroat.

11 **MYRTLE PT. TO COQUILLE** -plunk for winter steelhead January-February; troll for fall chinook Sept. through October, for searun cutthroat late summer and fall.

near Randolph, and at Riverton, Coquille, Arago, and Myrtle Point.

Non-boating anglers can fish for salmon and steelhead from an excellent fishing float at Sturdivant Park, and from the banks at the mouth of Ferry Creek in Bandon.

COQUILLE RIVER, EAST FORK A good trout and steelhead stream meeting the North Fork of the Coquille at Gravelford, about 5 miles east of Myrtle Point on Hwy. 42, paralleled by a good road throughout its 30-mile length. The upper river has good trout water, with plenty of good pools and boulder areas.

The first steelhead show here in November after rains raise the river level. Best steelhead angling is in January. Steelhead acclimation pens constructed at a site on Hantz Creek at Fronas Park near Dora will probably attract a concentration of returning steelhead to that area in years to come. Non-finclipped steelhead must be released unharmed, and anglers are required to use barbless hooks from December 1 through March 31.

Fall chinook are present in good numbers here in October, and coho in November, but most of these fish enter the East Fork ripe for spawning and should be left undisturbed.

COQUILLE RIVER, MIDDLE FORK A large fork of the Coquille, joining the South Fork just south of Myrtle Point, fished primarily for wild cutthroat. About 40 miles long, it is followed closely by Hwy. 42 throughout most of its length.

Angling is fair for native cutthroat trout. The salmon and steelhead runs are fairly small and lightly fished. Fall chinook move into the river in September, followed about a month later by coho. The small wild winter steelhead run usually peaks in January. All non-finclipped steelhead must be released unharmed. Barbless hooks are required from December 1 through March 31. The river is closed to angling above Myrtle Creek from September 15 through November 30 to protect spawning salmon.

COQUILLE RIVER, NORTH FORK A good steelhead and cutthroat stream, joining the mainstem just west of Myrtle Point after a 40-mile run. A county road follows the North Fork NE from Myrtle Pt. on Hwy. 42. The upper river can be reached by the Fairview Rd. from Coquille.

It offers very good angling for wild cutthroat trout in early spring and for returning sea-run in late fall.

Fall chinook appear here in October, and coho follow in November. Best steelheading is in January and February. Drift fishing is the most popular steelheading technique here. All non-finclipped steelhead must be released unharmed. Barbless hooks are required December 1 through March 31.

COQUILLE RIVER, SOUTH FORK A very productive fork of the Coquille River, featuring the most consistent steelheading in the area. Over 50 miles long, it is followed closely by a paved road from Myrtle Point on Hwy. 42 to Powers, about 20 miles upstream.

Once offering some of the best trout fishing on the south coast, the South Fork is now heavily stocked with, and managed primarily for, winter steelhead. A 12-mile section of the river from the Forest Service boundary above Powers to Coquille River Falls is an important salmon and steelhead spawning and rearing area and is closed to all angling. January and February are the prime months for steelhead.

Fall chinook are in the lower river in early October, and a few are caught. Though trout are not stocked, the river still offers good fishing for wild cutthroat in early season.

COW CREEK A large tributary of the South Umpqua, entering the river from the west about 8 miles south of Myrtle Creek. Over 80 miles long, it joins the South Umpqua between Riddle and Canyonville. Cow Creek contains wild cutthroat of good size, but they're hard to catch.

The creek's population of cutthroat and rainbow trout has soared in the Glendale area in recent years due to releases of cool water from the new reservoir on the stream. Future generations of anglers will have to decide if the enhanced trout fishery (and whatever profit results to the owners of the dam) were worth the destruction of the salmon spawning beds that are now inundated by the reservoir.

Cow Creek is closed to all angling from October 1 through November 15 to protect spawning salmon.

The creek is open for winter steelhead downstream from the Middle Creek Bridge, but few are taken (only 100 over the past 10 years). There are smallmouth bass in the lower creek up to Glendale. There are several BLM picnic areas on the creek south of Riddle and a small campground on Cow Creek Rd. 18 miles upstream from Azalea at Devil's Flat.

CROOKS LAKE A cutthroat lake about 10 miles south of Bandon on Hwy. 101. About 50 acres, 1 1/2 miles west of the highway, it is privately owned, with no access to public.

DAVIDSON LAKE Prominent on some maps, this 25-acre lake is about 7 miles south of Bandon on Hwy. 101. It is between the ocean and highway, near the sand dunes. It contains black bass and good size trout, but is privately owned, without public access.

DENMAN MANAGEMENT AREA PONDS An ODF&W angling and waterfowl development 6 miles north of Medford. The 20 small ponds here are managed for bass and panfish, and as waterfowl habitat. Legal rainbow are occasionally stocked in spring. The tract of land covers several thousand acres.

These ponds offer good bank fishing in spring before the ponds get slimy. Best fishing is in the six ponds near headquarters. Most of the ponds are only an acre or two. Whetstone Pond No. 1, a 10-acre pond near the management headquarters, is very popular. The ponds contain largemouth bass, bluegill, crappie and catfish. Bass have been taken up to 7 lbs. Early spring fishing produces brown bullhead to 2 pounds. Check with the resident manager for the best spots and for special regulations. Get a map of the area from at the ODF&W office, open weekdays. You'll have plenty of feathered company here. Watch for Canada geese, cinnamon teals, and mallards in summer. Egrets are here in winter and spring, as well as redtail hawks, black shoulder kites, and barn owls. Recommended for small fry.

DIAMOND LAKE (Douglas Co.) A large, extremely productive and popular rainbow lake in an attractive setting, 15 miles north of Crater Lake in the Umpqua National Forest. The lake is at elevation 5100 ft. with an eastern skyline dominated by 9,000 ft. Mt. Thielsen.

A lot of trout are caught here, as many as 342,000 in a single year, including many of good size. Trout to 8 pounds are landed, with 12-13 inch 2-pounders common. The average fish taken here weighs over one pound.

In past years, fish to 8 pounds were landed, with 6-8 pounders common. The decline in trout size is the result of an ongoing Tui chub problem. Chubs, which compete with trout for the lake's limited food supply, were introduced by thoughtless anglers using illegal live bait.

Diamond Lake is part of the Umpqua system but is more easily reached from the east. From Hwy. 97 in central Oregon, paved Hwy. 138 leads 20 miles west directly to the lake. The same highway can be taken east from Roseburg, following the North Umpqua about 90 miles to the lake. From the south, Diamond Lake is 108 miles NE of Medford by way of highways 62, 230, and 138. Roads to the lake are usually open by late May.

At over 2,800 acres, Diamond is one of the larger natural lakes in the state. It is rich in natural food, and fish put on weight fast. The trout fishery is sustained primarily by the introduction of rainbow fingerlings right after ice out. These fish reach legal size by fall, and are of good size by ice-out the following year.

Angling holds up throughout the season, but the most exciting time to be here is the first month after ice-out, when the inlets swarm with spawning trout. Smaller fish follow the large spawners in pursuit of eggs. Adding to the excitement is a very heavy midge that takes place simultaneously, giving an edge to fly anglers who can fish a chironomid nymph. This jamboree usually occurs in May, but can vary from spring to spring. Call the Forest Service Information Station at the lake for an update. The phone number is (503) 793-3310.

All methods of angling are used here, and all will produce at times. Bait angling takes fish in the shoal areas (depths 10-30 ft.). Single eggs and worms work well, and cheese bait or Power Bait on size 16 or 18 treble hooks is very popular. The north end of the lake is heavily worked by bait anglers and has picked up the name Velveeta Hole. The fish here have a reputation for leader shyness, so use the lightest line you can handle. Four pounds can be too heavy for still-fishing here.

Drifting worms through the weed beds at the south end produces the largest fish. Trolling in the deep areas near the center of the lake and parallel to the west and east shores near drop-offs can be profitable.

Fly anglers who can work small dark nymphs will always take fish here. Trolling with sunken wet flies can also be effective. The west shore, in 10-20 feet of water, is a good trolling area. Flies should be trolled very slowly with lots of line out. Small dry flies work well early and late in the day. Hint: when the lake water warms in late summer, the trout seek the cooler waters of the inlets at the south end of the lake. A long fine leader and a small dead drifted nymph can do the trick.

There are many facilities at the lake, including a resort at the NE end, several stores, boat and motor rentals, a boat ramp, lodging, and a restaurant. There are two Forest Service fish cleaning stations at the north and south ends by the boat ramps. The cleaning station at the lodge is also open to public use. Three of the four US Forest Service campgrounds around the lake also have boat ramps. Boat users should keep a weather eye out for high winds which sometimes rough up the lake mid-day. Be sure to have safety equipment aboard. Speed limit on the lake is 10 MPH during angling season.

Hearty anglers who enjoy breaking their own trail and getting away from the crowds might consider hiking and fishing Lake Creek, which flows from Diamond Lake to Lemolo (a good two day hike-and-fish). This adventure can be especially profitable in fall.

DUTCH HERMAN A 1-2 acre pond out of Wolf Creek. Largemouth bass, bluegill, and crappie are available. Rainbow trout fingerlings are stocked. Bluegill are particularly plentiful, and provide good fishing for youngsters. A rubber raft, float tube, or canoe would be helpful here. Recommended for small fry.

EEL LAKE A large coastal lake managed for cutthroat and rainbow trout, with good populations of largemouth bass and black crappie. Brown bullheads are also present, though not plentiful. Eel is about 10 miles south of Reedsport on Hwy. 101. The western arm of the lake is within William M. Tugman State Park.

A narrow, deep lake, shaped like a giant U about 2 miles long, Eel is about 350 acres and 60 feet deep in the center channel. Its water is fairly clear, and the lake stays productively cool throughout the summer. It is drained by Eel Creek at the SW end of the lake near the bottom of the U.

Eel provides good fishing for wild and stocked trout. Bank access is limited, but nice catches are made off the public dock. Fly-fishing can be good and saves on tackle. Bait fishing also produces consistently.

Largemouth bass fishing is growing in popularity here, with good catches made throughout the summer. Fish for them near the inlet and outlet, along the shoreline, near the docks, and in the shallows of the arms. Crawfish imitations can be productive, since the lake has a good population of the real thing.

A coho salmon stocking program at Eel is being discontinued. The last stocking was scheduled for 1994. Few returns are anticipated after 1995. Coho generally enter the lake in November and the fishery for them is open. The Eel lake coho fishery is specifically excluded from emergency closure.

There is a campground and boat ramp in the state park at the SW end of the lake. Supplies are available in Lakeside. The Lakeside airstrip is within a half-hour hike of the State Park camp.

ELBOW LAKE A pretty 13-acre lake in a forest setting west of Hwy. 101, about 13 miles north of Reedsport. Elbow receives a fair stocking of legal rainbow each spring, and panfish are available. Fishing pressure is moderate. There is a paved

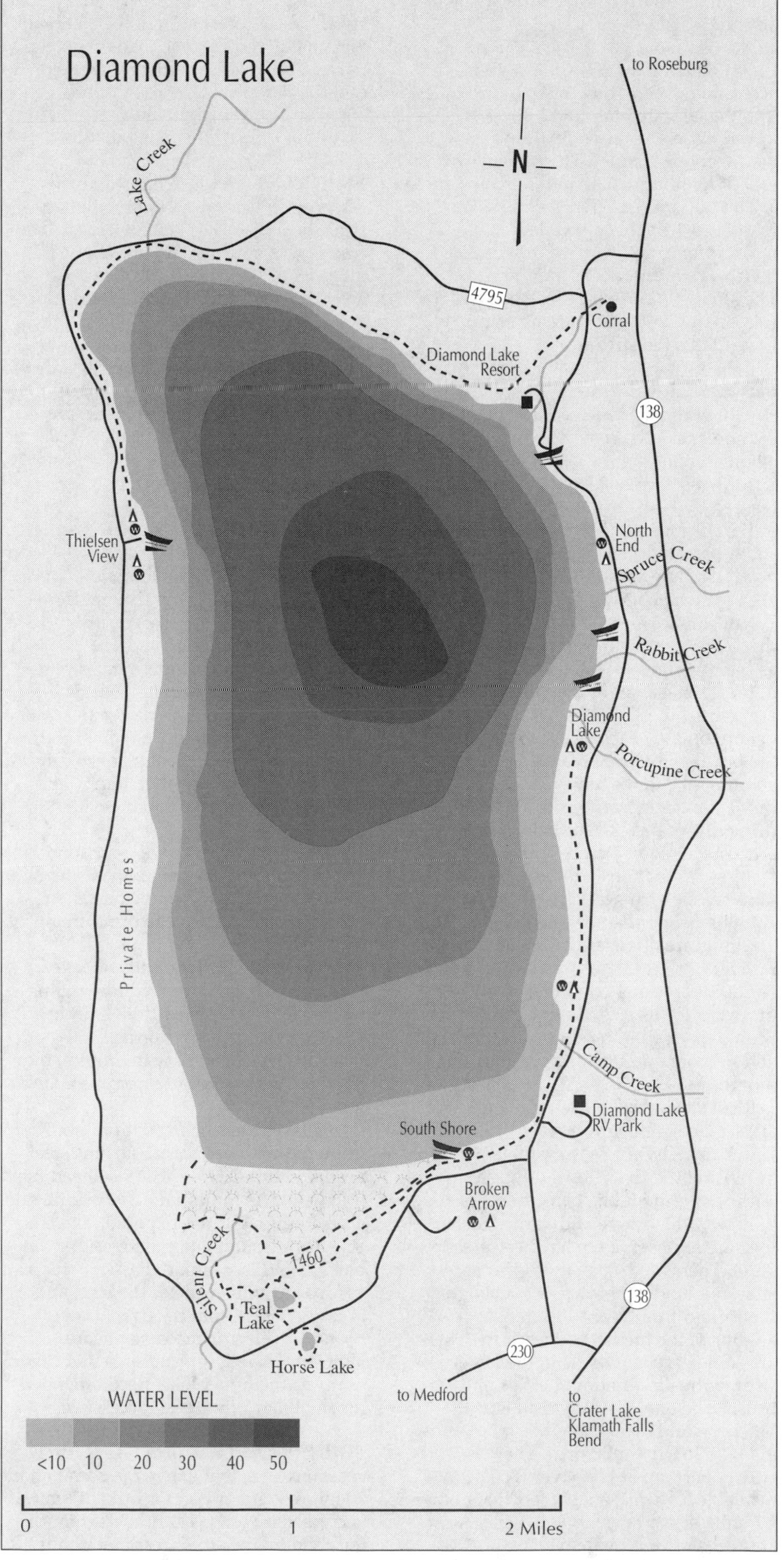

boat ramp, and picnic facilities are available at the lake.

ELK CREEK (Douglas Co.) A good, accessible stream, flowing about 35 miles into the Umpqua River at Elkton. It is followed closely by Hwy. 38 from Elkton to Drain, about 13 miles. The upper stream east of Drain turns SE and is crossed by I-5. The upper area is reached by several roads east from Scott's Valley.

Elk offers good early season fishing for both wild cutthroat and rainbow trout. The stream is closed to steelhead and salmon angling. There are no campgrounds on the stream.

ELK RIVER (Curry Co.) A south coast stream with fair steelhead and good salmon runs. The river flows west about 30 miles, entering the ocean north of Port Orford, just south of Camp Blanco. It's crossed by Hwy. 101 about 3 miles north of Port Orford. A paved road follows the south bank all the way up to the steelhead deadline at Bald Mt. Creek just above the hatchery.

Fall chinook fishing is very good in the lower section in October, or as soon as there is enough water for the stream to breach the dune at the mouth. The earliest fishing possible is actually a surf fishery on the beach. Walk south along the beach from Cape Blanco State Park, about a mile to the mouth. Fishing here can be fantastic, with some big fish taken through December. This fishery is governed by Oregon Ocean Salmon Sport Fishing Regulations and may be subject to in-season changes. In 1994 the fall chinook fishery here opened August 16. The runs are often late due to insufficient rainfall.

Elk River is a good winter steelhead producer for its size, though the run has been depressed in recent years. January and February are the best steelheading months.

Most steelhead and salmon angling takes place in the lower river. Unfortunately, access is a problem here, as most of the river flows through private land. The only public bank access is at the Hwy. 101 Bridge and at the hatchery (be sure to observe the hatchery area closure). There are some pay-to-fish access sites, but landowners seem to change their mind from year to year. Boat angling is the method of necessity. There are some excellent drifts in the lower river, with a minimum of snags and brush. The only public put-in is at the hatchery, and the only public take-out is at Hwy. 101, a 9-mile drift. There is a private boat ramp at Elk River RV Park, available for a reasonable fee, that allows a 6-mile drift to the Hwy. 101 site. A car shuttle service is available.

There are native cutthroat in the upper river, which flows through the Siskiyou National Forest, but the roads are steep, narrow, unpaved, and poorly marked (got the picture?). Carry a current Siskiyou Forest map if you venture far. There are campgrounds in the forest.

EMIGRANT LAKE A large irrigation reservoir in Jackson County with bass, panfish, and stocked rainbow trout. The reservoir is north of Hwy. 66 about 5 miles SE of Ashland. It can cover 800 acres, but actual size fluctuates considerably due to withdrawals.

Smallmouth bass fishing is popular here, with catches to 12 inches. Best bass fishing is around the dam rock face. There's also good fishing for crappie, largemouth bass, and bluegill. Largemouth bass to 5 pounds are caught around the willows in spring. A few brown bullhead are taken.

Legal rainbow are stocked in spring, with best fishing in spring and fall. Good catches are made in the Emigrant Creek arm near the inlet. Trout fishing drops off in summer when the lake warms and trout head for the bottom.

The county run campground on the lake is comfortably situated within an oak grove and provides trailer and tent spaces, a boat ramp, flush toilets, and hot showers. It's an excellent place to camp if you're planning to spiff up after the evening rise and take in a little Shakespeare.

Good bank access, eager and abundant crappie, and the attraction of a water slide for cooling down when the bite is off make this a good place to bring small fry.

EMPIRE LAKES Two artificial lakes which have been improved for angling by the city of Empire with help from ODF&W. Located just north of the road that runs from Coos Bay to Empire, they fluctuate with water use from a maximum 50 acres.

The lakes are stocked with rainbow trout and with occasional surplus steelhead and brood trout. The steelhead may be counted as trout in the daily limit, and a steelhead tag is not required. The lake also has sustaining populations of bluegill and largemouth bass.

A paved trail encircles the lake, and it is easily fished from the bank. Power boats with electric motors only are allowed. There is a picnic area and boat ramp on the upper lake. Recommended for small fry. Wheelchair accessible.

EUCHRE CREEK (Curry Co.) A small coastal stream that enters the ocean about 20 miles south of Port Orford at Ophir. It is crossed by Hwy. 101 near the mouth. A fair road follows the stream for about 7 miles. Another road follows a large tributary, Cedar Creek, to the south. Cedar Creek offers fair trout fishing.

The salmon runs on Euchre have not responded to enhancement efforts during the past ten years, and the run is thought to be extinct. Additional restoration efforts are being planned.

EVANS CREEK A fair size tributary of the Rogue River, entering from the north about 20 miles east of Grants Pass at the town of Rogue River. About 20 miles long, it is currently closed to all angling to protect juvenile steelhead and salmon.

EXPO PONDS Five ponds at the Jackson County Expo Center off I-5 at the Central Point Interchange. The ponds are open year-round. Largemouth bass, bluegill, crappie, and brown bullhead are available. Legal trout are occasionally stocked in early spring for Free Fishing Day. Recommended for small fry.

FISH CREEK (Douglas Co.) A wonderful trout fishery high up the North Umpqua River above an impassable barrier to salmon and steelhead. It enters the North Umpqua from the south one mile below Toketee Falls, about 40 miles upstream from Glide on the North Umpqua Highway. Several fair logging roads hit the upper stream, one heading south from Toketee Generator Plant, and the other following Copelands Creek near Eagle Rock.

The stream offers good early fishing for wild trout. Don't neglect the impoundments on the creek. Follow Watson Creek Rd. to the Fish Creek forebay for rainbow to 17 inches. There are forest campgrounds at Fish Creek and at Camas Creek, about 5 miles south of the highway.

FISH LAKE (Douglas Co.) A big, beautiful trout lake beneath Grasshopper Mt. in the Umpqua-Rogue Divide Wilderness. This 95-acre hike-in rainbow and brook trout lake is at elevation 3,500 ft., 1 1/2 miles (and 800 ft.) below, Buckeye and Cliff Lakes.

At Tiller on Hwy. 227, follow County Rd. 46 into the forest, where it becomes FS 28, the South Umpqua River Rd. Continue on Forest Rd. 28 about 4 miles past South Umpqua Falls Camp, where several roads branch off. Follow Forest Rd. 2823 to the right about 2 miles, then Forest Rd. 2830. Bear left at the fork. The Fish Lake Trailhead 2840 is a little over 2 miles further, at the next fork on the right. It's about a 3-mile hike to the lake.

Fish Lake has both rainbow and brook trout, with fish up to 20 inches caught each season. It is stocked from time to time, but wild fish make up most of the catch. It can be fished from shore, but a raft or float tube will increase your chances. All methods will take fish. There's an undeveloped camp at the lake, and good camping at Camp Comfort Campground on Forest Rd. 28 about 2 1/2 miles beyond your first right. Trail bikes are not allowed in the wilderness.

FISH LAKE (Jackson Co.) A large, very popular lake about 37 miles NE of Medford on Hwy. 140, head waters of the North Fork of Little Butte Creek. Take Hwy. 62 north from Medford, to its junction with Hwy. 140. From Ashland, take Dead Indian Memorial Rd. (east of the municipal airport) about 4 miles past Howard Prairie Lake to Big Elk Rd., a northbound gravel road which joins Hwy. 140 near Fish Lake. From Klamath Falls, take Hwy. 140 north past Lake of the Woods.

Covering 440 acres, Fish Lake has provided good fishing for stocked rainbow and brook trout. The lake has an increasingly serious rough fish problem. Past efforts to eradicate the rough fish through poisoning were unsuccessful and will not be repeated due to budgetary restraints and concern for the bald eagles that fish the lake. A hand trapping program might be attempted in the future.

The Pacific Crest Trail comes to within 1/2 mile of Fish Lake, and with good campgrounds and a fishing village-like resort, it is a popular stopover for hikers. There are two campgrounds at the east end of the lake, Doe Point and Fish Lake. North Fork Camp on Forest Rd. 3706 is about 3/4 mile west of the lake. There is a boat launch at Fish Lake Camp. The resort on the west shore has cabins, boat rentals, restaurant, and supplies.

FLORAS CREEK A short south coast stream with wild cutthroat, good for steelhead and fair for chinook. The creek is closed to coho angling. Hwy.101 crosses it about 15 miles south of Bandon. The upper stream is followed by road for about 5 miles, but the stream is usually in a gorge well below the road and bordered by mostly private property. The stream below the highway can be reached in several spots by car, but the area is swampy.

Cutthroat fishing is best in early season. Chinook show up in October or later, depending on the breaching of the outlet dune by high water. Steelhead show in December and are available through March. The creek is lightly fished due to difficulty of access.

FLORAS LAKE A large, popular lake west of Hwy. 101, about 17 miles south of Bandon. A good road just south of Langlois runs 2 miles west from Hwy. 101 to the lake. The lake covers 250 acres and in places reaches a depth of 50 feet.

Rainbow trout are stocked, and sea-run cutthroat are available if the run gets in after the spring opening.

The lake has a few largemouth bass 7-8 pounds, but it's slow fishing. There are quite a few weed beds. Try plugging into the open water near the beds to tempt these bass.

Chinook, coho, and steelhead all move through the lake into the upper tributaries. Both steelhead and chinook are caught here. The lake is closed to coho fishing.

Boice Cope County Park is located on the lake road and provides camping and a boat ramp. The lake is best fished from a boat, but keep a weather eye out, since it can get real windy here.

FORDS MILL POND A large pond with bass and panfish on Hwy. 225 near Sutherlin, about one mile west of the junction of highways. 225 and 99. About 100 acres, the pond is owned by Roseburg Lumber Co. Angler access is allowed at this time.

East, south, and west banks are accessible. A number of species are present in good numbers, including bluegill, crappie, perch, brown bullhead and bass. Four pound bass are not uncommon, and buckets full of fine crappie are taken in spring. Yellow jigs and cut bait are best for the crappie. Motorboats are prohibited, but bank fishing is easy anywhere. Accommodations and supplies are available at Sutherlin, 2 miles east of the lake.

GARRISON LAKE A large 134-acre lake with trout, a nice population of bass, and abundant yellow perch, just west of Port Orford off Hwy. 101. Up to 30 ft. deep in places, the lake is typical for the coast area, with partly sandy shores and a severe weed problem.

Garrison is stocked with hatchery rainbow and has some wild cutthroat. Yellow perch run to good size. The largemouth population is currently depleted, as the fish are slow to reproduce here and budget constraints have not allowed stocking on a regular basis. There is a one-fish bag limit on bass.

The lake is best fished by boat. There is a boat ramp and parking area provided by the state at the south end of the lake, and another provided by the county at the north end. The nearest public campground is at Battle Rock State Park in Port Orford. There is a private RV park at the lake.

GALESVILLE RESERVOIR An attractive 640-acre impoundment on Cow Creek, tributary to the South Umpqua, offering very good warmwater fishing and a unique fishery for landlocked coho. To reach it, take the Azalea Exit No. 88 off I-5 onto County Rd. 36.

Created in 1986 during the drought, the reservoir has finally filled and is providing excellent habitat for warmwater species. Fish the submerged trees along the NW edge for good size largemouth bass and crappie. A small boat or canoe will let you weave among the partially submerged timber.

The reservoir has spotty bank access along the road. There are two boat ramps here and a pretty picnic area.

GOLD RAY FOREBAY The 80-acre forebay to Gold Ray Dam on the Rogue River. Access is a problem due to the railroad tracks. There is no official boat access due to the danger of boats going over the dam (some have). A popular warmwater fishery here has diminished in recent years due to releases of cold water to benefit Rogue River salmon, steelhead, and trout.

GRASS LAKE A rich, self-sustaining brook trout lake in the Seven Lakes Basin of the northern Sky Lakes Wilderness, headwaters of the Rogue River Middle Fork, offering very good fly-fishing opportunities. It is accessible from both east and west. See Alta Lake for detailed directions.

Trail 981 accesses the basin from Forest Rd. 344, continuing past the cut-off to Alta, to the cut-off to Middle then Grass

Both trout and panfish are available in many coastal lakes.

Lake. Trail 3703 approaches the basin from Forest Rd. 3334 on the east at Sevenmile Marsh Campground, joining the Pacific Crest Trail after about 2 miles. The trail to Grass cuts off the PCT after about 2 miles.

Covering 30 acres, Grass supports some wild brook and is stocked every other year. Trout run to 15 inches, averaging 9 to 12 inches. Usually the most productive of the Seven Lakes group, it is quite shallow, and fly fishing is effective. There are natural campsites at Grass and at other nearby lakes. For trail information, check with the Butte Falls Ranger Station. See also Cliff, Middle, Alta.

GRAVE CREEK A fairly large tributary of the Rogue River, entering from the east, about 6 miles north of Galice. A spawning stream for Rogue River salmon and steelhead, the creek is closed to all angling.

HALL LAKE A small lake about 10 miles south of Reedsport on Hwy. 101, which is gradually being filled in by sand dunes. Private property surrounds the lake. It has a largemouth bass and a good population of cutthroat.

HERBERT LOG POND (a.k.a. Canyonville Pond) A good l0-acre mill pond purchased by the state for angling. It is located on Hwy. 227 in a county park about one mile east of I- 5 at Canyonville.

The pond produces good numbers of largemouth bass, black crappie, and brown bullhead. Bank fishing is ideal for youngsters. Motorboats are prohibited, but a float tube, canoe, or raft will help you reach the larger bass. Supplies and accommodations are available at Canyonville. Recommended for small fry.

HOOVER PONDS A series of four artificial ponds visible from Hwy. 140 north of Medford. They have naturally reproducing populations of largemouth bass, bluegill, crappie and brown bullhead. The ponds are small, 4-10 acres each, and most fishing is from the bank. Jackson Pond, at the County Sports Park, is just east of the Hoover complex and offers fishing for bass and bluegill.

HORSESHOE LAKE (Klamath Co.) A good hike-in brook and rainbow trout lake in the Blue Lake Basin of the Sky Lakes Wilderness, Rogue River National Forest. See Blue Lake (Klamath Co.). for road and trail directions. Horseshoe is about 1/2 mile SE of Blue Lake. Bear left at the trail fork. Other good lakes nearby include Blue Canyon, Pear, and Carey.

Horseshoe Lake is about 20 acres, with good shoal areas and cover for fish. The lake has good numbers of brook trout to 18 inches, and a smaller population of rainbow about the same size. The big brookies can be hard to catch. Fly fishing seems to be most productive here, though casting small lures from shore with a slow retrieve can be effective.

There are good natural campsites at the lake. Improved sites are available at nearby lakes. The Blue Rock Mt. Rd. usually opens in June.

HORSFALL LAKE An extremely shallow but (sometimes) large lake within the National Dunes Recreation Area north of North Bend. Like all dune lakes, Horsfall can vary dramatically in size from year to year depending on the water table. Some years they almost disappear.

From Hwy. 101, cross the Haynes Inlet of Coos Bay, turning onto the Bluebill Lake Rd. about half-way across the inlet. Horsfall Lake is NW of Little Bluebill Lake, part of a lake complex that includes adjacent Spirit Lake and Sandpoint Lake to the north. Horsfall contains yellow perch, largemouth bass, and brown bullhead.

HOWARD PRAIRIE LAKE One of southern Oregon's most popular lakes, a large irrigation reservoir in an alpine setting east of Ashland. Howard Prairie has a large trout population and grows fish very well. Depending on irrigation needs and rainfall, the reservoir varies from 2000-1500 acres.

From Ashland take Hwy. 66 to Dead Indian Memorial Rd. just past the municipal airport. Follow this paved road 22 miles to the reservoir. The route from Medford is circuitous but possible. Take Hwy. 62 to Hwy. 140, the Lake of the Woods Hwy. Turn south at Lake Creek, following Little Butte Rd. to Soda Creek Rd., then Conde Creek Rd. to Dead Indian Memorial Rd., emerging just west of Howard Prairie.

The reservoir is stocked annually with rainbows, which range 10-18 inches, and average over a pound, with 4 and 5 pounders not uncommon. Worms and eggs fished just off the bottom take fish in early season, and trolling with spinner/bait combinations works well. Good trout spots include the area south of the island, and the far north arm. Best trolling is in the deep water in the east inside channel. Fly anglers might try streamers on a slow troll, or cast to the shallows. A lot of the larger rainbow are taken late in the day on flies slowly trolled just under the surface.

While trolling is very popular, the lake can successfully be fished from its banks. The most popular area is between Klum Landing and the Dam.

Largemouth bass were introduced illegally some time ago and are an established and growing fishery. If you enjoy brown bullhead, there are plenty of them here. These fish average 8 inches and run to 11 inches. Worms are the favored bait. Pumpkinseed sunfish are also present.

There is a campground at Howard Prairie Resort, as well as at Willow Point on the west shore and at Klum Landing on the south shore. A horse camp, Lily Glen, is well back from the water at the far north end of the lake. Two group camps are available by reservation. Sugar Pine, a campground with drinking water, may be reserved by calling (503) 776-7001. Camp Asperkaha is managed by the Medford YMCA and is available for rental. Its facilities include covered sleeping shelters with bunks and an open air but fully equipped kitchen shelter.

Howard Prairie Resort offers supplies, boat rentals, and trailer rentals. It is open only during trout season. Recommended for small fry.

HUNTER CREEK A small coast stream that empties directly into the ocean just south of the Rogue River Estuary. Hwy. 101 crosses its mouth about 2 miles south of Gold Beach. After years of rehabilitation, the stream is once again supporting a winter steelhead fishery, though it remains closed to sea-run and salmon angling. Rehabilitation work continues.

HYATT RESERVOIR A large reservoir of about 9,000 acres, north of the Green Springs summit on Hwy. 66, which leads from Ashland to Klamath Falls. It is 5 miles from Green Springs, which is about 13 miles east of Ashland. Dead Indian Memorial Rd. accesses the reservoir from the north.

Hyatt was severely affected by the long drought, but it has recovered well. A 1989 treatment removed illegally introduced brown bullhead and bass, which were competing with the trout for limited food. The lake has been re-stocked with rainbow which are thriving in the less competitive environment, and trout to 20 inches are now available. Trolling the west shore and the northeast cove are especially productive. Bank access is good.

A BLM campground with boat ramp is at the south end of the reservoir. Howard Prairie Resort offers lodging, boat rentals a restaurant, and limited supplies. The reservoir is accessible in winter, and there is some ice-fishing.

ILLINOIS RIVER A major tributary of the lower Rogue River, joining it from the south at Agness, about 25 miles upriver from Gold Beach. Headwaters of the Illinois are in the Siskiyou National Forest east of Cave Junction, where there is good angling for wild trout in early spring. Winter steelhead are fished in the 25 miles from Pomeroy Dam at Cave Junction to Oak Flat.

A few anglers boat the 5-mile section between Kerby Bridge and Pomery Dam using small sleds, but the Illinois is primarily a bank fishery. All angling in the Illinois is now limited to catch and release, due to extremely low and warm water levels. This condition is the result of heavy irrigation withdrawals, intensive mining in past years, and overzealous timber harvests, further aggravated by years of drought. Barbless artificial flies and lures are required for all fisheries throughout the year.

To access the most popular section of the river, follow Hwy. 199 north from Cave Junction to Selma, then turn left on County Rd. 5070, which becomes Forest Rd. 4203. This road leads to Kerby Flat, then follows the river to Oak Flat, ending at Briggs Cr. Watch for roadside pull-offs indicating favorite river access points. At Briggs Cr., a Forest Service trail leads down to the river and follows it for about 5 miles to the Weaver Ranch, just beyond Pine Cr. This portion of the river is designated Wild and Scenic and is included in the Kalmiopsis Wilderness. There is no boat access here. There is boat angling in the lower river, with access from a ramp at Agness.

JORDAN LAKE A pond near the Weyerhaeuser paper mill west of Jordan Point on Coos Bay. It was severely affected by years of drought, and its warmwater fishery is currently depleted. In the past, it supported a good size population of yellow perch, and small numbers of big largemouth bass and brown bullhead.

JUMP OFF JOE CREEK A 20-mile tributary of the Middle Rogue River, entering the Rogue in the Merlin area NW of Grants Pass. It is crossed by Hwy. 99 about 10 miles north of Grants Pass and followed east by paved road for a good distance. It's not open for salmon or steelhead, but provides good early angling for wild trout. Fishing peters out with low water later in the season.

LAKE CREEK (Douglas Co.) The outlet stream of Diamond Lake, headwaters of the North Umpqua. The creek runs 10 miles north from the lake to Lemolo Reservoir. Roads follow within a mile throughout its length. Hwy. 138 crosses about 5 miles downstream from the lake at Thielsen Campground. The Umpqua National Forest map shows a rough track (Forest Rd. 4792) leading south from the Forest Rd. 60 junction with 138 near Thielsen, following the creek for almost 4 miles. North from Thielsen Camp, Forest Rd. 2610 to Lemolo Lake stays within a mile of the creek, though the creek runs through a deep canyon there.

The upper end of the creek near Diamond Lake contains good size rainbow to 2 pounds. The beaver flats below yield more brown and brook trout in a series of pools. Hearty anglers might like to try a 2-day hike-and-fish from Diamond Lake to Lemolo for the chance of a catch worth bragging about, especially in fall.

There are camping facilities at Diamond Lake, Lemolo Lake, and Thielsen Campground.

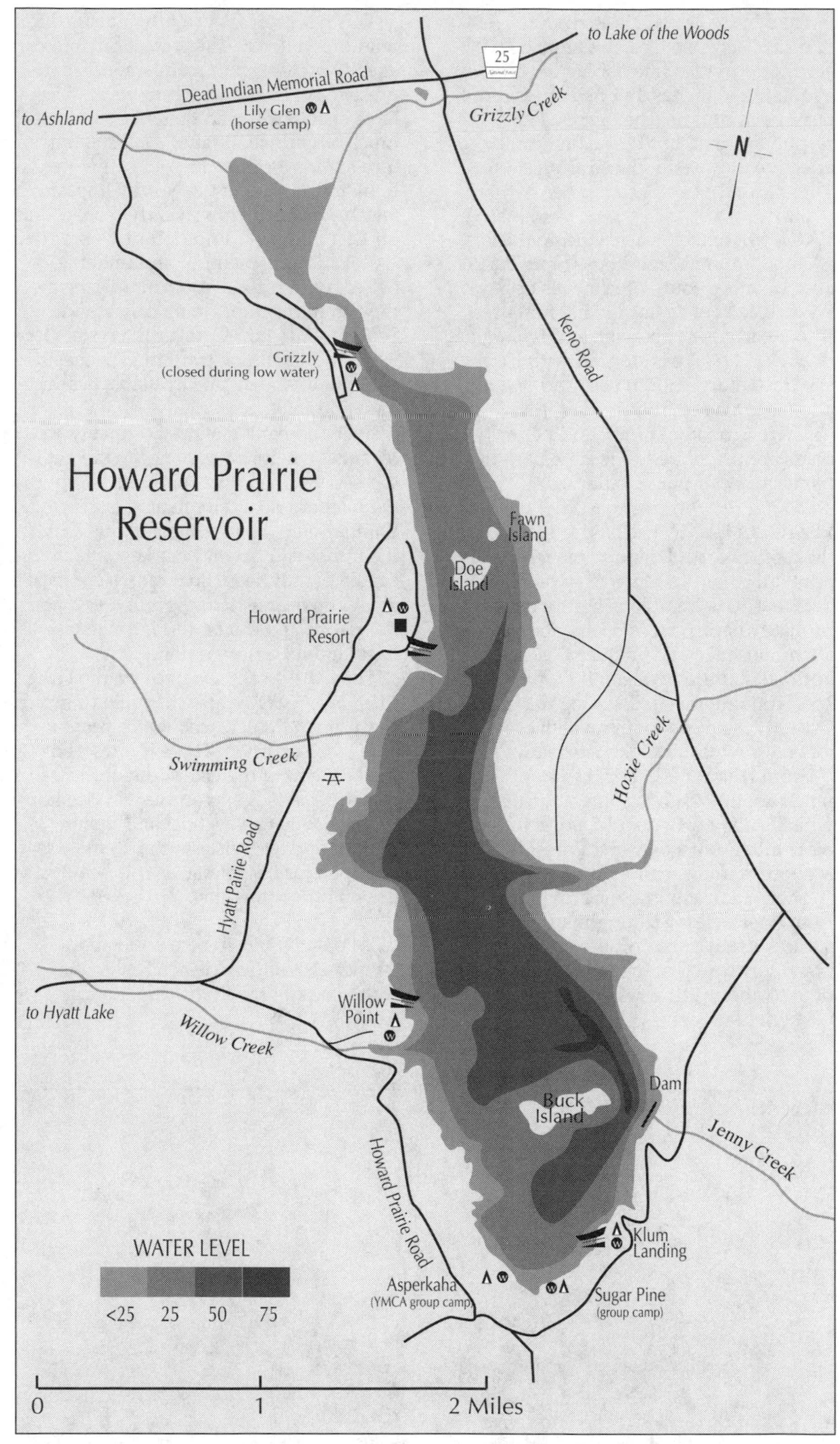

LAKE IN THE WOODS A small but easily reached lake in the Umpqua National Forest due east of Roseburg. It's about 24 miles to the lake from Glide. Take the North Umpqua Rd. to Glide, and the Little River Rd., Forest Rd. 27, to the lake.

Lake in the Woods is at elevation 3,000 ft. and is accessible early. Only about 4 acres, it provides fine fishing for rainbow averaging 10 inches, but fish to 19 inches have been caught. The biggest fish respond to bait, but fly-casting can be effective. It is easily fished from shore. There's a nice campground here.

LAKE MARIE A 5-acre cutthroat lake within Umpqua Lighthouse State Park, about 2 miles south of Winchester Bay off Hwy. 101. There's fair fishing for cutthroat early in the season, and fly anglers do well. The lake is stocked with hatchery trout. Largemouth bass and yellow perch are also present.

There is no boat ramp, and motor boats are prohibited. The state park has picnic and camping facilities.

LEMOLO LAKE The largest reservoir in the upper North Umpqua power development, covering 415 acres when not drawn down. Lemolo is lightly fished, probably because it is positioned between Diamond Lake and Toketee Reservoir, both outstanding waters. It's a scenic spot, though, situated among the pines with Mt. Thielsen looming above, and lots of browns and kokanee below.

From Diamond Lake take Hwy. 138 north about 7 miles to Forest Rd. 2610, which leads north about 5 miles to the reservoir. From Roseburg, Forest Rd. 2610 is about 80 miles east by way of Hwy. 138.

There's fair angling for brown trout from opening day through fall. Angling success usually falls off during midsummer. Drawdown in the fall reduces the pool to about 140 acres and severely limits angler success.

This reservoir is currently managed for wild brown trout. The typical catch averages 12 inches, and much larger fish are present. A few monster browns to 15 lbs. have been taken, and there are rumors of much larger fish. It takes a substantial lure to interest these big old carnivores. Look for browns in the North Umpqua and Lake Creek arms in early season, and off East Lemolo Campground.

Kokanee are plentiful and under fished, with a good opportunity to view the fish in their spawning colors mid-September to mid-October in crystal clear Spring River. Brook trout to 12 inches and a few rainbow are available near the dam and inlet.

Boat and bank anglers do equally well till June, when boats are needed to get to the best fishing. Float tubes are handy in the inlet areas, and fly fishing is very popular here. Boats are not allowed in the upper end beyond markers which can be plainly seen. Boat ramps are located at Poole Creek Campground and at the resort, and can be slid into the lake at East Lemolo Campground.

There are 4 campgrounds on the Lake. The Forest Service also maintains a group campsite at Poole Creek which is available by reservation. There is a resort at the NW end of the lake south of the dam. It features a lodge, groceries, tackle shop, dining room, cabins, boat and motor rentals, and a service station. Lemolo is not open for ice fishing, as it is heavily drawn down in winter.

LIBBY POND A 10-acre pond about 7 miles east of Gold Beach beside the south bank of the Rogue River off County Rd. 595.

Boats are needed to reach the fishing on Lemolo Lake after June.

It is stocked with legal trout in spring and hosts the annual Free Fishing Day Derby for youngsters. Brown bullhead are also available, but most fishing is for the trout.

Libby offers good bank access, but small boats and float tubes work well here. Best fishing is earlier in season, since the lake warms in summer.

Recommended for small fry.

LITTLE APPLEGATE RIVER A long trout stream flowing into the Applegate River about 3 miles south of Ruch. The river is closed to all angling.

LITTLE HYATT LAKE A pretty little 5-10 acre lake on BLM property just south of Hyatt Prairie Reservoir. From the reservoir, head south on Old Hyatt Prairie Rd., or drive north on Greensprings Hwy. 66. Meadows on the east and north shores allow good bank access. The west bank is forested. The lake is stocked with rainbow and has largemouth bass, brown bullhead, and crappie. There are no developed camps at the lake.

LITTLE RIVER A very nice tributary of the North Umpqua, joining the North Umpqua at Glide, about 20 miles east of Roseburg on Hwy. 138. It is followed east from Glide by paved road for about 15 miles, and by gravel road another 15 miles to the headwaters.

Fishing for wild cutthroat and stocked rainbows usually holds up until mid-summer. The upper river has some good fly water.

Little River has runs of summer steelhead and fall chinook. The river is currently closed to the taking of adult chinook during the spawning season from October 1 through November 30.

LOON LAKE A large, deep lake draining into the lower Umpqua River. Loon Lake offers good angling for trout in spring and fall, and fair angling for largemouth bass throughout the season. From Hwy. 38 (Reedsport to Darwin), a county road leads south about 6 miles to the lake. The turn-off is about 3 miles west of Scottsburg. Driving south on I-5, take the Drain Exit. The lake can also be reached from Coos Bay by very poor roads up the Millicoma River.

Loon Lake is 2 miles long, covers 275 acres, and is very deep with little shoal area. Wild cutthroat are present in good numbers, and rainbow are stocked. Rainbow fishing holds up for several months, with catches to 18 inches.

Largemouth black bass provide fair angling throughout the season. Anglers cast lures and plugs and use bait for bass to 8 pounds. The average bass is 2-4 pounds. Crappie to 12 inches and brown bullhead to 16 inches are available in fair numbers. Nice size bluegill are also present.

There are two resorts on the lake, and angling information and supplies can be obtained from them. Boats and motors are available. Loon Lake Recreation Site, an excellent BLM campground and boat ramp, is at the north end of the lake just south of the outlet crossing. The area is well protected from the wind, with pleasant sandy beaches and a wheelchair accessible dock. Camping and overnight accommodations are available at Loon Lake Resort. Several picnic areas are nearby on Hwy. 38. Recommended for small fry. Wheelchair accessible.

LOST CREEK RESERVOIR A 3,500 acre reservoir on the Rogue River that produced the state's record largemouth bass. Lost Creek is at river mile 157 just upstream from Cole Rivers Hatchery. In addition to bass, it offers good fishing for trout and a variety of panfish. It is open the year around. Located about 30 miles NE of Medford on Hwy. 62, it was built for flood control and to enhance downstream water flow for salmon and steelhead. First filled in 1977, it has a maximum depth of 322 feet with very little shallows.

Bass are a big fishery here. Lots of bass to 5 pounds are taken, and the success rate has been very good. In the spring, anglers work the shoal areas on the south side of the reservoir, and the willowy areas of the north shore's shallow coves. The state record bass, caught in 1988, and weighing 11 lbs. 4.64 oz., was caught in one of these coves 60 ft. from shore in about 4 ft. of water. The north shore warms first, attracting bait fish which draw the attention of the larger bass. Later in the season when the reservoir warms, the mouths of tributary streams on the south shore are productive. Good catches are also made above the highway bridge where there is a lot of submerged structure, and off the dam face. Bass fishing has been best when the reservoir is holding maximum water.

Lost Creek is stocked annually with legal and fingerling rainbow which reach 16 inches. It also has wild populations of cutthroat, brook trout, and brown trout. Still-fishing is limited to a few shoal areas. Trolling with spinner and worm or lures works most consistently, particularly at the upper end at the junction of north and south forks. Other good troll areas are along the dam and around the point of the island. Bank anglers fish beside the spillway, along the dam face, and in the cove off Fish Hatchery Rd. Cold sunny days in December, January, and February can produce surprisingly good catches on a troll here.

Smallmouth bass, bluegill, crappie, pumpkinseed sunfish, and bullhead also provide good fishing.

Camping facilities are available at Stewart State Park on the south shore. Boat ramps are located in Stewart Park and near the north abutment of the dam. There is a privately run moorage with store and boat rentals in the state park. Additional supplies are available at Prospect, Shady Cove, or Trail on Hwy. 62.

LOST LAKE (Douglas Co.) An 8-10 acre beaver pond in the Callahan Mts. near the town of Umpqua, with fine fly-fishing for wild cutthroat. Take the Hubbard Creek Rd. from Umpqua into the mountains, following the ridge crest. Turn right, and at about 100 yds., turn left to the creek. As you cross the creek, a trail leads off to the left about 300 yds. to the lake. Good luck!

LOST LAKE (Jackson Co.) A 10-acre lake at the head of Little Butte Creek, stocked by air with rainbow and brook trout. The lake is in the vicinity of the Lake Creek Rd., off un-named Medco and BLM roads. Check with the district ODF&W office in Central Point for directions.

LUCILLE LAKE An 8-acre hike-in lake in the Umpqua National Forest about 8 miles west of Lemolo Lake, 1/2 mile due west of Maidu Lake. The lake has very little cover and has consistently winterkilled. It is no longer stocked.

MAIDU LAKE A good eastern brook trout lake in the headwaters of the North Umpqua just off the Pacific Crest Trail. It's an 8-mile hike from Forest Rd. 958 west of the Bradley Creek Arm of Lemolo. A shorter hike begins at Miller Lake in the Winema National Forest. Take Trail 1446 (which follows the north shore of Miller) up to the Pacific Crest Trail. It's about one mile to the junction, and less then a mile further NW to Maidu.

At 20 acres, Maidu has good size brook trout to 16 inches, with a few larger. Any method takes fish, but fly fishing really pays off in the evening. The lake is stocked every year or two and has natural reproduction. It is usually accessible in late June.

MATSON CREEK A good little trout stream with wild cutthroat, about 10 miles long, tributary to the East Fork Millicoma River. Matson joins the east fork about 10 miles east of Allegany, which is about 10 miles east of Coos Bay. Roads here are primitive logging tracks. This is Weyerhaeuser timber country, and access is limited. There are several high falls in the upper stream and real rough going.

The upper stream offers good wild cutthroat fishing, and brook trout (which were stocked years ago) may still be present. Bait fishing is the usual method.

MEDCO POND An old 70-acre log pond between Prospect and Butte Falls, on the Prospect-Butte Falls Hwy. NE of Medford. From Medford, follow Hwy. 62 east to the Butte Falls Hwy. Follow this past Butte Falls to the junction with Prospect Road. Head north 15 miles. The lake is on the east side of the road.

Medco is owned by the Medford Lumber Co., which allows public use. It is stocked with legal rainbow and has a good population of bass and bluegill. The bass run to 5 pounds, and bluegill to 8 inches.

MIDDLE LAKE (Klamath Co.) A good fly lake in the Seven Lakes Basin of the Sky Lakes Wilderness, accessible from east or west. For directions, see Grass Lake, Alta Lake. Middle Lake is between Grass and Cliff lakes, less than 1/4 mile from each.

Middle Lake is stocked annually with fingerlings and has wild brook trout. The fish run to 16 inches and better, and angling holds up well all season. The west end seems to offer best fishing. Try wet bucktails and streamers in the morning and evening. There are good campsites here, as at other lakes in the basin.

MILLICOMA RIVER (NORTH FORK OF COOS RIVER) A major tributary of the Coos River, with a good run of shad, and good salmon angling. The main river is only about 7 or 8 miles long from Allegany to its confluence with the Coos. Above Allegany (which is head of tide) the river splits into East and West Forks. Access is by paved county roads off Hwy. 101 near Coos Bay.

Shad fishing is excellent at times, with best fishing in May and June. Best shad catches seem to be around the mid-section of the river near the tavern, especially on hot, sunny afternoons. It's a pretty stream, and a nice place to spend a summer day.

Trolling for fall chinook and coho occurs in September, October and November. The average year sees a couple hundred fall salmon landed. Most of the good steelhead angling takes place in the upper forks. Sea-run cutthroat are present from August through October.

Boats can be launched at Doras Ramp, 1/4 mile upstream from the confluence, and at Rooke Higgins, a facility with plenty of parking about 3 miles further upstream.

MILLICOMA RIVER, EAST FORK The East Fork is a good size stream with a fair steelhead run and cutthroat trout. About 25 miles long, it joins the main river at Allegany, about 10 miles east of Coos Bay. A road follows the East Fork another 10 miles, with logging roads branching off to follow the various tributaries.

A very good wild trout stream, it is heavily fished by local anglers in early season. Glen Creek, joining from the east about 6 miles upstream, has lots of cutthroat, too.

Stocked winter steelhead are picked up in good numbers.

MILLICOMA RIVER, WEST FORK Very good for hatchery-reared winter steelhead, about 30 miles long, joining the main Millicoma River at head of tidewater at Allegany. Allegany is about 10 miles east of Coos Bay, reached by paved county road from Hwy. 101. A paved forest road continues upstream following the river. The road ends at Stall's Falls, which is about 10 miles above Allegany. Headwaters are reached by a detour through Elliot State Forest.

The upper stream, an area called the Elkhorn Ranch, affords very good angling for wild cutthroat and is reached by hiking or pack trips. Fishing around Elkhorn Ranch provides a real quality angling experience. The fork provides outstanding cutthroat fishing starting as early as August.

The Dept. of Fish and Wildlife is currently stocking 35,000 steelhead smolts annually in the fork, and anglers have reaped good returns. The run hits its stride in December and holds through February. The West Fork has a high angler success rate for a small stream.

Bank access is limited along the lower river due to private property. Boats can be launched at the county bridge, 5.5 miles upstream from the confluence, but this is not novice water. There are many rapids between here and the take-out.

An interpretive center at the steelhead hatchery about 9 miles above Allagany is open to the public. It includes a rearing pond with an underwater viewing window. Best viewing is October through May. Educational programs for groups can be arranged by calling the ODF&W office in Charleston. This facility is recommended for small fry.

MYRTLE CREEK (Douglas Co.) A tributary of the South Umpqua, actually two forks, each about 20 miles long, entering the South Umpqua at the town of Myrtle Creek on Hwy. 99.

The stream offers very poor fishing for wild cutthroat. Many of the fish in the stream are young steelhead and salmon, which should be allowed to migrate to the ocean. Cutthroat are usually larger and can be identified by their heavy spotting.

Salmon and steelhead enter Myrtle Creek for spawning and should not be disturbed.

There are no campgrounds in the vicinity, although picnic areas are available. Most of the property along the lower stream is privately owned.

MUD LAKE A 3-acre lake in the Blue Lake Group, situated between Blue and Beale. Though it is not stocked, it has a naturally reproducing population of brook trout.

NATIONAL CREEK A small but scenic tributary of the upper Rogue, entering the river west of Crater Lake National Park, about 4 miles north of the junction of highways 62 and 230. About 5 miles north of the junction on Hwy. 230, take Forest Rd. 6530 to the right, which follows the stream for most of its 5-mile length. It offers fair early trout fishing for brook trout and rainbow, with best fishing in June.

Union Creek Campground, just south of the Hwy. 62/230 junction, is a popular camping spot beside the scenic Rogue Gorge. For other good nearby trout streams see Copeland Creek, Wizard Creek.

NEW RIVER The short but interesting outlet stream for Floras Lake. New River has been known to reverse its flow from year to year, breaching the dunes in new locations to empty into the ocean. The outlet appears to be moving north, and at this time there is public access to the river through a site purchased by BLM.

New River provides bank angling for sea-run cutthroat, salmon, and steelhead. The stream parallels the beach and connects Floras Lake to Floras Creek. It is approached by Croft Lake Rd. just north of the Curry/Coos County line.

The river offers pretty good chinook bank angling from September through October. A fair winter steelhead run takes place in December. Sea-run are in the river from July through fall. The river is closed to coho angling.

Boats can be launched at the Floras Lake outlet for a 6-7 mile float to the BLM access site. Though there's not a lot of good fishing water here, the tidewater drift is pleasant. Be warned that it can get windy here, turning this into a longer drift than anticipated. Motors are not allowed.

The BLM has large holdings along the stream and is trying to preserve the natural scenic values of the sand dunes. There's excellent surfperch fishing along the beaches across the dunes.

PEAR LAKE A good brook trout lake in the Blue Lake group of the southern Sky Lakes Wilderness. A long narrow lake, it is just east of Horseshoe Lake on Trail 982. See Blue Lake for complete directions from the west. It's a 4-mile hike, past Blue and Horseshoe lakes, to Pear.

To access the basin from the east, take Hwy. 140 (Lake of the Woods Rd.) to Forest Rd. 3651, about 6 miles NE of Lake of the Woods and 4 miles west of the junction of highways 140 and 62 near Upper Klamath Lake. Turn left on Forest Rd. 3659 toward Big Meadows about 1 1/2 miles north of the junction of Forest Rds. 3651 and 3458. Trailhead 3712 is at the apex of the hairpin curve on Forest Rd. 3659. From Trail 3712, cross over the Pacific Crest Trail at about one mile, and continue on Trail 3712 to the basin. At the next fork, follow Trail 982 SW around the south end of Island Lake to Pear. It's less than a 4-mile hike to Pear.

Stocked with fingerlings annually, this 25-acre lake supports a good population of brook trout to 14 inches. Catches are good in spring and fall. During the day, fish the deep water in the north end. In the evening the fish school and feed in the shallower southern end of the lake. A float tube or rubber raft would come in handy. Pear is usually accessible in early June.

PISTOL RIVER A south coast stream, quite small, with a small winter steelhead run and a greatly diminished run of fall chinook. It flows into the Pacific about 15 miles south of Gold Beach and is crossed near the mouth by Hwy. 101. Only 20 miles long, it is followed east by a good road about 8 miles upstream. Above that the only access is by logging roads or trails. Most of the river is bordered by private timber land holdings. Get permission before you cross private land.

Very little trout fishing takes place here, but sea-run cutthroat are fished in the estuary when the bar is breached in September or October. The Pistol mouth is bar-bound in the summer, and returning cutthroat are held out until late August or September most years. Check with the Department of Fish and Wildlife at Gold Beach for an update. The river has been closed for chinook fishing since 1991.

Fish runs in the Pistol have been hard hit by logging operations in the drainage. The river flows through an area of unstable gravel that is particularly vulnerable. Spawning gravel has been badly scoured and holding areas have filled in. Some local timber owners have begun to voluntarily participate in efforts to rehabilitate the stream.

PLAT I RESERVOIR A very productive 140-acre lake, 4 miles east of Sutherlin by the Plat I Rd. Built for flood control and irrigation in the late '60's, it now supports good populations of rainbow, crappie, bluegill, largemouth bass, and lots of brown bullhead.

Bank fishing is easy, with no brush or trees to interfere with casting. Water levels drop during the summer, and the reservoir is heavily drawn down in winter, calling a halt to bass fishing from November through February. Spring and early summer are the best times to fish. Bass to 6 pounds are common in the shallows on the east side. Plastic worms, nightcrawlers, and streamer flies are all effective. The reservoir is stocked with catchable rainbow in spring.

There is a good boat ramp, but a light boat with a short shaft motor will get you into the shallows where the bass tend to lurk. There are no campsites at the lake. Recommended for small fry.

POWERS POND An old mill pond at the edge of the community of Powers, about 21 miles upstream from Myrtle Point, that has been purchased by the county as a fishing and recreation area. It is surrounded by manicured grounds and covers about 10 acres. The lake is stocked with legal rainbow and has largemouth bass, black crappie, and brown bullhead catfish. Best fishing is in March, April and May before the water warms and the park gets crowded.

The pond offers good swimming, and the park has RV facilities, showers, and a picnic area. Recommended for small fry.

ROCK CREEK (Douglas Co.) A good wild cutthroat stream, flowing 20 miles to the North Umpqua. The creek enters the river from the north, about 27 miles east of Roseburg. From Roseburg, take Hwy. 138, which meets and follows the North Umpqua just west of Glide. A paved road, about one mile from Idleyld Park follows Rock Creek's west bank for about 14 miles.

There's good trout fishing here from early spring into summer. Wild cutthroat are available to 14 inches. Expect to lose a little tackle, however, as the stream is wide and rough. Rock Creek Hatchery is about 1/4 mile upstream from the mouth and is open to the public. Adult and juvenile chinook salmon are generally in the pools.

BLM maintains 2 nice campgrounds on the stream, and there are several county parks nearby on the North Umpqua. Susan Creek State Park, about 8 miles east of Rock Creek on the North Umpqua Hwy., has plenty of camping space.

ROGUE RIVER (Estuary) A narrow estuary with a difficult bar crossing that serves primarily as a point of access to the lower Rogue River's outstanding chinook and steelhead fisheries. Gold Beach is the major port town. Questionable secondary roads connect I-5 with the lower Rogue valley at Agness, but best direct routes are Hwy. 42 west from Roseburg and Hwy. 199 from Grants Pass. A dramatic but somewhat slower approach can be made by following Hwy. 101 from north or south. From Portland, it's slightly more than a 300-mile drive to Gold Beach. Allow at least 6 hours for the trip.

Some fall chinook are caught off Rogue River Bay's north jetty in July.

The Rogue River bar is not an easy one to cross. Small boats cannot get outside safely. The total ocean salmon sport catch out of Gold Beach is small in comparison with other south coast bays.

Spring chinook enter the bay in late March, but the major fishery for them begins up-bay, from Elephant Rock to head of tide at The Clay Banks. Peak catches are in May. By July, all the springers have moved through the bay and into the river.

Fall chinook first enter the bay in July, and fishing for them usually picks up in August. Anglers troll or mooch herring and anchovies above and below Hwy. 101 Bridge. A few are caught off the north jetty, and there is a good bank fishery for them on the sand spit near the south jetty. Popular spots are below Elephant Rock, at Johns Hole in the lower river, and at the Ferry Hole above the Clay Banks. The Clay Banks, head of tide, is a popular gravel bar access, with hog lines at the upper end just below the riffle, and fly-fishing for chinook at the lower end.

Summer steelhead hit the bay in good numbers in late July, and winter steelhead in November, but angling for them takes place upriver.

Perch and the occasional lingcod are caught off the north jetty in spring, and crab are available. Best crab catches are downstream from Doyle Pt.

Boats can be launched on the south side of the bay at the Port Commission Ramp in Gold Beach below the Hwy. 101 Bridge. Boats and equipment are available for rent nearby. On the north bank, small boats can be slipped into the river at the Ferry Hole, about 3 1/2 miles upstream, and larger boats can be launched at Canfield Riffle, 1 1/2 miles further up County Rd. 540. Private ramps with public access are numerous in the Gold Beach area, including Huntley Park, about 6 miles upstream on the south bank. The lower river is broad and provides easygoing boating.

Restaurants, motels, RV parks, and full-service resorts are plentiful in the Gold Beach/Wedderburn area. The nearest public coastal campground is about 20 miles north at Humbug Mt. State Park, but there's a large campground at Huntley Park, and there are Forest Service campgrounds at Lobster Creek and Quosatana upriver.

ROGUE RIVER (Grave Creek to Head of Tide) An extremely productive 60-mile segment of the Rogue, more than half of which is designated Wild and Scenic and accessible only by boat or foot trail. Challenging terrain helps maintain outstanding angling here year -round. Road access is limited to the stretch from tidewater up to Foster Bar, just above the settlement of Ilahee, about 27 river miles. Anglers fish this portion of the Rogue primarily for spring and fall chinook, summer and winter steelhead, and fin-

Peak chinook catches on the lower Rogue River are in August andSeptember.

clipped coho. The river also contains wild trout and wild coho in season, both of which must be released unharmed.

Rogue River steelhead are doing fairly well at this time, in comparison with their north coast cousins, perhaps because of localized ocean conditions. Steelhead are in the river all year, but fishing for them is best from September through February, with peak success in January and February. At this time, any steelhead within the bag limit (whether wild or finclipped) may be kept from December 1 through April 30. At other times of the year, non-finclipped steelhead must be released unharmed.

During the past ten years, the summer steelhead catch in this section of the river has fluctuated between 1,541 in 1991-92, and 4,470 in 1989-90. In the same time period, the winter steelhead catch has fluctuated between 298 in 1983-84, and

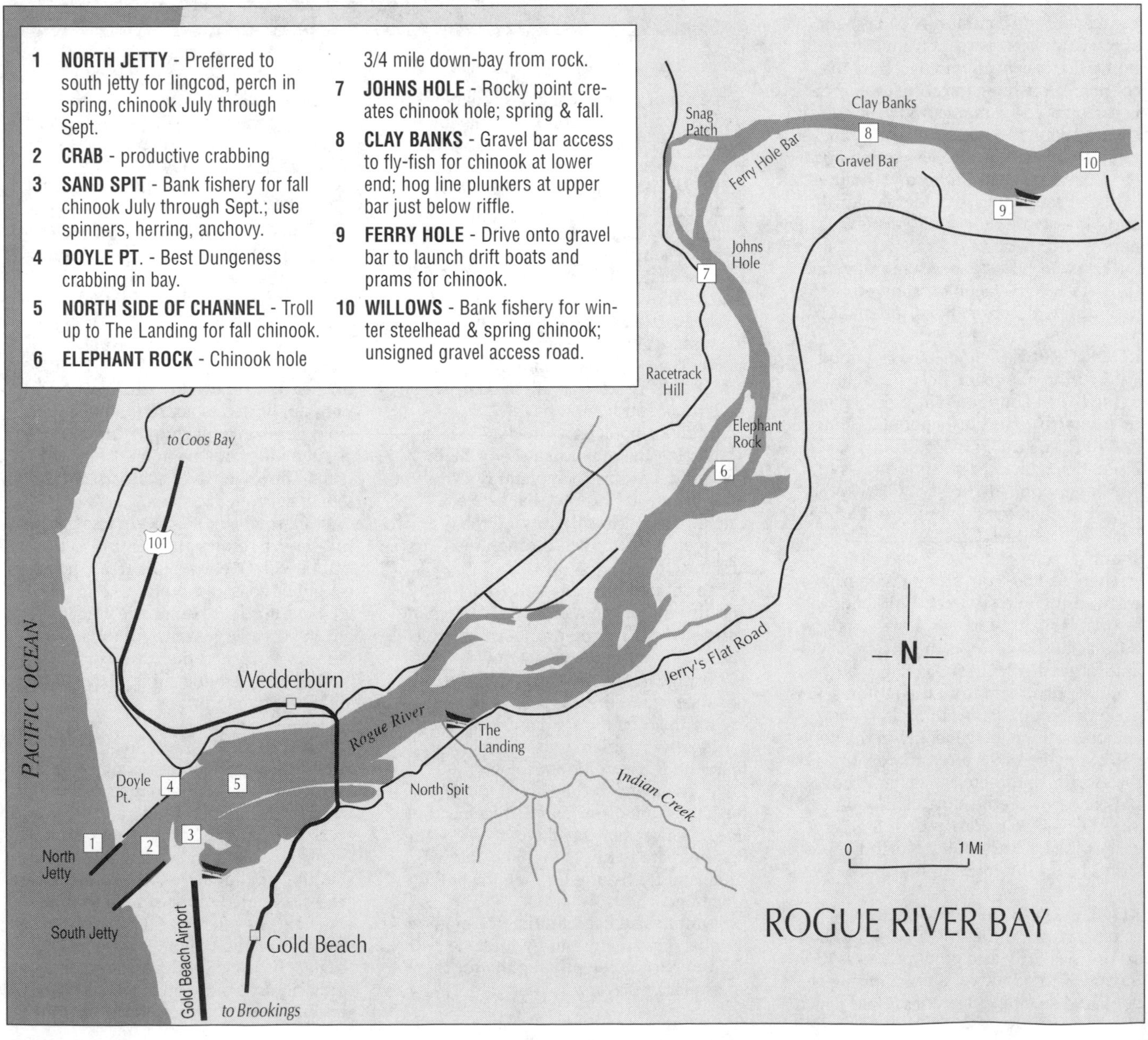

1 **NORTH JETTY** - Preferred to south jetty for lingcod, perch in spring, chinook July through Sept.

2 **CRAB** - productive crabbing

3 **SAND SPIT** - Bank fishery for fall chinook July through Sept.; use spinners, herring, anchovy.

4 **DOYLE PT**. - Best Dungeness crabbing in bay.

5 **NORTH SIDE OF CHANNEL** - Troll up to The Landing for fall chinook.

6 **ELEPHANT ROCK** - Chinook hole 3/4 mile down-bay from rock.

7 **JOHNS HOLE** - Rocky point creates chinook hole; spring & fall.

8 **CLAY BANKS** - Gravel bar access to fly-fish for chinook at lower end; hog line plunkers at upper bar just below riffle.

9 **FERRY HOLE** - Drive onto gravel bar to launch drift boats and prams for chinook.

10 **WILLOWS** - Bank fishery for winter steelhead & spring chinook; unsigned gravel access road.

Snag Patch
Clay Banks
Ferry Hole Bar
Gravel Bar
Johns Hole
Racetrack Hill
Elephant Rock
to Coos Bay
101
PACIFIC OCEAN
Wedderburn
Rogue River
The Landing
Jerry's Flat Road
N
Indian Creek
North Spit
Doyle Pt.
North Jetty
South Jetty
Gold Beach Airport
Gold Beach
to Brookings
0 1 Mi

ROGUE RIVER BAY

9,441 in 1989-90. The 1991-92 catch estimate is 3,629.

The Rogue hosts several distinct populations of chinook, including a run bound for the Applegate, one that heads for lower river tributaries, and one that continues into the upper river. These runs have been declining since the early 1980s, and special regulations are in effect. At this time, the river below the Illinois confluence is closed to angling for chinook from October 1 through December 1. Above the Illinois, the river is open to chinook fishing the entire year. Best chinook catches in the lower river have historically been from April through October, with peak catches in August and September.

During the past ten years, the spring chinook catch in this section of the Rogue has fluctuated between 57 in 1984, and 7,154 in 1989. The estimated catch for 1992 was 2,269.

Rogue River coho are stable, and fishing for finclipped coho has been permitted when other coho fisheries have been closed. Check for emergency closures before fishing, however. Coho enter the river in July, with best fishing in October. During the past ten years, the coho catch has fluctuated between 62 in 1982, and 810 in 1991. The 1992 estimated catch was 236.

Above Foster Bar, the river is bounded on all sides by the Wild Rogue Wilderness. This section contains a string of superior riffles and bars, most of which are popularly named. A riffle on the Rogue is a place where the river drops, usually in the presence of big boulders. The result is water that is both fast and white. Below a riffle, the tail-out offers good holding water for salmon and steelhead as they pause before the upstream challenge. Above the riffle is the head and pool, where salmon and steelhead linger for a little R&R before their next effort. Some anglers use an anchor on a quick-release pulley to stop mid-stream in order to fish the waters at the head of a riffle. Experienced rowers can hold a driftboat in the water at the head of a riffle just by oar power, while fellow anglers fish the head and pool.

Some anglers reach this stretch of the Rogue by jet boat from the lower river, but jet sleds are only allowed as far as Blossom Bar, about 15 miles above Foster Bar. This does provide access to a handfull of back-country lodges, including those at Marial, Paradise Bar, Half Moon Bar, and Clay Hill. A five-day drift from Grave Creek to Foster Bar often includes a stop at Black Bar Lodge, about half-way between Grave Creek and Marial. These lodges primarily support guided steelhead trips from August through October. The most popular fishery in this wild stretch is for summer steelhead in the fall.

There is a hiking trail from Grave Creek downstream to Illahe, which offers many angling opportunities, climbing high above the river in the canyons, but dropping down to riverside at the bars. The hike most popular with anglers is a 2-mile trek from Grave Cr. to Rainie Falls, where salmon and steelhead hold for long periods. Many anglers also hike the additional mile to Whiskey Creek. There is an un-maintained trail on the south bank from Grave Creek to Rainie. At Rainie Falls, anglers can find spring chinook, steelhead, fall chinook and shad. Rainie is the end of the line for shad, which reach the falls about July 4.

To reach Grave Creek from I-5 north of Grants Pass, take the Merlin Exit to the Merlin-Galice Rd. Grave Creek is about 7 miles north of Galice.

Access to the other end of the wilderness trail, and to the lower Rogue, begins

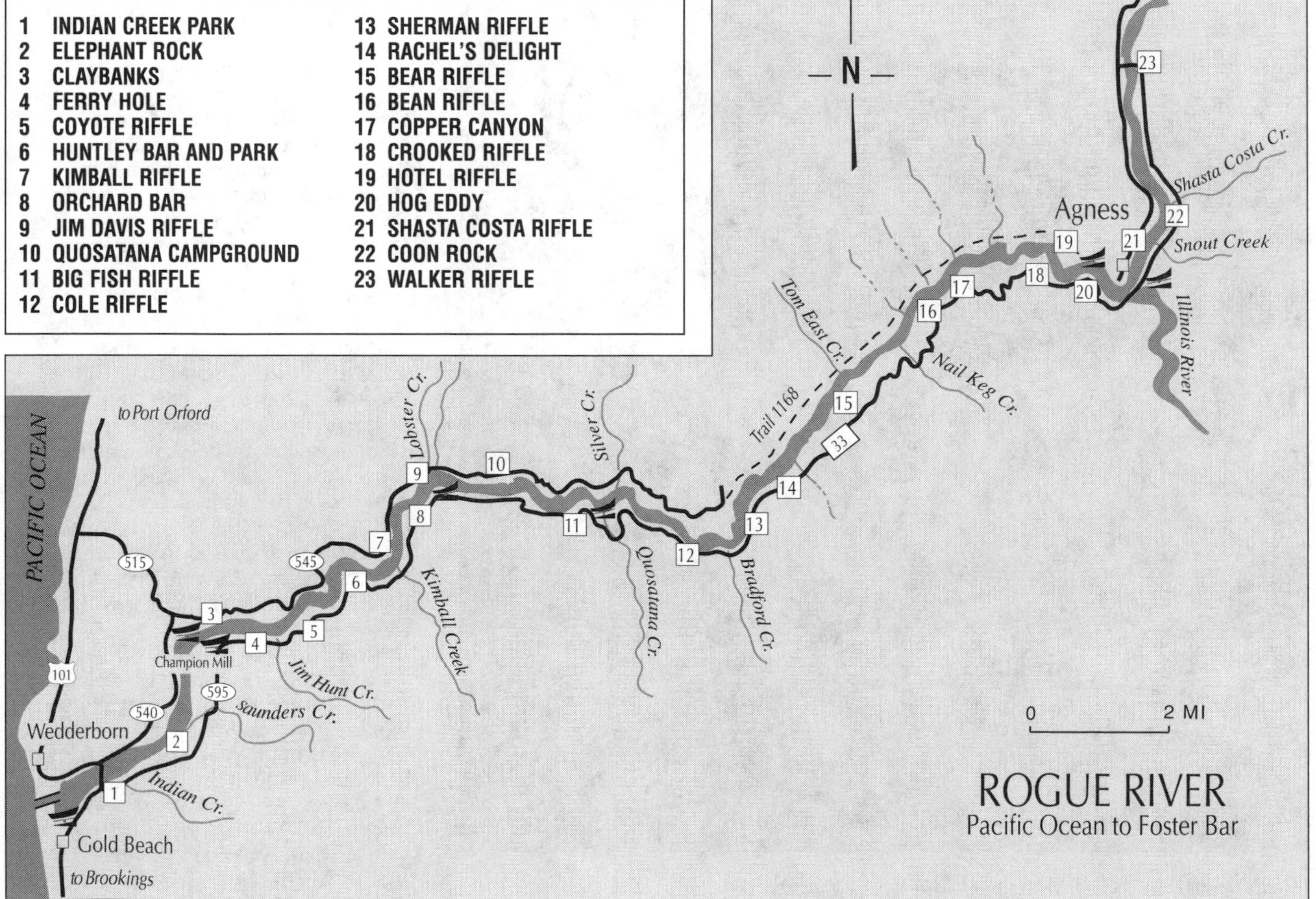

at Gold Beach on the coast. Follow County Rd. 595 from the south end of the Hwy. 101 Bridge across the estuary. This road becomes Forest Primary Rd. 33. It parallels the river's south bank closely for about 17 miles, then pulls back from the river through a deep canyon stretch known as Copper Canyon, crossing the mainstem Rogue about 3 miles above the confluence of the Illinois River. This bridge is known locally as Coon Rock Bridge. The trailhead at Illahe is about 7 miles further upstream at Illahe Campground. The little community of Agness is on the north bank, back downstream at the Illinois confluence.

Between tidewater and the bridge, the south bank road offers a number of access points. Indian Creek Park just a mile upstream from Hwy. 101, has a campground but doesn't access good fishing water. The first good fishing access is at the popular Ferry Hole about 3 miles upstream. You can fish from the gravel bar at Ferry Hole, or slip a boat into the water. You can also launch a boat off the Gold Beach Plywood gravel bar, or at Huntley Park, about 2 miles above tidewater. From these points, anglers drift down to fish Coyote Riffle or the Ferry Hole. Huntley also provides a half-mile gravel bar from which bank casters fish chinook and steelhead.

There's an improved ramp at Lobster Creek (about 3 miles further upstream off the south bank road). Boaters drift down, or jet up to Cole Riffle, about 5 miles up.

Quosatana Campground (pronounced Kwo-sate-na) has a paved ramp that is popular as a jet boat access to the Copper Canyon fisheries half-way to Agness. Steep, rough tracks lead down to the water both upstream and down from Quosatana. Look for pull-outs (little more than wide spots in the road). Cole Riffle, about 3 miles above Quosatana, has excellent fly fishing water. A trail leads down to the Cole Riffle at mile post 17. About seven miles above Quosatana, the road is carved out of the canyon wall, and there is no further bank access until the Illinois crossing.

About a quarter mile below the Illinois confluence, the Hotel Riffle offers good bank fishing. Just above, you can launch a boat from the camp at Hog Eddy, with permission from Cougar Lane Store. Both the Hotel Riffle and Hog Eddy are especially good steelhead spots. About two miles above the Illinois, Shasta Costa Riffles offer a challenge. Shasta Costa (upper and lower) is just above Cougar Lane Lodge. There is a pull-off and a short (steep) trail down to the riffles. Upper Shasta Costa is considerably more challenging than Lower.

About a half mile above Coon Rock Bridge, Walker Riffle generally holds steelhead during the prime season (August, September, and October). Walker is ribboned with bedrock and offers treacherous wading. Use a cut pole or wading staff to avoid sudden submersion.

Foster Bar is about three miles above Walker. It has an improved boat ramp and access to very good steelhead water. Boats with small motors drift down to the next riffle, then fish their way back up to Foster several times in a day. Foster Bar to Quosatana is a popular long day drift for winter steelhead. At low water, be advised that Two-mile Riffle (about 2.5 miles below Foster Bar) is Class 4 whitewater, for experienced boaters only.

Below Agness, access to the north bank of the Rogue (except by boat) is pretty much restricted to the lower 10 miles. County Rd. 540 heads up the north bank from the north end of the Hwy. 101 Bridge at Wedderburn. Pull-outs along the road generally indicate popular fishing spots. The north bank accesses some good water, including the Ferry Hole, Kimball Riffle, and Coyote. You can launch a boat from the old concrete ferry ramp (at high water only) or off the gravel bar at Coyote.

A bridge across the river at Lobster Creek (about 10 miles upstream), connects north and south bank roads. The north bank road continues across Lobster Creek, though it has been known to wash out after a hard winter. Dunkelburger Bar Access is off the north bank road about 3 miles upstream from Lobster Creek. There is good bank access at Dunkelburger for spring chinook and steelhead.

About 7 miles beyond Dunkelburger, the north bank road ends near Trailhead 1168 which leads to Agness, about 10 miles. Unlike the upriver trail (Graves Creek to Illahe), this trail is suited more to scenic enjoyment than to angling. Though well maintained, it remains high above the river and is cursed with rampant poison oak off-trail.

Below Agness, the Rogue is suitable for novice river boaters. Above, even experienced boaters would benefit from following a lead boat familiar with the river's treacheries.

Most drift trips from Grave Creek are 3-4 days. Anglers wishing to book guides and rooms at the back-country lodges would be well advised to make reservations early in the year. Fishing guides can be located through the Oregon Guides and Packers Assoc., or through the lodges. TuTuTun Lodge and several private RV parks provide the only overnight facilities on the North Bank Rogue River

Below Agness, the Rogue River is suitable for novice river boaters.

Rd. Camping is available on the south bank road at Huntley Park, Lobster Creek, and Quosatana below Foster Bar, and at Brushy Bar within the Wild Rogue Wilderness. Unimproved sites are plentiful all along the trail to Grave Creek, which passes through a forested terrain of mixed Douglas fir, madrone, and maple.

Tackle used in the Rogue above tidewater (the Ferry Hole Boat Ramp at river mile 5) is restricted to barbless hooks, except when bait angling. However, since non-finclipped coho, trout, and steelhead (most of the time) must be released unharmed, even bait anglers would be well advised to pinch down their barbs (or avoid bait altogether).

ROGUE RIVER (Grave Creek to Grants Pass) From Grave Creek downstream for about 35 miles there is no road access to the Rogue. At Grave Creek, anglers can launch a boat or pick up the Rogue River Trail on the north bank. A south bank trail at Grave Creek goes as far as Rainie Falls. From Grave Creek upstream, the river is very accessible. Roads follow and cross it all the way to Lost Creek Reservoir. Yet despite its accessibility, this portion of the river offers many good angling opportunities.

A summer run steelhead fishery gathers steam here in September, with peak catches in October and good angling through February and March. The winter run overtakes the summer run in December, with good catches into April. Non-finclipped steelhead must be released unharmed.

One of the most popular boat fisheries in this section is at Galice, where there's an improved boat ramp and a store with fishing supplies. Steelhead anglers drift to Rand or Almeda, a day's trip. Rocky Riffle immediately below Galice, and Galice Riffle immediately above, are very popular steelhead and half-pounder fisheries. This is the upper limit for half-pounders. The river from Almeda to Grave Cr. is only lightly fished, primarily for summer and winter steelhead.

To reach Galice from I-5 north of Grants Pass, take the Merlin Exit and follow the Merlin-Galice Rd. west. At Merlin, a county road also heads southwest to Robertson Bridge.

Robertson Bridge to Galice is a long day's drift (about 11 river miles), accessing some good gravel bars and steelhead drift water. The trip includes a float through Hellgate Canyon. Some anglers do shorter trips from the bridge, mounting small kicker motors on their drift boats to enable them to motor up to a favorite water and drift down again. This is a practical technique in the slower, quiet stretches of the river above and below the bridge (between Ferry Park on the east bank and Griffin Park on the west.) From Grants Pass, the Lower River Rd. offers a pretty drive to Robertson Bridge.

Higgins Canyon, Wild Rogue Wilderness.

Whitehorse Riffle, just below the mouth of the Applegate, is a good steelhead producer, with bedrock shelves and channels that hold the fish. There's an unimproved ramp at Whitehorse Park on the north bank. Whitehorse to Ferry Park is a good short drift.

Anglers fish the mouth of the Applegate for steelhead, and for fall chinook returning to the Applegate to spawn in late August and early September. These salmon are not in prime condition, but are still palatable. The Applegate marks the end of heavy recreational activity on the Rogue west of Grants Pass.

There's a lot of good bank access between Grave Creek and the Applegate. Anglers park and fish all along the Merlin-Galice Rd. between Galice and Grave Cr. Argo Riffle is a popular bank fishery, about 2 miles above Grave Cr. A mile above Argo Riffle, Almeda Park offers 1/2 mile of good beach fishing, with plentiful parking. Anglers also fish at Rand, and at the Chair Riffle just above. Rock Riffle above Galice is accessible to bank anglers, but there is little access at Galice itself. Ennis Riffle about 2 miles above Galice includes two gravel bars. Indian Mary Park, just below Taylor Cr. Gorge, offers quiet water for trout fishing, though it is no longer stocked. Bank anglers also fish above and below Hellgate Bridge for steelhead. And there is plenty of bank access at Ferry and Griffin parks.

Camping in this stretch is limited to Indian Mary Park, a popular tourist spot in a pleasant setting.

Tributaries of the Rogue in this section not listed by name in the regulations synopsis are closed to all angling.

ROGUE RIVER (Grants Pass to Lost Creek Reservoir) East of Grants Pass above Savage Rapids Dam, the Rogue flows through a broad valley, its banks lined with cottonwood and willow. East of the town of Gold Hill, Gold Ray Dam backs up the river, forming a small reservoir (Gold Ray Pool) and about 25 miles of slow but powerful flow tapped for multi-use withdrawals. Above Shady Cove, the valley narrows and confines the river again. Another 10-12 miles up is Lost Creek Dam, the end of the mainstem Rogue.

This section of the river includes major fisheries for spring and fall chinook, a strong hatchery coho run that is open to angling, summer steelhead, and an extraordinary opportunity to catch large wild trout on a fly.

Most spring chinook are caught above Gold Ray Dam April through July, but there are some opportunities to catch them lower in the reach. The first fishery for springers east of Grants Pass is at Pierce Riffle, about 3/4 mile below Savage Rapids Dam. Boats launch at Pierce Riffle County Park off Foothill Blvd. on the north bank. Jet sleds motor up through the riffle to fish the deadline below the dam. Drift boat anglers row up to Pierce Riffle. There is a bank fishery for springers at the dam deadline, accessed through property owned by We

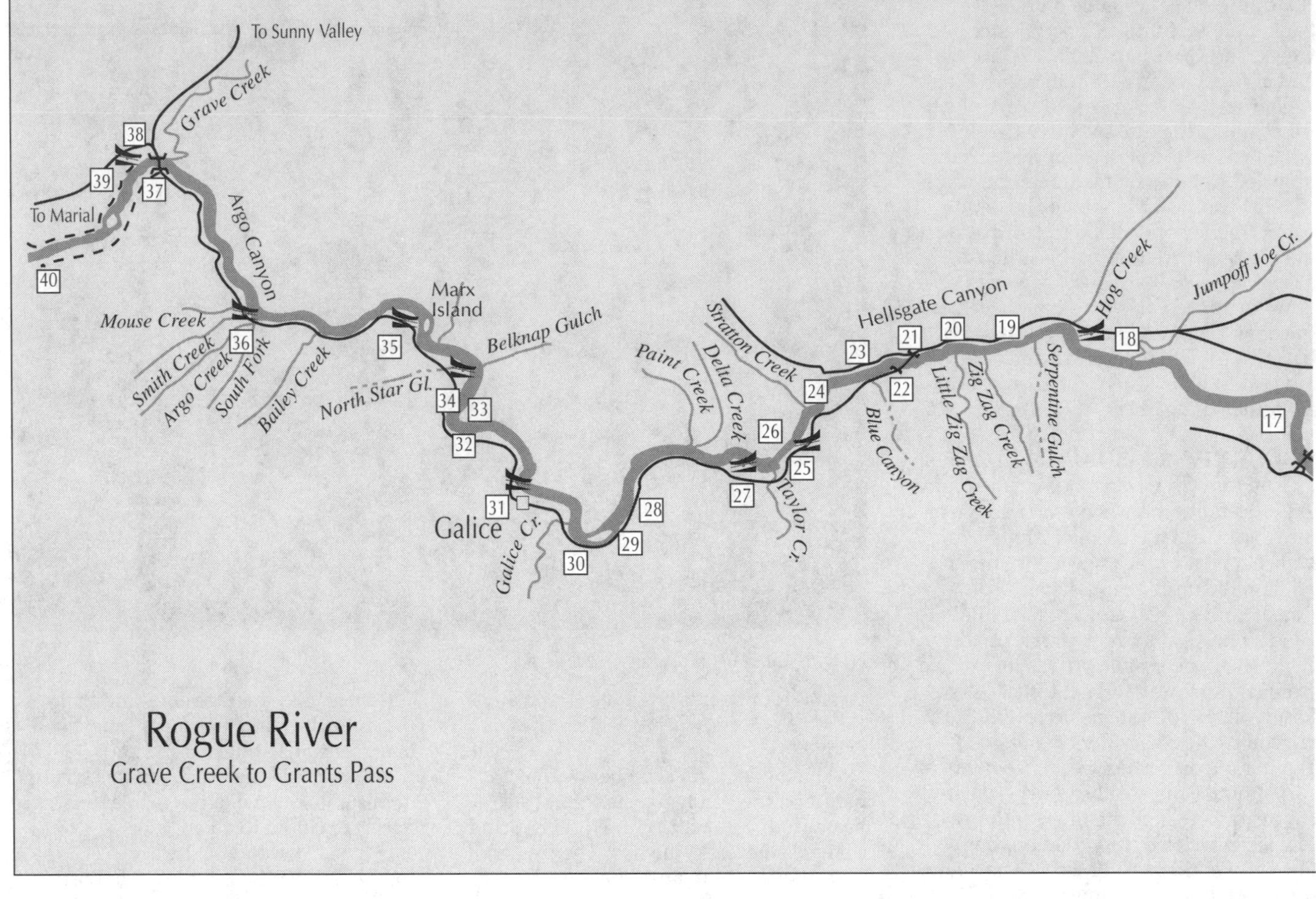

1 **PIERCE RIFFLE** -(different than Tom Pierce Park) - Paved ramp; nature trail; 1/4 mile of good salmon & steelhead water upstream.

2 **CHINOOK PARK** - Paved boat ramp with handicapped fishing dock & amenities; access to good steelhead water; walk up to fish Green Cr. Riffle.

3 **BAKER PARK** - Gravel bar launch; chinook & steelhead hole under bridge.

4 **TUSSY PARK**- Bank fishing at county park.

5 **SCHROEDER PARK** - Paved boat ramp, camping, handicapped fishing platform & bank access to salmon & steelhead.

6 **WHITE ROCKS** - Undeveloped access; fish from the rocks.

7 **LATHROP LANDIN**G - Paved ramp, a few rocks to fish from.

8 **WHITEHORSE RIFFLE** - Upper boundary for Wild & Scenic Rogue.

9 **WHITEHORSE PARK**- Gravel bar launch; walk up & fish mouth of Applegate; also good water downstream 1 mile.

10 **MATSON PARK**- Gravel bar launch; good bank fishing for steelhead & salmon.

11 **FINLEY BEND** - Hike down from the road to fish from rocks.

12 **GRIFFIN PARK** - Paved boat ramp,camping; fish the bend 3/4 miles; very good bank access to good steelhead water.

13 **FERRY HOLE PARK** - Paved boat ramp, bank fishing; popular put-in & take-out.

14 **FLANAGAN SLOUGH** - Old mine site, now BLM property; walk in on old road go fish salmon & steelhead.

15 **BRUSHY CHUTE**S

16 **ROBERTSON BRIDGE** - Paved boat ramp; popular steelhead bank fishery upstream.

17 **HUSSY HOL**E - Bank fishing.

18 **HOG CREEK LANDING** - Paved boat ramp, popular with rafters; good for fall chinook.

19 **HELLSGATE ACCESS** - Bank fishing.

20 **DUNN RIFFLE** - Bank fishing.

21 **HELLSGATE BRIDGE** - Bank fishing.

22 **SOUTH ACCESS**- Bank fishing.

23 **HELLSGATE PAR**K - Bank fishing.

24 **STRATTON CREEK**- Follow the river downstream to the fish the creek mouth; popular bank fishery for winter steelhead.

25 **TAYLOR CREEK GORGE**

26 **INDIAN MARY PARK** - Pay to use paved boat ramp, campground; gravel bar launch; some bank fishing for steelhead.

27 **RAINBOW ACCE**SS - Bank fishing.

28 **ENNIS PARK** - Paved boat ramp; long gravel bar offers access to Ennis Riffle; good for steelhead.

29 **CARPENTERS ISLAND**- Bank fishing.

30 **GALICE RIFFLE**

31 **GALICE RAMP** - Paved boat ramp, bank fishing.

32 **BLM ACCESS**- Fish anywhere along Merlin-Galice Rd.

33 **ROCKY RIFFLE**

34 **RAND ACCES**S - Gravel park launch, bank fishing.

35 **ALMEDA PARK** - Paved boat ramp, bank fishing.

36 **ARGO ACCESS** - Gravel bar launch, bank fishing, access to Argo Riffle.

37 **SOUTH ACCESS TRAIL**

38 **GRAVE CREEK LANDIN**G - Paved boat ramp, bank fishing.

39 **ROGUE RIVER TRAIL**

40 **RAINIE FALLS**

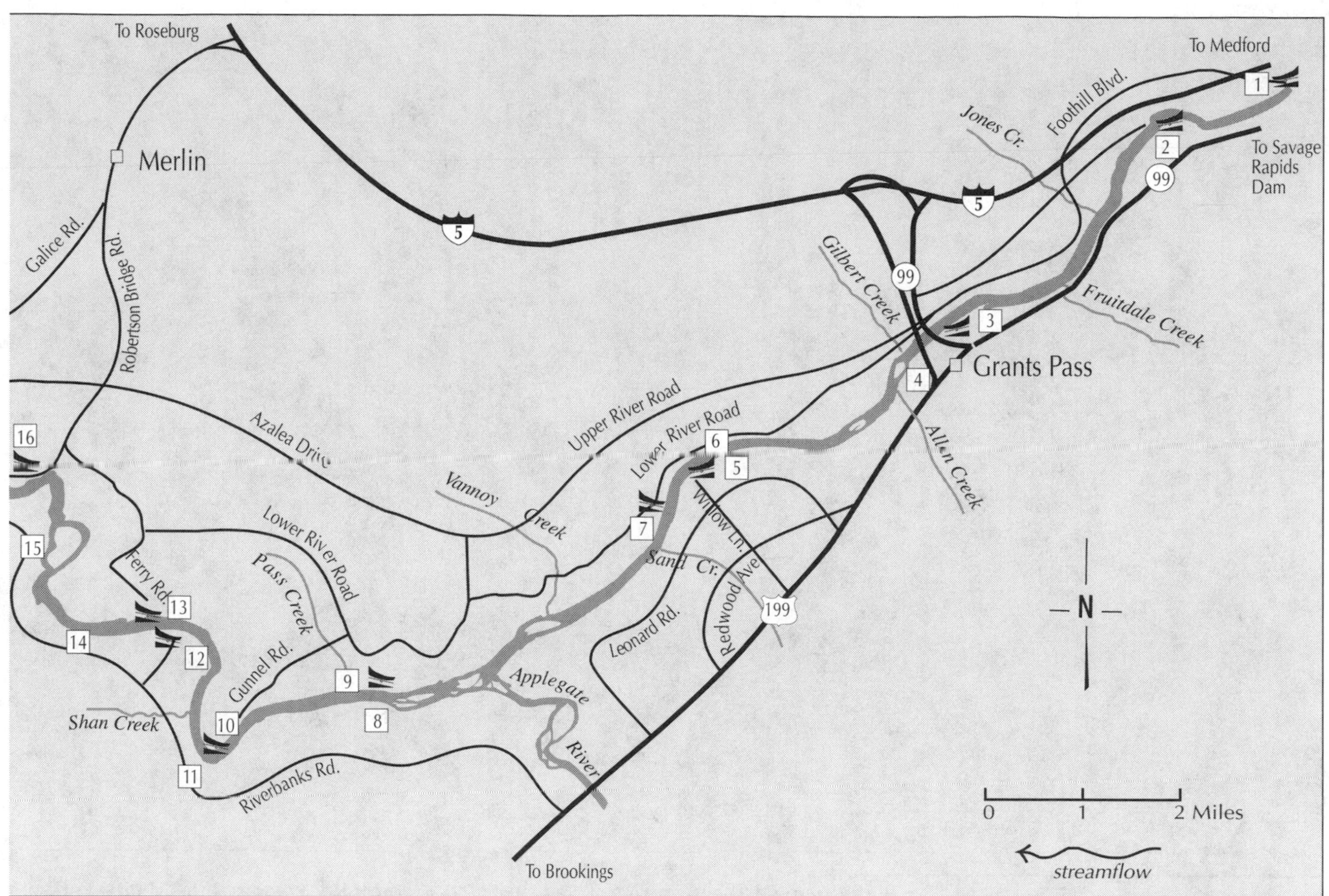

Asku Inn on the south bank off Hwy. 99. Ask permission at the inn before you fish.

Fall chinook are a popular fishery in this section of the river, particularly in the Grants Pass area in August and September, and coho heading home to Cole Rivers Hatchery reach this section in late October and November. The fishery for hatchery-reared coho in the Rogue has remained open despite general coho closures elsewhere.

There is a lot of private riverfront property on this stretch of the Rogue, so access is limited to a few parks and public easements. Boaters put in at Coyote-Evans Park in the community of Rogue River on Hwy. 99, and take out at the Savage Rapids pool. There is also a boat ramp at Valley of the Rogue State Park. The drift from there to Coyote-Evans, about 2 1/2 miles, is good for beginners (more current than whitewater). Anglers primarily drift fish for steelhead through this stretch. There is also bank fishing at Valley of the Rogue for steelhead and resident trout.

About 4 miles upstream, there's bank angling at Rock Point Bridge on Hwy. 99, and at Sardine Creek near the junction of the Gold Hill and Sardine Cr. roads. At Gold Hill on Hwy. 234, there is an improved boat ramp at Gold Nugget Park. Gold Ray Dam is a popular spot for spring chinook and summer steelhead. Boaters launch sleds and drift boats with motors at an unimproved boat ramp off a dirt road between the dam and Gold Hill on the south bank, then motor up to the deadline. The road also offers about 1 1/2 miles of bank access.

The water above Gold Ray Pool is especially productive for spring chinook. Boaters launch jet sleds at Tou Velle State Park on the south bank north of Medford. Anglers also bank fish for trout at Tou Velle. High Banks, just below Tou Velle, is a popular fly fishing spot for summer steelhead (boat access only).

Dodge Bridge Park, near the Hwy. 234 crossing of the Rogue, offers a nice long day's drift to Tou Velle, about 8 miles. There's good still water fishing for spring chinook and summer steelhead in this stretch, but there are rapids that should be scouted first, and attempted only by experienced boaters. An occasional chinook and steelhead are hooked from the bank at Dodge Bridge. There's also a fishing ramp that is wheelchair accessible.

Above Dodge Bridge on the west bank road to Shady Cove, Takelma Park offers a boat ramp and good bank access for spring chinook, steelhead, and trout. There's also a boat ramp at Shady Cove County Park, but bank access is limited to the area above Shady Cove Bridge. From Shady Cove to Lost Creek Dam, Hwy. 62 runs close to the river, with good access for bank anglers.

The mouth of Trail Creek is a popular bank access area. Anglers pull off and fish near the junction of highways 62 and 227. Rogue Elk County Park on Hwy. 62 is popular with boaters in pursuit of spring chinook and early summer steelhead. There is also a bank fishery for trout. Casey State Park, just west of the dam, has a boat ramp and excellent bank access for spring chinook, summer steelhead, and trout. Casey has a full service campground, and anglers will find it a

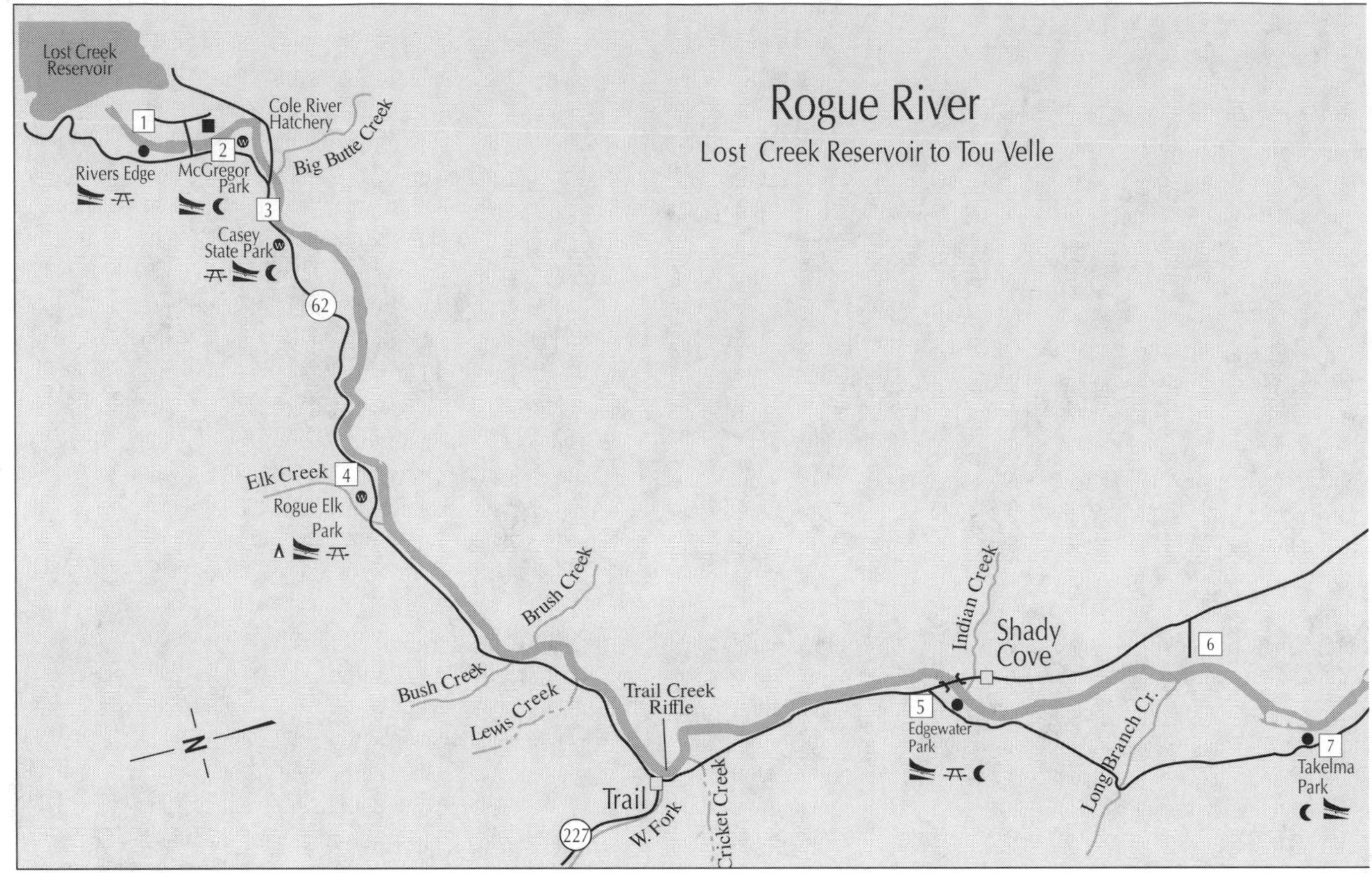

1 **HOLY WATER**- Rainbow to 18" in spillwater fishery between Lost Creek and Barrier dams; 3/4 mile of classic fly-fishing water accessible from both banks; Corp of Engineers park on south bank, gravel road on north; watch for fishing deadline signs near dams.
2 **MacGREGOR PARK**- Wheelchair accessible platform; bank access (north and south) to several good salmon holes and steelhead water.
3 **CASEY STATE PARK** - Good bank access to salmon & steelhead water; wheelchair accessible.
4 **ROGUE ELK PARK** - Bank access to Elk Creek bar, good for steelhead.
5 **EDGEWATER PARK** - Bank fishing for steelhead; wheelchair accessible.
6 **BROPHY ROAD** - Public acccess to half mile of bank fishing; good steelhead water.
7 **TAKELMA PARK** - Bank fishing; good steelhead hole.
8 **DODGE BRIDGE** - Steelhead hole & occasional opportunity for salmon; bank fishing and wheelchair accessible platform.
9 **GIVEN PARK** - Undeveloped public access off unmarked gravel road; park and walk to river.
10 **TOU VELLE STATE PARK** - Fish both banks 1.5 miles to Given Park; good steelhead water & occasional chinook; last take-out for 6 miles.

little crowded here during spring chinook season. Between Casey State Park and the dam, the river runs through public land where bank access is plentiful.

A notable catch and release fishery for wild rainbow has developed in a 3/4-mile reach below Lost Creek Dam. Cool water releases from the reservoir create spring creek-like conditions that grow exceptionally large trout. Encounters with trout 20 inches and larger are commonplace. Dubbed "The Holy Water" by anglers, this stretch is restricted to fly fishing. As with most "spring creek" fisheries, action here can be as exciting in winter as in summer, and this fishery is open year-round.

Campgrounds in this stretch of the Rogue are limited to Valley of the Rogue State Park on Hwy. 99, Rogue Elk County Park, and Casey State Park on Hwy. 62.

Tributaries of the Rogue below Cole Rivers Hatchery not listed by name in the regulations synopsis are closed to all angling.

ROGUE RIVER, MIDDLE FORK A fair spring and summer trout stream, flowing into the upper Rogue above Lost Creek Reservoir. From Medford take Hwy. 62 north to Prospect, about 45 miles, then follow Forest Rd. 37 from Prospect to the Middle Fork. Or follow the Butte Falls Rd. to its junction with the Middle Fork at Forest Rd. 37. About 3 miles after Forest Rd. 37 crosses the Middle Fork, a forest road on the left (before Imnaha Campground) leads to Trail 978, which follows the upper Middle Fork into its headwaters in the Seven Lakes Basin of the Sky Lakes Wilderness.

The upper portion of the stream is lightly fished for wild trout and migrants from the high lakes. See also Alta, Middle Grass, Cliff.

Campgrounds near the Middle Fork include a large campground at Joseph Stewart State Park on Lost Creek Reservoir, and three campgrounds just south of the Middle Fork on Forest Rd. 37 (Imnaha, Sumpter Creek, and South Fork).

ROGUE RIVER, NORTH FORK Forty-seven miles of premium trout water flowing into Lost Creek Reservoir. Highways. 62 and 230 more or less follow the river to its headwaters south of Diamond Lake, near the northern boundary of Crater Lake National Park. Forest roads access the stream at the mouths of many fine tributaries, and the Upper Rogue River Trail 1034 follows it from Prospect through the scenic Rogue National Forest to its headwaters. Early season road access is often limited by heavy snow, so check with the ranger station at Prospect. Roads are usually open by late May.

The North Fork supports good populations of wild rainbow, cutthroat, a few browns, and lots of brook trout. Fish

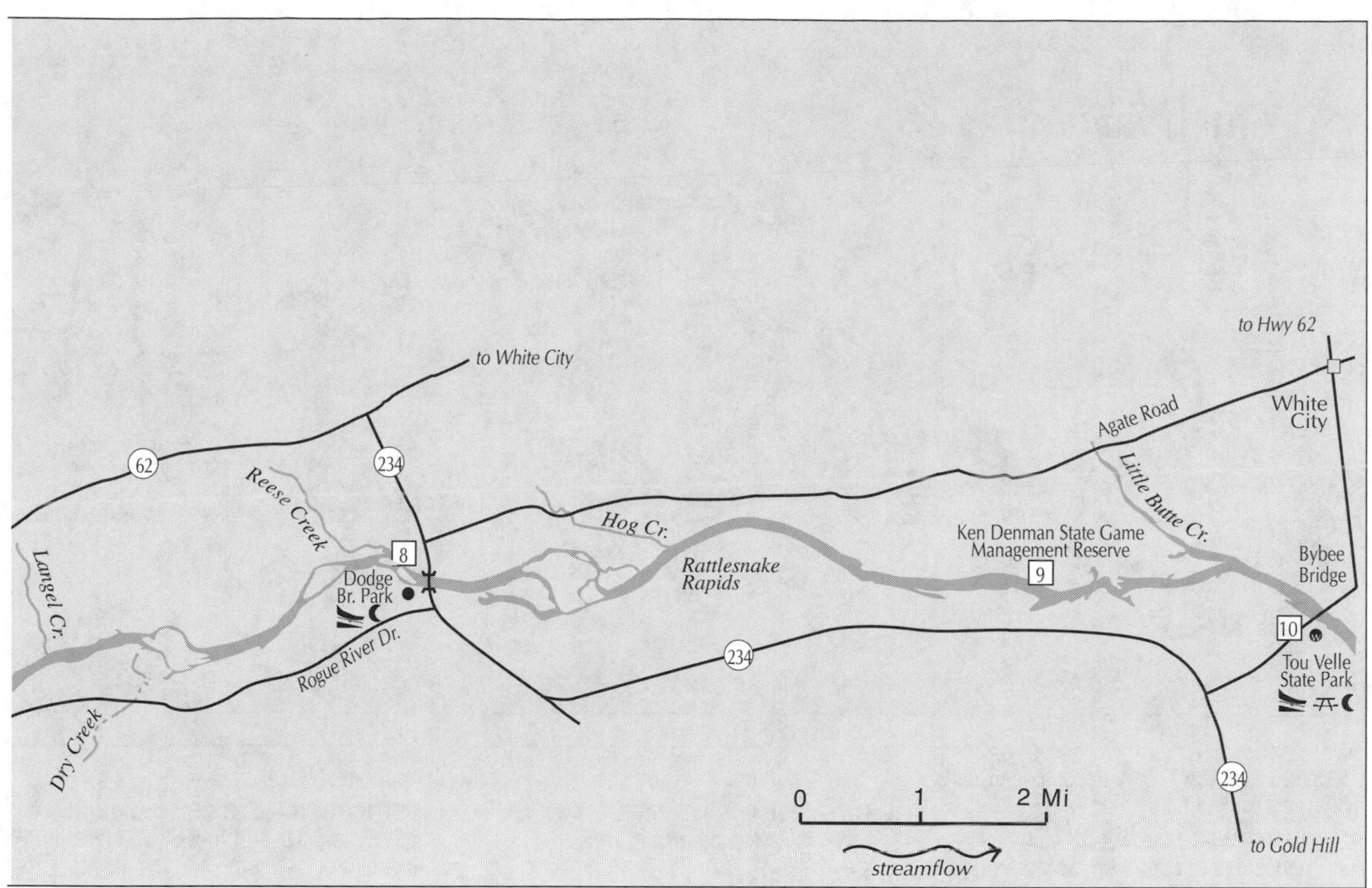

average 6-12 inches, with an infrequent brown taken in the 5-10 pound range. Beginning in late May, legal rainbow are stocked weekly between Natural Bridge Campground and Hamaker Meadows. Fish are released near all access points, including the campgrounds at Union Creek, Farewell Bend, and Hamaker Meadows, and near the Jackson/Douglas County Rd.

There's good fishing near the mouths of the North Fork's many tributaries, including Mill, Abbot, Union, Wizard, National, Foster, and Minnehaha. Most of the tributaries are best fished in early season before they get low, though Union and Mill are good all summer.

ROGUE RIVER, SOUTH FORK A nice trout stream flowing into Lost Creek Reservoir, best fished in mid-summer. From Medford take Hwy. 62 north to the Butte Falls Rd. Head north on the Butte Falls-Prospect Rd., turning onto Forest Rd. 34 toward Lodgepole, crossing the upper stream at South Fork Campground. Trail 988 follows the stream to Rogue Head Camp in the Blue Lake Group of the Sky Lakes Area. The upper stream is also accessed by forest roads from Prospect.

The upper portion is lightly fished and supports wild rainbow, cutthroat, and brook trout. A number of beaver ponds in the headwaters contain surprisingly big trout. Campgrounds near the South Fork include a large camp at Joseph Stewart State Park on Lost Creek Reservoir, Imnaha and South Fork camps off Forest Rd. 37, Parker Meadows, and Upper South Fork.

ROUND LAKE A five-acre lake in the south Sky Lakes Wilderness, Rogue River National Forest. Round Lake is off Trail 982 just before Blue Lake. See Blue Lake for directions. Round Lake is stocked by air with brook trout.

SAUNDERS LAKE An attractive and relatively deep coastal lake of about 55 acres west of Hwy. 101 about 15 miles south of Reedsport, offering fishing for stocked trout, largemouth bass, and panfish.

The lake is stocked several times in spring with rainbow trout, which are usually fished out in early summer. Bait fishing takes most of the trout, but a good mayfly hatch in spring provides an opportunity for good fly-fishing.

Yellow perch, crappie, bluegill, and bass are available the year around, with especially good bass fishing in fall.

There is a county park with boat ramp and bank fishing at the south end of the lake, but there is a lot of private property around the lake and no camping allowed. Campgrounds, accommodations, and supplies are available at Lakeside, 4 miles north.

SELMAC LAKE A record-breaking producer of largemouth bass, 23 miles SW of Grants Pass, with excellent facilities for family outings. Take Hwy. 199 to Selmac, and turn east. It's 4 miles to the lake. Covering about 160 acres, this artificial lake provides lots of angling opportunity.

Selmac is managed for trophy bass, and two state record bass have been produced here, including the current title holder at 11 lb. 7.4 oz., caught in 1991. (An unofficial 12 pounder was caught and released in 1974). Anglers are restricted to catching one bass per day. Rainbow trout are stocked in early spring, and there are many crappie, bluegill, and brown bullhead.

There is a county park here with boat rentals and ramp, tent sites, drinking water, picnic facilities, and a swimming area. Finger-like dikes have been constructed into the lake to provide better bank access. Recommended for small fry.

SHUTTPELZ LAKE A few acres in Oregon Dunes National Recreation Area, offering a rare wild cutthroat fishery. The lake is off Wildwood Drive west of Hwy. 101 at the Eel Lake turn-off.

Shuttpelz is deep with a lot of the submerged structure that trout appreciate. It grows fish to very good size. Angling is

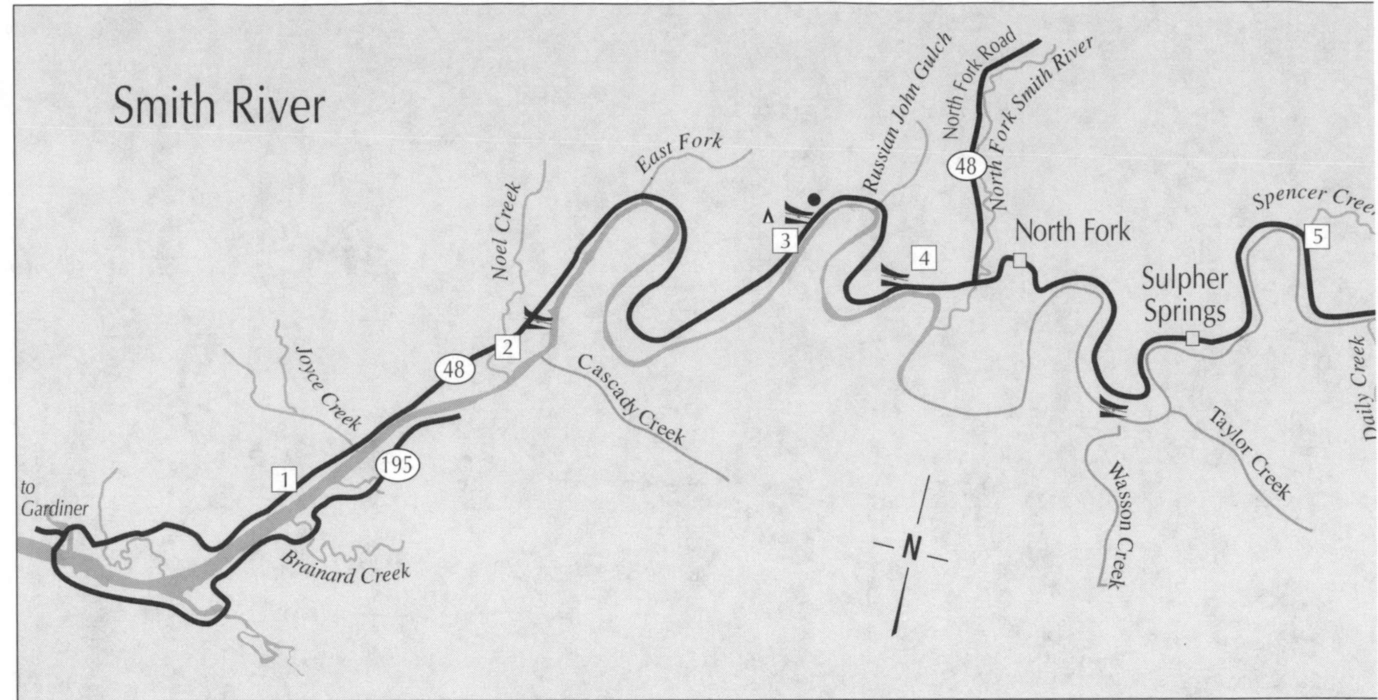

1 **SANDY BEACH** - Easy undeveloped put-in; good bank fishing.

2 **SMITH RIVER MARINA**- Private facility; modest fee to use ramp; accesses good salmon and striper water; rv & tent campsites.

3 **NOEL RANCH** - Paved public ramp; good bank fishing site; popular spot for shad in May and June.

4 **RIVERSIDE COUNTY PARK**- Paved ramps; good bank fishing, picnic area.

5 **HEAD OF TIDE**

6 **DAILEY RANCH**- Pole slide take-out at upper end of ranch; river access.

7 **FAWN CREEK** - Campground, river access.

8 **SMITH RIVER FALLS** - Highest developed put-in; popular drift to Dailey Pole Slide; campsites.

9 **VINCENT CREEK**- Campsites, river access.

10 **TWIN SISTERS** - Campground; river access.

restricted to barbless artificial lures and flies. This is an excellent float tube lake. Let's hope no one is foolish enough to dump warmwater fish in here and spoil this perfect little fishery.

SIXES RIVER A fairly good wild steelhead and salmon stream, entering the ocean just north of Cape Blanco. It is crossed by Hwy. 101 about 5 miles above the mouth, 22 miles south of Bandon. The stream is about 36 miles long, with a good road east to its headwaters. The lower section is reached by several secondary roads. Tidewater extends to 2 miles below the Hwy. 101 Bridge.

Wild trout are fished here in early season, but low water usually slows things down in June. After the fall rains, some sea-run cutthroat are taken in the lower river.

Steelhead angling starts in November and continues into March. Good size fall chinook are taken from late October through December.

A state park at Cape Blanco provides access to a lot of tidewater, including the mouth of the Sixes (walk through the picnic area). Chinook are caught here in early season. Be aware that the Sixes is closed to coho fishing.

Another popular spot is the Orchard Hole, 2 miles up from the mouth. To reach it, follow the road toward Cape Blanco, park adjacent to the wooden barn, and walk across the pasture to the river. Don't mind the sheep. Another popular spot, Squaw Bluff, is about a 3/4-mile walk upstream from Orchard Hole.

There is also a public access about 3 miles up from Hwy. 101. Watch for the triangular ODF&W sign. Boats can be launched at Edson Creek and taken out at mid-drift or at the Hwy. 101 Bridge behind Sixes Grange.

Nearest camping is at Humbug State Park, just south of Port Orford.

SKOOKUM LAKE (Douglas Co.) A 3/4-mile hike-in for brook trout in the Skookum Prairie area, about 10 miles west of Diamond Lake. From Hwy. 230, just south of Diamond, take Forest Rd. 3703 about 2 1/2 miles, then Forest Rd. 200 (a primitive track) to the right. Skookum is less than 1/4 mile from road's end.

Covering about 15 acres, Skookum provides good catches of brook trout to 10 inches, and quite a few to 18. The outlet, Skookum Cr., produces small (but mature) rainbow and browns. The lake is usually inaccessible until late June. There are natural campsites available.

SKOOKUM POND An artificial pond in the Umpqua National Forest that used to offer good fishing for rainbow trout. Illegally introduced brown bullhead have pretty much taken over here, and anglers are encouraged to catch as many as they can. (They're pretty good eating skinned and fried).

Take Forest Rd. 29 (Jackson Cr. Rd.) then Forest Rd. 2924 about 2 1/2 miles, and follow Forest Rd. 200 about 2 1/2 miles to the pond. There is no sign on the road indicating that the pond is here, so watch your odometer. The pond has a lot of submerged snags and an old clear cut which provide good habitat. Aquatic vegetation is heavy, but there is room for a small boat. Largemouth bass were illegally introduced, but didn't seem to take. There is an excellent population of crayfish here.

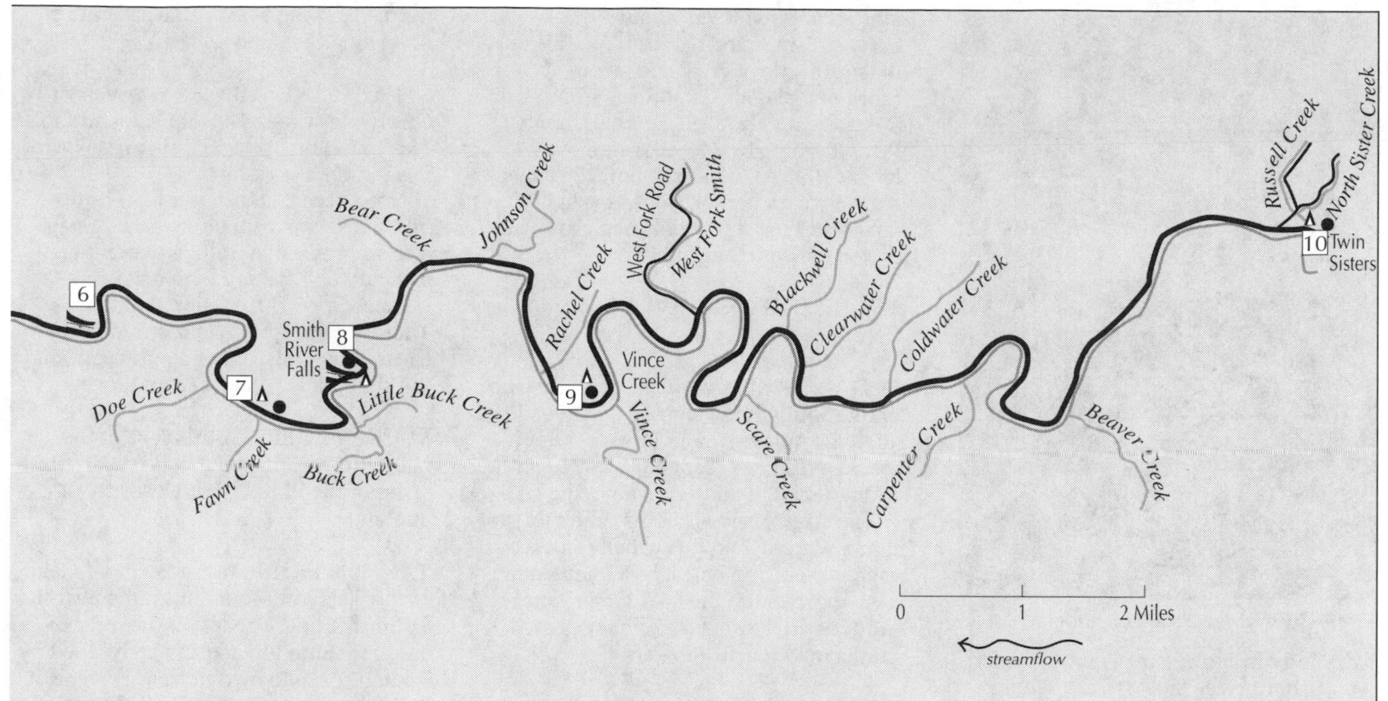

SMITH RIVER A major tributary of Winchester Bay (estuary of the Umpqua River), with a fair run of fall chinook, steelhead, and Oregon's best opportunity to hook a striped bass. After a 75-mile tumble through the Coast Range, the Smith enters the bay at Gardiner, just 9 miles from the sea.

From Gardiner, on Hwy. 101, a paved county road heads east to the river and follows it closely for 30 miles. A variety of gravel roads access its headwaters. The river can also be approached from the Eugene area by taking Hwy. 99 south to Drain, and Hwy. 38 west. County roads cut north to the Smith about 8 miles west of Elkton (just upstream of Sawyers Rapids on the Umpqua), and from the Wells Creek Guard Station about 3 1/2 miles upstream from Scottsburg. Tidewater extends to Spencer Creek, about 20 miles upriver.

Fall chinook in the Smith provide a good fishery, particularly in tidewater in early season and above Smith River Falls. The run has responded very enthusiastically to rehabilitation projects in the spawning beds area upriver. Coho are no longer stocked in the Smith, but the wild run (while diminished in recent years) is holding up better here than further north. The river is closed to coho fishing.

The Smith has a wild winter steelhead run and a hatchery run that is planted from Vincent Creek up to Smith River Falls. Non-finclipped steelhead must be released unharmed. Both salmon and steelhead fisheries are closed from October 1 through November 30 to protect spawning salmon.

Striped bass are reproducing modestly in the lower Smith, migrating seasonally between the river and Winchester Bay, following the food supply. In March, April, and May, striped bass are upstream in tidewater. Stripers return to the bay in late spring and summer to feed on marine fish, then return to the river to spawn in September and October. Best angling is upriver in spring and fall. This is a very q-u-i-e-t fishery. Stripers are easily spooked, and most anglers fish big plugs at night, either rowing or using electric motors. Most catches are in the 16-20 inch class and must be released unharmed, but some adults to 35 pounds are hooked here. The smaller fish are generally found in schools, while the larger fish are loners. Minimum length for a keeper is 30 inches.

Cutthroat trout are stocked for the spring opening, and most fishing for them takes place the first weekends in spring. Trout remain in the Smith throughout the summer, but the bite is off once the water warms (the Smith can get up to 70 degrees). Best summer trout fishing is in the cooler tributaries for smaller but hungrier fish. Few sea-run cutthroat are seen here anymore.

The Smith has a good shad run May through June, which extends up to head of tide at Spencer Cr. Shad are available to both boat and bank anglers, caught on troll and cast. A favorite shad spot is the Noel Ranch Boat Ramp at about river mile 8.

The Smith is very accessible to boat and bank anglers, primarily from the north bank road. The highest official put-in is at Smith River Falls (river mile 26), with a popular drift down to Dailey Pole Slide (river mile 11), a take-out only at the upper end of Dailey Ranch. There is a boat ramp and bank fishery at Riverside County Park about 11 miles up Smith River Rd., and at Noel Ranch, about 2 1/2 miles below Riverside. Sandy Beach, the lowest access on the river, has a good bank fishery, and boats can be launched from the beach.

Camping is available at Fawn Creek, a BLM camp a mile below Smith River Falls; and at Smith River Falls, Vincent Creek, and Twin Sisters. There are bank fishing opportunities at all the campgrounds.

Above the falls, boats can be launched from several access roads that were once low water crossings for logging operations. The old crossings are also good bank fishing sites.

SMITH RIVER, NORTH FORK A large, productive tributary of the Smith River, with a good run of wild winter steelhead. It joins the Smith 13 miles above its confluence with the Umpqua. A good county road cuts off from the Smith River Rd. at the community of North Fork, about 15 miles from Gardiner, and follows the North Fork for about 8 miles. The paved Smith River Rd. is accessible from Hwy. 101 north of Gardiner, and from Hwy. 38 by way of a cut-off about 2 1/2 miles NE of Scottsburg near the Wells Creek Guard Station.

Steelhead is the most popular fishery on the river. All are wild and must be released unharmed. The run usually peaks in December and January. Most anglers plunk for steelhead downstream

Fishing pier at South Tenmile.

from Culvert Hole, a treacherous waterfall at about river mile 6. Drift fishing from bank or boat is the favorite method above the falls. Bank access is very good, with most landowners granting permission to fish when asked. Be sure to ask. Several primitive roads approach the river above Culvert Hole, with drift boat launching adjacent to the bridge crossings. There is a primitive take-out right above the Hole (don't boat the Hole). When the mainstem is turbid, anglers will often find the North Fork clear.

Coho reach the North Smith late in the spawning run, and most are not in prime condition.

Sea-run cutthroat have been known to get up as far as a very high falls about 15 miles beyond the point where the road leaves the stream. These falls are approachable from Mapleton, a community on Hwy. 126, the Siletz River Rd. However, sea-run numbers are very depressed at this time, and non-finclipped cutthroat over 12 inches must be released unharmed.

SMITH RIVER, WEST FORK A beautiful wild trout stream, joining the mainstem Smith about 5 miles above Smith River Falls. Only about 10 miles long, the stream is paralleled by BLM Rd. 27.1 along its north bank almost to the headwaters. Closed to steelhead and salmon angling, it offers excellent fishing for wild cutthroat. It is best fished early in season while the water is cool.

SNAG LAKE About 30 acres, west of Hauser. It contains largemouth bass, yellow perch, and brown bullhead. The lake has been known to go dry.

SODA SPRING RESERVOIR A small reservoir with nice rainbows on the North Umpqua River, about 7 miles downstream from Toketee Lake. It is on the north side of Hwy. 138, about 40 miles east of Glide. Approach from Roseburg on Hwy. 138, or take County Rd. 200 from Hwy. 99 at Wilbur. No longer stocked, it has rainbow to 20 inches, brown, and brook trout. It is lightly fished and has a winter boat closure, due to danger from the spillway.

SOUTH UMPQUA RIVER See Umpqua River, South.

SQUAW LAKE (Coos Co.) A 2-acre lake on the South Fork Coquille River road, about 22 miles south of Powers. The river road leaves Hwy. 42 about 3 miles south of Myrtle Point and is paved to the lake.

The lake provides good angling for rainbow trout, and it is usually stocked each season. The Forest Service maintains a campground at the lake. Other campgrounds are located 3 and 5 miles back on the road toward Powers.

SQUAW LAKES (Jackson Co.) A good family recreation area in the upper Applegate drainage, about 4 miles east of Applegate Reservoir, 3 miles north of the California line.

From I-5 or Hwy. 99 take Hwy. 238 south to Ruch, then follow the Applegate River Rd. south to Applegate Reservoir. Cross the dam face to Forest Rd. 1075, which follows Squaw Creek to the lakes.

Big Squaw covers about 50 acres. Little (or Upper) Squaw Lake is about 1/4 that size, located about one mile SE of the large lake. There's no vehicle access to the lake shores, and motors are prohibited on the lake. There is a parking lot about 1/4 mile from Big Squaw. The road in can be rough in early spring.

Both lakes have good populations of wild cutthroat averaging 9 inches. There are lots of crappie, and brown bullhead to 10 inches. Fair size largemouth bass are well established.

The lakes are very popular and are fished heavily. Catches are good, especially in fall and early spring. Bait fishing is most popular, but trolling and casting will produce. A Free Fishing Day derby for youngsters takes place here in June each year.

Camping is by reservation only. Contact the Star Ranger District at the town of McKee on the Applegate River. Additional camping is available at Applegate Reservoir. Recommended for small fry.

STEAMBOAT CREEK A scenic tributary of the North Umpqua River, entering the mainstream at Steamboat Ranger Station about 21 miles east of Glide. Closed to all fishing, it is a designated sanctuary for Umpqua summer steelhead. Camping is available at Canton Creek and Steamboat Falls.

STUMP LAKE A 30-acre reservoir on Clearwater Creek NW of Diamond Lake. The lake is on Hwy. 138, 11 miles NW of Diamond Lake Resort.

Not a scenic lake, but it has plump brook rainbow trout to 15 inches. Snags and stumps make trolling or spinning difficult. Still-fishing with bait saves tackle. There's good fly action in the fall. There are improved campgrounds at Clearwater Falls, about 3 miles east, and at Whitehorse Falls 1 1/2 miles west.

SUCKER CREEK A tributary of the beleaguered Illinois River. Like all tributaries of the Illinois, it is closed to all angling.

TANNEN LAKE An 8-acre hike-in lake in the Siskiyou Mountains quite near the California line. The lake is just NW of Tannen Mountain and can be reached by hiking 1/4 mile by trail from Forest Rd. 041 south and east of Bolan Lake. From Cave Junction it's about 21 miles to Bolan Lake following Hwy. 46 to Holland, and Forest Rd. 4703 to a gravel road access to Bolan. The lake can also be reached by hiking the Thompson Creek Rd. north from Happy Camp, California. The hike is less than one mile.

Tannen is stocked as budgets allow, and fishing holds up well in spring and fall with brook trout to 15 inches. There's a natural campground at the lake. A one-mile trail leads up to East Tannen Lake, elevation 5,400 ft., which is also stocked but fairly brushy on three sides. The Tannens are usually accessible by early June.

TEAL LAKE A one-acre lake 8 miles south of Reedsport near Hwy. 101, several hundred yards south of Clear Lake. The lake has cutthroat trout, but is closed to public access.

TENMILE LAKES A premier largemouth bass fishery, world class for quantity of catch, if not for size . Big, rich, and productive, North and South Tenmile nestle in gorgeous coastal foothills. They offer miles of intricate shoreline with shallow bays, arms, and enticing fingers to explore for bass, brown bullhead, bluegill, rainbow, cutthroat, and the occasional steelhead. A striped/white bass hybrid is also present in waning numbers and is open to angling as long as they last, and coho move through the lakes but are closed to fishing at this time. There are even rumors of a landlocked behemoth of undetermined species whom the locals have affectionately named "Tillie," and while the lakes lack the depth generally associated with land-

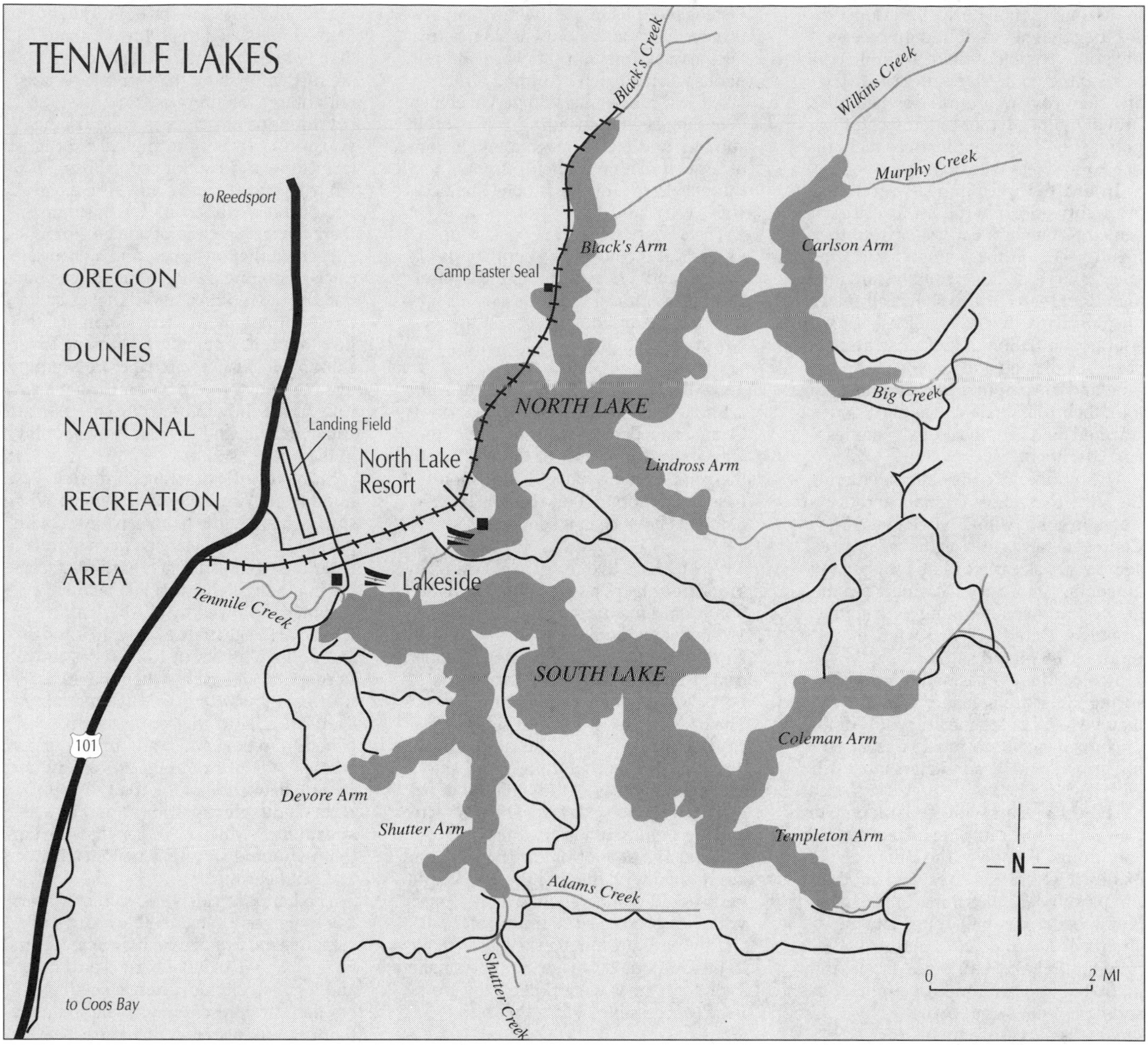

TENMILE LAKES

OREGON DUNES NATIONAL RECREATION AREA
to Reedsport
to Coos Bay
101
Landing Field
North Lake Resort
Lakeside
Camp Easter Seal
Black's Creek
Black's Arm
Wilkins Creek
Murphy Creek
Carlson Arm
Big Creek
NORTH LAKE
Lindross Arm
Tenmile Creek
SOUTH LAKE
Coleman Arm
Devore Arm
Shutter Arm
Templeton Arm
Adams Creek
Shutter Creek
N
0 2 MI

locked sea monsters, it isn't that hard to imagine such a presence on a fog-draped morning at Tenmile.

The two lakes are tucked off to the east of Hwy. 101 at Lakeside, about 12 miles south of Reedsport. North Lake is a bit under 1,000 acres, and South Lake is several hundred acres larger. Their average depth is about 15 feet, and neither lake has any real deep areas.

Bass tournaments are frequently held here, and the pros are known to catch 20 to 50 largemouth in a day in the 2-5 pound range, with bass to 8 pounds common in late spring. Bass to 10 pounds are available.

Tenmile bass are catchable the year around, but best fishing is May through September, or once the water warms to 70 degrees. In May and June when the bass spawn, Spinnerbait are effective around the willows and docks (dark at night, chartreuse during the day). The shallow shoreline (over 170 miles of it) is always productive, with abundant aquatic weeds as well as the willows, docks and other structures that bass favor. Plastic worms, weedless spoons, and topwater lures are popular. Favorite areas in South Lake are the Coleman and Templeton arms. In North Lake, a lot of bass are caught near the railroad trestles and in Lindross and Black's arms.

The state record hybrid bass (15 lbs. 4 oz.) was taken from Ana Reservoir, but bass to 15 lbs. have been caught at Tenmile. Hybrid bass were last stocked here in 1987 in an experiment to control the bluegill population and should still be available through 1996. The hybrid is a cross between striped and white bass, both very big fish. It is a handsome, deep

bodied fish with an obvious resemblance to stripers. Its tendency to wander (as far as the Willamette River in Portland) led to discontinuation of the program.

Bluegill aren't as abundant here as they once were, but there are still enough to keep the youngsters interested. Try any calm cove or around downed trees. Brown bullhead are numerous off the points. Look for them in areas that are deeper and less weedy.

Trout are stocked annually, and there are plenty of fish in the 2-4 lb. class with some to 20 inches. For larger trout try fishing deep off the points, or dragging a lake troll. These days, rainbow are more abundant than cutthroat. Tenmiles were once primarily a cold water fishery, with a large population of cutthroat, and good size runs of coho and steelhead. As logging and development around the lake took their toll, the lake has filled and warmed, and the traditional fisheries have declined.

The number of coho salmon entering the lakes these days is small, and the lake closes to coho fishing November 15. Coho generally enter as the water rises, some years as early as late October, but November and early December see the greatest numbers. Trolling with spinners, wobblers, Daredevils or Kwikfish can produce 5-6 pound salmon .

Steelhead are occasionally hooked in spring. Most are hatchery reared and may be kept, but some are wild. All non-finclipped steelhead must be released unharmed. Steelhead anglers must fish with barbless hooks.

There's a resort with RV park on North Tenmile, public camping across the highway from Lakeside in the Dunes National Recreation Area, and another campground 2 miles north at Eel Lake. Flying fishermen will appreciate the airstrip at Lakeside, a 10 minute walk from South Lake. Lakeside Marina, right in town, has a full range of supplies, gas, and boat rentals, and owner Roby Breaker is a treasure trove of wisdom about how, where, and what to fish. There's a nice public fishing dock in Lakeside that accesses very productive water. All species are caught from the dock, which is wheelchair accessible.

TOKETEE RESERVOIR One of several power system reservoirs on the upper North Umpqua, occupying several hundred acres. It is successfully managed for brown trout. Located about 60 miles east of Roseburg, 40 miles east of Glide, it can be approached from both east and west on the North Umpqua River Rd., Hwy. 138. From the east, take Hwy. 97 to the Hwy. 138 (Diamond Lake) cut-off. Toketee is about 23 miles west of Diamond Lake.

The reservoir has good numbers of browns and a few brook trout. The browns run to 11-13 inches and are taken on bait, Kwikfish-type lures, and flies. Fishing nymphs in the shallows can also be effective, and the browns do rise to take mayfly imitations on warm afternoons when a hatch is coming off the lake. Float tube anglers do very well here.

Fishing is good in spring, tapers off in summer, and picks up again in fall. Some of the best fishing is often February through April. Toketee is open and accessible year-round.

There are two Forest Service campgrounds at the north and south ends of the lake and a boat ramp on the eastern shore. Good forest campsites are also available up and down river on the North Umpqua Rd.

TRUMIS & BYBEE PONDS Four small artificial ponds owned by the Jackson County Fair Board. Adjacent to the freeway at the community of Central Point, the ponds contain bluegill, largemouth bass, and crappie. A few bass as large as 6 pounds have been taken here.

TWIN LAKES (Douglas Co.) Two nice brook trout lakes between the North and South Umpqua drainage systems, just 1/2 mile hike from the road. Take the North Umpqua Hwy. 138 about 32 miles east of Glide to the Wilson Creek Rd., Forest Rd. 4770. Bear right at the forks. The trailhead is on the west side of the road, about 7 miles in. The lakes are also approachable by trail from Twin Lakes Mountain, by way of the Little River Rd.

The larger, lower lake is about 12 acres, and the smaller twin is half that.

Both have brook trout to 15 inches and are stocked with fingerlings. Bait or spinners should work well in early season, with flies good in late summer and fall.

The Twins are among the last to thaw in the Umpqua drainage, and the smaller Twin sometimes winterkills. They are usually accessible by late June.

UMPQUA RIVER ESTUARY (a.k.a. WINCHESTER BAY, from Winchester Bar to Scottsburg Park) Oregon's number one coastal sturgeon fishery, with offshore opportunities for halibut and bottom fish, and bay fishing for spring and fall chinook, striped bass, perch, crabs, and softshell clams. There are three port towns on the bay, Winchester Bay (which is closest to the bar), Reedsport, and Gardiner.

The bay is approached by a good road, Hwy. 38, which cuts through the Coast Range south of Cottage Grove. From Eugene on I-5, it's about 90 miles to Reedsport. From Florence on the coast, it's 15 miles south by Hwy. 101.

Winchester Bay is one of Oregon's top ten offshore ports. Its charter fleet pursues bottom fish year-round, and schedules halibut and chinook trips as ocean regulations allow. Offshore anglers heading out on their own for big rockfish and lingcod may need to go further than they're used to, since Winchester's reefs are further offshore than reefs associated with other Oregon bays.

Within the bay there is good fishing year-round. In Spring, anglers dig clams, trap crabs, and fish for striped bass, white sturgeon, perch, and spring chinook (as regulations allow). In summer, there are spring chinook, green sturgeon, stripers in the lower bay, and a chance to catch migrating chinook bound for points north (but who turn into Winchester briefly in pursuit of bait fish). In Fall (late July through September), Umpqua River chinook linger in the bay before heading upstream toward the South Umpqua and Cow Creek. In winter, white sturgeon are still available, and stripers can be found in the upper estuary.

Sturgeon are attracting a growing number of Winchester Bay anglers. White sturgeon are in the bay year-round, with peak catches mid-March. Green sturgeon enter the bay in summer. Earliest catches are in the Big Bend area just below Gardiner, followed by a fishery at Reedsport beneath the Hwy. 101 Bridge and at the bluff about 1 1/2 miles above Reedsport. The fishery then moves upstream toward Little Mill Creek at Scottsburg Park, where sturgeon are fished from boat and bank. Bank anglers access the river from pull-offs on Hwy. 38, at the junction of the road to Loon Lake (2nd highway bridge), and downstream from Mill Cr. Anglers fish the bottom with mud shrimp, smelt, herring, and sand shrimp.

The Umpqua tidewater salmon fishery has undergone considerable change in recent years. Coho, which once made up 90% of the catch, have been closed to angling. Fall chinook, once a small fishery here, are present in growing numbers thanks to releases of hatchery-reared juveniles at the head of tide. Both wild and hatchery runs tend to linger in the estuary and are available for harvest, providing good fall fishing. Fall chinook average 14-18 pounds, while coho are generally 8-9 pounds. Spring chinook arrive as early as March and are fished through September. Peak catches in the bay are often in April and May, with momentum picking up again in August.

Chinook are caught by boat anglers between the jetties below the town of Winchester Bay, and up-bay in the main channel north of Steamboat Island between Gardiner and the Point. There are also salmon fisheries off the mouths of the Smith and Umpqua. Bank fisheries for salmon include the south jetty, Training Jetty and extension, and the public docks in Reedsport.

There is some trolling for jack salmon and for sea-run cutthroat in the fall, espe-

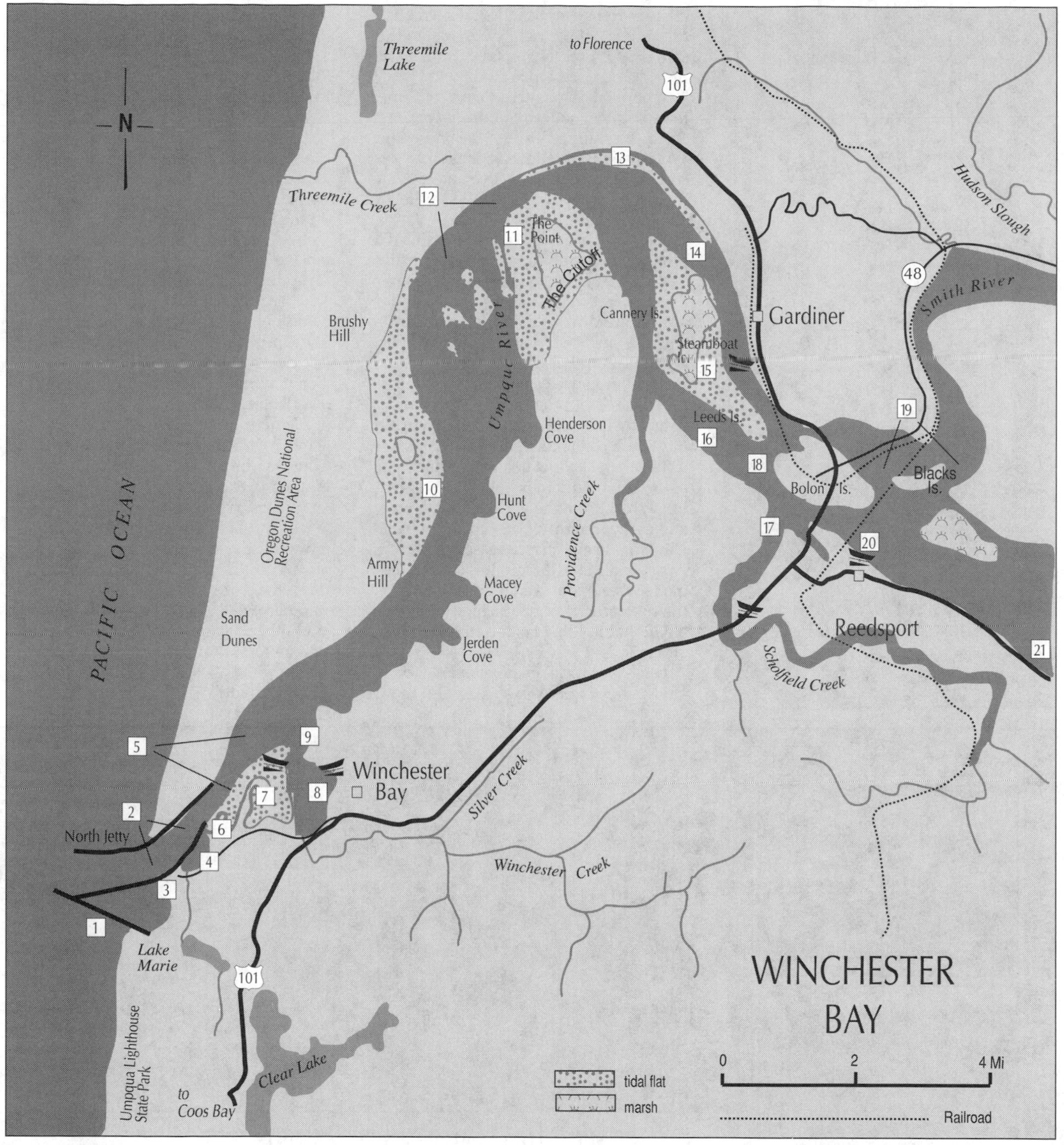

1 **SOUTH JETTY** - Fish for salmon, perch, rockfish.
2 **LOWER BAY** - Fish from boat and bank for salmon, perch, rockfish.
3 **TRAINING JETTY** and extension - Public access for salmon, perch, rockfish, crab.
4 **SOCIAL SECURITY BAY** - Shore access for perch, striped bass.
5 **CRABBING**
6 **COAST GUARD DOCK** - Public access for perch, rockfish, Dungeness crab
7 **WINCHESTER PT.** - Gravel fill access to bank fishery for rockfish, perch.
8 **PUBLIC DOCKS** - Charter boats, public moorage, and dock fishing for tomcod, perch, rockperch.
9 **COAST GUARD PARK** - Bank fishing from rock crib for perch and rockfish.
10 **NORTH SPIT** - Softshells; shad in channel May-June.
11 **THE POINT** - Softshells.
12 **CHANNEL** - Salmon, striped bass, sturgeon, pinkfin perch (July & Aug.); shad May-June.
13 **THREE MILE FLATS** - Softshell clams.
14 **STURGEON**
15 **STEAMBOAT ISLAND** - Softshell clams.
16 **STRIPED BASS**
17 **SEA-RUN CUTTHROAT**
18 **BOLON ISLAND** - Most popular softshell digging.
19 **MOUTH OF THE SMITH** - Striped bass, salmon, sea-run.
20 **REEDSPORT** - Public boat ramp and docks; fish for striped bass, sturgeon, salmon.
21 **MOUTH OF THE UMPQUA** - Striped bass, salmon, sturgeon.

cially in the lower Scholfield River, but they are usually caught incidental to the salmon. All non-finclipped cutthroat must be released unharmed.

A population of striped bass continues to reproduce modestly in the lower Smith, migrating between the Smith and Winchester Bay, following the food source. These large bass live and grow a long time (up to 27 years), and thrillers to 45 pounds have been taken. In the bay, stripers are primarily caught on trolled plugs or bait from June to October, with best catches in September and October. Popular baits include herring, anchovies, sea and mud worms, and fresh or frozen smelt. A smelt wrap on a large Kwikfish-type lure could also be effective. In late summer, try surface plugs or fly-fishing for a heart-stopping thrill. Stripers are fished by boat anglers in Social Security Bay south of the town of Winchester Bay, in the main channel below Gardiner, just below the mouth of Scholfield River near Reedsport, from the docks at Reedsport, and at the mouths of the Smith and Umpqua. Prime striper season is March, April, and May. Best catches seem to be made when there is a lot of sediment in the river after freshets. Stripers are generally found holding behind big boulders and in holes.

Perch and rockfish are available to anglers boating the lower bay, and there are good bank fisheries for them at South Jetty, the Training Jetty and extension, the Coast Guard Dock south of Winchester Bay, Winchester Point gravel fill, and the public docks and Coast Guard Park in Winchester Bay.

Softshell clams can be dug in many of the coves and flats on both sides of the bay. The flats off Bolon Island are most popular, but good numbers are also dug in the North Spit Flats, off the Point, and above Steamboat Island. Crabs are available in good numbers, with best catches in spring off Winchester Point.

There are public boat ramps in Gardiner, in Reedsport at the mouth of the Umpqua and on Scholfield River, at the docks in Winchester Bay, and at Scottsburg Park about 12 miles above Reedsport.

Campgrounds are available at Windy Cove in Winchester Bay, Lake Marie just south of the lighthouse, at William Tugman State Park south at Eel Lake, and at forest service campgrounds at Eel Creek just south of Tugman Park on Hwy. 101. Seven miles north of Gardiner at Tahkenitch Lake and also at Siltcoos Lake there are additional Forest Service campgrounds. RV parks, motels, moorages and other accommodations and supplies can be found throughout the bay area.

UMPQUA RIVER (Scottsburg Park to

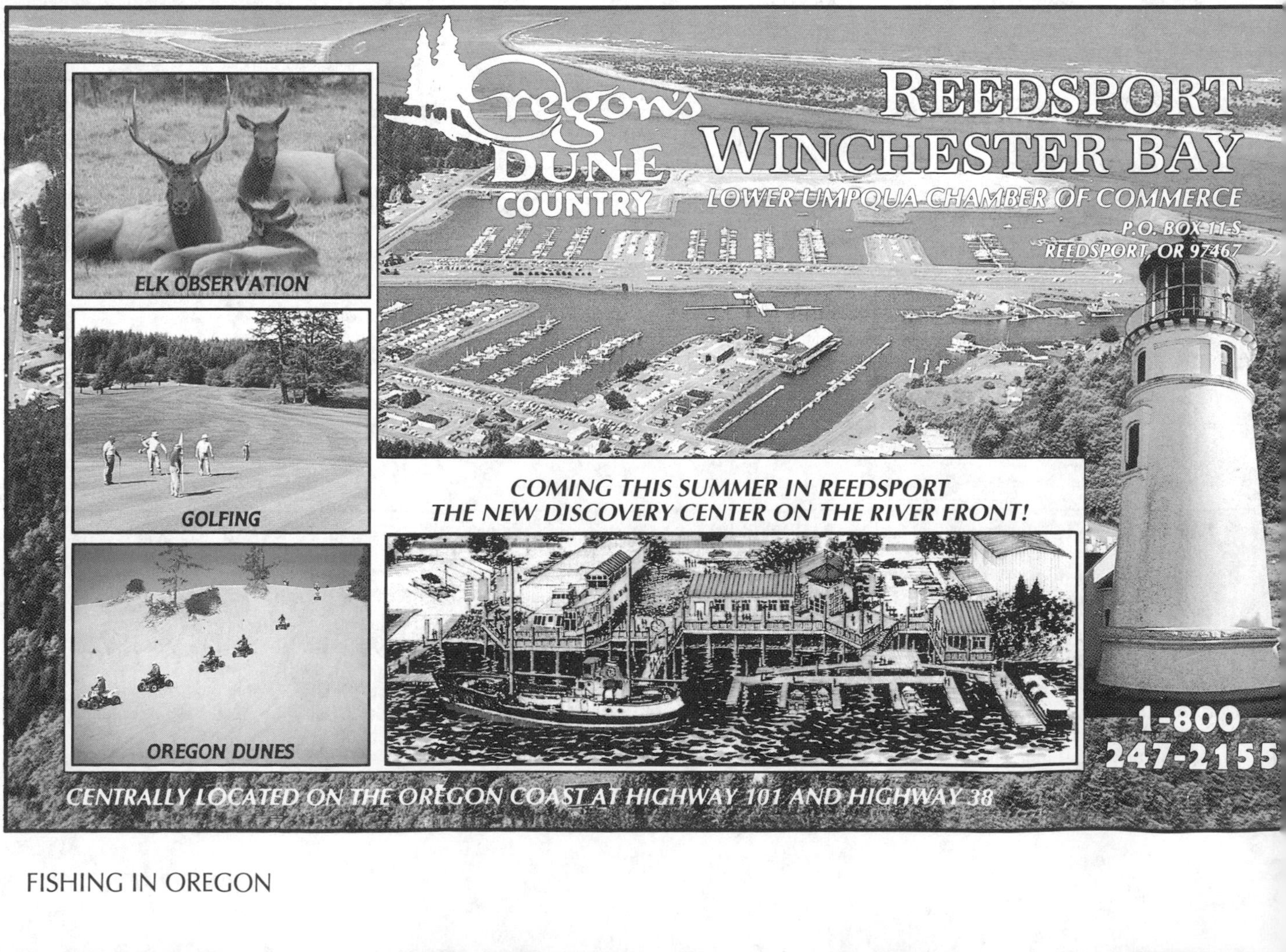

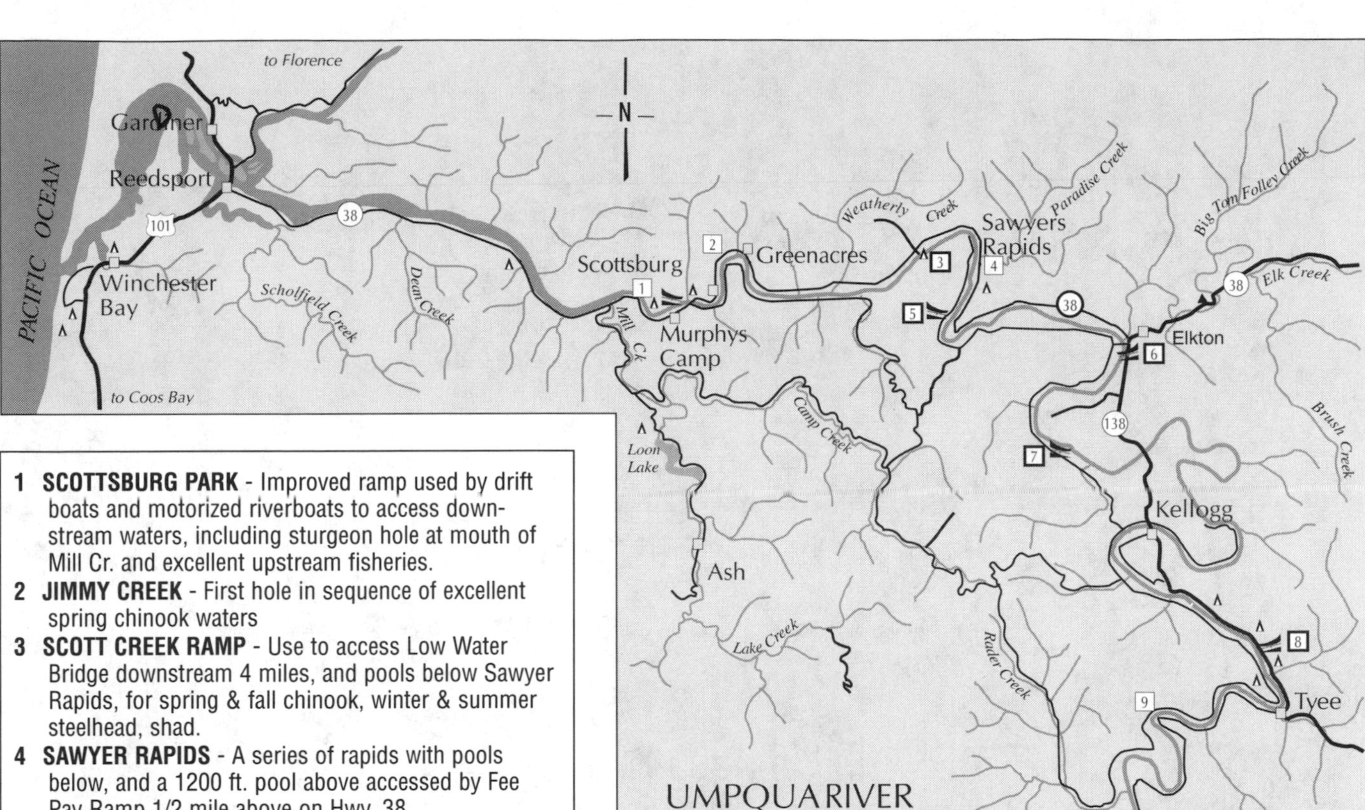

1 **SCOTTSBURG PARK** - Improved ramp used by drift boats and motorized riverboats to access downstream waters, including sturgeon hole at mouth of Mill Cr. and excellent upstream fisheries.
2 **JIMMY CREEK** - First hole in sequence of excellent spring chinook waters
3 **SCOTT CREEK RAMP** - Use to access Low Water Bridge downstream 4 miles, and pools below Sawyer Rapids, for spring & fall chinook, winter & summer steelhead, shad.
4 **SAWYER RAPIDS** - A series of rapids with pools below, and a 1200 ft. pool above accessed by Fee Pay Ramp 1/2 mile above on Hwy. 38.
5 **BUNCH BAR** - Day-use park with primitive ramp and bank fishing on first riffle above Sawyer Rapids upper pool. Excellent for winter steelhead.
6 **ELKTON BRIDGE** - Fish from bridge and both banks for spring chinook, winter steelhead. Excellent smallmouth bass water from here to the forks.
7 **MEHL CREEK RD.** - Drift boat slide at myrtle grove.
8 **YELLOW CREEK BOAT RAMP** - Improved ramp accesses shad, spring chinook, winter steelhead.
9 **POWELL BAR** - Drift boat access.
10 **MACK BROWN COUNTY PARK** - Primitive boat ramp accesses spring & fall chinook water, smallmouth bass, winter steelhead, shad.
11 **UMPQUA BOAT RAMP** - Improved ramp and picnic area; fish for spring chinook, summer & winter steelhead, shad.

the Forks) A handsome and productive river, second largest on the Oregon Coast. It flows over 100 miles from The Forks, 10 miles NW of Roseburg, to Winchester Bay. Its base is gravel and bedrock carved into underwater channels and shelves that provide ideal habitat for migrating salmon, summer steelhead, and a large run of winter steelhead. Its fine and feisty population of smallmouth bass attracts a lot of attention, and it hosts the largest shad run in the state.

Hwy. 38 follows the river from Reedsport east about 36 miles to Elkton. Gravel and paved county roads follow the river closely to the town of Umpqua, where paved roads continue to The Forks. The lower Umpqua meanders through relatively flat land, bordered by a mix of BLM timber and private ranch land. The river varies in width from 100 to 200 yards, dropping only 400 feet in the 100 miles from Roseburg to the bay. Smallmouth bass provide the number one summer fishery here from Elkton to Tyee (river mile 48 to river mile 80) from May through October, with best catches in the summer months. Most bass anglers use worms, but plugs, rubber worms, spinners, and flies are also effective. The most heavily fished pools are near the boat ramps, with popular floats from just below Tyee to just above Kellogg Bridge. Below Kellogg the river bank is private with no public access, but bass fishing may actually be best there. To fish Tyee to Elkton, anglers put in at Yellow Creek Boat Ramp, or at Hutchison Wayside State Park where there is a natural gravel bar put-in at river mile 72 just above Kellogg. Get permission from the landowners to access private land there. Boaters also find good smallmouth water below Mack Brown County Park, which has a boat ramp. Catch rate is very good.

Spring chinook are in the mainstem Umpqua from mid-March to July, with highest catches in April and May. Fall chinook are present in August and September, and are the strongest run at this time. Most fishing is from anchored riverboats (flat bottoms only are suitable for the Umpqua), with anglers running spinners or herring. Earliest fishing for chinook takes place at Jimmy Creek, the first rapids above Scottsburg Bridge, featuring an excellent chinook hole. Anglers launch at Scottsburg Park and motor up about 3 miles to the rapids, or launch at Scott Cr. Boat Ramp and drift down. Scott Cr. Ramp is also used to access Sawyer Rapids about a mile upriver. Sawyer is a series of rapids with pools below and a large pool above, accessed from a fee-pay ramp 1/2 mile further up on Hwy. 38. Bank anglers can fish the Sawyer Rapids upper pool from Bunch Bar, a day-use park about 5 miles west of Elkton. Other popular spring chinook access points are Elkton Bridge, Yellow Cr. Boat Ramp, Mack Brown Park, and Umpqua Boat Ramp.

Steelhead are a very popular fishery on the mainstem, though nothing to compare with the North Fork. Summer-run fish are present in May, June, July, and August. Peak catches are taken in June and July, and boat and bank anglers use everything to catch them from flies to nightcrawlers. Most popular boat launches for summer steelhead are at Yellow Creek, Umpqua, and at The Forks. Bank anglers find best access above Yellow Creek, where there is a complement of

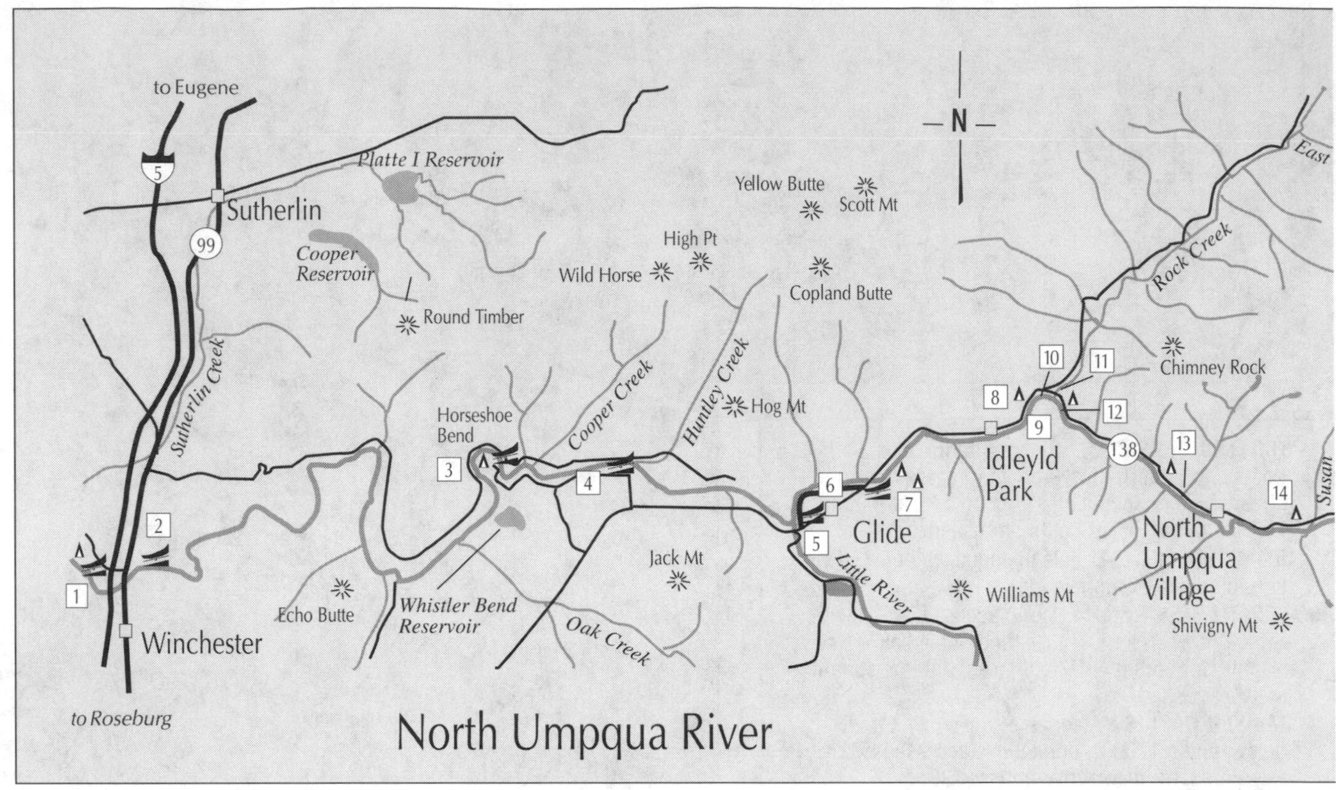

public (BLM) land. Look for turn-outs off County Rd. 33 below Tyee.

Winter steelhead provide a good fishery in the mainstem beginning after the first fall freshets, usually in October, and lasting through March. Scottsburg to Elkton sees the earliest angling, with high quality catches to 20 pounds. Below Sawyer Rapids there's a good bank fishery accessed through private land, open to public use by the landowner. The Elkton area offers good bank access from Mehl Canyon Rd., and there is drift boat fishing throughout the stretch. Popular day drifts include Elkton to Sawyer Rapids (fee-pay), the Myrtle Grove dirt skid on Mehl Canyon Rd. to Yellow Creek Boat Ramp, Yellow Creek to Hutchison Wayside (a primitive ramp at mile post 9 on Hwy. 138W), The Forks to Umpqua, and Umpqua to just below Mac Brown Park on the Tyee Rd. The standard method is to run plugs in front of the drift boat. These same drifts can be used to fish summer steelhead. The annual catch of winter steelhead on the mainstem Umpqua usually fluctuates from 3,000-5,000.

A famous mailbox on the North Umpqua.

A huge run of shad appears in the river in May and June from Scottsburg to the forks. Shad to 4 pounds are commonly caught, and 5 pounders have been taken. Popular fishing spots include the areas around Yellow Creek Boat Ramp, Umpqua, and The Forks. Yellow Creek attracts a large number of bank anglers. But any of the winter steelhead drifts can also be fished for shad in season. Shad anglers use light tackle with small spinners, darts, or shad flies.

The only campground on the mainstem is the Tyee BLM camp on County Rd. 57 between Elkton and Umpqua. Shad fishery recommended for small fry.

UMPQUA RIVER, NORTH One of Oregon's most treasured streams, beloved for its pristine quality and picturesque setting, and for its large run of summer steelhead. Spring chinook, coho and wild winter steelhead also return to the river to spawn. Native cutthroat trout and good size browns can be found above Rock Creek, and catchable rainbows are planted throughout the river. A significant and productive stretch of the North Umpqua is restricted to fly fishing only.

The North Umpqua originates high in the Cascade Mountains at Maidu Lake, and is fed by the outflow of big Diamond Lake and by snow melt and springs on a tumultuous 100-mile journey through a steep forested canyon. It joins the South Umpqua just NW of Roseburg to form the mainstem Umpqua.

The North Umpqua offers a pleasant lesson in how big fish navigate their home stream, where they pause before attempting a chute, where they rest after they've made it to the upper pool. Here, historically, anglers have been able to find fish where the books say they should be. And each riffle, tail-out, chute, and pool seems to have been lovingly (or ruefully) named by local anglers.

For the past several seasons, summer steelhead returns to the North Umpqua have been very low (though only five years ago the run was far surpassing historical numbers). The mixed run of wild and hatchery stock enters the North Umpqua in June and is pursued through October. At this time, both wild and hatchery fish are available for harvest, but anglers may keep only one non-fin-clipped steelhead per week. Barbless hooks are required for all angling from June 1 through October 31.

Spring chinook are in the river from April through October, with peak catches in May, June, and July. Below the fly boundary, all adult chinook must be released unharmed. Within the stretch restricted to fly-fishing, only jack salmon

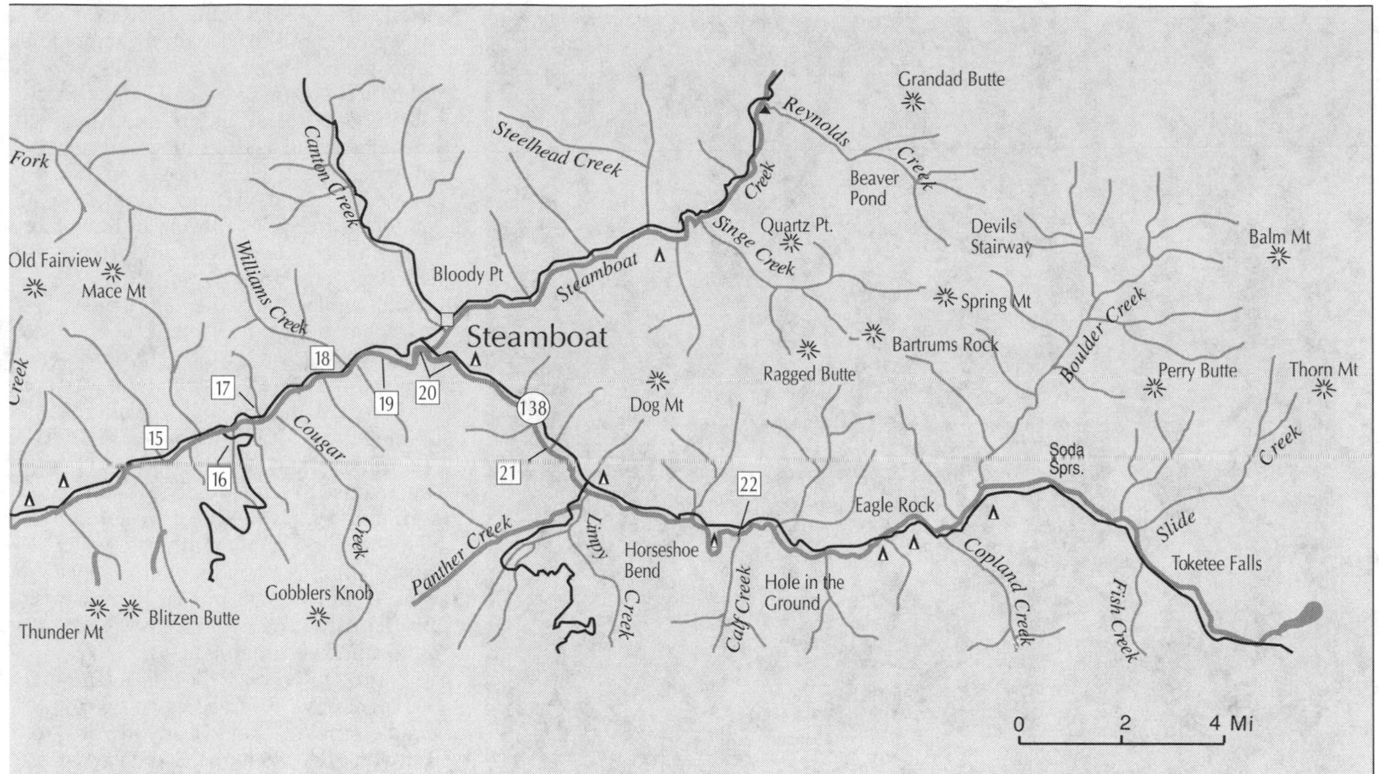

may be kept. The entire river has been closed to coho fishing during the normal coho season.

Catchable hatchery-reared rainbow trout are planted from Amacher Park on up from just before opening season until July 4, or until the river warms above 70 degrees. Contact the Dept. of Fish and Wildlife at Roseburg for a calendar of stocking dates and locations.

Hwy. 138 follows the river all the way from the forks to Lemolo Lake. Above Lemolo, as the highway swings south toward Diamond Lake, Forest Rd. 60 leads to the Kelsay Valley Trailhead, which tracks the North Umpqua to its headwaters at Maidu. West of the trailhead, forest roads follow the North Umpqua inlet of Lemolo Lake, including a stretch between Crystal Springs and the Lake that offers excellent opportunities for late season fishing for brook trout and browns to 1 1/2 pounds.

The lower 35 miles of the North Umpqua are less accessible, fished primarily from boats, since the surrounding land is mostly private. From The Forks County Park, about 6 miles north of Roseburg, anglers boat about 1/2 mile upstream. Jet sleds can navigate the 5 miles up to Winchester Dam (few jet the river beyond the dam). There is also a productive bank fishery at The Forks for salmon, steelhead, smallmouth bass, and shad. The most popular stretch on the lower river is from Amacher Park to just below Winchester Dam for stocked rainbow, steelhead, and salmon. There is 1/4 mile of good bank access at Amacher.

1 **AMACHER PARK** - To just below Winchester Dam, most popular fishing on the river; productive bank access for 1/4 mile above boat ramp.

2 **PAGE ROAD TAKE-OUT** - Pole slide above dam.

3 **WHISTLER'S BEND** - County park with boat ramp, camping; one mile of good bank fishing.

4 **ROCK PIT BOAT ACCESS** - Drift boats only.

5 **COLLIDING RIVERS** - Boat ramp; good steelhead holes downstream.

6 **BARN HOLE** - One major hole in two miles of good water accessed by the old Glide Rd. off Hwy. 138; bank fishing along road.

7 **LONE ROCK** - Pole slide boat ramp; deadline for boat angling.

8 **NARROWS** - chute is one of the best spring chinook holes on the river.

9 **MAC PLACE** - Drift fishing for spring chinook, summer and winter steelhead, coho.

10 **SWIFTWATER BRIDGE** - Fish 200 yds. of good water on north and south banks.

11 **ROCK CREEK** - Huge pool where fish congregate prior to running up to hatchery; summer steelhead and stocked trout only available from here upstream;fly-fishing only above this point.

12 **FAMOUS** - Bedrock tail-out

13 **LOWER HONEY** - Pocket water and some gravel

14 **SUSAN CREEK** - Long classic steelhead run; tail-out, riffle, bedrock, shelf; BLM campground.

15 **FAIRVIEW** - Dead drift through a deep chute and around big boulders.

16 **WRIGHT CREEK** - Wide tail-out of bedrock ledges where steelhead rest above major rapids.

17 **LOWER & UPPER ARCHIE** - Two 20 ft. deep pools between major rapids.

18 **WILLIAMS CREEK** - Half-mile classic run.

19 **THE LEDGES** - Shallow water featuring series of ledge slots where steelhead lie.

20 **STEAMBOAT CREEK** (Camp Water) - At least 25 named holes where steelheaders and summer steelhead congregate bridge accesses south bank; Steamboat Creek is closed to angling.

21 **REDMAN CREEK** - Gravel tail-out above major rapids.

22 **CALF CREEK** - Pocket water.

Above Winchester, Whistler's Bend County Park offers a mile of good bank fishing for salmon and steelhead in a fine stretch of classic water, including tail-out, riffle, bedrock chutes, and pockets.

The North Umpqua offers a pleasant lesson in how steelhead navigate their home stream.

Boat and bank access picks up from Glide east, with a boat ramp at the confluence of Little River (Colliding Rivers) accessing a string of good steelhead holes downstream. Anglers bank fish off the Old Glide Rd. off Hwy. 138, with the Barn Hole just one of many in a 2-mile string of good water. The deadline for boats on the North Umpqua is at Lone Rock Boat Ramp, about 3 miles west of the community of Idleyld Park. There's a lot of good water in the Idleyld area, but not a lot of bank access. A 200 yd. stretch is accessible from the north and south banks at Bridge to Nowhere, off Hwy. 138. Rock Creek joins the river about one mile east of Idleyld. There is a hatchery about 3/4 mile up the Rock Creek Rd., and fish congregate in a huge pool at the confluence prior to running up. A large concentration of stocked legal rainbow is also available there.

From Rock Creek up to Soda Springs Power House, only fly-fishing is permitted. Fly anglers in pursuit of steelhead use heavy gear in order to make long casts, and to break through the canyon winds. Named holes follow even more closely upon one another, many of them associated with the North Umpqua's plentiful tributaries. Among them are Susan Creek, Fairview, Wright Creek, Lower & Upper Archie, Williams Cr., The Ledges, and Steamboat. Steamboat Creek itself is a steelhead spawning ground, closed to angling. But the bend of river that includes the Steamboat confluence attracts anglers from throughout the world. Called the Camp Water by familiars, this 400 yard stretch of pocket water includes at least 25 named holes where summer steelhead and steelheaders gather under the protective eye of an organization of fly anglers called the Steamboaters.

Whistler's Bend County Park offers the only campground on the lower river, but campgrounds are plentiful east of Idleyld on Hwy. 138 and at the reservoirs. At Susan Creek there is a long, classic steelhead run—tail-out, riffle, bedrock, shelf, as well as a full-service BLM camp. Other large facilities are at Bogus Creek, and Island. There are two small camps on Steamboat Creek (Canton Creek and Steamboat Falls). There are large camps at Apple Creek, Horseshoe Bend, and Eagle Rock; a small camp at Boulder Flat; and large camps at Toketee and Lemolo. There are also two BLM campgrounds on the Rock Creek Rd. (County Rd. 78) about 5 miles above the hatchery.

UMPQUA RIVER, SOUTH A big river, flowing over 95 miles from headwaters in the Rogue-Umpqua Divide Wilderness, joining the North Umpqua at The Forks about 10 miles NW of Roseburg to form the mainstem Umpqua. The South Umpqua features some of western Oregon's best smallmouth bass water, and maintains a good winter steelhead run. Trout fishing is primarily for hatchery rainbow. The river is closed to chinook and coho angling.

South of Roseburg the South Umpqua is flanked by I-5 and accessed by county roads from Winston to Canyonville. From Canyonville, where the river bends east, it is followed by Hwy. 227 to Tiller, then by County Rd. 46 into the Umpqua National Forest. Forest Rd. 28 continues along the stream past South Umpqua Falls to Camp Comfort.

Forest land along the South Umpqua was heavily logged in the 1950s and '60s, with maintenance of the river's fisheries a low priority. Today, reforestation, better logging practices, and sensitive management within the several impacting agencies have allowed the South Umpqua to stage a comeback. The construction of Galesville Dam has also helped, providing a better summer stream flow for the river's salmon and steelhead.

The lower 30 miles offer the best angling for smallmouth bass, though bass are present up to Days Creek east of Canyonville. Good bass angling begins whenever river temperature hits 65 degrees, generally from May through September. Above Canyonville, the smallmouth population decreases and is lightly fished. Anglers access the best bedrock pockets from driftboats in spring, and fish from the banks and bridges around the boat ramps when the river drops too low for drifting in summer. Urban anglers can fish the mouth of Deer Creek from the banks at Stephens St. Park in Roseburg, or at the foot of Lane St. up from the Oak St. Bridge. The Fairgrounds south of town also offers opportunity for smallmouth bass as well as spring chinook, shad, and both winter and summer steelhead. The area around Winston, including the vicinity of Lookinglass Creek, is popular with smallmouth bass anglers. Coon Hollow and

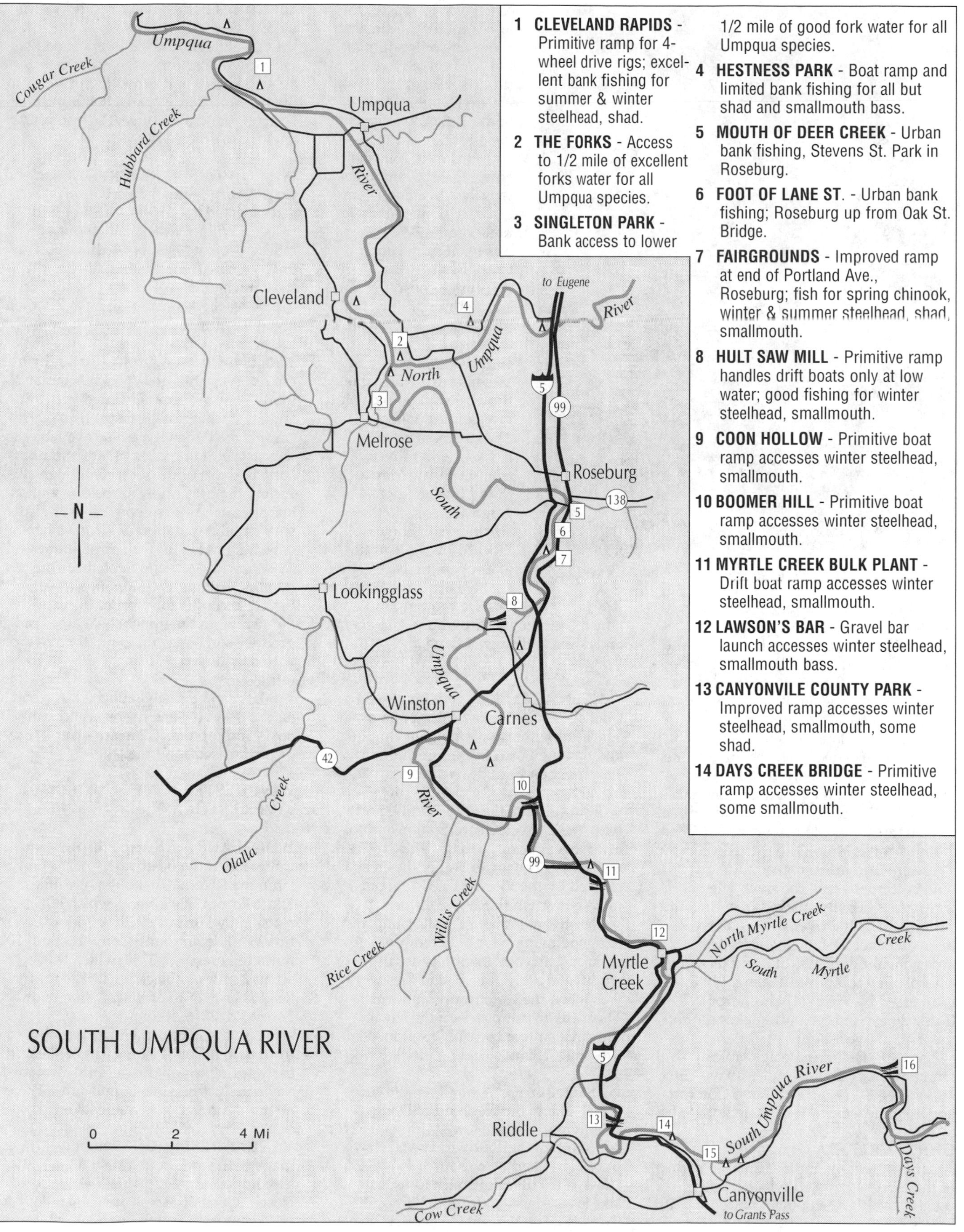

1 **CLEVELAND RAPIDS** - Primitive ramp for 4-wheel drive rigs; excellent bank fishing for summer & winter steelhead, shad.

2 **THE FORKS** - Access to 1/2 mile of excellent forks water for all Umpqua species.

3 **SINGLETON PARK** - Bank access to lower 1/2 mile of good fork water for all Umpqua species.

4 **HESTNESS PARK** - Boat ramp and limited bank fishing for all but shad and smallmouth bass.

5 **MOUTH OF DEER CREEK** - Urban bank fishing, Stevens St. Park in Roseburg.

6 **FOOT OF LANE ST**. - Urban bank fishing; Roseburg up from Oak St. Bridge.

7 **FAIRGROUNDS** - Improved ramp at end of Portland Ave., Roseburg; fish for spring chinook, winter & summer steelhead, shad, smallmouth.

8 **HULT SAW MILL** - Primitive ramp handles drift boats only at low water; good fishing for winter steelhead, smallmouth.

9 **COON HOLLOW** - Primitive boat ramp accesses winter steelhead, smallmouth.

10 **BOOMER HILL** - Primitive boat ramp accesses winter steelhead, smallmouth.

11 **MYRTLE CREEK BULK PLANT** - Drift boat ramp accesses winter steelhead, smallmouth.

12 **LAWSON'S BAR** - Gravel bar launch accesses winter steelhead, smallmouth bass.

13 **CANYONVILE COUNTY PARK** - Improved ramp accesses winter steelhead, smallmouth, some shad.

14 **DAYS CREEK BRIDGE** - Primitive ramp accesses winter steelhead, some smallmouth.

Access to the N. Umpqua improves below Colliding Rivers.

Round Prairie, off Hwy. 99, both have good bedrock bass pools.

The South Umpqua has both early and late arriving winter steelhead runs. The first run usually appears in the river in late November (depending on the arrival of fall freshets) and continues into December. The late run shows in late December with good catches till tax time. The river is open for steelhead up to Dumont Creek, and a lot of angling takes place in the area right below the deadline.

Trout are available from Dumont Creek (about 7 miles NE of Tiller) to the Forks. These are primarily stocked rainbow, but wild cutthroat are in the river. The South Umpqua is heavily stocked in spring and summer until the river warms above 70 degrees. Several of its good size tributaries, including Days, Elk, and Jackson creeks, offer good trout fishing. Elk Creek is accessed by Hwy. 227 south from Tiller. (Keep an eye out for rattlesnakes around the river above Tiller.)

Camping facilities are available at Dumont Creek about 7 miles above Tiller, at Boulder Creek, and at Camp Comfort, about 7 miles above South Umpqua Falls.

UNION CREEK A very good trout stream, extremely popular among anglers of the North Rogue, of which it is a productive tributary. About 15 miles long, it enters the North Fork from the east about 10 miles north of Prospect, upstream from Natural Bridge. From Medford, follow Hwy. 62 about 58 miles north and east. Hwy. 62 crosses the lower end of the stream about one mile south of the junction of Hwy. 62 (to Crater lake) and Hwy. 230 (to Diamond Lake). Forest Rd. 6230 follows the creek for about 7 miles from Rt. 230, and Forest Rd. 900 continues to its headwaters. There is a trail along the creek for several miles upstream from Union Creek Resort.

Fishing is best from late spring through July, but the creek holds up well all season. Brook trout, cutthroat, rainbow, and browns are all available. Browns to 10 pounds are rare but not unknown. The stream is heavily stocked with rainbow trout from late May through the end of August. Access to the stream is sometimes blocked by snow until after opening day.

There is a large Forest Service campground at Union Creek and campgrounds upstream and down, at Farewell Bend and Natural Bridge.

VINCENT CREEK A very good wild trout stream in the lower Umpqua drainage, heading north of the main Umpqua and flowing north to join the Smith River. The upper end can be reached by road from Hwy. 38, 1 1/2 miles east of Scottsburg. Take the road leading north from Wells Creek Guard Station and follow it over the ridge to the Vincent Creek watershed. The lower end of the creek is reached by the Vincent Cr. Rd., about 4 miles above Smith River Falls.

The stream is about 12 miles long and has good angling for wild cutthroat. A spinner/bait combination is usually effective in early season, and flies work well when the water drops and warms. There are no campsites on the stream. This area suffered terribly from forest fires in 1967, but is healing nicely.

WASSON LAKE A small remote cutthroat lake in the west end of Douglas County north of the lower Umpqua River and south of Smith River. The lake is on public land and is the source of Wasson Creek, a tributary of Smith River. The lake is best reached from the Vincent Creek Rd. See Vincent Creek. But the new sections of the road are not usually passable until mid-summer. A paved road now passes immediately beside Wasson Lake.

Only about 5 acres, it offers good fishing for wild cutthroat. They average about 8 inches and run to 15 inches. Spinner and bait work well, but the lake is snaggy, and a lot of gear is lost. A fly angler can do well here.

WILLOW CREEK RESERVOIR (Jackson Co.) A very popular reservoir of 340 acres located about 9 miles SE of Butte Falls on Willow Creek, and about 41 miles north and east of Medford by way of Hwy. 62. From Ashland, later in the season when the roads are passable, it can be reached by the Fish Lake Rd. then about 8 miles of dirt road north from Fish Lake.

Rainbow trout reproduce naturally in the reservoir and grow to 18 inches and more. They are supplemented with an annual stocking of legal size fish. Black crappie to 10 inches are also available, as well as a good number of largemouth bass. Because of the reservoir's high elevation, the bass rarely surpass 4 pounds, but the catch rate is good. There is also a very small population of kokanee here.

Fishing holds up well throughout the season, with May and September the best months. Trolling is common, but bait fishing accounts for most of the catch. Fly-fishing in the upper shoal areas can produce some nice rainbow (try a nymph with a sunken line, using a slow jerky retrieve).

Boats can be easily launched. A resort on the reservoir has supplies and rents boats and motors. There are several nice picnic areas around the lake.

WINCHESTER BAY (See UMPQUA RIVER ESTUARY)

WOLF LAKE An 8-acre hike-in brook trout lake in the headwaters of the South Umpqua River. It is about a one-mile hike SE from Black Rock, which is reached by Forest Rd. 2780. Follow Forest Rd. 28 NE from Camp Comfort about 10 miles to Forest Rd. 2780, which leads about 2 miles to Black Rock. The trailhead is just south of the junction with Forest Rd. 2716.

Wolf offers good angling for brook trout to 16 inches. Fishing can be great in early spring if you can get in. The roads are usually accessible in mid-June. There are no improvements at the lake.

YANKEE RESERVOIR Prominent on maps of the area, a privately owned 30-acre impoundment on Yankee Creek, closed to public access. It is one mile upstream from Antelope Creek Rd. about 6 miles from White City.

COLUMBIA RIVER ZONE

The Columbia River Zone is all waters of the Columbia River upstream from a north-south line through buoy 10 at the mouth, and includes those portions of tributaries downstream from the main line railroad bridges near their mouths except for the Willamette, Sandy, Hood, Deschutes, and Umatilla River systems.

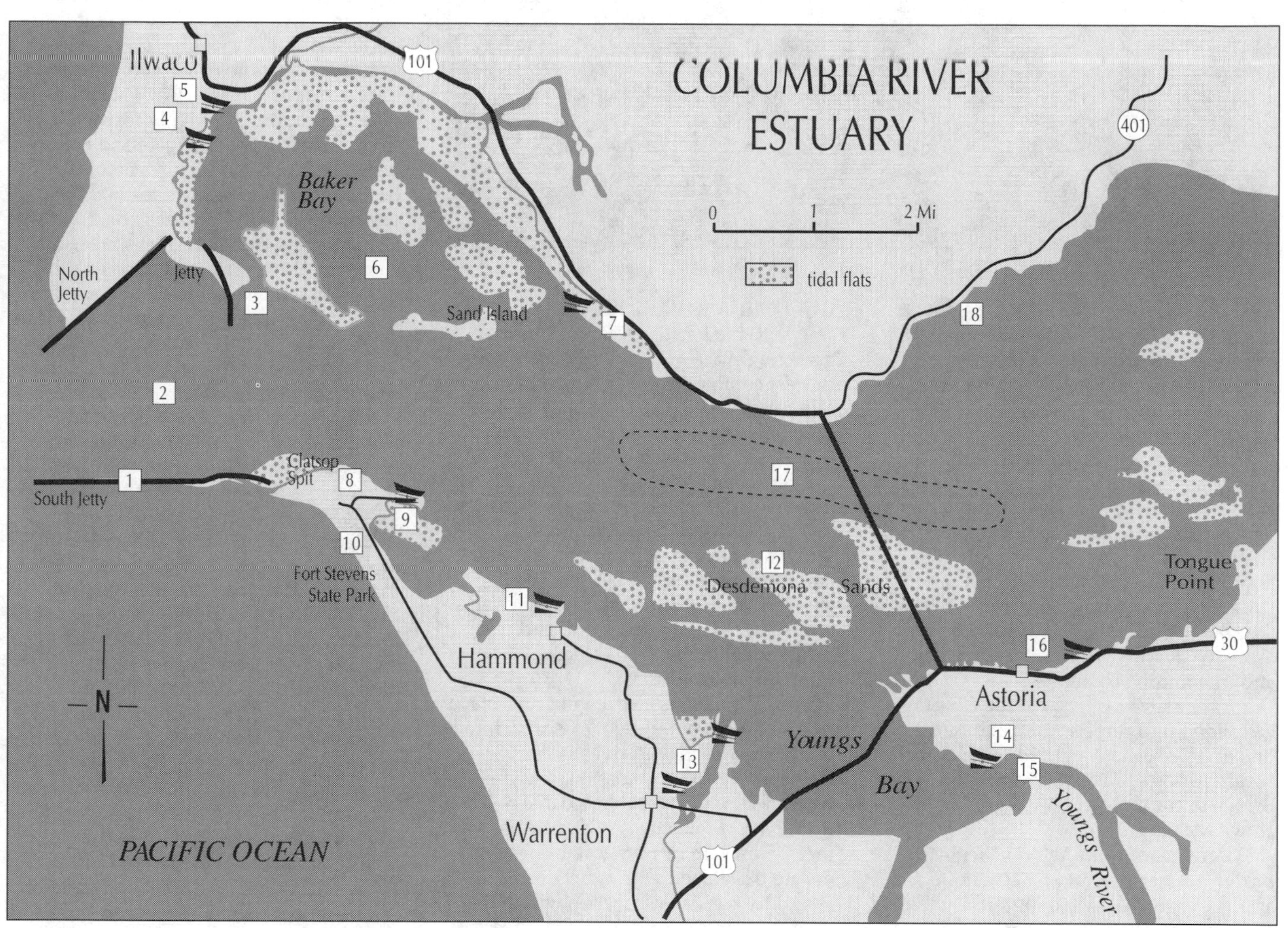

1 **SOUTH JETTY FISHERY** - Fish for salmon at end of black; black rockfish and bottomfish mid-jetty, surf perch nearest spit.

2 **BUOY 10** - Active fall chinook and coho feeding area; give way to commercial traffic.

3 **CRAB**

4 **FT. CANBY ST. PARK**

5 **ILWACO HARBOR**

6 **CRAB, FLOUNDER, STURGEON**

7 **CHINOOK**

8 **BANK FISH** for crab, salmon, surfperch, flounder.

9 **JETTY SANDS** - Unimproved boat launch off beach.

10 **CLATSOP SPIT** - Fish the surf for perch; most productive razor clam digging in Oregon.

11 **HAMMOND BOAT RAMP** - Improved ramps.

12 **DESDEMONA SANDS** - Submerged sand bar; sturgeon.

13 **WARRENTON BOAT RAMP** - Improved ramp

14 **YOUNG'S BAY** - Improved boat ramp

15 **STURGEON**

16 **EAST END BASIN** - Improved ramp

17 **STURGEON**

18 **STURGEON**

Buoy 10 on the Columbia River is an active salmon feeding spot in late summer.

REGULATIONS ON THE COLUMBIA. When the fishing season is open in both Oregon and Washington, a license of either state is valid for Columbia River angling except when fishing from the other state's shore. Anglers must follow the rules of the state they are fishing in. When the Oregon season is closed, a Washington fishing license is not valid on the Oregon side of the state line (mid-channel), and vice-versa. Though most regulations are concurrent at this time, rules have been known to vary between the states. Check the relevant state synopsis for the final word on season, bag, and maximum size limits.

For regulatory purposes, the Columbia is divided into three sections: Buoy 10 line up to Astoria-Megler Bridge, Astoria-Megler Bridge to I-5 Bridge, and I-5 Bridge to the Oregon/Washington border above McNary Dam.

Downstream from Astoria-Megler Bridge ocean catch and length limits apply. Oregon and Washington usually adopt the regulations determined annually by the Federal Pacific Fisheries Management Council. The Council has jurisdiction over waters from 3 miles to 200 miles offshore. Regulations are established each year in April.

For regulation and management purposes, sloughs and other backwaters of the Columbia are included in ODF&W's Northwest Zone. The following Columbia sloughs are described in the Northwest section of this book: Beaver, Blind, Bradbury , Brownsmead, Clatskanie , Deer Island, Dibblee, Goat Island, Magruder, Mayger, Prescott, Rinearson, Sandy Island, and Westport.

COLUMBIA RIVER, ESTUARY (Astoria Bridge to the Pacific Ocean) Primary gathering place of the Northwest's water, the last confinement of a flow that drains more than 250,000 acres of land over a 1200 mile journey. It is a gathering place of life as well. The Columbia estuary is the permanent home of greenling, perch, lingcod, and rockfish. A variety of panfish inhabit its many backwaters. Sturgeon move in and out with the tides and the runs of baitfish. Coho; spring, summer, and fall chinook; summer and winter steelhead; and sea-run cutthroat trout move through the estuary on their migration journeys.

The Columbia is also a gathering place of many races of migratory fish, each race unique to a particular river system. Dams, tributary degradation, and (in recent years) unfavorable oceanic conditions have diminished each of these races. Some are relatively stable, but others are threatened with extinction.

Tightly regulated fisheries within the mainstem and the curtailed fishery off the Columbia River mouth are efforts to allow enough fish from each of these races to return to their home streams—to fulfill Native American treaty obligations, to provide traditional sport fisheries, and to regenerate the populations. Anglers should anticipate that sport fisheries on the Columbia, for salmon in particular, will be in a state of flux for years to come as regulatory and management agencies attempt to strike a balance between the demands of nature and those of business, politics, and competing concepts of progress.

Offshore Fisheries. The mouth of the Columbia was once Oregon's number one access to ocean salmon fishing. Experienced anglers and charter boats out of the ports of Hammond, Warrenton, and Astoria would start taking big spring chinook just beyond the bar in May. In early summer anglers pursued the smaller coho, followed by an intense fall chinook fishery from mid-August through Labor Day. For years this fishery has been tightly regulated. In April 1994, in response to anticipated record low returns of coho salmon, all salmon fishing off the Columbia bar was closed for the year. Coho have a history of wild population swings, and as ocean conditions improve, it is very likely that coho populations will rebound, and the Columbia offshore fishery will re-open.

The Port of Astoria, near the river's mouth, is home to a highly respected fleet of charter fishing boats and continues to be a popular starting point for ocean salmon trips, with destination waters beyond the closure area. The fleet also operates year-round bottom-fishing charters . Some offshore bottom-fishing occurs around the south jetty, but most activity takes place from Tillamook Head south.

A powerhouse (literally), the Columbia rushes toward the ocean on an average summer day at a rate of 400,000 cubic feet per second. Its meeting with the ocean is NOT pacific. The Columbia River bar is the most dangerous on the Oregon coast. Only 25 feet deep, though dredged to 60 feet in the channel, and relatively narrow, it is subject to swells that can rise higher than the average water depth. More often the exchange of fresh and salt water takes place beneath a smooth surface, but boaters must be ever alert, mindful of the tide, time, and weather. A craft at least 18 ft. long is recommended for bar crossings, and boaters are urged to cross in flood and slack tides only, and to beware of the ebb tide.

Salmon. "Buoy Ten" is the name given to the most popular fishery in the Columbia estuary. Charter and private boats traditionally gather to fish fall chinook and coho salmon between buoys 10 and 14, with the majority of boats fishing as close as possible to the Buoy 10 line.

This is an active salmon feeding area and, on busy weekends in late summer, over 2,000 boats might gather along the buoy line, drifting or trolling herring or anchovies through the flood tide. Anglers fish coho closer to the surface, and seek chinook somewhat deeper. Electronic gear is handy for locating salmon, but the presence of rips (the meeting of conflicting currents), and concentrations of bird activity are also good detectors. Bank anglers also participate in the Buoy 10 fishery off Clatsop Spit, where coho catches predominate.

The Buoy 10 season traditionally opens in early August after summer salmon (bound for upper river tributaries) have passed through. The season usually extends through Labor Day. In 1994, a very low-return year, the Buoy 10 season was closed by emergency regulations. It was feared that too many upriver chinook would be caught in this "mixed race" gathering place. The fishery re-opened in mid-September, when it was determined that Idaho-bound fall chinook had left the buoy area.

Spring chinook bound for the lower tributaries (the Willamette and Sandy rivers in Oregon, the Cowlitz, Kalama, and Lewis in Washington) enter the Columbia from January through May. Fish bound for the middle and upper tributaries enter beginning in March. Traditionally, the estuary has been open for spring chinook fishing from whenever the fish arrive until March 31. Though this fishery was open in 1994, very low returns may well lead to a closure in 1995.

As with salmon fisheries throughout Oregon, anglers are urged to read the annual regulation synopsis carefully, and be prepared for the possibility of emergency closures, re-openings, and even extensions in some years. For a Columbia River salmon update, call the ODF&W information line in Portland; the Columbia district ODF&W office; or charter outfits, tackle shops and marinas on the river. Information is also printed in *The Oregonian* and in local newspapers.

Sturgeon. In the late 1800s, Columbia River sturgeon were fished almost to extinction. Today, the Columbia is host to what may be the world's largest concentration of white sturgeon. Less common green sturgeon are also present.

Conservative regulations and a growing understanding of the sturgeon life cycle are responsible for the come-back. Today we know that the largest sturgeon are generally pregnant females. Minimum and maximum catch lengths protect juveniles and spawners, and there is a daily bag limit.

With an estimated life expectancy of 100 years or more, sturgeon have been known to reach lengths of up to 20 feet and weigh up to 1,500 pounds. While the average sturgeon catch at this time is about 41 inches, catch and release opportunities for over-size fish have attracted anglers from all over the world. Unfortunately, suspicion is growing that the mortality rate of caught-and-released over-size sturgeon may be high. While it is not illegal to fish for them at this time, anglers should think twice before targeting this big game fishery.

To avoid hooking over-size sturgeon, anglers should use lighter line and smaller hooks, smaller bait, and lighter line. If your electronic fish-finding gear tells you you're over larger fish, go somewhere else. If you do hook an over-size fish, get your hook out as soon as possible, with minimum handling. Single barbless hooks are required for all sturgeon fishing.

Sturgeon migration patterns have yet to be determined. At this time it is only known that sturgeon migrate freely and frequently between ocean and estuary, and roam far from their home waters. Tagged Columbia River sturgeon have shown up as far north as Alaska, and as far south as San Francisco Bay. The estuary is open to sturgeon fishing the year around, but spring and summer seasons are most popular with anglers. Increased catches generally coincide with the appearance of anchovies in the river from April to August, with peak catches in June and July. Check with local bait shops to determine when the anchovies have arrived, and to place your order for bait. Fresh bait is essential for this fishery, and should be ordered at least one day in advance to insure a supply. Normally 12 to 18 baits per person will suffice.

During the peak season, several hundred boats may gather on a single day in the area from Desdemona Sands to Grays Bay Point, with the best bite occurring from low slack to several hours into the flood tide. Tides and thieving sculpin often drive anglers to try several locations per trip.

Anglers fishing sturgeon in the estuary should be especially watchful for barge traffic. It is unlawful, not to mention suicidal, to impede vessels that are restricted to the deep draft channel. To fish for sturgeon, anglers must purchase a sturgeon tag in addition to their regular fishing license, though a sturgeon tag is not required for anglers who purchase a daily fishing license.

Sea-run Cutthroat Trout. Sea-run cutthroat trout appear at the mouths of estuary tributaries from July to October, but most angling for them takes place further up the tributaries. Ideal tide, time and conditions are low water at dawn with cloud cover, light rain, and a breath of wind. Here as elsewhere throughout the Oregon coast, the sea-run population is extremely diminished.

Bottom-Fishing. The Columbia Estuary offers varied opportunities for bottom-fishing from both boat and bank. The jetties on both north and south sides of the bay provide access to bottom and surf fish such as greenling, rockfish, surfperch, and lingcod. Lingcod may weigh over 20 pounds, and the perch sometimes reach 3 pounds or better. Best catches occur during incoming tide, using cut herring, shrimp, or clam necks. The surf along the Clatsop beaches south of the estuary is very productive for perch.

Clams. The Clatsop beaches from the south jetty to Seaside offer the best razor clam digging in the state. There is a season, though, and catch rules, so check the regulations before you plan a trip. You'll also want to check the tide tables. Minus tides below one foot at low water are usually necessary for good clam digging in general, and spring minus tides are best for razor clams. Clamming in Oregon is free, and beaches throughout its 300-mile length are open to the public.

Tidal information is published daily in the newspapers, and tables for the year are available free at many tackle shops. The Long Beach Peninsula north of Ilwaco, Washington is also famous for razor clams, but Washington regulations are changeable, and a non-resident license is required.

Most boat anglers anchor to fish for summer steelhead in the lower Columbia.

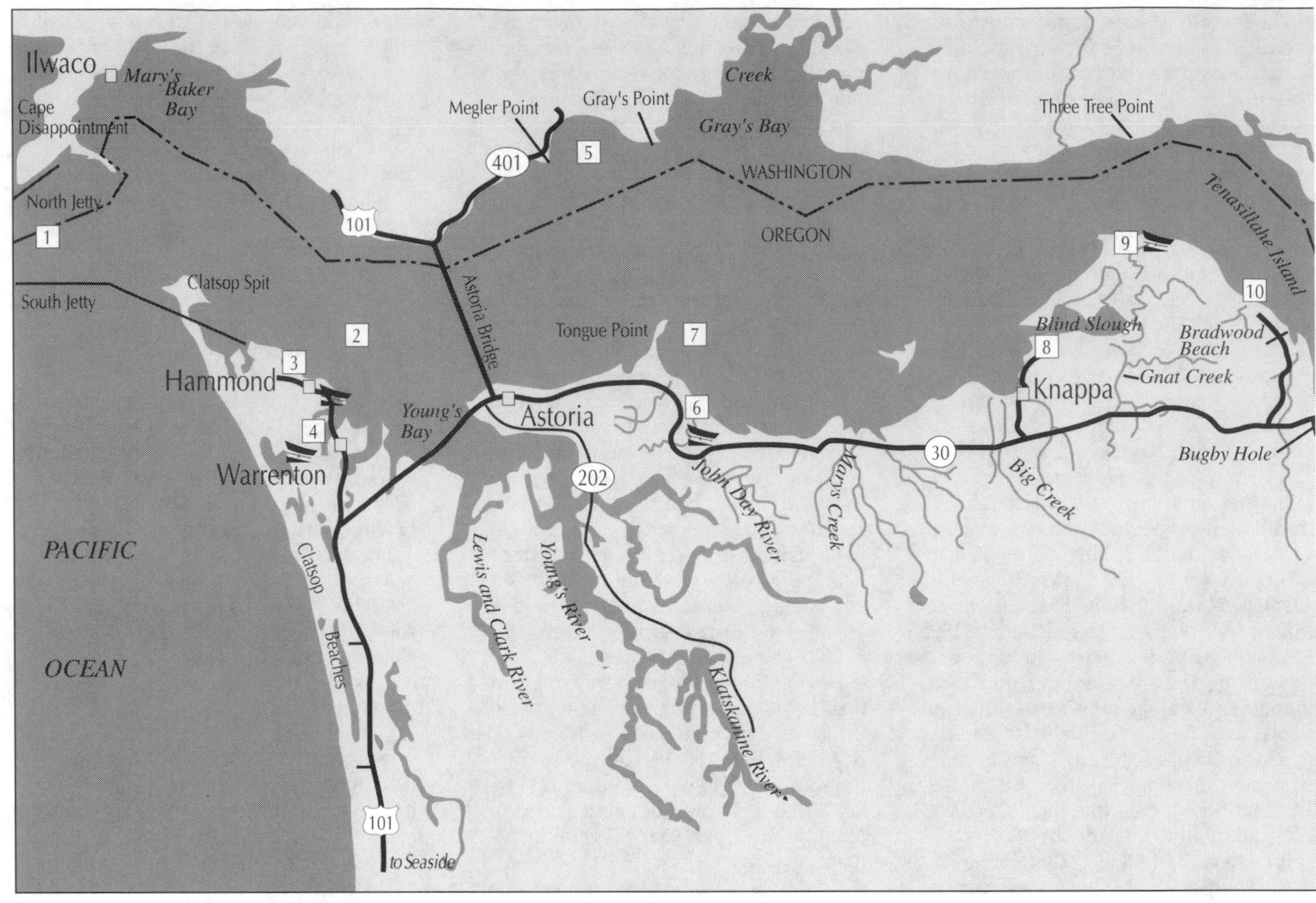

1 **BUOY 10** Active fall chinook & coho feeding area.

2 **DESDEMONA SANDS** - Fish troughs north and south of sandbar for early spring chinook when anchovies are running.

3 **HAMMOND BOAT RAMP** - Improved public ramp and moorage; major access to Buoy 10 fishery and to sturgeon through summer.

4 **WARRENTON BOAT RAMP** - Improved public ramp and moorage; accesses Buoy 10.

5 **MEGLER PT. TO GRAY'S BAY** - Best sturgeon fishing in estuary.

6 **JOHN DAY BOAT RAMP** - Improved public ramp is major access to sturgeon in estuary above bridge.

7 **TONGUE PT.** - Fish for sturgeon along islands just off shipping channel.

8 **BLIND SLOUGH** - Hot spot for yellow perch in Mar. & April when anchovies run.

9 **ALDRICH PT. BOAT RAMP** - Take Brownsmead turn-off to improved single ramp to access Clifton Channel and Blind Slough.

10 **CLIFTON CHANNEL** - Fish through March for spring chinook when water is clear and low.

11 **WESTPORT BOAT RAMP** - Improved single ramp accesses lower Clifton Channel.

12 **SEINING GROUNDS** - Fish wing jetties for salmon to just above Wallace Is.

13 **WALLACE TO CRIMMS IS.** - Spring chinook along Oregon shore; bank access at Jones Beach.

14 **BARLOW PT.** - Fish for coho jacks, sea-run, some sturgeon.

15 **LORD ISLAND** - Fish north side from boat and bank for spring chinook, summer steelhead.

16 **DIBBLEE BEACH** - Year-round bank plunking for chinook, steelhead; day-use only.

17 **RAINIER BEACH** - Plunk for summer steelhead from high dredged ash banks.

18 **COWLITZ RIVER** - fish the mouth for sturgeon, summer steelhead, fall chinook, coho, sea-run cutthroat.

19 **LAUREL BEACH** - Plunk for spring chinook, summer steelhead, fall chinook.

20 **PRESCOTT BEACH & SLOUGH** - Plunk from beach for summer steelhead, spring chinook; launch hand carried boat in slough west of beach entrance for bass & panfish; best near mouth & below bluff.

21 **KALAMA RIVER** - Fish the mouth for spring chinook, summer steelhead, fall chinook.

22 **TROJAN HOLE** - Deep hole (up to 100 ft.) for sturgeon; give way to commercial traffic.

23 **DEER ISLAND** - Boat fishery for spring chinook, summer steelhead, fall chinook.

24 **MARTIN BLUFF** - Sturgeon

25 **COLUMBIA CITY** - Fish for sturgeon, or the jetties for salmon;give way to commercial traffic.

26 **SHELL ISLAND** - Fish wing jetties for salmon, anchor or troll to mouth of Lewis River.

27 **ST. HELENS** - Improved public ramp accesses lower Multnomah Channel.

28 **SCAPPOOSE BAY MARINA** - Public ramp accesses lower Multnomah Channel; fish bay for crappie, bass, perch, carp; small bank fishing area.

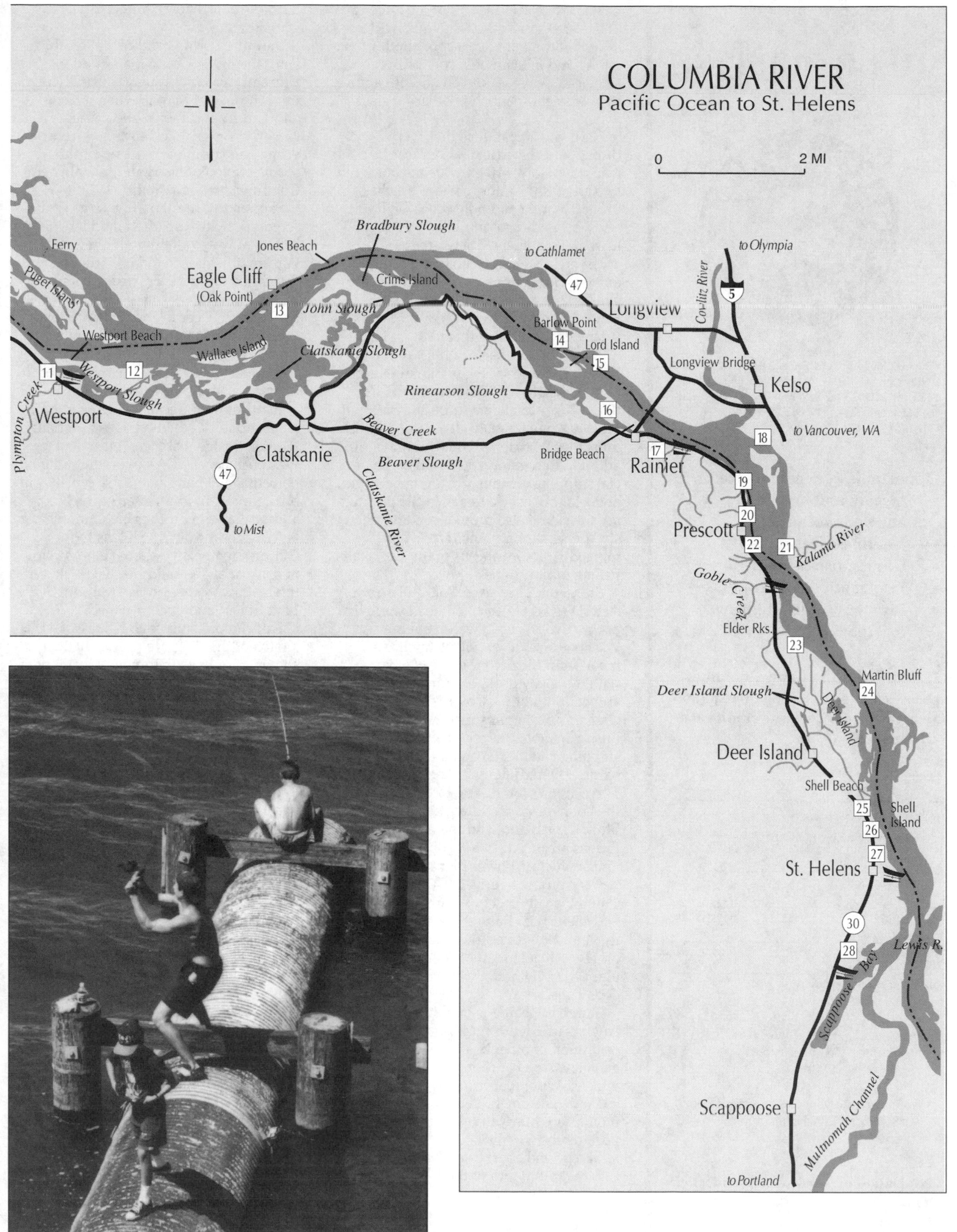
COLUMBIA RIVER
Pacific Ocean to St. Helens
N
0
2 MI
Ferry
Puget Island
Jones Beach
Bradbury Slough
Eagle Cliff
(Oak Point)
Crims Island
John Slough
13
Westport Beach
Wallace Island
Clatskanie Slough
11
12
Westport Slough
Plympton Creek
Westport
Clatskanie
Beaver Creek
Beaver Slough
Clatskanie River
47
to Mist
Rinearson Slough
to Cathlamet
47
Longview
Barlow Point
14
Lord Island
15
16
Bridge Beach
17
Rainier
Cowlitz River
to Olympia
5
Longview Bridge
Kelso
18
to Vancouver, WA
19
20
Prescott
22
21
Kalama River
Goble Creek
Elder Rks.
23
Martin Bluff
24
Deer Island Slough
Deer Island
Deer Island
Shell Beach
25
26
Shell Island
27
St. Helens
30
28
Scappoose Bay
Lewis R.
Multnomah Channel
Scappoose
to Portland

COLUMBIA RIVER (Astoria Bridge to St. Helens) A 73 mile long, mile-wide swath offering anglers opportunities for spring and fall chinook, coho, sturgeon, steelhead, walleye, and shad, with abundant bass and panfish in adjacent slack water.

Highway 30 parallels the river throughout this reach. Secondary roads lead down to the river, which is bordered by agricultural lands, narrow beaches, private marina and houseboat facilities, and a sprinkling of industry and small town development. There are many access points for both boat and bank anglers. Boat ramps, tackle, and bait are available at Astoria, Rainier, Goble, St. Helens, and other points along Hwy. 30. (Many gas stations sell bait).

Navigational charts of the Columbia River, produced by the National Oceanic and Atmospheric Administration (NOAA) are available through retail map outlets. An up-to-date chart (in hand) is a must for all boaters of the Columbia. In addition to helping you avoid commercial shipping channels, running aground, and losing your way back to the parking lot, the charts also provide a comprehensive presentation of the river's submerged structure and its many backwater fishing opportunities.

Sturgeon. The lower Columbia from Astoria to St. Helens includes extremely productive sturgeon water. On the Washington side, excellent catches are made from Megler Pt. to Gray's Bay. within the bay itself, off Barlow Pt., and at the mouth of the Cowlitz. On the Oregon side, anglers fish from Tongue Pt. upstream along the islands just off the shipping channel (keep an eye out for barges). Other popular spots include Three Tree Point, Bugby Hole, Oak Point, the Longview area, Elder Rock, Martins Bluff, Deer Island, and the entire St. Helens area. A deep hole opposite the Trojan Nuclear Power Plant at Goble can be very productive, as can the water off Columbia City just downstream from the St. Helens Boat Ramp. The boat ramp on the John Day River (the *other* John Day, off Hwy. 30 just west of Astoria) is a popular access point to the lower river sturgeon fishery.

Sturgeon fishing is mainly a boat show. Anglers use depth finders (and the concentration of other boats) to locate sturgeon lays, then anchor and fish the bottom. Most popular baits are herring, fresh anchovy and smelt. The most productive months are May through August, with peak catches in June and July. In 1993, the total reported sport catch between the estuary and mouth of the Willamette was 5,500.

Anglers are urged to avoid fishing for over-size sturgeon. To avoid hook-up, use lighter line and smaller bait and hooks. Barbless hooks are required for all sturgeon angling.

Salmon. Spring chinook generally enter the lower Columbia in mid-February, and the fishery is usually open until the end of March, when it closes to allow upriver chinook safe passage. Mid-season closures do occur in low-return years, and complete closures of the spring chinook fishery in the mainstem Columbia are a possibility.

Salmon use the shoreline to navigate, so good catches are often made in 10 to 20 feet of water along both Oregon and Washington shores and on either side of the various islands. Favorite spots include the waters just off Shell Island, Shell Beach, Deer Island, Sandy Island, Prescott Beach, Lord Island, Crim's Island, Westport Beach, Puget Island, Tenasillahe Island, and the mouths of the Lewis, Kalama, and Cowlitz rivers.

Bank angling (locally called *bar fishing*) is most popular at Shell, Prescott, Laurel, Rainier, Bridge, Dibblee, Jones, and Westport, beaches. An overwhelming percentage of bar anglers use No. 4 Spin-N-Glo lures. In low-water years, bank and boat angling for spring chinook can be very good from St. Helens to the Clifton Channel. Most boat anglers troll herring or anchor and use Kwikfish type lures. Prawns are also used productively, both trolled and anchor-fished.

Fall chinook and coho fisheries in this stretch of the river are primarily boat shows. Hog lines (regimental formations of anchored boats) form at the mouths of the Lewis, Kalama, and Cowlitz Rivers on the Washington side, with anglers preferring either Kwikfish type lures or some kind of spinner. The water just off Shell Island is productive, as is Barlow Point just below the Cowlitz mouth. A bar fishery for chinook jacks occurs at Prescott, Laurel, and Dibblee beaches in years of good returns.

In 1994, the fall chinook fishery in this stretch (from Tongue Point upstream) was closed to sport fishing in order to promote safe passage for the endangered race of Snake River fall chinook. The coho fishery remained open. All anglers are urged to use barbless hooks when fishing an area with mixed regulations.

Steelhead. Summer steelhead runs in the Columbia River during the last five years have been outstanding. In 1993, the estimated catch in the lower river was 9,800. Most boat anglers anchor to fish, using Kwikfish-type lures and rainbow blade spinners. Bank anglers seem to prefer the old standard, Spin-N-Glo.

Winter steelhead run up the lower Columbia from November through March. However, the fishery for them here is minor. Most anglers prefer to intercept them higher in the river system rather than tough it out on the blustery

Columbia. There is some winter fishing from the beaches, including Shell, Prescott, Laurel, Rainier, Bridge, Dibblee, Jones, and Westport,.

All non-finclipped steelhead must be released unharmed. Anglers are urged to use barbless hooks for all Columbia River steelhead fishing.

Sea-run Cutthroat Trout. The sea-run population on the lower Columbia is now at such a low ebb that there is no longer an identifiable fishery for them. For many years, as the wild population was diminishing, the fishery was inflated by huge releases of hatchery fish. Sea-run are no longer stocked in the Columbia, except for a single hatchery program associated with the Cowlitz in Washington.

Traditionally, sea-run were fished from July through November, with a peak in August through October. The majority were taken from the Washington shore, but good Oregon spots included Shell Beach, the mouth of Goble Creek, and Prescott, Diblee and Jones beaches. Over 50% of the Oregon catch was taken at Jones Beach. Anglers plunked worms and used the incidental catch of chub and squawfish, which they slice into strips for bait.

Shad. Shad migrate through the lower Columbia heading upriver from mid-May through June. Anglers tap into the run as it passes Shell Island on the Washington side near the Lewis River, and off the wing jetties near Goat Island on the Oregon side of the river. Wing jetty numbers 62, 70, and 72 are especially productive. To identify these jetties, check the Columbia River NOAA chart. Average annual catch here is 2,000.

Bass and Panfish. The Columbia River is home to an enormous population of bass and panfish, which inhabit its hundreds of sloughs and intertidal marshlands. Largemouth and smallmouth bass, white and black crappie, bluegill, yellow perch, channel cats, and brown bullhead are all richly represented.

COLUMBIA RIVER, MIDDLE (St. Helens to Bonneville Dam) This 58-mile stretch is the most heavily fished in the river and provides the greatest variety of angling.

About 20 miles upstream from St. Helens, the Columbia is separated from mainland Oregon by Sauvie Island and Multnomah Channel, a long slough that carries a significant flow of the Willamette River to its confluence with the Columbia at the downstream end of Sauvie Island. Anglers in the lower portion of this reach access the Columbia at the town of St. Helens by launching boats at various points along the Channel and motoring to the Columbia, and from beaches on the east shore of Sauvie Island. When giving directions in this reach, remember that the Columbia makes a hard right at the Willamette River; after a long westward flow, it turns north.

Upstream of Sauvie Island, the mid-section of this reach is accessed from Kelley Pt. Park in North Portland at the confluence of the Willamette and Columbia rivers; from boats launched into the Willamette at the north end of the St. Johns Bridge in North Portland; and from public and private marinas off Marine Drive, which follows the Columbia's south bank to Blue Lake Park east of Portland. Chinook Landing on the Columbia near Blue Lake has four large paved ramps and lots of parking.

Beyond Blue Lake, the river is followed closely by I-84 to Bonneville and beyond. Interstate exits allow access to the river at Sundial Beach, Dalton Pt., Dodson (5 miles south of Bonneville Dam), and at the dam.

Salmon. Angling for spring chinook in this stretch of the Columbia is limited to the area below the I-5 bridge that links Oregon and Washington at Portland/Vancouver. A closing date of March 31 further focuses angling effort on the early run, which is composed primarily of fish bound for the Willamette River. The primary bank fishery here takes place in March off the Sauvie Island beaches. Most popular are Reeder Beach (private, fee required), Willow Bar, and Walton Beach (at the end of pavement on Reeder Rd.). Spring boat anglers fish throughout the open area, as well as in Multnomah Channel and the Willamette.

The fall salmon season (chinook and coho) generally opens just before the fish arrive (August 1) and ends after they pass through. Best fishing is found at tributary mouths where the salmon congregate to enjoy the cooler water in August and September. On the Washington side, anglers fish the mouths of the Cowlitz, Kalama, and Lewis rivers. On the Oregon side, the best fishing is from the mouth of the Sandy River downstream as far as Government Island. Fall chinook are also fished in the vicinity of Hamilton Island near Bonneville Dam.

During the past ten years the estimated spring chinook catch on the lower Columbia has fluctuated between a low of 765 in 1985, and a high of 8,851 in 1990. The 1993 catch estimate was 1,865. The estimated fall chinook catch for the same time period fluctuated between 1,097 in 1983, and 17,540 in 1988-90. The 1993 catch was estimated to have been 4,206. The lower Columbia coho catch has fluctuated between an estimated 603 in 1993 and 84,914 in 1991.

In 1994, the fall chinook fishery in this stretch was closed to sport fishing in order to promote safe passage for the endangered Snake River fall chinook. The coho fishery remained open. It is always a good idea to call for an update on the regulations before planning any salmon fishing trip. Anglers are urged to use barbless hooks when fishing in areas where regulations are mixed.

Sturgeon. Sturgeon are fished the year around in this stretch, and catch numbers are quite high. The most productive angling in the Bonneville area occurs from February to March in conjunction with the arrival of smelt. Boat angling at Bonneville begins at the boating deadline and continues downstream about 12 miles to Rooster Rock. Other productive spots include Lady Island at Troutdale, near the I-5 bridge in NE Portland, at the mouth of the Willamette, and across from

Columbia river commercial catches are often available for sale along the highway.

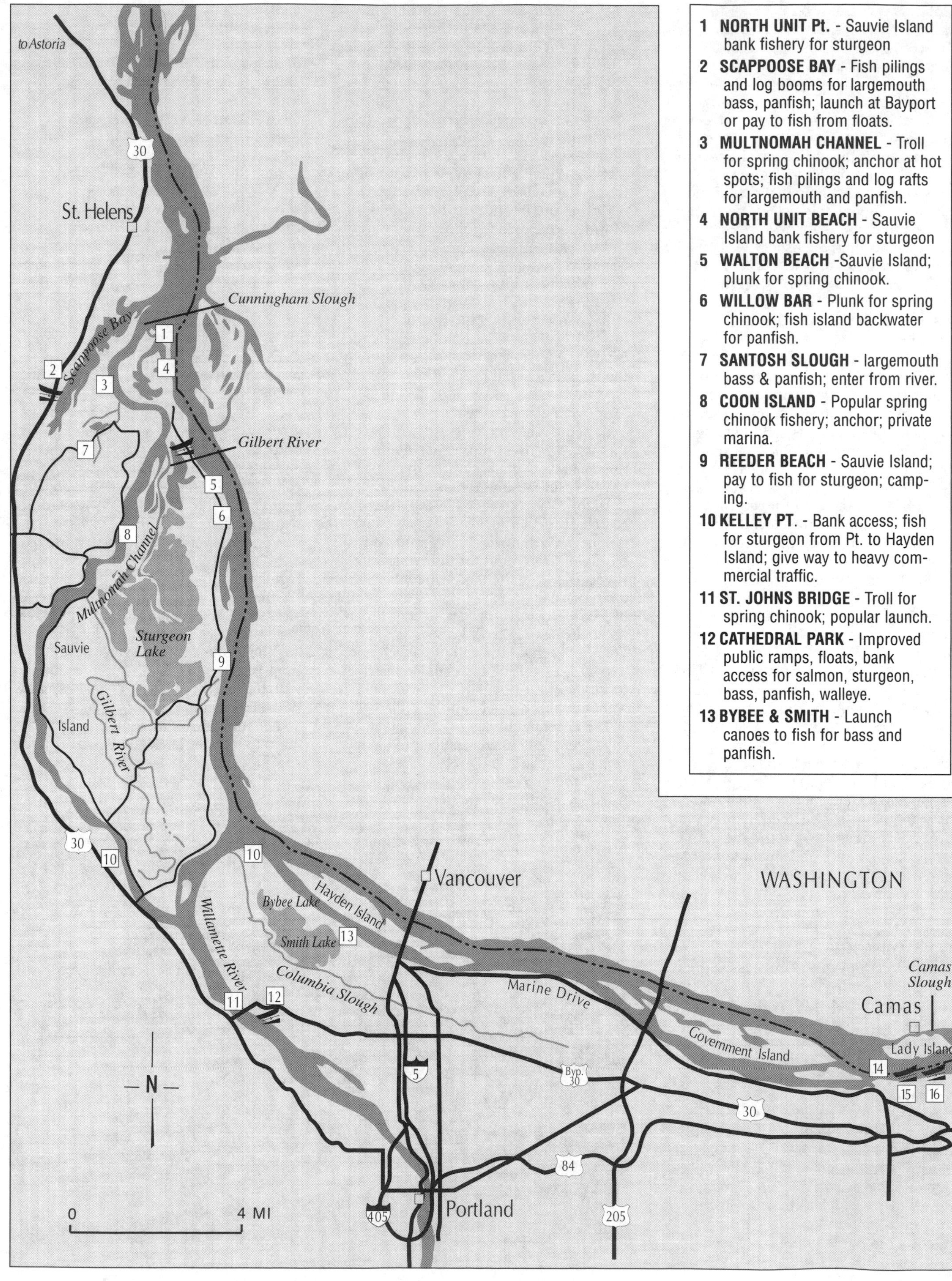
to Astoria
30
St. Helens
Cunningham Slough
Scappoose Bay
1
2
3
4
Gilbert River
5
6
7
8
Multnomah Channel
Sturgeon Lake
Sauvie
Island
Gilbert River
9
30
10
10
Vancouver
WASHINGTON
Bybee Lake
Hayden Island
Smith Lake
13
Willamette River
Columbia Slough
11
12
Marine Drive
Camas Slough
Camas
Government Island
Lady Island
14
15
16
N
5
Byp. 30
30
84
0
4 MI
405
Portland
205
1 NORTH UNIT Pt. - Sauvie Island bank fishery for sturgeon
2 SCAPPOOSE BAY - Fish pilings and log booms for largemouth bass, panfish; launch at Bayport or pay to fish from floats.
3 MULTNOMAH CHANNEL - Troll for spring chinook; anchor at hot spots; fish pilings and log rafts for largemouth and panfish.
4 NORTH UNIT BEACH - Sauvie Island bank fishery for sturgeon
5 WALTON BEACH -Sauvie Island; plunk for spring chinook.
6 WILLOW BAR - Plunk for spring chinook; fish island backwater for panfish.
7 SANTOSH SLOUGH - largemouth bass & panfish; enter from river.
8 COON ISLAND - Popular spring chinook fishery; anchor; private marina.
9 REEDER BEACH - Sauvie Island; pay to fish for sturgeon; camping.
10 KELLEY PT. - Bank access; fish for sturgeon from Pt. to Hayden Island; give way to heavy commercial traffic.
11 ST. JOHNS BRIDGE - Troll for spring chinook; popular launch.
12 CATHEDRAL PARK - Improved public ramps, floats, bank access for salmon, sturgeon, bass, panfish, walleye.
13 BYBEE & SMITH - Launch canoes to fish for bass and panfish.

14 GOVERNMENT ISLAND - Good fishing up to mouth of Sandy; anchor and spin-fish for coho and chinook jacks in fall; summer steelhead, fall chinook, coho, walleye.

15 CHINOOK LANDING

16 SUNDIAL BEACH - Improved private ramp popular access to summer steelhead, sturgeon, fall chinook.

17 WASHOUGAL REEF - Fish the rocks for walleye.

18 CAPE HORN - Poplar sturgeon hole (especially in winter) beneath rocky cliff; give way to barge traffic.

19 MULTNOMAH FALLS - Fish for walleye.

20 OUTLAW ISLAND - Fish around for sturgeon and walleye.

21 DODSON - Most popular sturgeon fishing on the river.

22 WARRENDALE - Plunk from beach for summer steelhead, fall chinook.

23 IVES ISLAND - Fish for walleye; anchor for shad on south side of island.

24 HAMILTON ISLAND - Fish both sides of channel for fall chinook, summer steelhead.

25 TANNER CREEK - Fish cautiously in heavy water from Bradford Is. to mouth of Tanner for sturgeon, walleye, summer steelhead, shad; bank access at mouth.

26 BRADFORD ISLAND - Fish lower end for sturgeon; only known shad bank fishery.

Sauvie Island on the Washington side of the river between navigation light numbers 15 and 23.

Bank angling for sturgeon is best below Bonneville Dam at Bradford Island and the mouth of Tanner Creek; and off Sauvie Island beaches, particularly Reeder Beach (privately owned, fee required to fish) and North Unit Beach at the very end of Reeder Rd. (public property, about 3 miles beyond the end of pavement).

Bank angling for sturgeon demands sturdy gear: a 9-l2 ft. rod, size 4/0+ reel, and 40-80 lb. line. Lighter gear is suitable for boat angling, except in the fast water just below Bonneville Dam. Lamprey eels and sand shrimp are the favored bait. They stay on the hook well and are the primary natural bait below the dam throughout most of the year. Smelt are effective in season. and anglers also use salmon, pickled herring, and shad strips.

Steelhead. The steelhead fishery on the lower Columbia is open from May 16 to March 31 from the I-5 Bridge downstream, and from June 16 to March 31 between Bonneville Dam and I-5. (The brief closure is to promote safe passage of upriver salmon.). Summer steelhead make up the bulk of the catch, which is understandable if you've ever been out in the Columbia Gorge in winter.

Steelheading is concentrated near the tributary mouths. On the Oregon side of the river, most fish are caught from Government Island to the mouth of the Sandy, near Warrendale, and at Hamilton Island and Tanner Creek near the dam.

In 1993 the estimated reported catch was 9,847 summer steelhead, and 100 winter fish (a record low). During the past 10 years, the estimated winter steelhead catch has been as high as 1,284 in 1987-88. The summer steelhead range during the past ten years has been a low

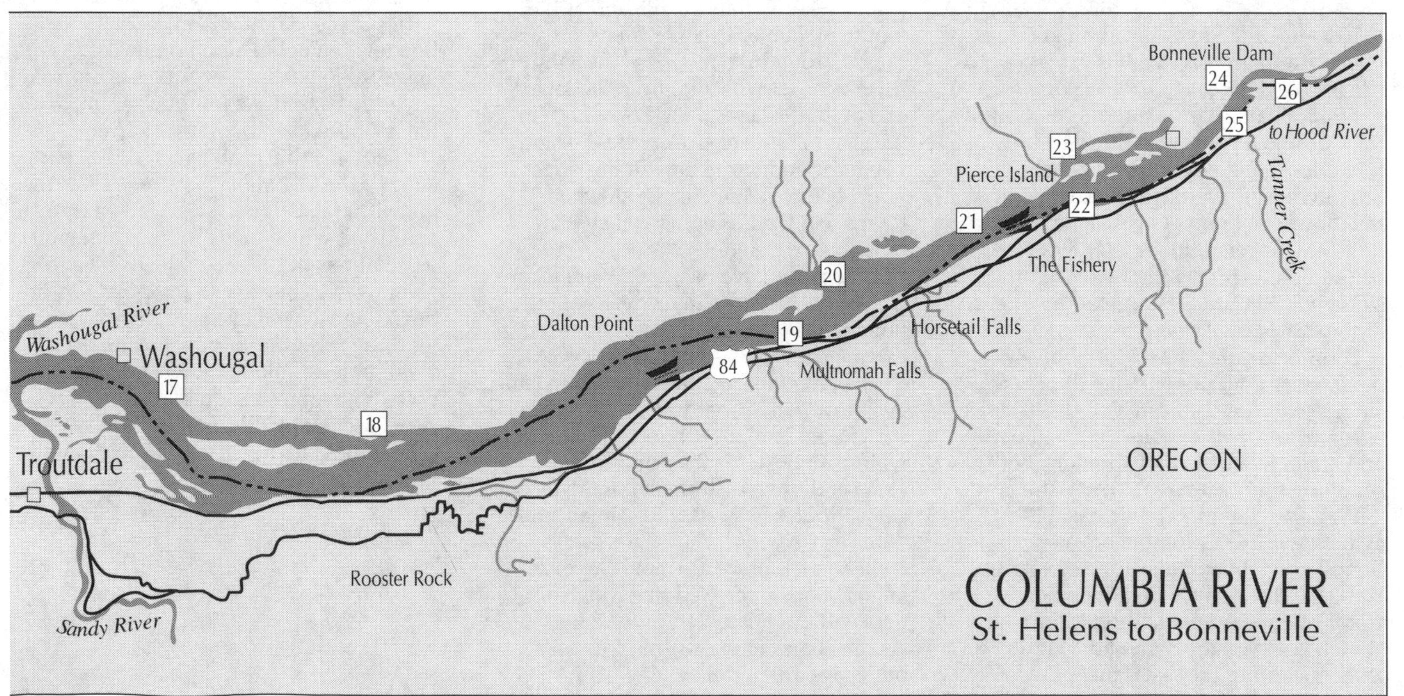

Above Bonneville, the Columbia is transformed into reservoirs.

of 1,654 in 1983-84, and a high of 7,344 in 1986-87.

Non-finclipped steelhead must be released unharmed. Anglers are urged to use barbless hooks.

Shad. Shad migrate into this section of the Columbia from May through early July. Most bank angling occurs at Bonneville, off Bradford Island, and at the mouth of Tanner Creek. Boat anglers favor the waters off Ives Island (3 miles below Bonneville on the Washington side), and in Camas Slough at the mouth of the Washougal River.

Estimated runs of 2 to 4 million shad have passed over Bonneville dam in a single year. A record catch of 111,400 was reported in 1993. Anglers use shad darts and small wobblers and spinners. Both plunking and casting are successful.

Walleye. Walleye are increasingly available in the Columbia below Bonneville. The popular time of year is late June through the end of September. Good catches are made throughout the stretch between the dam and Multnomah Falls, including the water just off Multnomah Falls, inside Ives and Pierce Island, near Outlaw Island, and at the mouth of Tanner Creek. Walleye are also caught around the mouth of the Sandy River near Lady Island, from the lower end of Reid Island to Big Eddy, and on the channel side of Government Island. The most popular fishery in this stretch is just below Bonneville Dam, where forage fish (and foraging walleye) are most concentrated.

Though walleye below Bonneville are generally smaller than upriver populations, some nice size fish are caught in this stretch. Serious anglers use NOAA river charts to locate the flats where walleye prowl, and sonar to study submerged structure where these ferocious predators wait in ambush for their natural prey (shad and squawfish smolts, and the occasional trout, steelhead, and salmon smolt).

In early season, when the water is colder and walleye are more sluggish, anglers fish Super Wedding Ring spinners with nightcrawlers and 1.5 oz. sinkers. Later in the season, 1 to 1.5 oz. bullet jigs are popular.

Anglers also troll plugs that resemble the natural forage fish, trolling fast in summer and fall when walleye are most active, and slower earlier in the season. Popular plugs include Power Dive Minnows and Hot Lips Express in blue, chartreuse, and silver (red and orange heads are popular in late summer and early fall when salmon eggs are around). Most walleye forage fish are between 5 and 8 inches, though smaller plugs may be more effective on brighter days and in shallower water.

Bass and Panfish. Most angling for bass and panfish in this section of the river occurs in Scappoose Bay, Santosh Slough, Multnomah Channel, and the lakes and sloughs of Sauvie Island, including Cunningham Lake, Cunningham Slough, the Gilbert River, Haldeman Pond, Big and Little McNary, Pete's Slough, Pope Lake, and Sturgeon Lake. Columbia Slough in Portland also contains bass and panfish. These waters are described in the Willamette section of this book.

Campgrounds. There are few camping opportunities in this increasingly urbanized area. There is a small campground at the northwest end of the reach, off Hwy. 30 near the Scappoose Airport. And there are camping facilities at The Fishery, at the opposite end of the reach (5 miles below Bonneville at Dodson). The Fishery also serves as an informal angler's information center for the salmon, sturgeon, walleye, and shad fisheries in the upstream portion of this section.

COLUMBIA RIVER, UPPER (Bonneville to Lake Wallula) Four dams obstruct the flow in this portion of the Columbia, transforming the mighty river into a string of reservoirs 147 miles long—Bonneville Pool behind Bonneville Dam, Lake Celilo behind The Dalles Dam, Lake Umatilla behind the John Day Dam, and Lake Wallula behind McNary Dam.

The dams drastically altered the character of the Columbia here, as well as the life within it. Salmon, steelhead, sturgeon, and trout, which made up the dominant populations of the pre-dam river, have given way to burgeoning populations of bass, panfish, walleye, and the warmwater forage fish that support them.

For a description of the fisheries in each of Oregon's Columbia River reservoirs, see Bonneville Pool and Celilo in the Central chapter, Umatilla and Wallula in the Northeast chapter.

WILLAMETTE ZONE

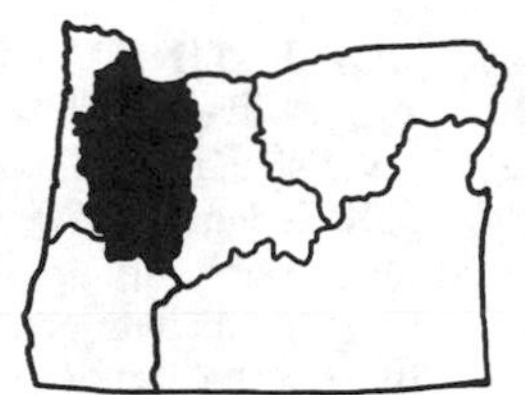

The Willamette Zone is all waters draining to the Columbia River between the city of St. Helens and Bonneville Dam, except for those portions of the Sandy River which are downstream from the Union Pacific Railroad line. Includes all waters on Sauvie Island except the Columbia River.

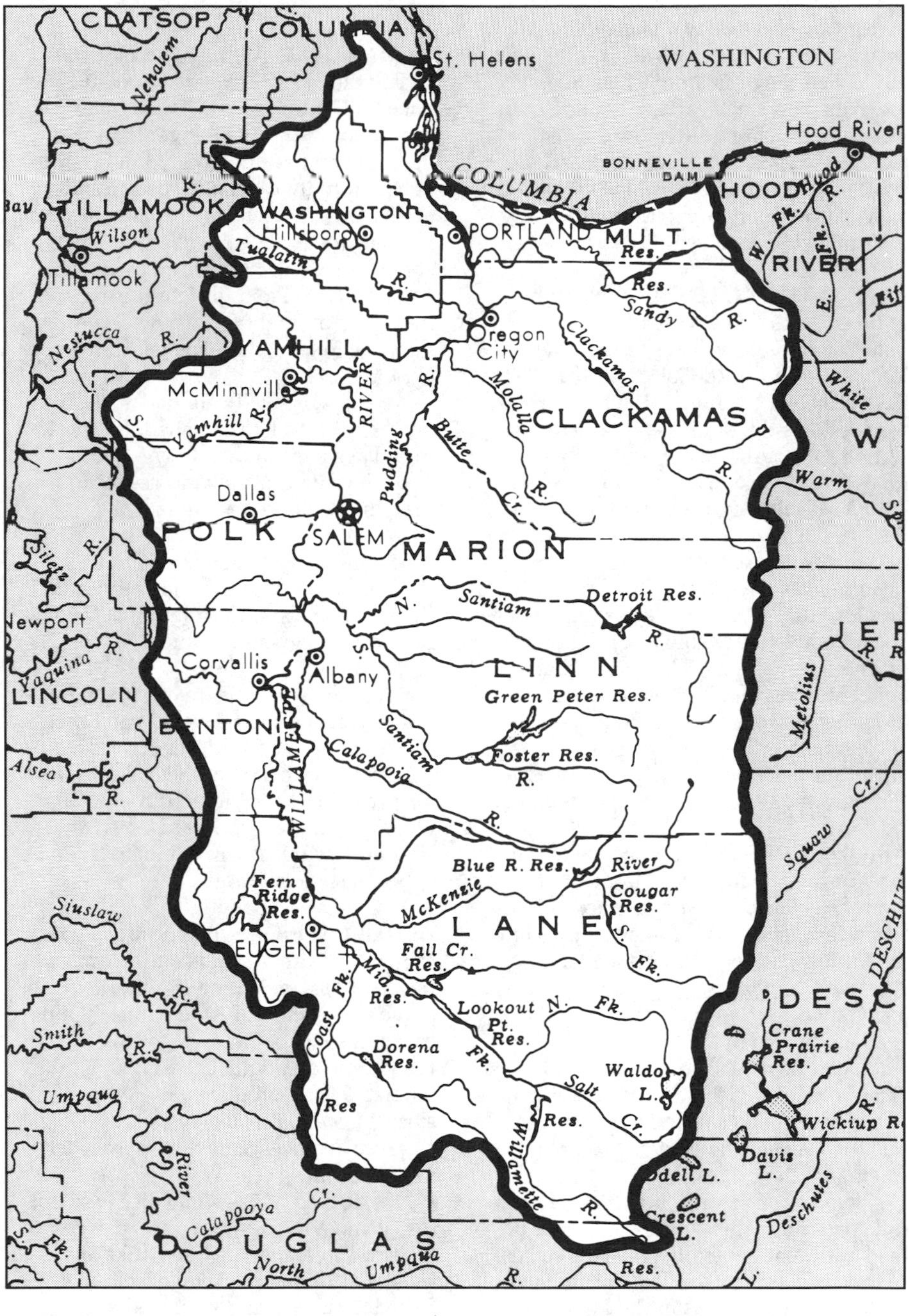

Four out of five Oregon anglers live within the Willamette Zone. This region is defined by the reach of the Willamette River and its tributaries, which drain the east slope of the Coast Range and the west slope of the Cascades for 150 miles north to south.

The Willamette Zone is blessed with an abundance of water, in the form of rain at lower elevations, and snow at higher. The result is plentiful and varied fishing.

In addition to the highly productive Willamette itself, the zone offers fine fishing for summer and winter steelhead and for spring and fall chinook salmon in the Clackamas, Luckiamute, McKenzie, Molalla, Salmon, and Sandy rivers and in the Middle, North, and South Santiams. Also yielding large numbers of chinook is Multnomah Channel, a bucolic detour for salmon between Columbia and Willamette rivers.

Trout are stocked in many rivers and creeks near roads, parks, and campgrounds, and in most high lakes of Mt. Hood and Willamette National Forests.

This zone boasts some fine wild trout fisheries as well, including the McKenzie River, Middle Santiam, South Fork Clackamas, and upper Willamette. Big Willamette cutthroat are also taken in Luckiamute, Marys, and Yamhill rivers.

Reservoirs on the Clackamas, Santiams, and Willamette offer additional fishing for trout and for some warmwater species. Detroit, Green Peter, Timothy, and Harriet are especially popular.

Bass and panfish are plentiful in the Willamette's many un-named sloughs, as well in the lower Long Tom River and in Hagg Lake, which yielded the state record smallmouth bass.

Aside from the rain, the Willamette Zone offers an idyllic climate. At lower elevations, temperatures rarely reach the freezing point in winter, or above 90ºF in summer. The air is cooled and freshened by marine breezes. By mid-June, most trails in the Cascades are cleared of snow, and eager brook trout rise to any offering. You can drive to many of the lakes south of Mt. Hood, or hike-in for solitude and alpine angling in Mt. Jefferson or Three Sisters wilderness areas. East of Eugene, the Taylor Burn and Mink lake basins offer additional high country fishing.

I-5 provides easy north-south access throughout the zone, and paved two-lane roads follow each river and many of the major tributaries. Some forest roads are also paved, though most are gravel (and some are ungraded).

Campgrounds are abundant in the national forests. Accomodations are available in the I-5 corridor, but are somewhat sparse along the river roads and near lakes and reservoirs.

ABERNETHY CREEK A very accessible wild cutthroat stream with small runs of coho and steelhead. Abernethy joins the Willamette River on the east side of Oregon City. About 12 miles long, it flows from the Highland Butte area, SE of Oregon City. In Oregon City the creek is crossed by several bridges right in town and is followed and crossed by county roads throughout its mid-section. The upper waters are reached from Hwy. 213 by turning east through Beaver Creek.

Abernethy is not stocked, and it is usually fished down in a month or two. A few coho and steelhead are hooked each year. Non-finclipped steelhead must be released unharmed. Except for road right-of-ways and bridges, the creek flows through private land, so ask permission before you fish.

ABERNETHY LAKES A couple of hike-in brook trout lakes with a lot of little fish. The trail to the lakes is about a mile long. Take Forest Rd. 5899 NW from West Bay, at the west end of Odell Lake. This road follows the railroad track to a derail station called Abernethy, a little over 2 miles from Odell. Follow Deer Creek Trail 3670 south and watch for the sign to the lakes. The trail is well blazed, and the upper lake is just NW of the lower.

Both lakes have naturally reproducing brook trout. The lower lake covers about 2 acres and is fairly shallow. It loses fish during hard winters. The upper lake is about 16 acres and 20 feet deep. Its brookies run to 13 inches. Both lakes are at elevation 4,950 ft. You can camp at the lakes, but there are no facilities. There are campgrounds and supplies at Odell Lake.

ABIQUA CREEK A very nice wild cutthroat trout stream with a fair run of wild winter steelhead. The stream heads in the Cascades east of Silverton and flows into the Pudding River. It is crossed by Hwy. 213 about 24 miles south of Oregon City, just 2 miles north of Silverton. Its mouth is about 3 miles to the west.

Abiqua flows about 30 miles, and gets pretty low in the upper stretch in summer. A good road follows the stream east for 9 miles, then leaves the stream, staying on the ridges.

Abiqua opens at the end of May to protect spawning wild winter steelhead. Its wild cutthroat generally run 6-12 inches. Abiqua is no longer stocked with rainbow.

Steelheading here is limited to catch and release, with best fishing from February through April. The creek is open to steelhead fishing up to the Silverton Water Supply Dam. It is closed to all salmon angling.

Abiqua flows through private land throughout its run, with public access at road crossings only.

ADAIR POND A 6-acre pond south of Adair Village on Hwy. 99W chock full of good size bluegill, bass, and channel catfish. Redear sunfish are also present, but they rarely bite. Bass to 8 pounds are taken, and channel cats are currently in the 4 pound range. The pond is immediately behind the ODF&W regional office. Park in the ODF&W parking lot. Stop by the office if you have any questions. Enthusiastically recommended for small fry.

AERIAL LAKE A hike-in brook trout lake in the Horse Lake area west of Elk Lake off Century Drive. The trailhead is across from Elk Lake Ranger Station on the north end of Elk Lake, 35 miles from Bend. From the Elk Lake Forest Service Station on the west shore, follow the trail west to Horse Lakes. At the trail junction about 4 miles in, turn south. In less than 1/4 mile two side trails join the main trail. Take the right fork to Aeriel, less than one mile further. The left trail leads to Sunset Lake.

Aerial Lake is only about 3 acres, but fairly deep and lightly fished. Its brook trout have been known to show some size. The lake is usually accessible in July. Bring mosquito repellent.

AGENCY CREEK A fair size trout stream, tributary to the South Yamhill River. It flows into the Yamhill at Grande Ronde Agency, about 3 miles NW of Valley Junction on Hwy. l8. A BLM road parallels the creek upstream from Grande Ronde Agency and provides good access. It can also be reached from Hwy. 22.

Agency is stocked with legal rainbow in spring and has wild cutthroat to 10 inches. It's a good early-season stream but gets low quickly in summer. It can be fished at several bridges.

ALDER CREEK A wild cutthroat and rainbow stream. Alder is a tributary of the Sandy River, joining it from the south at the community of Alder Creek, 9 miles east of the city of Sandy. It is crossed by Hwy. 26 at its mouth. Only about 5 miles long, it doesn't produce very long in the spring. Several dirt roads from the Cherryville area access the upper reaches of the stream.

Not stocked, it has some nice wild cutthroat and a few rainbow. The fish run 6-l0 inches, averaging 8. The banks are brushy, with bait producing best. It is closed to salmon and steelhead angling.

ALFORJA LAKE A consistent producer of fair size brook trout in the headwaters of the North Santiam near Duffy Butte, Mt. Jefferson Wilderness. A 4-acre lake, not very well known, it is off the trail and lightly fished. See Duffy Lake for directions into the basin. Alforja is about 3/4 mile SW of Duffy. Cincha Lake is north of Alforja.

The naturally reproducing brook trout back here run to 13 inches and will usually hit anything early in season. In late summer and fall, flies work best in morning and evening. The lake is brushy, but not hard to fish.

ALICE LAKE This is a tiny lake, about an acre, right on Trail 3422, 1 1/2 miles north of Duffy Lake just south of Red Butte. See Duffy Lake for directions. There are usually lots of fair size brook trout here in early season, but fishing tapers off in fall because the lake's so small. There are good campsites all along this part of the trail.

AMOS AND ANDY LAKES Two small high lakes in the southeast corner of the Willamette National Forest, a bushwhack from Indigo Lake. See Indigo Lake for directions. From Indigo, hike cross country 1 1/4 miles NE, skirting a butte which projects NW from Sawtooth Mt. and divides the Indigo basin from the basin holding Amos and Andy. Hold your elevation, as Amos and Andy are just slightly higher than Indigo.

Is it worth it? The lakes are stocked by air from time to time, but at 6,000 ft. and only 10 ft. deep, they frequently winterkill. On the other hand, a lot of 6-10 inch brook trout might just be hungrily waiting for you.

ANN LAKE A good brook trout lake of about 20 acres just north of Marion Lake. See Marion Lake for road and trail directions. Ann is on the Marion Lake Trail about one mile in, on the left.

It provides excellent angling in early season for eastern brook trout to 15 inches. A good fly lake, it usually holds up well throughout the season, though it may go slack in late summer. There's a lot of vegetation around the shore, so a float tube would very handy. There are no improved campsites. It is usually accessible by late May.

AVERILL LAKE A good 11.5 acre brook trout lake in the western portion of the Olallie Lakes group about 95 miles SE of Portland. Quickest route is by trail from the west.

Follow the Breitenbush River Rd., Forest Rd. 46, from Detroit Reservoir to the Mt. Hood National Forest boundary. Turn east onto the Breitenbush Lake Rd., Forest Rd. 42, then go left at the fork onto Forest Rd. 380 about 1/2 mile further. About .1/4 mile from where 380 passes under the power transmission lines, pick up Trail 719, which leads east about 1 1/2 miles to the lake. The trail first passes Red Lake. Averill can also be reached by way of trails leading into the basin from Olallie Lake on the east.

Averill is an excellent fly-fishing lake, but other methods will work. Brook trout here run 6-12 inches. There are fair unimproved campsites at the lake. It's usually not accessible until late June. Be prepared for mosquitoes.

BAKER CREEK A small trout stream, about 9 miles long, located just north of McMinnville. It flows into the North Yamhill River from the west. Baker Creek is crossed just above its mouth by the paved Carlton-McMinnville Rd. Several good roads follow and cross the creek. These are reached by going west from the north end of McMinnville.

Baker contains wild cutthroat to 12 inches and is not stocked. It is fished heavily in early season and doesn't hold up long. Rainbow Lake Education Center, an educational facility operated by ODF&W, is on the creek. An old water supply dam currently blocks fish passage to the upper stream. Above the dam, the creek flows through BLM land, and hiking is permitted.

BAYS LAKE A 10-acre brook trout lake in the picturesque and popular Jefferson Park of the Mt. Jefferson Wilderness. This natural alpine parkland of meadow and wooded hummocks is on a saddle dominated by Mt. Jefferson to the south.

There are several approaches to Jefferson Park, all at least a 5 mile hike. One approach is from the north by way of the Pacific Crest Trail from Breitenbush Lake. It's about a 4-hour hike with fair elevation gain, but the view is great all the way in. Another popular approach is from the west by a trail which follows Woodpecker Ridge to the PCT, and the PCT north to the Park.

Take North Santiam Hwy. 22 to Pamelia Creek Rd. 2246, about 7 miles south of Idanha. At the first fork, bear left onto Forest Rd. 040 and follow it about 4 miles to its end. A trail leads east 1 1/2 miles to the Pacific Crest Trail. Follow the PCT north to Bays.

Bays Lake is quite deep and easy to fish, with a rocky shoreline and many arms or bays. It offers good fly angling, particularly along the western shore. The lake is stocked by air with brook trout. This area is high, and the fish don't put on much growth, but by August they come readily enough. Scout Lake to the east holds some good size brook trout, but you'll work harder for them.

Unfortunately, the beauty and accessibility of this area has lead to heavy use, especially on weekends. Camping permits are required. This is a wilderness area, and campers are urged to use no-trace methods and to camp well back from the water in order to assist in the regeneration of fragile plant life.

Benson Lake is fished for stocked trout, panfish, and largemouth bass.

BEAR CREEK (Lane Co.) A small wild cutthroat stream, about 8 miles long, joining the Long Tom River about 3 miles west of Junction City at Hwy. 99. It flows from the west and is followed and crossed by Hwy. 360 as well as by several county roads. Bear Creek is not stocked but has some fair spring angling. It is usually fished down by June. It is mostly fished by local anglers, and there is not much public access.

BEAR LAKE (Mt. Hood National Forest) A nice little 2-acre hike-in brook trout lake in the Mt. Hood Forest SW of Hood River. The lake is about 2 miles NE of Rainy Lake.

From the community of Dee, drive north about 2 miles towards Punchbowl Falls, and pick up Forest Rd. 2820, which twists and winds its way west. The trailhead is on the north side of the road about 2 miles beyond the intersection of Forest Rd. 2821. If you get to Rainy Lake, the trail's a mile behind you. The lake is on a spur trail off the Defiance Mt. Trail 413. The trailhead described here leads north less than 1/4 mile to Trail 413, which you take to the east. A bit over 1/4 mile brings you to the Bear Lake Trail, cutting off to the north and leading 1/2 mile to the lake.

Though small, Bear Lake is fairly deep and hardly ever winterkills. At elevation 3,800 ft., it is stocked by air with fingerling brook trout. The catch ranges in size from 8-12 inches. The road in usually opens by late June.

BEAR LAKE (Willamette National Forest) Across the ridge from Firecamp Lakes, one mile south of Slideout. See Slideout Lake for directions. Bear covers 9 acres and is 24 ft. deep. It is stocked every other year with brook trout. You might need orienteering skills to find it.

BENSON LAKE (Lane Co.) A nice brook trout lake of about 25 acres, 1 1/2 miles by trail from Scott Lake on McKenzie Pass Hwy. 242. The McKenzie Hwy. is usually the last Cascade crossing to open each spring. The trailhead is at the Scott Lake campground, and the trail leads NW to Benson Lake then on to Tenas Lake and Mt. Scott.

There's a mixed bag of trout here, with some to 18 inches. Best fishing is in early season as soon as the road is open. There are no improved campsites at the lake, but there are campgrounds at Scott Lake and along the highway close by.

This is a great introductory hike-in lake for kids. The trail is easy, the scenery is pretty, and the fish are plentiful. Recommended for small fry.

BENSON LAKE (Multnomah Co.) A 23-acre lake in Benson State Park, adjacent to the Columbia River on the south side of I-84 just before Multnomah Falls. The lake has populations of brown bullhead, white crappie, pumpkinseed sunfish, and largemouth bass. It is stocked from April through June with catchable rainbow.

There is no boat ramp, but anglers can hand launch rafts and car-tops. The banks are quite flat, offering unimproved access for less-abled anglers. The lake itself is open for year around fishing, but the park closes after Labor Day. Anglers can still park on the access road and hike in. Wheelchair Accessible (unimproved).

BERLEY LAKES Two small trout lakes north of the Santiam Hwy. near the summit. Take the Pacific Crest Trail north from Santiam Pass at Hwy. 20, and hike 1 1/2 miles north to the junction of Trail 3491, which ultimately leads to Duffy Lake. Follow 3491 two miles north to Lower Berley Lake. Upper Berley is off the trail about 1/8 mile NW of Lower.

The lakes are both about 7 acres. They are air stocked with either cutthroat or brook trout every other year. Any method will take fish here. There are no improved campsites at the lakes.

BETH LAKE An interesting lake to find and to fish. It's located near the upper Collawash River in the Bull of the Woods area, some 50 miles SE of Portland. Five acres and 35 ft. deep, it sits at an elevation of 4,450 ft.

Follow the Clackamas River Hwy. 224 to Ripplebrook Ranger Station, then take Forest Rd. 63 south along the Collawash River. About 10 miles south, in the Toms Meadow area, take Forest Rd. 6340 SW to where Forest Rd. 6341 forks off to the right. Take 6341 about 5 miles south, and where the road crosses Pansy Creek and switches back to the north, you'll hit Trail 551. In about 1/2 mile, Trail 549 intersects from the left (east). Follow 549 to its junction with 550, then cross over 550 and head up the ridge. Keep bearing NE, and you'll hit a small stream which enters the lake.

There are wild brook trout to 13 inches here, and the lake is easy to fish from the bank. Caddis, coachman, or bucktail will take fish if you sink them. There's one good campsite on the NW side.

BETHANY LAKE A fair size lake with a warm water fishery just west of Portland at the community of Bethany. Turn north off Hwy. 26 just before the Cornelius Road junction, or take Cornelius Road to West Union, then go east to Bethany.

The lake is about 500 ft. wide and 1/2 mile long. It features bluegill, largemouth bass, and large brown bullhead. The bass grow to respectable size, with some to five pounds. There has been a charge for access at times. Check locally for details.

Good-size largemouth bass are taken at Blue Lake near Troutdale.

BETTY LAKE A 40-acre rainbow lake high in the Cascades that is lightly fished and offers very good angling. The lake is at an elevation of 5,500 ft. one mile SE of the south end of Waldo Lake. Fish to 23 inches are available here.

Take Hwy. 58 from Oakridge about 20 miles SE to Waldo Lake Rd. 5897. Five miles NE on this road there is a sign for the Betty Lake Trail 3664 on the west side. It's an easy 1/2 mile hike to the lake.

The rainbow average 10 inches. A float tube or raft is useful here. Bait or lures will work well anytime, and flies will take large fish early in the day and near dusk. There are no improved campsites. Remember the slogan, "Waldo Lake, Famous Mosquitoes." There are several other small lakes within a mile of the Betty, and many hold fish.

BIG CLIFF RESERVOIR About 150 acres on the North Santiam River, built about the same time as Detroit Reservoir. The dam is located several miles below Detroit Dam.

Eclipsed by the popularity of Detroit, Big Cliff is lightly fished but offers good catches of rainbow and very large whitefish (up to 33 inches). There is a poor boat ramp near the Detroit Reservoir Dam. Keep in mind that this is a re-regulation reservoir, subject to extreme and rapid water level fluctuation (up to 6 ft.). After launching a boat, be careful to park well away from the shore, or you may be inundated.

Nearest campgrounds are upriver off Hwy. 22.

BIG LAKE Over 225 acres, south of Santiam Hwy. 20 near the summit of the Cascades. It is about 8 miles SE of the junction of North and South Santiam highways. The lake is 4 miles down Forest Rd. 2690, which leads south from Hwy. 20 near the Santiam Lodge. Continue south past Hoodo Ski Bowl.

Speed boaters and water-skiers offer fisher folk plenty of competition here. But Big Lake has some large brook trout, as well as stocked kokanee, rainbow, and cutthroat. The lake can get rough in the afternoon, so plan to fish early or late.

There are several nice campgrounds on the lake, and good boat ramps. Open all year, it is a available for ice fishing.

BIG SLIDE LAKE, UPPER A pretty little one-acre hike-in with brook trout in the headwaters of the Collawash River. Located in the Bull of the Woods area, it is at least a 3-mile hike from the nearest road. Several trails will get you there. The lakes are less than 1/2 mile NE of the Bull of the Woods Lookout.

From Estacada drive up the Clackamas River on Hwy. 224 to Ripplebrook Ranger Station, then take Forest Rd. 63 south along the Collawash River. About 10 miles south, in the Toms Meadow area, take Forest Rd. 6340 SW several miles to Trailhead 550 near the end of the road. Three miles on this trail south will take you to Bull of the Woods Lookout. Big Slide Lake is 1/2 mile NE on Trail 555. The lake is at an elevation of 4,300 ft.

Stocked by air (in odd number years), the brook trout here average 9 inches with a range from 6-11. It does occasionally winterkill. It's easy to fish, and any method works when they're hitting. Fly angling is good late in the season in the evening. It is surrounded by tall timber with some talus slopes. There are three nice campsites here. Supplies are available at Estacada or at Detroit if you come in from the south. Other lakes nearby are stocked with brook trout. See Welcome, Pansy, and Lenore.

BINGHAM LAKE (Linn Co.) A small cutthroat lake in the Mt. Jefferson Wilderness Area 1/2 mile west of the Pacific Crest Trail in the Bingham Basin, south of Mt. Jefferson. It is about a 6-mile hike from Marion Lake and about 5 miles south from Pamelia. There is no blazed trail. The lake feeds Minto Creek, a tributary of the North Santiam River.

Bingham is about 4 acres and has cutthroat that exceed 15 inches. It is lightly fished (rarely found?) and can provide good fly-fishing for the pathfinding angler.

BINGO LAKE A shallow lake 1/2 mile west of the southern tip of Waldo Lake at the head of Black Creek, reached best by boat from Shadow Bay Campground on Waldo. It can also be approached by trails leading from Waldo Lake, and from the north from Black Creek or Salmon Creek roads out of Oakridge.

About 4 acres and shallow, it frequently winterkills. Nevertheless, it is stocked periodically with cutthroat. Bongo Lake is about a 3/4-mile bushwhack NW. Bongo covers 9 acres and has naturally reproducing brook trout. This here's 'skeeter country in late spring to early summer, so be prepared.

BIRTHDAY LAKE A small hike-in brook trout lake 3 miles south of Waldo in the Island Lakes Basin. See Island Lakes for the best trail route to the basin. Birthday Lake is less than 1/2 mile south of Lower Island Lake, reached by Trail 3674.

Birthday is about 3 acres, just north of the trail. Its brook trout are small, from 6-10 inches, but usually hit well in spring and fall. Fly angling here is usually good. An occasional lunker is taken. There are natural campsites here, with good campgrounds at Gold and Waldo lakes. The roads up are usually accessible by late June. Other lakes within 1/2 mile of Birthday are stocked. See Verde, Island Lakes, and Lorin Lake.

BLAIR LAKE A 35-acre trout lake in the Willamette National Forest at the head of Salmon Creek, NE of Oakridge on Hwy. 58. From Oakridge, take the Salmon Creek Rd., Forest Rd. 24 (look for the salmon hatchery signs) about 9 miles NE to the signed Blair Lake turnoff. Follow Forest Rd. 1934 north about 8 miles to the lake.

The naturally reproducing brook trout at Blair run 6-16 inches, averaging 10 inches, and there are plenty of them. There are several nice campsites near the lake outlet a very short hike from the road. Evening fly angling is generally excellent, with mosquitoes, blue uprights, caddis and gray hackles good bets. Motorboats are prohibited.

About 1 1/2 miles east is Devil's Lake, which has no trail access. It is only about 5 acres but has nice brook trout to 14 inches.

The Blair Lake Rd. takes you past the small but pleasant Wall Creek Warm Springs, suitable for a soak on a summer day. The springs are shown on the Forest Service map and are located about 1/4 mile in on a trail which follows Wall Creek. The trailhead is on the first hairpin turn, about 1/2 mile from the junction of Forest Rd. 1934 with the Salmon Creek Rd. There are good camps along the Salmon Creek Rd.

BLOWOUT CREEK A good trout stream in the North Santiam area of Willamette National Forest. Take Hwy. 22 to Forest Rd. 10, about 3 miles south of the community of Detroit. Forest Rd. 10 crosses the North Fork of the Santiam River and follows the south shore of the reservoir to Blowout Creek, then follows the creek to its headwaters.

Blowout has a population of wild rainbow and cutthroat. Bait and spinner work best in early season, and fly angling is productive when the water warms in late spring. There are no camps on the upper stream, but there is a good campground at Stahlman Point on Detroit Reservoir, and there are other camps on the north shore along Hwy. 22.

BLUE LAKE (Lane Co.) A good secluded brook trout lake on the western border of the Diamond Peak Wilderness Area, Willamette National Forest. It is a good introductory hike-in experience for youngsters.

From Oakridge, drive south on Hwy. 58 a mile or so to the Hills Creek Reservoir turn-off. Follow Forest Rd. 21 around the west shore of the reservoir and up the upper Middle Fork of the Willamette, about 26 miles (from the dam) to where Forest Rd. 2145 forks NE. Take 2145 about 5 miles to a fork where Forest Rd. 2149 turns east then south. Follow 2149 about 4 miles to the Blue Lake Trailhead. It's an easy 1/2 mile hike east to the lake on a well marked trail. The roads usually open in late June.

Blue Lake covers 20 acres and is 33 ft. deep. It has naturally reproducing brook trout that run 6-16 inches, with a few larger taken at times. The average size is 10-12 inches. Bait and lures are best during the day, and fly angling is effective in early morning and evening. A good lake for a float tube. Don't forget the mosquito repellent.

BLUE LAKE (Linn Co.) A 12-acre brook trout lake in the Eight Lakes Basin of the Mt. Jefferson Wilderness. Blue Lake is 1/4 mile NE of Jorn Lake in the northern part of the basin, south of Marion Lake.

Blue Lake is over 40 ft. deep, and though its fish tend to be short, they are usually deep bodied. They average 6-11 inches, with most on the small side. Any method will take fish. Several other lakes are close by, and all are fishable. See Jorn, Bowerman, Teto and Chiquito.

BLUE LAKE (Multnomah Co., Mt. Hood National Forest) About 50 acres at the head of the Bull Run River, in Portland's water supply reserve. Closed to all recreational use.

BLUE LAKE (Multnomah Co. near Troutdale) A 62-acre lake east of Portland, 3 miles west of Troutdale. The lake is north of Hwy. 30 and 1/2 mile south of the Columbia River. A paved road leads to the north end, where there is a county park. The rest of the lakeshore is privately owned.

Blue Lake has good size largemouth bass that are taken on bait and lures, and angling for crappie, green sunfish, and bluegill can be very good.

The park is large and has plentiful picnic facilities, but no camping. Rental boats are available in summer, with private boats allowed only in winter and restricted to no larger than 14 ft. in length (17 ft. for canoes), and maximum 3 hp motors. Facilities include a wheelchair accessible fishing dock.

BLUE RIVER A good size tributary of the McKenzie River in the Willamette National Forest, flowing into Blue River Reservoir about 43 miles east of Eugene off Hwy. 126. A good road, Forest Rd. 15, leaves the highway about 5 miles east of the community of Blue River and follows the middle and upper stream more than 10 miles.

The main catch consists of stocked rainbow trout in the first 5 miles above the reservoir, although wild cutthroat and rainbow are present in small numbers. The catch rate for bank angling is on a par with the main McKenzie. The fish usually run 8-12 inches, but a few larger are taken. Bait is best in early season. Later there is fair fly angling.

Camping is available at Blue River Reservoir, and there are numerous camps near McKenzie Bridge on the highway to the east.

BLUE RIVER RESERVOIR A 935-acre flood control lake on a major tributary of the McKenzie River, offering fair to good angling for stocked rainbow. Non-finclipped trout must be released unharmed.

Blue River is located north of Hwy. 126, about 45 miles east of Eugene in the heart of the McKenzie Recreational Area. The dam is about 2 miles above the mouth of Blue River.

By mid-August the reservoir is drawn way down, driving the fish to sulk in the depths and limiting boat ramp accessibility. (Few things are uglier than a drawn down reservoir). There is a ramp and campground at the NE end of the lake. To get there, follow Hwy. 126 east past Blue River Ranger Station, about 3 miles to the Forest Rd. 15 cut-off on the left.

BLUEGILL LAKE A lightly fished 7-acre bass and panfish pond on the eastern edge of Salem. It is located in Cascade Park, across the creek from Walter Wirth Lake, which is also in the park. The lake is just west of I-5, between the airport road and Turner Rd.

It has good populations of crappie and bluegill, and a fair number of largemouth bass and carp. Bait fishing is the most popular method.

BOND BUTTE POND A 35-acre pond south of Albany. The lake is east of I-5 at Bond Butte Overpass, 15 miles south of town. It contains channel cats, white crappie, and a few largemouth bass.

BONGO LAKE A 9-acre brook trout lake near Waldo Lake. See Bingo Lake for directions.

BOOT LAKE Usually a good brook trout lake in the Mink Lake Basin of Three Sisters Wilderness, about 1/2 mile due east of Cliff Lake. See Cliff Lake for directions from the Bend area by the way of Elk Lake. From Cliff Lake you can test your compass skills on this 5-acre target.

Boot Lake is quite deep for its size, a good lake for lures, spinners, or bait, as the bottom drops off quickly in most spots. Fly-fishing can be good at dusk. There are nice campsites at the lake. The early summer mosquitoes up here are legendary.

BOWERMAN LAKE Usually a good producer of brook trout, at the north end of the Eight Lakes Basin. It is reached by 6 miles of trail from the Duffy Lake Trailhead, just 3 miles off Hwy. 22. Bowerman is just east of Jorn Lake. It can also be approached from the north by a 5-mile hike from Marion Lake.

Bowerman is shallow and covers only about 6 acres. The lake is a consistent producer of brook trout 6-12 inches, averaging 8-9. The outlet runs into Little Bowerman Lake, which is only several acres and is not stocked, since it winterkills. Fly-fishing is usually good, although bait and lures will take fish, too. There are good campsites throughout the area. This is a scenic spot, and there are many other lakes to explore.

BREITENBUSH LAKE (Confederated Tribes Warm Springs) A fine big lake at the southern end of the Olallie Lake area north of Mt. Jefferson. The lake is about 105 miles from Portland. Take Hwy. 26 about 8 miles south of the Hwy. 35 junction to Forest Rd. 42, which cuts south. Stay on 42 until you reach Forest Rd. 4220, following signs to Olallie Lake. Continue past Olallie to Breitenbush Lake, about 3 miles south.

It can also be reached from Detroit Reservoir by following Forest Rd. 46 up the North Fork of the Breitenbush River to Forest Rd. 4220. Watch for signs to the lake. Neither road is usually open before late June, so check with the Forest Service for conditions. Both approach roads are rough, with the way in from the north either muddy or dusty, and from the west, rocky.

Breitenbush is on a plateau area near the western boundary of Warm Springs Reservation. Tribal permits are generally required to fish waters on reservation land, however a permit is not required to fish Breitenbush. Other good lakes off the road to the north, not on CTWS land, include Olallie, Monon, and Horseshoe.

Breitenbush is a nice family lake and has excellent fishing at times. The lake is stocked from time to time, and has natural reproduction of brook trout and rainbow. About 75 acres with quite a bit of shoal area, it offers good fly-fishing in fall. August and September are the best months. The fish usually run 6-12 inches with a few larger. There is a campground at the north end of the lake. Boats can be easily launched, but motors are prohibited.

BREITENBUSH RIVER A stocked trout stream in Willamette National Forest, flowing down the slopes of Mt. Jefferson some 30 miles to Detroit Reservoir. The lower stream is crossed by Santiam Pass Hwy. 22 at the point where it enters Detroit Reservoir just north of Detroit. A good road, Forest Rd. 46, follows the stream NE to the Mt. Hood Forest boundary. A poor road, Forest Rd. 42, branches off and follows the North Fork to its source, Breitenbush Lake.

The lower 12 miles are stocked with rainbow, and there are a few wild cutthroat and rainbow. The rainbow run 7-12 inches, though good fly anglers can taker larger rainbow in the lower river late in the season. There are also whitefish present.

The lower end of the stream in the Breitenbush arm of Detroit Reservoir can be fished by boat until the water drops. All of the stream above can be reached from the road, but the bank in most areas is steep and brushy. Worms and eggs usually work well throughout the season, and there is good fly water available. There are four nice campgrounds between the reservoir and Breitenbush Hot Springs (private), about 12 miles upstream.

BRICE CREEK About 16 miles long, joining Laying Creek to form Row River about 22 miles SE of Cottage Grove. From Cottage Grove take Hwy. 99 SE past Dorena Reservoir to Disston, where a gravel road follows the stream to its head.

The creek is not stocked, but wild cutthroat are present. Most angling is confined to the lower 8 miles, but some fish are taken in the upper stretch. There is a campground at Cedar Creek about 4 miles up from Disston. Another park area is located a few miles upstream.

BRIDAL VEIL CREEK A nice little stream for wild cutthroat in the Columbia Gorge area, about 7 miles long. It flows into the Columbia at Bridal Veil, 29 miles east of Portland, and is crossed by Hwy. 30 and the scenic route. Angling is confined to the stream above the falls. A poor dirt road follows the creek south, and the upper end is accessed by branch roads from the Larch Mountain Rd.

A 10 -inch fish is a whopper in this little stream, but Bridal Veil has some feisty little wild cutthroat. Bait angling is the best bet, but flies should work well in late summer and fall using sneak tactics. State Park picnic areas are located on Hwy. 30 near the mouth, but there are no campgrounds.

BRITTANY LAKE A small but deep hike-in brook trout lake in the Taylor Burn area north of Waldo Lake. From North Waldo Campground at the NE end of Waldo, take Trail 3590 west. At slightly over one mile, a trail cuts north and reaches Rigdon Lakes in one mile. Brittany is about a 1/4-mile bushwhack NE of Lower Rigdon.

Though only about 4 acres, Brittany is almost 30 feet deep. It is at elevation

5,600 ft., a good little lake that's lightly fished. Any method works, but flies are always productive.

BROOK LAKE (Confederated Tribes Warm Springs) A small brook trout lake just east of Olallie Meadows Campground, 3 miles north of Olallie Lake. See Breitenbush Lake for road directions. One of a group of three good lakes, including Jude and Russ, in a line 1/2 mile SE of the camp by easy trail.

About 4 acres, Brook has brook trout from 7-16 inches, averaging 10 inches. It's pretty brushy for shore fishing. A rubber boat or float tube comes in handy here. Bait or bait and spinner will usually take fish. Fly angling is good in evenings, especially in the fall.

Brook and its two neighbors are on reservation land, but tribal fishing permits are not required at this time. It is usually inaccessible before early June. Camping at the lakes is prohibited due to fire danger.

BROWN-MINTO ISLAND COMPLEX On the Willamette River south of Salem, a network of borrow pits and sloughs near the east bank that contain largemouth bass, white crappie, bluegill, brown bullhead, and stocked channel cats. The closest public boat ramp is at Wallace Marine Park in Salem on the west bank, just north of the Hwy. 22 Bridge. Recommended for small fry.

BUCK LAKE A 9-acre brook trout lake off the upper Clackamas Rd. just west of Timothy Lake, about 42 miles south of Estacada. It can be reached from the Shellrock Creek Rd., Forest Rd. 58, by turning right onto Forest Rd. 5810 about one mile north of Shellrock Campground. Drive 5 miles to Forest Rd. 210. Trailhead 728 is about one mile up this road on the left. It's a 1/4 mile hike south to the lake. If you are at Timothy Lake, head west on Trail 5810 to reach the spur.

Buck is stocked with brook trout that generally average 9-10 inches with some to 12 inches. All methods are used, but fly angling produces consistently after the first month or two. Though accessible in early June, there may still be some snow here since the lake is at 4000 ft. Supplies are available at Estacada or Government Camp.

BULL RUN RIVER A large tributary of the lower Sandy River flowing in from the east about 16 miles up from the mouth, crossed by the east side Sandy River Rd. about 1 1/2 miles above its mouth. The upper stream is in the Bull Run watershed reserve. Not much angling takes place below in the open area because of water level fluctuations. A few trout are taken in this stretch, but it is not stocked. The lower 1 1/2 miles are also open during winter season, and a few spring chinook and summer and winter steelhead are taken.

BUMP LAKE A 3-acre drive-in lake at 4300 ft. in the Olallie Lakes group. The road is accessed by a series of spur roads off Forest Rd. 46 north of Breitenbush. It is stocked with brook trout. Check the Mt. Hood National Forest Map for directions.

BURNT LAKE This is a favorite lake of many hiking anglers, as it is fairly accessible and close to Portland. The lake is about 8 acres and contains brook trout. Take Hwy. 26 east from Zigzag to an unnumbered forest road heading north about one mile east of Tollgate Campground. At about 4 miles, the road ends at Trailhead 772. Burnt Lake is 3 miles NE by trail, just to the east of East Zigzag Mountain. The trail passes 2-acre Devil's Lake about half-way. There are also brook trout in Devil's.

The brookies in Burnt average about 9 inches, with a size range 6-14 inches. Some years the fish run generally large, but there are off seasons. All methods are used, with flies working well in summer and fall. The lake is a pretty thing, in high alpine country at 4,100 ft. and is usually inaccessible until early June. There are pleasant campsites at the lake.

BURNT TOP LAKE (a.k.a. Top Lake) A fairly good 20-acre cutthroat lake in the Three Sisters Wilderness, north of the Horse Lake area on the west side of the Cascade summit. It's a long hike from the west side McKenzie drainage. Best way in is from the east. From Bend, take the Cascade Lakes Hwy. south toward Bachelor Butte. About 5 miles past the ski resort and just past the Devil's Lake Campground, a trail leads west to Sister's Mirror Lake. Burnt Top is 1 1/2 miles west, about 1/2 mile east-northeast of Burnt Top Peak. There is no trail to the lake.

Fly-fishing is good here, though lures and bait can be worked easily from shore as well. Angling is consistently good due to light pressure, with trout 8-11 inches. There are pretty campsites here and one mile east at Sisters Mirror Lake. It is usually accessible by early July.

BUTTE CREEK (Marion Co.) A fair wild cutthroat stream with a small run of wild winter steelhead. Roads follow both sides of the stream, but in the upper reaches the roads are not close to the creek.

Float tubes are a good way to fish many hike-in lakes.

Butte Creek forms the boundary between Clackamas and Marion counties, about 20 miles from the Salem area and 40 miles south of Portland. It flows NW over 30 miles from the lower Cascade range into the Pudding River near Woodburn. Hwy. 213 crosses it about 5 miles north of Silverton.

Fishing is pretty much confined to the area above Scott's Mills, just 2 miles east of the highway. Steelhead fishing is catch and release only.

BYBEE LAKE A 200-acre warmwater lake in a large bottomland complex that also includes Smith Lake, as well as smaller ponds, sloughs, swamps, and marshes. The complex, which is on a peninsula between Columbia Slough at Oregon Slough near the confluence of Willamette and Columbia rivers, has been designated a Metropolitan Greenspace. It contains largemouth bass, crappie, bluegill, and bullhead catfish. Bass to 4 pounds have been taken here.

Access to Bybee is either by canoe or foot trail. Trailheads are on Marine Drive west of Heron Lakes Golf Course near the Multnomah County Expo Center, and on Columbia Blvd. on the north side of the bridge that crosses Columbia Slough near Kelley Point Park.

Canoe access to Bybee is by way of the Columbia Slough, Smith Lake, or the small pond complex off Marine Drive between Smith and Bybee lakes. Canoes can be launched into the Columbia Slough off Columbia Blvd., at the Columbia Slough crossing near Kelley Pt. (paddle east), or near the former St. Johns Landfill.(paddle west). Some portaging between the slough and Bybee is required.

Bybee is a gem of a little wilderness in the heart of Portland's industrial sector. Wildlife is abundant, including mosquitoes in season. Dress appropriate to blackberry brambles and nettles.

CALAPOOIA RIVER Flows 65 miles into the Willamette at Albany from its head in the Cascade range between South Santiam and McKenzie rivers. Trout fishing is confined to the upper half of the stream, with a run of wild steelhead available for catch and release angling. Largemouth and smallmouth bass and panfish can be found near its mouth.

The Calapooia is usually well stocked with rainbow trout from just above Brownsville to just above Dollar, and wild cutthroat are present. Trout average about 9 inches with a range of 7-12. The upper stretch is usually a good bet in late season, with fewer, but larger fish, available. From Holley, which is south of Sweet Home on Hwy. 228, a good road follows the stream for 9 miles to Dollar, and a fair road continues upstream another 12 miles to the North Fork. The lower river is followed and crossed by many roads from Holley to Albany.

The Calapooia is managed for wild steelhead, which are generally in the river from February through April. The river is closed to salmon angling.

CAMP CREEK (Clackamas Co.) A tributary of the upper Sandy River in the Mt. Hood National Forest. Though only 7 miles long, it provides fair fishing for wild cutthroat. Camp Creek joins the Zig Zag River one mile east of Rhododendron. Hwy. 26 parallels the creek to the north from Rhododendron to Government Camp, but access is good only in the lower stretch.

Rainbow trout are no longer stocked, but wild cutthroat are scattered throughout. Bait is best early in the year, when the stream is silty from glacial run-off. Fly anglers can do well in summer and fall.

There are two campgrounds along the stream, Tollgate just east of Rhododendron, and Camp Creek 2.5 miles further east. Both are off Hwy. 26.

CAMPERS LAKE A fairly consistent producer of cutthroat trout located just east of the McKenzie Pass Highway 242 about one mile north of the Scott Lake turnoff. The lake has about 13 acres, mostly shallow, with the deepest area (the north end) about 15 feet. It's a good fly-fishing lake if you can get out beyond the shoal area, with fish to 14 inches, but it doesn't hold up well late in the season. The lake has been known to dry up.

There are no improved campsites at the lake, but there are campgrounds on the highway south. A good lake for float tubes.

CANBY POND About one acre, in Canby City Park at the western edge of the town off Hwy. 99E. It can be fished for largemouth bass, crappie, and bluegill.

CANIM LAKE An easy to find brook trout lake just north of Waldo Lake, south of the Taylor Burn area. Canim is 2 miles west of the North Waldo Campground on Trail 3590. The lake winterkills easily and is only occasionally stocked.

CARMEN RESERVOIR (a.k.a. Beaver Marsh Reservoir) On the upper McKenzie River, built by the Eugene Electric and Water Board. Unlike a lot of power reservoirs, this one provides good fishing. It has about 65 acres and puts out a lot of fish.

Carmen is about 2 miles south of Clear Lake on Hwy. 126, about 21 miles north of the McKenzie Hwy. It's in a scenic area and is easily reached. Fishing is primarily for rainbow 7-12 inches, but larger rainbows are available. A few brook trout and cutthroat are also caught. Trolling takes most fish, but any method will work. You'll have to row since motorboats are prohibited. There is a nice campsite near the north end of the lake.

CAST CREEK A small trout stream in the Mt. Hood National Forest about 5 miles NE of Zigzag on Hwy. 26. It flows north from Cast Lake into Lost Creek. To reach it, take the Lost Creek Rd., Forest Rd. 18 north from Zigzag about 5 miles to the Riley and McNeil campgrounds turnoff. Cast Creek is crossed by Forest Rd. 382 about 1/2 mile past Riley Campground.

It provides fair fishing for wild cutthroat and brook trout from 6-10 inches. There are three forest camps nearby, Riley, McNeil, and Lost Creek.

CAST LAKE A good hike-in brook trout lake on the west slope of Mt. Hood within the Mt. Hood Wilderness. From Hwy. 26 about 1 1/2 miles east of Rhododendron, take the Devil Canyon Rd. north about 5 miles to Trailhead 772. Hike to Devil's Lake, about 1 1/2 miles, then take Trail 774 north 1/2 mile then west another 1/2 mile to the lake. Burnt Lake is just 1 1/2 miles east. Cast can also be approached from the north by Cast Creek Trail 773, which heads at Riley Campground on the Lolo Pass highway.

Dumbell shaped, this 7-acre lake is 17 Ft. deep at elevation 4,450 ft. It has had some very good catches of trout from time to time, but can be slow. Brook trout here run 6-13 inches, averaging 9. All angling methods can be used, as the lake is easy to fish. Spinner and bait combinations do well in early season, and fly anglers take some large fish in late fall. There are no campsites at the lake, but Devil's Meadow has a good camp. The lake is usually accessible in early June.

CEDAR CREEK A tributary of the middle Sandy River entering from the east just north of the city of Sandy, about 27 miles from Portland. The upper stream is crossed by Hwy. 26 near Cherryville, and the lower section is followed for a way by county roads.

There is a salmon hatchery located near the mouth, and no angling is allowed on hatchery grounds or below the dam to the mouth of the stream. There is a false outlet at the head of an island, so make sure you're not in the closed area. Watch for signs. Many unhappy anglers have been given tickets catching coho in what they thought was the Sandy River.

Cedar Creek isn't stocked, but wild cutthroat and rainbow 6-10 inches are caught in the upper stream. There is some private property along the creek, so be wary of trespassing.

CERVUS LAKE A 12-acre brook trout lake in the popular Taylor Burn area, 2 miles north of Waldo Lake. From North Waldo Lake Campground, drive 7 miles north on a rugged dirt road to Taylor Burn Campground. This road may be impassable to low-riding vehicles.

Cervus Lake is 1/2 mile south of Torrey Lake, which is just south of Taylor Butte, a tall pinnacle on the south side of the road as you enter the area. It can also be approached from Taylor Burn Camp by the Olallie Trail going south. Follow around the south side of Wahanna Lake and head 1/2 mile SE. The area is brushy, and you should have a forest map along, but there are good landmarks.

Cervus is lightly fished and shallow, and frequently winterkills, though some brook trout usually survive. The brookies run 6-14 inches, with an average of 10 inches. All methods work, and fly fishing is excellent when the shadows hit the water. Bucktails and streamers will usually take fish. There are no campsites nearby, but there's a good camp at Taylor Burn. The lake is usually accessible by the end of June.

CHAMPOEG CREEK A small wild trout stream about 12 miles long, flowing through agricultural land into the Willamette near Champoeg State Park. The creek has been severely degraded by development in the area and is not stocked. There remains a small population of wild cutthroat. Access is limited to the state park.

CHEHALEM CREEK A small trout stream that heads in the Chehalem Mts. north of Newberg in Yamhill County. Tributary to the Willamette, it is crossed just above its mouth by Hwy. 99W at the east end of Newberg. Land development in the area has taken its toll on this small stream, though a few small wild cutthroat can be caught early in the year. Adjacent property is all private, except for road crossings.

CHETLO LAKE A large good brook trout lake one mile west of the north end of Waldo Lake. It's over a 4-mile hike from North Waldo Lake Campground. Take Trail 3590 west 2 1/2 miles to the outlet stream, which is the head of the Middle Fork of the Willamette. Some anglers take boats across the north end of Waldo Lake to this point. Here you pick up Trail 3583 and follow it south 1 1/2 miles to Chetlo.

Chetlo is about 19 acres and can be finicky about producing at times. Brook trout are stocked by air, and the catch generally runs 6-16 inches with an average of 11 inches, but a few larger have been reported. A rubber boat or float tube would be handy. Best angling is in August and September. Try a double blade spinner with a worm trailer fished slowly for the larger trout during the day.

In late spring mosquitoes in this area are awesome. Be prepared. There are natural campsites here and other good lakes are within a mile or two. The area is usually inaccessible until late June.

CHIQUITO LAKE A fair size brook trout lake at the north end of the Eight Lakes Basin, SW of Mt. Jefferson. Chiquito is 1/4 mile NE of Bowerman Lake. Chiquito's fish are a naturally sustained population, with catches ranging from 6-11 inches. All methods are generally productive. There are good campsites near Jorn Lake and other good lakes to the south.

CINCHA LAKE A small brook trout lake south of the Duffy Lake Trail in the Mt. Jefferson Wilderness. Hard to find, it is lightly fished and has been known to put out some big fish. From North Santiam Hwy. 22 about 5 miles north of Santiam Junction, take Forest Rd. 2267 to the Duffy Lake Trailhead. About 1 3/4 miles along the trail, a trail intersects from the north. Cincha is due south of the trail intersection about 1/4 mile. (Sounds easy, but it's not).

It's a small lake and has a little sister just to the west. Cincha is about 2 acres and shallow, while Little Cincha is smaller but deeper. Both lakes are stocked by air every few years. There are good campsites at the larger lakes in the basin.

CLACKAMAS RIVER A favorite of anglers in the greater Portland area, always among the top ten producers of salmon and steelhead in the Columbia River system. Spring chinook, a large run of summer steelhead, a good run of winter steelhead, and small runs of coho and fall chinook, all come home to this major tributary of the Willamette River.

The Clackamas heads in the Olallie Lake Basin between Mt. Hood and Mt. Jefferson, and flows 83 miles through Mt. Hood National Forest to enter the Willamette just north of the I-205 Bridge at Oregon City. A beautiful mountain river, the Clackamas has carved high rock cliffs out of the steep Douglas fir forest, rushing past giant boulders, its shoreline strewn with smoothly tumbled river rock. The river has three major tributary streams, the North and Oak Grove Forks, and the Collawash River.

The Clackamas is closely followed for over 40 miles by Hwy. 224, from one mile north of Carver near Oregon City to Ripplebrook Ranger Station in the Mt. Hood National Forest. From there upstream, it's followed by Forest Rd. 46 all the way to its headwaters in the Olallie Lake basin.

There are three dams on the river, beginning with River Mill Dam at river mile 23, which is considered to be the dividing line between the upper and lower river. Though all dams on the mainstem have fish bypass facilities, there is high mortality rate associated with all of them, especially for juvenile fish during their downstream migration. A collection facility at North Fork Dam attempts to gather in seaward steelhead and release them below River Mill. There are two salmon hatcheries on the river, at McIver State Park and on Eagle Creek, which produce both salmon and steelhead for the Clackamas and for other rivers in the Columbia system.

Salmon catches in the upper river have been small since construction of the dams. At this time, the upper river is closed to salmon angling during the fall salmon season, and to steelheading from January 1 through May 27.

The river's spring chinook population is doing well. Fishing takes place from January through October in the lower river, with peak catches in April and May. Only a small number of spring chinook are caught above the dams. During a recent ten year period the lower river catch of spring chinook fluctuated between 2,237 in 1985, and 7,171 in 1990. The 1992 catch was 4,043.

The river's several different populations of steelhead return in overlapping runs. Steelhead are fished in the lower Clackamas throughout the year, with peak catches from December through April. In 1992, greatest tag returns were in December and January, but well over a hundred fish were caught every month. It is estimated that wild fish make up 30% of the total population. All non-finclipped steelhead must be released unharmed.

During a recent 10-year period, the estimated summer steelhead catch in the lower river fluctuated between 1,330 (in 1985-86) and 4,300 (in 1982-83). The 1992-93 catch estimate was 2,123.

The estimated summer steelhead catch in the upper river during the same time period fluctuated between 1,456 (in 1991-92) and 7,185 (in 1984-85). The 1992-93 catch estimate was 4,832. The winter steelhead catch in the lower river was 2,227 in 1991-92, and 6,930 in 1984-85.

There is a popular fishery for stocked trout in the upper river, which receives about 160,000 rainbow from the 4th Saturday in May till the end of October. Fish are released near all campgrounds and road turn-outs between the head of North Fork Reservoir and the June Creek

Small motor boats can be used to fish the lower Clackamas.

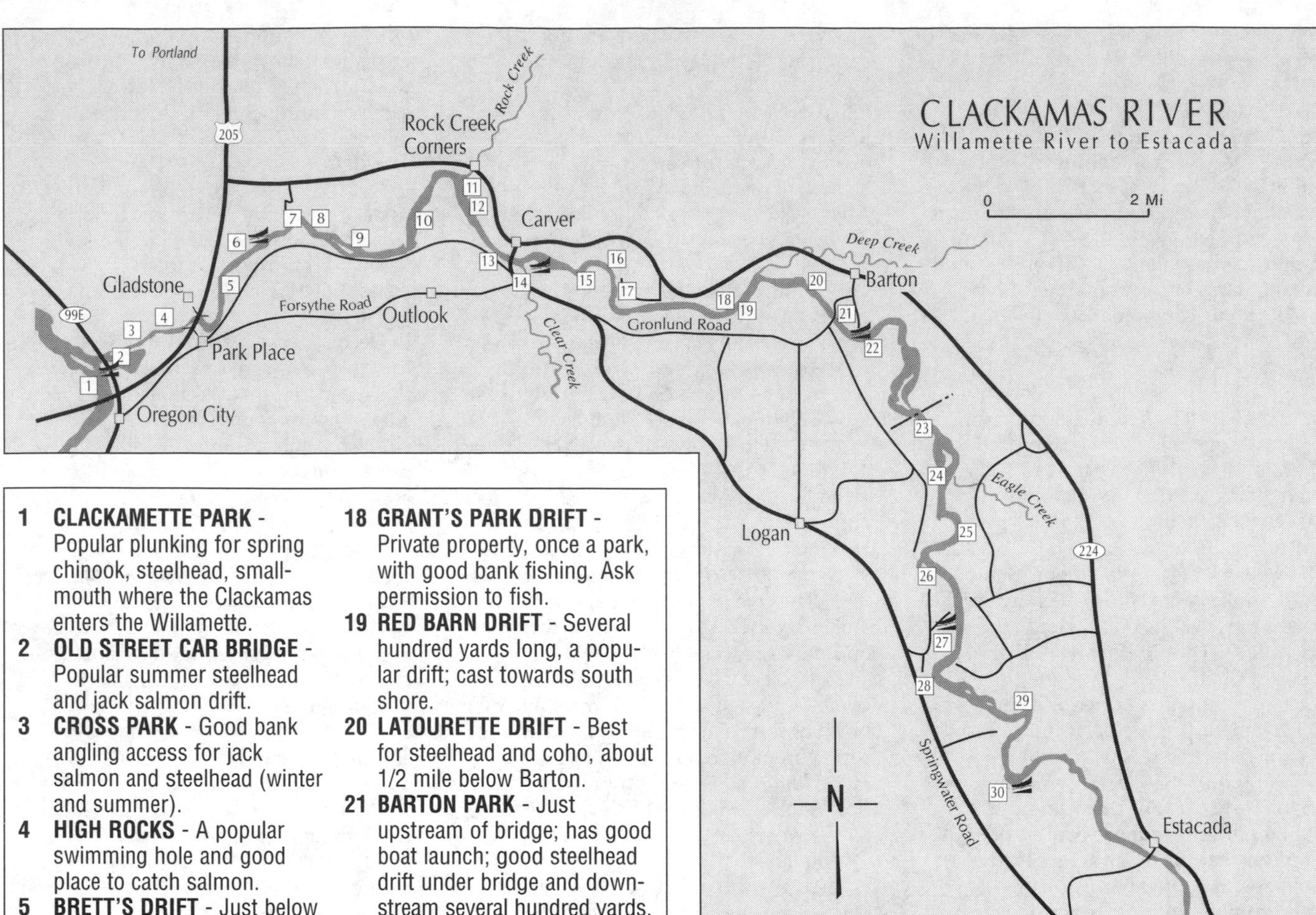

1 **CLACKAMETTE PARK** - Popular plunking for spring chinook, steelhead, small-mouth where the Clackamas enters the Willamette.
2 **OLD STREET CAR BRIDGE** - Popular summer steelhead and jack salmon drift.
3 **CROSS PARK** - Good bank angling access for jack salmon and steelhead (winter and summer).
4 **HIGH ROCKS** - A popular swimming hole and good place to catch salmon.
5 **BRETT'S DRIFT** - Just below Riverside Park and around the corner.
6 **RIVERSIDE PARK** - Good boat launch.
7 **ERICKSON'S EDDY** - A half mile above Riverside park, a popular salmon role.
8 **CAPE HORN DRIFT** - Around the corner and against the high bank.
9 **COFFEY'S DRIFT** - Another popular bank area down over a short riffle from Steven's.
10 **STEVEN'S** - A popular bank area one mile below Rock Creek at the highway.
11 **ROCK CREEK DRIFT** - Long and good for salmon and steelhead.
12 **SMITH'S DRIFT** - Shallow, but a good producer.
13 **CARVER BRIDGE DRIFT** - Just downstream from bridge; good steelhead drift up against the clay bank.
14 **CARVER BOAT RAMP** - On south shore, just upstream from Carver Bridge.
15 **BIG FISH HOLE** - Just around the corner from Larry's; cast toward high bank.
16 **LARRY'S** - Fast and shallow
17 **DOG HOLE** - Long and good for salmon, steelhead.
18 **GRANT'S PARK DRIFT** - Private property, once a park, with good bank fishing. Ask permission to fish.
19 **RED BARN DRIFT** - Several hundred yards long, a popular drift; cast towards south shore.
20 **LATOURETTE DRIFT** - Best for steelhead and coho, about 1/2 mile below Barton.
21 **BARTON PARK** - Just upstream of bridge; has good boat launch; good steelhead drift under bridge and downstream several hundred yards.
22 **CLARK'S EDDY** - A deep salmon hole, 2 miles below Power Line Hole.
23 **POWER LINE HOLE** - Several sets of power lines here; cast toward high clay bank.
24 **MOUTH OF EAGLE CREEK** - A good run of salmon and steelhead heading' for home at Eagle Creek Hatchery.
25 **SWINGING BRIDGE** - No bridge here, but good fishing about a mile below Eddy.
26 **FISH WITH EDDY** - A mile below Feldheimer's, a long drift against a high clay bank.
27 **FELDHEIMER'S** - Gravel boat ramp; Old Barlow Trail used to cross here on ferry.
28 **PARADISE PARK** - Below Eagle's Nest river splits into several channels; these come together against high clay bank, forming this popular drift.
29 **EAGLE'S NEST DRIFT** - Good bank drift at lower end of McIver Park.
30 **McIVER PARK** - Two boat ramps, one beside hatchery intake, one just below dangerous rapids; good salmon, steelhead drift just off second ramp.

Bridge above Austin Hot Springs. Above June Creek the river offers high quality catch and release angling for wild trout in an exquisite pristine environment.

The good thing about the Clackamas is that is offers superior angling for large fish in a beautiful setting within an hour's drive of Portland. The bad thing is that, just an hour's drive from Portland, most of the land adjacent to the lower river is privately owned. Consequently, the lower Clackamas is primarily a boater's show.

The river is suited to riverboats only (drift boats and jet sleds) except near the mouth and in the big pool at McIver Park near Estacada. From the mouth, anglers in standard motorboats can fish good water up to the first riffle above the Hwy. 99 Bridge. Be aware that spring chinook season typically brings on hoglines at the mouth, with boats anchored and tied in tight formation. At McIver, small motor boats can launch to fish the Big Flats, a 1/2 mile pool of relatively slow water below a major rapid, the Minefield.

The most popular drifts on the Clackamas are below this rapid, named for the sharp protruding rocks that stud the riverbed there. Even experienced driftboat handlers, and jet boat operators who value their hull, avoid this stretch. From McIver to the mouth the Clackamas offers fairly easy drifting, interspersed with rapids that are real enough, but not overwhelming for beginning driftboat operators. It is very popular with rafters.

There are 5 improved boat ramps on the lower river, and one natural gravel put-in. McIver Park, about 21 miles above the mouth, offers the last two improved boat ramps upstream. To reach McIver, take I-205 to Hwy. 224 just north of Gladstone. Follow 224 east to Carver, turning right at Carver Store and crossing the bridge over the river. Turn left onto Springwater Rd., and drive about 7 miles to the park. Feldheimer's, the gravel bar launch, is off Springwater Rd. just 2 miles before you reach McIver (if you pass the tavern, you've missed Feldheimer's). The next ramp downriver is at Barton Park. Follow Hwy. 224 toward Estacada to Barton Store, then turn right onto Baker's Ferry Rd., which leads to the river. Carver Boat Ramp is immediately across the bridge from Carver store, down the first driveway on the left.

The last ramp above the mouth is at Riverside Park in Clackamas. Follow the merged highways 212/224 east, one stoplight past the 82nd St. junction, turning right onto Evelyn St. (watch for the green ODF&W sign. The Clackamas District headquarters is on this road, with some river frontage for bank angling). Follow Evelyn through an industrial warehouse district to the park.

At the mouth of the Clackamas is Clackamette Park, off Hwy. 99E at the north end of Oregon City. Clackamette has a huge boat ramp that offers access to both the Willamette and the Clackamas. This is where a 55-pound chinook was landed in 1983.

Bank angling on the lower river is restricted primarily to the parks and bridges. There's some bank angling at Clackamette Park, with good angling at Cross Park and High Rocks. To Reach High Rocks, a popular salmon and swimming hole, take the Park Place-Mollala Exit off I-205 and head west. The road ends at High Rocks on the east bank. There is a bridge across the river to Cross Park on the west bank. Riverside Park also offers a strip of bank for salmon and steelhead angling, and there is bank access on the south bank River Rd. just above the river gauging station downstream from Carver.

ODF&W owns a strip of bank from Carver Bridge up to Clear Creek, purchased on behalf of Oregon anglers. There is bank angling at Barton Park, and at Bonnie Lure Park, off Hwy. 224 about 6 miles below River Mill Dam. Bonnie Lure, an undeveloped state park, accesses the fishery at the mouth of Eagle Creek. Park at the gate and walk in along a path to the river. The river bank is also accessible from McIver Park to below River Mill Dam. From the dam up to Mt. Hood Forest most bank access is owned by Portland General Electric and is open to public use. Anglers pull off Hwy. 224 and fish at will.

There's lots of good steelhead water in the upper river. There's a nice long steelhead drift accessible from the bank near Memaloose Log Scaling Station about 10 miles above Estacada, with some off-road parking available. Anglers also fish near the PGE Towers, a power line crossing about 2 miles further up.

Carter Bridge (not to be confused with Carter Store), about one mile above Big Eddy Picnic Area, offers access to nice pools and tail-outs downstream from the bridge, as does Lockaby Campground. Roaring River Campground features good holding water below a big cliff. At Three Links Power Station, about 22 miles above Estacada, there are good pools above and below the chute. Park off the road. And this is only the beginning. Steelhead run all the way up to the Big Bottom country above Austin Hot Springs, as well as into the Collowash and the forks.

The likelihood of catching fish on the Clackamas, as on many rivers in western Oregon, is heavily influenced by water level. Water level on the Clackamas is primarily affected by snow-melt in the mountains and by rainfall. To find out the water level prior to heading for the river, call (503) 261-9246 for a river gauge reading. The best reading for fishing the Clackamas is considered by many to be 4.5 ft., with readings as low as 3.6 and as high as 5.4 still worth the trip. Flood level on the Clackamas is 18 ft.

Camping facilities are available below the national forest at Barton Park and McIver. Within Mt. Hood National Forest, campgrounds are numerous along Forest Rd. 46, including many near good steelhead water (Lazy Bend, Carter Bridge, Lockaby, and Sunstrip to name but a few).

There are few stores and no motels, resorts, or full service RV facilities in this part of the national forest. Supplies can be purchased at Oregon City, Estacada, and at Barton and Carver stores. For information about fishing the North Fork Dam pool, see North Fork Reservoir.

CLACKAMAS RIVER, NORTH FORK A good size tributary of the Clackamas, entering the river from the east about 15 miles SE of Estacada. Forest Rd. 4610 follows the fork from the east end of North Fork Reservoir upstream, rarely straying more than 1/4 to 1/2 mile from the fork. Forest Rd. 4613 crosses the stream near Whiskey Creek. There are many falls on the North Fork. Boyer and Winslow creeks, both good tributaries, join the North Fork at North Campground, about 9 miles upstream.

Fishing here is primarily for wild cutthroat, which run 6-11 inches. The road is usually open by late April. For information about fishing the reservoir, see North Fork Reservoir.

CLACKAMAS RIVER, OAK GROVE FORK A good size tributary of the upper Clackamas, affording fair trout fishing. About 25 miles long, it heads in the Big Meadows area in the NW corner of Warm Springs Reservation. It flows 7 miles to Timothy Lake, and 16 miles below the reservoir to its confluence with the Clackamas just above Ripplebrook Ranger Station, about 31 miles east of Estacada.

Both banks of the lower 5 miles are followed by forest roads east from Ripplebrook to Lake Harriet, a small reservoir on the fork. Above Harriet the roads meet, and Forest Rd. 57 continues upstream about a mile beyond Timothy. Shortly thereafter, the river enters the reservation, where a tribal fishing permit is required.

The Oak Grove Fork is stocked with legal rainbow from April through July in the vicinity of Ripplebrook and Rainbow campgrounds. Above Harriet there are

There's wheelchair access to the Clackamas at Fish Creek.

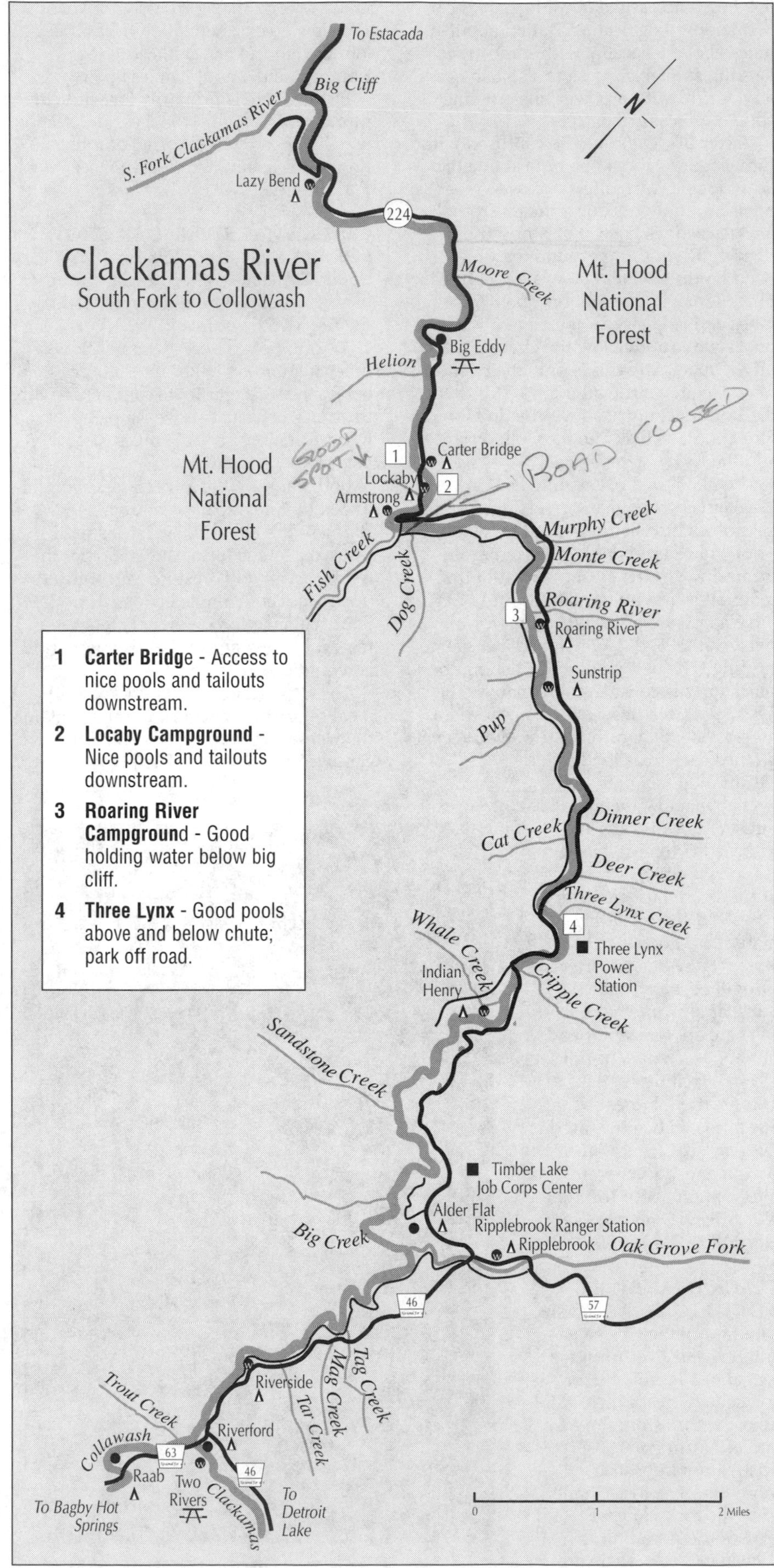

good populations of wild cutthroat, with brook trout in the highest reaches. A few browns, spawners from Lake Harriet, are occasionally hooked. Size range of all fish is 6-14 inches, with the larger fish hooked within a few miles above the reservoirs.

Size limits, 8-inch minimum and 12-inch maximum, are in force here. Anglers are also restricted to the use of barbless artificial flies and barbless lures.

There are campgrounds at Ripplebrook, Rainbow, Lake Harriet, Shellrock Creek and in the Timothy Lake area. Supplies are available at Estacada and North Fork Reservoir.

CLACKAMAS RIVER, SOUTH FORK
A nice stream entering the main river near Memaloose log scaling station at the east end of North Fork Reservoir. Long a water source for Oregon City and closed to all angling, the South Fork is now open, offering some exciting trout angling for the energetic.

Most of the river flows through deep canyon, with a number of natural barriers. Best trout fishing is above these barriers. Memaloose Creek joins the South Fork just above its confluence with the mainstem Clackamas.

One way to approach the South Fork is by way of Trail 516. In Estacada, turn off Hwy. 224 and cross the Clackamas, heading south along DuBois Creek toward Dodge. Forest Rd. 45, the Hillockburn Rd., approaches and parallels the South Fork canyon. About 2 miles past the spur road to Hillockburn Spring (about 2 1/4 miles east of Dodge), Trail 516 leads down to the river. The 1956 USGS topographic quadrangle map shows this trail crossing the river and connecting with another trail that crosses over to Memaloose Creek and follows it to the mouth.

CLAGGET LAKE **See Firecamp Lakes**

CLEAR CREEK (Clackamas System)
A large tributary of the lower Clackamas River, flowing from the south into the main stream at Carver, about 6 miles east of Clackamas. The creek is about 24 miles long and heads in the low hills west of the Clackamas River south of Viola. It is followed by county roads south of Hwy. 211, and the upper end can be reached by going east from Hwy. 213 in the Mulino area.

Primarily a wild cutthroat trout stream, a few steelhead do enter during January and February. Most fish are taken by bait in the lower end. Many of the small fish hooked early in trout season are young steelhead or coho moving downstream. These fish will produce a lot more excitement on their return journey if anglers will release them carefully, or better yet, fish heavier water and avoid them.

CLEAR FORK A tributary of the upper Sandy River above Brightwood Bridge which provides good late spring and summer trout angling in its lower stretch. From Portland, take Hwy. 26 east to Zigzag, a distance of 43 miles. Turn north on Forest Rd. 18, the Lolo Pass Rd., which parallels Clear Fork about 1/4 mile or so to the north of it. Five miles north of Zigzag, at McNeil Campground, the road comes very close to the creek. It then follows the creek almost to the headwaters.

Small wild cutthroat are present in good numbers. Because of its low temperature, it's not a good early stream. The cutthroat start biting in late May. Some of the Sandy system steelhead get up here and can be caught, but the stream is closed to salmon angling. Barbless hooks are required in November and December.

Riley, McNeil, and Lost Creek campgrounds are all located near the midsection of the stream. Supplies are available in Zigzag and Welches.

CLEAR LAKE (Linn Co.) The very scenic and geologically fascinating headwaters of the McKenzie River, created only 3,000 years ago by a lava flow that formed a natural dam on the stream. The impoundment inundated a standing Douglas fir forest, which the lake's cold waters have preserved. The Underwater Forest, as it is named on Forest Service maps, can be viewed by boaters through Clear Lake's crystalline lens.

The lake is just off Hwy. 126, about 3 miles south of the junction of Hwy. 126 with Hwy. 20.

Clear Lake contains a large self-sustaining population of brook trout and some wild cutthroat, and is stocked with easier-to-catch rainbow trout. It covers 148 acres and is deep throughout, reaching 175 ft. near the south end. The only shallows are near Cold Water Cove.

Still-fishing and trolling are the predominant angling methods here, with fly-fishing near shore. There is a campground at Cold Water Cove on the east shore, and a resort with rustic cabins, docks, and rental boats on the west shore. The resort is run by the Santiam Fish and Game Association, a mid-valley sportsman's club, and is open to public use. There is a pole slide boat ramp at Cold Water Cove. Motor boats are prohibited on the lake.

CLEARY POND A 4-acre pond in Fern Ridge Wildlife Management Area. It is west of Neilson Rd. about 1/2 mile south of Hwy. 126. It contains largemouth bass.

The upper Clackamas offers many good bank fishing opportunities.

CLIFF LAKE (Lane Co.) A 40-acre brook trout lake in the popular Mink Lake Basin of the Three Sisters Wilderness. It is off the Pacific Crest Trail 1 1/2 miles east of Mink Lake (there is a trail between the two). The trail up to the PCT heads on Hwy. 46 at a turn-around between Elk Lake and the Hosmer Lake junction south of Elk.

The stocked trout in Cliff average 9-10 inches and run to 15 inches. Fished rather heavily, it still produces on all methods of angling.

There is a shelter at the lake, and other nice natural campsites. The area is usually accessible in late June, with angling good then and again in late summer and fall. Closest supplies are at Elk Lake Resort and at McKenzie Bridge. There are a lot of other good lakes close by. See Porky, Mink, Moody, Vogel.

COLLAWASH RIVER A beautiful tributary of the Clackamas River, flowing completely within the Mt. Hood National Forest, entering the Clackamas about 35 miles SE of Estacada. The Collawash and its tributary, the Hot Springs Fork, feature a nice size run of summer steelhead and fair to good trout angling.

The Collawash heads in Marion County north of the Breitenbush drainage and flows north to the Clackamas. From Estacada, follow Hwy. 224 to Ripplebrook Ranger Station, then head south on Forest Rd. 46 to Two Rivers Camp at the confluence of the Collawash and Clackamas. A good road, Forest Rd. 63, follows the stream south for 9 miles to Tom's Meadow. About 4 miles south of Two Rivers a branch road, Forest Rd. 70, turns west and follows the Hot Springs Fork for about 7 miles. Trails access the upper reaches of both forks, as well as a number of lakes in the area.

Rainbow trout are the main catch near the road, with legal rainbow stocked in season. Further upstream, the catch consists of rainbow and an occasional brook trout, with Bull Trout scarce but occasionally hooked in all sections. The taking of bull trout is prohibited.

Steelhead are available throughout the river, in the many pools carved by this rushing mountain stream. Best results are in October or November. Steelhead season closes at the end of December. The river is closed to salmon angling to protect late steelhead spawners.

Plentiful trout of good size are taken by anglers willing to hike up the Hot Springs Fork to Bagby Guard Station and above. Trail 544 to Bagby Hot Springs and beyond heads about one mile south of Pegleg Campground. There is a large parking area at the trailhead, and it is well signed. The hot springs are a real treat after a day's angling. In recent years a rough crowd has been frequenting the hot springs, which traditionally was a place of great tranquillity. It would probably be best not to go there alone, and don't leave anything valuable in your car.

The main river upstream from Tom's Meadow to Oh Boy Camp (about 5 miles south at the confluence of Elk Lake Creek, shown on topo but not forest map) is accessed by trail or bushwhack, and offers good fishing. Average size is about 9 inches with a range 7-15 inches.

Bait and lure angling will produce well, but there's beautiful fly water on both forks. In late summer and fall, dry fly anglers take big rainbow from the riffles using light leaders and small dries, (number 14 or smaller), with Blue

Uprights, McGinty, and Mosquito patterns effective.

There are four campgrounds in the lower 4 miles between the Hot Springs Fork and the Clackamas River, and two campgrounds on the Hot Springs Fork.

COLLINS LAKE A tiny rainbow and brook trout lake of about one acre, just south of the old highway at the west end of Government Camp on Hwy. 26. The lake is formed by a block on one fork of Camp Creek. This is a private lake but it is open to public use. It is stocked with rainbow and has some wild brook and rainbow. Camping is not permitted at the lake.

COLORADO LAKE A 30-acre private lake 2 miles east of Corvallis, open to public use for a fee. The lake contains largemouth bass, white crappie, bluegill, and brown bullhead catfish.

COLUMBIA SLOUGH A long back eddy of the Columbia River which borders North Portland from Kelley Point to east of Parkrose. Deceptively innocent-looking with its cottonwood fringe, plentiful wildlife, and good population of warmwater fish, it is considered by some to be one of the most polluted waters in the west. Mercury, PCBs and other industrial poisons are present, as well as raw sewage. Signs throughout the slough warn visitors not to swim or eat any fish taken from the water.

In 1994 the first steps were taken to restore the slough when the city of Portland agreed to reroute its sewage so that the overflow would not drain into the slough. There is also the possibility of an infusion of federal dollars to the clean-up project.

Meanwhile, the slough continues to provide habitat for largemouth bass, crappie, bullhead, bluegill, perch, crawfish, and many species of rough fish that provide food for the bass. Occasional sturgeon and steelhead are also spotted, as well as salmon smolts. Catch and release angling, while not required by regulation, is a must here.

Access to the slough is best from NE 17th Ave. west to the Willamette. Canoes can be slipped into the water here, or at other points all the way to Parkrose. Columbia and Sandy boulevards parallel the slough, and many roads cross it, providing right-of-way access to its narrow shore. The Four Corners area between NE 158th and 185th avenues features a narrow channel with overhanging trees, shrubs, and submerged structures that are attractive to bass. This upper area may be less contaminated than the lower slough.

Remember, industrial pollution can be very poisonous. Don't even wade in the water.

COPEPOD LAKE A good brook trout lake in the Mink Lake Basin at the head of the South Fork of the McKenzie River. The lake is just north of the Goose Lake/Corner Lake Trail, 1/2 mile west of the junction of that trail with the Pacific Crest Trail. See Cliff Lake for directions into the basin.

About 20 acres, Copecod has nice brook trout from 6-16 inches with the average 8-10 inches. Fly angling is good here, with wet flies working well most of the time. Bucktail coachman or caddis and most streamer flies will take fish. There are good natural campsites here and at other lakes in the basin. There is a shelter at Cliff Lake, a little over one mile south by trail. Copepod is usually accessible in late June, but the mosquitoes can be fierce. Best angling is in the fall.

CORNER LAKE A 60-acre brook trout lake in the northern Mink Lake Basin, at the head of the South Fork McKenzie. It is about 2 trail miles north of Mink Lake and just north of Goose Lake, which flows into it. See Cliff Lake for directions into the basin.

Corner usually produces fair to good fishing for wild brook trout through most of the season. The fish range from 6-18 inches, averaging 10 inches. All methods will take fish. The catch limit is 10 fish. Goose Lake, a shallow lake to the SE, has good angling early in the year, but gets very low in fall. There are many fine natural campsites throughout the basin.

COTTAGE GROVE PONDS Six bass and panfish ponds with stocked rainbow trout available in spring. Follow Row River Rd. to the truck scale, where the road crosses the Row River across from the car lot. Signs point toward Dorena Dam. A paved bicycle path leads to the first pond. Park near, but do not block, the scales.

COTTAGE GROVE RESERVOIR A large flood control reservoir on the Coast Fork of the Willamette River, managed primarily for bass and panfish, with catch-and-release regulations on trophy bass (over 15 inches). It is located about 6 miles south of Cottage Grove. Just south of town, a paved road heads SW to the reservoir, and roads follow both shores. It covers about 1,000 acres at high level, through the spring and summer months, and is drained down later in the year.

Catchable rainbow trout are stocked annually in the spring, but largemouth bass are the prime catch. Bluegill, black crappie, and brown bullhead catfish are also present.

Be aware that fish taken from this reservoir frequently contain levels of mercury that can be poisonous. The longer a fish lives in the reservoir, the more likely it is to absorb and retain mercury. To play it safe, eat only the catchable trout, and the earlier in the season the better.

The reservoir is popular for diverse recreational water activities, especially boating. Boat landings and ample parking space are provided. Overnight camping is available at Pine Meadow Campground (Corp. of Engineers) on the lake. There are three picnic areas here as well. Accommodations and supplies are available in Cottage Grove.

COTTONWOOD MEADOWS LAKE Located south of the High Rock lakes area of the Mt. Hood National Forest, north of the Oak Grove Fork of the Clackamas River. From Estacada take Hwy. 224 to Ripplebrook Ranger Station, about 30 miles. From there, follow the Oak Grove Fork Rd. (Forest Rd. 57) to the Shellrock Creek Rd. (Forest Rd. 58). About 2 1/2 miles north of Shellrock Campground turn west onto Forest Rd. 5830 and drive to Hideaway Lake. Continue on 5830 about 1 1/2 miles to the crossing of Trail 705, just past a creek crossing. Follow the creek to the lake.

Cottonwood Meadows Lake is about 8 acres and shallow, ideal for fly angling if it doesn't get too low, and capable of growing good size fish. It has a lot of shoal area and deeper channels, and though it has its ups and downs, it's usually consistent for cutthroat 8-12 inches. In some years, fish to 16 inches have been taken in good numbers. Natural campsites are available. It's usually accessible in early June.

COUGAR LAKE (Clackamas Co.) A small brook trout lake near the headwaters of the North Fork Molalla River. Privately owned by a timber company, it is closed to public use.

COUGAR RESERVOIR (Lane Co.) A large reservoir on the South Fork of the McKenzie River, 50 miles east of Eugene. Used both for power and flood control, it fluctuates considerably but provides fair fishing for stocked rainbow trout. To reach it, take Hwy. 126 east from Eugene. Four miles past the community of Blue River turn south on the South Fork Rd., and follow it 3 miles to the lake.

Cougar covers about 1,200 acres when full and is 6 miles long. The primary catch is rainbow trout, but a few bull trout to 5 pounds are present and available for catch and release angling. Trolling with a Ford Fender or a silver or gold lure can be effective. Bank fishing at the upper end at the bridge also produces. Boat anglers should try fishing the coves, where there are usually large concentrations of trout.

Cougar Hot Springs is an added treat for visitors here, located on Rider Creek about 1/4 mile west of the reservoir. About 4 miles south of the dam, the west shore road bisects an embayment at the mouth of Rider Creek. There you will find a small parking area. Follow the trail along the north shore of the creek to the hot springs. In recent years, a rough crowd has been frequenting the springs. Best advice may be to avoid them in July before and after the county fair. This is no longer the tranquil wilderness experience it once was.

There are several forest campgrounds in the vicinity. Echo is on the East Fork Rd., Forest Rd. 1993 near the lower end of the reservoir. Slide Creek is on the east shore near the southern end, and French Pete is one mile south on Forest Rd. 19. There are additional campgrounds along the South Fork McKenzie.

CRABTREE CREEK A trout and wild steelhead stream east of Albany, flowing from the Cascade foothills south of the North Santiam River into the South Santiam River near Scio. The lower end is crossed by Hwy. 226 about 9 miles north of Lebanon. Both paved and gravel roads follow and cross the lower end, and from Lacomb upstream a fair road follows it to the headwaters some 35 miles from the mouth. The extreme upper portion is sometimes closed to access by a logging concern during fire season.

A popular stream, it is stocked with rainbow trout, and has some wild cutthroat. The success rate is high for trout 6-12 inches, with a few larger fish taken at times. All methods of angling will work, but bait is usually best in early season. The creek also presents opportunities for catch and release steelheading.

CRAIG LAKE This is a hard to find brook trout lake, though not a long hike. Because of its location, it's easily missed and lightly fished, but it puts out a lot of medium size trout. Craig is on top of Craig Butte at elevation 5,300 ft. It is across the canyon west of the head of Lost Lake Creek, and is 3/4 miles due south of Lower Berley Lake.

Take the Pacific Crest Trail north 1 1/2 miles from the Santiam Lodge area to the junction of Trail 3491. Take 3491 about one mile north, and look for a fair trail which goes up the NE side of Craig Butte. It is about 1/2 mile to the lake by this trail.

Craig Lake is about 5 acres and is 14 ft. deep. Fly-fishing is usually the best bet. There are good natural campsites at the lake.

CRESWELL PONDS Freeway ponds east of Creswell, containing largemouth bass, bluegill, brown bullhead, and black crappie.

CRIPPLE CREEK LAKE A very good 15-acre hike-in brook trout lake at the south end of the High Rock Lakes group in Mt. Hood National Forest. The lake is at elevation 4,300 ft.

From Estacada, follow Hwy. 224 just past Ripplebrook Ranger Station, then turn NE on Forest Rd. 4631 toward Silvertip. About 4 miles from Ripplebrook, Forest Rd. 4635 cuts sharply back to the NW. Follow it 10 miles. Just after crossing Cripple Creek, the head of Trail 702 to Cache Meadow is on the east side of the road. (The road dead ends a mile or so beyond the trailhead, if you miss it.) Follow the creek upstream about a mile to the lake, an elevation gain of 300 ft.

By late June the High Rock Rd. is usually open, and the lake can also be reached by a 2-mile hike SW from Frazier Mt. From Frazier turn-around, take Trail. 517 to Cache Meadow, and follow the stream south for 1/2 mile.

Brook trout in the lake run 7-13 inches, averaging 9-10 inches. All methods can be used. It gets very heavy pressure in years when the fish are running large. Natural campsites are available.

CUNNINGHAM LAKE A 200-acre bass and panfish lake near the north end of Sauvie Island, NW of Portland. The lake is at the head of Cunningham Slough near the narrow neck of the island. Subjected to flood waters in the spring and affected by tides, it has a good selection of the warm water fish found in Willamette and mid-Columbia.

From St. Helens or Scappoose Bay the lake can be reached by boating up Cunningham Slough, which is just across Multnomah Channel from the Crown Paper Mill south of St. Helens. An alternate route is to boat south 3 miles from the mouth of Scappoose Bay to the east side of the channel at a point opposite Jackson or Santosh Slough. Walk several hundred yards to the shore of the lake.

Brown bullhead angling is very good at times if you have a boat to get to them. Largemouth bass, crappie and perch move in and out of the lake with the tidal action. Best angling is in June and July when the water is up.

Tackle and rental boats are available at commercial marinas on Multnomah Channel, Scappoose Bay, and at St. Helens.

CUNNINGHAM SLOUGH A good bass and panfish fishery south of St. Helens at the north end of Sauvie Island. A boat is required to fish it. The slough is about 5 miles long and serpentines out of Cunningham Lake, flowing into Multnomah Slough across from the mouth of Scappoose Bay. It has a double mouth with an island located at the entry. By boat from St. Helens, it's about a 2-mile run upstream. From the public ramp at Scappoose Bay north of Warren, it's 1 1/2 miles down the bay and across. Scappoose Bay is about 25 miles north of Portland (and offers good warm water angling itself).

The main catch in the slough is brown bullhead, which are very plentiful at times. These catfish run 8-12 inches with an occasional larger one. A number of good size perch are picked up in the lower slough, and crappie respond to cut bait, jig flies, and spinners. Best spots to fish are at the mouths of the smaller sloughs. Angling is best on the ebb tide, according to the experts, but some fish can be caught at any time.

Angling can be very good for bass to 5 pounds. Areas near the mouth and at the outlets of the smaller streams produce best results. All methods are used, a good spot to test everything in your tackle box. Bass seem to hit best at the tide changes.

Boats, tackle, and supplies are available at marinas on Multnomah Channel and Scappoose Bay.

DAIRY CREEK, EAST FORK (Wash. Co.) A popular and heavily fished trout stream just 25 miles west of Portland, crossed by Hwy. 26. The stream flows from the north and joins West Dairy Creek, entering the Tualatin River near Cornelius.

Trout angling is largely confined to the area north of Hwy. 26. A good road turns north off the highway toward Mountaindale just before Hwy. 26 crosses the stream. A paved and gravel road follows the stream up about 10 miles. The lower creek has quite a bit of private property, so don't trespass.

East Dairy is managed as a wild cutthroat stream and is no longer stocked. Single eggs, worms, and caddis nymphs will all work well, and flies will take fish when the stream drops and clears. There is no camping in the area.

DAIRY CREEK, WEST FORK (Wash. Co.) A good wild cutthroat stream in Washington County, tributary to the Tualatin River, with headwaters north of Hwy. 26. It flows south along Hwy. 47 out of Vernonia, then at Staleys Junction flows east along 26 to the Hillsboro junction at Banks. From there, it flows SE through farmland to join East Dairy Creek and the Tualatin River.

This is an excellent wild cutthroat stream. Fishing usually holds up until early summer, but best catches are made early. The stream is fairly brushy and has

Over 100,000 catchable trout are stocked in Detroit Lake each year.

a lot of cover for fish. Bait angling is best, but a small spinner/bait combination will work well. Black Gnats, brown hackles, and McGintys flicked off the brushy overhangs will take nice size cutthroat. Small crayfish tails will also attract the big ones. There's some private property along the stream, so avoid trespassing.

DALY LAKE Cupped in the headwaters of the Middle Fork of the Santiam River, 11 acres, with excellent angling for brook trout and cutthroat, and not too remote. From Hwy. 22, the North Santiam Rd., turn west on the Scar Mt. Road (Forest Rd. 2266) at a point about 22 miles SE of Idanha. Don't take the wrong turn and get onto Forest Rd. 1164, which will take you too far north. About 4 miles from Hwy. 22, Forest Rd. 2266 goes right between Daly and Parrish Lakes. Daly is on the north side.

Daly Lake has a lot of cutthroat 6-10 inches, with a few larger. A fair number of brook trout are caught, from 6-12 inches. Both of these trout are sustained by natural reproduction. All methods will take fish, with fly-fishing especially good in late summer and fall. The east side of the lake has the best fly water. There are good natural campsites here. Riggs Lake, also good for brook and cutthroat, is west along the same road. Parrish is also close by. The road may still be snowbound in early June.

DAVIS LAKE (Linn Co.) A lightly fished (hard to find) 3 acre brook trout lake between Marion Lake and the old Santiam Rd., located within the Mt. Jefferson Wilderness. It is 4 miles south of Marion Falls Ranger Station on North Santiam Hwy. 22. Forest Rd. 2261 leads east to the Pine Ridge Scout Camp. From the camp, take Trail 3443 SE about 2 miles. The trail stays 1/4 mile south of the lake, crossing an inlet stream which can be followed to Davis.

The lake is very shallow, good for fly-fishing, but it sometimes loses fish to winterkill. When it gets by for a few years without winter loss, it grows some good size brook trout. Fair natural campsites are available.

DEEP CREEK (Clackamas Co.) A wild cutthroat stream with a small wild steelhead run, tributary to the lower Clackamas River. The stream is about 15 miles SE of Portland and enters the Clackamas River near Barton. The upper North Fork is crossed by Hwy. 26 south of Orient, and the main upper stream is crossed by Hwy. 211 SW of Sandy. Other county roads cross and follow the stream from the mouth eastward.

The creek is open to angling above the fish ladder at Sizemore Dam. Trout angling is good from late April through May and June, but the stream gets low in summer. It offers fair fishing for wild cutthroat. Bait angling is most popular.

Angling for steelhead here is catch and release only. Be sure to use a barbless hook. Most are hooked from January through March. An occasional coho is taken in the early fall.

There's private property along the creek, but some owners will allow you to fish if you ask permission. There's no camping in the area.

DEER CREEK (Yamhill Co.) A wild cutthroat stream about 17 miles long, flowing into the South Yamhill River about 3 miles east of Sheridan off Hwy. 18. The mouth is about 5 miles SW of McMinnville. The creek is crossed by the highway just east of Sheridan, and followed north by good roads for about 11 miles up Gopher Valley.

Fishing is best in the portion north of the highway. As in all west valley streams, best fishing is in spring. Average catch is around 9 inches, with few larger. There's a lot of private land along this stream.

DELTA PARK PONDS Offering bass and panfish opportunities in the Portland metropolitan area. From I-5 North take the Delta Park Exit, just after crossing Columbia Slough. The city-owned park is west of the freeway.

Unfortunately, fishing seems to be losing ground to other park activities. The golf course ponds are closed to angling. However, there are a half dozen lakes and sloughs here, many of which are still accessible when the horses and cars aren't running! The four largest lakes contain bass, perch, catfish, and bluegill. All can be easily fished from the bank.

DELTA PONDS Offering 200 acres of bass and panfish water east of Delta Hwy. and north of Valley River Center in North Eugene. This is a network of ponds in a former gravel pit, with good bank fishing, though it does get brush. Fish for largemouth bass, white crappie, brown bullhead, and bluegill. Plenty of blackberries to nibble on in August. Recommended for small fry.

DENUDE LAKE A scenic 9-acre brook trout lake in the Sisters Mirror Lakes Basin of the Three Sisters Wilderness, NW of Elk Lake near the Cascade summit. The Pacific Crest Trail crosses the basin, which is about 5 miles NNW of Elk Lake. One of several approaches begins at Elk Lake Resort, about 35 miles SW of Bend on the Cascade Lakes Hwy. 46. Take the Horse Lake Trail 1.1/2 miles west to its intersection with the PCT, and turn north onto it. Hike 4 1/2 miles north to the Sisters Mirror area. Another route, about 3 miles to the lake, is by Trail 20, which leads NW from Hwy. 46 1/2 mile north of Sink Creek, which is about 2 miles north of the Elk Lake Resort turnoff. Denude is the western-most lake in the basin.

The Mirror Lakes are on a picturesque plateau in an alpine setting. Most are quite shallow and don't provide much fishing. The brook trout in Denude average 9 inches, ranging 6-14 inches. They are easily fished from shore by all methods. Good natural campsites are available. This is designated wilderness, so no-trace camping guidelines should be followed.

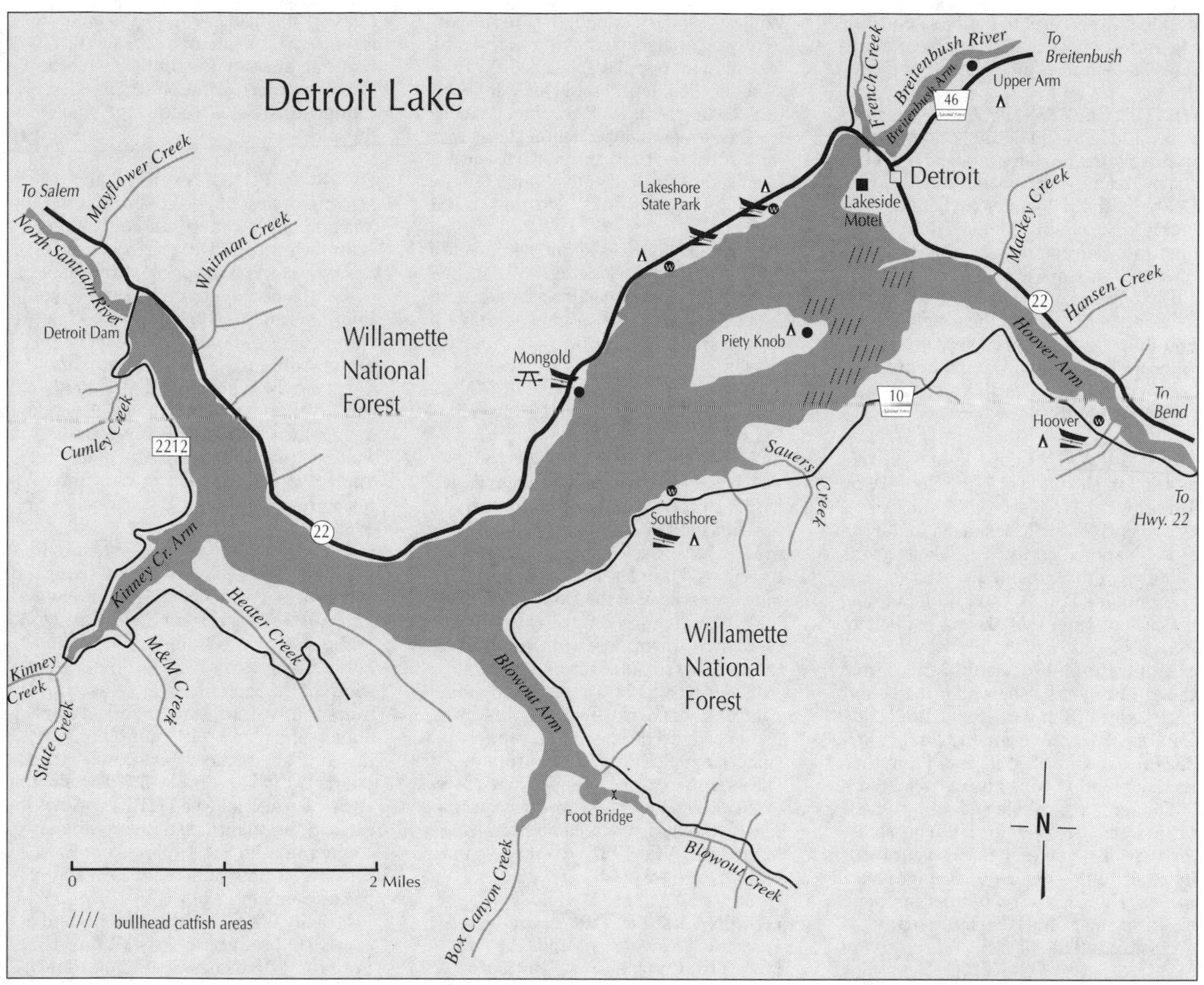

DETROIT LAKE A large popular reservoir on the North Fork Santiam River that has been providing good angling since it was first filled with water. It's about 100 miles from Portland, 50 miles east of Salem, off Hwy. 22. The town of Detroit is located near the upper (east) end of the lake.

Detroit Dam is used for flood control and power, so water level in the reservoir fluctuates during the year, though it's usually full in spring and summer, covering over 3,000 acres. In fall the water is lowered, but fishing can still be good in the pools and near the dam.

About 100,000 catchable trout are stocked throughout the season. Fingerling rainbow, kokanee, and chinook fingerlings are added in late spring. Detroit also has a few wild brook trout and cutthroat that drift in from Breitenbush and North Santiam Rivers and from Blowout and Kinney Creeks. Most of the trout caught are the stocked rainbows, averaging about 12 inches, though a good number reach 16 inches.

Brown bullhead, though not stocked by the state, have increased in number and provide quite a fishery. They run to 14 inches and are taken with nightcrawlers on the bottom. Try the NE end of Piety Island, just south of Lakeside Motel on either side of the peninsula, and near the NE shore below Hoover Arm. The tributary arms are also good producers.

Kokanee anglers use downriggers to fish as deep as 80-100 ft. in July and August, or troll deep around the island and towards the dam. Kokanee grow well in Detroit, but not a lot are taken. The landlocked chinook, on the other hand, are gaining popularity with anglers. They are taken throughout the reservoir, but in the spring the dam seems to be a good spot.

All methods of fishing are used here, with trolling the most popular. One popular trout set-up is a rudder-flasher with 2 ft. leader, followed by a small Kwikfish-type lure or worm. Triple Teasers and small Spin-n-glo's behind large flashers

also work well, but remember to troll very slowly. Still-fishing and lure casting also take lots of fish. Best angling is in the river arms and shoal areas. Catches have been good through Labor Day, with the best fishing in spring and after Labor Day.

There is a boat ramp at Mongold State Park on the north shore near the east end of the lake. Mongold and Lake Shore State Park offer camping facilities on the north shore off Hwy. 22. Hoover and South Shore Campgrounds are on the south shore, on Forest Rd. 10. (From Hwy. 22 at Detroit, turn right onto Forest Rd. 10.) There is also a boat-in campground on Piety Knob, an island in the main pool at the east end of the reservoir. Hoover campground has a flat area beside a steep bank that offers good fishing and is wheelchair accessible. Restaurants and supplies are available in Detroit.

DEXTER RESERVOIR A fair size reservoir on the lower Middle Fork Willamette with no attractions for anglers. It is just downstream from Lookout Reservoir. Dexter is about 20 miles east of Eugene on Hwy. 58, about 140 miles from Portland. The community of Lowell is on the north side of the lake.

Dexter is heavily infested with squawfish, and is not part of the squawfish bounty program. It is heavily used by water-skiers and sailboaters. Camping, boating, and picnic facilities are on the north and south shores.

DINGER LAKE A good little trout lake at 4,000 ft. elevation, 2 1/2 miles NW of Timothy Lake (a reservoir on the Oak Grove Fork of the Clackamas) in the Mt. Hood National Forest. The lake is about 77 miles from Portland.

From Pine Point Campground on the SW arm of Timothy Lake, drive NW on Forest Rd. 5820 toward Black Wolf Meadows Trailhead. About 3 miles from the campground a short spur road cuts back to the NE. If you see the trailhead for Trail 724, you've gone 1/2 mile too far. Take the spur road to its end. From there the lake is a 1/3 mile bushwhack NW.

Dinger is very shallow and in some years loses fish to winterkill. This shallowness also makes it an excellent fly lake for trout 7-14 inches, average size 10 inches. There are good natural campsites and a spring at the lake. It is usually accessible in late May.

DIXIE LAKES A couple of small brook trout lakes at the southern end of the Eight Lakes Basin in the Mt. Jefferson Wilderness. Easy to find, they're fished lightly by anglers passing through on the way to more popular spots. See Duffy Lake for directions. From Duffy, take the trail leading SE toward Santiam Lake. At the meadow trail intersection about 1/2 mile down the trail, turn north toward Jorn Lake. The Dixies are about 3/4 mile from this junction on the west side of the trail.

North Dixie covers about 3 acres and is 8 ft. deep. It has brook trout to 12 inches. The South lake is smaller, shallower, and is not stocked. It may or may not have fish. There are lots of adequate campsites nearby.

Dorman Pond offers bass and bluegill.

DON LAKES These trout lakes are hard to find. In fact, the Forest Service map does not show their location correctly, which doesn't make finding them easier. Upper Don Lake is about 1/2 mile due north of Parrish Lake and 1/2 mile NW of Daly Lake. See Daly Lake for road directions. From Daly, it's about a 1/2-mile bushwhack to the Don Lakes, bearing NW and descending slightly. The maps show them closer, but you'll have to cross two stream beds on your way.

Lower Don Lake is about 3 acres and over 20 ft. deep. Upper Don is 1/4 mile or so north up the stream bed and is smaller but also deep. Brook trout in both lakes grow to 12 inches, and there are lots of them. The lower lake also has quite a few cutthroat. There are good campsites in the area. A float tube would be handy but not necessary.

DORENA RESERVOIR A large reservoir on the Row River, 7 miles east of Hwy. 99 at Cottage Grove south of Eugene. Used mainly for flood control, it covers around 1,800 acres of water when full and holds its water level pretty well throughout spring and summer. Two good roads follow the north and south shoreline.

The reservoir is stocked with rainbow trout and has a good population of largemouth bass. It also has wild cutthroat, brown bullhead, bluegill, and black crappie. Angling has been generally good here. It is open for year-round angling and affords some good opportunities from September through January.

The trout range 6-14 inches, averaging 10 inches. Trolling accounts for most of the catch, but bait fishing from boats and shore is very popular. The upper end of the lake seems to be the most productive. There's good bass angling for fish to 8 pounds or more.

There are good boat ramps on both north and south shores, a picnic area, and restrooms with showers. The reservoir has a low-water boat ramp that permits launching year around. Rental boats and motors, and a limited selection of supplies are available at a concession on the reservoir. There are two parks with camping areas on the south side road. This is a peaceful and pretty place. Campsites are in a wooded area next to the lake.

DORMAN POND A very popular 12-acre pond west of Forest Grove at the junction of highways 8 and 6. The pond is on the south side of the road. Legal rainbow stocked in spring attract a lot of early attention. Later in the season, you'll find more solitude to fish the good populations of largemouth bass, bluegill, brown bullhead, and black crappie.

An old, high borrow pit, privately owned but open to public use, its banks have returned to natural vegetation. Motors are prohibited on the pond, but anglers can launch car-top and rubber boats from the shore.

DUFFY LAKE One of the best lakes in the Eight Lakes Basin of the Mt. Jefferson Wilderness. From North Santiam Hwy. 22, drive 3 miles east on Forest Rd. 2267 to the Duffy Lake Trailhead. Turn off Hwy. 22 (sign says Big Meadow) just south of the Santiam River crossing, 8 miles south of the Marion Forks Ranger Station and about 4 1/2 miles north of the Santiam junction. Hike 3 miles east on the Duffy Lake Trail 3427. The old Pacific Crest Trail (the PCT has been relocated closer to the crest) meets here also, coming in from Santiam Pass on Hwy. 20. This trail is now numbered 3491 and passes Santiam Lake.

Heavily used, Duffy is 30 acres and a consistent producer of brook trout. The trout run 6-15 inches, averaging 10 inches. Rainbow have also been stocked and make up a quarter of the catch, running to 12 inches. The brook trout are most easily taken while trolling, especially in early season, but you'll have to carry in that rubber raft. It's easy to fish from shore. Fly angling is good in fall from late afternoon till dark. There are good small lakes in all directions and nice campsites at Duffy. It is usually accessible by June, but it tends to get early snow.

DUMBELL LAKE One of the northernmost lakes of the Mink Lake Basin, holding stocked brook trout. From Elk Lake Resort take Trail 3517 west 2 1/2 miles to the Pacific Crest Trail, then hike south about 3 1/2 miles to the lake. An alternate approach is from the south by the Six Lakes Trail which heads one mile south of Elk Lake. This route will take you past Davis and Blow lakes. The Pacific Crest Trail touches the eastern shore of Dumbell, and the lake gets fished pretty hard.

Dumbell covers 6 acres and doesn't hold up well under the angling pressure. Its brook trout run 6-14 inches, averaging

9 inches. There are several unnamed lakes to the west of Dumbell that might provide surprises for the adventurous. Supplies are available at Elk Lake Resort.

EAGLE CREEK (Clackamas Co.) A very good winter steelhead stream with a traditionally strong run of coho and some wild cutthroat. It enters the lower Clackamas River just west of the community of Eagle Creek on Hwy. 211, 5 miles north of Estacada. From Portland, take Hwy. 224 through Carver. From Eagle Creek, county roads follow the creek east. The upper 10 miles of stream is accessible only by trail.

Eagle Creek heads in the Cascade foothills near the Salmon River divide. There is a hatchery operation on the stream which rears coho and winter steelhead. There is an occasional down year, but the winter steelhead catch is typically 1,000-2,000. The estimated 1991-92 catch was 1,150. The coho catch often exceeds 1,000, though only 246 were caught here in 1992. Spring and fall chinook are present in small numbers.

Steelhead start up the creek in December and are available through March, with angling activity from the Scout Camp at the mouth up to the hatchery. The creek is closed to salmon and steelhead angling above the hatchery intake. Coho start to show in the stream in late September and peak around November. Coho jacks are picked up in good numbers in late fall. Bait or spinners and small Kwikfish-type lures will take them.

The creek received its last stocking of hatchery rainbow in 1994. Wild cutthroat are present, and there's lots of good fly water here. Young steelhead which fail to go to sea, about 10 inches long, may also be present. Mostly males, they are already mature and will put up a good scrap, but they are dark like spawners. If released, they will probably go to sea the following spring.

There are no overnight campsites on the creek, but Eagle Fern Park near the mouth has a nice picnic area.

EAST McFARLAND LAKE This is a lightly fished brook trout lake 2 miles north of Irish Mt. about 6 trail miles north of Irish Lake. About 10 acres and over 30 ft. deep, it's very difficult to get to. The best route is to hike north on the Pacific Crest Trail from Irish Lake about 6 miles, passing Dennis and Lindick lakes. About 1/4 mile north of Lindick, bushwhack about 1/2 mile west, and you'll find the lake. The road to Irish is very rough. Watch your oil pan.

East McFarland is stocked by air, and there is usually some carry-over each year. It is usually inaccessible until late June.

A hatchery on Eagle Creek rears coho and winter steelhead.

EASTERN BROOK LAKE A good 11-acre lake in the Taylor Burn area. It is very close to Taylor Burn Forest Camp, north of Waldo Lake. From Oakridge on Hwy. 58 drive 20 miles east, turning north on the Waldo Lake Rd., Forest Rd. 5897. When you get to North Waldo Campground, head north on the old road which meets the Taylor Burn Rd. in about 4 miles. From Bend, take the Cascade Lakes Hwy. to Little Cultus, or cut west off Hwy. 97 onto any of the roads to Crane Prairie or Wickiup Reservoir, and follow the signs to Taylor Burn. From Taylor Burn Camp, go south 1/2 mile on the Wahana Trail, then head west down a side trail through a meadow about 1/4 mile to the lake. There are good campsites and water at Taylor Burn Camp.

Eastern Brook Lake is deep and usually holds a lot of fish, but it has its slack periods. Alternate your methods for better luck. Spinner and bait fished slowly will usually produce. The brook trout run 6-18 inches, with most around 10 inches. The road in usually opens near the end of June.

E.E. WILSON POND An 8-acre pond stocked with legal rainbow trout and large brood fish when available from the hatchery. Redear sunfish are also present, but elusive.

The pond is in the E.E. Wilson Wildlife Management Area of Camp Adair, off Hwy. 99W. The management area also provides habitat for deer, waterfowl, and pheasant. Anglers are urged to show consideration for nesting waterfowl in spring by staying on the path to the pond and confining activity to the angling area only. The management area is closed from October 1 through January 31 for waterfowl hunting season.

The half-mile trail leading from the parking lot to the pond is not paved, but it is wheelchair accessible. Recommended for small fry.

EDDEELEO LAKE, LOWER A large brook trout lake in the Taylor Burn area of the Central Cascades, about 1/2 mile north of Upper Eddeeleo Lake. See Upper Eddeeleo for directions. Lower Eddeeleo covers about 160 acres and produces consistently.

It's a good deep lake suited to any angling method. It can be fished from shore, but a float tube would be very useful. Angling is for naturally reproducing brook trout from 6-14 inches with a 10-inch average. Rainbow have not been stocked for some time, but a remnant might show up.

Fly angling is good, early and late in the day. Bucktails fished wet with a slow retrieve have been successful on larger fish. Other good flies are the blue upright, mosquito, black gnat, spruce fly and the reliable gray and brown hackles. If things get dull, try Long Lake to the north of Upper Eddeeleo and Round Lake to the south. There are lots of good campsites in the area, usually accessible by late June.

EDDEELEO LAKE, UPPER A good brook trout lake 2 miles NW of Waldo Lake in the headwaters of the North Willamette River. About 63 acres, the lake is approached from Taylor Burn Campground, 7 rough road miles north of the North Waldo Lake Campground. The area is usually accessible in late June. The Indian-sounding name for this lake is actually a combination of the first names of Ed Clark, Dee Wright, and Leo

McMahon, three early forest service workers who first stocked the lake.

From Taylor Burn, take Trail 3553 west from camp, down through the Willamette canyon, and up to the Quinn Lakes Trail junction. Go south on Trail 3597 for 3 miles past Long and Lower Eddeeleo lakes.

Upper Eddeeleo can also be reached from the Wehanna Trail 3590, which skirts the NW shore of Waldo Lake. Some anglers camp at North Waldo and boat across to the outlet at the NW corner of Waldo. From there it's only a 1 1/2 mile hike into the Eddeeleos.

The brook trout average about 10 inches and range 6-14 inches. The lake holds up well all season. The shore is quite brushy, making fly angling difficult from the bank, but flies work well early and late in the day. Bait and lures are effective any time. Other lakes close by are Lower Eddeeleo and Round Lake. Chetlo Lake is about one mile to the south.

EDNA LAKE A small trout lake just a few hundred yards west of Taylor Burn Campground, 7 miles by rough road north of North Waldo Lake Campground. Take the Olallie Trail (leading to the Erma Bell Lakes) west out of Taylor Burn. In about 1/4 mile, the trail passes Edna Lake.

Edna is only 3 acres, but is lightly fished and holds up well. The brook trout range 6-10 inches. It's easy to fish from shore or from logs extending into the water.

ELBOW LAKE (Lane Co.) A 10-acre brook trout lake near the NW edge of Waldo Lake, about 1/2 mile south of Chetlo Lake. It's about 5 1/2 trail miles from Taylor Burn or North Waldo Lake campgrounds. The easiest way in is by boat from Waldo Lake. See Chetlo Lake for directions.

Elbow has its ups and downs from year to year. Brook trout average 10 inches and range 6-13 inches. It can be fished from shore, and all methods will work when the fish are hitting. Try a Mickey Finn, casting out and letting it lie, bringing it in with short twitches. If this doesn't work, use nymph patterns or lures.

ELK LAKE (Marion Co.) A lightly fished 60-acre trout and kokanee lake at the head of Elk Creek, one of the main forks of the upper Collawash River. It can't be reached by road from the Mt. Hood Forest. Best approach is from Detroit on Hwy. 22. Take Forest Rd. 46 four miles NE from Detroit to Forest Rd. 4696, which intersects from the north. Follow 4696 for one mile, then take Forest Rd. 2209 left for 6 ferociously rough, steep miles to the lake. This road is usually impassable until late June.

Elk Lake usually provides good fishing for brook trout 7-10 inches and cutthroat. A population of kokanee reproduces naturally here, and the average fish caught is 8-9 inches. Though it's easy to fish from shore, a boat would be handy. All methods are used, but bait angling and trolling are best in early season. Fly angling picks up in late August and September. There's a good size campground, but no room for trailers. This is a good base camp for pack trips to lakes to the north. See Twin Lakes, Pansy, Big Slide.

EMERALD LAKE A privately owned 4-acre trout lake 19 miles east of Molalla on the North Fork Molalla River. Owned by a logging company, the lake is now closed to public use.

ERMA BELL LAKES A series of three very good rainbow lakes in the northern part of the Taylor Burn area. The lakes are along the Olallie Trail 3563. The northernmost is Lower Erma Bell.

According to Lewis McArthur, these lakes are named for what must have been one of Oregon's earliest automobile victims. Miss Erma Bell, employed by the Forest Service as a statistician, died in an automobile accident in April of 1918, and the Forest Service named these lakes for her.

The lakes can be approached from the north by driving to Skookum Creek Campground in the headwaters of the North Fork of the Middle Fork of the Willamette, by way of the North Fork Rd. Take Trail 3563 south 2 miles to Lower Erma Bell. An alternative approach is from Taylor Burn Campground, 7 miles by rough road north of North Waldo Lake Campground. Take Trail 3563 north about 2 miles to Upper Erma Bell.

Upper Erma Bell is the smallest of the three, covering 25 acres. Middle and Lower are each around 60 acres. Each of the lakes is fairly deep.

Lower and Middle have wild rainbow. Lower's rainbows run 6-15 inches with an average of 10 inches. They can be fished from shore. All methods will take fish, with fly angling good in mornings and evenings. Nymph patterns and deep fished wet flies should do well.

Middle Erma Bell is 1/4 mile south and slightly higher. It is a little larger and is very consistent for rainbow to 14 inches. All methods will work, and an occasional large trout is taken.

The upper lake is 1/2 mile further south and west of the trail. The fish here are brook trout, which average around 10 inches.

There are no improved campsites in the area, but there are good camps at Skookum Creek and Taylor Burn. At this time there is a 2-fish daily limit. The area is usually accessible near the end of June, depending on depth of snow pack.

ESTACADA LAKE The pool behind River Mill Dam on the Clackamas River at Estacada, reached from Hwy. 224. It is stocked with legal trout each season.

EUGENE REST AREA PONDS A series of ponds on the west side of Hwy. 99W between Eugene and Junction City, just north of Clear Lake Rd. The ponds were contaminated by chemicals from a plant across the road. Do not fish here.

FAIRVIEW CREEK A 5-acre urban stream, fed by springs SE of Grant Butte in Gresham and flowing five miles across East Multnomah County before entering Fairview Lake. The creek once provided habitat for cutthroat trout and steelhead. Much degraded by development and pollution, it is presently in the care of the Fairview Creek Watershed Conservation Group, among whose goals is the restoration of the creek's fish population.

For more information about Fairview Creek, or to participate in the restoration project, call the Fairview Creek Watershed Conservation Group at (503) 231-2270.

FAIRVIEW LAKE A bass and panfish lake of more than 200 acres, north of Hwy. 30 and west of Troutdale. Adjacent to Blue Lake, it has a mixed population that includes a lot of rough fish. The lake is completely surrounded by private lands and is currently closed to the public.

FALL CREEK (Lane Co.) This beautiful stream offers good trout angling and is quite popular. About 30 miles long, it heads in the Cascades between the McKenzie and Middle Fork Willamette drainages, and flows into Fall Creek Reservoir just NW of Dexter Reservoir. Above the reservoir it is followed by a hiking trail throughout much of its length.

From Eugene, drive SW on Hwy. 58 to Dexter Reservoir, then turn east onto the Lowell Rd. The reservoir is 3 miles past Lowell, and the creek empties into the eastern arm. Hwy. 126 from Springfield also leads to the reservoir, a 12-mile drive SE. From the town of Fall Creek, a paved road follows the stream east for 11 miles to the Willamette National Forest Boundary, where forest roads and a hiking trail follow the creek to its headwaters.

Fall Creek is heavily stocked with rainbow trout and has some nice wild cutthroat in the first 13 miles above the reservoir. Average size is about 9 inches with some going to 12. The best area for angling is from the head of the reservoir below the forest boundary to Sunshine Creek above Puma Camp. Bait and spinner are most effective in early season, with fly angling picking up in summer and good through the fall.

Spring chinook and summer steelhead are occasionally caught here. Angling for them is permitted up to Fall Creek Dam. In 1992, anglers caught 25 steelhead from October through January. Twenty-three chinook were caught in April and May. The Creek is closed to salmon angling from August 16 through October 31.

There's a lot of private land in the lower section, but the upper creek is all on public land. This is a fine recreational area, with four National Forest campgrounds in a 7-mile stretch. The upper creek has several good swimming holes favored by Eugene residents.

FALL CREEK RESERVOIR A fair size reservoir about 12 miles south of the Eugene-Springfield area. About 1800 acres when full, it is used mainly for flood control and is drawn down low in late fall. It is located just north of Lowell, which is reached from Hwy. 58 by crossing Dexter Reservoir. Two streams, Fall Creek and Winberry Creek, flow into it. The dam is just below the junction of the two streams.

Most angling is for stocked legal rainbow. The primary management objective for the reservoir is the rearing of juvenile chinook to smolt size. Consequently, no fingerling rainbow are stocked. Trout angling is best early in season and late fall, with trolling the best producer. There are several boat ramps and picnic areas on the reservoir, with campgrounds on the Fall Creek Rd. All roads are good in this area.

FANNO CREEK An urban stream meandering 14 miles through residential, commercial, and industrial lands in west Portland, Washington County, and Clackamas County. It empties into the Tualatin River at the city of Durham downstream from Cook Park.

A network of little parks, private woodlots, and urban wetlands have helped keep the creek alive. There is still a small breeding population of cutthroat trout here, occasionally fished by neighborhood kids. If you're one of them, you know how to find the creek. Remember that a trout has to be at least 6 inches long to be a keeper. Fanno opens for trout fishing the fourth Saturday in April.

The creek is now being cared for by Fans of Fanno Creek, a citizen's watershed protection group dedicated to preserving the creek and its fish and wildlife. For more information about Fanno Creek or to participate in restoration efforts, write Fans of Fanno, PO Box 25835, Portland, OR 97225 or Call Watershed Partners, United Sewerage Agency, (503) 648-8621.

FARADAY LAKE A popular and accessible 25-acre reservoir on the Clackamas River about 2 miles SE of Estacada by way of Hwy. 224. It is used for power purposes but provides fair angling. To reach it, turn off Hwy. 224 at the bridge, crossing the river.

Faraday is stocked with rainbow. An occasional steelhead enters the lake through the diversion canal and may be caught as a trout (no steelhead tag necessary). Most anglers use bait, but spinners and other lures will produce from the bank.

FAY LAKE A fairly good brook trout lake just off North Santiam Hwy. 22, in the Big Meadows area. About 4 1/2 miles north of Santiam Junction, take Forest Rd. 2267 for approximately one mile, then go left on 2257 for 2 miles into Big Meadows. The lake is about one mile north of Big Meadows Campground on the east side of the road. There are more roads in this area than show on the current maps, but if you find Big Meadows, you'll find the lake.

Fay Lake is only about 7 acres but holds up well even with heavy pressure. Brook trout run 6-15 inches, averaging 9 inches. Stocked rainbow about the same size make up half the catch. Formerly a fly-fishing only lake, it is now open to all methods. It's a hard lake to fish, shallow and clear, and if there is no wind on the surface the fish spook easily. The Forest Service has felled and submerged a number of big trees to enhance fish cover. The lake is brushy and hard to fish from shore, but it is easily waded. A light cartop or rubber boat would be useful here. There are good campsites at Big Meadows.

FERN RIDGE RESERVOIR A large flood control reservoir on the Long Tom River, 12 miles west of Eugene. It covers 9,000 acres when full. Primarily used for general water sports, it does support a small population of warmwater fish and some cutthroat. To reach it, follow Hwy. 126 west to the Territorial Rd. junction at Perkins Peninsula and Veneta. The Territorial Rd. passes through Elmira and leads to the dam at the north end of the reservoir.

Fern Ridge is very popular for general water recreation, especially sailing. There are 6 boat ramps, several boat docks, and 3 picnic areas as well as developments at Richardson Point on the NW shore and Perkin's Peninsula on the south. There is only one campground.

East of Perkins Peninsula Park, the Coyote Creek bypass leads to a lightly fished slough area that looks very promising for bass and panfish, with submerged trees and overhanging brush. To reach it, turn left just below the highway bridge. Crappie are plentiful at the inflow of the Long Tom River, and in the cement spillway structures below the dam (this area is especially good in winter). Bluegill are available in the shallows and the weedy areas. Largemouth bass can be found prowling the weedy slopes mornings and evenings.

Draw-downs of the reservoir have inhibited spawning and fry survival for all species. Plans are afoot for some habitat enhancement which might improve the fishery here. Check back in five years.

FIR LAKE Once a real sleeper, difficult to reach, with anglers in the know making terrific catches and keeping mum. It's not a big lake, only about 6 acres, but it's quite deep and puts out some really good brook trout. Most of the fish run 10-12 inches, but there are larger ones to 18 inches.

It used to be a brushy hike by compass to the lake, but there is now a blazed trail. To get there, first drive to Fay Lake. See Fay Lake for directions. Go north past Fay for about 1/4 mile to a turnout. A blazed trail takes off to the east from here, and it's about one mile to Fir (past Pika Lake, which has brook trout in it). Fir is fairly brushy but can be fished easily from logs if you don't have a rubber boat.

FIRECAMP LAKES A group of three lakes NW of Mt. Jefferson, near the head of the South Fork of the Breitenbush River. From Detroit on Hwy. 22, take Breitenbush Forest Rd. 46 for 10 miles (one mile past the Hot Springs), then take Forest Rd. 4685 to road's end. Crown Lake, the largest of the group, is 2 miles east on Trail 3361, at elevation 4,852 ft.

Crown is about 16 acres and quite shallow. It is stocked, but has a tendency to winterkill. The next lake, just a few hundred yards SE is Clagget Lake. This is a small but deep lake of several acres and is the most reliable lake of the three. The third lake, Sheep, is brushy, shallow, and hard to fish, but it produces larger trout.

This is an old burned-off area, great for huckleberries in late fall. Just over the ridge to the east are three other lakes which have good fishing at times. See Slideout Lake.

FIRST LAKE A 3-acre cutthroat trout lake accessed by road just north of Olallie Lake. It is the first lake south of Lower Lake Campground. The Olallie Lake Basin is about 100 miles from Portland by way of highways 26 or 224 and a network of forest roads. First Lake is west of the road. See Olallie Lake.

First Lake is stocked every other year now. It doesn't have a large trout population, but cutthroat 8-13 inches are available, and it is lightly fished. Spinner and bait and small lures cast from shore are effective. Campsites are available at Lower Lake Campground to the north and all around Olallie Lake to the south. Other lakes in the area include Head and Monon.

FISH CREEK (Clackamas Co.) A 15-mile long tributary of the Clackamas River, completely within Mt. Hood National Forest. It joins the Clackamas from the south about 9 miles upstream from North Fork Reservoir. From Estacada drive SE 16 miles on Hwy. 224 past the reservoir. Forest Rd. 54 crosses the Clackamas just past Lockaby Campground, immediately passes Fish Creek Campground, then follows the creek along its eastern bank for much of its length. Several trails lead down to the creek.

The creek has been closed for some time as part of a Forest Service study, but it may re-open soon. If so, you may anticipate finding wild cutthroat and a few brook trout. Wild rainbow also show up in the lower section. There's some good fly water in the upper stretch. There are four campgrounds near the mouth. Several lakes are located in the headwaters. See Skookum and Surprise.

FISH LAKE (Clackamas Co.) A 20-acre lake NW of Olallie Lake, featuring small stocked cutthroat and a few brook trout. From Lower Lake Campground on Olallie Lake Rd. (Forest Rd. 4220), follow Trail 717 NW just over one mile to the lake.

Though the trout only run 6-11 inches, good catches are made using all methods of angling. Bait, small lures, and spinners work well, with wet flies effective in the evening. This is a very deep lake, and a float tube would be useful. There are primitive campsites at the lake, but a power transmission line mars the scenery. There's a good camp at Lower Lake.

FISH LAKE (Hood River Co.) A small brook trout lake in the Mt. Hood National Forest about one mile by trail north of Wahtum Lake, 25 miles SW of Hood River. Trail 408 leads north from the Wahtum Lake parking area about 2 miles to the lake. When road conditions are suitable, you can follow a primitive road just over one mile around the east side of Wahtum then NW. This road intersects the trail and saves one mile of hiking.

Fish Lake is just 2 acres with few large fish. It is occasionally stocked with brook trout 6-12 inches, averaging 9-10 inches. The lake is shallow, and in severe winters the fish may all be lost to winterkill. Fly angling works best due to the shallowness of the lake. There are no good campsites here, but there are a few at Wahtum Lake to the south. The road usually opens late in spring.

FISH LAKE (Linn Co.) A shallow cutthroat lake north of Clear Lake, just off the South Santiam Hwy. 20. It's about 72 miles from Albany, 3 miles west of the Santiam junction.

About 50 acres, Fish Lake drains into Clear Lake. It has an unusually short open season (late April till June 1) because it tends to dry up, making its fish too vulnerable for sporting angling. Cutthroat from 6-14 inches are caught during the season, with fly-fishing very effective. There's a small campground here, and supplies can be obtained at Clear Lake Resort. Motorboats are prohibited on the lake.

FISHER LAKES Two small lightly fished trout lakes in the Horse Lake area of the Upper McKenzie watershed. See Horse Lake for directions. From Upper Horse Lake, take the McBee Trail SW for 1 1/2 miles. The trail goes right by Fisher Lakes. The fish here are small, 8-10 inches, both brook trout and cutthroat.

East Fisher is about 2 acres and 20 feet deep. It's shaped like a dumbell and is easily fished from shore by standing on the logs that line its bank. There are many good campsites in the Horse Lake area.

FOSTER RESERVOIR A 1,200 acre reservoir on the Santiam River near the town of Foster, about 3 miles east of Sweet Home, just north of Hwy. 20. It backs up the South and Middle Forks of the Santiam River, offering fishing for trout, bass, and bluegill.

Foster is stocked in April and May with catchable rainbow. Unauthorized plants of largemouth bass and bluegill have established themselves. Smallmouth bass appeared in the pool in 1988. The reservoir is lowered in April and May to allow young steelhead to escape. For water level information, call (503) 367-5124.

There are boat ramps at Gedney Creek Access, Sunnyside Park, and Calkins Park. Campgrounds are at Sunnyside Park and Meare Bend. Recommended for small fry.

FRAZIER LAKE (Clackamas Co.) A 3-acre lake in the High Rock Lakes area, one mile NE of Shellrock Lake. From High Rocks Lookout, reached by the Squaw Mt. Road (Forest Rd. 4610) or by the Shellrock Creek Road (Forest Rd. 58) from the Clackamas River on the south, head west on Forest Rd. 240 toward Frazier Mt. About 2 1/2 miles west there is a switchback from which the lake can be seen. It's a half mile hike from the road to the lake. There are other approaches to the lake as well. Check the Mt. Hood National Forest map.

Frazier is about 8 ft. deep, at an elevation of 4,100 ft. It contains brook trout 6-11 inches. All methods seem effective, with bait best early in the season and flies in summer and fall. The road in is usually snowbound until late June.

FREEWAY PONDS Trout ponds along I-5 about 9 miles south of Albany. Take the State Police Exit and follow the frontage road south. The ponds are stocked with legal rainbow in spring. Later, they offer pretty good fishing for bluegill and largemouth bass. Recommended for small fry.

FROG LAKE RESERVOIR Given the redundant name to distinguish it from another Frog Lake in the Clackamas River drainage. This Frog Lake is associated with the Three Lynx Power Station on the Oak Grove Fork of the Clackamas, and is notable for its population of large rainbow and brown trout, both of which migrate to the reservoir through a pipeline from Harriet Lake. About 16 acres, it can be reached from the Three Lynx Rd., off Hwy. 224. Frog Lake Reservoir is on the right. Boats are prohibited. Parking is plentiful.

This is an undeveloped recreation site, without camping or picnicking facilities, but Harriet Lake fish grow to nice size in this relatively non-competitive environment. There's not much shoal here, so plan to fish deep. There's a good chance the big trout stick around to feast on Frog Lake's plentiful sculpin population, so choose your offering accordingly.

GALES CREEK A steelhead and trout stream close to west Portland, major tributary of the Tualatin River, which it joins just south of Forest Grove. Gales Creek heads in the coast range near the headwaters of the Wilson River. The upper creek is followed by Hwy. 6, and the lower water by Hwy. 8 NW of Forest Grove. From Portland take Hwy. 26 west to the junction of Hwy. 6, then follow the highway to the stream.

Gales Creek is managed for winter steelhead, and the run was looking good for a while, but fewer than a hundred fish have been caught each year for the past five years. December through February are usually offer the best steelheading. Wild cutthroat trout are also available. A late trout opening on Gales Creek protects downstream steelhead migrants.

GANDER LAKE A fair size rainbow and brook trout lake at 5000 ft. elevation, 3 air miles NW of Waldo Lake. Forest roads have crept up on this lake and cut the hiking distance from 9 miles to a little over one, increasing the pressure and reducing the catch. Better have your forest map in hand when you set out for Gander, as you must navigate through a maze of roads to get to the trailhead.

From the south end of Oakridge on Hwy. 58, take the Salmon Creek road east, Forest Rd. 24. Watch for the salmon hatchery signs to locate the road. At about 11 miles, take Forest Rd. 2417 east roughly 12 miles, almost to its end. At the last fork (about 3/4 mile before road's end) follow Forest Rd. 256 to the left 1/2 mile to its end. Pick up a trail running due south. After 1/2 mile this trail intersects the Gander Lake Trail 3591. Take this trail to the right (west) and follow it 1/2 mile to the lake.

Gander covers 58 acres and is stocked with rainbow and/or brook trout. The average fish is around 10-11 inches, and they run to 16 inches. It's a good fly-fishing lake and can be fished from shore, but you'll do better if you get out on the lake. Good natural campsites are available.

GIFFORD LAKES Two beautiful little stocked rainbow lakes in the Olallie area about one mile west of the Skyline Rd. just north of Olallie Lake. It's most easily reached by hiking from Lower Lake Campground, around the north shore of Lower Lake to the junction of Trail 706, then south 1/2 mile. Upper Gifford is just east of the trail.

The upper lake covers about 8 acres and is quite deep. It is easily fished from shore, with plenty of casting room. All methods are effective. The rainbow run to 14 inches, averaging 10. Lower Gifford just north and has some good size brook trout. A float tube would be ideal. Feel free to keep fish from these stocked lakes.

Finley Lake perches on a rock cliff above the talus slope at the east shore of Gifford. Though no longer stocked, it makes a very scenic campsite. There's also a prime campsite on the peninsula and other undeveloped sites between upper and lower lakes. The area is not accessible until late June.

GILBERT RIVER A bass and panfish slough on Sauvie Island, about 10 miles NW of Portland off Hwy. 30. The property surrounding the slough is managed by ODF&W, and angling is only restricted during duck season. Sauvie Island offers a welcome respite from urban life for both wildlife and humans. See Sturgeon Lake, McNary Lake, Pete's Slough, and Cunningham Lake for other fishing opportunities on the island.

Gilbert heads near the south end of the island and is crossed by Reeder Rd. near its upper end. After crossing the Sauvie Island Bridge, turn left and drive west on Reeder Rd.

Gilbert River provides pretty good fishing for largemouth bass, crappie, bluegill, and brown bullhead. Canoes or small motor boats are appropriate for this quiet backwater in its bucolic setting.

The upper slough is followed by Oak Island Rd. several miles to Sturgeon Lake. The slough leaves the lake on the NW side and meanders another 5 miles NW, where it flows into Multnomah Channel. The upper and lower ends are accessible by road and some walking.

To reach the lower slough area, continue on Reeder Rd. for another 8 miles along the Columbia until you see the waterfowl checking station. Turn left, and one mile west puts you at the main dike. In summer you can proceed over the dike and drive on dirt roads to McNary Lakes at the north end of Sturgeon Lake. In order to reach Gilbert, leave your car on the east side of Pete's Slough, which parallels Gilbert, and cross on one of the footbridges. Gilbert is several hundred yards to the west.

The extreme lower end of the slough can be reached by going north past the checking station for 2 1/2 more miles and turning left on the dike road. This puts you at the mouth, where there is a gravel boat ramp.

You will need to purchase a recreation permit to park on the island. Day or seasonal passes are sold at the market on the island just north of the bridge. Refer to the Appendix for a map of the island.

GNAT LAKE A good 3-acre brook trout lake in the Mink Lakes Basin. Gnat is about 1 1/2 miles west of the Pacific Crest Trail near the Goose and Corner lakes trail. Gnat Lake is stocked with fingerling cutthroat trout every few years and provides good catches of 10-inch trout. You can fish from shore, but a float tube wouldn't hurt. See Corner Lake and Cliff Lake.

GOLD LAKE A very good trout lake for fly anglers. It's just north of the Willamette Pass summit off Hwy. 58, 23 miles SE of Oakridge. You can drive right to it. It is restricted to fly angling only, and no motorboats are allowed.

To reach Gold Lake, drive 23 miles SE from Oakridge on Hwy. 58. About 2 miles south of the Waldo Lake turn-off, Forest Rd. 500 turns off to the east and leads 2 miles to the campground at the SW corner of the lake. The turn-off is signed. The road is usually open by June, but may be rough and muddy.

The catch is at least 2 to 1 brook trout to rainbow. Rainbows must be released unharmed. The lake isn't stocked, but holds up well because of the short season and restricted tackle. Trout taken here are all wild, ranging in size from 6-20 inches.

Gold is about 1/2 mile long and covers slightly over 100 acres. Although it can be fished from shore, it's pretty brushy, and a boat is strongly recommended. The shallower water at the NE end of the lake always seems to be livelier. Slow trolling a wet fly or nymph will stir up action when the hatch is off. Fly anglers will have a good time trying to match the hatch. Most standard patterns will do the trick if used at the right time. Bring plenty of tippet material.

There's a nice campground here, with boat ramp and shelter, and much waterfowl activity. Supplies are available at the Odell Lake resorts. The Marilyn Lakes, good for brook trout, are just south of Gold by trail. All tributaries of the lake are closed, and Salt Creek, the outlet stream, is closed down to the Hwy. 58 Bridge.

GOODFELLOW LAKES A series of three lakes in the closed area of the Bull Run Watershed, the water supply for the city of Portland. Gates on the roads leading to the area are locked. We mention it here to prevent anglers from walking into an illegal area.

GOOSE LAKE A 9-acre bass and panfish lake 7 miles north of Salem. Access is through Willamette Mission Park off the Wheatland Ferry Rd. Largemouth bass and white crappie are available.

GORDON CREEK This small tributary of the Sandy River provides interesting fishing for wild cutthroat and rainbow trout. The stream is about 12 miles long and joins the lower Sandy from the east. The Sandy River Rd. crosses its mouth about 7 miles south of Hwy. 30. No road follows the stream, but the upper reaches are accessible from several dirt roads that cut south off the Larch Mt. Rd.

Rainbows predominate in this rather steep stream. Average size is 9 inches with a few fish larger. Beaver ponds in the upper tributaries have been known to have fair size cutthroat.

GORDON LAKES Two small cutthroat lakes south of South Santiam Hwy. 20, about 15 miles east of Cascadia. Take Forest Rd. 2044 south from Hwy. 20 at House Rock Campground. It's a bit over 3 miles to Forest Rd. 230, which cuts off to the SW. Follow 230 about 2 miles to road's end. The lakes are about 1/4 mile NW. The area is usually accessible in June.

These are wild cutthroat lakes, each about 7 acres and fairly deep. Both lakes have fish 6-15 inches, with an average length 10 inches. Bait angling with eggs or worms will take them early, and spinner and bait combinations should attract some large fish. Fly angling is good late in the season.

The lakes are connected by stream and trail, with the further lake larger and at slightly lower elevation. It is also considerably deeper and have a brushy shore that makes casting difficult. An old growth log extending into the lake serves as a natural pier. Both lakes offer pleasant swimming in late summer.

GOVERNMENT ISLAND LAKE (a.k.a. Beer Can Lake) At the west end of state-owned Government Island, in the Columbia River just east of Portland. It supports a portion of the I-205 Bridge across the river but can only be reached by boat. Landing on the island is prohibited, but when the river is high you can take a boat up a slough (Beer Can Slough) on the north side of the island. At low water, it may also be possible to fish the lake within the high water zone around the lake's perimeter.

The 40-acre lake contains crappie, brown bullhead, perch and a few largemouth bass. Angling is usually fair before spring high water and again for a few months after. Bait, spinners, and plugs are all used with success, with bait most popular. The island is owned by the Port of Portland, which has eliminated public access following repeated acts of vandalism.

GREEN PEAK LAKE A brook trout lake which is lightly fished and hard to find, located near the Eight Lakes Basin in the Mt. Jefferson Wilderness Area. Best approach is from Blue Lake. See Blue Lake for directions. Green Peak is a steep bushwhack one mile due west of Blue.

The lake is about 6 acres and 12 ft. deep. It puts out fair catches of 10-12 inch brook trout, but some large ones should show up due to light pressure. There are good natural campsites.

GREEN PETER RESERVOIR A flood control reservoir on the Middle Santiam River offering fishing for rainbow, kokanee, and largemouth bass. It is east of Sweet Home and Foster, north of Hwy. 20. Quartzville Creek and the Middle Santiam form a pool of over 3,700 acres at high level.

A naturally reproducing population of kokanee is well established and draws a lot of angler attention. Catches have been quite heavy, with fish usually closer to the surface than at Detroit Reservoir. Anglers jig Buzz Bombs at about 40 ft., going deeper later in the year. The kokanee run 10-11 inches. The largemouth bass fishery here is growing in size and popularity. Catchable rainbow trout are stocked in April.

There is a boat ramp, but it's difficult to use at low water. When the reservoir is drawn down, lighter boats can be launched at Thistle Creek Boat Access and at Whitcomb Creek Park. There are overnight camping facilities at Whitcomb Creek Park upstream on the reservoir.

GREEN POINT CREEK A small trout stream heading near Wahtum Lake SW of Hood River, flowing into the West Fork Hood River near Dee. To reach Green Point, cross the West Fork downstream from Dee off Hwy. 281, and follow the signs west. The stream is about 10 miles long and is followed by a dirt road throughout most of its length. It has fair angling for wild trout.

GROSSMAN POND A privately owned 2-acre pond near Independence, open to public enjoyment by permission of the owner. Follow Monmouth St. to Talmadge Rd. Turn south 0.6 mile. Bluegill and largemouth bass are available. The landowner encourages anglers to release all bass.

HAGG LAKE Source of the current state record smallmouth bass, a Bureau of Reclamation reservoir on lower Scoggins Creek about 7 miles SW of Forest Grove. Hagg Lake is a popular general recreation area for communities SW of Portland and has been attracting smallmouth anglers from throughout the metropolitan area and its suburbs. From Hwy. 47, just south of Dilley near Forest Grove, a paved road runs about 7 miles west to the reservoir. A second road from Gaston also reaches the lake. The reservoir holds 1,100 acres of water when full. It is drawn down in late fall.

Smallmouth activity picks up when the lake temperature reaches 60 to 65 degrees. Early in the season the bass are attracted to the warmer shallower areas, especially the Tanner Creek Arm at the northeast end of the lake. Later in the season, smallmouth move into the cooler water of the Seine Creek Inlet Arm on the east, and the deep south end of the lake near the dam and Scoggins Creek outlet.

In spring, lures that imitate trout fingerlings (optimistically planted by ODF&W) are effective bass attractors. In fall, try plastic worms. The record-making smallmouth was caught here in September 1994 using a green plastic worm with split shot.

Yellow perch are also a popular fishery. Tanner Creek and the litttle cove north of A-Ramp (east shore at the end of Herr Rd.) are good spots. Bluegill and crappie are also plentiful in the cove

Hagg Lake was originally intended as a trout lake. Today, warmwater species are far more plentiful. Legal rainbow trout are planted each April and the lake does have a self-sustaining population of cutthroat which spawn in the tributaries. Best trout fishing is in the Scoggins Creek Inlet Arm at the northwest end of the lake, and in the Seine Creek Arm. Best trout fishing is in spring and early summer before the lake warms. Largemouth bass are present in small numbers, and only a few seem to be caught each year.

There are two boat ramps on the lake, A-Ramp off Herr Rd. on the west shore, and B-Ramp off West Shore Drive. Portions of the lake have speed limits that boating anglers will appreciate. Don't come here expecting a wilderness experience. This place can be very busy summer. In fact, boats are required to move in a counter-clockwise pattern to minimize the possibility of collisions.

There are four developed picnic areas, including a group picnic area at the southwest end of the lake. A wheelchair accessible fishing facility is located near the Elk Point Picnic Area at the south end of the lake. There are no campgrounds.

HALDEMAN POND A small pond on Sauvie Island built by the Dept. of Fish and Wildlife. It's on Oak Island in Sturgeon Lake. After crossing the Sauvie Island Bridge from Hwy. 30, turn left then right onto Reeder Rd. The Oak Island Rd. will be on the left.

The pond is only about 4 acres, but deep. Originally stocked with bluegill and largemouth bass, it now has rainbow trout as well. Best success is with single eggs. Rubber boats and canoes can be launched, but nothing larger. The trout average 10 inches and run to 15 inches. Try spinners with bait in early season. The pond is closed to angling during waterfowl season, but open the rest of the year.

You will need to purchase a recreation permit to park on Sauvie Island. Day or seasonal passes are sold at the market on the island just north of the bridge. Refer to the Appendix for a map of the island.

HANKS LAKE A small scenic trout lake high in the Mt. Jefferson Wilderness south of Mt. Jefferson, west of Cathedral Rocks. Located in a cove-like meadow beside Hunts Lake. It is best reached by a short, steep trail from Pamelia. For directions, see Hunts Lake. Hanks offers consistent fishing for brook trout. There are beautiful natural campsites at both lakes.

HARRIET LAKE A reservoir on the Oak Grove Fork of the Clackamas River, about 60 miles from Portland. Narrow and deep, it is 23 acres and contains three varieties of trout. Rainbow predominate, but some lunker brown and brook trout lurk here.

From Estacada, take Hwy. 224 SE into the Mt. Hood National Forest and continue to Ripplebrook Ranger Station. About one mile beyond the ranger station, follow Forest Rd. 57 toward Timothy Lake. The road follows the south bank of the Oak Grove Fork. At about 6 miles, the road crosses the fork, and Forest Rd. 4630 cuts back west a mile to Harriet Lake.

The fishing runs hot and cold at Harriet. It is stocked with legal rainbow in spring and summer and contains wild fish from the streams above. Best angling is at the upper end, where large rainbow and browns to 4 pounds are taken each spring by anglers who know the lake. Most of the catch consists of rainbow 8-15 inches. The action usually slows in summer and fall. Most fish are taken by trolling large spinners and worms. Anglers also cast small lures and spinners along the shore line.

There is a campground and picnic area at the head of the lake.

HARVEY LAKE (Lane Co.) A rainbow trout lake in the Taylor Burn area north of Waldo Lake. Harvey is 1 1/2 miles south of Taylor Burn Campground off Olallie Trail 3583, 1/4 mile south of Wahanna Lake and a bushwhack west of the trail. Taylor Burn campground is reached by 7 miles of rough road leading north from North Waldo Lake Campground.

The lake is 22 acres and up to 24 feet deep. It is stocked regularly with small rainbow. The fish do well and range in size from 6-18 inches, averaging 10 inches. Harvey can be fished from shore, and any method will take fish when they're hitting. There are no good campsites at the lake.

HEAD LAKE A 2-acre cutthroat trout lake off the Skyline Rd. just north of Olallie Lake. Head Lake is just west of the road, about 1/4 mile south of Lower Lake Campground.

It can be fished from shore and is fairly productive for fish ranging 7-14 inches, averaging 10 inches. Spinner and bait are usually best. Fly angling is generally good around evening later in the season. There is no camp at the lake, but camps are available all around Olallie Lake to the south. Other good lakes in the area include Fish and Monon. The road is rarely open before late June.

HEART LAKE (Linn Co.) A 13-acre brook trout lake south of South Santiam Hwy. 20, about 7 miles west of the Santiam Junction. About 3 miles west of Lost Prairie Campground on Hwy. 20, take Forest Rd. 60, which cuts back sharply to the east. After 2 miles the road crosses Indian Creek and turns north. Stay on 60 and proceed east a little over a mile to where the road dips to cross a stream. This stream is the outlet of Heart Lake, and the lake is upstream an excruciatingly steep 1/2 mile.

Heart Lake usually holds up well into the season. The brook trout average about 9 inches and run 6-12 inches. Heart is 13 acres and fairly deep. All methods of angling will take fish, with flies usually good in fall.

HELEN LAKE A 6-acre lake in the Taylor Burn area north of Waldo Lake, offering good rainbow trout fishing at times. A quarter mile trail leads north to the lake from the very rough Taylor Burn Rd., Forest Rd. 517. Watch your oil pan on this one. The trailhead is at Taylor Butte, about one mile east of the Taylor Burn Campground.

Helen can be easily fished from shore. It's deep throughout, and lures or spinners cast and retrieved slowly bring up the fish. Flies work nicely in the evening. The trout average 8-10 inches with a few to 14 inches. The lake is usually accessible in late June.

HIDEAWAY LAKE A 12-acre lake stocked with cutthroat, in the upper Clackamas River area near the head of the South Fork of Shellrock Creek, elevation about 3,00 ft. Once a dandy hike-in lake, it is now accessed by road and is heavily fished. From Estacada follow Hwy. 224 to the Timothy Lake Rd., turning north at Shellrock Creek. At about 3 miles, follow Forest Rd. 5830 to the left. In 4 miles you'll be at the lake.

There's some natural reproduction of trout here, and the lake is stocked, but pressure is high. It's shallow enough to provide good fly fishing, but all methods work. The trout are 7-13 inches with most around 10 inches. A nice campground has been provided courtesy of an Isaak Walton League chapter. Anglers can show their appreciation by helping to keep the grounds and facilities clean. The lake is usually snowbound until late May.

HIDDEN LAKE (Lane Co.) A good 11-acre wild cutthroat lake, 3 miles south of Cougar Reservoir. Not as well hidden as it was before the roads came in, it will still take your attention to find it.

From McKenzie Hwy. 126, take the South Fork of the McKenzie Rd. past Cougar Reservoir to Forest Rd. 1980, 1/2 mile past French Pete Campground. Drive west on 1980 about 3 miles, crossing Buoy Creek to a right angle intersection with Forest Rd. 231. Stay on 1980, which is the hard left, and you will again cross Buoy Creek, the outlet from Hidden Lake. There is no trail, and the lake is difficult to spot from the road, about 300 yards west, but you can always follow the stream. The snow usually melts by early June.

The cutthroat here are all wild and run 6-16 inches, averaging 10 inches. Bait or spinner combinations are best early in the season, and wet flies are effective. Supplies are available at Blue River or McKenzie Bridge on Hwy. 126. All tributaries are closed to angling.

HIGH LAKE (Clackamas Co.) A little pocket near the top of the mountain, usually worth the hike. It is on the Fish Creek Divide south of the upper Clackamas River. From Estacada drive SE on Hwy. 224 to where Forest Rd. 4620 crosses the river and heads south. This cut-off is signed for Indian Henry Campground and is about 3 miles before Ripplebrook Ranger Station. Follow 4620 about 8 miles to Forest Rd. 210 cutting west. Take this spur about 1/2 mile to an intersecting road. Turn north on this road and follow it to a hairpin turn about 3/4 mile distant. Ignore a fork to the left before the hairpin. Cold Spring Trail 541 heads north from the hairpin. This is a very steep trail which gains 1,200 ft. in about 1 1/2 miles. Near the summit of Fish Creek Mountain, a trail drops down

Large rainbow and browns are taken at the upper end of Harriet Lake.

1/4 mile or so to the lake. It is on the east side of the mountain.

High Lake has a lot of brook trout 6-11 inches. The lake is about 3 acres and 12 feet deep. All methods can be effective. There are some nice natural campsites here. It is accessible in early June.

HILLS CREEK (Lane Co., upper Willamette) A large tributary of the upper Middle Fork of the Willamette River, emptying into Hills Creek Reservoir about 4 miles SE of Oakridge. About 18 miles long, the creek heads in Diamond Peak Wilderness. Forest Rd. 23 follows it from the reservoir upstream.

The lower 3-4 miles are stocked with legal rainbow in summer. A few wild cutthroat show up in the catch, but rainbow predominate, running 10-12 inches. There are campgrounds at the reservoir.

HILLS CREEK RESERVOIR A multipurpose reservoir 3 miles south of Oakridge, offering consistently good winter fishing for rainbow trout. Cutthroat and crappie are also available. The reservoir was created by the damming of Hills Creek and the Middle Fork of the Willamette. To get there take Hwy. 58 SE from Eugene to Oakridge. About one mile beyond Oakridge, follow the signs. The reservoir is about 8 miles long and covers 2,735 acres. It is heavily fished due to easy access.

It is kept well stocked with rainbows and picks up cutthroat from its tributaries. Most of the rainbows are 8-12 inches, but quite a few grow larger, with some to 20 inches. All methods can produce, though trolling is most popular. Its variable crappie fishery is concentrated in the Hills Creek Arm at the upper end of the reservoir. Crappie fishing can be quite good some years.

The Forest Service and Corps of Engineers have provided good recreational facilities here. Packard Creek Campground, on the west bank about 3 1/2 miles upstream from the dam, has a paved boat ramp and RV and picnic facilities. There is another ramp at the C.T. Beach Picnic area, about 2 miles from the dam on the Hills Creek arm. Supplies and accommodations are available in Oakridge.

HONEY LAKES A couple of nice brook trout and cutthroat lakes in the Three Sisters Wilderness Area, 6 miles due west of South Sister and 6 miles south of Linton Lake. It's at least a 6-mile hike from the nearest road to this basin.

Just east of McKenzie Bridge Ranger Station on Hwy. 126, take the Foley Ridge Rd., Forest Rd. 2643, about 12 miles to the end where it meets the Substitute Point Trail 3511. About a 5-mile hike takes you past Substitute Point to the intersection of Trail 3520, which you follow south 1 1/2 miles to the basin. It's also possible to approach from the east by a side trail leading from the Pacific Crest Trail.

There are two main lakes in this group. Honey is the larger at about 12 acres. Brook trout here range 6-15 inches, averaging 10 inches. Kidney Lake is the other good lake. It's 1/2 mile to the west of Honey, and is good for trout to 16 inches, averaging 10. Kidney Lake is about half the size of Honey. Both lakes are exceptionally cold. There are several smaller pothole lakes in the area, but they produce little but mosquitoes. There are good natural campsites in the basin. Users are urged to follow no-trace camping guidelines.

HORSE CREEK A large tributary of the upper McKenzie River, entering the river at the community of McKenzie Bridge on Hwy. 126. About 24 miles long, the stream heads in the Horse Lake area north of the Mink Lake Basin and flows NW to McKenzie Bridge. Forest Rd. 2638 follows the lower 10 miles of the stream to the boundary of the Three Sisters Wilderness.

Horse Creek has a population of wild cutthroat. The water is clear, swift, and cold, and fishing can be slow. The average catch is 9-12 inches, with all methods of angling used. Horse Creek Campground is on the creek about a mile above McKenzie Bridge.

HORSE LAKES Several good hike-in trout lakes in the Three Sisters Wilderness Area at the head of Horse Creek, a tributary of the McKenzie River. Trails coming into the area from the west are all very long. Best access is from Elk Lake on the Cascade Lakes Hwy. 35 miles SW of Bend. Trail 3517 heads at the Elk Lake Guard Station and leads 4 miles west to Upper Horse Lake.

The upper lake covers 60 acres and contains naturally reproducing brook trout, including some of good size. It can be fished from shore, but more water can be covered from a raft or float tube. It offers good fly angling in late summer and fall.

Middle Horse Lake is about 1/2 mile west, but a little longer by the Horse Creek Trail, which is easier than beating brush. Middle Lake is about 5 acres, with small brook and cutthroat trout 6-10 inches.

Lower Horse Lake NW of Middle Lake, is shallow and about 25 acres. It has a population of wild cutthroat and some brook trout. The cutthroat are small but eager and are a lot of fun on light fly tackle. It really takes a rubber raft or float tube to fish this area decently.

There are many other smaller lakes in the area, such as Sunset, Moonlight, Herb, Park and Mile lakes. Most are stocked with brook trout or rainbows.

HORSESHOE LAKE (Lane Co.) A good hike-in rainbow lake on the Pacific Crest Trail in the Mink Lake Basin west of Elk Lake. For trail directions, see Cliff Lake. Horseshoe Lake is about 1 mile south of Cliff Lake on the Pacific Crest Trail. The first lake you pass on the west side of the trail is Moody Lake. It has cutthroat and rainbows. Horseshoe is 1/4 mile further south, on the east side of the trail.

Horseshoe is 60 acres and fairly shallow, and it grows exceptionally large trout for a high mountain lake. Its rainbows average 6-20 inches. All methods can produce, with fly-fishing good in the evenings. There are good campsites nearby, and a shelter at Cliff Lake. Some of the many nearby fishable lakes include Mink, Mac, Cliff, Porky, Merrill.

HORSESHOE LAKE (St. Paul area) A classic oxbow lake formed when the Willamette river punched through a bend and shifted course. It offers a variety of Willamette species. The lake is about 40 miles SW of Portland between Dayton and St. Paul, 1/2 mile east of the Willamette River and 2 miles west of St. Paul by a good road. From Newberg on 99W, go south on Hwy. 219 to St. Paul. From 99E at Hubbard, turn west on Hwy. 214.

Horseshoe covers about 25 acres and is surrounded by private land. There's a small charge for parking, and boat rentals are available. It has good populations of crappie, bluegill, perch, brown bullhead and largemouth bass. A few large bass are taken on plugs each season. It's a good spot for relaxed summer bait fishing.

HORSESHOE LAKE (Olallie Lake area) A pretty, 14-acre brook and rainbow lake between Olallie and Breitenbush Lakes on Forest Rd. 4220. You can drive right to this scenic beauty, and there is a campground here. A spit of land juts into the lake from the west shore giving the lake its characteristic shape. It's easy to fish from shore.

HUNTS LAKE A small scenic trout lake in the Mt. Jefferson Wilderness south of Mt. Jefferson, west of Cathedral Rocks. The Pacific Crest Trail passes above the lake 1/3 mile to the east. Best approach is from Pamelia Lake by taking the trail that follows Hunts Creek upstream (south) for 3 miles to the junction of Trail 3430. Follow this trail east past Hanks Lake and north to Hunts Lake, a total distance of about one mile.

Hunts Lake is about 6 acres and offers both rainbow and cutthroat. The cutthroat average 9 inches with a few to 12 inches. The rainbow average 8-10 inches. All methods of angling will work.

Hanks Lake, 1/4 mile south, is slightly larger and contains brook trout about the same size as those in Hunts. It's a beautiful alpine area with attractive natural campsites. Both lakes are consistent and easy to fish.

INDIAN PRAIRIE LAKE A good rainbow lake just outside the Willamette National Forest, south of the North Santiam Hwy. in the headwaters of Thomas Creek. The lake is between the head of Neal Creek and Indian Prairie Creek. The quality of roads in this area depends on logging status. There are no signs to the lake. Contact the State Forestry Department for the Linn County Fire Patrol District map for help in locating it. Indian Prairie lake is owned by a logging company which allows public access. There are two gates. The first is about 3 miles from the lake and may be locked. Foot access is permitted.

Indian Prairie is stocked with rainbow trout. Bait or spinner/bait combinations work well. Fishing from a motor propelled boat is prohibited.

INDIGO LAKE A pretty hike-in trout lake with good fishing in the SE corner of Willamette National Forest, 5 miles south of Summit Lake. This is a fine place that would make a good get-away. An easy trail begins at the south end of Timpanogas Lake Campground and climbs 700 feet in 1 1/2 miles directly to the lake. See Timpanogas.

Indigo is at 6,000 feet in a basin directly below Sawtooth Mountain, which dominates the view when you reach the lake. The south end is a talus slope which offers plenty of backcasting room for fly anglers at the deepest end, over 30 feet just 100 feet from shore. The forest runs right up to the lake along the rest of the shore except at the extreme north end. The north half of the lake is under 10 feet deep.

Trout average 8-10 inches with some to 14 inches. Rainbow, cutthroat, and brook trout are often in residence. The lake isn't heavily fished, and almost any method will take fish when they're feeding. There are improved campsites at the south end of the lake. Timpanogas Lake has a fully developed campground. The road to Timpanogas usually opens in late June.

ISLAND LAKE (Mink Lake area) A 3-acre lake offering fair fishing for rainbows. It's located in the north Mink Lake Basin, east of Elk Lake. For trail directions, see Dumbell Lake. Island is 1/2 mile south of Dumbell on the west side of the Pacific Coast Trail.

The lake is stocked by air. Trout average 9 inches and run to 11 inches. Best fishing is early in the season and again in late fall. Though a little too accessible for good angling, it usually produces a few fish. There are natural campsites in the area.

ISLAND LAKES (Gold Lake area) Two small brook trout lakes which provide good fishing for a few months during spring and fall. About 14 miles SE of Oakridge on Hwy. 58, just past the railroad trestle crossing over the highway, Forest Rd. 5883 cuts north. Follow 5883 about 9 miles to its end, where a short spur trail leads to the Fuji Mt. Trail 3670. A quarter mile north on 3670 brings you to an intersection with the Island Lake Trail, which you follow SE a bit over 1/2 mile to the intersection of the Waldo Lake Trail 3586. Hike 1/2 mile NE on 3586 to Island Lakes.

Lower Island is on the south side of the trail and is about 7 acres. Upper Island Lake, on the north side of the trail, is about 9 acres.

The trout average 10 inches, with a few to 13 inches and better. All methods will work, with fly angling especially good in the evening. There are nice natural campsites at the lakes and a developed campground at Gold Lake.

JEFFERSON JUNCTION BORROW PIT A 5-acre pond north of Albany, west of Hwy. 99. It contains largemouth bass, bluegill, and brown bullhead.

JOHNSON CREEK (Multnomah Co.) An urban trout stream, popular with neighborhood youngsters, which heads near Boring and flows 24 miles past Gresham and through SE Portland, entering the Willamette River just north of Milwaukie. Roads follow the creek, and it's crossed many times by bridges. Johnson Creek is one of the region's last free-flowing urban streams, and though severely degraded by development and by agricultural and industrial pollution, it does still support fish and light angling activity.

Access is difficult because of private homes along the stream, but there is open water in the upper creek, and angling is possible throughout at public road crossings. If you live in the neighborhood, you know where these crossings are. Other access points are Tideman Johnson Park off SE Berkeley Way in Eastmoreland, and Johnson Creek Park between Sherrett and Marion in Sellwood. The city of Milwaukie owns land along the bank from the mouth upstream one mile, open to public access from Hwy. 99E.

ODF&W encourages youngsters to fish Johnson Creek. The creek is stocked with catchable rainbow trout through May from Johnson Creek Park just west of McLoughlin almost to 82nd St. Unfortunately the stream gets too warm to permit stocking later in the season. Some wild cutthroat are also caught in the spring. An occasional coho is seen in the fall, and Johnson Creek has a small (very small) run of winter steelhead which may be fished. All non-finclipped steelhead must be released unharmed. Barbless hooks are required for all fishing from November 1 through the fourth Saturday in April. The stream is usually pretty high and muddy when the steelhead come up.

In 1994 50,000 tule chinook smolts were released into Johnson Creek. This race of chinook was selected because its fry emerge in winter and only need to spend about four months in fresh water before migrating to sea. Any later, and Johnson Creek gets too warm for fry survival.

Unfortunately, the tule will be past their prime for angling purposes by the time they make it back to Johnson. If the tules return, they should be enjoyed as a wildlife viewing opportunity rather than as an opportunity for angling.

From summer through fall, bass and panfish are taken in the lower few miles. A few good size bass are taken near the mouth each year. Waterfront Park Boat Ramp on the Willamette at the Johnson Creek confluence offers some access to the lower bass water.

For more information about Johnson Creek or to participate in restoration efforts, write Friends of Johnson Creek, 11820 SE Foster Pl., Portland, OR 97266.

JORN LAKE A heavily fished lake in the Eight Lakes Basin of the Mt. Jefferson Wilderness. Take Trail 3422 four miles south from the western shore of Marion Lake to Jorn. This is beautiful hiking country.

The brook trout here average 10-12 inches with a few to 15 inches. All methods of angling will work at times, and the lake can be easily fished from shore. This 35-acre lake is hit hard because of its central location in the basin and pretty campsites. Fly-fishing in the late afternoon and evenings usually pays off.

There are many good lakes in the basin. See Bowerman, Teto, Chiquito, Blue lakes. The area can also be reached from Duffy Lake to the south. It is usually accessible in early June depending on snow pack.

JUDE LAKE (Confederated Tribes Warm Springs) One of a group of three hike-in brook trout lakes east of the Skyline Rd. and north of Olallie Lake. The trail begins at Olallie Meadow Campground, 3 miles north of Olallie Lake. It's a 1/2 mile hike to Jude.

Jude is about 2 acres and quite brushy. Bait or spinner and bait are effective early in the season, and fly angling works well later. The fish run 8-12 inches, averaging l0 inches. A tribal permit is not required to fish Jude, or nearby Russ and Brook lakes. Overnight camping is prohibited at these lakes due to fire danger. The nearest campground is at Olallie Lake.

JUNCTION CITY POND An 8-acre pond on the west side of Hwy. 99 about 3 miles south of Junction City, 0.9 miles south of the Hwy. 36 junction. The pond is heavily stocked with rainbow trout and an occasional brood fish. It also contains crappie, brown bullhead, and largemouth bass. A former gravel pit, and not at all picturesque, it can nevertheless offer lively fishing in spring.

JUNCTION LAKE A pretty 50-acre hike-in lake amongst old trees at a trail junction in the Mink Lake Basin west of Elk Lake. It is l/2 mile NW of Mink Lake and at least 6 miles by trail from the nearest road. See Mink Lake.

Junction contains rainbow and cutthroat from 8-11 inches, with a few to l5 inches. A float tube would be helpful. This is an on again, off again lake. Inquire at the Elk Lake Guard Station for current conditions. Good natural campsites are plentiful throughout the basin. Other good lakes in the basin include Mink, Porky, Corner, Cliff .

JUNE LAKE A shallow 11-acre lake in the headwaters of the Middle Fork Willamette, south of Summit Lake. It is stocked with rainbow trout, but it occasionally winterkills.

KELLOG CREEK An urban stream flowing through SE Portland from Johnson City near Milwaukie to the Willamette River. The creek originates in a little wetland upstream from Lake Lenore. Near the Willamette, it enters Kellog Lake, which can be seen from Dogwood Park. Though flowing through intensely developed, primarily residential land, the creek is shaded by what urban planners call a linear forest and may support some forms of aquatic life. However, it is doubtful that gamefish can survive here due to heavy winter flows and reduced, warm summer flows. The creek is being monitored, and restoration studied by a citizen interest group,

For information about Friends of Mt. Scott/Kellogg Watershed or to participate in restoration efforts, write the Friends at PO Box 22112, Milwaukie, OR 97269.

KIRK POND A 10-acre fishery on the north side of the main road immediately below Fern Ridge Dam. It contains white crappie, largemouth bass, bluegill, and brown bullhead.

KIWA LAKE A good rainbow and brook trout lake in the heart of the Taylor Burn area north of Waldo Lake. To reach Taylor Burn Campground follow a rough road 7 miles north from North Waldo Lake Campground.

Kiwa is 2 miles south of Taylor Burn Campground by way of Olallie Trail 3583, on the east side of the trail. An easier drive, but slightly longer hike, begins at North Waldo Lake Campground. Hike west along the northern shore of Waldo Lake on Trail 3590, then north on Trail 3583 past the Rigdon lakes to Kiwa.

Deservedly popular, Kiwa is consistent year after year for good size rainbow and brook trout. It covers about 40 acres and reaches a depth of 25 ft. The trout average l0 inches and run to l6. All methods of angling work, and you can easily fish from shore. Bait angling is always good. Lures trolled or cast from shore work well. Fly-fishing with wet patterns produces mornings and evenings. There are good natural campsites here, and several other small fishable lakes nearby. Be warned that mosquitoes are fierce here in summer until the first frost. There are campgrounds at Taylor Burn and North Waldo Lake.

LAKE OF THE WOODS (Linn Co.) A 5-acre rainbow lake 2 miles NE of Marion Lake. Take the trail running north from the NE shore of Marion. It's about 2 miles to Lake of the Woods.

The lake is stocked by air with rainbow, and average catch is 8-10 inches, but a few get larger. All methods work well, with spinner and bait preferred early in the season. The lake is lightly fished and holds up well. It is usually accessible by mid-June.

LAMBERT SLOUGH A Willamette River slough 19 miles downstream from Salem. About 3 miles long, it contains bass and panfish. Most anglers reach it from the boat ramp at San Salvadore Park near St. Paul.

LAYNG CREEK A wild cutthroat stream, tributary of Row River SE of Cottage Grove. It joins Brice Creek at Disston, 22 miles from Cottage Grove. From Cottage Grove, take the highway leading east past Dorena Reservoir and Culp Creek. Logging roads follow Layng to its head about 15 miles up. Bait is most effective for taking fish here, with single eggs and nightcrawlers equally successful. There are no camping areas along the stream.

LENORE LAKE Shown on some maps as Leone Lake. This is a good hike-in brook trout lake tucked away in the Pansy Lake Basin, Bull of the Woods area of the upper Collawash River. A beautiful spot, Lenore offers good fishing for wild 7-inch overcrowded and hungry brookies. It's about a 5-mile hike by trail from any road. The area is accessed by several trails, and there are other lakes worth visiting in the area. See Big Slide, Welcome, West lakes.

Hike in to Bull of the Woods Lookout (See Big Slide Lake for one approach), then take Trail 554 (Battle Creek and Welcome Lake) SE 1/2 mile to its intersection with Trail 555, which comes in from the NE. Follow 555 about 2 miles to Big Slide Mt. A short, steep spur trail leads from the NE side of the mountain to the lake, which is due north of the mountain. Check at Ripplebrook Ranger Station for latest road and trail information.

Brook trout 7-10 inches are thick here. The lake is about 5 acres and shallow with a rocky shore, and can be easily bank fished. Flies will work best.

LEONE LAKE This is a good but difficult to find brook trout lake in the North Santiam area NE of Detroit Reservoir. Take Forest Rd. 46 NE from Detroit to the Boulder Ridge Rd., Forest Rd. 223l at Breitenbush Hot Springs. Follow 2231 about 3 miles to a short spur road, Forest Rd. 916, entering from the south 1/3 mile west of the Hill Creek crossing. Trail 3367 leads from the end of the spur west abut 1/2 mile to the lake. Bring your forest map.

Leone brook trout average 9-l2 inches with a few larger. An occasional brown trout is taken. Spinner and bait and still-fishing both work well, and flies are good mornings and evenings. There are good natural campsites in the vicinity.

LINTON LAKE A 75-acre brown trout lake off the old McKenzie Pass Hwy., easily reached, yet holds up well. Rainbow and brook trout may also be present. The lake was formed when a wall of lava flowed across Linton Creek, perhaps as recently as 3,000 years ago. The trail to the lake leads through a classic lava field before diving into the forest.

To reach Linton drive l5 miles east from McKenzie Bridge on McKenzie Pass Hwy. 242 to Alder Springs Campground. A trail begins on the south side of the highway just before the campground and leads SE to the lake. Linton covers 70 acres and reaches a depth of 82 ft.

It is one of the few lakes in the Oregon Cascades that has a reproducing population of brown trout. These fish are thriving and range l0-l6 inches and larger. Small flatfish-type lures or flashing lures from one to two inches may fool them. A rubber raft is advisable for effective fishing.

In addition to the browns, there are brook trout and rainbow 10-l4 inches. Bait is effective with any of these, and flies are especially good in the evening. The catch rate isn't high here, but the fish are worth the effort. There are nice natural campsites at the lake and a campground at Alder Spring.

LITTLE FALL CREEK A fair trout stream with a respectable run of winter steelhead, flowing west from the Cascades between the McKenzie and Middle Fork Willamette drainages. About 20 miles long, it flows into Big Fall Creek at the town of Fall Creek, 5 miles north of the community of Lowell at Dexter Reservoir. A good gravel road follows the stream east to its headwaters.

The creek is open to steelhead fishing year-round, from the mouth to the concrete fish ladder 12 miles upstream. Winter steelhead show up in March and April. A fair number of summers return later in the year. Cutthroat 6-10 inches are also available. The creek is only lightly fished and has some fair fly water. There are no camping areas along the stream.

LITTLE LUCKIAMUTE RIVER See Luckiamute River, Little.

LITTLE NORTH SANTIAM RIVER An accessible little fork of the North Santiam, with good wild winter and summer steelhead runs for its size, and fishing for wild and stocked trout. There's some good fly water on the stream. It enters the North Santiam at Mehama, about 30 miles east of Salem off Hwy. 22. A paved road up Little North soon turns to gravel. This road follows the river into Willamette National Forest, where it becomes Forest Rd. 2207. It runs close to the stream in many places. At Shady Cove Campground, Cedar Creek enters the stream, and Battle Ax Creek joins the flow about 6 miles higher. Road access ends at a locked gate about 4 miles above Shady Cove. The area above the gate is known as "Jaw Bone Flats."

The Little North winter steelhead run arrives in November and provides fishing through March. All non-finclipped steelhead must be released unharmed, but hatchery strays from the North Santiam may be taken. The Summer steelhead hatchery program here has been terminated, but there may be strays from the Santiam.

Spring chinook enter in late May, but they seem to hold in water that is only accessed from private property closed to public use. The river may soon be closed to chinook fishing due to the depressed state of the run.

The river receives a good stocking of legal rainbow several times each spring, and angling holds up through July. All of the stocking, and most of the fishing, takes place below Elkhorn at the forest boundary. Within the forest, wild cutthroat are available.

There is a campground at Shady Cove on the river road. Other undeveloped sites are available and accessible to vehicles. Recommended for small fry.

LONG LAKE (Lane Co.) Consistently good for naturally reproducing brook trout and cutthroat, 3 miles NW of Waldo Lake in the headwaters of the North Fork of the Willamette. From Taylor Burn Campground take Trail 3553 west about 2 miles to Fisher Creek, where you pick up Trail 3597 heading south to the Quinn Lakes. Long Lake is a bit over 1/2 mile from the trail junction, about 1/4 mile south of middle Quinn Lake.

True to its name, Long Lake is 3/4 mile long and only a few hundred yards wide, covering a total of 50 acres. It can be fished from shore. The trout range 6-16 inches, averaging 10 inches, and fishing holds up well through the season. There are good lakes north and south along the trail. The area is generally inaccessible until late June.

LONG TOM RIVER A long stream originating west of Eugene near Siuslaw Hwy. 36, and flowing south into Fern Ridge Reservoir. It offers very good trout fishing as well as bass and panfish opportunities. Downstream from the reservoir, it flows north past Junction City and along Hwy. 99W to join the Willamette about half-way between Corvallis and Monroe.

Above the reservoir Long Tom is primarily a trout stream, with a good population of wild cutthroat. Below, trout, bass, and panfish are caught. Some nice size cutthroat, which fatten in Fern Ridge Reservoir and the Willamette, are taken above and below the reservoir on spinner and bait. Spring, early summer, fall, and winter are best for the large trout.

Largemouth bass, white crappie, and brown bullhead catfish are taken in the lower area. There is a good spring fishery for white crappie below Fern Ridge Reservoir. Best crappie catches are in March. When the reservoir is drawn down in fall, the crappie are flushed out.

There is reputed to be a sturgeon hole at the mouth.

The Long Tom is open the year around, with catch and release fishing for trout from November 1 till the Friday before the fourth Saturday in April.

The Long Tom is not driftable due to structures in the river below Fern Ridge Dam. These structures, called "drop structures," provide gradient control, creating a series of little lakes in the river. The lake is also armored with rip-rap to control erosion. There is a State Park picnic area on the upper stream, and many facilities are available at Fern Ridge Reservoir. There are no campgrounds along the lower stream.

LOOKOUT POINT RESERVOIR This is one of the largest artificial impoundments in the state, stretching 14 miles along Hwy. 58 from 21 miles east of Eugene to within 6 miles of Oakridge. It is formed by a dam on the Middle Willamette and when full, covers over 4,300 acres.

The lake is heavily infested with suckers and squawfish but still produces good bank and troll catches of rainbow and landlocked chinook. Illegally introduced crappie are also present, as well as a small population of largemouth bass.

The reservoir is heavily drawn down from late July until early May, but the boat ramps remain functional. An excellent ramp is located at the north end of the dam. Black Canyon Campground at the SW end has good camping facilities and a boat ramp, though the ramp is above the water line in winter.

LORIN LAKE A bushwhack rainbow trout lake in the Gold Lake area north of Willamette Pass. About 14 miles SE of Oakridge, and just past the railroad trestle over Hwy. 58, Forest Rd. 5883 cuts north. Follow 5883 about 9 miles to its end, where a short spur trail leads to the Fuji Mt. Trail 3670. About a quarter mile north on 3670 is the intersection with the Island Lake Trail, which you follow SE a bit over 1/2 mile to the intersection with Waldo Lake Trail 3586. A 1/2 mile hike NE on this brings you to the Island Lakes. Lorin Lake is 3/4 mile due east and slightly lower than the Island Lakes.

Ten acres and 17 feet deep, Lorin is at about 6,000 ft. and rarely thaws before late June. It can be fished from shore, but a rubber raft would be handy. Try a Mickey Finn or bucktail caddis, and you might tie into a lunker. Natural campsites are available. Jo Ann Lake is below Lorin 1/2 mile to the SE and contains cutthroat. Both Joann and Lorin can be tricky to find.

LOST CREEK (Clackamas Co.) A tributary of the upper Sandy, joining it about 4 miles NE of Zigzag. From Hwy. 26, turn north at Zigzag on the Lolo Pass Rd. At McNeil Campground, about 4 1/2 miles, take Forest Rd. 1825, which begins to parallel Lost Creek within 1/2 mile. About one mile upstream, at Lost Creek Campground, Forest Rd. 109 branches south and continues to follow the creek another 2 miles upstream.

The creek has some nice wild cutthroat and a few brook trout (probably migrants from Cast Lake in the headwaters).

Lost Creek Campground has a wheelchair accessible fishing structure. Riley and McNeil campgrounds are on the Sandy within 1/2 mile of the confluence.

LOST CREEK (Lane Co.) A wild cutthroat stream about 15 miles long, joining the Middle Willamette just below Dexter Reservoir. A paved road cuts SE off Hwy. 58 at Dexter and follows the stream for 10 miles. The stream is no longer stocked and flows primarily through private property There is no camping along the creek.

LOST LAKE (Linn Co.) A trout lake with Atlantic salmon and an opportunity for ice fishing, on the north side of Santiam Hwy. 20, two miles east of Santiam Junction. The lake is fed by several streams and though it has no visible outlet, its water leaks through lava cracks. In some years, such as 1987-88, it has gotten very shallow. The lake generally covers about 50 acres at the beginning of the season. It always closes after Labor Day.

It is stocked annually with rainbow and Atlantic salmon, and contains wild brook trout 6-15 inches. The primary catch is rainbow 9-11 inches. Trolling and bait fishing work best early in the year, and fly-fishing is good in summer and fall. The fish tend to concentrate in two or three holes, so watch where the anglers bunch up. Fishing from a motorboat is prohibited.

The lake usually builds up a solid ice cover by early spring. Ice fishing is a possibility here, but parking is limited. There is a large developed campground on a spur road on the west shore of the lake.

LOWER LAKE A good trout lake, very accessible, just west of the Skyline Rd., Forest Rd. 4220, about one mile north of Olallie Lake. Take Hwy. 26 east, then Forest Rd. 4220 south to the area, about 100 miles from Portland.

Lower Lake is 14 acres and very deep. A lot of water can be covered from shore, and all angling methods can be effective. Fly anglers will find good water along the north shore. Trolling with small lures or spinner and bait works well.

Stocked cutthroat range 7-14 inches, averaging 10 inches. Rainbows are occasionally stocked as well. Evening angling in late spring and fall produces nice fish.

There is a good size campground at the east end of the lake. The road in is usually inaccessible until late June.

LUCKIAMUTE RIVER (Pronounced Lucky-mute) A large stream heading in the coast range near Valsetz, offering quality opportunities for catch and release winter trout and steelhead fishing. The Big Lucky flows into the Willamette River at a point south of Independence. About 5 miles south of Monmouth it is crossed by Hwy. 99W, and further upstream by Hwy. 223 about 12 miles south of Dallas. A fair road parallels the river from Hoskins about 7 miles upstream, with several road crossings providing access. The river then flows about 10 miles through private forest land, with a private road paralleling the north bank. This road provides generally good angler access and is only occasionally closed during fire season.

Rainbow trout are stocked for 3 weeks in spring, and for Free Fishing Day, in the 7 mile stretch above Hoskins. There is a good population of wild cutthroat throughout the river, with best fishing in the upper stretch. Rainbows dominate the catch 2 to 1, averaging 8 to 11 inches.

The Luckiamute is a good early season stream, with bait angling, and spinner and bait working well. Wild trout are available well into summer for the persistent angler, with some good fly-fishing possible after the crowd thins out. Some nice fish can be taken late in fall after the water cools. From November 1 through the Friday before the last Saturday in April, trout fishing is catch and release only.

The stream offers good steelhead habitat, but its early winter run receives little pressure (late January to early March). Large Willamette cutthroat migrating into the river to spawn in winter provide an additional catch and release fishery.

LUCKIAMUTE RIVER, LITTLE Often a very good trout stream for the first 3 months of the season. Fished quite heavily, it produces well. The river heads in the coast range near Valsetz and joins the Big Luckiamute just south of Monmouth.

To reach it from Hwy. 99W at Salem, head east 16 miles to Dallas, then 5 miles south. Good roads follow the stream up through Falls City, but there is very limited access due to private property. A 4 mile stretch from Falls City upstream is easily reached from the highway and is stocked with rainbow in spring. Above this point, anglers can hike to the river from a logging road that follows about one mile north of the stream. This road is open, except during fire season. Wild cutthroat are available in the upper waters. All fish run 6-13 inches, with rainbow dominating.

Large trout from the Willamette migrate into the river below Falls City on an early spawning run in winter. The falls are a natural barrier to these fish. The Little Luckiamute is open for trout fishing the year around, but trout fishing from November 1 through the Friday before the fourth Saturday in April is catch and release only.

MAC LAKE A rainbow lake near the Pacific Crest Trail in the southern portion of the Mink Lake Basin, west of Elk Lake. Mac Lake is 1/2 mile SE of Mink Lake and 1 1/2 miles south of Cliff Lake and the Pacific Crest Trail. It is one mile east of Packsaddle Mt. For a good overview of the basin, climb Packsaddle. You'll be able to pick out the various lakes from your map.

Mac Lake covers 70 acres and is stocked by air with fingerling rainbow. Average size is 10 inches, with some to 15 inches. The lake can be fished from shore using all methods, with flies effective mornings and evenings. There are good natural campsites available.

MARIE LAKE (Lane Co.) A rainbow trout lake in Diamond Peak Wilderness NW of Summit Lake. The lake is just north of what is known as the Diamond Rockpile south of Diamond Peak. Take the Pacific Crest Trail north from where it crosses the road just west of Summit Lake Campground. About 2 miles north, the PCT intersects Trail 3672. Follow this trail west about 1/2 mile to Marie.

Marie is easy to fish from shore. The brook trout run 6-14 inches, averaging 10 inches. In some years, larger fish have been taken. Spinner and bait usually work well any time, and late summer evening fishing with bucktails can be effective. There are good natural campsites available. The area is usually inaccessible until late June.

MARILYN LAKES Two good hike-in brook trout lakes near Gold Lake in the Willamette Pass area. These lakes are tailor-made for fly-fishing. They are about one mile north of Hwy. 58, 23 miles SE of Oakridge. Take the Gold Lake Rd. 2 miles to Gold Lake Campground, and follow the Marilyn Lakes Trail an easy 10-minute walk south.

The lakes are each about 25 acres and drain into Salt Creek. Brook trout here run 6-16 inches, averaging 10 inches. The upper lake has smaller but more plentiful fish. The lower has larger fish in small numbers. They are lightly fished, as most fly anglers in the area are trying for Gold Lake's feisty rainbows. Late fall fly anglers can take some real lunkers here. Ice fishing is also a possibility. Drive to the Sno-Park on Waldo Lake Road and ski or snowshoe in. There are no campsites near the lakes.

MARION CREEK Also known as the Marion Fork of the North Santiam, a cold, fast trout stream. Lightly fished, it flows from Marion Lake in Mt. Jefferson Wilderness. A good road, Forest Rd. 2255, leaves Santiam Pass Hwy. 22 at the Marion Forks Ranger Station (about 15 miles south of Detroit at Detroit Reservoir) and follows the stream to Marion Falls, about 2 miles downstream from Marion Lake. Between the falls and the lake the stream is closed to angling.

Cold and clear, Marion is difficult to fish. Anglers might try single eggs or other bait, with fly-fishing effective late in the season. The stream is seldom productive early in the year. If you are in the area, pay a visit to the salmon hatchery on the south side of the stream near Hwy. 22. There's a good forest campground at the creek mouth.

MARION LAKE A large hike-in lake with large trout, both stocked and wild. It is at the head of Marion Creek within Mt. Jefferson Wilderness. Take the Marion Forks Rd., Forest Rd. 2255, SE from Hwy. 22 at Marion Forks Ranger Station, about 16 miles from Detroit. At the end of the road, follow Trail 3436 about 2 miles to the lake.

Marion is about 350 acres and holds some nice fish. The catch rate is variable, but size makes up for it. Brook trout and rainbows are equally plentiful, averaging 11-14 inches, with a good number of 3-4 pounders taken each season. A rubber boat or float tube are useful here, although the lake can be fished from shore. Bait angling and lures will take fish throughout the season. Cutthroat are also present and will put up a good fight on light gear. Other smaller lakes nearby offer good angling. See Ann Lake.

MARY'S RIVER A fair trout stream flowing into the Willamette River at Corvallis. It heads on Mary's peak, highest point in the Coast Range, and flows over 30 miles to the Willamette. Hwy. 20 follows the river from Corvallis to Blodgett, where a good forest road heads north, accessing the upper forks. Private property restricts access in the lower river.

Mary's River has a good population of wild cutthroat, typically from 7-12 inches, and a small winter steelhead runs. Big Willamette cutthroat (to 2 pounds plus) migrate into the stream to spawn in winter, providing an additional catch and release fishery. From November 1 through the Friday before the last Saturday in April, the trout fishery is catch and release only. Non-finclipped steelhead must be released unharmed as well. Whitefish are abundant and available through the winter. These whitefish reach 2 lbs., will take a fly, offer good sport on light tackle, and are good eating.

There are no camping areas along the river.

McDOWELL CREEK A small wild cutthroat stream entering the South Santiam River about 9 miles SE of Lebanon. Take Hwy. 20 south from Lebanon to McDowell Creek Rd., about 3 miles south of Hamilton Creek. A road follows the stream closely for about 5 miles, but only one mile of this lower stretch is open to public access. The upper stream is in private forest land, which may be accessible.

Wild cutthroat 6-12 inches make up most of the catch. McDowell Creek Park (which features some pretty water falls) offers trails along the creek. There is no camping along the stream.

McFARLAND LAKE A 39-acre trout lake north of Irish Mt. about one mile west of the Pacific Crest Trail. You'll work to get here, but the hike sure does thin out the crowd. Take Trail 3307 west from Forest Rd. 1958, a 4-5 mile hike.

Stocked with rainbows, McFarland is a good, deep lake for lure fishing, and all methods of angling will take trout when they're hitting. Some lunkers are taken each season. The catch runs 6-16 inches, averaging 13 inches. There are good natural campsites available. Several other small fishable lakes are nearby. It is usually inaccessible until late June.

McKAY CREEK (Washington Co.) A good early-season trout stream only 20 miles west of Portland, crossed by Hwy. 26. The creek flows into the Tualatin River just south of Hillsboro, heading in the West Hills, north of North Plains near the Multnomah County line. From North Plains, the stream is followed north by gravel roads for about 9 miles. Most anglers fish the stretch north of the highway.

McKay is primarily a wild cutthroat stream. Angling is good for a few weeks after opening, but slows up early. Bait is the most popular method. Some warmwater species are taken near the mouth. Watch for private property along the stream.

McKENZIE RIVER One of the finest trout streams in Oregon, namesake of the McKenzie River drift boat, the boat that draws so little water it can float on dew, or over clawing rapids. The McKenzie River features plump and spunky redside rainbow trout, a few brook trout from Clear Lake in the upper waters, a good run of summer steelhead, and spring chinook. The river flows past giant boulders and through forested canyons at a grade that delights rafters, and with an iridescence that inspires poetry. It has, by the way, only one major (Class 4) rapids in its boatable stretch, and is a good river for less experienced riverboat anglers.

The McKenzie is one of those rivers that weaves its magic around an angler. In the last glimmer of light, an unexpected steelhead takes the fly. Out of mere inches of water, a big cutthroat suddenly materializes. Into the silence of an emerald pool, a huge spring chinook leaps and slams. Then there's the quality of sunset on shimmering water, the honey scent of cottonwood, a sudden storm of mayflies on a summer evening.

The McKenzie is 89 miles long and is followed for most of its length by Hwy. 126. The river heads in Clear Lake near the Santiam Pass, then flows south 14 miles to Belknap Springs, where it swings west. This upper water is very cold and swift, and the fishing is slow. By Blue River, 18 miles further downstream, the valley begins to open up and the slope is moderated. From here downstream to its junction with the Willamette River at the north end of Eugene, water conditions for trout fishing are excellent. Reaching the best water can be a chore without a boat, however, as the river runs through primarily private land in the lower 50 river miles. Most bank access is at the boat ramps.

There are almost 3-dozen public boat ramps on the McKenzie, with the lowest at Armitage State Park north of Eugene. To reach, it drive north from the city on Coburg Rd., or take I-5 to the Coburg Exit, just south of the McKenzie. Most of the park stretches west of I-5. Anglers can also cross the McKenzie on Coburg Rd. and fish the north bank about 200 yds. upstream and down from the I-5 Bridge. Park on McKenzie View Drive and make your way down to the river, keeping an eye out for stinging nettles. Despite its proximity to one of Oregon's largest cities, not to mention the freeway, this is a rural spot, and an angler streamside is caught up in the world of the river. Be aware that this stretch of water is within the catch and release portion of the McKenzie, with tackle restricted to artificial flies and lures on barbless hooks. These restrictions are in effect from the river mouth up to Hayden Bridge in Springfield. Bait is permitted on barbless hooks 1/2 inch or larger from April 23 through July 14, however, in deference to salmon anglers.

There is also bank access at Deadmond Ferry Slide on the south bank at the end of Deadmond Ferry Rd. To get there take the Belt Line Hwy. east to Game Farm Rd. Turn left then right onto Deadmond. Harvest Lane is a potential boat ramp site in Springfield. Follow 6th St. north to Harlow Rd., turn right on Harlow, then left on 14th St. to Harvest Lane. Hayden Bridge in Springfield, Hendricks Bridge State Wayside north of Cedar Flat on Hwy. 126, Emmerich Co. Park just east of Walterville (bank access only, no boat ramp), and Greenwood Drive Ramp east of Leaburg all offer access to good water, as does Deerhorn Co. Park on the south bank. To reach Deerhorn, turn right onto Deerhorn Rd. before crossing Hendricks Bridge on Hwy. 126. Helfrich Landing on the north bank right below Marten Rapids offers interesting trout fishing, as does Ben and Kay Dorris State Park right above the rapids. Silver Creek, Finn Rock, and Forest Glen Boat Ramps (all off Hwy. 126) are good trout bank fisheries. Above Forest Glen (at Blue River) the river picks up speed, and bank fishing is more difficult.

The highest boat ramp on the river is at Olallie Campground, about 12 miles east of McKenzie Bridge, but the most popular fishing drifts are between Blue River and Leaburg Lake, a 17-mile stretch within which anglers can select a combination of put-ins and take-outs suitable to their time schedules.

The river below Leaburg Dam has a lower gradient that offers easy drifting, but the upper river is more challenging and includes one Class 4 rapids (Marten Rapids) between Dorris State Park and Helfrich Landing. All other runs on the McKenzie are rated class 1 or 2. This is good water for beginning drift boat operators, but it is always beneficial to follow a lead boat familiar with a river's peculiarities first time through. Licensed river guides are available through the Oregon Guides and Packers Association, and through Eugene and Springfield fly and tackle shops, many of which also offer informal streamside introductions to various fisheries on the river, and are glad to share practical tips and information about current river and fishing conditions.

Trout are plentiful throughout the season, but best fishing for wild cutthroat and rainbows is in March and April when March Brown mayfly hatches take place. Cutthroat populations are heaviest in the area down from Bellinger. The river is heavily stocked with hatchery rainbow from early spring through summer between Hayden Bridge and Paradise Campground. Over 126,000 are released annually at intervals. Above and below these points, anglers have a better chance of hooking the river's true prize, the native McKenzie rainbow, known as the redside.

In an effort to preserve these native beauties, regulations require that all non-finclipped trout over must be released. Hatchery rainbows are marked with a ventral fin clip. (Hatchery steelhead are adipose finclipped). Redsides are also distinguished by their bright orange spots. Hatchery stocked trout rarely last through the season, with those not caught generally dying within a few months from the rigors of life on a wild stream. Most fish over 10 inches are wild. The average fish hooked runs 7-11 inches, with many larger fish (2-3 pounders) in the river. Cutthroat and whitefish are plentiful below Leaburg. Bull trout are also in the river and must be released unharmed.

McKenzie River spring chinook enter the river in May, with peak catches in middle or late June. Anglers fish from boat and bank using bait and lures. Most chinook angling takes place in the 2-mile stretch from Leaburg Dam down to Greenwood Dr. Boat Ramp. Chinook anglers use the bank access at Greenwood and both banks below the

1 **ARMITAGE PARK** - take-out for pleasant drift from Deadmond Ferry; good bank fishing.

2 **McKENZIE VIEW**- public access to 200 yds of good water upstream and down from I-5 bridge; park on road and scramble down to river.

3 **DEADMOND FERRY** - boat slide to steep for good take-out; pleasant evening's drift to Armitage; access to good fishing on both banks.

4 **RODAKOWSKI BOAT RAMP** - paved ramp;some bank access; good fishing below the bridge.

5 **HAYDEN BRIDGE** - steep paved ramp; bank fishing on both sides of bridge.

6 **BELLINGER LANDING** - paved ramp with limited bank access; better fishing on opposite shore.

7 **HENDRICKS BRIDGE WAYSIDE** - paved ramp with good bank access.

8 **PARTRIDGE LANE** - put-in only; steep dirt slide on Partridge Lane off Hwy. 126

9 **WALTERVILLE LANDING** - near Walterville school; paved ramp near canal entrance.

10 **DEERHORN BOAT RAMP** - put-in and take-out.

11 **DEERHORN COUNTY PARK** - paved ramp with some bank access; good fishing below the bridge.

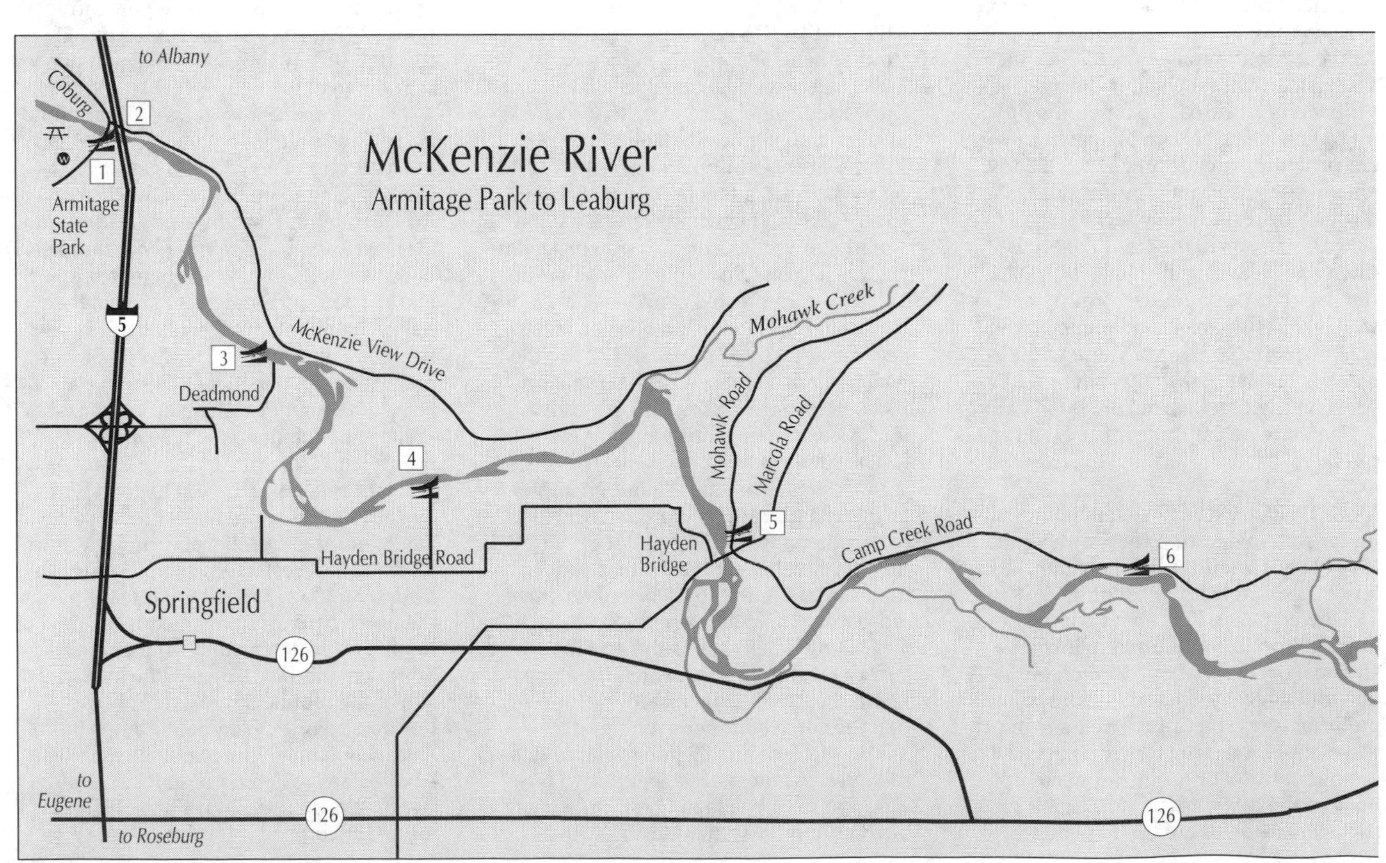

dam. Watch for the deadline at the dam. The Hayden Bridge vicinity is popular with boat anglers, who use drift fishing and back bouncing techniques. The current run size is estimated at between 3,000 and 4,000. Over 1,000 spring chinook are generally caught each year, primarily in the lower river. The estimated 1992 catch was 1,195.

A good run of hatchery-reared summer steelhead returns to the McKenzie in May, with best catches from July on. The season closes December 31. In most years over 1000 steelhead are taken. Despite poor ocean conditions, the 1992-93 estimated catch was 2,058. These fish move quickly through the lower river, heading for the hatchery at Leaburg Dam. Fishing for them is concentrated from the town of Leaburg up to the dam, but there are good fishing opportunities from Hendricks Bridge up to Leaburg as well.

Developed camping and picnic sites are limited along the river below the National Forest. Armitage State Park north of Eugene offers camping, as does Ben and Kay Doris State Park just east of Vida. Above Blue River the McKenzie flows through Willamette National Forest, where there are streamside campgrounds about every 5 miles. Delta, McKenzie Bridge, and Paradise are right on the McKenzie. Limberlost is about 2 miles up the Lost Creek Rd. just before Belknap Springs. Additional camps are available in the headwaters area from Trail Bridge to Clear Lake.

McKENZIE RIVER, SOUTH FORK A popular trout stream flowing into the upper McKenzie between Blue River and McKenzie Bridge. It joins the mainstem McKenzie about 3 miles upstream from the community of Blue River. The river is dammed to create Cougar Reservoir about 3 miles above the confluence. Cougar covers about 5 miles of stream channel. A good forest road, Forest Rd. 19, follows the river upstream for the next 12 miles. Here the river splits into two forks, Elk Creek and Roaring River.

Elk Creek can be followed upstream 3 miles on Forest Rd. 1964 to Trailhead 3510, which leads into the Mink Lake Basin. Forest Rd. 19 follows Roaring River Creek then McBee Creek over a divide to the SW, then drops into the headwaters of the North Fork of the Willamette.

The South Fork is stocked with legal rainbow downstream from Frissel Crossing throughout spring and summer. Wild redsides, cutthroat, and bull trout are also available for catch and release angling. All non-finclipped trout must be released unharmed. The catch rate is high for such a popular stream, but the fish don't run large. Average size is 8-11 inches. There's lots of good fly water, especially above the reservoir.

There are six campgrounds on the upper stream. Tributaries enter the fork at several of these camps, providing good fishing and additional angling opportunities along the creeks, accessed only by trail. Wild cutthroat are the main fare in these creeks, with light leaders and stealth required. French Pete Creek, which enters from the east at French Pete Campground, offers many miles of hiking through superb old growth timber. The water in the creek is cold, swift, and clear. Augusta Creek, which drains a considerable area, enters the river from the south at Dutch Oven Campground.

Spring chinook fishing on the lower McKenzie.

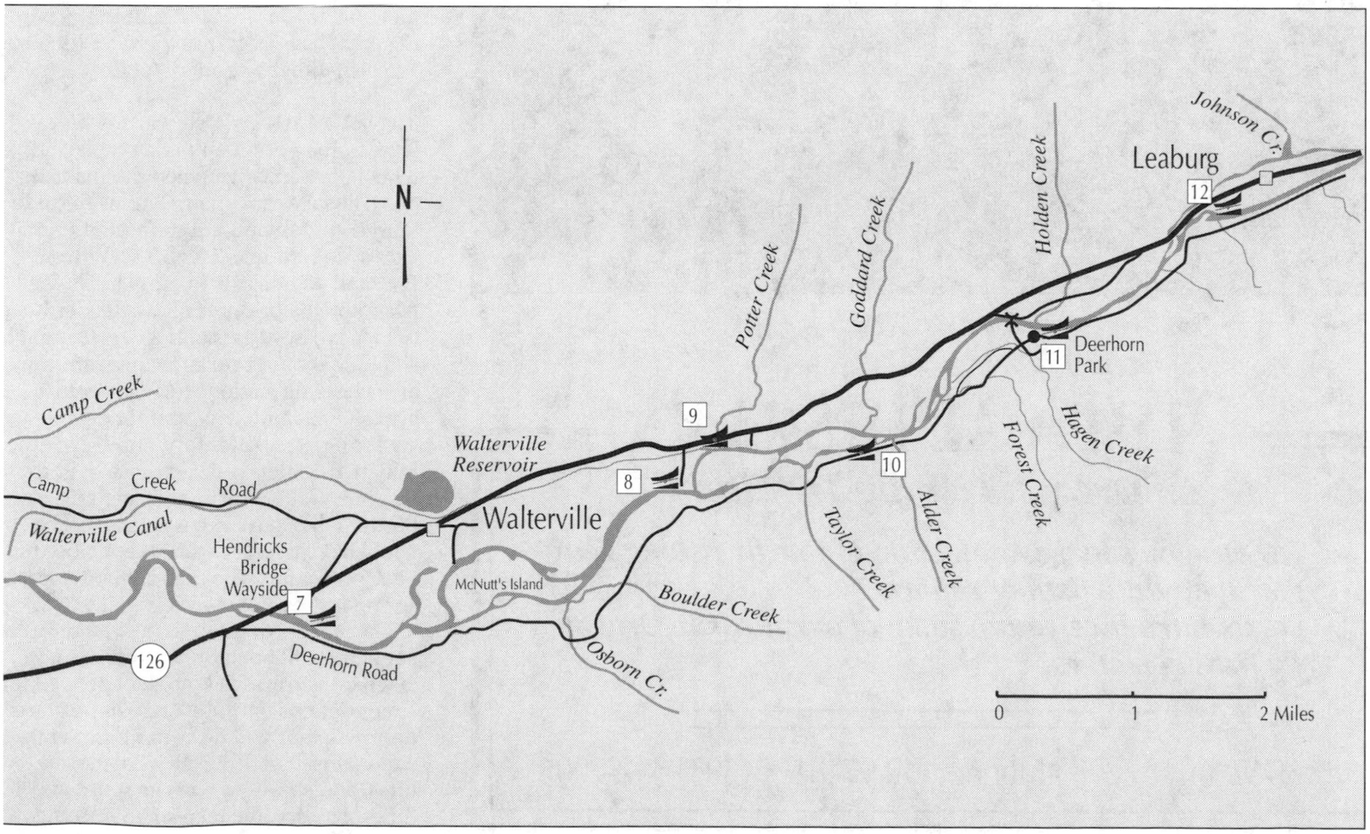

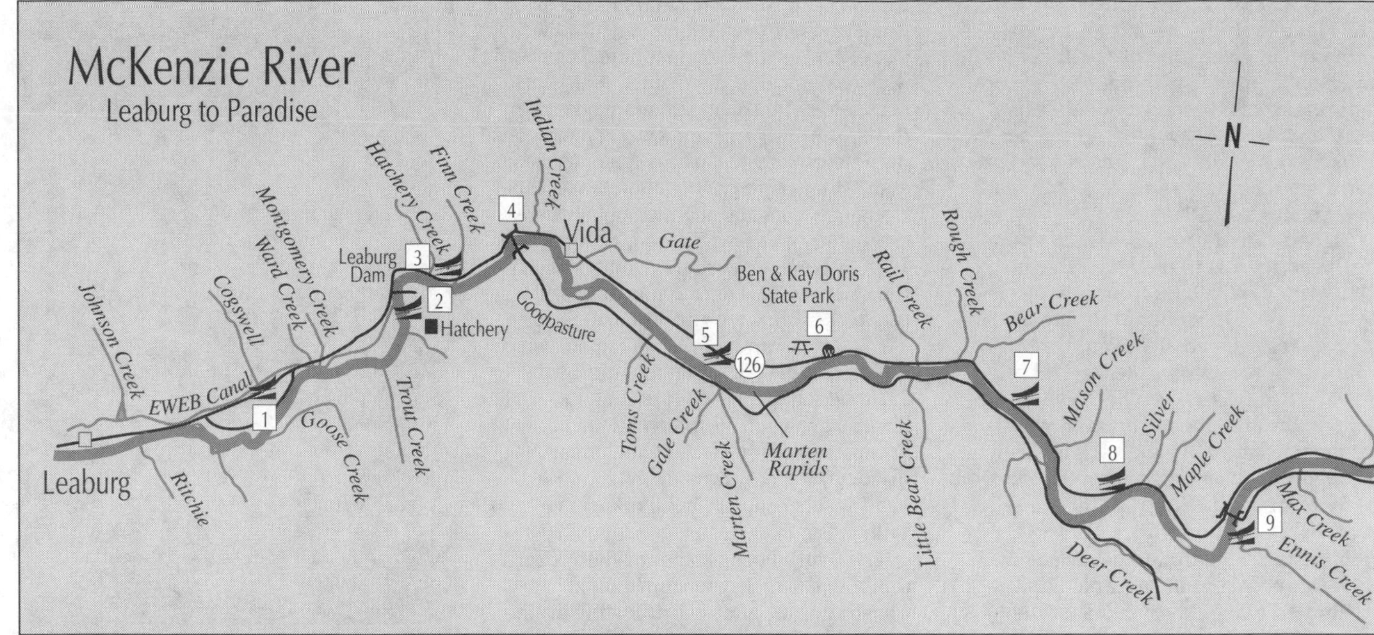

Best fishing for the McKenzie's wild rainbows is in March and April.

When studying a map of the South Fork, you will probably notice reference to Cougar Hot Springs. These are located about a 1/4 mile west of the reservoir near Rider Creek. There is a parking area on the reservoir side, and a short trail follows Rider to the hot springs. Unfortunately, though the springs have lost none of their natural beauty, they have lost much of their innocence. A rough, unsavory, crowd has discovered the springs. Enough unpleasant and downright dangerous incidents (not to mention vandalism and theft in the parking area) have occurred there to discourage visitation by prudent folks.

McNARY LAKES Two warm-water lakes at the north end of Sauvie Island, to which one can drive when the roads dry out. The lakes are about 2 miles north of Sturgeon Lake and are connected to it by Pete's Slough. Take Hwy. 30 NW from Portland 10 miles, then cross to Sauvie Island by the bridge. Follow Reeder Road (which crosses the island to the Columbia side) for about 11 miles to the waterfowl area checking station. Turn left onto a gravel road, and drive about one mile to a parking area. After July, and before the May high water, you can drive over the dike then follow dirt roads one mile north to the lakes. If the gate is locked you'll have to walk, as it's kept closed for your protection. The area is flooded each spring for several months.

There's lots of room to fish, either from bank or small boat. Brown bullhead are taken on worms. Bass anglers do well for a month or so once the high water starts dropping, but will do better in moving water after that. Plugs, Kwikfish-type lures, and spinning lures all work at times. The crappie take small flashing

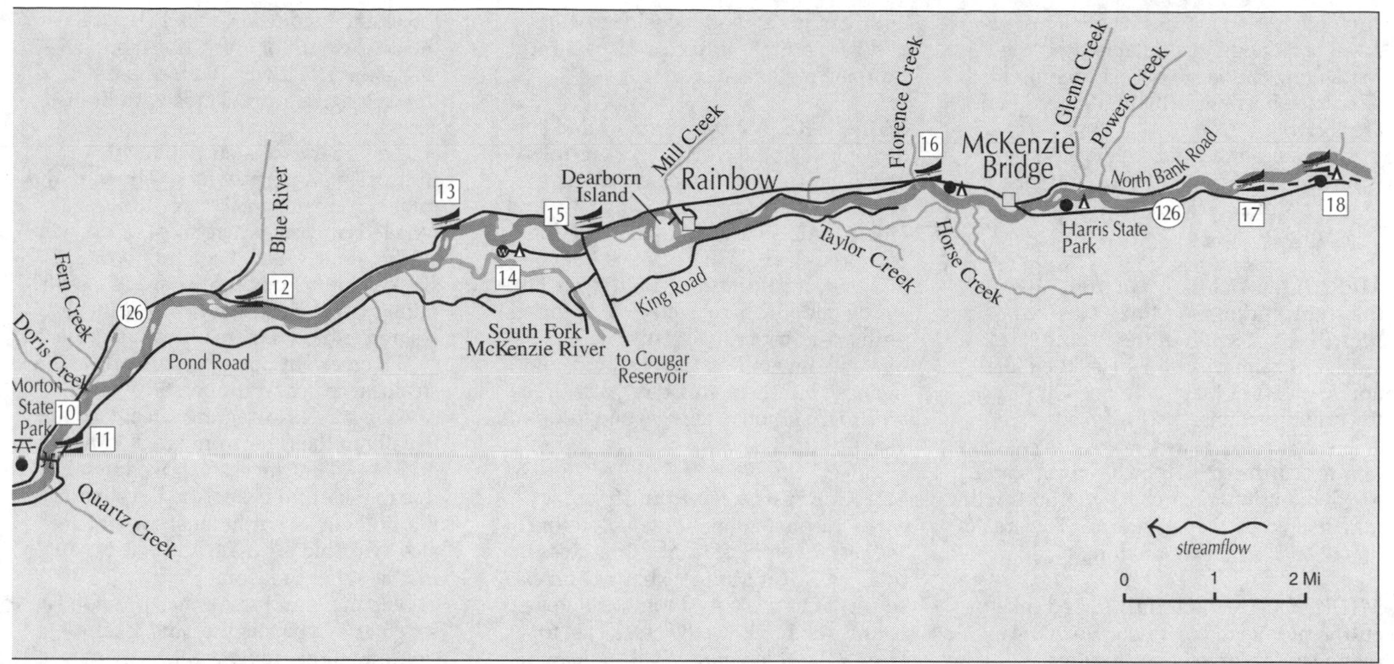

1 **GREENWOOD LANDING**- Popular take-out for drift from Leaburg Dam; access to Curry Holes for salmon & steelhead just upstream.

2 **WATERBOARD PARK** - Good boat and bank access for stocked trout.

3 **IKE'S LANDING** - Take-out on a busy highway.

4 **GOODPASTURE COVERED BRIDGE** - Bank fishing.

5 **HELFRICH LANDING** - Off Thompson Lane; county park take-out below Martin Rapids; put-in for about 5 miles of good water without bank access.

6 **BEN & KAY DORRIS STATE PARK** - Popular take-out to avoid Martin Rapids (Class 3-4); bank fishing.

7 **RENNIE LANDING** - Paved ramp; some bank access; good drift includes Browns Hole (white water pocket near south bank).

8 **SILVER CREEK LANDING** - Paved ramp with bank access; nice water between here and Rennie.

9 **ROSBORO LANDING** - Unimproved put-in; several rapids here to Silver Creek (1.5 miles) but good fishing; some bank access.

10 **HOWARD J. MORTON STATE PARK** - Limited fishing access, but pretty picnic spot.

11 **FINN ROCK**- Major raft put-in for popular drift to Helfrich; good flat take-out.

12 **FOREST GLEN LANDING** - Upper limit of heavy trout stocking.

13 **HAMLIN LANDING** - Lightly stocked; fish mostly for catch & release wild redsides.

14 **DELTA CAMPGROUND** - Bank fishing

15 **BRUKHART BRIDGE LANDING** - Steep paved ramp, best for launching.

16 **McKENZIE BRIDGE CAMPGROUND** - Unimproved dirt ramp at west end of campground; some bank access.

17 **McKENZIE RIVER TRAIL** - Popular hiking trail along fast water; fish pocket water for wild redsides with some brook trout near Clear Lake.

18 **PARADISE CAMPGROUND**- Unimproved ramp; popular take-out for advanced river runners who launch at Whitewater Slide or Olallie Campground; water above Paradise is shallow and fast with many rapids.

lures, pork rind, and even maribou flies if retrieved very slowly.

For other waters close by, see Pete's Slough, Gilbert River, Haldeman Pond, Sturgeon Lake. No overnight camping is allowed. Fishing on Sauvie Island is restricted during waterfowl season. You will need to purchase a recreation permit to park on Sauvie Island. Day or seasonal passes are sold at the market on the island just north of the bridge. Refer to the Appendix for a map of the island.

McNULTY CREEK A small trout stream, about 7 miles long, flowing through Columbia County south of St. Helens. It is crossed by Hwy. 30 about 25 miles NW of Portland and is accessible primarily at road crossings.

The creek provides fair early season trout fishing, mainly for wild cutthroat, but a few rainbow show up. It is not stocked, and the fish are mostly under 10 inches. Bait works best, or spinner and bait in the larger holes. The creek gets too low for angling after the first month or two. At its Columbia River confluence there is fair fishing for bass, perch, and brown bullhead.

MELAKWA LAKE A 35-acre rainbow and cutthroat lake west of the McKenzie Pass Hwy. 242, SW of Scott Lake. A scout camp is located here, and the boys fish it hard. The trout run 6-12 inches, averaging 9 inches. Motor boats are prohibited on the lake.

MELIS LAKE A small brook trout lake mid-way between the Eight Lakes Basin and Marion Lake in Mt. Jefferson Wilderness. It is just south of Jenny Lake, about 2 miles south of Marion, and the same distance north of Jorn Lake on the Jorn Lake Trail. See Jorn Lake for trail directions.

Not a very rich lake, its brook trout run small, 6-11 inches, averaging 9. Only 5 acres, the lake doesn't hold up long. It does have some fair natural campsites.

MERCER RESERVOIR On Rickreall Creek, 10 miles west of Dallas on Allendale Rd. It serves as the water supply for the city of Dallas but has been open to public angling.

This 60-acre reservoir on Boise Cascade land is fished primarily for wild cutthroat, which run to 12 inches. Boats are allowed, but no motors. There's lots of good bank angling available from the road along the west shore. Largemouth bass have been illegally introduced and are thriving.

The gate on the road to the reservoir is locked at this time, though anglers may walk or bicycle in. Best fishing is in spring.

MERRILL LAKE A small trout lake in the south end of the Mink Lake Basin. Merrill is just south of the Pacific Coast Trail, 1/4 mile west of Horseshoe Lake and just east of Mac Lake. See Cliff Lake for trail directions.

Though only 7 acres, Merrill is consistent for cutthroat 9-10 inches with some to 15, though not many. All methods will take fish when they're hitting. The area is usually accessible in late June.

MICKEY LAKE A lightly fished hike-in cutthroat lake in the Taylor Burn area, managed for large trout. Angling is restricted to barbless lures and flies only. To reach it, head south from Taylor Burn on Olallie Trail 3583, or north from Waldo Lake on the same trail. Mickey is 1/4 mile NE of Lower Rigdon. See Rigdon Lakes for trail directions. Mickey Lake is just a short way NW of Brittany, another good lake.

About 5 acres and deep, over 40 ft. in places, it has turned out some lunkers. The trout don't spawn here, so it is stocked every few years. A good rocky shoal in the center of the lake is a consistent producer on flies. There are no good campsites here.

MIDNIGHT LAKE A good rainbow trout lake west of Odell Lake and south of Hwy. 58, just off the Pacific Crest Trail. Pick up the PCT from a spur road at the NW end of Odell, and hike about one mile SW to the lake.

Midnight covers about 12 acres and is quite deep. It is well stocked with rainbow 6-13 inches. It gets fairly heavy use but holds up well, best in early season and again in the fall. Camping and supplies are available at Odell Lake.

MILDRED LAKE A 3 acre brook trout lake in the headwaters of Breitenbush River NW of Mt. Jefferson in the Mt. Jefferson Wilderness. Mildred is 1 1/2 miles NE of the Firecamp Lakes See Firecamp Lakes for directions. No trail leads to the lake, which is in a basin separated by a ridge from the Firecamps. Hike east-northeast from Crown Lake in the Firecamps, crossing the ridge at the saddle.

Mildred reportedly contains brook trout to 12 inches, with fall the best season. There are several other lakes nearby, including Slideout (just south) Swindle, and Bear. It's a good Huckleberry area and has natural campsites. Use no-trace camping methods.

MILE LAKE A 7 acre rainbow and cutthroat lake in the Horse Lake group NW of Elk Lake in the Three Sisters Wilderness. It is between Horse Mt. and Horse Lake Guard Station. A trail due west from Horse Lake reaches Mile in one mile, then continues on to Park Lake.

The rainbow here average 9-10 inches, with a 6-13 inch range. This lake has its ups and downs, hot one year and cold the next, but there are other lakes in the area to try if you catch this one on an off year.

MILK CREEK A fair trout stream for early season angling, flowing into the Molalla River SE of Canby. It is crossed by Hwy. 213 at Mulino, about 11 miles south of Oregon City. From Mulino a county road follows the creek east to Hwy. 211, which parallels the stream to near its headwaters in the Colton area. It is only accessible at the road crossings due to private ownership throughout.

Milk Creek has a fair population of wild cutthroat. Bait is most often used, but it's a good spinner stream. The best section to fish is west and east of Colton. It is not open for salmon and steelhead fishing.

MILL CREEK (Marion Co.) A long stream with opportunities for viewing (but not fishing) a sizable fall chinook run in the heart of Salem. The creek flows from the east near Stayton, and joins the Willamette River at the capital. Pringle Park, behind Salem Hospital, is a popular viewing area during the spawning migration in September and October.

The creek is closely followed by Hwy. 22 and the paved road from Aumsville to Salem. Private land throughout makes access difficult, though it can be fished at road crossings. Mill Creek supports a small wild trout population, and is lightly stocked with rainbow early in the season at Cascade Park, but stocking may be discontinued . Most angling is with bait or spinner and bait. The lower end of the creek below Turner offers some fishing for bluegill and crappie. The entire creek is closed during the chinook spawning season.

MILL CREEK (Yamhill Co.) A good rainbow and cutthroat stream, with winter steelhead and big Willamette cutthroat available. A tributary of the South Yamhill River, it joins the Yamhill from the south about half-way between Willamina and Sheridan. Hwy. 18 crosses the creek a short way above the mouth, and Hwy. 22 crosses it about 5 miles above that. Harmony Rd. follows the lower end, and Mill Creek Rd. parallels the creek south of Hwy. 22. About 20 miles long, its lower 10 miles pass through agricultural lands with limited access.

The upper end is on Willamette Industries property, which is open to the public. Here the creek runs through a wooded canyon, where most of the wild cutthroat are taken. Legal rainbow are stocked in this upper area as well. Both rainbow and cutthroat run 9-12 inches. Fishing usually tapers off by late June.

The creek supports a small wild winter steelhead run and is open for winter catch and release angling. Steelhead are usually in the river from late February to mid-May. Few are seen above Hwy. 22 due to a natural barrier on the stream. Big Willamette cutthroat spawners are also available for catch and release during the winter season.

Willamette Industries has provided several day use facilities and a campground on the upper creek.

MILTON CREEK A fair size stream, entering the Columbia near the town of St. Helens, about 30 miles NW of Portland. It provides good early season trout angling and supports a small run of wild winter steelhead.

Eighteen miles long, Milton heads in the hills west of St. Helens and meanders east, flowing through the west end of town and into Scappoose Bay near its mouth. County roads access the upper waters. There's lots of private property along the stream near St. Helens, but open water above. When in doubt as to whether land is privately owned, be sure to ask. Some of the upstream farmers will give permission to cross their property.

Milton is no longer stocked, but it has wild cutthroat. Bait angling is the most commonly used method, but you can find good fly riffles in the upper area. Trout angling usually falls off in late June, and the water gets fairly low. The creek is open for winter steelheading, but the run is spread throughout the winter. All non-finclipped steelhead must be released unharmed.

There is fair bass angling in the late spring near the mouth, though it seems to take a lot of casting to connect. There is no camping along the stream.

MINK LAKE The largest lake in the Mink Lake Basin, 180 acres at 6,000 ft. elevation. Mink Lake is at the head of the South Fork of the McKenzie River.

Trails enter the area from all directions. To approach from the west, drive into the headwaters of the South Fork on Forest Rd. 19. At Frissel Crossing Campground, head east on Forest Rd. 1964 about 2 1/2 miles to a short northern spur which accesses Trail 3510. This trail leads about

7 miles to Mink Lake. Two popular eastern approaches are from Elk Lake on the Pacific Crest Trail, about 11 miles, or on the Six Lakes Trail by way of Blow Lake, about 8 miles. Trails surround the lake, and there are other good lakes in every direction.

Mink Lake is stocked with lots of rainbow and cutthroat, and it usually produces fair catches. The fish average about 10 inches, running 6-20 inches. A float tube would be handy, as the lake is large, and the fish are sometimes hard to find. All methods of angling are used. There are good natural campsites all around the lake. Mosquitoes are very fierce in spring. See also Cliff, Moody, Porky lakes.

MIRROR LAKE (Clackamas Co.) A popular lake with a spectacular view of Mt. Hood, reached by a short hike from Mt. Hood Hwy. 26. It offers good brook trout angling despite heavy pressure. Most visitors are sightseers and hikers. The lake is about 53 miles from Portland, just west of Government Camp. Trail 664, the Tom, Dick, and Harry Mountain Trail, leads just over a mile to the lake. The trailhead is on the south side of Hwy. 26 at Yocum Falls, about one mile west of Multipor Ski area. It's fairly steep, gaining 650 ft. between the highway and lake.

Mirror Lake is stocked with rainbow and brook trout. Most of the catch runs 6-9 inches. Some larger fish remain each year, and good anglers can do well, especially on flies. Best fishing is early in June and again in fall, when the crowd thins out. The lake is 8 acres, with some improved campsites. A boat is not necessary.

MIRROR POND (Multnomah Co.) One of the I-84 ponds adjacent to the Columbia River, featuring bass and panfish. It is about 8 miles east of Troutdale, south of I-84 across from Rooster Rock State Park. The pond is directly under Crown Point State Park.

Mirror Pond is fed by several small streams and receives water from the Columbia during the freshet in May and June. It is almost one mile long and 1/4 mile wide in spots. Largemouth bass 3-4 pounds have been taken on plugs or spinning lures. Weedless lures fished in the shallows in June are effective. There's a large population of crappie, and brown bullhead, perch, and bluegill are available. Bullhead fishing is best when the water drops.

There is limited parking at the pond off a dirt access road right before Rooster Rock. Camping is available at the state park.

MISSION CREEK RESERVOIR A 130-acre reservoir with good populations of bass and panfish north of St. Paul, 5 miles south of Newburg. Public access is limited to the south end of the reservoir, which can be reached by Hwy. 219 from Newburg. There is limited parking on the road shoulder, and car-top boats can be launched.

Most anglers fish from the highway shoulder. Good catches of bluegill to 8 inches are made in early spring, though weeds become a problem later in the season. After June you'll need a boat to get to open water. There's good bass water here if you can get to it.

MISSION LAKE A 19-acre oxbow lake along the Willamette River in Willamette Mission County Park, one mile south of Wheatland, about 8 miles north of Salem. Take the Brooks Exit off I-5 and drive towards Wheatland, or take the ferry from Wheatland to the east bank of the Willamette.

The lake has a good population of bass and panfish, including largemouth bass, white crappie, brown bullhead, and bluegill. There is a boat ramp in the park and a speed limit on the lake. A trail in the park leads to Goose Lake, a 9-acre oxbow offering the same species as Mission Lake.

MOHAWK RIVER An important tributary of the lower McKenzie River, joining the main stream at Springfield. It is the primary provider of the McKenzie's cutthroat population and provides fair fishing for wild cutthroat early in the season.

The river is followed NE from Springfield by a paved road to Marcola, which is about half-way up the stream. From there, gravel roads access the upper river. Mill Creek, a fair tributary, comes in from the east, just north of Marcola. Most angling takes place in this area. The lower stream has much private land and almost no access. It is best fished early in the season, as the river gets pretty low by July. There is no camping along the stream.

MOLALLA RIVER A 45-mile tributary of the Middle Willamette, home river to many Portland area steelheaders. When the Molalla's good, it's very good. The river heads in the Cascades of the southern Mt. Hood National Forest and flows into the Willamette just up from Molalla State Park near Canby.

The lower stream is followed and crossed by paved backroads in the vicinities of Canby, Liberal, Union Mills, and Molalla. Above Molalla, a paved road closely parallels the river south and east. This road is through BLM property, and bank access is public.

The Molalla has a late wild winter steelhead run. Surprised trout anglers occasionally hook up with them after trout season opens, some still bright. The winter fish begin showing up in December and generally run through April. The winter fishery, though predominately wild, is currently supplemented by some earlier run Big Creek hatchery-reared fish, as well as by lingering summer steelhead. From February to mid-April, almost all steelhead in the river are wild.

The summer steelhead fishery in the Molalla is totally hatchery produced. The first summer smolts were stocked in the Molalla in 1984, with first returns in 1986. The catch rate has fluctuated between 1,488 in 1988-89, and 410 in 1992-93. Summers first appear in the river in May, and fishing is good through June and early July. By mid-summer, the river temperature gets too high to encourage new entries. Steelhead already in the river may be fished higher in the system, and in the cool deep pools. Additional summers probably enter after the river cools off in early fall, mingling with the early winter run.

The river is most accessible from drift boats, with the best run from Molalla down to Canby. Keep your eyes open for sweepers (partially submerged fallen trees). From Canby downstream the river can be handled by novice boaters. The stretch from Liberal to the state park provides a long day's drift, with a few steelhead holes and some classic slicks before the Pudding River muddies the water. If you take out at the state park, take time to enjoy the long easy trail along the river and the extensive heron rookery in the trees just back from water's edge. The take-out here is steep and often silted, so four-wheel drive with plenty of horse power is advisable.

Though there are few wild trout in the main river, legal rainbow are stocked from the Liberal area 4 miles north of Molalla, to Horse Creek, about 20 stream miles south of the town. Wild cutthroat are available in several tributaries. The lower 10 miles, west of Hwy. 213, are generally less productive than the upper waters, though nice fish are occasionally taken on spinners or bait. There's a lot of private land in this area, but paved and gravel roads access the stream in many places. Fishing holds up well into summer, and all methods of angling can be used with success.

Spring chinook from the early Willamette run show up from late January through March, and there are some fall run tule chinook in the river, too. However, most Molalla chinook are taken in the Willamette just before they turn up their home stream. The Molalla's chinook population has been supplemented with hatchery stock, though this may be discontinued in the future to encourage more wild production.

Boats can be launched at Feyrer Park east of Molalla (gravel ramp), the Hwy.

211 Bridge (pole slide), Hwy. 213 Bridge at Liberal (a gravel bar, also known as Wagonwheel Park), Logging Bridge at Macsburg (gravel bar), Goods Bridge just south of Canby (private access to gravel bar; gate may be locked), City Park just off 99E at the west end of Canby (gravel ramp), Knight's Bridge at the NW edge of Canby just outside the city limits (gravel ramp), and Molalla State Park on the Willamette about 1/2 mile below the Molalla mouth (paved ramp).

There are no campgrounds on the river.

MOODY LAKE A 5-acre brook trout lake just west of the Pacific Coast Trail in the Mink Lake Basin. See Cliff Lake for directions. Moody is one mile south of Cliff Lake. The trout average 8-9 inches, but some go to 12. There are fish here, but they're hard to catch. They will take flies late in the day. Mosquito imitations are always a good bet in the Mink Lake Basin.

MOOLACK LAKE A good hike-in brook trout lake 2 miles SE of Moolack Mt. and west of the Taylor Burn area. Moolack was a Chinook jargon word for elk. Shortest way in to this lake is from Taylor Burn Campground, which is best approached by the road from North Waldo Lake Campground. Hike west on the Blair Lake Trail 3553 about 2 miles, then take the Moolack Trail north 1/2 mile to the lake. This last trail is poorly marked, so keep a sharp eye. It's also possible to hike in from the west, starting on Trail 3594 just east of Etta Prairie on Forest Rd. 2417 in the headwaters of Furnish Creek, a tributary of Salmon Creek. Bring your map.

About 14 acres, Moolack puts out some nice rainbow and cutthroat averaging 11-12 inches. All methods of fishing produce, and fly angling can be excellent in the fall. There are a few good natural campsites. The area is usually accessible by late June.

MOONLIGHT LAKE A very productive small lake with lots of brook trout, just under 2 miles NW of Horse Lake. It is lightly fished due to its location. The best route is by way of Bend and the Cascade Lakes Hwy. to Elk Lake. Take the Horse Lakes Trail 3517 west to Upper Horse Lake. From there, head NW on trail 3514, the Horse Cr. Trail, and continue 2 miles. Keep watch to the left, and you'll spot the lake.

Moonlight Lake covers 8 acres and reaches a maximum depth of 14 feet. There's a lot of brush along the edges, so a rubber boat or float tube will really help. The brook trout average 8-10 inches, but a few to 16 inches are caught. Any method usually works here. There are no good campsites at the lake.

MOSBY CREEK A lightly-fished trout stream, over 20 miles long, located in southern Lane County. It enters Row River just below Dorena Reservoir, east of Cottage Grove. The headwaters are in the hills just west of the NW corner of the Umpqua National Forest.

From Hwy. 99 at Cottage Grove, turn east towards Dorena Reservoir, then south. A gravel road follows the stream closely for about 15 miles, then a dirt road takes over. A private timber company gate prevents vehicle access to several miles of the upper river, but anglers can continue on foot.

The creek has a fair catch rate for rainbow and cutthroat trout, though there's a lot of inaccessible private land. There is no camping along the stream.

MOTHER LODE LAKES In the Pansy Basin area of the Collawash River headwaters, hard to reach but worth the effort for fine scenery and good fishing. The lakes are about half-way between Pansy Lake and the Twin Lakes. See Pansy Lake for trail directions. The Mother Lodes are west of the trail, on the east side of Mother Lode Mountain. Trail No. 558 will get you closest.

These are a series of 3 small lakes, each about an acre or two at an elevation of about 4,000 ft. Currently only Ercrama Lake, the largest, is stocked. The state usually stocks cutthroat. It can easily be fished from shore.

MT. HOOD COMMUNITY COLLEGE PONDS Trout ponds on the Stark St. campus in Gresham, east of Portland. The ponds are stocked with legal rainbow in early season, but the water quality is poor due to run-off from nearby golf courses. Fishing falls off when the water warms in summer. Recommended for small fry.

MOWICH LAKE A large and very good rainbow and brook trout lake in the Eight Lakes Basin of Mt. Jefferson Wilderness. Mowich is the Chinook word for deer. The largest lake in the basin, it covers 54 acres and reaches a depth of 45 ft. It is 1/2 mile north of Duffy Lake by Trail 3422, and can be reached from Marion Lake by good trail.

Its brook trout run 8-16 inches, averaging 12 inches. Bait fishing with worms, or eggs and lures will take fish almost any time, and fly-fishing is effective early and late in the day. The lake is usually accessible by June.

MUDDY CREEK (Benton Co.) This stream lives up to its name during the spring. It is south of Corvallis, west of 99W, with headwaters in the hills west of Monroe. It flows over 20 miles north to join Mary's River at Corvallis. Many roads follow and cross the creek.

Muddy is a slow moving creek with a mud bottom. The stream is not stocked, but offers angling for bass, crappie, and a good population of wild cutthroat averaging 8-11 inches. Angling is good in early season and again when the fall rains begin. Large cutthroat may migrate up from the Willamette and Mary's River.

Access is a problem due to private land holdings. There is no camping along the stream.

MUDDY FORK (Sandy River) A small fork of the upper Sandy River which contains wild cutthroat, joining the main Sandy and the Clear Fork about 5 miles NE of Zigzag and just north of McNeil Campground. To reach it, drive north from Zigzag on Forest Rd. 18, the Lolo Pass Rd. Follow Forest Rd. 100 from Lost Creek Campground about 2 miles to its end. There Trail 797 leads north about 1/2 mile to cross Muddy Fork. There is no road access to Muddy Fork.

Muddy Fork has some wild cutthroat of fair size, and anglers can do well in spring after the water warms and before the glacial silt starts flowing. There are several forest campgrounds in the vicinity.

MULTNOMAH CHANNEL (a.k.a. Willamette Slough) This long channel near the mouth of the Willamette carries a significant flow of the main river and offers spring chinook angling that rivals the popular Oregon City fishery. It forms the southern boundary of Sauvie Island, a large delta island about 9 miles NW of Portland, and flows into the Columbia River at St. Helens. See Columbia River (St. Helens to Bonneville) for a map showing the channel's relationship to the Columbia. The Sauvie Island map in the appendix provides a larger scale presentation.

Hwy. 30 parallels the channel's west shore for most of its length, with plentiful bank access on Sauvie Island. Cross the Sauvie Island Bridge to pick up county roads that follow a good stretch of the channel's east bank. Much of the land along the channel on the island is publicly owned. Private land is well marked.

Anglers start fishing for salmon as early as mid-February if the water is clear, but few are caught until well into March. In late March and throughout May, the channel is literally filled with boats anchored or trolling for the elusive springers. Occasionally a steelhead is picked up, but if you hear "fish on!" bellowing across the water, chances are someone's got a hefty chinook in tow. The average catch weighs 18 pounds, but a few fish over 40 pounds are landed each spring. The middle of April is the best time to try.

Chinook anglers here are mostly trollers, although you'll find anchored boats at hot spots when the tide is running. Trollers move very slowly and fish the bottom, except in deep water, where they troll at 10-15 ft. Herring bait takes the overwhelming number of chinook, but lures also prove worthy. When the water is murky, hardware trollers use good size spinners or wobblers (copper finishes are especially effective at this time), changing to smaller lures as the water clears. Plugs and Kwikfish-type lures in silver, gold, and other light finishes are generally effective. Favorite spots include the mouth of Scappoose Bay, the Santosh Slough area, Coon Island, the Tank Hole, Rocky Point, and the head of the channel at the Willamette. Remember to keep an eye out for tow boats, whose vision is often impaired by barge loads.

From July through September, many channel anglers bring home a mess of catfish, largemouth and smallmouth bass, perch, and crappie. A tremendous number of panfish are taken around the log rafts, pilings, and abandoned docks, and at the mouths of streams. Boat angling is easiest, but a number of these areas can be reached from road and bank on both sides of the channel.

The channel also offers western Oregon's greatest sport catch of crayfish. Try baiting these with shad, which are available near Coon Island in June. A few sturgeon are picked up in the lower and upper channel. In late fall occasional large cutthroat are taken by bait anglers. The cutthroat are heading for spawning grounds in the short mainland tributaries, though few are seen these days due to habitat degradation.

Moorages are located all along the channel, accessible from Hwy. 30. There are boat ramps on the channel at Burlington Ferry off Hwy. 30 across from Sauvie Island, at Brown's Landing 3 miles east of Scappoose on Dike Rd., and at the Gilbert River mouth on Sauvie Island. Channel boaters also put in at Cathedral Park on the Willamette, at Scappoose Bay, and at St. Helens.

MULTNOMAH CREEK A 7-mile stream flowing into the Columbia Gorge, forming the beautiful Multnomah Falls east of Portland. It drains into Benson Lake at Hwy. 30. The only trout fishing is in the upper stream. Cut south off the scenic road at Bridal Veil, and drive 6 miles to the creek. A trail follows the creek both ways from the road's end. Wild cutthroat 6-9 inches dominate the catch, with a few to 12 inches.

NASH LAKE A naturally reproducing brook trout lake in the Three Sisters Wilderness, 6 air miles NW of Elk Lake.

Multnomah Channel provides a bucolic detour for Willamette-bound chinook.

Best access is from the east side of the Cascades. Take the Cascade Lakes Hwy. to Sisters Mirror Lake Trailhead, about 1/4 mile north of Sink Creek, which is about mid-way between Devil and Elk lakes. Follow Trail 20 to the Sisters Mirror Lake group, then continue west 3 more miles.

Nash Lake covers 33 acres and is at 4,900 ft. elevation. The lake is heavily fished for an isolated lake, but still produces consistently. The trout average 10 inches and get as large as 15. A few cutthroat are also present. Fly fishing is exceptional here late in the year. There are good natural campsites.

NIGHTSHADE LAKES Two little brook trout lakes off the beaten path in the Mink Lake Basin, offering rather poor fishing. The west lake usually has the larger fish. There are no campsites available. If you still want to give it a try, bushwhack NW from the north end of Dumbell Lake. A half mile will get you to Krag Lake, and the Nightshades are just 1/4 mile west of there.

NORTH FORK RESERVOIR A large, accessible power reservoir on the Clackamas River, covering 350 acres when full, located 7 miles south of Estacada off Hwy. 224. It's about 35 miles SE of Portland. The reservoir is formed by a PGE dam on the mainstem at the confluence of the North Fork and the Clackamas River.

The pool is 4 miles long, quite narrow and deep. It isn't very productive for wild fish, but it is stocked with legal rainbow every few weeks during the season and attracts a lot of anglers. Cutthroat, bull, brook and brown trout occasionally drop in from the river above the dam and are caught at times. Best fishing is at the upper end near the in-flow and near the resort, where fish are stocked. Best angling is with bait or troller/spinner combinations. Bank angling is possible in quite a few places. A flat bank area near the mouth is an especially good place for kids.

PGE has provided boat ramps, picnic, and camping facilities. There is a concession with supplies, tackle and boats at the upper end of the pool. A portion of the reservoir 2.3 miles above the dam has a 10-mph speed restriction to protect angling in the resort and park area.

NOTCH LAKE A 4-acre brook trout lake in the headwaters of Hills Creek, just west of Diamond Peak Wilderness. Follow the Hills Creek road, Forest Rd. 23, to Forest Rd. 2145, continuing 2 miles to Trail 3662, which follows the north bank of upper Hills Creek one mile to the lake. The brook trout and rainbow here run 6-11 inches. In most years the lake is accessible by early June. There are no improvements.

ONEONTA CREEK A small stream entering the Columbia River in the picturesque Columbia Gorge, dropping from the cliff between Benson State Park and Dodson several miles east of Multnomah Falls. Only 5 miles long, it is followed by trail through its own scenic gorge, and offers good fishing for small rainbow and a few cutthroat in the spring and summer.

OPAL LAKE (Douglas Co.) A fairly good trout lake in the Willamette National Forest just west of the southern boundary of Diamond Peak Wilderness. Follow Forest Rd. 211 from the SW end of Crescent Lake, then turn left on Forest

Many high mountain lakes in the Willamette zone are stocked with brook trout.

Rd. 398. Opal is about 13 miles from Crescent Lake. Timpanagos Lake is just south of Opal.

About 15 acres, the lake supports both rainbow and brook trout. The rainbow average 9 inches and run 6-13 inches. Brook trout predominate, averaging 8 inches. All methods are used here. The lake can be fished from shore. There's a small campground here and another at Timpanogas Lake, one mile south.

OPAL LAKE (Marion Co.) A brook trout lake 6 miles north of Detroit Reservoir at the head of Opal Creek. Take the Little North Santiam River Rd. past the Pearl Creek Guard Station on Forest Rd. 2207 to Shady Cove Campground. Cross the bridge on Cedar Creek Rd., taking the left fork uphill and switching back at the next right. Opal Lake is a half-mile bushwhack, at the bottom of the ridge. It is at elevation 3,476 ft., covering 11 acres, and is 40 ft. deep, with a self-sustaining population of brook trout.

OSWEGO CREEK Once known as Sucker Creek, it flows out of Lake Oswego south of Portland and is crossed by Hwy. 43 near the mouth. There is only about a mile of stream between the lake and the Willamette.

An occasional cutthroat is spotted here in winter, but most fishing is for warmwater fish in the lower half mile. A lot of crappie are picked up near the mouth. Small runs of winter steelhead and coho return to the creek each year. Non-finclipped steelhead must be released unharmed. Minimal parking is available at the Oswego City Park near the mouth.

OSWEGO, LAKE A large private lake just south of Portland, whose outlet at the town of Lake Oswego drains into the Willamette River. The lake is about 3 miles long and 1/3 mile wide. Its shores are completely developed, and almost exclusively residential. A private corporation controls access and polices the lake against trespassers. There is no public access. It is fed by the Tualatin River and is privately stocked. The lake was originally called Sucker Lake, but the name offended the residents of this posh district, so they renamed it. You can fish the outlet stream, Oswego Creek, as long as you don't trespass.

OTTER LAKE A very productive 17-acre trout lake at the north end of the Taylor Burn area, one mile NE of Erma Bell Lakes. Approach the lake from the north, from Skookum Creek Campground at the end of the Box Canyon Rd. (Forest Rd. 1957). The campground can be reached from the North Fork of the Willamette or the South Fork of the McKenzie. Head south 1/2 mile from Skookum Campground, then take Trail 3558 to the lake.

To approach from the south, take the Williams Lake Trail north from Taylor Burn Campground 3 miles to the lake. The Williams Lake Trail parallels the Olallie Trail, but is on the east side of Erma Bell Lakes.

Otter Lake is a consistent producer of rainbow and brook trout, with sizable fish available. Late fall is the best time for success. The lake is very brushy around the shore, so carry in a rubber boat or float tube. There are good natural campsites at Otter Lake and a small camp at Skookum Creek. It is usually accessible in late June.

PALMER LAKE A 15-acre lake NE of Larch Mt. on the Latourell Prairie Rd. It is in the closed area of the Bull Run watershed and is not open for angling.

PAMELIA LAKE A large lake with small cutthroat in the Mt. Jefferson Wilderness directly in front of the SW flank of the mountain. About 7 miles south of Idanha, take Pamelia Rd., Forest Rd. 2246, east 4 miles to Trail 3439. The lake is 2 miles down the trail over easy terrain.

Pamelia covers about 50 acres but gets low in late summer and fall. It has excellent spawning habitat and suffers from a classic case of over-population, teeming with stunted, eager cutthroat 6-8 inches. A special bag limit of 30 fish per day is an effort to encourage catch and keep angling in order reduce the population and increase average size. All methods will take fish here, and there are no size restrictions. The road is accessible during winter, and the is lake open, so anglers could do a little snowshoe ice fishing.

There are several good natural campsites at the lake, and there are other good lakes in the neighborhood. See Hanks and Hunts. Supplies are available at Idanha or Detroit. The lake is often ice-free by late May, but there is usually lots of snow left.

PANSY LAKE In the Pansy Basin near the head of the Hot Springs Fork of the Collawash River. Take Hwy. 224 past Estacada 34 miles to the mouth of the Collawash. From there, follow Forest Rd. 63 up the Collawash to Tom Meadows, then Forest Rd. 6340 and Forest Rd. 6341 to the Pansy Trail 551. Hike south for one mile to Pansy Basin. Bear right, and cross the meadow to the rock slide. Hike 1/2 mile up the ridge by trail. The lake is just west of Bull of the Woods Lookout, The trails are well signed.

Pansy covers about 6 acres and is very shallow. It is stocked with brook trout and supports some natural reproduction as well, offering consistent catches of 8-9 inch fish, with some to 12 inches. Fly angling or small lures work best due to the lake's shallow depth. Fall is the best season to fish here.

PANTHER CREEK A small wild trout stream flowing into the North Yamhill River, just north of McMinnville off Hwy. 18. The lower end of the stream is crossed by the paved road north from McMinnville to Carlton. A paved road west from Carlton accesses the upper stream. Panther provides good angling the first few months of trout season, but gets low in the summer. A few fair size cutthroat are occasionally hooked.

The creek flows entirely through private agricultural land, with public access only at road crossings.

PARRISH LAKE A good brook trout lake west of the North Santiam River, about 9 miles NW of Santiam Junction. From Hwy. 22, turn west 7 miles south of the Marion Forks Ranger Station onto Forest Rd. 2266. Follow this road west about 5 miles. The road runs between Daly Lake on the north, and Parrish Lake on the south.

Parrish is about 7 acres and produces brook trout 6-13 inches, averaging 9 inches. The lake is usually good early and late in the season. All methods are used to take fish. Spinner and bait are effective in early season. There are good natural campsites available. It is usually accessible in late May.

PATJENS LAKES A group of three small lakes south of Big Lake along the Cascade Summit, SW of Santiam Pass Hwy. 20. At Hoodoo Ski Bowl, turn onto Forest Rd. 2690. It's 4 miles to Big Lake, and the Patjens are 2 miles south by Trail 3395. The upper and deepest lake covers about 3 acres and has brook trout 6-12 inches. The middle lake covers 6 acres and has rainbow trout. The lower lake is just a shallow pot hole and doesn't hold fish. The lakes are lightly fished. There's a good camp at Big Lake.

PENN LAKE A trout lake in the north Mink Lake Basin, at the head of the South Fork McKenzie, west of Elk Lake. See Corner Lake for directions. Penn Lake is lightly fished due to it's position in the basin. It is about 1/4 mile NW of Corner Lake by a good trail.

It contains naturally reproducing cutthroat and brook trout. About 26 acres and very shallow, it occasionally winterkills. Best fishing for brook trout is early in the year and again in fall.

PETE'S SLOUGH A Columbia River backwater on Sauvie Island at the north end of Sturgeon Lake, fished for bass and panfish. After crossing Sauvie Island Bridge 10 miles west of Portland off Hwy. 30, follow Reeder Rd. for 11 miles to the checking station. Drive left about one mile and cross the dike, where several dirt roads head west to the slough. The dike crossing is closed from late May through June, as the area is flooded.

Pete's Slough connects McNary and Sturgeon lakes and is fishable all along the shore. See McNary Lake. Three or four footbridges cross it, and these are heavily used by anglers. Good catches of crappie, brown bullhead, and other panfish are taken. Bait is most popular, but small lures and streamer flies take large crappie. An occasional largemouth bass is caught, but they're not numerous. Try plugging the few shallow oxbows. The entrances to the many duck lakes are also frequent bass hang-outs. Overnight camping is not permitted on the island. Minimal supplies are available at the island store near the bridge.

You will need to purchase a recreation permit to park on Sauvie Island. Day and seasonal passes are sold at the market on the island just north of the bridge. Refer to the Appendix for a map of Sauvie Island.

PIKA LAKE A small brook trout lake, lightly fished but not too hard to reach. It's in the Big Meadows area off the North Santiam. See Fay Lake for directions. Continue past Fay for 1/4 mile, then follow a blazed trail south. It's 1/2 mile to the lake. Pika is very brushy and hard to fish, so a rubber boat or float tube is helpful. It's about 3 acres and shallow, and the fish bite well on almost anything once you get out to them. Brook trout here run 8-10 inches. There are no good campsites at the lake.

PINE RIDGE LAKE Also known as Pine Lake, adjacent to a heavily-used Scout camp. It can be reached from Marion Forks on Hwy. 22 by turning east onto Twin Meadows Rd. (Forest Rd. 2261) about 4 miles south of Marion Forks. From this point it's five miles to the lake. The lake is restricted to use by juveniles (under 18 years). It's a fine lake for youngsters. Cutthroat and rainbow run to 13 inches. Trails lead to other lakes in the area. See Temple, Davis. Public camping is prohibited. Recommended for small fry.

PIPER LAKE A lightly fished 5-acre brook trout lake in the Irish Mt. area north of Irish and Taylor lakes. See McFarland Lake for directions. Piper is a few hundred yards west of McFarland. Although small, the lake has a maximum depth of 24 ft. deep. It's not very productive, but some nice brook trout catches have been reported. It's a good lake to try while in the Irish Mountain area.

PLATT LAKE An 8-acre trout lake in the Horse Lake area west of Elk Lake. See Horse Lake for directions. Platt Lake is 2 miles SW of Upper Horse Lake. Take the Horse Mt. Trail 3530, which goes right to the lake. Platt has some nice brook trout around 10 inches. All methods of angling will take fish at times, and the lake is easily fished from shore. There are good natural campsites at the lake. Other small lakes to the south are also stocked. See Mile Lake.

PLAZA LAKE A 5-acre hike-in brook trout lake east of Hwy. 224 near Squaw Mt., in a setting of rare old growth forest. The lake drains into the South Fork of the Salmon River from elevation 3,650 ft. The hike in is about 20 minutes.

From Estacada follow Hwy. 224 about 6 miles to the North Fork Rd. (Forest Rd. 4610). At about 6 miles Forest Rd. 4610 crosses Winslow Creek then cuts right sharply, while Forest Rd. 4613 continues straight ahead to North Fork Crossing Campground. Stay on 4610 (known as the Squaw Mt. Rd.) 11 miles to Twin Springs Campground. About one mile past the camp, Trail 788 to Plaza Lake heads east. The trail is 3/4 mile downhill, although the lake is only 1/2 mile or less from the road.

Though small, Plaza produces a fair number of pan-size brook trout 6-10 inches. All methods of angling will take fish here. It's usually not open until late June.

PLUMB LAKE A brook trout lake in the Mink Lake Basin, 1/2 mile NE of Junction Lake on the trail to Corner Lake. See Mink Lake and Junction Lake for directions. One of the smaller lakes in the Mink Lake Basin, it covers 15 acres and reaches a maximum depth of 17 ft. Brook trout reproduce naturally here, and fishing for them is generally good. It's a good fly-fishing lake, with best catches late in the day.

POPE LAKE A Sauvie Island lake containing brown bullhead, crappie, bass, some carp, and chubs. To reach the lake, take Hwy. 30 north from Portland to the Sauvie Island Bridge. Cross to the island and follow Reeder Rd. for about 10 miles to a slough with moorage on the right. The lake is about 300 yards directly west. The surest way to find the lake is to proceed to the waterfowl checking station, then walk due south for 1/2 mile. This is Dept. of Fish and Wildlife property, which is open to public access except during duck season. A piece of land at the south end of Pope Lake is private property, so watch the signs.

Pope covers about 10 acres and is easily fished from shore. Fair size bass are taken on plugs and spinners, and crappie will hit the smaller lures. Angling for brown bullhead is fair throughout the summer. There is no camping in this area.

You will need to purchase a recreation permit to park on Sauvie Island. Day or seasonal passes are sold at the market on the island just north of the bridge. Refer to the Appendix for a map of the island.

PORKY LAKE One of the most productive and consistent lakes in the Mink Lake Basin. See Cliff Lake and Mink Lake for directions. It covers about 38 acres, located 1/2 mile east of Mink Lake, halfway to Cliff Lake.

Porky is a very rich body of water with a lot of naturally reproducing brook trout. It usually holds up throughout the season. All methods will catch fish, with fly-fishing especially good in late summer. There are good natural campsites at the lake.

PRESLEY LAKE A shallow drive-in 3-acre lake 3 miles NW of Marion Lake. About 1/2 mile south of Marion Forks Ranger Station, turn east onto Forest Rd. 2257. Follow this road about 2 miles to Forest Rd. 515, a left fork which goes to Horn Creek Unit 2. At about 1/2 mile, you can see the lake to the north. A spur road runs down to Presley. The lake is stocked with catchable rainbow. There are no camping facilities.

PRILL LAKE A small brook trout lake in the Marion Lake Basin. See Marion Lake for directions. From Marion, follow the trail around the east bank to Mist Creek. Prill is about one mile east by very steep trail. It covers 8 acres and is 20 feet deep. Brook trout 8-14 inches will hit anything. There are a few natural campsites.

PUDDING RIVER A fairly long stream with headwaters east of Salem, flowing through the center of Marion County north into Clackamas County, where it joins the Mollala River near Canby. It is crossed by Hwy. 99E outside of Aurora. A number of paved and gravel roads in the Silverton, Mt. Angel, and Woodburn areas cross the stream. Most bank angling takes place at the road crossings.

The Pudding isn't stocked, but its main tributaries (Drift, Butte, Silver, and Abiqua creeks) keep the upper waters fairly populated with trout. Most trout anglers use bait or spinner/bait combinations. Cutthroat dominate the catch, with a few rainbow taken.

Winter steelhead, most of which are heading for Abiqua and Butte Creeks, are fished up to the mouth of Silver Creek, but only a few are hooked in the Pudding each year. All non-finclipped steelhead must be released unharmed.

The lower stream offers fair bass angling on plugs or spinners, with panfish taken on bait. The extreme lower river can be drifted in small boats, and some anglers motor up from the Willamette when the water is high. The lower river is sometimes navigable into June.

PYRAMID LAKE (Clackamas Co.) A cutthroat lake in the High Rocks area of the Clackamas drainage. At elevation 4,000 ft., it is usually accessible several weeks earlier than the rest of the mountain lakes. It's only 1/2 mile by trail to this 4-acre lake.

From Estacada, take Hwy. 224 about 30 miles SE to Ripplebrook Ranger Station, and continue another 8 miles to the Shellrock Rd. (Forest Rd. 58). A little over 4 miles north past Shellrock Campground, Forest Rd. 140 branches off to the left. Follow Forest Rd. 140 about 2 miles to road's end at Pyramid Lake Trailhead.

Formerly stocked with brook trout, the lake is now stocked with cutthroat, which put on more size here. Fishing holds up well, producing fish 6-13 inches. Bait and spinner work best in early season, with good fly angling later on. There are natural campsites at the lake.

PYRAMID LAKE (Marion Co.) An up and down lake for brook trout, with occasional winterkills. Some years have produced fine, plump brookies. The lake is 1 1/2 miles west of Breitenbush Lake. See Breitenbush Lake for directions. The trail to Pyramid takes off south at the bridge over the Breitenbush Lake outlet, following the creek up 1/2 mile, then traversing a steep slope. Pyramid is on a flat, 1/2 mile west of Pyramid Butte.

The lake is about 5 acres and shallow. When the fish are there, fly-fishing is excellent. There are some pretty, natural campsites.

QUARTZVILLE CREEK An excellent trout stream, also known as the Quartzville Fork of the Santiam. It enters Green Peter Reservoir from the north about 12 miles east of Sweet Home. From Hwy. 20, follow a paved road that runs north about 3 miles east of Foster. This crosses the upper end of Foster Reservoir and follows the north shore of Green Peter. Quartzville is about 25 miles long, and the paved road follows it most of the way, with gravel roads continuing to the headwaters.

The creek has a lot of productive water, most on BLM or National Forest land. It's stocked with rainbow trout each spring and early summer, and some nice wild cutthroat are present. All methods of angling are used, with light gear usually best. Fly-fishing can be good when the water warms. Best catches are from Canal Creek down to the Forks Canal.

Camping is available at Whitcomb Creek Campground, on the reservoir just west of the creek mouth, and at Yellowbottom BLM Campground about 6 miles upstream from the reservoir.

QUESTION MARK LAKE A good trout lake in the Mink Lake Basin. It receives a lot of pressure but still produces well. The lake takes its name from its unique shape, and not from puzzled fly anglers trying to match the hatch. The lake is on the east edge of the basin. From the junction of the Six Lakes Trail and the Pacific Crest Trail, which meet at Ledge Lake Meadow, it's 1/4 mile NW through the trees to Question Mark.

The lake is about 10 acres and deep in spots, but with a lot of shoal area for easy fly-fishing. It's a very easy lake to fish. The rainbow and cutthroat trout here run 7-12 inches, with a few larger. There are excellent campsites here. It's hard to reach before late June.

QUINN LAKES Two trout lakes west of Taylor Burn Campground across a canyon carved by the North Fork of the Willamette. It's about a 2-mile hike, down and up, on Blair Lake Trail 3553. Lower Quinn Lake is just south of the trail at the head of Fisher Creek. The Quinns can also be reached from North Waldo Camp or from the Oakridge area by the Salmon Creek Rd. and Forest Rd. 2417. See Eddeeleo Lakes for trail details.

Lower Quinn is 12 acres and has rainbow trout. The shore is a little brushy, but it can be fished in places. A rubber boat would be handy. Upper Quinn Lake is 1/4 mile south, covering 17 acres. Upper has brook trout and, like most brook trout lakes, it slows up for periods during the season. Both lakes are heavily fished.

RED BUTTE LAKE A scenic 6-acre lake in the Eight Lakes Basin of the Mt. Jefferson Wilderness. It is to the west of the trail running south from Jorn Lake, about 1/2 mile south of Jorn, 2 miles north of Duffy, on the east side of Red Butte, a prominent landmark. See Jorn and Duffy for directions.

Red Butte is long, narrow, and fairly deep for its size. Being on the trail, it's fished frequently. Stocked by the state every other year, the brook trout average 8-9 inches, with a few to 12 inches. It's easily fished from shore. There are good natural campsites near the lake, and additional sites at Jorn. There are other good lakes north and south.

This is a heavily used wilderness area. Camp well back from the lake to help preserve the fragile vegetation.

RIGDON LAKES A pair of inconsistent trout lakes in the Taylor Burn area north of Waldo Lake, with both rainbow and cutthroat trout. From Taylor Burn Campground, 7 miles north of the North Waldo Lake Campground by poor road, take the Olallie Trail 3583 south to Kiwa Lake, and turn east off the trail just south of Kiwa. The Rigdons are 1/2 mile east of the trail, just east of Rigdon Butte. From North Waldo, take the trail along the north end of Waldo Lake about 2 miles, then head north by trail about 1/2 mile to the Rigdons.

Upper Rigdon offers fair brook trout angling on its 50 acres. The fish run 6-13 inches, averaging 10 inches. Lower Rigdon is just a few hundred yards to the south. About the same size as Upper, it sometimes holds rainbow and brook trout to 15 inches. Both lakes can be fished from shore. Bait, lures, and flies can all work here depending on conditions. These lakes are at their best in late summer and fall.

ROARING RIVER (Clackamas Co.) A tributary of the upper Clackamas River, offering good hike-in angling for wild trout and summer steelhead. About 15 miles long, it heads in the High Rock area of Mt. Hood National Forest about 4 miles NW of Timothy Lake. It joins the Clackamas just upstream from Fish Creek at Roaring River Campground on Hwy. 224.

Anglers must hike to reach the stream. Bring your forest map. The canyon is very deep, and the hiking tough. Some anglers hike up from the forest camp at the mouth. The central creek can be reached by a 3-mile hike on a trail south from Lookout Spring Camp on the Squaw Mt. Rd. A dirt road, Forest Rd. 4611, can be followed from about one mile south of North Fork Crossing Campground to a trailhead which takes at least 2 miles off this hike.

For rugged hikers, the upper river can be reached by a trek into the canyon about 2 miles by trail from Twin Springs Camp, which is several miles further east on Squaw Mt. Rd. Cutthroat run 6-12 inches. If you like fishing in solitude, this is the spot. Summer steelhead are found in the lower 3 miles of river below the falls and may be fished from June 1 through December 30. There's a nice pool below the falls that often holds steelhead.

There are several camps on the Squaw Mt. Rd. and near the mouth on Hwy. 224, and there are natural sites in the canyon.

ROARING RIVER (Linn Co.) A small trout stream, tributary to Crabtree Creek, 20 miles east of Albany. From Hwy. 99E, turn east at Jefferson, continue through Scio, then follow the Crabtree Creek Rd. Roaring River is only about 8 miles long, and most of it runs close to the road.

A trout and steelhead hatchery near the mouth is a nice spot to visit. Bait is probably most consistently effective, but flies will work when the water warms up. Small spinners with bait should also do well. Some wild cutthroat of small size are caught at times. A county park below the hatchery is stocked with legal rainbow from May through June. The catch runs 7-12 inches, with a few larger fish occasionally caught near the mouth. There are no campgrounds on the river, but there is a nice little day-use park near the fish hatchery which includes a wheelchair accessible fishing pier.

ROBINSON LAKE A good cutthroat lake on the western border of Mt. Washington Wilderness. To reach the lake take Robinson Rd. east from Hwy. 126, the McKenzie River Hwy. The turn-off is about 2 miles south of Clear Lake. Follow this road about 4 miles to the end, where a trail leads 1/4 mile east to the lake.

Robinson is only 5 acres and mostly shallow, but runs to 20 ft. deep in spots. It offers good trout angling using any method, with most fish averaging 12 inches and some beauties to 16 inches. Campsites are available on Clear Lake Rd.

ROCK CREEK (Clackamas Co.) A fair early-season wild cutthroat stream, flowing into Butte Creek about 5 miles south of Canby and east of 99E. The head of the creek is about 10 miles south of Molalla. The stream is crossed by Hwy. 213 a few miles south of Molalla, and by paved and gravel roads throughout its length.

The cutthroat run 6-12 inches. Bait is the best method, with spinner and bait effective in the larger holes. Bear Creek, flowing into Rock Creek near Marks Prairie, has some fair cutthroat angling, too. Best fishing is in May and June. Most land along the creek is privately owned, so get permission. There are no campsites on the stream.

ROCK LAKES (Clackamas Co.) Three good lakes in the High Rock area, north of Hwy. 224, offering a variety of trout for the hiking angler. Upper Rock features cutthroat, Middle has rainbow, and Lower offers brook trout.

The lakes are just over 50 miles from Portland. The shortest hike in is by Trail 512, which heads between Frazier Fork and Frazier Turnaround campgrounds. Follow Hwy. 224 from Estacada to the Shellrock Rd. Forest Rd. 58, and drive 7 miles to High Rock Springs Campground. Just north of the campground, take Forest Rd. 240 five miles west to Frazier Forks Campground. The lakes are one mile west on Serene Lake Trail 512. Lower Rock Lake is to the north. Signs mark the trail junctions.

The lower lake is about 9 acres and 13 ft. deep. Middle Rock is 15 acres and 34 ft. deep. Upper Rock is only 3 acres, but 22 ft. deep. All the lakes have reproducing populations of brook trout, as well as stocked fish. Average catch in all the lakes is 8-9 inches, and some brook trout over 12 inches are taken.

The lakes are fished rather heavily since they are so close to the road. One or more of the three is usually putting out catches. All methods of angling can be used, from boat or bank. Spinner and bait are usually good in early season, fly-fishing in late summer and fall.

There are good campsites at the two larger lakes. They are usually inaccessible until early June, except by hiking west from Shellrock Lake. The road to Frazier Mt. is sometimes snowed in until late June.

ROCKPILE LAKE A scenic cutthroat trout lake in Diamond Peak Wilderness at 6,100 ft., just east of a peak called Diamond Rockpile. It is a few hundred yards SE of Marie Lake. See Marie Lake for trail directions.

This 6-acre lake is fished heavily, but it produces some nice brook trout. The fish average 10 inches and run to 14 inches. The lake is easily fished from shore, and all methods can be used. There are good natural campsites here, and a full-service campground at Summit Lake. It is usually snowbound until late June.

ROOSTER ROCK SLOUGH A Columbia River backwater, about 5 acres, north of I-84 at Rooster Rock State Park. The slough contains brown bullhead, yellow perch, white and black crappie, and largemouth bass.

ROSLYN LAKE A trout lake about 26 miles from Portland, 2 miles NE of Sandy. From Hwy. 26 at the east end of Sandy, turn north onto Dodge Park Rd. It's about 3 miles to the lake.

Catchable rainbow trout are stocked annually. Best fishing is on the east side, where the stream comes in.

There's a nice developed area with picnic and recreational facilities here. No motorboats are allowed, but car-top or rubber boats and canoes can be launched. A naturally flat bank permits wheelchair access. The lake is controlled by PGE as part of the Bull Run Power Plant.

ROUND LAKE (Lane Co.) A good brook trout and rainbow lake in the Eddeeleo group south of Taylor Burn, NW of Waldo Lake. See Eddeeleo Lakes for directions. Round Lake is just east of Upper Eddeeleo, 100 yards from the trail to North Waldo.

The catch averages 8-11 inches, with some fish to 16 inches. All methods of angling are used with good results. Fish reproduce naturally here. The lake covers 20 acres and is easily fished from shore. There are good natural campsites available, and excellent fishing in other lakes north and south.

ROUND LAKE (Marion Co.) A productive brown trout lake high in the southern Mt. Hood National Forest, popular with float tube anglers and restricted to barbless artificial flies and lures. Take Hwy. 224 from Estacada past Ripplebrook Ranger Station, then follow the Collawash River Rd. south to Forest Rd. 6370. Follow this road to Round Lake Campground. It's an easy hike down to the lake.

Round Lake is 9 acres and about 20 ft. deep. It has naturally reproducing brown trout, supplemented by stocked brook trout. The brook trout have been running

The spring chinook run is the largest of three salmon runs on the Sandy River.

8-14 inches, and the browns 8-16 inches, averaging 12 inches. It's a tough lake to fish from shore because of weeds along the shoals. Bring a float tube for best results. All methods will produce, but the browns are wary, so use light gear. There is a small campground above the lake.

ROW RIVER A wild cutthroat stream NE of Cottage Grove, a major tributary of the Coast Fork of the Willamette River. The river forms Dorena Reservoir, and a good road heads north along the lower stream, around the reservoir, and on up to the Forks at the confluence of Brice and Layng creeks. The distance from the mouth to this point is about 20 miles.

Average catch is around 10 inches, ranging from 6-13 inches. Fishing is best above the reservoir. A spinner will work best in early season, with good fly-fishing later. There are no improved campsites along the stream, and access is difficult due to private property. Ask permission before crossing private land.

RUSS LAKE (Confederated Tribes Warm Springs) A 6-acre brook trout lake east of Olallie Meadows Campground on the Skyline Rd. A 1 1/4 mile easy going trail reaches the lake after passing two other small, good lakes. See Jude and Brook.

The fish run 6-15 inches, averaging 10 inches. The bank is brushy, so a float tube would be helpful. Angling with wet flies is usually good in the morning and late in the day. Spinner and bait will work well almost anytime.

Although the lake is on Warm Springs Reservation, tribal permits are not required. Overnight camping is prohibited due to fire danger.

SALMON CREEK A good trout stream, tributary of the Middle Fork Willamette, flowing 26 miles from headwaters in Waldo Meadows to its confluence with the Middle Fork at Oakridge. Salmon Creek originates in Upper and Lower Salmon Lakes in the high lakes area west of Waldo Lake. It is fed by many small tributaries and two good size creeks (Furnish and Black), all of which have wild cutthroat. Salmon Creek itself has a lot of wild cutthroat, some wild rainbow, and is stocked with rainbow in the lower 15 miles from the mouth to the Black Creek confluence. It has better trout habitat than nearby Salt Creek (less steep gradient, slower flow, more pools), and consequently has a better population of wild fish.

The name Salmon Creek derives from a run of spring chinook that once spawned here. The run was destroyed when the Army Corps of Engineers failed to construct fishways over Dexter and Lookout Point dams on the Middle Fork Willamette. To mitigate the loss, the Corps has built a fish trap at Dexter Dam, where the Oregon Dept. of Fish and Wildlife collects salmon eggs for rearing in a hatchery on Salmon Creek. The Creek is closed to salmon angling.

To reach Salmon Creek, follow Hwy. 58 east from Springfield through Oakridge. The road to the hatchery, one mile east of town, joins Forest Rd. 24, which follows the creek for about 10 miles. Logging roads access the upper stream and many of the tributaries. There is a Forest Service campground on the creek at Salmon Creek Falls.

SALMON RIVER (Clackamas Co.) A fine tributary of the upper Sandy River with wild cutthroat and a good run of summer steelhead. It has excellent water for steelhead fly-fishing. The Salmon joins the Sandy from the south at Brightwood, a community on Hwy. 26 about 4 miles west of Zigzag.

At Wildwood on Hwy. 26, a road leads south to a BLM recreation area on the river, about 3 miles upstream from the mouth. Roads due south from Wemme and Zigzag Ranger Station join the Salmon about 6 miles from the mouth and continue south as Forest Rd. 2618, which follows the river about 5 miles upstream to Trail 742. The trail keeps pace with the river for 11 miles in a wilderness-like setting. The upper river can be reached by trails which head from forest roads south of Trillium Lake. These are clearly shown on the Mt. Hood National Forest map.

The Salmon River heads on the upper slopes of Mt. Hood, carrying snow melt down from Palmer Glacier. It flows 31 miles, 24 through national forest. Thirteen miles above the mouth a series of scenic waterfalls form a barrier to salmon and steelhead passage. Above the falls there is a good population of wild cutthroat.

Summer steelhead reach the Salmon River in June, and good fishing is available through December. The stretch of river from the bridge on Forest Rd. 2618 to the falls, about 4 miles, is restricted to fly-fishing only. The Salmon River Trail begins at the bridge. This charming wooded stretch, dotted with deep pools, offers a quality angling experience. Most steelhead in the Salmon are finclipped, however there is some natural reproduction, and non-finclipped steelhead must be released unharmed. Barbless hooks are required throughout the river from November 1 through December 31. The estimated catch during the past 10 years has fluctuated between a high of 6,368 in 1984-85 and a low of 911 in 1991-92.

The Salmon also contains spring chinook and coho, but all salmon angling is prohibited in order to protect spawning fish. The mouth of the Salmon is a popular Sandy River angling site for both salmon and steelhead.

There are camping facilities at the Wildwood Recreation Site on Hwy. 26 and at Green Canyon Campground on Forest Rd. 2618, about 5 miles south of Zigzag. The fly shop in the shopping center at Welches is a good source of information as well as supplies.

SALMONBERRY LAKE A 3-acre put'n'-take rainbow fishery near St. Helens, formerly a city water supply. From Hwy. 30 at St. Helens, head west on the Pittsburgh-St. Helens Rd. about 9 miles, turning left onto a gravel road soon after the main road itself turns to gravel. The access road leads directly to the pond.

SALT CREEK A large and powerful tributary of the Middle Fork Willamette River. It flows 28 miles through Willamette Pass from its source at Gold Lake to its confluence with the Middle Fork at Oakridge. It is closely followed by Hwy. 58 to the Gold Lake cut-off and is a popular tourist fishery, due more to its proximity to the highway than to its productivity. Steep and tumultuous throughout much of its run, it offers little fish habitat and, consequently, has only a small wild trout population. The Forest Service has made some efforts to enhance trout habitat in the lower 10 miles. The creek is stocked with hatchery rainbow from the mouth to South Fork Bridge (about 7 miles above Blue Pool Campground).

The most productive stretch for small but feisty wild trout is the few miles from Hwy. 58 Bridge down to Salt Creek Falls. Here the creek flows at a diminished gradient, meandering prettily through meadows. It is brushy and hard to fish, but wild rainbow and brook trout are plentiful. Salt Creek Falls is a handsome 286 ft. falls which can be viewed from a paved trail on the south side of Hwy. 58 about 20 miles east of Oakridge.

Salt Creek flows within Willamette National Forest. There is a Forest Service Ranger Station at Oakridge. There are campgrounds on the creek at Blue Pool (a nice swimming hole) about 8 miles east of Oakridge, and at Salt Creek Falls. McCredie Hot Springs, an undeveloped natural hot spring pool beside the creek, is less than one mile from Blue Pool. There is a large gravel parking area above the springs, but no sign. Most bathers soak au naturelle. There are no facilities of any kind here, so users are urged to carry out all trash and respect the delicate sanitation situation. The nearest outhouses are at Blue Pool. As with all hot springs in Oregon which are within easy reach of population centers (this one is right below busy Hwy. 58), users are urged to be wary. Daylight soaks are probably safest. Things can get rowdy here at night, especially on weekends. Don't leave valuables in your car.

The Sandy above Marmot Dam.

SANDY RIVER An excellent steelhead and salmon river, located conveniently close to Portland. Most of fish are caught within an hour's drive of the city. The Sandy heads in the glaciers of Mt. Hood and flows 50 miles west to join the Columbia River at Troutdale.

The majority of steelhead and salmon angling takes place in a 23-mile stretch between the river mouth, which can be reached from I-84 just east of Troutdale, and the town of Sandy on Hwy. 26. Good county roads cross and parallel the lower river, and Hwy. 26 leads to the river and its upper tributaries, including the Salmon River.

The Sandy has three salmon runs. The spring chinook run is the largest. Springers enter the river in April, and fishing holds up through June. During the past ten years, the estimated spring chinook catch has fluctuated from a high of 1,897 in 1990, to a low of 537 in 1992.

Fall chinook appear in late August, and the run peaks in October. These fish spawn in the lower river and are rarely seen above the town of Sandy. The catch has fluctuated from a high of 549 in 1989-90, to a low of 236 in 1992-93. An annual Salmon Festival celebrating the return of the fall chinook to the river takes place the third weekend in October at Oxbow Park. The Festival, organized by Oregon Trout, offers educational programs and guided tours of salmon spawning areas.

Coho are present from early September through October, but low returns in recent years have prompted emergency closures. Call the Columbia Region Office of ODF&W for a season update. In the past ten years, the estimated catch rate has fluctuated from a high of 2,200 in 1991, to a low of 524 in 1987. The 1992 catch was 1,176.

Popular salmon lures used on the Sandy include small spinners, fluorescent wobblers, Kwikfish-type lures, and Hotshots. See the regulations synopsis for special hook and weight restrictions.

Steelhead are in the river year-round, and not a month passes without a catch. In good years, more than a hundred steelhead are taken each month. In 1991-92, several months had catch rates of less than 50 fish.

Winter steelhead provide the biggest fishery by far. During the past ten years, the estimated catch has fluctuated from a high of 10,449 in 1984-85, to a low of 5,252 in 1991-92. Fishing picks up in late November and remains very good through April. Fewer than 300 fish are generally caught above Marmot Dam.

Summer steelhead are present in force from late May through August. The catch rate is good both above and below Marmot. During the past ten years, the estimated catch has fluctuated between a high of 3,557 in 1988-89, and a low of 1,839 in 1991-92. The 1992-93 catch was

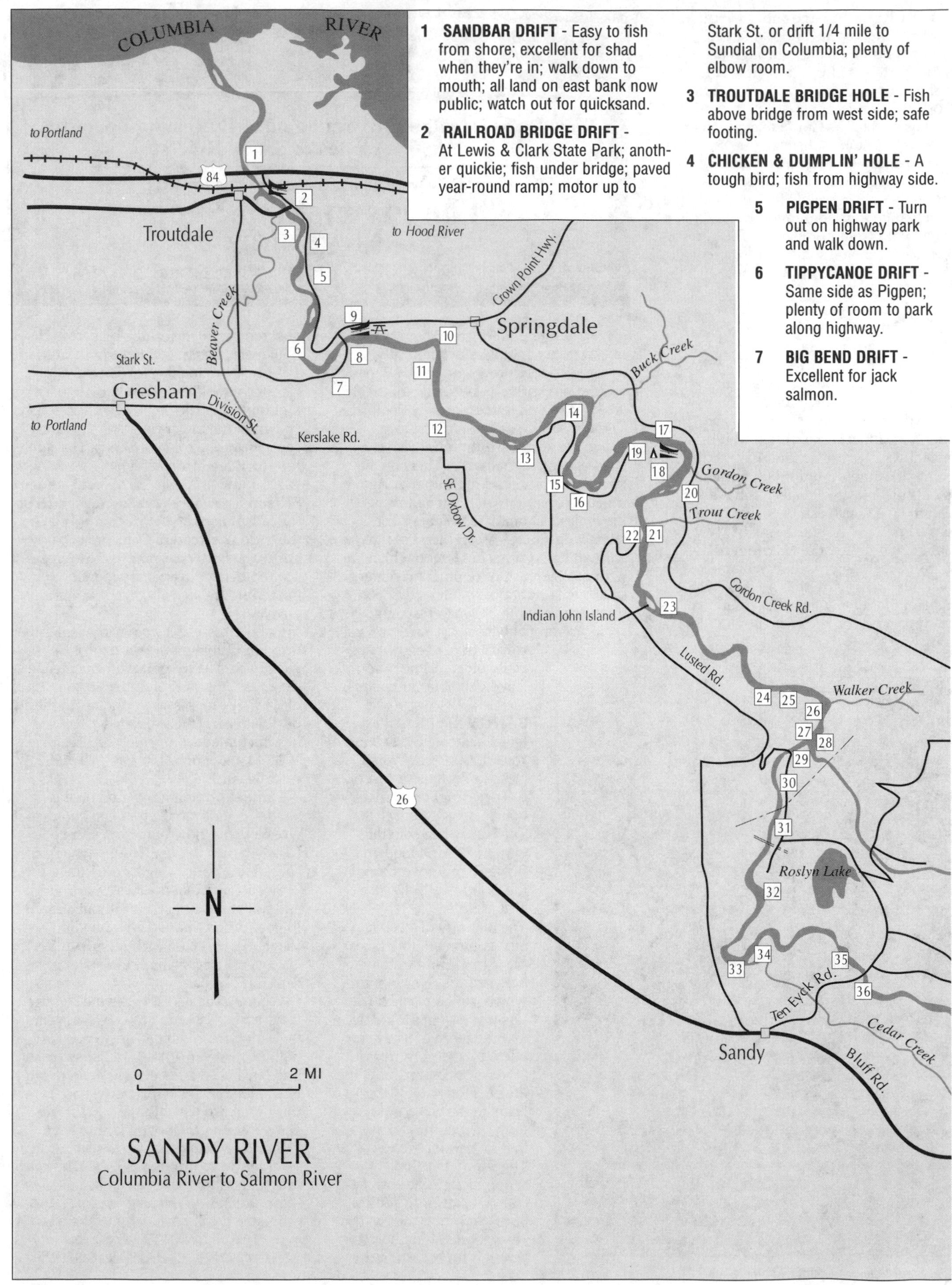

SANDY RIVER

Columbia River to Salmon River

1 **SANDBAR DRIFT** - Easy to fish from shore; excellent for shad when they're in; walk down to mouth; all land on east bank now public; watch out for quicksand.

2 **RAILROAD BRIDGE DRIFT** - At Lewis & Clark State Park; another quickie; fish under bridge; paved year-round ramp; motor up to Stark St. or drift 1/4 mile to Sundial on Columbia; plenty of elbow room.

3 **TROUTDALE BRIDGE HOLE** - Fish above bridge from west side; safe footing.

4 **CHICKEN & DUMPLIN' HOLE** - A tough bird; fish from highway side.

5 **PIGPEN DRIFT** - Turn out on highway park and walk down.

6 **TIPPYCANOE DRIFT** - Same side as Pigpen; plenty of room to park along highway.

7 **BIG BEND DRIFT** - Excellent for jack salmon.

8 STARK ST. BRIDGE DRIFT - Very deep hole below bridge, park side; launch at Dabney; no fishing from boats above bridge.

9 DABNEY PARK DRIFT - Seasonal unimproved launch area available (Oct. 1 - April 30); good place to take the family.

10 FILL YOUR WADERS DRIFT - A long cast, hard to fish; boats only.

11 GOOD PLUNKING HOLE

12 SPRINGDALE HOLE - Fish from north bank at leaning log; boats only.

13 COLLINS HOLE - Good plunking; drift fish tailout; boats only.

14 YMCA DRIFT - Big long click.

15 HOSSNER DRIFT - Deep plunking hole; tailout and 300 yds. of good drift water below.

16 UPPER HOSSNER DRIFT - Good drift-fishing.

17 SAWMILL DRIFT - Also known as Stump Hole; real good drift water; the tackle snatcher on the river; fish from north side.

18 OXBOW LAUNCH - Park extends almost to Gordon Creek.

19 TURNAROUND HOLE - Long drift, good boat access; watch for quicksand below Buck Cr.

20 GORDON CREEK DRIFT - Long, deep riffle; drift it with floating lure; easy access.

21 TROUT CREEK DRIFT - This one can be waded at low water.

22 BIG ROCK HOLE - Deep drift, good in low water; long walk in.

23 INDIAN JOHN ISLAND DRIFT - Good water above island, Oxbow side; walk up from Oxbow Park.

24 BUTLER'S EDDY - Walk here from Gauge Hole, fish bottom of rough water.

25 BLUE HOLE - Below Gauge hole; good for spring chinook; fish tailout for steelhead.

26 GAUGE HOLE - Walk from Pipeline Hole (rough road); fish deep water close to bank on pipeline side.

27 SWIMMING HOLE - Girl Scout Camp; upper end is good.

28 PIPELINE HOLE - Downstream from mouth of Bull Run; big deep hole, excellent for plunking or drifting.

29 DODGE PARK BRIDGE HOLE - Just downstream from bridge.

30 GARBAGE PIT HOLE - Plunking and drifting; fairly easy access and good parking.

31 ALDERS HOLE - Long and deep; hard to get into.

32 SOAPSTONE DRIFT - Fairly deep hole drifts down to gravel bar; walk up from Alders.

33 MOUTH OF CEDAR CREEK - Plunking hole on Cedar Cr. side, drift-fishing on opposite side; accessible from Cedar Cr.

34 OKIE DRIFT - Long fast drift, good for floating lures, just above mouth of Cedar Cr.

35 REVENUE BRIDGE - Fish south side of stream below bridge.

36 LOWER CANYON HIKE - Park at bridge and hike up lower canyon.

37 AIRPORT HOLE - Park on road and walk downstream into canyon.

38 POWER LINE HOLE - Long walk in.

39 UPPER CANYON HIKE - Walk into canyon and fish to below dam; road parallels stream to dam.

40 MARMOT DAM - Excellent bank angling access for winter steelhead; good for summer steelhead & spring chinook.

41 MOUTH OF SALMON - Good for summer steelhead, spring chinook; closed to winter steelheading.

2,333 summer fish.

Sandy River steelhead average 6 pounds, but 15 pounders have been taken. Eggs, yarn, sand shrimp, and lures are all used, and in significant quantities, since this boulder-strewn river is a real tackle-grabber.

For regulation purposes, the Sandy is divided into waters above and below Brightwood Bridge, about 12 miles east of the town of Sandy at the confluence of the Salmon River. The river below Brightwood Bridge is currently open to steelhead fishing the entire year. The steelhead season above the bridge is from the last Saturday in May through December.

There is a boat angling deadline at the powerline crossing about a mile below Oxbow Park. Above this point, plenty of good water is accessible from the bank. Those who do choose to use boats as a means of transportation above the deadline should disconnect tackle while in transit.

The most popular boat drifts on the river are from Oxbow County Park to Dabney State Park, and from Dabney to Lewis and Clark State Park near the mouth, each a good day's run. The Sandy is only navigable by riverboats.

Excellent steelhead and salmon water is accessible to bank anglers throughout

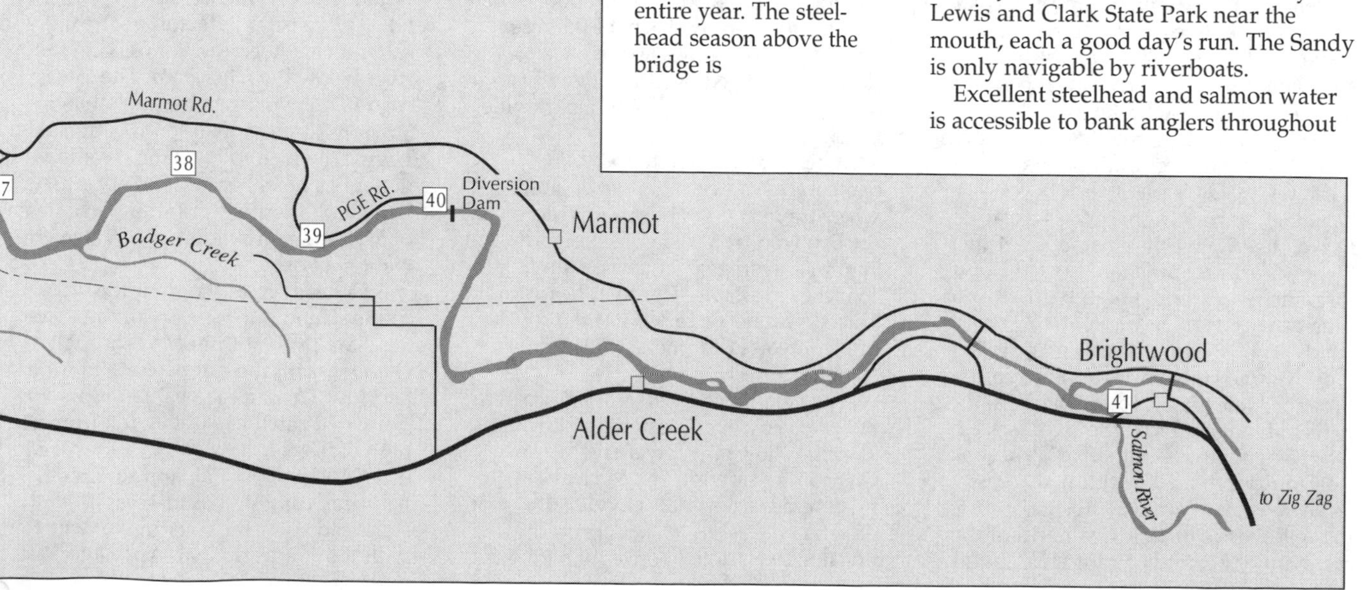

much of the river. From the bank at Lewis and Clark, anglers can fish the Sandbar and Railroad Bridge drifts. To reach Lewis and Clark, follow I-84 to the Lewis and Clark Exit just east of Troutdale. There is also a good hole above Troutdale Bridge (off Crown Point Hwy.) that can be fished from the west bank. Crown Point Hwy. crosses the river and follows the Sandy's east bank to Springdale, providing access to Chicken & Dumplin Hole, Pigpen Drift, Tippycanoe Drift, and Big Bend Drift. Anglers can park along the road. At Springdale, follow Hurlburt Rd. east to the road junction near Big Creek, and turn onto Gordon Creek Rd, which follows the Sandy's north bank. Gordon Creek and Trout Creek drifts can be reached off this road.

The term drift, by the way, is used in several different ways when discussing steelhead fishing in the northwest. It is used to refer to the distance covered by a day's float downstream in a riverboat (a good day's drift), or to a stretch of the river favored by steelhead (Pigpen Drift), sometimes interchangeable with the term hole. It is also used to distinguish the steelhead angler who moves from place to place on the river (drift fisherman) from the angler who fishes one spot hour after hour (plunker).

Dabney State Park offers bank access, and is a good place for non-fishing family members to play and relax. To reach Dabney, follow Stark Street east from Gresham, crossing from the south to the north bank on the Stark St. Bridge (a.k.a. Viking Bridge) just below the park. There is a good deep plunking hole below Stark St. Bridge. Above Dabney, Fill Your Waders Drift, Springdale Hole, and Collins Hole are accessible only to boat anglers.

Oxbow Park offers excellent access to many good holes and drifts, including the YMCA Drift, Hossner Drift, Upper Hossner Drift, Sawmill Drift, the Crusher Hole, and Big Rock Hole. To reach Oxbow, follow Division St. east from Gresham, turning right onto Oxbow Dr., then left on Oxbow Parkway.

Dodge Park also provides outstanding bank angling opportunities. To reach the park, follow Division St. east beyond Gresham, turning right onto Oxbow Drive, then right onto Lusted Rd at the Oxbow Parkway junction. Lusted Rd. follows the river along a high bluff, dropping down at Dodge and crossing to the Sandy's north bank. Buttler's Eddy, Blue Hole, Gauge Hole, Swimming Hole, and Pipeline Hole are all accessible from the bank at Dodge. Across the river from Dodge by way of Dodge Park Bridge, Lusted Rd. provides additional access.

There is also excellent steelhead water in the Revenue Bridge area north of the community of Sandy. From Hwy. 26 turn north onto Ten Eyck Rd., crossing Cedar Creek and following signs to the ODF&W Hatchery. Park in the lot and walk down to the river to fish a good hole at the mouth of Cedar Creek Fishing is prohibited in Cedar Creek itself. Okie Drift is just above the creek mouth, and there is often good fishing below the bridge.

Upstream there is a lot of good water available for bank fishing off a private PGE road on the north bank. Cross Revenue Bridge, turning right onto Marmot Rd. and climbing Devil's Backbone, then dropping down onto the PGE road, which is usually open to public use. There is also good fishing above the Diversion Dam and below the road, for anglers willing to do some hiking.

Shad occasionally enter the Sandy from the Columbia, usually in June if the Columbia is high. Most anglers fish for them from boats below I-84. Smelt enter the Sandy when they feel like it. Only the smelt seem to know exactly which years and when, and they aren't talking. Anglers can call the ODF&W Columbia Regional Office for a smelt update in March or April. When smelt do enter the Sandy, they are caught by dipping hand nets from the bank in the area from Stark St. Bridge to the mouth, with heaviest concentration around the old Troutdale Bridge.

Trout are not stocked in the Sandy, and the river is generally too turbid for good trout fishing.

The only campground on the lower Sandy is at Oxbow County Park. Other parks along the river have picnic facilities only. Additional campgrounds are available in Mt. Hood National Forest off Hwy. 26.

SANTIAM RIVER, MIDDLE A fine trout stream, major tributary of the South Santiam, flowing about 30 miles to its confluence in the Foster Dam pool, where it forms the northeast arm of the reservoir. Only a few miles above Foster its flow is obstructed by Green Peter Dam to form Green Peter Lake with Quartzville Creek.

Above Green Peter, the Middle Santiam flows free for about 20 miles, where it offers one of Oregon's more productive wild trout fisheries. Rainbow and cutthroat average 6-9 inches, with fish to 15 inches available. The river heads in the Three Pyramids area west of the southern Mt. Jefferson Wilderness, Willamette National Forest.

A private Weyerhaeuser road (open to public use except occasionally during fire season) follows the lower river from Green Peter through an old clear-cut. To reach it, head north off Hwy. 20 at a spot designated Cascadia Damsite on the Willamette National Forest map (about 1 1/2 miles west of Cascadia State Park). This road leads to the south bank of Green Peter. Turn east at the reservoir and continue about 7 miles before crossing to the north bank at the upper end of the dam pool. The Weyerhaeuser road closely follows the Middle Santiam about 6 miles upstream, providing access to good trout water.

Beyond this road, the Middle Santiam flows through a 7-mile roadless area, a wooded canyon that beckons adventurous anglers. Near its headwaters, the river is again accessed by roads. Forest Rd. 2041, which heads north from Hwy. 20 at Upper Soda (1 mile past Fernview Campground) crosses the Middle Santiam just above Pyramid Creek. There is some very nice fly-fishing water near the crossing, with broad flat banks and good gravel. Forest Rd. 2047 heads north from Hwy. 20 at House Rock Camp, following Sheep Creek and meeting the river just below Iron Mt. Lookout. This road follows the Middle Santiam about 3 miles downstream. These roads are snowbound until May or June.

The only developed campground on the Middle Santiam is on the north bank of Green Peter. Weyerhaeuser discourages camping along the lower road due to fire danger. However, there are natural campsites in the Willamette National Forest along the upper river.

SANTIAM RIVER, NORTH One of two equally productive and popular forks of the Santiam River, a top producer of summer and winter steelhead, with a good run of spring chinook and plenty of trout angling. Over 60 miles long, this major tributary of the Willamette River is accessible from boat or bank, providing good angling the year-round.

North and South Santiam meet near Jefferson, east of Hwy. 99E about 5 miles north of Albany, just 12 miles from the Willamette confluence. Most angling takes place from Jefferson upstream, with salmon and steelhead confined to the river below Big Cliff Dam. The lower river is followed east by the Jefferson-Stayton Rd. From Stayton it is tracked by Hwy. 22, which follows the river to within 8 miles of its headwaters at Santiam Lake in the southern Marion Lake Basin of Mt. Jefferson Wilderness, Willamette National Forest.

Steelhead are in the river the year-round. Good numbers of summer steelhead are present from May through October, with the run peaking in June and July. During the past ten years, the estimated catch has fluctuated from a high of 5,399 in 1986-87, to a low of 840 in 1991-92. In 1992-93, almost 2,500 fish had been caught by mid-season. Winter steelhead enter the river in November, with the run peaking in April and May.

Red and yellow fluorescent lures are popular with both boat and bank anglers. Non-finclipped steelhead must be released unharmed.

The North Santiam is a favorite river for fly-fishing steelheaders. Anglers use a floating greased line, skating steelhead flies on the surface. Naturals on the river include stoneflies, caddis, green drakes, and mayflies. Popular imitations are Purple Matukas, Green-Butted Skunks, Macks Canyon, and Golden Demon. Bait anglers use eggs, sand shrimp, and nightcrawlers. Popular lures include Corkies (pink pearl, red, and chartreuse), No. 4 Bud's Spinner (gold or silver, especially effective in fast water), Wee Warts, Wiggle Warts, and Hot Shots.

Spring chinook enter the river in mid-May, with peak catches in June. Most fishing takes place in the area from Stayton to Mill City. The annual catch rate is currently up to 1,400.

There's fair angling for rainbow and cutthroat trout below Detroit Reservoir, with some big fish available (and the chance of incidentally hooking a steelhead). Rainbows are stocked several times each year between Mill City and Mehama. Catchables are launched in the river from boxes pulled behind drift boats, with releases made over several miles of stream. But the best trout fishing is above the reservoir. From Idanha to above Marion Forks the river is well stocked with legal trout, and there are good size wild fish as well. The water above Marion Forks is especially productive for fly-fishing. Above the last highway bridge in the Big Meadows area, small wild cutthroat are available, as well as some brook trout which have migrated from the lakes above. Late season angling in this section is usually productive.

Below Big Cliff Dam, the North Santiam offers a challenge to drift boat anglers. Boaters launch at Packsaddle County Park about 4 miles below Big Cliff Dam, Kimmel Park in Mill City, Fishermen's Bend BLM Campground just west of Mill City, North Santiam State Park 3 miles east of Lyons, John Neal County Park and Mehama Bridge in Lyons, Stayton Bridge, Buell Miller Access north of Shelburn, Green's Bridge east of Jefferson (natural gravel bar), and the Jefferson Boat Ramp. (See map for details). Popular one-day drifts are from Packsaddle County Park to Kimmel (rough rapids below Packsaddle), Fishermen's Bend to North Santiam State Park, State Park to John Neal Park or Mehama Bridge, Stayton Bridge to Buell Miller, and Green's Bridge to Jefferson. The river is laced with formidable rapids, and boating experience and advance scouting are recommended.

Bank anglers have good access to salmon and steelhead at Packsaddle Park, Minto Park, Fishermen's Bend, North Santiam State Park, John Neal, Mehama Bridge, Stayton Bridge, Green's Bridge, and Jefferson Boat Ramp.

The North Santiam is fed by many good tributaries. See also Breitenbush, Marion, Blow-out, Little North Santiam. Several dams obstruct the flow in the mid-section of the river, the largest forming Detroit Reservoir.

Below Detroit Reservoir, camping facilities are available at Fishermen's Bend BLM Recreation Area west of Mill City. Willamette National Forest campgrounds are located at Detroit Lake, and off Hwy. 22 east of Idanha at Whispering Forks and Marion Falls.

SANTIAM RIVER, SOUTH FORK One of two equally popular and productive forks of the Santiam River, a top producer of summer steelhead and spring chinook. The South Santiam joins the North Santiam near Jefferson, about 5 miles north of Albany, just 12 miles from the Willamette confluence. It flows about 80 miles from its headwaters in the Cascades of Willamette National Forest, interrupted by two dams, one at Lebanon and the other near Sweet Home. The lower dam creates Foster Reservoir. The second dam, a few miles upstream, forms Green Peter Reservoir.

Hwy. 20 roughly follows the river from Albany to Sweet Home. River crossings are on Hwy. 226 just east of Albany, at Lebanon on the Grant St. Bridge, and at Sweet Home on the Pleasant Valley Bridge. Above Foster Reservoir, Hwy. 20 follows the river very closely to its headwaters.

Summer steelhead offer the most popular sport on the South Santiam. A hatchery fishery, summers are in the river year-round, with heavy catches made from May through August. The run (which has been up to nearly 7,000 fish some years) peaks in June and July. During the past ten years, the estimated catch has fluctuated from a high of 6,478 in 1988-89, to a low of 514 in 1983-84. During the first half of the 1992-93 season, almost 3,000 fish were caught. The river's winter steelhead are a wild run, in the river from January through May. All non-finclipped steelhead must be released unharmed.

Both summer and winter steelhead returning from sea after two years average 8 pounds, while three year salt steelhead weigh in at about 12 pounds. Steelhead to 15 pounds are not uncommon. Sand shrimp and eggs are the common bait, with drift fishing techniques effective when the river is low. Fly-fishing for steelhead is very popular on the South Santiam, with Green Butted Skunks and Muddler Minnows among the favorite patterns.

Most steelhead angling takes place in the Sweet Home and Foster Dam areas. The most popular bank fishery is at Wiley Creek Park just below Foster, where heavy concentrations of anglers fish heavy concentrations of steelhead from March to August.

The South Santiam's chinook run has been thriving, with the run estimated to be up to 10,000 fish some years. Chinook are in the river from April through July, with peak catches in May. For the past five years, the annual catch has been between 1,400 and 2,400 fish. The 1992 catch was 2,166. The most popular chinook fisheries (with access from bank and boat) are at the Cable and Waterfall holes below Foster Dam from May through August, downstream from the Pleasant Valley Bridge at Sweet Home, and below Lebanon Dam from mid-May to Mid-June. The chinook average 13-17 pounds, with fish to 30 pounds available.

Favorite angling techniques include bobbers and jigs, and back-bouncing eggs, or egg and shrimp combinations. When back-bouncing, Corkies or Spin-N-Glos are used to float the set-up, which usually includes 4-5 ounces of weight on about 8 inches of leader. Smaller baits are usually best when the water is running fast. Boat anglers pull Hot Shots for steelhead, and Kwikfish for chinook.

The South Santiam is a popular river for drift boats and jet sleds. Its less challenging whitewater makes it especially good for beginning boaters. Boat ramps are available at Wiley Cr. Park (accessing the most popular drift on the river), and at Sweet Home on the south end of Pleasant Valley Bridge. There are fee-pay gravel bar access sites at Sanderson's Bridge 10 miles south of Jefferson and at McDowell Cr. Boaters can take out at Waterloo-Linn Co. Park right before Lebanon Dam.

There's good fishing for trout in the South Santiam above Foster Dam. Wild cutthroat are available, and the stream is stocked with legal rainbow from mid-May through July. Wild trout make up about 25% of the catch. Fly-fishing is very good up here, with light gear a necessity for all angling later in the season. The trout average 8-11 inches.

Smallmouth bass are available in the river from Thomas Creek downstream about 4 miles. Bank angling for them is restricted due to private land holdings, but boat anglers reach the fishery in jet sleds, or by putting in at Sanderson's and drifting to Jefferson. The smallmouth average one pound.

Camping facilities are available at Foster Reservoir, at Cascadia 5 miles east of Foster, and at four campgrounds on Hwy. 20 in the Willamette National Forest (Trout Creek, Fernview, House Rock, and Yukwah). There are wheelchair

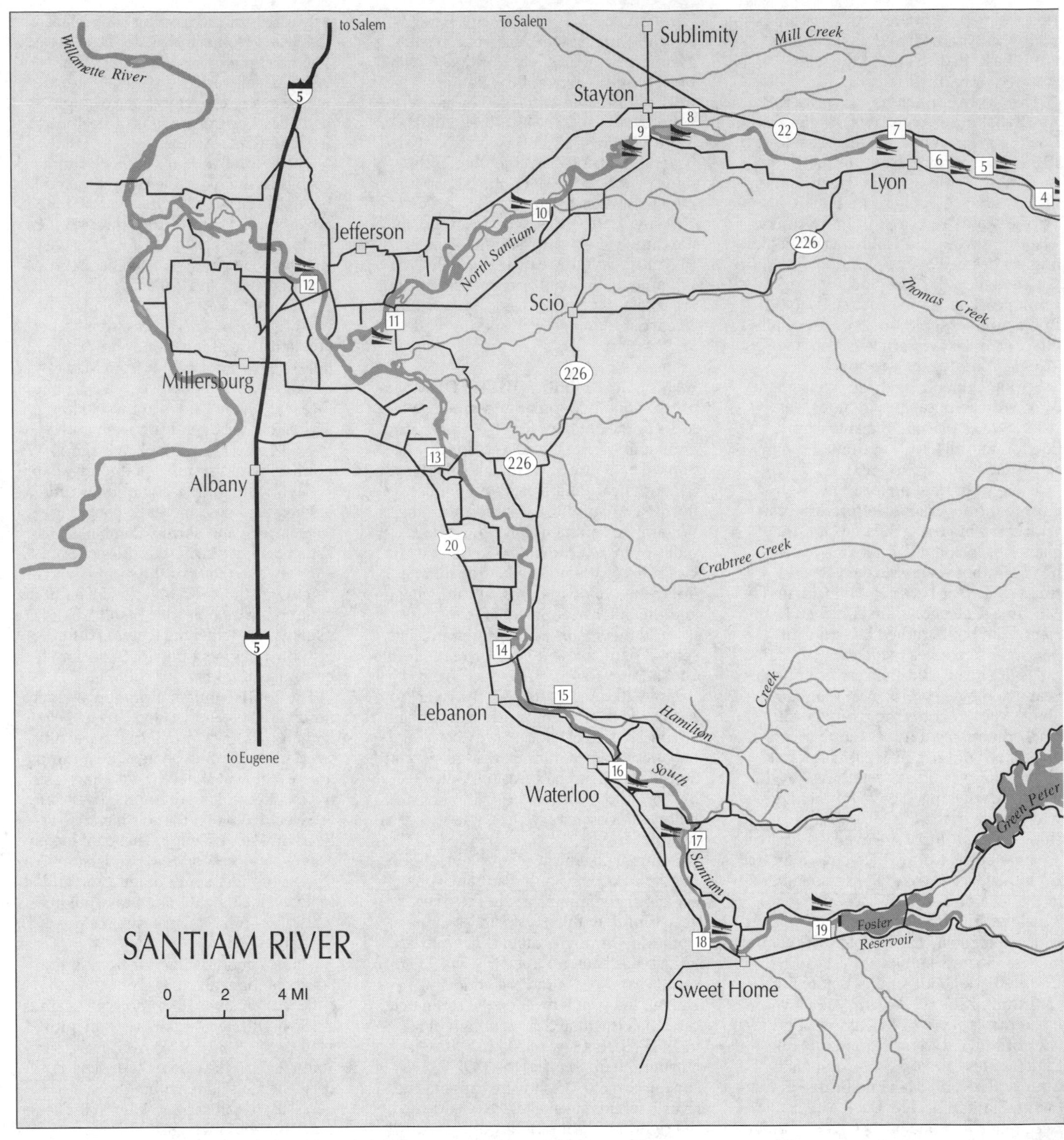

accessible piers at Yukwah and downstream from Fern View Camp.

SANTOSH SLOUGH A Columbia River Slough off Multnomah Channel, offering good fishing for bass and panfish. Take Hwy. 30 through Scappoose, turn right at the airport sign, then left onto Honeyman Rd. The slough access is beyond the airport and gravel operation. Park at the metal dike gate and walk in along the dirt road. Vehicle access has been closed due to abuse of the site. A 2,000 ft. bank area is open to the public.

There are crappie, bass, perch, and bullhead catfish here, with some crappie to 3/4 pound and bass to 2 pounds. Rafts and canoes are best suited to the narrow slough, though boats occasionally squeeze in from Multnomah Channel.

SCAPPOOSE CREEK A good early-season trout stream in Columbia County, only 20 miles NW of Portland. Following Hwy. 30 from Portland to Scappoose,

1 **PACKSADDLE CO. PARK** - Concrete slab launch; rough rapids for experienced boaters only; next take-out 4 1/2 mi. at Kimmel on south side; bank angling at lower end of park for summer steelhead, chinook in June & July.

2 **MINTO CO. PARK** - Take-out only, suitable for rafts; good bank access for salmon & steelhead.

3 **KIMMEL PARK** - Pole slide put-in and winch take-out; falls below boatable

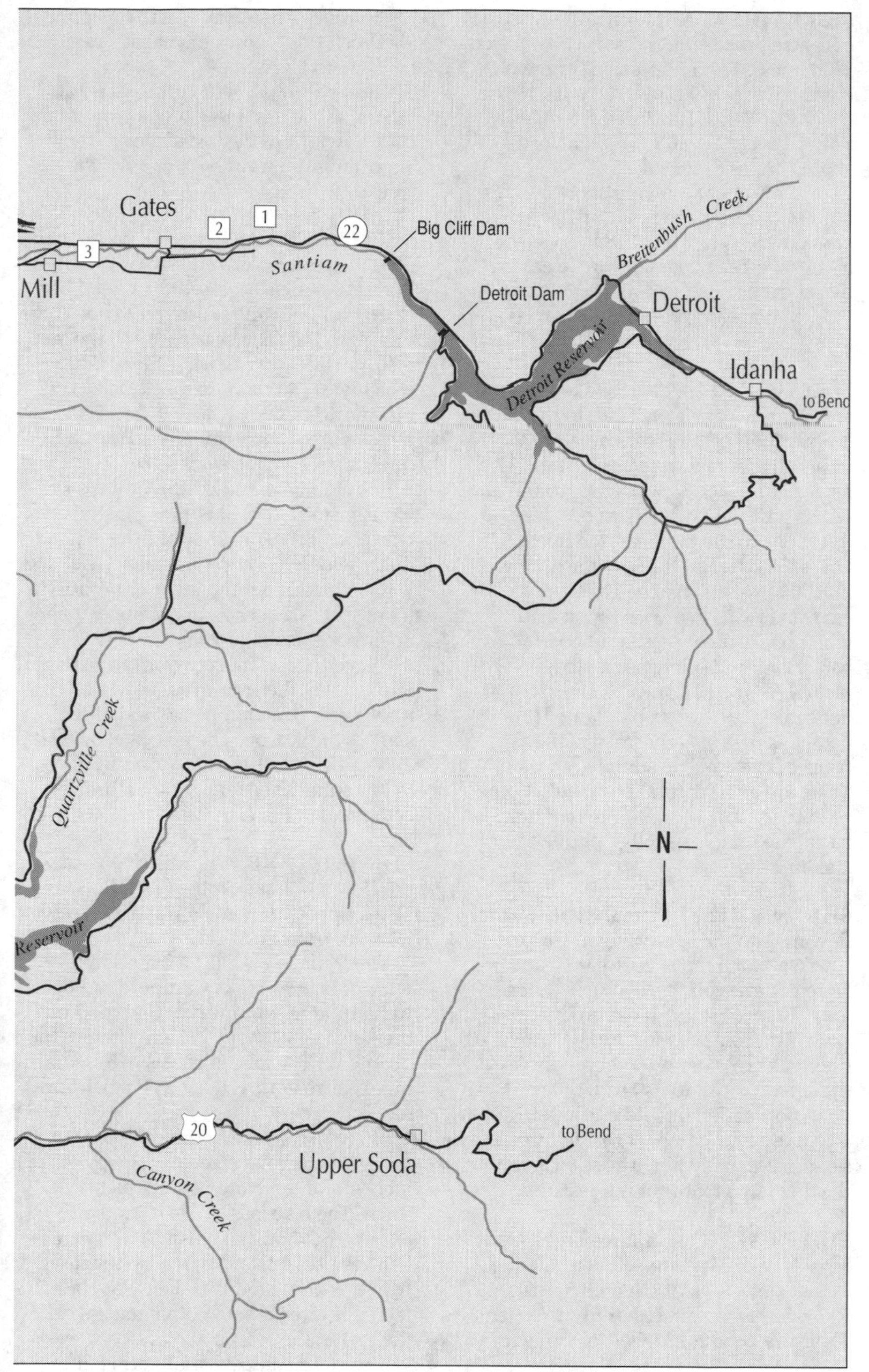

in high water only; check special regs. for Mill City Bridge area.

4 FISHERMEN'S BEND - BLM park, campground, good ramp; prior to park opening, launch boats off bank west of park entrance; drift 4 mi. to next take-out (moderately experienced boaters); good bank access for summer steelhead, spring chinook; stocked rainbow.

5 NORTH SANTIAM STATE PARK - Unimproved launch from gravel road west of parking lot; drift 1+ miles to Neal Park or 2+ miles to Mehama Bridge (intermediate boaters); good bank access for summer steelhead, spring chinook, stocked rainbow.

6 JOHN NEAL CO. PARK - Easy one-mile drift from improved ramp to Mehama; good holes with bedrock ledges near mouth of Little No. Santiam; good bank access for all fisheries.

7 MEHAMA BRIDGE - Fish above bridge on south bank and good water upstream 1/2 mi.; paved ramp on so. side accesses 7 mile drift to Stayton Is. with many holes and drifts; verify accessibility of next take-out.

8 STAYTON IS. - Tricky take-out; in high flows use wooden slide to portage over upper & lower Bennet dams; otherwise, check with City of Stayton Police for key to old water supply bridge access from right channel.

9 STAYTON BRIDGE - Improved public ramp at so. end of bridge for easy 5 mi. drift to next take-out; good chinook holding water; some bank angling on no. side.

10 BUELL MILLER BOAT RAMP (Shelburn) - Improved ramp, limited parking; beware of impassable log jams in main channel; channel braiding; 7 mi. to next take-out.

11 GREEN'S BRIDGE - Public boat and bank access from gravel bar; popular drift for winter steelhead in March & April to confluence with So. Santiam and Jefferson ramp.

12 JEFFERSON BOAT RAMP - Improved ramp with good bank angling from bridge for chinook and steelhead among rock ledges.

13 SANDERSON'S BRIDGE - Gravel bar access at end of old highway right-of-way; bank angling above & below bridge; drift 10 mi. to Jefferson beyond N. Santiam confluence; accesses smallmouth fishery at mouth of Thomas Cr.

14 GILL LANDING - Seldom used ramp above Grant. St. Bridge; shallow drift over gravel bars.

15 LEBANON DAM - Popular bank angling for spring chinook mid-May to mid-June, 200 ft. below dam.

16 WATERLOO-LINN CO. PARK - Last developed take-out before Lebanon Dam; good bank fishing above bridge at rapids where fish hold below cascades, upstream from ramp.

17 MCDOWELL CR. - Private (fee pay) access to unimproved gravel bar upstream of bridge; next take-out 4 mi. at Waterloo.

18 SWEET HOME BOAT RAMP - Steep improved ramp at so. end of Pleasant Valley Bridge; next take-out a slow 6 mi. to McDowell Cr.; good bank fishing chinook hole downstream of bridge; park along highway.

19 WILEY CR. PARK - Intensive bank fishery for heavy concentrations of summer steelhead below Foster dam April-Aug.;' winter steelhead March-April; spring chinook May-Aug.; improved ramp accesses most popular drift on river.

you'll cross the two forks of the stream just west of the town. They join just north of the highway, and the creek flows into Scappoose Bay a few miles downstream. To get to the upper North Fork, take the paved road south. This road crosses and follows the creek to its headwaters. The South Fork is reached by the Dutch Canyon Rd. which heads west from the highway just south of town. Lots of private property on the South Fork creates a real access problem, but the North Fork has plenty of available water.

The creek is no longer stocked, but both forks have a fair number of wild cutthroat. Sea-run are occasionally seen here in April. Some good size cutthroat are taken in December by steelheaders.

Both forks are open for winter angling, with small runs of steelhead in each. Most fishing takes place below the forks. The fish enter the creek in December and remain until March. All non-finclipped steelhead must be released unharmed. There are several picnic areas on the North Fork, but no campgrounds.

SCOGGINS CREEK This is a fair early-season trout stream in the Tualatin River drainage south of Forest Grove. It heads at the Tillamook Co. line and flows east for 13 miles, paralleling and south of Gales Creek.

The upper section empties into Haag Lake Reservoir. It is not stocked, but contains wild cutthroat. A gravel logging road follows it upstream quite a ways. Angling usually slows up by June, and the creek gets quite low in late summer.

The lower section is crossed near the mouth by Hwy. 47 about 4 miles south of Forest Grove, and is followed upstream by a good road. Trout run 6-11 inches. There is no camping in the area.

SCOTT LAKE Two connected lakes off Hwy. 242 offering stocked cutthroat and a beautiful view of the Three Sisters. There is a primitive campground here and some good walk-in campsites. Scott makes a good base camp for day hikes to Benson and Tenas lakes. Campers Lake is just up the road.

SCOUT LAKE (Marion Co.) A good lake in a beautiful natural alpine park at the base of Mt. Jefferson. See Bays Lake for trail directions into Jefferson Park. Scout Lake is 1/4 mile east of Bays Lake.

Seven acres and 30 ft. deep, it is stocked by air with fingerling brook trout. These fish are not easily caught, but they run to 3 pounds. Try a grasshopper in late August. Heavy use has impacted the land along the lakeshore, and the Forest Service is discouraging camping within 100 feet of the shore to allow regeneration of the vegetation. Please cooperate.

SEPARATION LAKE A relatively isolated 5-acre brook trout lake in Three Sisters Wilderness. From McKenzie Bridge on Hwy. 126 east of Eugene, take the Horse Creek Rd. Forest Rd. 2638 SE 8 miles to Roney Creek. A trail from there leads about 7 miles to the lake.

Separation Lake is only about 5 acres but has had good angling for 10-14 inch brook trout. A few trout 18 inches or more have been taken. It can be easily fished from shore, and all methods can be effective. Natural campsites are available.

SERENE LAKE A 20-acre hike-in brook and rainbow lake at 4,350 ft. in the western part of the High Rock area of the upper Clackamas watershed. Trail 512 begins at Frazier Forks Campground and winds past the Rock Lakes. For detailed directions to the trailhead see Rock Lakes. Signs point the way for the easy 3 mile hike west to Serene Lake.

Serene is stocked with brook trout, which are usually present in good numbers. Fish run 6-15 inches, averaging 9-10 inches. All methods can be effective depending on the season. Bait or lure fishing is best in early season, and fly-fishing is best in late summer and fall. There are good natural campsites. Some pasture is available if you're on horseback. The road is usually not open until late June.

SHARPS CREEK A small trout stream flowing into the Row River at Culp Creek, about 5 miles upstream from Dorena Reservoir. It's about 12 miles long. To reach it, turn east on the Row River Rd. from 99W at Cottage Grove. At the creek crossing, a gravel road follows the stream south to its head. Sharps has a good population of wild cutthroat, and it is stocked with rainbow early in trout season. It usually offers good bait fishing the first few months of the season.

SHEEP LAKE One of three brook trout lakes NW of Mt. Jefferson near the head of the South Fork of the Breitenbush River. See Firecamp Lakes for directions. There are good huckleberries up here.

SHELLROCK CREEK A small accessible trout stream in the upper Clackamas drainage. Shellrock flows south from the High Rock area and enters the Oak Grove Fork several miles above Harriet Lake. From Estacada, follow Hwy. 224 to Ripplebrook Ranger Station. From there take Forest Rd. 57 up the Oak Grove Fork. About 2 miles east of Harriet Lake, this road crosses the mouth of Shellrock Creek and turns north to follow it upstream. At this point the road becomes Forest Rd. 58, and you'll almost immediately pass Shellrock Creek Campground. It's 38 miles from Estacada to this point. Shellrock Rd. follows the creek's east bank up to High Rock.

The stream has wild cutthroat 6-10 inches, as well as a few brook trout that drift down from the lakes above. There are campgrounds at both ends of the creek.

SHELLROCK LAKE A very pretty, popular 20-acre brook trout lake in the High Rock lakes area, accessed by a good but steep trail one mile south of Frazier Forks Campground. The easier way to the lake is from Hideaway Lake to the south, which you can drive to. Shellrock is 1/2 mile north of Hideaway by Trail 700, which circles Hidaway Lake. For road directions see Hideaway Lake.

Both rainbow and cutthroat were previously stocked in Shellrock, but survival was poor. Brook trout hold up well, and that's what you'll find here now. The lake is fished hard, but manages to produce a lot of fish 6-13 inches, averaging 9 inches. Shellrock is a shallow lake, and fly-fishing is very good mornings and evenings. Sunken wet flies retrieved slowly often work well. Bait angling is good at the start of the season. The lake is at 4,200 ft., and snow usually limits access until mid- to late June. There are good natural campsites at the lake.

SHINING LAKE A productive 12-acre rainbow trout lake in the High Rock area of the upper Clackamas watershed, about 55 miles from Portland.

The trailhead is a little over 3 miles west of Frazier Forks Campground on Indian Ridge Rd. It leaves that road on the north side, about 1/2 mile before the dead-end. The lake is an easy 15-minute hike. For road directions to Frazier Forks, see Rock Lakes.

Shining is stocked with rainbow trout that grow to good size, averaging 6-13 inches, and there are usually plenty of them. The lake is 24 ft. deep, and all angling methods take fish. A lot of crayfish are present, and the tails attract big fish. This is a good fly lake in late fall, in fact, it is often a hot spot in general near the end of the season.

There is a campsite and spring at the lake, and a camp on the road above. This area is excellent for huckleberries.

SHORT LAKE A small but deep brook trout lake one mile north of Breitenbush Hot Springs. To reach it, follow the Breitenbush River Rd. from Detroit to Breitenbush Campground, take the first road to the left, then the next right. This is Forest Rd. 46-040. It heads north up the west side of Short Creek and reaches Short lake in 2 miles. You can see the lake just south of the road. There used to be big brook trout to l8 inches here, but since the road came in, the size has dropped. It is stocked by air and truck.

SILVER CREEK (Marion Co.) One of the main forks of the Pudding River, about 25 miles long, heading east of Silver Creek Falls State Park. The 2 upper forks meet in the State Park, and the main creek joins the Pudding River east of Silverton after flowing through the city. A reservoir on the creek is about 2 miles above Silverton. From Silverton, Hwy. 214 follows the creek above the forks. Distance from Salem is about 25 miles.

A fair number of wild cutthroat trout are taken in both the forks and mainstem below. Both cutthroat and rainbow can be found below the reservoir. Fish range 6-11 inches.

Silver Creek Park is very big, with a well developed network of trails along the creek, as well as camping and picnic facilities. Anglers can access the lower creek at Silverton City Park

SILVERTON RESERVOIR A 65-acre water supply reservoir for Silverton which drains into Silver Creek. It's stocked with legal size trout early each season and has wild cutthroat and brown bullhead. This one is hard to fish from the bank, so it helps to bring a boat or float tube. No motors are allowed. Unlike most reservoirs in the state, Silver Creek is only open to angling from the fourthSaturday in April through October.

SILVER KING LAKE A nice brook trout lake, still fairly isolated, in the upper Collawash River headwaters west of Silver King Mountain. Shortest way in is by Trail 544 from Elk Lake. It's about 4 miles by ridge walk north to the lake. See Elk Lake for road directions.

A longer but interesting approach is by trail up the Hot Springs Fork of the Collawash River. You can look forward to a good soak in the waters of Bagby Hot Springs. Take Hwy. 224 to the Collawash River Rd. (Forest Rd. 63). Follow this to the Bagby Hot Springs Trailhead. The route up the Hot Springs Fork is fairly long, about 8 1/2 miles, but you can fish the stream. After 8 miles on Trail 544 south, you will reach a sign reading Silver King Mt. A quarter mile further, watch for a trail leading up to the lake.

The lake is only 4 acres and 8 feet deep, at about 4,100 ft. There's good angling for brook trout 7-14 inches. All methods take fish here.

SKOOKUM LAKE (Clackamas Co.) A small trout lake with campground in the headwaters of Fish Creek, a bit over 30 road miles SE of Estacada. Skookum is at elevation 3,800 ft. The lake covers only 4 acres but is fairly deep.

From Estacada drive SE on the Clackamas River Rd., Hwy. 224, into Mt. Hood National Forest. About 8 miles inside the forest, at Fish Creek Campground, Forest Rd. 54 crosses the Clackamas River and heads south along Fish Creek. Six miles south, Forest Rd. 5440 branches SW. Six miles down 5440 near Bracket Mountain, Forest Rd. 5420 cuts back to the east. Follow this winding road a bit over 2 miles to Forest Rd. 350, which turns SW and leads about 2 miles to the lake.

Skookum has a good supply of brook trout 6-12 inches, averaging 10 inches. The lake is stocked with fingerlings by air every other year. Fly fishing can be very good in late fall.

SKOOKUM LAKE (Marion Co.) A bass and panfish lake in northern Marion County, 3 miles south of Newberg. The lake is 1/2 mile south of Hwy. 219, which goes from Newberg to St. Paul. The road into the lake is private, and there's a charge for access. About 25 acres and lightly fished, it maintains the usual assortment of panfish, including bluegill, crappie, and brown bullhead. A few largemouth bass are also taken. There's a parking area and a few boats for rent.

SLIDEOUT LAKE A fair brook trout lake high in the headwaters of the Breitenbush River, east of the Firecamp Lakes. See Firecamp Lakes for trail directions. Slideout is a hard mile's bush-whack over the ridge to the east of the Firecamp area. It is downstream and north about 1/2 mile from Swindle Lake.

A fairly deep lake, Slideout is about 10 acres and lightly fished. The brook trout run 6-11 inches, but there may be a few sleepers in here. It can be fished from shore using any method.

SMITH LAKE (Lane Co.) An 8-acre brook trout lake one mile north of Irish Mt. Smith Lake is about 1/4 mile SW of McFarland Lake. See McFarland for trail directions. Any method will take fish here almost any time. Natural campsites are available. McFarland Lake offers more exciting fishing.

SMITH LAKE (Multnomah Co.) A 60-acre lake between Marine Drive and North Portland Rd. west of Heron Lakes Golf Course and the Multnomah County Expo Center. It is part of a wetland complex that includes the Columbia Slough, Bybee Lake, and several smaller ponds and marshes.

More a wetland itself than a lake, Smith does offer fishing for white crappie, brown bullhead, bluegill, yellow perch, and largemouth bass. Canoes can be launched from a site at the north end of the lake off Marine Drive. The wetland complex is being developed as an urban wilderness by the Portland Bureau of Parks and Recreation.

SMITH RIVER RESERVOIR A narrow deep reservoir in the upper McKenzie area. It can be reached by following the McKenzie Highway 71 miles to Carmen Bridge at Trail Bridge Reservoir. From there, Forest Rd. 730 heads north for several miles, ending at Smith Dam.

The reservoir is stocked with legal rainbow, and fishing is usually good. Most fish are taken by trolling or still-fishing. They run 9-13 inches, though a few good size cutthroat show up in the catch, and brook trout to 12 inches are occasionally taken.

More wetland than lakes, Smith and Bybee support largemouth bass and panfish.

There is a good boat ramp at the dam. A speed limit of 10 mph is in effect, so anglers get a break from speedboats. There is a very nice boat-in camping area at the north end of the reservoir. Additional campsites are available at Trail Bridge Lake just south.

SPINNING LAKE A good brook trout lake just off the road in the Breitenbush Lake area. The trail begins about 1 1/2 miles west of Breitenbush Lake, where the outlet of Pyramid Lake crosses Forest Rd. 4220. It's 1/4 mile north to the lake. See Breitenbush Lake for road directions.

Spinning Lake is only 3 acres and shallow, but it's lightly fished and holds up well. Brook trout run big here, with most from 10-18 inches and some bigger. The lake loses fish in severe winters, but some fish usually survive. There are no campsites available, but there's good camping at Breitenbush Lake.

SPIRIT LAKE A good 12-acre brook trout lake in the headwaters of Salmon Creek about 5 miles west of Waldo Lake. From Oakridge, take the Salmon Creek Rd., Forest Rd. 24, all the way up to the Black Creek Branch road (Forest Rd. 2421). About 1/2 mile up Forest Rd. 2421, Forest Rd. 2422 cuts to the north. Follow Forest Rd. 2422 about 7 twisting miles to the Spirit Lake Trailhead. Trail 3584 offers an easy 1/4 mile hike to the lake.

The brook trout in Spirit Lake are in good shape and average about 10 inches, with some to 15 inches. All methods can be used effectively. Recommended for small fry.

SPY LAKE A small trout lake north of the Mink Lake Basin, well off the beaten track. See Corner Lake for directions. From Corner Lake, take Trail 3517 north one mile. Spy Lake is 1/4 mile to the east. Only 3 acres but 20 feet deep, the lake is lightly fished, with a population of 6-9 inch cutthroat. Nice natural campsites are available.

SQUAW LAKES (Clackamas Co.) A series of small brook trout lakes east of the Clackamas River near Squaw Mt. The three main lakes total only about 7 acres, and all are quite shallow. They are at elevation 3,550 ft.

From Estacada, take Hwy. 224 SE 6 miles to North Fork Reservoir, then head east on Forest Rd. 4610, the North Fork Rd. Follow Forest Rd. 4610 about 14 miles east to the lakes, which are located just north of the road. Twin Springs Campground is about 2 miles further along the road, so if you miss the lakes, backtrack from there. There is some private property in the area which may be fenced. The western shores of the lakes are in the Mt. Hood National Forest.

The lakes have all produced well, with naturally reproducing 6-14 inch brook trout. Things can get slow here in midsummer, but fall angling is usually good. Squaw Lakes only run about 5 feet deep, so fly-fishing can be effective. Sunken wet flies or nymphs have produced some big fish. There are a few natural campsites at the lakes, and a campground at Twin Springs.

ST. LOUIS PONDS A group of seven constructed ponds offering an interesting variety of panfish near the community of Gervais, south of Woodburn. From I-5 take the Woodburn Exit west to Gervais Rd. Head south, then west on Jenson Rd. This is a rural area well out of range of freeway sights and sounds. The ponds are in an attractive setting of natural undergrowth. They are located to the left of the railroad. A large parking area is provided out of sight of the ponds.

The ponds have been open to angling since 1980, and there is a little of everything in them, including bass, channel cats, bluegill, black and white crappie, and green- and red-ear sunfish. Unfortunately, weed growth has been a problem, and though fish are plentiful, they are small.

The seven ponds have a combined area of 55 acres. They were excavated by the State high Dept. in a maze design, and offer an impressive 7 miles of bank fishing. This is strictly a bank fishery, as floating devices are prohibited. A float on Pond No. 3 is wheelchair accessible.

The ponds are open all year except during pheasant and duck seasons. No camping is allowed here, but there is a small picnic area. Recommended for small fry.

ST. PAUL PONDS The Oregon Dept. of Fish and Wildlife rearing ponds for bass and panfish. Closed to fishing.

STILL CREEK A fair wild trout stream in Mt. Hood National Forest, flowing into the Zigzag River about 2 miles east of the community of Zigzag. The creek heads near Hwy. 26 in the Government Camp area and loops around south of the highway to meet the Zigzag. Forest Rd. 2612 follows the creek quite closely throughout its length. The upper road is usually snowbound until late May.

The creek is not stocked with trout, but it offers fair fishing for wild cutthroat in a pristine mountain setting. Hatchery-reared summer steelhead are released near the lower end.

Still Creek's clear water can be challenging, but steelhead fishing with a fly is often effective here.

STURGEON LAKE A 3,500 acre bass and panfish lake in the center of Sauvie Island, so named because many years ago it was thought to be the spawning ground for sturgeon. Actually, very few sturgeon are found in the lake and surrounding water, and most are too small to keep. Roads almost encircle the lake, but you cannot drive around it because of the Gilbert River outlet at the north end. In recent years the lake has begun to silt in, and efforts to flush it with a channel from the Columbia River have been only marginally successful.

From Portland drive NW 10 miles on Hwy. 30 to the Sauvie Island Bridge. Follow Sauvie Island Rd. north after crossing to the island. Turn right on Reeder Rd. to reach the Oak Island access to the lake, or continue on Reeder about 1 1/2 miles past the Oak Island Junction to Coon Pt., where there is a parking area beside the road. The point offers good bank angling opportunities just over the dike. Reeder Rd. continues west to the junction with Gillihan Loop Rd., then turns north, following the Columbia River toward the north end of Sauvie Island.

The west bank of Sturgeon Lake can be accessed through Game Management land at several points along Reeder. Anglers can also boat into the lake from the Gilbert River. There is a public boat ramp on Sauvie Island at the Gilbert River confluence with Multnomah Channel, and another at Brown's Landing (fee pay to park) just up the channel. It is about 5 miles from the Gilbert River mouth to Sturgeon Lake.

Crappie are the most abundant species in the lake, which also contains brown bullhead, perch, bluegill, and largemouth bass. Some fairly large bass are available in the shoal areas in June and July. Anglers seem to prefer using surface plugs. Other species are primarily taken on bait, with fishing best on the incoming tide, especially near the sloughs and streams. The crappie get big here and will hit spinner and bait, or pork rind and feathered jigs.

The lake is closed to angling during duck hunting season. You will need to purchase a recreation permit to park on the island. Day or seasonal passes are sold at the market on the island just north of the bridge. See also Haldeman Pond, Gilbert River, and McNary Lakes.

SUNSET LAKE (Lane Co.) A good trout lake in the Horse Lake group west of Elk Lake. The easiest route to the lake is by the Island Meadow Trail from Elk Lake Lodge. The junction with the Pacific Crest Trail is about one mile west. Follow the PCT west one mile to a side trail cutting to the north. This trail leads to Sunset Lake in about a mile, then continues to Horse Lake.

Sunset is about 40 acres and fairly shallow. It can be fished from shore using all methods. Rainbow and brook trout here average 9-12 inches. The lake has slow periods but is usually good. There are good natural campsites here and at other lakes to the west. See also Horse Lakes.

SURPRISE LAKE (Fish Creek Area) Mt. Hood National Forest has a few Surprise Lakes. This one is south of the Clackamas River on the west side of the Fish Creek divide. The lake is about 5 acres and contains a good supply of very nice rainbow. It is quite shallow, at elevation 4,050 ft., and grows nice size fish.

From Estacada, take Hwy. 224 16 miles SE to Fish Creek Campground. Follow the Fish Creek Rd. (Forest Rd. 54) for 6 miles to Forest Rd. 5440. Follow 5440 about 8 miles to the lake. Distinctive Camelback Mountain is visible north of the lake across the canyon.

The fish here run 8-16 inches, averaging 10. This is a very shallow lake with little cover, so stealth is in order. The lake occasionally loses fish to winterkill, but produces consistently most years. There are fair natural campsites at the lake, and a good big camp at the mouth of Fish Creek.

SURPRISE LAKE (Olallie Area) A hike-in cutthroat lake in the Olallie Lake area, west of the Skyline Rd. The 2-mile trail to Surprise heads at Lower Lake Campground 1/2 mile north of Olallie Lake. Take Trail 717 north, reaching Surprise 1/4 mile past Fish Lake.

Cutthroat here range 6-12 inches and are feisty. There aren't many fish, but good anglers are successful. There are some fair natural campsites here, and a developed campground at Lower Lake. Skyline Road is usually snowbound until the end of June.

SWINDLE LAKE A 2-acre brook trout lake in the headwaters of the Breitenbush River NW of Mt. Jefferson. The lake gets too warm to support trout and is no longer stocked.

TANNER CREEK A short stream in the Columbia Gorge, flowing north into the Columbia River just below Bonneville Dam. It joins the Columbia about 41 miles east of Portland off I-84. The creek is about 8 miles long and is followed by a dirt road several miles, with a trail continuing up the creek beyond road's end. The upper creek has a few wild cutthroat but is fished down quickly.

This lower end of the creek has two small steelhead runs. The winter run peaks in December, and the summer run in July. All non-finclipped steelhead must be released unharmed.

The mouth of Tanner Creek offers one of the few bank access points for the Columbia system's shad fishery. Anglers walk down to the creek from the Bonneville Dam access road. Shad usually appear in May.

The stream below the railroad bridge is in the Columbia River Regulation Zone. Check current regulations for seasons and closures. Camping facilities are available at Eagle Creek, several miles east on I-84.

TEMPLE LAKE A good hike-in rainbow lake in the upper North Santiam area west of Marion Lake. Best access is from Pine Ridge Lake by Forest Rd. 2261, the Twin Meadows Rd. south of Marion Forks. If the road is snowbound early in the season, you may have to hike up to the Scout Camp at Pine Ridge. Follow Trail 3443 east about 2 miles to a spur trail that leads north 1/4 mile to the lake.

Temple covers 7 acres and is quite shallow. It is stocked by air with rainbow, and they hold up well. Most fish caught run 9-11 inches, with some over 15 inches. Almost any method works, with flies a good bet early or late in the day.

TENAS LAKES Three heavily-fished trout lakes 2 miles NW of Scott Lake Campground on the McKenzie Pass Highway. These are especially good lakes for a family outing, only a 2-mile hike from Scott Lake Camp. Take Trail 3502 and head north from Benson Lake.

One lake has brook trout, one cutthroat, and one rainbow. Damifino which is which. They all seem to produce lots of action for small fish. The first or Lower Tenas is about 3 acres and quite deep. The middle and upper lakes (just a bit north) are only an acre or so but are 15-20 ft. deep. They are usually inaccessible until late June. Recommended for small fry.

TETO LAKE A fair brook trout lake at the northern end of the Eight Lakes Basin SW of Mt. Jefferson. Teto is about 1/2 mile NE and several hundred feet below Jorn Lake. See Jorn Lake for trail directions. Covering 12 acres, Teto is just west of Chiquito Lake and has lots of small brook trout. It's a fairly deep lake, and all methods are used with success.

THOMAS CREEK (Linn Co.) A good size tributary of the South Santiam River with opportunities for smallmouth bass, wild cutthroat, and catch and release winter steelhead. It joins the South Santiam near Scio. The creek is about 35 miles long and flows from the east slope of the Cascades near Mill City. Hwy. 226 follows it from Scio to Jordan, and a gravel road continues east upstream about 10 miles further. A hiking trail follows the extreme upper end. Access is somewhat restricted.

Smallmouth bass are well established in the lower 8 miles below Scio. Quite a few wild cutthroat are caught, and there's good fly-fishing here when the water warms and clears.

Thomas has a wild steelhead run which peaks in March and April. All non-finclipped steelhead must be released unharmed. A remnant chinook run spawns in this river, but angling for them is prohibited most of the season.

There is no camping along the creek. Supplies are available at Scio and Lyons.

TIMBER LAKE A 15-acre lake in the compound of the Timber Lake Job Corps Center, open to public fishing for stocked legal rainbow and small brown bullhead. To reach it, take Hwy. 224 east from Estacada. The compound is just west of Ripplebrook Ranger Station.

TIMOTHY LAKE (Timothy Meadows Reservoir) A productive 1,400 acre reservoir featuring three varieties of trout, kokanee, and quantities of crayfish, located on the upper Oak Grove Fork of the Clackamas River. It's about 80 miles to

Kokanee provide good sport on popular Timothy Lake.

Timothy from Portland by way of Hwy. 26 and Forest Rd. 42 (the Skyline Rd.). It can also be reached from Estacada by Hwy. 224 along the Clackamas River, a route which appears to be shorter, but is slower.

For the Skyline route, follow Hwy. 26 about 11 miles east of Government Camp, and turn west onto Forest Rd. 42 about 2 miles past the Clear Lake turnoff. Seven miles south at Joe Graham Campground, Forest Rd. 57 forks off to the west and leads 2 miles to the reservoir.

Timothy has brook, rainbow, and cutthroat trout. Brook trout are very plentiful, with some over 5 pounds and challenging to catch. Catchable rainbow are stocked. Kokanee provide good sport from spring through early summer. When the water warms they move down to the thermocline, and the success rate drops off. The kokanee are 8-11 inches.

Most angling is from boats, with bait fishing and trolling both effective. Bank anglers favor spinning gear and small lures. Fly angling can be excellent near the mouths of the tributaries in late summer and fall. Although the lake gets heavy use, it is productive throughout the season, with catch rate increasing as the season progresses.

The reservoir supports a large population of crayfish. In fact, crayfish (a.k.a. crawdads, crawfish) are so plentiful here that the state licenses commercial fishing for them as long as the supply holds out. They are found in all the shallows, including right off the campgrounds. Fish for them with traps baited with pieces of fish or chicken. Crayfish tails can be very tempting to the lake's big brookies.

There are 5 large campgrounds around the lake, each within sight of a boat ramp. The Pine Point ramp is usable even when the reservoir is drawn down. Meditation Point Campground on the north side can be reached only by boat or trail. Several smaller lakes are within easy hiking distance. See Dinger and Buck. Wheelchair accessible.

TIMPANOGAS LAKE A very nice drive-to brook trout lake, headwaters of the Middle Willamette. It can be reached by road from Oakridge or Crescent Lake. Neither of these approaches is open until late June in most years. The Crescent Lake approach is a bit rougher, but quicker if you can tolerate it.

From Oakridge, drive south on Hwy. 58 a mile or so to the Hills Creek Reservoir turnoff. Follow Forest Rd. 21 around the west shore of the reservoir and up the upper Middle Willamette about 33 miles (from the dam) to Forest Rd. 2154. Take Forest Rd. 2154 about 5 miles to its junction with Forest Rd. 398/399, just before Opal Lake. Follow Forest Rd. 399 one-half mile south to Timpanogas.

From the town of Crescent Lake on Hwy. 58, follow Forest Rd. 244 around the NW shore of the lake 6 miles to the junction with Forest Rd. 211 (Summit Lake Rd.), which enters from the NW. Take this road 6 miles to Summit Lake Campground, then head south on Forest Rd. 398 about 4 miles to the lake.

Timpanogas is a pretty 40-acre lake at 5,300 ft., in a setting of thick fir forest and abundant huckleberries. It's a little over 100 feet deep near the center, with most of its shoal water near the NW shore. It contains brook trout and is easily fished. Trolling is quite popular, but motors are prohibited.

There is a small but pleasant campground on the SW shore close to Lower (or Little) Timpanogas Lake, but mosquitoes can be awesome throughout much of the summer. Little Timpanogas, just west of the large lake, is 7 acres and offers fair fishing for brook trout. There are several hike-in lakes to the south, and Opal Lake is one mile north and a bit off the road. See also Indigo, June.

TORREY LAKE A large lake with fair angling for rainbow, brook, and cutthroat trout in the Taylor Burn area north of Waldo Lake. To reach it, follow a one mile trail from the trailhead on the awful Taylor Burn Rd., 2 miles north of North Waldo Campground.

Torrey covers 70 acres and can be fished from shore, but a rubber boat would help. Brook trout averaging 10 inches make up the principal catch, with some to 16 inches plus. Rainbow are fewer but generally a bit larger. Cutthroat are also stocked. All methods are effective here, with fly angling good in the evenings. The nearest campground is Taylor Burn. It is usually accessible in late June.

TRAIL BRIDGE RESERVOIR A 90-acre reservoir in the upper McKenzie area. From Hwy. 126 about 14 miles south of the Santiam Junction, follow Forest Rd. 730 around the northern shore of the reservoir. Forest Rd. 2655 leads to the dam.

The primary catch here is stocked rainbow 8-16 inches. A very few cutthroat and brook trout are also taken. Bull trout are present and must be released if hooked. Most anglers still-fish or troll very slowly along the shoal areas. There is a boat launch at the north end beside a large campground. Wheelchair accessible.

TRILLIUM LAKE A trout lake on the south slope of Mt. Hood, just 3 miles from Government Camp. Forest Rd. 2656 cuts south off Hwy. 26 opposite the road to Snow Bunny Lodge. The road leads directly to Trillium Lake Campground.

Trillium is formed by the damming of the headwaters of Mud Creek. It covers about 60 acres, with lots of shoal area. Pressure is very heavy on this drive-in lake so close to Portland. The lake is stocked with fingerling and legal rainbow, with a catch range 6-14 inches, averaging 9 inches. Fly-fishing is quite good in late summer and fall. There is a large campground that accommodates trailers, and a boat ramp, but motors are prohibited on the lake. Kids can fish from the dam, and there is a pier at the campground. Recommended for small fry. Wheelchair accessible.

TUALATIN RIVER A meandering valley stream, about 75 miles long, flowing from the west across populous Washington County. It enters the Willamette River several miles above Oregon City. The Tualatin is fed by a number of good tributaries, including Gales Creek, Dairy Creek and Scoggins Creek. The main river is crossed and followed by many roads SW of Portland and in the Hillsboro-Forest Grove area.

Long-suffering from the effects of intense agricultural and residential development along its banks, the Tualatin is being closely monitored for water quality.

Best trout angling is in the upper river above Gaston, which is on Hwy. 47 south of Forest Grove, but this part of the river is almost inaccessible due to private land holdings. For this reason, it is no longer stocked. Gravel roads follow the upper stream through the Cherry Grove area, west of Gaston.

The river below Gaston has some wild cutthroat but is primarily bass and panfish water. Most angling is confined to the bridges, though it is possible to boat stretches of the river in a small craft, with put-ins and take-outs at the bridges or with landowner permission. A few salmon and steelhead are seen in the lower river in November and December.

TUMBLE LAKE A fairly good 20 acre hike-in brook trout lake about 3 miles north of Detroit Reservoir at the head of Tumble Creek. Best approach is by the French Creek Rd. (Forest Rd. 2223) leading north from Hwy. 22 at Detroit. About 8 miles from the highway take the Dome Rock Trail east, then hike south to the lake.

Tumble has naturally spawning 6-11 inch brook trout averaging 9 inches. Trout are usually plentiful and can be caught using all methods. There are a few natural campsites around the lake. The outlet stream drops off a sheer cliff to the stream bed below.

TWIN LAKES (Marion Co.) Two good brook trout lakes in southern Mt. Hood National Forest near the head of the

Collawash River. Best approach is by trail from Elk Lake north of Detroit. See Elk Lake for directions. The road is generally snowbound until June.

Twin Lakes are a pleasant 4-mile hike north from Elk Lake by Trail 544. The two 12 acre lakes lie in an east/west line just south of Mother Lode Mt. and are connected by a stream flowing east.

They have excellent natural reproduction, with fish from 6-13 inches. Both lakes are deep, and all methods of angling can be effective. A float tube would be helpful. Fly angling is excellent late in the year, mornings and evenings. West Twin, which is fished most heavily, has three campsites. East Twin has one campsite. The lakes can also be reached by about 12 miles of trail from the north by way of Bagby Hot Springs. See Mother Lode Lakes for trail details.

VEDA LAKE A 3-acre hike-in lake which is very good for small brook trout. On the south slope of Mt. Hood about 5 miles south of Government Camp, it produces consistently despite its small size and accessibility. From Hwy. 26 turn south about 1/4 mile east of the Timberline Lodge turnoff onto Forest Rd. 2613. From Fir Tree Campground about 5 miles south, follow Trail 673 directly to the lake, an easy mile downhill.

Brook trout are stocked by helicopter, and there are a few wild trout. Size range is 6-13 inches, averaging 9-10 inches. All methods can be used, as the lake is easily fished from shore. Bait angling is best early in the season, with fly-fishing good in the fall, mornings and evenings. Wet flies or nymph patterns retrieved slowly are especially effective. There is a natural campsite at the lake. Roads usually open about the end of June.

VIVIAN LAKE A 20-acre brook trout lake on the NW slopes of Mt. Yoran in Diamond Peak Wilderness. To reach it, hike south on Trail 3662 from Salt Creek Falls, about 4 miles.

The lake is fairly deep, at elevation 5,500 ft. A float tube would be handy. The lake is stocked by air every few years. There are several good natural campsites. Bushwhacking 1/2 mile north along the lake's outlet creek will bring you to Lopez Lake, which also has brook trout and doesn't see a lot of traffic.

VOGEL LAKE A 25-acre brook trout lake in the Mink Lake Basin west of Elk Lake. For trail directions, see Cliff Lake and Mink Lake. Vogel is 1/4 mile SE of Cliff Lake, east of the Pacific Crest Trail. Quite shallow, it frequently winterkills. There is an island in the lake with the remnants of an old trapper's cabin, and there are good natural campsites around the shore.

WAHANNA LAKE A rainbow lake within short hiking distance of Taylor Burn Campground, north of Waldo Lake. Taylor Burn Camp is 7 miles north of Waldo Lake by rough road. Wahanna lies along Wahanna Trail 3583 about 1 1/2 miles south from Taylor Burn Camp.

About 60 acres, it generally offers good fishing for rainbow averaging 10 inches and up to 4 pounds. It can be fished from shore in places, but a float tube is helpful. All methods are effective at times. Try trolling a red and white flash bait for the large fish during the day. Fly-fishing is good in the evenings, especially late in the year.

WALDO LAKE A sparkling blue gem, a giant alpine lake whose water ranks among the purist in the world. It covers almost 10 square miles and is over 400 feet deep in places. The water is so clean that the bottom can still be seen at depths well over a 100 ft. Waldo is usually Oregon's second largest natural lake, following Upper Klamath.

It stretches along the backbone of the Cascades almost in the center of the range, the source of the North Fork of the Middle Fork of the Willamette River. To reach it drive about 23 miles SE of Oakridge on Hwy. 58. At a well signed intersection, Forest Rd. 5897 forks off to the NE and follows the east side of Waldo about one mile from the lake, with three spur roads leading west to the lake. The spurs at the south and north ends have lakeside campgrounds. From the east, Forest Rd. 5897 leads to North Waldo Camp by way of various connecting roads from Crane Prairie, Wickiup and Davis Lakes. Trails lead into Waldo Lake from all directions.

Waldo has a fair supply of brook trout and an occasional kokanee, but in a lake of over 6,400 acres, it's a job to find them. It isn't easy fishing, but brook trout to 5 pounds are there for the angler who learns this lake's secrets. Fall is definitely the best time to try, and you'll beat the mosquitoes as well.

Waldo can be fished from shore, but most angling is done from boats. Speed limit is 10 mph. Trolling is probably the most productive method, but bait angling and fly-fishing are profitable when feeding fish are located. Productive areas include the shoal areas at the north and south ends. The lake is very deep, so be careful not to get below the fish. Catching is usually confined to morning and evening hours. When the wind comes up, this water gets really rough. Small boats should stay near the shoreline.

There are beautiful campgrounds at north and south ends of lake, and many picturesque natural campsites on rocky promontories, but the mosquitoes of Waldo Lake are legendary, and throughout much of the season the campgrounds are almost deserted. In spring and early summer, persistent campers often take to their boats to escape the blood thirsty hordes, as mosquitoes seldom attack beyond about 100 ft. offshore. Bring lots of repellent.

WALL LAKE A fairly good brook trout lake at the west end of the Olallie Lake group, about 100 miles from Portland by way of Hwy. 26 and the Skyline Rd. From Lower Lake Campground one mile north of Olallie Lake, take Trail 706 SW one mile to Trail 719. Follow 719 west 1/2 mile to Wall Lake. Averill and Red Lakes are further west on Trail 719. Easy to fish, Wall Lake brook trout run 6-13 inches, averaging 10 inches. Small lures or spinners usually work well, and evening fly-fishing is effective. There are good natural campsites here.

WALLING POND An old gravel pit that is open for largemouth bass year-round and is stocked with legal rainbow in spring. It is within Salem city limits west of I-5. To reach it, follow Turner Rd. or Mission St. The lake is south of Hines St. Public access is on 16th St. north of McGilchrist. The larger pond is private. Most anglers use bait to catch the pond's 10-12 inch trout. There are no facilities of any kind here.

WALTER WIRTH LAKE A trout, bass and panfish lake on the east edge of Salem. It is fed by Mill Creek and is within Cascade Gateway Park, just west of I-5 at its junction with Hwy. 22. The lake can be reached from the airport road or Turner Rd. Largemouth bass, white crappie, brown bullhead, and channel catfish are available, as well as stocked legal rainbow and an occasional brood trout. Recommended for small fry. Wheelchair accessible.

WALTERVILLE POND A very shallow 66-acre bass and panfish lake east of Springfield. It contains largemouth bass, black crappie, and brown bullhead.

WARREN LAKE A 5-acre brook trout lake at the head of Warren Creek. The creek flows north 3 miles into the Columbia River about 9 miles west of the community of Hood River. Warren is 1/4 mile by trail from the end of a primitive road SE of Mt. Defiance. You might want to walk the last mile of the road, too.

To reach the trailhead, follow the directions to Bear Lake, but take Forest Rd. 2821 (to the left) at the forks, heading NE on Forest Rd. 2820. Here is where you might begin to consider the capabilities of your vehicle. At the next T intersection, turn right, away from Mt. Defiance.

The road ends in 1/3 mile, and the trail heads west to Warren Lake.

Warren Lake is about 5 acres and only 8-ft. deep. It is at an elevation of 3,750 ft. and is fished quite heavily, yielding good catches of small brook trout. Most of the fish are 8-10 inches with a few to 12 inches. All methods can be used effectively, with flies working well in late summer and fall.

There is no camp at the lake. The nearest developed campground is at Rainy Lake, 3 miles west of the Forest Rd. 2821 turnoff on Forest Rd. 2820. It is normally accessible in June.

WAVERLY LAKE A panfish and bass lake along Hwy. 99E just north of Albany. The lake was formerly restricted to angling by children under 18 years old, but is now open to general public use. About 10 acres, it offers good angling for largemouth bass and bluegill, with crappie and catfish also available. The lake is easily fished from shore.

WELCOME LAKES Two brook trout lakes in the headwaters of the Collawash River east of Bull of the Woods Lookout. Several trail lead into this area. The most direct route is by way of Elk Lake Creek Trail 559 to Trail 554, which follows Welcome Creek to the lakes. This is a hike of 3 1/2 miles. To reach the trailhead, follow the Collawash Rd., Forest Rd. 63, south a twisty four or five miles past Toms Meadow to Forest Rd. 6380. Follow Forest Rd.. 6380 about 2 miles to a T-intersection where a short spur road leads in from the south. Trail 559 begins at the end of this spur.

The largest lake, Lower Welcome, is about 6 acres, and West Welcome is about 3 acres. Both of these are shallow and rich. Upper Welcome Lake is only one acre and has no fish, campsites, or trail directly to it. Lower and West Welcome both have some natural reproduction, and Lower Welcome is stocked each year.

Brook trout in Lower and West run to 12 inches, averaging 8-9 inches. There are good populations of fish in both lakes. Fly-fishing is the best method after early season. There are no campsites at West Welcome, but good campsites at Lower Welcome. The lakes are accessible in early June from the north, if you don't mind hiking through snow. However, don't underestimate the challenge of keeping track of the trail (through dense forest) when it is intermittently covered by snow.

WHIG LAKE A brook trout lake in an area well sprinkled with good lakes. Whig is located in the Taylor Burn area north of Waldo Lake. It is 1/2 mile south of Taylor Butte, a prominent landmark along Forest Rd. 517 leading to Taylor Burn Campground. To reach the campground, head north from North Waldo Campground on Forest Rd. 514 to its intersection with Forest Rd. 517, then turn west on Forest Rd. 517. Both roads are rough. If you park at Taylor Butte, circle the Butte and you'll come to long, narrow Whig Lake. It's at the west end of Torrey Lake.

Its shape makes it easy to fish from shore. The lake covers about 17 acres and is 10 feet deep. The catch ranges 10-16 inches. Lures and bait are usually effective, but fly-fishing mornings and evenings, especially in the fall, will really take fish. Bucktail coachman, caddis fly, mosquito, blue upright, and March brown are all good pattern choices. There's a good camp at Taylor Burn.

WIDGEON LAKE A good 3-acre eastern brook trout lake in the Big Meadows area east of Hwy. 22. See Fay Lake for directions. Go north past Fay for 1/4 mile, and take the blazed trail east about 1/2 mile past Fir Lake. Widgeon is small but fairly deep and lightly fished. The brook trout run 8-13 inches. The shore is pretty brushy, so a float tube is useful. It is a good late season lake.

WILEY CREEK A tributary of the South Santiam joining the river at Foster, east of Sweet Home. The creek is followed throughout its length by a gravel road. It is managed for wild steelhead and is open to steelhead angling from June 1 to January 31. Steelhead from the hatchery across the Santiam from Wiley sometimes wander up Wiley and are available for catching. Non-finclipped steelhead must be released unharmed.

Wild cutthroat are present in the upper creek, but most trout-size fish in lower Wiley are juvenile steelhead.

WILLAMETTE RIVER (Columbia R. to Oregon City) One of the few rivers in the world that provides salmon and steelhead angling in the midst of a major metropolitan area. The Willamette is the Number One producer of spring chinook in Oregon. Bass and panfish are also available near islands, log rafts, and the many structures in this section of the river (bridges, sea walls, docks, pilings), as well as in the sloughs. The largest slough in this portion of the river, Willamette Slough (a.k.a. Multnomah Channel), adds 33 additional river miles to the spring chinook fishery. It is treated separately in this book. See Multnomah Channel.

If you consider the Columbia to be an interstate for salmon and steelhead, the lower Willamette River is like a good four-lane highway. Salmon and steelhead are just passing through on their way home to spawning grounds in its tributaries. The Clackamas River is the primary tributary of the lower Willamette, joining the Willamette just north of Oregon City. The mouth of the Clackamas is a popular spring chinook fishery. Willamette Falls, an impressive cataract spanning the river at Oregon City, creates another concentration of fish and fishing activity.

In this section, the Willamette flows a quarter-mile wide and quietly powerful. Its current is fed by six major tributaries—the Coast Fork, Middle Fork, North Middle Fork, McKenzie, North and South Santiams, and Clackamas (each a major river system in itself) and by many smaller rivers and streams. These drain the snow-melt of two major mountain ranges (the Coast Range on the west, and the Cascades on the east) as well as the smaller Callapooya Mts. of Southern Oregon. The Willamette flows more than 200 miles to its meeting with the Columbia River just 4 miles north of Portland.

Salmon. Chinook angling on the lower Willamette heats up in March, April, and May along a stretch of 25 river miles, from the Columbia confluence near St. Johns to Willamette Falls at Oregon City. The main fishery in this stretch is from the Sellwood Bridge up to the falls, and from St. Johns Bridge down to the Columbia.

Portland Harbor, which has been dredged to 50 feet from bank to bank to permit passage of commercial freighters, has little to offer weary salmon in search of a resting place from strong currents. The addition of six acclimation ponds in Portland Harbor below the Ross Island Bridge (near the Oregon Museum of Science and Industry) may encourage more salmon to linger "downtown." Acclimation ponds have also been built at the mouth of the Clackamas. It is hoped that returning chinook, recognizing their old nursery, will spend some time in Clackamette Cove just east of Clackamette Park.

Once feared to be a dying race, Willamette system spring chinook have been growing in strength as a result of increased hatchery production and vigilant efforts to limit losses at PGE's Willamette Falls hydro-electric facility. PGE has upgraded the migrant bypass system to direct fish away from the turbines, which are shut down during peak passage. Though the current population is down from its high in 1988, it was still estimated to be a strong 64,000 in 1993. As with all anadromous fisheries, the run varies in size in response to ocean conditions. During a recent ten year period, the estimated catch has fluctuated between a high of 39,289 in 1991, and a low of 13,952 in 1986. The estimated catch for 1992 was 14,733.

The first spring chinook show up in February, with a few picked up at the mouth of the Clackamas. In March they come on steadily, and the catch is good if the water isn't too murky. April is usually the hottest month near the Clackamas mouth, with best catches at Oregon City made in late April and early May. Chinook are still being caught at Oregon City during the June shad run.

The average weight of a 3-year old Willamette springer is 15 pounds. The earlier arriving 5 year olds average 21 pounds. A 56-pounder was landed in 1983 at the Clackamas mouth, but fish that size are extremely rare here.

Most anglers fish from boats, but there are very productive chinook bank fisheries at Clackamette Park at the mouth of the Clackamas River on the east bank, and at Meldrum Bar just north of Gladstone on the east bank. Chinook are also taken from the catwalk behind the West Linn Municipal Building, from the sea wall and fishing platform at Oregon City, at Dahl Park on the north bank of the Clackamas mouth, at the Swan Island Lagoon float in North Portland, and at Cathedral Park in North Portland.

The most popular boat fishery is from Meldrum Bar to Willamette Falls. This area includes the two major chinook gathering spots—the mouth of the Clackamas, and the pool below Willamette Falls. Always an imposition to salmon and steelhead, the falls became an obstruction when a concrete lip and power turbines were installed. A large fishway on the west side of the river now enables fish passage. The fish are observed and counted as they swim up the fishway. Anglers can obtain the daily count over the falls by calling the Oregon Dept. of Fish and Wildlife Information number. The schooling of fish at the base of the falls has resulted in the most competitive chinook fishery on the river.

When the chinook are in, boaters at the Clackamas mouth and at Willamette Falls traditionally anchor side by side to form a hogline. Near the falls, the water is swift and turbulent. Anglers must use caution and observe posted boat deadlines. The turbulence of the water, the roaring of the falls, as well as the intense concentration of fish and anglers create a charged atmosphere here that may be unnerving to some. If you can't find a place in the line-up, or prefer a less pressurized environment, try your luck in Multnomah Channel, where the Coon Island fishery is reputed to be more relaxed, though equal in productivity to that at the falls.

Throughout this stretch of the Willamette, boating anglers are advised to keep an eye out for tow boats, whose vision is often impaired by loaded barges. When in doubt, weigh anchor.

Chinook boat anglers prefer to use herring and prawns as bait in early season, both fishing at anchor and trolling. Most bank anglers seem to prefer prawns or Spin-N-Glos, frequently using double hook-ups with 4-6 ounces of weight. Both bank and boat anglers switch to hardware later in the season. Common lures include wobblers, plugs, Clamshell Spinners, and Kwikfish-type lures.

Chinook follow the shoreline during their run upriver, generally staying within 25 ft. of the surface in the deeply dredged portion of the channel. On cloudy days, they are often found as shallow as 10 ft. Effective trollers troll s-l-o-w-l-y. Some use a spinner to gauge speed. In deep water, they fish the 12-16 ft. level, just above cruising chinook. In addition to Multnomah Channel, the most popular trolls in this section are from Milwaukie to the Sellwood Bridge, and from the St. Johns Bridge to the mouth.

Salmon follow fairly definite current movements. Anglers try to locate these routes and troll through them, or troll an S-curve through water whose current is broken by tied up ships, log rafts, and bridge abutments. Salmon sometimes lie in the slack water pocket beside or just downstream from these obstructions.

The Willamette is strongly affected by tidal flows. Low slack to high tide provides the best fishing. Adjust Astoria tide readings (printed in the daily newspaper or available on cards at sporting goods stores) for the lower Willamette by adding 6 hours to the Astoria time for a correct Oregon City reading, 4 hours for Sellwood Bridge angling, and 2 hours for Multnomah Channel angling.

Best chinook fishing on the Willamette is generally when the river stage level is at about 6.5 ft., with clarity between 3.5 and 5.2. A river clarity reading is available from ODF&W at 657-2059 (Willamette Falls Information).Call the National Weather Forecasting Service at (503)261-9246 for stage level.

Sturgeon. Sturgeon provide a year-round fishery. Quite a few are taken below the falls, and some are picked up by bank anglers casting from shore in the Sellwood to Oregon City reach. A depth finder is helpful to identify the deep holes frequented by sturgeon. Keep your bait on the bottom. To avoid hooking over-size sturgeon, use lighter line, and smaller hooks and bait.

Shad. The lower Willamette shad fishery is primarily a boat show, beginning in early May and extending through the July 4 weekend, with a peak in June. Thousands of shad are taken in the main channel from the mouth of the Clackamas to Willamette Falls, and in the Coon Island vicinity of Multnomah Channel. There is some bank angling for shad at Clackamette Park.

Steelhead. Modest numbers of winter and summer run steelhead are taken in this stretch of the river from late December through June, primarily in the vicinity of the Clackamas mouth and near the falls. Non-finclipped steelhead must be released unharmed. The 1992-93 catch of summer steelhead was 282. The catch of winter steelhead was 194, though over a thousand winter steelhead have been caught in the lower Willamette in better years.

Bass and Panfish. The Willamette River provides excellent and extremely varied habitat for bass and panfish throughout its length. In this reach, in addition to islands and sloughs, there are man-made structures that attract concentrations of warmwater fish. Look for them near bridges, sea walls, docks, pilings, and log rafts.

There is good bank fishing for bass, crappie, perch, and crayfish at Oaks Bottom in Sellwood, particularly below the log booms (though standing on the booms themselves is extremely dangerous). Other good bank fisheries are at

Spring chinook fishing in downtown Portland.

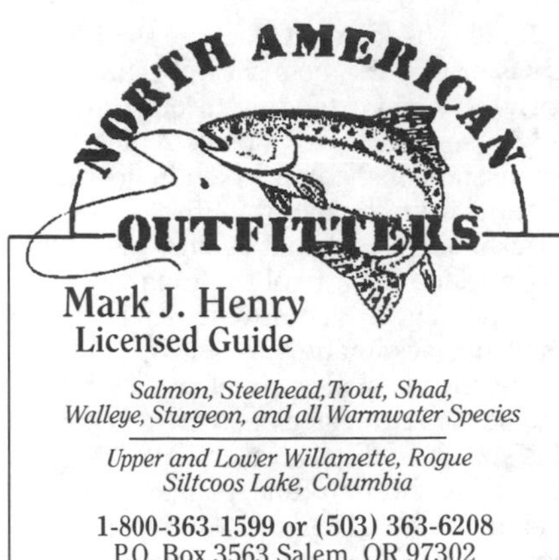

Ross Island, with its blue heron rookery mid-river in South Portland; Swan Island in north Portland; Elk Rock Island near Milwaukie; and Cedar Island north of Gladstone. Swan Island Lagoon can be fished from floats, with best catches downstream from the cross street between Basin and Lagoon Avenue. Bass and panfish are also fished at Cathedral Park, Willamette Park (plunk the shallow water south of the ramp), the harbor wall at Waterfront Park, and Milwaukie Boat Ramp (Fish the bay). The mouth of Johnson Creek offers excellent crappie fishing and smallmouth bass. It can be reached from the Milwaukie Boat Ramp by wading during low water.

Facilities. Fishing supplies are available in Sellwood and in Oregon City. Public boat ramps are located at Sauvie Island on Multnomah Channel, Cathedral Park in North Portland, Swan Island, Willamette Park in SW Portland, Milwaukie off Hwy. 99E, Meldrum Bar Park, and Clackamette Park. There are numerous private moorages and boat ramps throughout this stretch, open to public use for a modest fee. Rental boats are available at some of these facilities.

There are locks at Willamette Falls, operated by the Army Corps of Engineers, which enable passage for boats traveling upstream and down. The locks are open to public use at no fee from 7 a.m. to 11 p.m. daily. Boaters should tie up at the Corps dock on the west bank, and pull the signal cord to alert the operator. Vessels should have fenders to protect their hulls from the lock walls. Allow about 35 minutes for passage through the 5 chambers.

WILLAMETTE RIVER (Oregon City to Eugene) This 100-mile portion of the Willamette serves as a highway for thousands of migrating spring chinook and summer and winter steelhead bound for their spawning grounds on the McKenzie, North and South Santiams, and the forks of the Willamette. The river is also year-round home to largemouth bass, smallmouth bass, panfish, channel catfish, and sturgeon. Trout and whitefish grow more numerous from Harrisburg upstream.

The Willamette can be reached by secondary roads off Hwy. 99E and Hwy. 99W. It can be boated by all manner of craft launched from many improved, primitive, and natural sites on both banks of the river. Anglers commonly motor upstream from a ramp, and fish and drift their way back. Boat ramps popularly used by Willamette anglers in this section are located at Willamette Park and Bernert Landing in West Linn, Molalla River State Park off Hwy. 99E north of Canby, Hebb Park 1/2 mile north of Canby Ferry Rd., Rodgers landing just outside of Newberg, San Salvador Park two miles south of the Yamhill confluence, Willamette Mission State Park next to the Wheatland Ferry off Hwy. 221 between Dayton and Keizer, Wallace Marine Park off Hwy. 221 in West Salem, Independence Riverview Park off Hwy. 51 at Independence, Buena Vista Ferry south of Monmouth, Bryant Park in Albany, Hyak Park on Hwy. 20 west of Albany, Pioneer Boat Basin off 99W at Corvallis, Willamette Park off Hwy. 99W south of Corvallis, Peoria Park in Peoria, McCartney Park north of Harrisburg, Hileman and Whitely landings off River Rd. north of Eugene, Alton Baker Park in Eugene, and Island Park in Springfield. The river is also used heavily by pleasure boat operators during the summer.

Salmon. Chinook angling activity in this stretch of the Willamette has traditionally been light despite the fact that tens of thousands of adult chinook make it over the falls. In 1993, about 30,000 adult chinook were counted at the top of the falls. Anglers in this stretch must be willing to learn some new tactics, and to locate the holes and slots where salmon linger.

From Willamette Falls to the Yamhill confluence, the Willamette is moderately slack, and trolling is the most effective chinook tactic. Wobblers such as the No. 4 Slow Sam and No. 3 Manistee trolled in a zig-zag pattern work well. Brass/chrome or silver are the most popular colors. The most popular anchor fishery is at the mouth of the Molalla, where spinners are generally effective.

1 **MOLALLA RIVER STATE PARK** - Steep paved ramps into Willamette also provide access to lower Molalla; fish for crappie, bass, bullheads, and occasional channel cats as well as trout, salmon, steelhead; also accesses lower Pudding for bass and panfish in spring.

2 **MOUTH OF THE MOLALLA**- Fish for winter steelhead late Jan. through March, chinook in April.

3 **ROCK ISLAND SLOUGHS** - Fish submerged rocks, log booms & sunken trees for bass & panfish; explore inside and outside sloughs; park adjacent to 99E or launch boat at Willamette park (West Linn).

4 **WEST LINN MUNICIPAL BLDG**. - Bank fish from catwalk for sturgeon & spring chinook; park behind building.

5 **WILLAMETTE PARK** (West Linn) - Bank fish from catwalk for sturgeon & spring chinook; park behind building.

6 **OREGON CITY TO MELDRUM BAR** - Three miles of intensive bank fishing; hoglines and trolling for summer and winter steelhead, spring chinook, and sturgeon; bank fishing in Oregon City from 99E sea wall and platform 1/2 mi. below falls.

7 **CLACKAMETTE PARK** - Very popular improved boat ramp at mouth of Clackamas,south bank; intensive bank fishery for shad, summer steelhead, and chinook; boat access to lower Clackamas.

8 **DAHL PARK** - North bank of mouth of Clackamas; bank fish for summer steelhead & spring chinook.

9 **MELDRUM BAR** - Improved boat ramp; largest bank fishery for summer steelhead & spring chinook; parking permitted on gravel bar.

10 **MILWAUKIE BOAT RAMP** - Improved public ramp with some bank angling for bass & panfish in bay; cast to submerged stub pilings, logs, and stumps; wading access to mouth of Johnson Creek during low water for smallmouth and crappie; intensive spring chinook trolling in deep water.

11 **MILWAUKIE TO SELLWOOD BRIDGE** - Very popular troll for spring chinook.

12 **OAKS BOTTOM** - Fish from bank for plentiful bass, crappie, perch, crawfish; fish water below log booms but do not venture onto logs.

13 **WATERFRONT PARK**- Plunk the length of harbor wall in downtown Portland for sturgeon, bass, crappie, perch, and occasional salmon and steelhead; bass & panfish lurk close-in here and at sea walls on east shore beneath freeway ramps.

14 **WILLAMETTE PARK** (Portland) - Fish weekdays and early to avoid motorized summer crowd; plunk the shallow water south of ramp for bass and panfish; use float to access deeper holes; popular launch for spring chinook trollers concentrating beneath Sellwood Bridge.

15 **SWAN ISLAND LAGOON** - Fish for crappie, bullhead, yellow perch, and numer-

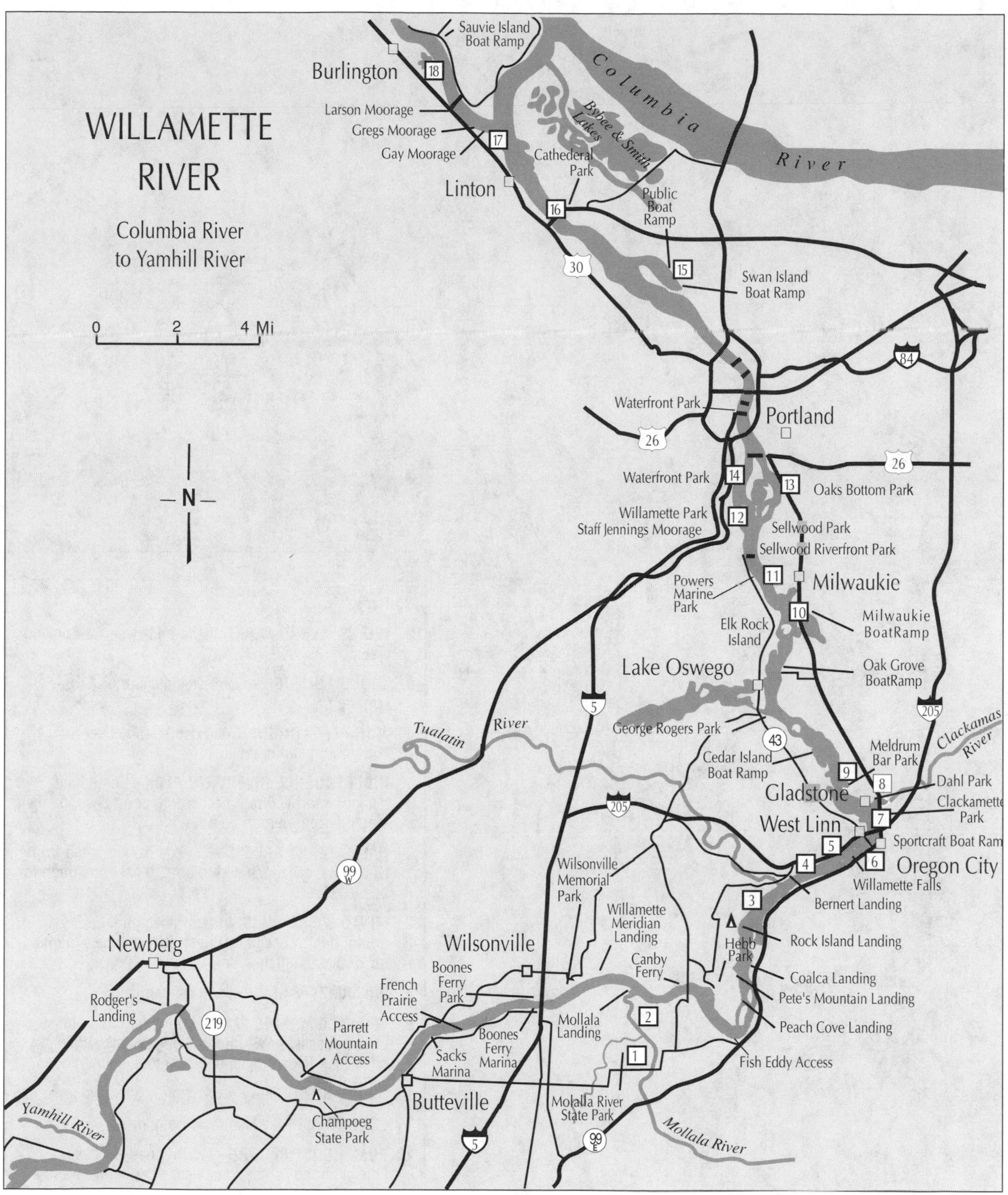

ous bluegill; best fishing downstream from cross street between Basin and Lagoon avenues and in main Willamette from Channel Ave.; floats and improved ramp at east shore of lagoon; popular access for lower river spring chinook and sturgeon. Beware of heavy commercial traffic.

16 CATHEDRAL PARK - Improved public ramps, floats, bank access for salmon, sturgeon, bass, panfish, walleye, channel cats.

17 ST. JOHNS BRIDGE - Troll from bridge of Willamette mouth for spring chinook; anchor at hot spots; fish pilings and log rafts for largemouth and panfish.

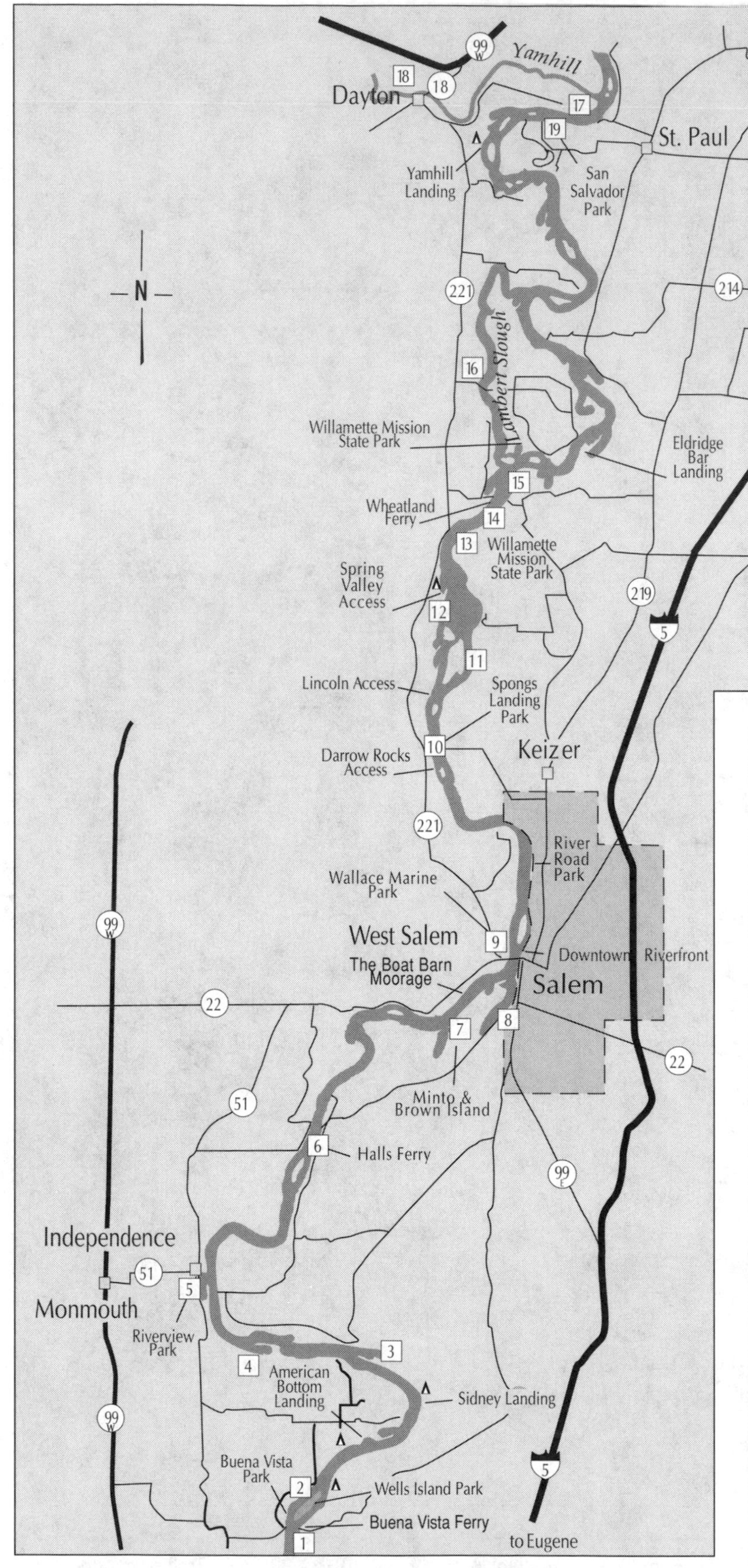

1 BUENA VISTA FERRY - County park & improved boat ramp provides downstream take-out for floating the Santiam from I-5 bridge; motor upstream for smallmouth bass, largemouth, crappie, bluegill; good holding water at mouth of Santiam; beware of strong currents downriver of ferry.

2 WELLS ISLAND PARK - Camp mid-river; no drinking water.

3 JUDSON SLOUGH - Good bluegill, crappie, some largemouth.

4 MURPHY SLOUGH - Good depth and cover for largemouth and crappie.

5 INDEPENDENCE RIVERVIEW PARK - Some bank fishing; improved ramp accessing good bass, panfish sloughs from here to Salem.

6 HALLS FERRY ACCESS - Limited bank angling from Greenway, or launch cartop boat to access slough for bass, panfish.

7 MINTO & BROWN ISLAND - Public park on River Rd. South, not accessible by river; fish several sloughs for bass & panfish.

8 WILLAMETTE SLOUGH - bass, panfish.

9 WALLACE MARINE PARK - Improved ramp above bridge accesses Willamette Slough; bank angling in main river for spring and fall chinook below bridge.

10 SPONG'S LANDING - Bank angling at public park.

11 LONE TREE BAR - Fish for bass, panfish.

12 PUMPHOUSE SLOUGH - Fair to good for bass, bluegill; good cover along west side; bank access at Spring Valley.

13 WILLAMETTE MISSION STATE PARK - Improved boat ramp next to Wheatland Ferry slip accesses several warmwater sloughs; cut-off oxbow lake in park refills with Willamette fish following high water, including bluegill, bass, bullhead, crawfish, crappie; good bank access or launch boat.

14 WHEATLAND FERRY - Improved public ramps east and west provide access to Lambert Slough, Jackson Bend, Windsor Is. sloughs; bank fishing on west for occasional summer steelhead and non-game fish.

15 JACKSON BEND - Fish for largemouth bass, panfish, smallmouth bass.

16 LAMBERT SLOUGH - Six-seven miles from any ramp, but popular for largemouth bass, panfish; watch for gravel bars on the way; no bank access.

17 MOUTH OF YAMHILL - Fish for largemouth, smallmouth, panfish at mouth, or motor up to Yamhill Locks Park; large crappie hold inside abandoned lock structure; bass, bluegill, perch, catfish, trout, salmon also available; check big eddy below locks and cascade.

18 DAYTON BOAT RAMP - Improved ramp provides best access to Yamhill.

19 SAN SALVADORE PARK - Improved ramp, bank fishing in deep water from gravel beach.

Above the Yamhill, the current is generally too strong for trolling, though some anglers backtroll Kwikfish-type lures. Bait, however, is useless here due to the large number of non-game fish looking for an easy hand-out. Mid-stream current edges and drop-offs can be productive places to anchor and fish, but you must keep a sharp eye out for large drifting debris and be prepared to disengage quickly from your anchor. For safety, boating anglers in this section should use a bow slide with chocks, cleats, and an anchor buoy. A 25-pound rocking chair-type anchor on 200 ft. of stout rope is best for dealing with the shallowness of the river in this section and its hardpan bottom.

Most anglers prefer to anchor close to the bank, fishing spinners in 4-6 ft. deep slots. Keep the spinner in the slot until a salmon wanders in. Anglers generally use a 17-21 inch lead dropper line with a slightly longer leader. Amount of lead can vary from 1-8 ounces, depending on current and depth. You'll need to experiment. The most effective spinner sizes are numbers. 3, 4, or 5. Vary the color according to the light and clarity of the water.

The most productive chinook fishing in this reach often takes place the first 20 days in May. If you follow the fish counts over Willamette Falls, calculate that the fish will reach the Yamhill in about 7 days.

Summer run steelhead are moving upstream during this time as well and can be fished with the same lures as salmon. About 20% of the spring catch in this reach is summer steelhead. Most of the summer run are finclipped. Winter steelhead are all wild and must be released unharmed.

Bass and Panfish. This section of the Willamette is also the domain of warmwater fish. The river is laced with sloughs that offer quiet refuge for largemouth and smallmouth bass, crappie, bluegill, and catfish. Its channel is broken by islands mid-stream that divide and slow the flow to either side. Look for largemouth in the sloughs under logs and brush piles, casting plugs or spinning lures along the shore where there's lots of cover to draw them out. Smallmouth are present in good numbers from Salem to Corvallis, found primarily at the mouths of the sloughs and at the edges of the main current. Best bass fishing takes place when the river drops in summer and fall.

This portion of the Willamette beckons the adventurous bass and panfish angler, for whom exploration is part of the sport. Try Rock Island Sloughs off 99E near West Linn, which offer good habitat among submerged rocks, log booms and sunken trees. There are two sloughs (inside and outside), and both can be productive. Lambert Slough, about 4

Willamette River, Oregon City.

miles long, is 6-7 miles from boat ramps upstream or down, but nevertheless attracts a lot of interest among bass and panfish anglers. There is no bank access, and boaters should be wary of gravel bars throughout the slough. Best access is from Wheatland Ferry Boat Ramp, which is also used to reach Jackson Bend and Windsor Island sloughs.

One of the few slough areas in this section with bank access is Minto & Brown Island near Salem. There's a lot of good boatable bass and panfish water between Independence and Salem, including Murphy and Judson sloughs. Luckiamute Slough, just upstream from the Luckiamute River confluence, offers good boat fishing for largemouth, crappie, and bluegill until June. The 12-mile drift from Peoria Park to Corvallis offers many promising sloughs and holes, including the waters around McBee, John Smith, Kiger, and Fischer islands.

Sturgeon. Sturgeon are available in this stretch, though they don't make it over the falls on their own. A number of sturgeon were transplanted here in the early 1950s. Since 1989, an additional 37,000 sturgeon fingerings have been planted near Harrisburg and between Corvallis and Newburg. Sturgeon probably do not spawn naturally above the falls. Fish the deep holes and eddies with bait well on the bottom. Large gobs of nightcrawlers, crawfish tails, or pieces of scrap fish make good bait. Use smaller bait and hooks, and lighter line to avoid hooking over-size fish. ODF&W encourages anglers to help them monitor the sturgeon fishery by reporting catches to their Corvallis office. Log books are available for anglers who would like to participate in the sturgeon study program.

Trout. There is some fishing for rainbow and cutthroat trout in the Corvallis area, but trout fishing is best from Peoria upstream, where there are more gravel bars, channels, and other structure that provide good trout habitat. From Harrisburg to the McKenzie, all non-finclipped trout must be released unharmed. Barbless artificial flies and lures must be used except when fishing bait for salmon or steelhead.

Cutthroat head up the tributaries each winter and return in early spring. The areas near the mouths of good cutthroat tributary streams are usually best in April. Cutthroat are scattered throughout the river in summer. In the Eugene area, the river above and below the I-5 Bridge offers excellent fly-fishing early in the season.

Trout fishing drops off in this stretch as the water warms, and whitefish predominate by June. Whitefish actually present a year-round angling opportunity in the Middle Willamette. Look for them in the same places as trout. In winter, whitefish are often quite active.

Facilities. Natural campsites are available on many of the islands in the river, and there is a developed campground on Wells Island below Buena Vista Ferry. Most of the parks that have boat ramps or fishing access do not have camping facilities, but there are campgrounds at Spring Valley Access on the west bank upstream from Wheatland Ferry, Sidney Landing on the east bank about 5 miles below Independence, American Bottom Landing on the west bank 2 miles above Sidney, Luckiamute Landing at the Luckiamute confluence, Riverside Landing on the east bank SW of Albany, Half Moon Bend Landing downstream about 4 miles from Corvallis on the west bank, Buckskin Mary Landing 4 miles above Peoria Park on the west bank, and Harkens Lake Landing 3 miles below McCartney Park on the west bank.

WILLAMETTE RIVER, COAST FORK

Least productive of the major Willamette tributaries. It heads in the vicinity of Black Butte in the Calapooya Mts., flowing 7 miles to Cottage Grove Reservoir, closely followed by a road. The upper portion supports wild cutthroat trout. There is some good fishing near the dam. The lower river is stocked with rainbow trout in early season in the Cottage Grove area.

WILLAMETTE RIVER, MIDDLE FORK

The largest tributary of the upper Willamette, joining the Coast Fork to form the main river just south of Springfield and Eugene. Highways 58, 99 and 126 meet near it's mouth. From Springfield to Lowell (at Dexter Reservoir) a paved county road follows the north bank of the river's lower 18 miles. Hwy. 58 then follows it past Lookout Pt. Reservoir to just above Oakridge. About 3 miles SE of Oakridge, Forest Rd. 21 cuts off to the south and follows the river past Hills Creek Reservoir and far into the headwaters. The river is easily accessible at most points.

This fork of the Willamette offers a variety of water. From Dexter Reservoir downstream it resembles the mainstem Willamette, flowing through mostly flat agricultural lands. Most anglers fish this stretch for summer steelhead and spring chinook, though some trout are present. Above Lookout Point Reservoir the Middle Fork is a fast big river, much like the McKenzie.

Above Hills Creek Reservoir the Middle Fork is stocked with legal rainbow. Wild rainbow and cutthroat trout are also in the river in fair numbers. Fishing for wild rainbow is especially good in June and again in the fall. In summer, the river gets low.

From Lookout Point Reservoir to Hills Creek Dam, the river is restricted to the use of barbless flies and lures. The Middle Fork is open the year-round, with a 2-fish limit during trout season, and catch and release for trout the balance of the year.

A fair spring chinook fishery has developed in the lower river between Springfield and Dexter Dam. The catch averages about 1,000 fish per year, though the 1990 catch was about 3,000 chinook. Fishing with spinners or Kwikfish-type lures is the usual method. Most chinook are caught in June and July.

In 1981 the Dept. of Fish and Wildlife began an experimental summer steelhead stocking program in the lower river. The estimated catch from this program has fluctuated from a high of 534 in 1986-87 to a low of 148 in 1987-88. The 1992-93 catch estimate was 366. Additional steelhead smolts have been released.

There are boat ramps at Clearwater Lane in Springfield and at Jasper Bridge, and there are 2 ramps below Dexter Dam on both sides of the river. Pengra Greenway Boat Ramp is about 4 miles below the dam.

Campgrounds are available at Lookout Pt. and Hills Creek reservoirs, on Hwy.

WILLAMETTE RIVER

Buena Vista Ferry to Harrisburg

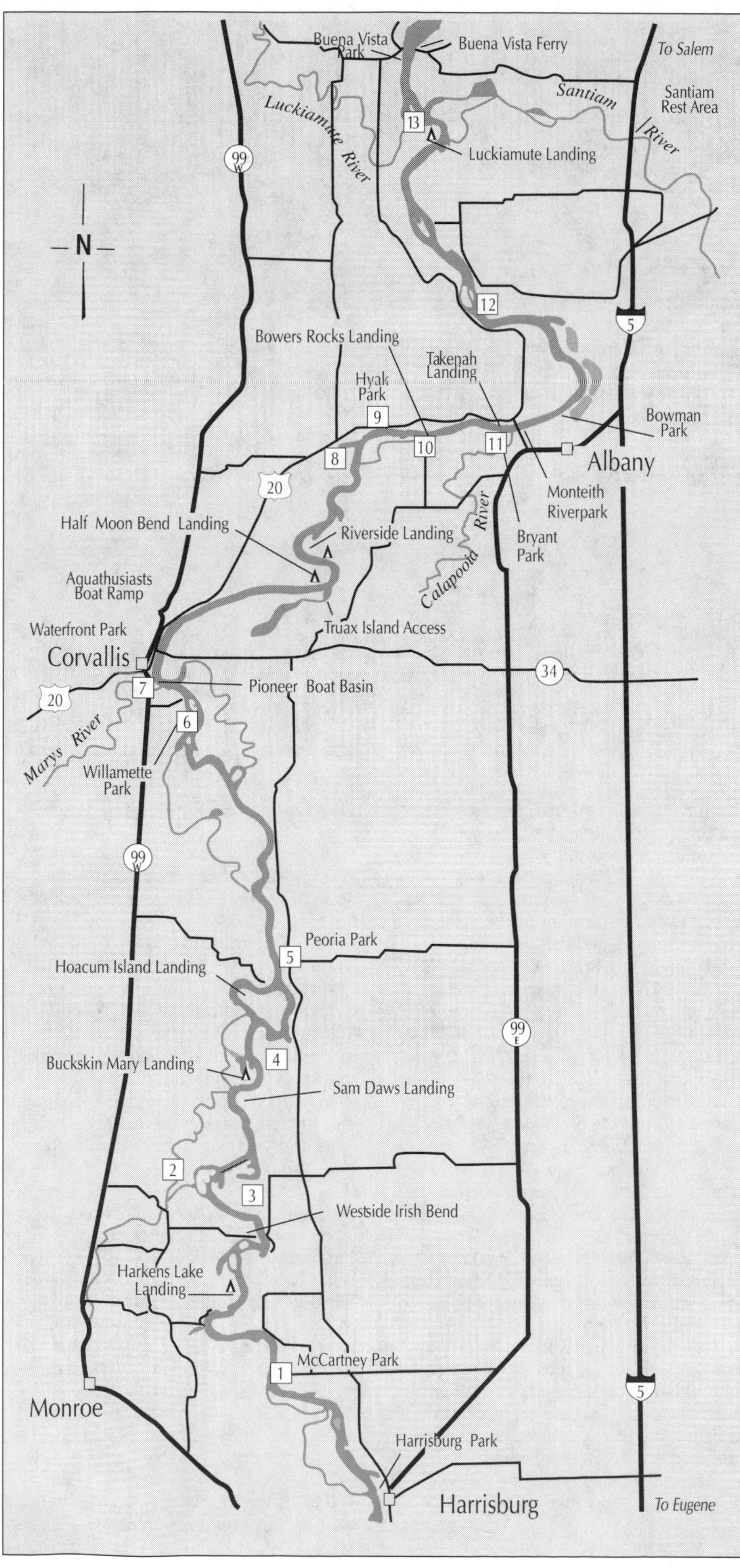

1 **McCARTNEY PARK** - Improved ramp accesses good bass, panfish sloughs here to Peoria; some early season native cutthroat.

2 **MOUTH OF LONG TOM** - Sturgeon hole at confluence; old mouth just upstream forms promising slough with deep water in lower half, good cover in upper for largemouth, crappie.

3 **SLOUGH** - Deep slough with good cover on east bank.

4 **SLOUGH** - Promising for bass & panfish, on east shore at head of Hoacum Island.

5 **PEORIA PARK** - Many sloughs and holes here to Corvallis, a 12 mile drift; try waters around McBee, John Smith, Kiger, and Fischer islands for bass, panfish; improved ramp.

6 **WILLAMETTE PARK** (Corvallis) - Improved ramp with large bank angling access.

7 **PIONEER BOAT BASIN** - Take-out for 12-mile drift from Peoria.

8 **COLLINS BAY** - Nearly circular slough with shallow neck holds abundant crappie, bluegill.

9 **HYAK PARK** - Improved ramp accesses nearby sloughs.

10 **BOWERS ROCKS** - Large slough with good bank cover, good for crappie and largemouth in spring, shallow in summer.

11 **BRYANT PARK** -Improved ramp is difficult at low water; bank angling from dock.

12 **BLACK DOG SLOUGH** - Bluegill, largemouth, crappie.

13 **LUCKIAMUTE SLOUGH** - Just upstream from Willamette confluence; good boat fishing until June for largemouth, crappie, bluegill.

Willamette Falls is a popular spot to anchor and fish for spring chinook.

58 west of Oakridge, and roughly every 5 miles on Forest Rd. 21.

WILLAMETTE RIVER, NORTH FORK The North Fork is a good size, very attractive stream, managed for wild trout. It is restricted to barbless artificial flies and lures from the mouth to the railroad bridge at Westfir, and is fly-fishing only from Westfir upstream. About 40 miles long, it joins the Middle Fork 2 miles west of Oakridge, about 35 miles SE of Eugene.

The river heads in Waldo Lake and skirts the Taylor Burn Lakes area. A good road, Forest Rd. 19, follows the river from the community of West Fir far into the headwaters. Forest Rd. 19 turns to gravel the last 10 miles to Box Canyon Guard Station, after which it joins the South Fork McKenzie Rd. The last 8 miles of the stream to Waldo Lake is off the beaten track, though it is crossed once by trail.

There are good populations of wild rainbow and cutthroat trout in the North Fork. The fish range in size from 8-12 inches, with some to 17 inches. The lower 12 miles has excellent fly-fishing water from July through the fall. Angling pressure is generally light.

This is a lovely forest stream, and official recognition of its merit has won the North Fork state designation as a Wild and Scenic river. Its water is crystal clear and quite cold, too cold for good angling in the spring. But a sunny summer day on this sparkling river is inevitably memorable. The only campground on the river is Kiahane, about 20 miles north of Westfir on Forest Rd. 19. Other camps are located on Hwy. 48 east and west of Oakridge.

WILLAMINA CREEK A good little trout stream on the east side of the coast range, flowing into the upper Yamhill River. From McMinnville on Hwy. 18 head north through Sheridan on the old highway to Willamina. From Willamina, at the mouth of the creek, a paved road heads north, and gravel roads follow the upper stretch.

Willamina has a nice run of winter steelhead, which are available from late January through April. All non-finclipped steelhead must be released unharmed. Best steelhead water is in the lower portion where the creek runs through agricultural lands, but access is a problem there. The upper creek is on tree farm land, and the public is allowed. Abundant wild cutthroat are available in the 7-11 inch range. Migrant cutthroat to 13 inches are probably available in winter. There are no campgrounds along the creek.

WILLAMINA POND A 5-acre abandoned log pond in Huddeston Park in the town of Willamina. Take the Hwy. 18 business loop through Sheridan into the community of Willamina. Turn left just past the Rocket Gas Station onto Polk (which runs behind the high school), and follow Polk to the park. The pond is stocked with catchable rainbow each from mid-March through Free Fishing Day, and it supports populations of largemouth bass, black crappie, brown bullhead and yellow perch. Recommended for small fry.

WILLIAMS LAKE A 4-acre brook trout lake just north of Taylor Burn Campground north of Waldo Lake. See Whig Lake for road and trail directions. The one mile trail heads north from the east side of the campground to Williams Lake. Williams is SE of Upper Erma Bell Lake. The trail goes on to Otter Lake.

Williams is stocked with brook trout 6-12 inches. It is easily fished from shore, and all methods will take fish at times. The area is not accessible until late June.

WILSONVILLE POND A 3-acre pond west of I-5, south of the Wilsonville Rest

Area. From Butteville Rd., take Boones Ferry Rd. north about 1/2 mile. The pond contains largemouth bass and bluegill.

WIND LAKE A small hike-in brook trout lake about 2 miles SW of Government Camp as the crow flies. You'll envy the crow when you hike this one. Wind Lake is on the south side of Tom Dick and Harry Mt. There are two ways to reach it. You can hike one mile to Mirror Lake on Trail 664, then continue on this trail for an additional 1 1/2 miles, crossing the western flank of Tom Dick and Harry above timberline. From there hike about 3/4 mile due east, staying above timberline, and you will see the lake about 100 ft. below you. A trail leads down to the lake. This hike is about 4 miles and is strenuous.

The second route begins at the parking area of the Multipor ski area. A trail leads SW, following a ski lift to timberline. (Don't confuse this with the trail that follows another lift SE up Multipor Mt.) The trail crosses to the south side of the mountain and ends at Wind Lake. This route reaches the lake in a little over 2 miles, but is even steeper than the first.

Wind Lake is stocked with brook trout by air and offers pretty good fishing for fish 6-12 inches. Fly-fishing is the best method, as the lake is extremely shallow. In some severe winters most of the fish are lost, and it takes a year or two to rebuild the population. It is usually accessible in early June, with some snow left to struggle through.

WITHEE LAKE A fair warm water lake not far from McMinnville, just east of the Yamhill River. From Amity on 99W, head west about 2 miles. The state has an access agreement with the owner of the property, and if anglers act responsibly, the lake will remain open. A sign marks the area. Strictly a bank fishery, Withee supports good size largemouth bass and some crappie. After a big flood you can find all Yamhill species in here. The lake is usually good in spring and summer until the weeds get thick.

WOODBURN POND A highway borrow pit adjacent to I-5 north of Woodburn. Take the Woodburn Exit and head east on Hwy. 214 to Boones Ferry Rd., north on Boones Ferry about 2 miles, and west on Crosby Rd. Just before the Interstate overpass, turn north onto Edwin Road, which parallels the expressway and leads to the pond. There are 14 acres to fish for largemouth bass, bluegill, crappie, and channel cats to 18 inches. The water gets weed choked by late spring. Anglers can launch a car-topper here, but motors are prohibited.

There is a parking area, and anglers are encouraged to use it, hand carrying boats to the water. This pond has been badly abused by anglers who insist on driving right up to the bank, destroying the fragile lake-side vegetation that holds back erosion and provides habitat for insect life that, in turn, feed the fish. There is no garbage collection here either, so take home whatever you bring. Irresponsible angler behavior may result in closure.

YAMHILL RIVER A pretty, rural tributary of the Willamette, flowing 60 miles from the Coast Range to its confluence near Dayton. It offers good spring fishing for wild cutthroat in its upper forks, bass and panfish primarily in the mainstem, and big Willamette cutthroat spawners throughout the system in winter.

The river splits into two forks just east of McMinnville. The North Fork flows south from the mountains above Yamhill. The South Fork flows north from the Willamina area. Among the first Willamette tributaries to clear, the Yamhill is a good choice for the year's first trout outings.

From the lower end, the river can be reached by paved and gravel side roads leading south from Hwy. 99W and north from Hwy. 233. From McMinnville upstream, the South Fork is skirted on the north by Hwy. 18 and is followed through Sheridan and Willamina by the old highway. The North Fork is accessed by Hwy. 47 between Yamhill and Carlton, and is closely followed by a road NW of Yamhill in the vicinity of Pike.

The river and its forks are not stocked but have a good population of wild cutthroat, plus the odd stocked rainbow that drifts down from upper tributaries. There's good bank access for trout on the North Fork between Pike and the Flying M Ranch.

Bass and panfish angling is excellent from the McMinnville area down to the mouth. Some large crappie are caught each summer with spinner and bait, small flash lures, and streamer flies. The Yamhill is navigable by small motorboats from the mouth to the old locks above Dayton. There is also bank fishing at Yamhill Locks Park, where large crappie have been known to hold inside the abandoned lock structure. Check the big eddy below the lock and cascade as well. Bass, bluegill, perch, catfish, trout, and even salmon have been taken here on occasion. The sloughs in the lower river have excellent crayfish populations.

The Yamhill is open for winter angling. Steelhead migrate through the river into the forks and other tributaries, where they spawn in the upper reaches. Steelhead angling takes place from mid-January through April. Anglers can also fish for the big migrating Willamette cutthroat that head up the Yamhill in winter to spawn in the forks. Some anglers drift the upper river in pursuit of this quarry. A popular drift on the South Fork is from Ft. Hill to Willamina, and on the North Fork, from Pike to the West Side Rd.

ZIGZAG RIVER A high gradient tributary of the Sandy River, flowing mostly within the Mt. Hood National Forest. The ZigZag offers exciting summer steelhead fishing for nimble anglers. About 12 miles long, the Zigzag joins the Sandy River at the community of Zigzag, which is located on Hwy. 26 about 43 miles east of Portland. Hwy. 26 follows the north bank all the way to its headwaters near Government Camp.

The ZigZag has recently been stocked with summer steelhead, and the fish have been returning. Hooking a steelhead in this fast-moving mountain stream can result in quite a chase. This is exclusively pocket water fishing. A few small wild cutthroat are also available.

CENTRAL ZONE

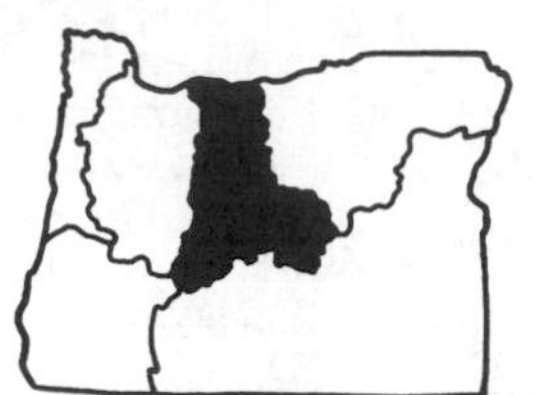

The Central Zone is all waters draining into the Columbia River from Bonneville Dam up to and including the Deschutes River.

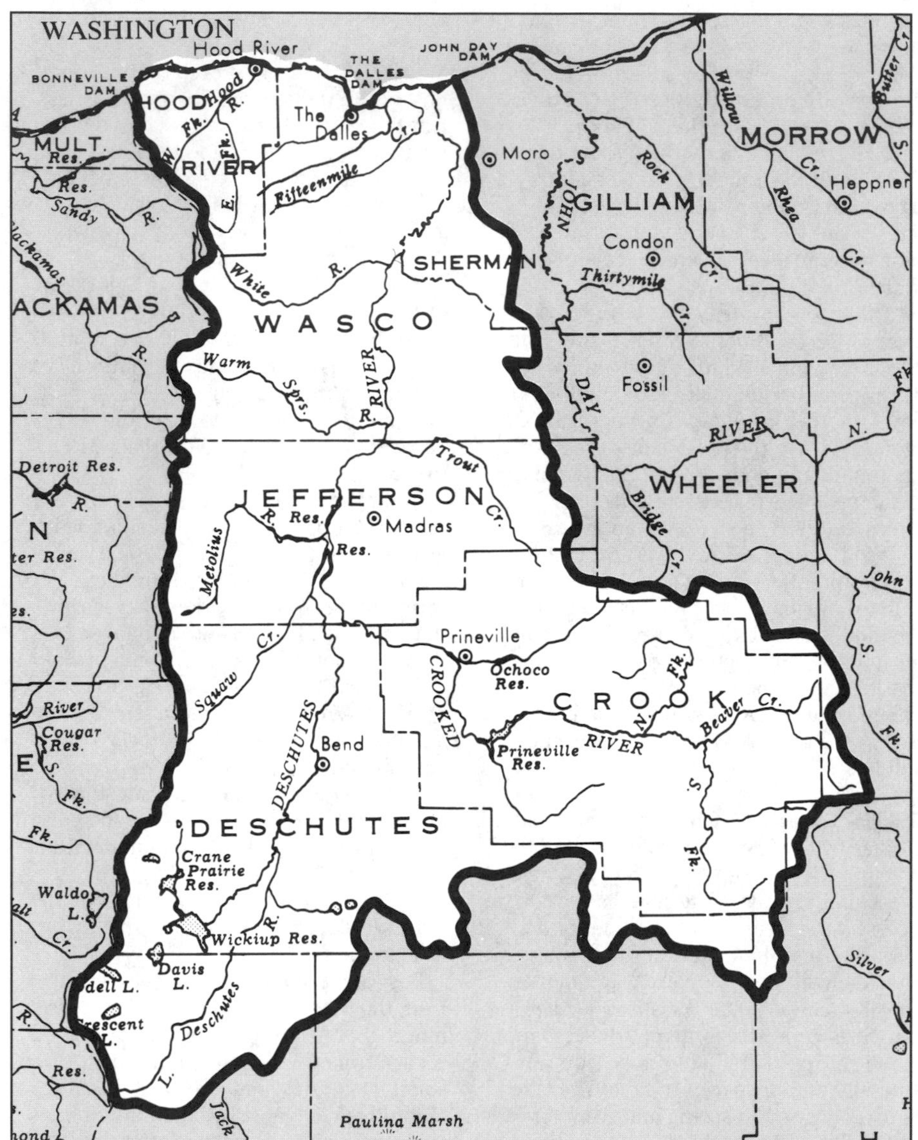

The Central Zone reaches deep into Oregon's heartland where it draws forth all the waters that feed the state's premiere trout river, the Deschutes. These sources include lovely snow-melt pools and their icy outlets, crystalline rivers that pour full-blown out of fern banked springs, meandering desert streams, and a treasure trove of handsome volcanic lakes.

Here are many of Oregon's richest angling opportunities in settings of varied and astounding beauty.

The Deschutes itself offers year-round fishing for large rainbow trout, and a strong run of summer steelhead. Other large-trout stream fisheries include the Metolius and Crooked rivers.

Reservoirs on the Deschutes (Crane Prairie and Wickiup) offer additional opportunities for superior trout fishing, as do the big natural lakes of Central Oregon's high desert plateau (Crescent, Cultus, Davis, East, Elk, Hosmer, Lava, Odell, and Paulina). Big lake trout, and tasty land-locked salmon (sockeye, coho, and Atlantic) are also available in many of the area's lakes.

Warmwater fishing can be found in the string of productive ponds and sloughs along the Columbia River between Hood River and The Dalles. Good catches of smallmouth bass are made in Lake Billy Chinook and Lake Simtustus, and largemouth are plentiful in Crane Prairie and Pine Hollow reservoirs. Lake Celilo, one of two Columbia River impoundments in this zone, offers a growing fishery for large walleye.

Highways 26 and 97 provide primary access to the region, with additional paved primary roads leading in from the mid-Willamette valley. Paved or graded two-lane secondary roads lead to most of the big lakes. Most river roads are unpaved but graded. Steep ungraded roads connect basins and lead to smaller lakes, streams, and trailheads.

Access to Central Zone fisheries includes an excellent network of trails. Trails are well-signed both at their head and in the back-country. Three Sisters Wilderness, Diamond Peak Wilderness, and the newly designated Paulina National Monument are all here.

The Central Zone encompasses a generous amount of publicly owned land, including much of the Deschutes and Ochoco national forests, and BLM holdings along the Deschutes and Crooked rivers.

Well-maintained campgrounds are plentiful around the big lakes and reservoirs and along most rivers. Primitive campsites are available in the backcountry, and any piece of off-road public land (unless specifically designated to the contrary) may be used for overnight stays.

The community of Bend offers the most complete and sophisticated services and accomodations for visiting anglers. Sisters, Camp Sherman, Redmond, Prineville, Madras, Maupin, and Warm Springs also serve fishing visitors. Many of the big lakes of Central Oregon have one or more resorts on their shore. As elsewhere in the state, these are mostly pleasant and comfortable, but modest establishments.

This is high country, with serious winters and cool evenings even in summer. The climate is considerably dryer than on the west side of the Cascades, but a good snowpack accumulates and lingers in the back country well into June.

ALLEN CREEK RESERVOIR A large hike-in lake with good views of the Ochocos, in the NW corner of Summit Prairie. A mix of BLM and private ranchland surrounds the 200-acre reservoir, which offers good fishing for 6-12 inch redband trout. The road into the lake is currently closed to motor vehicles. It is about a 1 1/2 mile hike from the parking area.

To negotiate the spur roads that lead to the reservoir you will need an Ochoco National Forest map. From Prineville, follow Hwy. 26 east about 7 miles beyond Ochoco Reservoir, then take County Rd. 23. At the Ranger Station, this road becomes Forest Rd. 22, which leads to Walton Lake. About 2/3 mile beyond Walton, where the road degenerates, take a sharp right heading south, and get out your forest map. Allen is about 9 miles from this point.

This is a remote spot with no facilities. Allen Creek Campground is nearby.

ANTELOPE FLAT RESERVOIR A medium size reservoir in the Maury Mt. area of Ochoco National Forest, 30 air miles SE of Prineville. From Prineville take the highway toward Paulina, turning south onto Forest Rd. 17 about 8 miles east of the community of Post. The reservoir is about 9 miles south at the head of Bear Creek, about 2 miles beyond Pine Creek Campground. It is wheelchair accessible.

Antelope covers about 170 acres when full, but is sometimes heavily drawn down. During the extreme low-water years of 1987-92, the reservoir was drawn down to 40 acres, its dead storage level, leaving its trout vulnerable to the harsh winter of 1992. All the fish were lost. A desert reservoir, Antelope is known for growing large trout quickly. The reservoir was restocked in 1993, and fish to 18 inches were available by the end of the season. Unusually high growth rates for the new population are anticipated through 1995. Under ordinary conditions, the average trout at Antelope is about 12 inches, with 18 inchers not uncommon. Through 1995, anglers can anticipate a higher percentage of large trout.

The single campground at Antelope Flat is one of the largest in Ochoco National Forest. Set amongst the pines above the reservoir, it offers picnic tables, fire rings, and out houses, but no water. Camp and boat ramp are at the west end of the reservoir. There are additional campgrounds north at Elk Horn and east at Double Cabin and Wiley Flat.

Antelope Flat is in a big game winter range area. Anglers are urged to be respectful of elk and mule deer, and of adjacent private property in order to keep access open to the public. The reservoir is currently open for year-round angling, and winter fishing can be good in dry years. The road in is not plowed, however, so in normal years access is limited to snowmobiles and skis.

BADGER CREEK A nice trout stream in the White River system, featuring a unique strain of rainbow trout. The creek flows out of Badger Lake on the SE slope of Mt. Hood, entering Tygh Creek one mile west of the town of Tygh Valley. Tygh Creek empties into White River 3 miles to the east. A falls about 3 miles above the mouth of Badger keeps the creek's rainbow isolated.

About 25 miles long, Badger is accessible by road throughout its lower half. It is crossed by Hwy. 197 at Tygh Valley, and by secondary roads and Forest Rd. 47 east of Tygh Valley. The upper 10 miles is reached by road only at Bonney Crossing Campground and at Badger Lake. A good trail follows the stream through this section.

Bait or spinner and lures will take fish early, and flies do well in summer and fall. A little hiking can result in good fishing. There are campgrounds at Bonney Crossing and at Little Badger Creek. Forest Rd. 2710 connects the two camps.

BADGER LAKE A good rainbow trout lake on the lower SE slope of Mt. Hood, accessible by car. From Portland follow Hwy. 26 east 58 miles, then Hwy. 35 (the Mt. Hood Loop Road) to Bennett Pass. Take Forest Rd. 3550 SE to Camp Windy. Turn east on Forest Rd. 4860 then north on Forest Rd. 140 to the lake. Watch for signs. Check with the Forest Service for road conditions. This route is usually inaccessible until late June. Two other routes generally clear 2 weeks earlier. From the east, heading into the forest from Wamic, follow the road toward Rock Creek Reservoir, turning south on Forest Rd. 48 before reaching Rock Creek. Take the Forest Rd. 4860 cut-off, heading north to Badger. To reach the lake from the south, take Hwy. 26, Hwy. 216, then a network of forest roads. A navigator with a Mt. Hood Forest map is essential for this one.

Badger is stocked with rainbow, and has wild brook trout to 14 inches. Average catch size is 10 inches. There's fair fishing on bait or troll in early summer. Fly-fishing is the best technique in fall, and the fish are larger. There's a good camp at the lake. The Badger Lake Rd. is one-lane with no turn-outs. Trailers are prohibited from using the road, and. no motors are allowed on the lake.

BAKEOVEN CREEK A small stream entering the Deschutes River just below Maupin, where Hwy. 197 crosses the river. The lower stretch usually contains some nice fish early in the year. The upper stream is accessible from highways 97 and 197. The lower stream is reached by the Eastside Deschutes Rd. Deep Creek, a tributary, also provides some good early fishing. A road follows Bakeoven a short way from the mouth. The stream gets dry in summer and fall, but in spring, rainbow to 15 inches can be taken on bait or spinner combinations.

Bakeoven flows through mostly private land, and permission to cross private land should be secured. A note on the distinctive name of this creek and other features and sites in the area: according to Lewis McArthur, the name Bakeoven derives from an incident in 1862, during Canyon City gold days. A Dalles trader with a pack train of flour was ambushed by Indians in the night. They drove off his horses but left his supplies. He built a rough oven of clay and stone on the spot, made bread, and sold it to the miners. The abandoned oven remained on the site for years.

BAKER POND A 4-acre pond 2 miles south of Bend in the Deschutes River

The descent to Lake Billy Chinook is about 700 ft.

Kokanee are the major fishery in Billy Chinook.

Woods subdivision. Currently closed to private access.

BIBBY LAKE A 16-acre reservoir west of Hwy. 97 at Kent, in Sherman County. It is used chiefly for irrigation and is fairly shallow, except near the dam face. Bibby supported an unproductive fishery for brown bullhead until 1991, when the lake was chemically treated and re-stocked with rainbow trout. Rainbow to 14 inches are now available.

A tributary of Buck Hollow Creek flows into the reservoir in winter only. Motor boats are allowed for transportation only. Regulations require anglers to shut off their boat motors while fishing. There is a day-use area at the reservoir, but no campground or water.

BIG FINGER LAKE A 5-acre alpine lake in the Deschutes National Forest, off the beaten path and lightly fished. Only 16 feet deep, it is air stocked with brook trout and sometimes winterkills. There are lots of fallen logs around the shoal area. To reach it from the Mink Lake Basin, head SE toward Cultus Lake by way of Trail 33 to Snowshoe Lake. From the west end of Cultus, head NW on Trail 16, cutting north on Trail 33 past Winopee Lake to Snowshoe. See Cultus for complete directions. Big Finger is 1/4 mile east of Snowshoe Lake. There is no trail between them. Little Finger Lake, about 2 acres, is another 1/4 mile east.

BIG HOUSTON LAKE An 88-acre lake near Powell Butte, privately owned with no public access. It contains largemouth bass, bluegill, brown bullhead, and channel catfish.

BIG MARSH CREEK A nice wild trout stream and wetland in south central Oregon SE of Crescent Lake, which is being restored through the efforts of public and private groups. It joins Crescent Creek just south of Hwy. 58, 14 miles NW of the junction of highways 58 and 97. Forest Rd. 5825, which heads SW from Hwy. 58 just south of Odell Butte, follows the stream's marshy headwaters. Forest Rd. 6020 crosses it east of the railroad crossing at Umli.

The upper creek runs through a large marsh, making the main channel hard to find in places. The stream is not stocked, but has predominantly brook trout and a good supply of brown trout. Don't expect to catch big the fish up here, but it's a pleasant stream.

The main fishery is in the meadow, where restoration efforts have been focused. The meadow has been closed to cattle grazing, the man-made canals have been blocked, and the stream is now flowing in its original channel. Willows are returning streamside, and beaver are making a comeback. It is anticipated that fishing will continue to improve.

There is also nice fishing above and below the marsh, including 1 1/2 miles of good dry fly water between the marsh and the railroad trestle, with lots of beaver ponding (watch for bank holes). The water below the trestle is good but brushy. This stream is in best shape between May and July, after which the water warms and fishing drops off.

BIKINI POND One of the I-84 ponds adjacent to the Columbia River, located at hwy. mi. 75.7. Covering 4 acres, it is immediately west of Mayer State Park's access road, between the railroad and the river. Access is from Exit 76. It may contain any of the Columbia River warmwater species. See p. 206 for Columbia River Ponds map.

BILLY CHINOOK RESERVOIR (a.k.a. Lake Billy Chinook) A large reservoir, partially administered by Confederated Tribes Warm Springs, in the scenic high desert canyon country east of the Cascades, about 8 miles SW of Madras. Created by Round Butte Dam on the Deschutes River, it covers over 6 square miles and backs up three major Oregon rivers—the Deschutes, Metolius and Crooked. Long arms of slack water reach up each stream. The fishery on the Metolius Arm is administered by CTWS. The dam itself is operated by Portland General Electric.

The major fishery here is kokanee, but trout (brown, redband, and bull) make up a portion of the catch. A good population of smallmouth bass and a much smaller number of largemouth are well established, though the bass do not grow to great size here. A few landlocked chinook are also present, but few are taken.

To reach Billy Chinook from Madras, drive south on Hwy. 97. Near Culver take the road west to Cove Palisades State Park. The route is well signed. The descent to the lake is about 700 ft. From Sisters, follow Forest Rd. 63.

Kokanee are thriving in Billy Chinook. In fact, overpopulation has lead to a drop in average size and a bonus bag limit of 25 fish per day. Kokanee are caught throughout the reservoir much of the year, with best fishing in late spring (May and early June) and again in August and early September when kokanee return to the tributaries to spawn.

The most popular kokanee fisheries are at the confluence of the Crooked and Deschutes rivers, and around Chinook Island in the lower Metolius Arm in midsummer. In late August and early September kokanee begin schooling in the upper reaches of the tributaries, with the Metolius Arm turning in the greatest number of catches. (Kokanee in spawning condition are best eaten smoked). Angling methods include trolling flashers (the Ford Fender has been popular), and jigging in late summer with white corn and grubs. From mid-season through October, anglers find kokanee at deeper levels.

Billy Chinook is the only place in Oregon with a trophy fishery for bull trout. Elsewhere in the state, bull trout must be released unharmed. Bulls to 20 lbs. are in the reservoir, and anglers are encouraged to release all bull trout less than 24 inches. (Size limits may be instituted, but are not currently in effect). There is a one-fish bag limit. Good size bull trout are hooked in the upper end of the Metolius Arm along with an occasional brown trout. The state record bull trout was caught here in 1988, weighing 20 pounds 8 ounces.

To fish for the big bulls and browns, anglers commonly troll large lures that imitate the movement of crippled fish. Best fishing is along the shoreline in spring. Anglers catching tagged bull trout are asked to return the tag along

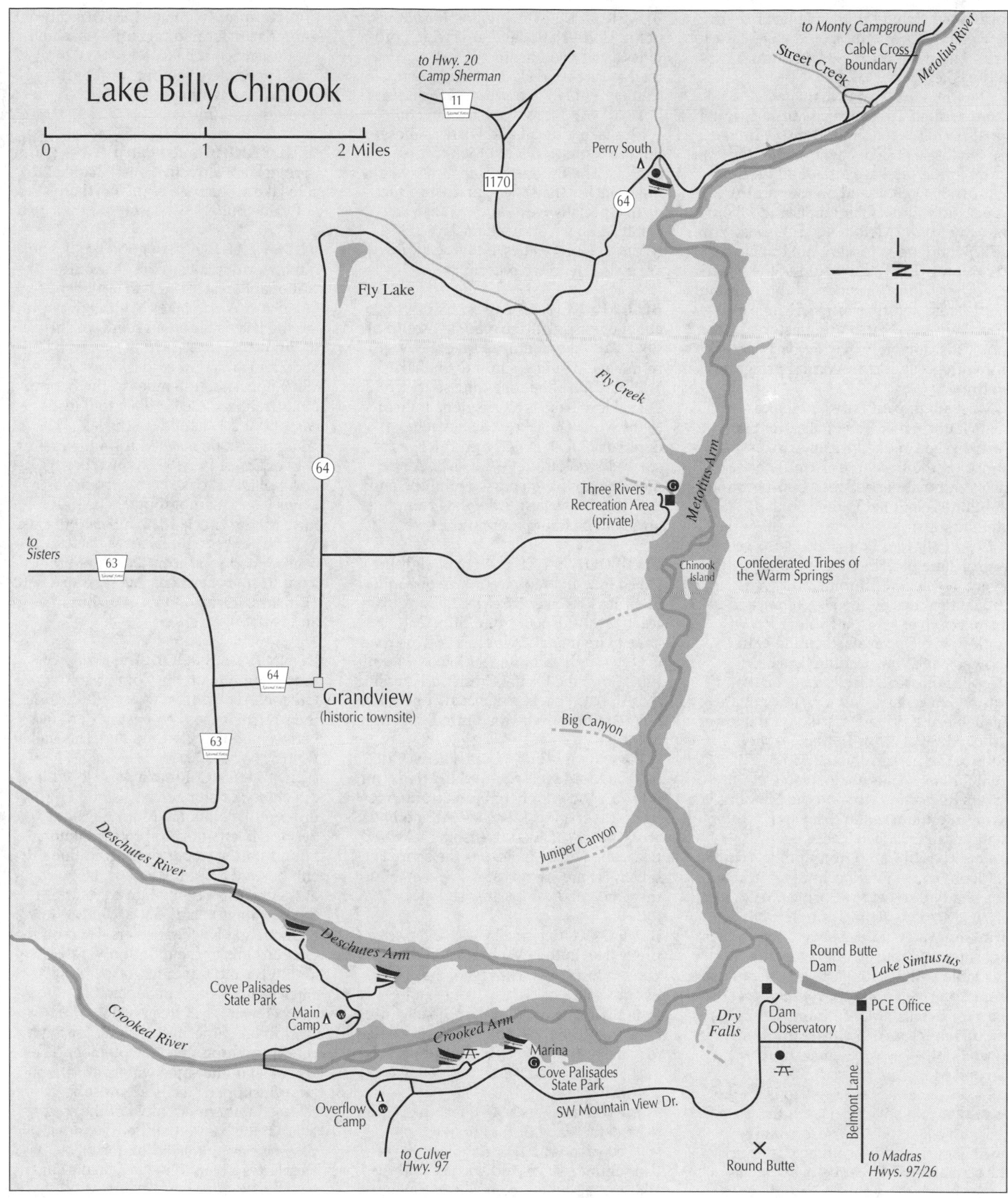

with date caught, location, and length to the Oregon Dept. of Fish and Wildlife office in Prineville. The best trout habitat on the lake is upstream from the Island in the Metolius Arm. The Deschutes and Crooked River arms are open throughout the year, and anglers occasionally hook good size bull trout in mid-winter. The Metolius Arm opens March 1. When the surface water temperature hits 55 degrees, bull trout go deep, and smallmouth bass may be found in the habitat vacated by the bulls.

Smallmouth bass are caught near the shore after the water warms, especially in the upper reaches of the Deschutes and Crooked River arms (be aware of a speed limit above the bridges in both arms). Some anglers troll for bass, but most cast plugs and lures toward the rocks. There is some bank angling opportunity for bass in the vicinity of the picnic area and between the boat ramps on the Deschutes Arm. There are very few largemouth bass in the lake.

The Metolius Arm is managed by Confederated Tribes Warm Springs, and a tribal permit is required. Daily permits are modestly priced, cover fishing for the entire family, and are also valid on Lake Simtustus. Do not land on the (north) reservation shore. Chinook Island (about midway up the Metolius Arm) is also CTWS land, open for day use but closed to camping. Permits are sold at the general store in Camp Sherman, at the sporting goods store and fly shop in Sisters, at Cove Palisades State Park, in stores at the top of the canyon above the park, and from other vendors in Warm Springs and Madras.

Most angling on Billy Chinook is from boats launched at Cove Palisades State Park on the Crooked River Arm, and at ramps on the Deschutes Arm. There is also a ramp at Perry South Campground, Deschutes National Forest, on the Metolius Arm.

Cove Palisades State Park is the second largest state park in Oregon. It has extensively developed camping and recreational facilities on the Deschutes and Crooked River arms, including R.V. hook-ups, picnic areas, running water, showers, and a swimming beach. Supplies (grocery, tackle, gas), boat and equipment rentals, and a restaurant are available at a private marina on the lower Crooked River Arm. To make reservations at the park, call (503) 546-3412. Rental house boats are available at Three Rivers Recreation Area on the Metolius Arm (minimum rental 3 days). For information call (503) 546-2939.

Perry South Campground in Deschutes National Forest offers primitive camping in a shady draw at the Spring Creek inlet on the Metolius Arm. Though it has no drinking water, it does have picnic tables, fire rings, outhouses, and a serenity not available at the State Park. Best access is from Camp Sherman or from Sisters (See map for details). Monty Campground is about 5 miles further upstream from Perry South. The road ends shortly beyond Monty.

Lake Chinook State Airstrip is on the west plateau above the Deschutes Arm. This is a 5,000 foot dirt strip running north/south within walking distance of the arm about 700 feet below. Watch out for strong drafts from the canyon in the afternoon.

BINGHAM LAKES (Klamath Co.) A series of three hike-in lakes 2 miles south of Crescent Lake. There are no fish in the lakes at this time.

BLACK LAKE A 4-acre brook trout lake in Mt. Hood National Forest which provides some good fishing. It's about 18 road miles SW of Hood River, one mile south of Rainy Lake, west off the Rainy Lake Rd. See Rainy Lake for directions.

This lake is small and fairly shallow but has some excellent brook trout angling. The fish are 7-14 inches, averaging 10 inches. Bait will usually produce well, especially early, and spinner-bait combinations work well for large fish if retrieved slowly. Flies, either wet or dry, are good late in the season.

BLOW LAKE A 45-acre brook trout lake about one mile off the road just south of Elk Lake. Take Century Drive (Hwy. 46) from Bend 37 miles south to Six Lakes Trailhead 14, about one mile south of Elk Lake. Blow Lake is an easy one mile hike to the west. The lake, which reaches a depth of 23 feet, is fairly productive for stocked brook trout 9-12 inches. All methods can be effective, with June and the fall months best. Adequate camping areas can be found around the lake.

BLOWDOWN LAKE A small, lightly fished hike-in brook trout lake one mile SE of Taylor Lake. Take the Taylor Burn Rd. (Forest Rd. 600) from Little Cultus Lake to Irish and Taylor Lakes. This road is very rough and often snowbound until June. From the Pacific Crest Trail crossing at Irish Lake, backtrack exactly one mile. Hike south from the road uphill 1/4 mile to the lake.

Blowdown is only about 4 acres, but has produced well. Stocked lightly by air, it has a good supply of brook trout 8-14 inches, averaging 12 inches. All methods work, but it's a good fly-fishing lake. A float tube will be handy, as the shore is brushy. There are no campsites here, but there are good camps at Irish Lake.

BLUE LAKE (Jefferson Co.) A very deep, pretty lake in the Deschutes National Forest about 16 miles west of Sisters. It lies just south of Hwy. 20 and can be seen from the highway as you approach Suttle Lake from the west. Take the Suttle Lake turnoff south from Hwy. 20, and proceed past Suttle to road's end at Blue Lake Resort.

The lake is 65 acres, 300 feet deep, and extremely clear. Legal rainbow are stocked each year. Best fishing is in the late summer, since cold springs and the lake's great depth keep the trout inactive earlier in the season. Rainbow run 10-12 inches with a few larger. A few small kokanee are caught, primarily by trolling.

Part of the lake shore is privately leased, and there is a fee to launch a boat. Some angling can be done from shore, but it's not easy. The resort at the east end has supplies, boat rentals, and a campground. Two Forest Service campgrounds are located on Suttle Lake and another at Scout Lake, all within 2 miles. Ling Creek, between Blue and Suttle Lake, is a spawning area closed to angling at all times.

BLUE LAKE (Confederated Tribes Warm Springs) An attractive pear-shaped 26-acre lake at the base of the northern slope of Olallie Butte. It is closed to public use.

BOBBY LAKE A very good brook and rainbow trout lake in the Deschutes National Forest about half-way between Odell and Waldo lakes. Although popular, the lake is far enough into the brush to produce consistently. From Hwy. 58 take the Waldo Lake Rd. (Forest Rd. 5897) north about 6 miles to the Bobby Lake Trailhead (3663). This trail leads east about 2 1/2 miles to the lake. The lake can also be reached from the east by way of Forest Rd. 4652, which begins just north of Davis Lake across from North Davis Creek Campground. The trail follows Moore Creek 4 1/2 miles to the lake.

Bobby Lake, with 85 acres, has always been a good producer. There are brook trout to 16 inches here. Average size is 10-11 inches. It's a good fly lake, but lures and bait will work.

BONNEVILLE POOL The lowest of four reservoirs on the Columbia River in Oregon. About 20 miles long, it includes the stretch of the river east of Portland between Bonneville Dam and The Dalles Dam.

In 1994, the Columbia was closed to fall chinook fishing in this stretch by order of the National Marine Fishery Service, in an effort to protect salmon bound for the upper river. Traditionally, chinook have been fished in the plumes at the mouths of the main tributaries on the Washington side—the Wind, White Salmon, and Klickitat rivers—and on the Oregon side, at the mouth of Eagle Creek and in the old Cascade Locks. Most catches were made in September.

Steelhead reach this portion of the river in late June, and angling for them continues through late September. They are taken in the same waters as salmon. Non-finclipped steelhead must be released unharmed. Most of the steelhead in this section of the river are just passing through, heading for the Deschutes River, John Day, Snake, and Eastern Washington streams.

Sturgeon are fished from boat and bank in the pool. Favorite boat fisheries are between Cascade Locks and Stevenson WA, at the Dalles below the Interstate Bridge, and in a few scattered areas throughout the pool. Bank anglers fish from rocky points off I-84 where there are safe pull-offs on the highway shoulder. To avoid hooking oversize sturgeon, anglers should use lighter line, and smaller hooks and bait.

Walleye anglers concentrate below the Interstate Bridge at The Dalles, above Hood River Bridge near the Washington shore (you don't need a Washington license), and in the Rowena area just west of The Dalles. Launch at Mayer State Park.

Shad are fished primarily in the area below the Interstate Bridge in May and early June. Most bass and panfish in this stretch of the Columbia are caught in ponds adjacent to the river. See Appendix for a map of Columbia River ponds from Hood River to the Deschutes.

The Columbia is accessible from shore in many places throughout this section, but parking can be a problem due to the divided highway. Parking on the shoulder of I-84 is discouraged except in emergency situations. Alternative parking suggestions are included in the Columbia Ponds write-up. Public boat ramps are available at the Port of Cascade Locks, Port of Hood River, Port of The Dalles, and at Mayer State Park. All ramps are concrete.

BOOTH LAKE A fair brook trout lake in the Mt. Jefferson Wilderness on the SE slope of Three Fingered Jack. Take the Pacific Crest Trail north from its crossing of Hwy. 20, one mile east of the Hoodoo Ski Bowl turnoff in the Santiam Pass area. A quarter mile north of the highway, Square Lake Trail 65 heads off to the east. Booth Lake is about 2 miles beyond and about 1 1/2 miles north of Square Lake to the left of the trail.

The lake is about 8 acres and is usually accessible in June. Most of the fish are about 9 inches, with some to 12. An easy lake to fish.

BOULDER LAKE (Confederated Tribes Warm Springs) A good hike-in brook trout lake 1/2 mile south of Trout Lake on the west edge of Warm Springs Reservation. The lake is accessible only by unimproved trail which begins at the Trout Lake Rd., about 1/4 mile east of Trout Lake Campground.

Boulder is a round, 50-acre lake at elevation 4,780 ft. It has a maximum depth of 29 ft., with about a third of its area shoals. There are just under 2 miles of shoreline, most of which is quite brushy. The lake is aptly named for the very large boulders that cover most of its bottom. It produces plump brook trout. A permit is required and may be purchased at the market in Warm Springs. No overnight camping is allowed due to fire danger.

BOULDER LAKE (Wasco Co.) A fair rainbow trout lake in the Mt. Hood National Forest on the SE slope of Mt. Hood. It's about a half-mile hike to the lake from Bonney Camp, which is reached by 6 miles of poor road from Bennett Pass. The roads are usually snowbound until July. Approaches from the west are clear earlier.

Boulder Lake covers about 20 acres. A talus pile on the west side of the lake makes a good platform for fly-casting. The fish here don't get large, averaging 8 inches. Little Boulder Lake, about half as big, is a half-mile bushwhack SE and provides good angling for brook trout at times. Both lakes are stocked with fingerlings. There are natural campsites at Boulder Lake.

BRAHMA LAKE A nice 10-acre brook trout lake off the Pacific Crest Trail in the Deschutes National Forest, north of Irish and Taylor lakes. From the south on Hwy. 58, take the Davis Lake Rd. past Crane Prairie to Forest Rd. 600, which is intersected by the Pacific Crest Trail at Irish and Taylor Lakes. Brahma is an easy 2-mile hike north.

It offers good angling for brook trout to 15 inches. Average size is around 10 inches. Fly-fishing is good, as the lake is quite shallow. Wet bucktails fished with a slow retrieve can be effective. A few natural campsites are available. In early season the mosquitoes in this area are unbelievable. Be prepared. An army surplus mosquito helmet can be a godsend here.

BUTTON POND A one-acre pond associated with the Columbia River at hwy. mile 65 two miles east of Cascade Locks. It is immediately south of the freeway with limited vehicle parking on an unimproved road paralleling the freeway. Access is from exit 64. See map p. 206.

CABOT LAKE A small lake in the Mt. Jefferson Wilderness on the northern edge of the Deschutes National Forest. Six acres and shallow, it has had a tendency to winterkill. ODF&W is currently experimenting with a stocking of cutthroat trout.

CACHE LAKE A good fly-fishing lake which is trying to turn back into meadow in the Deschutes National Forest SW of Suttle Lake on the Jefferson-Deschutes County line. From Hwy. 20, 2 miles east of the Suttle Lake turn-off, follow Forest Rd. 2066 west 2 miles to Forest Rd. 2068, and continue west on 2068 a bit over 2 miles to a short spur which leads to the lake. Look for the spur just before the road makes a sharp hairpin east.

Cache Lake is just north of Cache Mountain. It's a shallow lake and offers excellent fly-fishing until weeds choke access in mid-summer. Fish size fluctuates from year to year, but brook trout average 10 inches and get as large as 15 inches. A few cutthroat of good size show up now and then. Cache is usually accessible in early summer. There is no campground. Motorboats are prohibited.

CARL LAKE A good size trout lake in the Metolius River watershed on the eastern edge of Mt. Jefferson Wilderness. From Hwy. 20 about one mile east of the Suttle Lake turn-off, take Forest Rd. 12 north about 4 miles to Forest Rd. 1230, which branches north at Jack Creek Campground. Follow 1230, the Abbot Butte Rd., 8 miles north to its end, where you will find Trailhead 68. The trail leads 2 miles west to Cabot Lake. Carl is about 2 miles beyond Cabot by way of Trail 68.

Carl is not a rich lake, and its population of stocked cutthroat average 9-11 inches. Brook trout are no longer being stocked, but a remnant may be available for a few more years. A long deep lake, it can be effectively fished using any technique.

CELILO, LAKE (a.k.a. The Dalles Pool) One of four power impoundments on the Columbia River east of Portland, offering the most productive angling of the four. Fairly shallow and only about 15 miles long, Lake Celilo offers good habitat for walleye, plentiful food sources for resident sturgeon, and features the powerful attraction of the Deschutes River mouth.

In 1994, the Columbia River was closed to fall chinook angling by order of the National Marine Fishery Service, in an effort to protect salmon bound for the upper river. Traditionally, there has been a popular chinook fishery immediately below the mouth of the Deschutes, where Deschutes salmon (as well as others) enjoy the cool water after their passage over The Dalles Dam. This is a boat fishery, with boats launched at Celilo Park downstream of the mouth, and at Heritage Landing just above the mouth on the Deschutes. Salmon are most abundant at the Deschutes mouth in August and September.

Angling for summer steelhead in Lake Celilo begins July 4th weekend, primarily at the mouth of the Deschutes. There is also a small bank fishery just below John Day Dam. All non-finclipped steelhead must be released unharmed.

Sturgeon are fished by boating anglers throughout the pool, and there is a very popular sturgeon bank fishery at French Giles Park below John Day Dam. About 50% of the sturgeon catch for all the reservoirs is made in Lake Celilo. To avoid hooking oversize sturgeon, use lighter line and smaller hooks and bait.

Walleye are a big fishery here year around. Mostly a boat show, the best catches are made at the mouth of the Deschutes, and around Rufus up to the deadline below John Day Dam, a 3-4 mile stretch. There is a small bank fishery for walleye from French Giles Park below the dam down to the Rufus gravel pits.

Shad are taken at French Giles Park during June and early July. Most bass and panfish angling takes place in ponds adjacent to the river. See p. 206 for a map of Columbia River ponds from Cascade Locks to the Deschutes. Bass and panfish are also fished in the Rufus gravel pit complex, a network of sloughs and ponds where anglers can walk out on the flats at low tide from access roads off French Giles Park.

CHARLTON LAKE A large brook trout lake on the Pacific Crest Trail 2 miles east of Waldo Lake. Best reached by the Waldo Lake Rd. (Forest Rd. 5897), a paved road leading north from Hwy. 58 about 3 miles west of Odell Lake. Near the north end of Waldo Lake, the road turns sharply to the east and gives way to gravel. This is easy to miss, as a paved road continues north to North Waldo Lake Campground. The 1/4 mile trail into the lake is within one mile of the transition to gravel.

Charlton is big, and sometimes the fish are hard to find. Watch out for rough water during the day. Brook trout here average 10-12 inches with some to 16 inches. Spinners or lures do well, but fly-angling will out-fish both in fall. Peak fishing is just after ice-out and late in the season. The former is hard to catch, as snow often blocks the roads. There are excellent blueberries around the lake in late summer and some improved campsites. Motorboats are prohibited.

CHENOWETH CREEK A small, lightly fished stream about 10 miles long, entering the Columbia at the west end of The Dalles. It is followed by gravel road west to the headwaters. Not stocked, it offers fair cutthroat fishing in late fall and early spring. Bait angling or spinner/bait combinations work well. There's a lot of private property, so ask permission to fish.

CLEAR CREEK (Wasco Co.) A fair trout stream flowing from Clear Lake east into the White River in Mt. Hood National Forest. The creek is crossed by Hwy. 26 about 14 miles SE of Government Camp. Several forest roads follow and cross the stream as well.

Clear Creek is not stocked but has good populations of rainbow and brook trout, some from Clear Lake. Fishing is usually good from early season through the summer in the upper section. Irrigation water is diverted from the lower stream. Bait is usually most effective for fish 7-12 inches. A small portion of the creek is on Warm Springs Reservation land and is signed to that effect.

CLEAR LAKE (Wasco Co.) A good trout lake in Mt. Hood National Forest, drained by Clear Creek of the White River system on the east side of the Cascade Range. The lake is 67 miles from Portland by Hwy. 26. Turn off at a well signed intersection to the right, about 11 miles past Government Camp. It's a short mile to the lake. A good road follows the lake shore about half-way around it.

Clear Lake covers just under a square mile most of the season, but is heavily drawn down for irrigation by fall. Stocked rainbow trout supplement the lake's self-sustaining population of brook trout. Rainbow outnumber the brook trout about 5 to 1 in the catch. Both species average 8-12 inches, with some fish to 18 inches. Trolling and bait fishing are popular, and flies are good early and late in the day. Crawfish are abundant. Poor snow packs in recent years may have been hard on the fishery.

There is a nice campground with boat ramp on the east shore of the lake. When the reservoir is low, the ramp is only usable by smaller boats.

CLIFF LAKE (Wasco Co.) An I-84 pond adjacent to the Columbia River, located at hwy. mi. 74.6. Only one acre, it is immediately east of McClures Lake south of the freeway. There is limited unimproved parking for eastbound traffic only at the east end of the lake. The pond may contain any of the Columbia River warmwater species. See p. 206 for map of Columbia River Ponds.

CODY PONDS Three small ponds west of Tygh Valley offering bass and panfish. From Hwy. 197 south of the Dalles, head west 5 miles to the community of Wamic. From there continue west 4 miles on Rock Creek Reservoir Rd. Between 2 small ponds on the right, a road turns north. Follow this a short way to the first 5-acre pond. For the second pond, stay on the main road to Rock Creek Reservoir, and head north on Forest Rd. 466. After one mile, turn right to the pond, which covers 6 acres. The third, covering 5 acres, is on the north edge of the Reservoir road, about 1 1/2 miles from Rock Creek.

The ponds are all on ODF&W land, but the second has only a 10-foot public easement around the shore. All are shallow, with good populations of bluegill and bass. The bass are rather small, with an occasional 16-inch fish tops. A rubber boat or float tube would be handy on the lakes, but they're easily fished from shore. There are no facilities here, but there's a campground at Rock Creek Reservoir. Recommended for small fry.

CRANE PRAIRIE RESERVOIR A large, very rich reservoir fed by the waters of the upper Deschutes River. Beautiful and productive for large rainbow, brooktrout, and largemouth bass, it is one of Oregon's premier fisheries. Relatively shallow water, abundant cover, and dense insect populations make this a fly angler's paradise. It covers over 5 square miles, with many interesting arms and bays, historically maintaining a fairly constant water level.

When Crane Prairie was flooded in 1920, most of its timber was left standing. Though many of the old stands have deteriorated, silver skeletons of the old forest still rise from the water, their bark long since weathered away. The fallen timber forms intricate and extensive log jams. Approximately ten percent of the lake is covered by these stands, which provide excellent fish habitat and, with the bottom ooze and pond weed, produce an endless supply of damselflies, mayflies, leeches, and other trout delights. Average depth of the reservoir is 11 ft. at full pool, and maximum depth in the old river channels is 20 ft.

Crane Prairie is a Wildlife Management Area. Osprey, Canadian geese, great numbers of assorted ducks, grebes, blue heron, bald eagles, and an occasional sandhill crane are among the many birds that frequent the area. The osprey and eagles nest in the snag forests and do their own share of fishing with consummate skill. Deer, elk, mink, porcupine, and otter can be seen at the water's edge.

Crane Prairie is just east of Century Drive about 46 miles from Bend, a beautiful drive on paved road past other fine Cascade lakes. Alternately, one can drive south from Bend about 18 miles on Hwy. 97 to County Rd. 42, Fall River Hwy. Turn off 2 1/2 miles past the Sunriver junction, and continue west approximately 20 miles to Forest Rd. 4270, which is signed for Crane Prairie. Turn right. It is only 4 miles to the east side of the lake. From the Willamette Valley, Eugene offers good access by way of Hwy. 58 to the Davis Lake cutoff (Hwy. 61), which is 3 miles south of the Crescent Lake junction. Take Hwy. 46 north past Davis Lake to the junction with Hwy. 42. Here one may go east to reach Crane Prairie's eastern shore, or proceed north to the campground on the west or the resort on the north shore.

The reservoir offers excellent angling for both amateurs and experts. These waters are very rich, and trout put on poundage quickly here. In good years, trout average 12 inches, with many big fish taken daily. Rainbow to 18 3/4 pounds and brook trout to 6 pounds have been landed. Five pounders don't even raise eyebrows at the resort.

Crane Prairie offers outstanding conditions for all types of trout angling, and

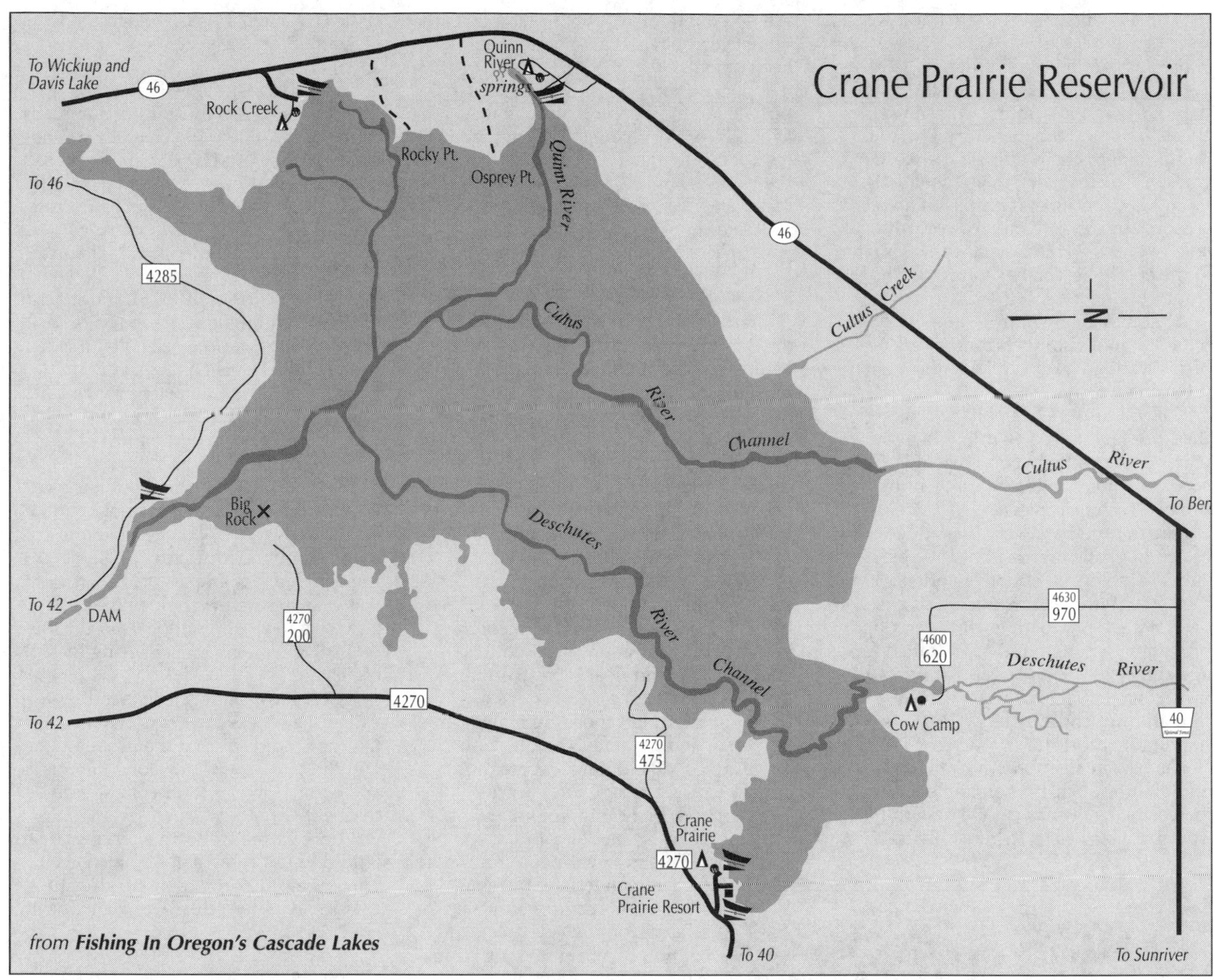

from **Fishing In Oregon's Cascade Lakes**

two or three methods may be producing fish at the same time. In early season, before weed growth is excessive, many large rainbow are taken on trolled woolly worms or big streamers, including some developed especially for Crane Prairie (available at the resort store and at area fly shops).

Dry and wet fly anglers do well with*Callibaetis*, damselfly, midge, leech, caddis, and scud imitations. Callibaetis hatch from late spring through summer, gradually diminishing in size. Damsel nymphs are especially effective in late June and July. Midges are a good choice in September and October.

Trout of all sizes may be taken with a variety of bait (either fishing from the bottom up in less timbered areas, or with a bobber). Live dragonfly nymphs are a favorite for still-fishing, using a bobber or quill float to detect the soft bite. Power Bait and nightcrawlers are also popular. Spin anglers favor Panther Martins, Kwikfish, Roostertails, and spinner and worm combinations. Check in at the resort store for advice on tackle and hot spots.

In spring and early summer and when the reservoir is high, fish the area close to shore and among the submerged trees. As the water lowers, head for the channels. Early in the summer you can sometimes locate the channels by sight, but a depth finder is helpful once the weeds thicken. The biggest fish are usually landed in May and June, but there is no off-season here. In 1994 the reservoir did get so low that the lake was closed to angling at the end of September to protect the trout from over-fishing.

Although Crane Prairie rainbow dominate the trout fishing, fair numbers of brook trout are also available throughout the reservoir.

Kokanee are well established, though their population grows thin when low water prevents them from reaching their spawning areas in the Quinn, Cultus, and upper Deschutes rivers.

Largemouth bass were illegally introduced in Crane Prairie about 10 years ago. Illegal introductions are often a biological nightmare, introducing disease, or destroying a productive fishery through predation or competition for limited forage and space. So far, Crane Prairie's trout seem to be holding their own, though trout anglers and ODF&W are holding their breath.

The bass are thriving in Crane Prairie, and their popularity with anglers is increasing as the bass move toward trophy size. Catches have generally been in the 4-5 pound range, but 7-pound fish are not uncommon, and a 9-pounder has been caught.

In low water years bass are spread throughout the reservoir, though they avoid the cooler channels. When the reservoir is higher, they generally favor the very shallow eastern shore and its backwater. Bass are also found near the southern shore and along the dam. Top water plugs, such as the Rappala or Rebel, (favored in silver or gold with a black back) are popular

Crane Prairie is so large it can be a bit overwhelming at first, but likely looking habitat is more obvious here than at most big lakes. Fishing near concentrations of other boats is an acceptable scouting tactic, though be sure to position yourself a generous cast away from the casting range of others . Fishing guides are available through fly and tackle shops throughout Central Oregon and at the resort on the north shore.

Because the locus of action on the reservoir shifts frequently, it is best fished by boat. Trolling, however, is rarely the best method. A 10-mph speed limit is in effect. Canoes and float tubes work fine, but be sure to keep a weather eye out. Boats, motors, and canoes are rented at the resort, and gasoline is available there. There are good boat ramps at the resort, at Rock Creek. and at Quinn River Campground. The campground just south of the resort has 2 boat ramps.

Crescent Lake grows Mackinaw trout to 33 pounds.

There is a very poor ramp (not recommended) by the dam. There are 4 campgrounds on the reservoir. Rock Creek and Quinn River campgrounds on the west shore are large and have boat ramps. The campground just south of the resort is like a small city, with 140 spaces. The campground at Cow Meadow on the north shore is very small. The road into this is a bit rough, and there is no ramp, though you can slip in a shallow draft cartopper or canoe. A campground shows up on the forest map at the dam, but there are no developed sites there. All these camping areas get crowded on weekends and holidays, and individual sites are not very secluded. Cow Meadow sometimes offers the best bet for solitude. For more information, see *Fishing In Oregon's Cascade Lakes.*

CRESCENT CREEK A fair trout stream which meanders 40 fishing miles through Deschutes National Forest from Crescent Lake to the Little Deschutes River. Though moderately swift, it's an easy stream to fish using any method.

Crescent Creek flows east out of Crescent Lake and away from any roads for its first 2 miles. The creek then swings south, paralleling Hwy. 58 for about 3 miles, where it flows through mostly private land. It then turns east again, crossing and leaving Hwy. 58, entering a steep valley in the Deschutes National Forest. Within the forest the creek is followed from above by Forest Rd. 61, the shortcut to Lapine and main route to Davis Lake. Crescent Creek is intersected by this road just past the Davis Lake turn-off and trends east through mostly private land until it joins the Little Deschutes River about 5 miles north of the town of Crescent on Hwy. 97.

The creek is not stocked but has nice populations of brown and rainbow trout. The browns run 8-14 inches and are found throughout the stream. Rainbow run a bit smaller. In past years, Crescent was known to grow some of the largest browns and stream rainbows in the forest. Anglers are no longer seeing these big fish.

Best fishing on the creek is in the steep valley. It isn't easy to get down there, and the bank is brushy, but the fish are there. You can park anywhere along the road and climb down, or bull your way in from either road crossing. Fly angling wet or dry can be effective. Evening fishing is red hot when a good hatch is on. There is a campground at the stream crossing on Forest Rd. 61, and lodging on Hwy. 58.

CRESCENT LAKE (Klamath Co.) A large deep lake in the Deschutes National Forest, 3 miles south of Odell Lake, offering fair fishing for hefty Mackinaw, brown trout, and rainbow, as well as kokanee and whitefish. Just under 6 square miles, with a depth of 280 ft., it's a popular general recreation area, with clear sparkling water and miles of wooded shoreline.

Crescent Lake is about 75 miles SE of Eugene by Hwy. 58, about 18 miles NW of the junction of highways 58 and 97. A small community, Crescent Lake Junction, is on Hwy. 58 at the turnoff to the lake, Forest Rd. 60. The forest road reaches the lake in about 2 miles and hugs the western and southern shore for about 5 miles. Forest Rd. 6015 follows the eastern shore.

This big, deep lake grows big, deep-bodied lake trout from 5-10 pounds, with some over 20 pounds occasionally landed. A 33-pound Mackinaw was landed in 1993.

Ice-out finds the big trout cruising the shallows, and anglers have good success casting spoons from shore, particularly in the Simax Beach area on the NE side of the lake. Fly anglers participate in the action at this time of year using big leach patterns and dragonfly nymphs. The trick is spotting the fish and casting directly to them. Wearing polaroid glasses helps.

By July, the Mackinaw begin to school and are running in deep water. Deep trolling with downriggers and lead line along the summer home area (NW shore), and along the ledges off Spring and Contorta Point campgrounds (southern shore), is often productive. A depth finder is useful to locate the ledges. If you don't have one, the area offshore from the scout camp, one mile east of Contorta Point, has a straight ledge at 80 feet that is easy to track. Trollers favor lures that resemble kokanee, the Mack's favorite forage. Kwikfish-type lures or fish-imitation plugs like the Rebels or Rappala are effective. Fly anglers use big streamers. In spring and fall, trollers often work at depths of 20-30 ft. In summer, they go deeper.

A big lead jig, like the Luhr Jensen Nordic, might be effective here, as they have been at nearby Odell. With these jigs, anglers can avoid all the special downrigging gear. The only catch is, of course, being (and knowing you be) directly over the fish in order to get results.

Kokanee are the most popular fishery on the lake. Though less abundant in Crescent than in nearby Odell Lake, they tend to be larger. Fingerling kokanee are planted annually and generally grow to 13-14 inches, with some catches to 20 inches. Kokanee move in schools throughout the lake, ending their migration in fall at Crescent Creek near the resort. Check at the resort to learn where the schools have been located and at what depth to fish. Kokanee are generally taken by jigging, or by trolling spinner and bait. Light-weight gear with a downrigger offers the best sport. Dodgers and lake trolls are also popular, though they require a heavier rod and line and (consequently) a lighter touch in order to keep the hook from pulling out of the comparatively diminutive kokanee.

Brown trout continue to be stocked and grow to respectable size in Crescent. Fish to 12 pounds have been taken, though the catch has fallen off during the drought. Rainbow reproduce naturally here, and additional rainbow from the Deschutes hatchery are stocked each year. All angling methods are used, with good success near the creek inlets on the southern shore. Whitefish also show up in the catch. Some anglers regard them as a nuisance, but they make fine eating, especially if smoked. Bank angling opportunities are available on the northwest shore near the road, and near the west side campgrounds.

The Crooked River grows large trout.

Drought has hit Crescent's fisheries pretty hard. Though a natural lake, Crescent is heavily drawn down for irrigation. In recent years, kokanee have been unable to reach their spawning areas. Rainbow and brown trout habitat has been diminished. The Mackinaw catch rate is considerably lower than in pre-drought years.

Crescent Lake Resort is located at the northern tip of the lake. Rundown in recent years, it is scheduled for refurbishment by new management. In the past, the resort has provided boat rentals, supplies, cabins, and a snack bar. Supplies are also available on Hwy. 58 at Crescent Lake Junction.

There are three Forest Service campgrounds on the lake shore—Crescent Lake, Spring, and Contorta Point. Each has a boat ramp. Picnic facilities are available at Simax Beach, Tandy Bay, and Tranquil Cove. For more information, see *Fishing In Oregon's Cascade Lakes.*

CROOKED RIVER A large productive tributary of the Deschutes River, carving canyons through the central Oregon desert. The Crooked joins the Deschutes in Lake Billy Chinook. The North Fork heads in the Ochoco Mts. about 75 miles east of Prineville. The South Fork heads in the high desert NE of Brothers on the G.I. Ranch.

Spring fed, the north and south forks of the Crooked are consistently cool despite the desert heat, growing good size trout. The mainstem above Prineville Reservoir suffers from riparian degradation and heavy irrigation withdrawals. Trout survival in this section is poor during drought years.

The river above the reservoir is followed for some distance by the Post-Paulina Hwy. Below the reservoir, Hwy. 27 follows the river to Prineville.

Though much of the South Fork flows through BLM land, access is limited by private ranchland holdings. The only drive-in access is a rough road leading south about 4 miles east of the BLM office on the Post-Paulina Rd. The road shows up on the Ochoco National Forest Map. Driving toward Paulina (east) look for a small sign on the right. The road ends at a BLM site, known as Congleton Hollow, which offers river access and undeveloped campsites. The access is not named on Forest maps. For best fishing, head upstream about 2 miles. Most of the land along this stretch is managed by BLM.

The South Fork trout average 12-18 inches, and the river is capable of growing fingerlings to 10 inches in a single season. Fly-fishing is excellent in spring and fall. The South Fork is restricted to angling with artificial flies and lures. The fishery has been down in recent years as a result of the drought.

The North Fork also grows trout to good size. A rough road heading north off the Post-Paulina Rd. about 4 1/2 miles west of the BLM office leads to the only public access on the lower river. The upper Fork is approached by Forest Rd. 42 in the Ochoco National Forest west of Prineville. Follow Forest Rd. 42 to Deep Creek Campground, then get out your topo map. This stretch offers anglers a quality fishing experience, more for the

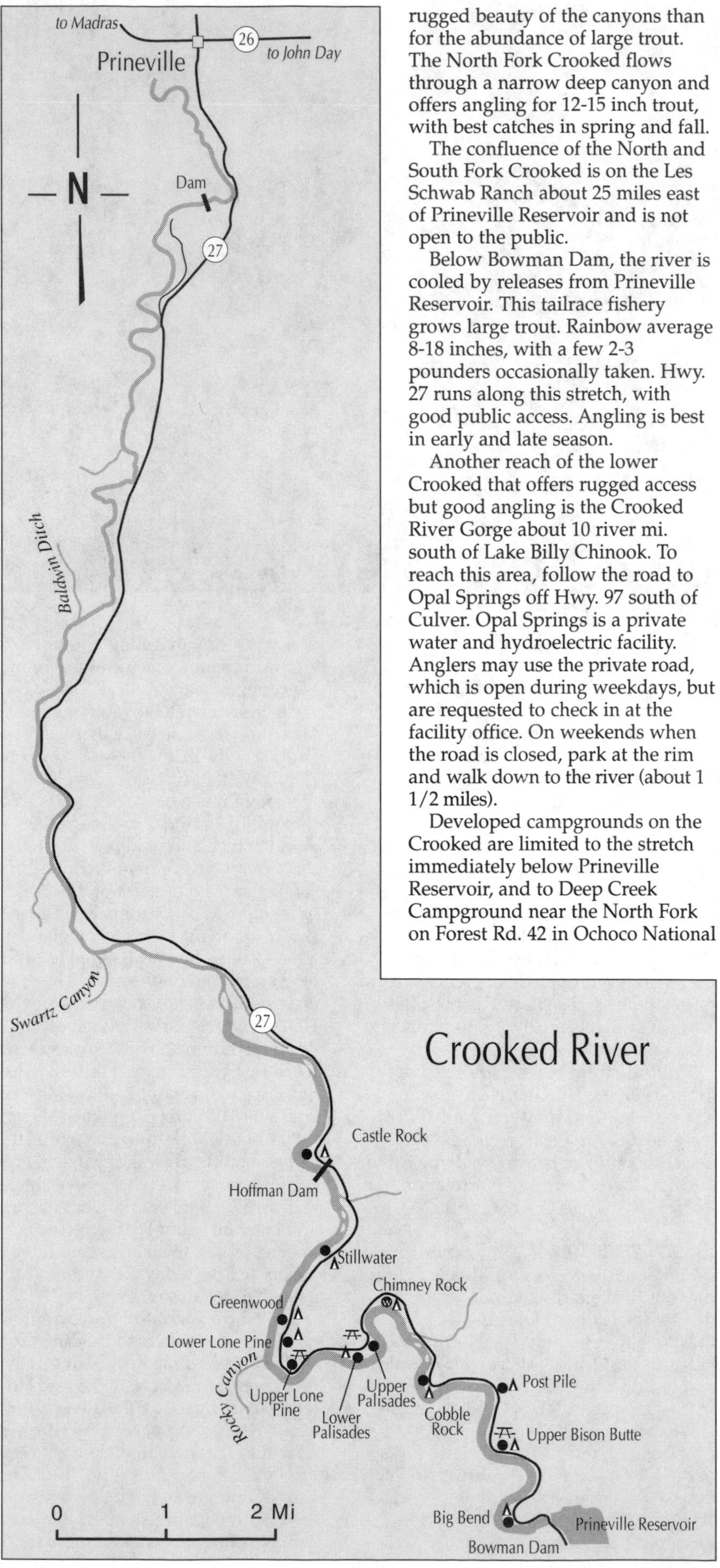

rugged beauty of the canyons than for the abundance of large trout. The North Fork Crooked flows through a narrow deep canyon and offers angling for 12-15 inch trout, with best catches in spring and fall.

The confluence of the North and South Fork Crooked is on the Les Schwab Ranch about 25 miles east of Prineville Reservoir and is not open to the public.

Below Bowman Dam, the river is cooled by releases from Prineville Reservoir. This tailrace fishery grows large trout. Rainbow average 8-18 inches, with a few 2-3 pounders occasionally taken. Hwy. 27 runs along this stretch, with good public access. Angling is best in early and late season.

Another reach of the lower Crooked that offers rugged access but good angling is the Crooked River Gorge about 10 river mi. south of Lake Billy Chinook. To reach this area, follow the road to Opal Springs off Hwy. 97 south of Culver. Opal Springs is a private water and hydroelectric facility. Anglers may use the private road, which is open during weekdays, but are requested to check in at the facility office. On weekends when the road is closed, park at the rim and walk down to the river (about 1 1/2 miles).

Developed campgrounds on the Crooked are limited to the stretch immediately below Prineville Reservoir, and to Deep Creek Campground near the North Fork on Forest Rd. 42 in Ochoco National Forest. Camping on BLM land is permitted wherever you can find a flat spot free of sage brush and rocks. Be aware that rattlesnakes are a fact of life in canyon country, particularly in summer.

CULTUS LAKE, BIG A large deep lake with fair fishing for Mackinaw (lake trout), about 50 miles SW of Bend in Deschutes National Forest. Take Century Drive (Hwy. 46) south from Bend to the Cultus Lake turn-off, about 10 miles past Elk Lake. Forest Rd. 4635 leads to the lake. The road is paved and there is a sign for Cultus Lake Resort at the turn-off. From the Willamette Valley, take Hwy. 58 SE from Eugene to the Davis Lake cutoff (Hwy. 61), which is 3 miles south of the Crescent Lake junction. Then take Hwy. 46 north past Davis Lake and Crane Prairie to the Cultus turn-off.

Cultus covers 785 acres and is exceptionally deep and sparkling clear. In places its blue waters reach a depth of 200 feet. Lurking in these depths are hefty lake trout from 3 to 7 pounds, with 15 pound fish available. There are fewer Mackinaw here than at Odell or Crescent, but there are also generally fewer anglers.

In the first few weeks after ice-out you can find lake trout in the shallows, and even tempt them with a fly (try big dragonfly nymphs and leach patterns). Mackinaw fishing is best in May and from mid-September on.

In July and August Macks head for deeper water. Their primary quarry is whitefish. Trolling flashers with Kwikfish-type lures near drop-offs is a good method. Trollers use lead core line or 6 ounces of lead to get down to the fish, and a fish-finder really helps. The deepest area is from about 1/2 mile northwest of the lodge (which is located on the southeast shore), right down the middle of the lake. The shallow west end is least productive.

A downrigger is the best way to get to the Mackinaw without weighting your line. If you want to try this fishery without investing in a lot of special gear, you might look into a leaded jig like the Luhr Jensen Nordic. There is some indication that these jigs are taken more readily than a trolled lure if you're over the fish. With a fish finder, that's not hard to accomplish.

Cultus also offers fair fishing for rainbow trout, which are stocked annually. Most run 8-12 inches, but a few reach 18 inches. Trolling accounts for most of the rainbow. The SE shoreline is a popular area, and sticking close to shore is good advice anywhere on the lake. You might also try working the shelves along the NW shore. Fly casting along shore can be effective in late summer and fall. A few brook trout show up around the mouth of Winopee Creek at the NW end of the lake. Whitefish are abundant and tasty when smoked.

This is a popular general recreation lake in a beautiful setting, though without spectacular mountain views. It has nice swimming areas and is one of the few lakes in the area without a speed limit, so water-skiing and large boat cruising are popular, as is sailing.

Cultus Resort is a pleasant place, with restaurant, boat and motor rentals, cabins, supplies and gas. West Cultus Campground just north of the resort, has a boat ramp. There are also three boat-in or hike-in campgrounds. On the north shore, Little Cove is about 3 miles by water from the resort, and Big Cove is near the lake's mid-point. Trail 16 from Cultus Lake Campground reaches these campgrounds and continues on to Teddy Lakes. West Cultus Campground is at the extreme west end of the lake. Other trails at the west end lead to Teddy Lakes, and Corral Lakes. For more information, see *Fishing In Oregon's Cascade Lakes.*

CULTUS LAKE, LITTLE A very nice trout lake in the Deschutes National Forest SW of Bend on the east slope of the Cascade Range. Don't let the "little" fool you. The lake covers 170 acres. It is about 50 miles from Bend by way Century Drive (County and Forest Rd. 46). From Forest Rd. 46, take Forest Rd. 4635 toward Big Cultus. At a little over 1/2 mile, turn left on Forest Rd. 4630. When the road forks, keep going straight. You are now on Forest Rd. 4636, which reaches Little Cultus in a little over 1/2 mile. Later in the season, you can approach Little Cultus from Waldo Lake by way of the infamous Forest Rd. 600, which passes Irish and Taylor Lakes. See Irish and Taylor for a description of this road.

Little Cultus offers good angling for stocked brook trout 9-10 inches, with an occasional fish to 14 inches. Smaller, naturally reproducing rainbow can be found near the springs in the meadow at the west end of the lake. Best fishing is in early season and again in fall.

Though shoal area predominates, there is a deep hole (50 ft.) toward the west end, and an interesting variety of underwater environments to fish. Trolling the west end is popular, but there's good fly- and spin-fishing throughout the lake. Nymphs, or bucktails fished wet can be especially effective late in the season.

There is a boat ramp off Forest Rd. 4636 toward the east end of the lake. A primitive campground a bit further east from the boat ramp has drinking water, tables, fire rings, and outhouses. Other campsites are scattered along the south shore. There is a 10-mph speed limit for motorboats. For more information, see *Fishing in Oregon's Cascade Lakes*.

CULTUS RIVER A very short stream in the Deschutes National Forest, about 50 miles SW of Bend. The river rises from a large spring about 2 miles north of Crane Prairie Reservoir and flows into the north end of the reservoir. The road to Cultus Lake crosses it about mid-way, near Round Mountain. It is rather brushy but carries a lot of water.

There are very few trout of legal size in the stream. Not recommended for angling except where it enters Crane Prairie.

DARK LAKE (Confederated Tribes Warm Springs) The middle lake in a chain of five, which also includes Trout, Island, Long, and Olallie. It is accessible only by unimproved trail from either Olallie Lake on the east, or Trout Lake on the west. From Trout Lake Campground, it's about a 1 1/2 mile hike. The first 1/4 mile of trail is a fairly steep uphill grind, but the remaining distance is more easily traveled, passing Island Lake on the way in. The trail from Olallie Lake begins at the SE end of Olallie and is most easily reached from Olallie Peninsula Campground.

With a maximum depth of 52 feet, Dark Lake is the deepest lake in the chain. It occupies a glacial cirque, its west and south shores abutting a steep talus slope 200 feet high. The shadow of this cliff over the lake and the lake's depth are responsible for its name. Dark Lake is at 4,690 ft. and has a surface area of about 22 acres. There isn't a lot of shoal area around the lake. It contains brook trout. A permit is required to fish. No overnight camping is allowed due to fire danger.

DARLENE LAKE A small, deep hike-in brook trout lake in the Windy Lakes area SW of Crescent Lake. See Crescent Lake for road directions. The trail is 1/2 mile west of the entrance to Spring Camp, sharing a trailhead with the Windy Lake Trail. It is about 4 miles to Windy. Darlene is about one mile further on Trail 46. The trail continues east to eventually meet the Pacific Crest Trail.

Darlene covers 11 acres and is 48 feet deep. All angling methods can be used. There are some fair natural campsites at the lake.

DAVIS CREEK Inundated by Wickiup Reservoir, it is a major cold water inlet to the reservoir, attracting large numbers of whitefish. See Wickiup Reservoir.

Fly-fishing is excellent on the Crooked in spring and fall.

DAVIS LAKE (Deschutes Co.) Regulated for fly fishing only, a large, shallow lake in the Deschutes National Forest that has a proven capacity to grow large and abundant trout. Since 1987, its fishery has been drastically depleted by drought.

Davis Lake is located about 8 miles south of Crane Prairie in the Deschutes National Forest, about 60 miles south of Bend by way of Century Drive (County and Forest Rd. 46). From the Willamette Valley it is best reached by way of Hwy. 58. From Eugene, follow Hwy. 58 east. About 3 miles past the turn-off to Crescent Lake, turn left onto County Rd. 61. At about 3 more miles, turn left onto Forest Rd. 46. Turn left at the junction of roads 46 and 62. At the T-intersection, turn right to reach Lava Campground at the north end of Davis. Turn left to reach East and West Davis campgrounds. Neither East or West Davis are on this road, but spur roads to the camps are well signed. Davis Lake is about 220 miles from Portland.

Davis was created when volcanic action (less than 3,000 years ago) sent a mile-wide, 100 ft. high wall of lava across the bed of Odell Creek. This natural dam has formed a roughly round lake almost 3 miles across, but quite shallow. It offers about 5 square miles of fishable water, all of it under 25 feet deep even in the best of times. Water from Davis seeps through the lava dam (and into Wickiup Reservoir) at a fair rate. The lake is rich with vegetation and consequently, thick with insects. It is also rich with small

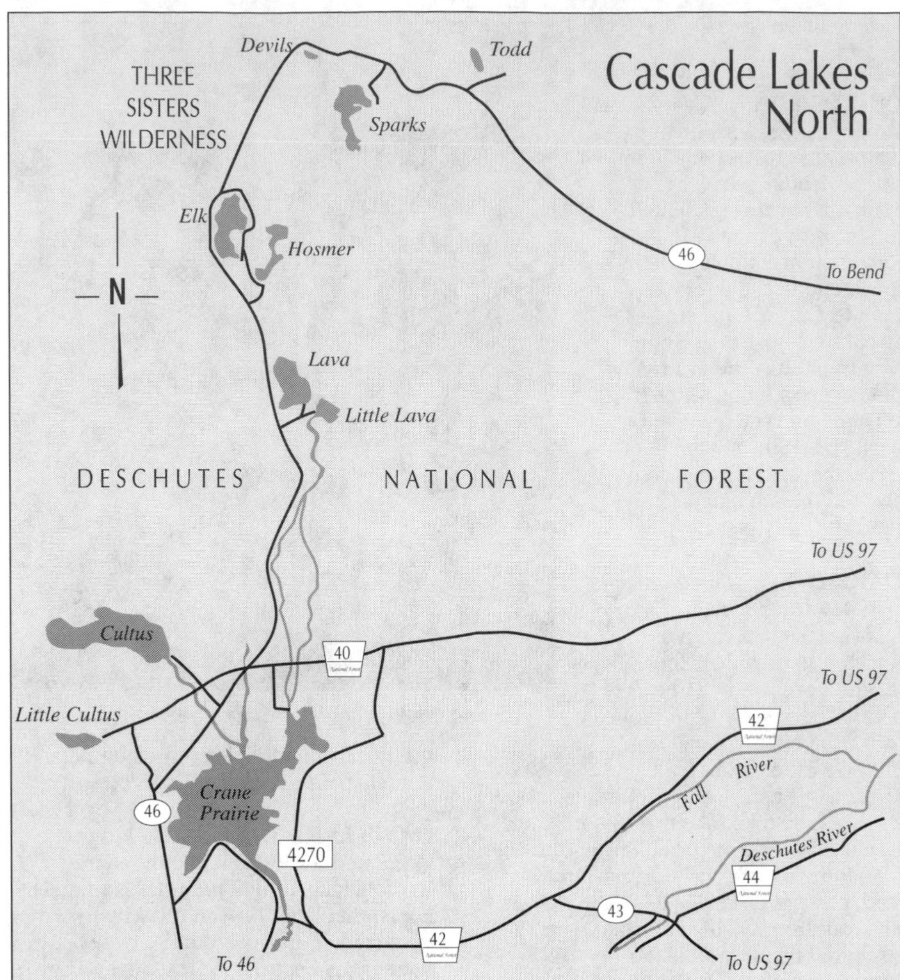

shiner-like rough fish called roach. Roach thrive in the aquatic vegetation and provide an excellent food source for trout.

This lake is ideally suited to fly angling and, except for one five-year period, it has been so regulated since 1939. The lake is too thick with vegetation for effective trolling. It's not deep enough for dependable still-fishing. And it's much too cold for bass. Don't even think about it.

The Davis management plan calls for development of a trout fishery where average angler success would be one fish for every three hours of effort, and where most fish landed would exceed 15 inches. Davis has met and exceeded this goal in past years. But since 1987, drought has had a severe effect on the lake, which is fed primarily by snowpack. By summer, 1992, the lake had lost much of its trout population. A good snowpack in winter 1992-93 encouraged ODF&W to restock Davis. By summer 1994, however, the lake was almost completely dry again, its trout clinging to life in Odell Creek and near the dam.

The fishery at Davis has had other problems as well. For reasons unknown, Davis Lake trout have been susceptible to disease. ODF&W has been experimenting with various trout stocks. The Deschutes hatchery rainbow appeared to resist infection but did not control or take advantage of Davis's primary food source, the abundant roach. Klamath Lake rainbow and Atlantic salmon were stocked in 1993. Either or both could rebuild the Davis fishery once the lake refills. The Atlantic salmon are from the same stock as those at Hosmer Lake. They are known to be robust, trout-like in behavior, and to take a wet fly enthusiastically. They could grow to 20 inches in Davis's rich water. Landlocked coho may also be stocked in the future.

Keep in mind that it will take just one good winter to replenish Davis and restore its fishery, so capable is this water of growing big fish. Once restored, Davis will continue its history of challenging fly anglers. Five square miles is a lot of water to cover. Regulations prohibit fishing while using a motor, though anglers may motor from spot to spot. Summer winds can rapidly turn the center of the lake into a character building outdoor experience. Since most anglers here practice catch-and-release, over time many of its trout will have tasted a fly and grown wary.

In early season, fish are scattered throughout the lake. As the season progresses and the water warms, they seek out the cooler water near the inlets and in the depths near the lava dam. When the water is very low, the lava dam often has the only productive fishery on the lake. The largest inlet is Odell Creek, which enters Davis between East and West Davis campgrounds. Other inlets are Ranger Creek to the northwest and Moore Creek, northeast of Lava Campground. By late June, dragonfly and damselfly nymph patterns would normally be effective near the reed beds along shore. A black leech pattern is usually effective anywhere on the lake, and roach imitations may take some large trout.

There are three campgrounds on the lake, each with a boat ramp. West Davis ramp has been high and dry in recent years, and East Davis ramp has been usable only in spring. The Lava Campground ramp is usually usable all summer. All three campgrounds have pleasant primitive sites among lodgepole pine (well into recovery from past years of beetle damage). Drinking water is available at all three camps. Supplies can be purchased at Twin Lakes or Crane Prairie resorts to the north.

The large size of the Davis rainbow has always been due in part to the voluntary catch-and-release practices of anglers. Your support is encouraged. For more information, see *Fishing In Oregon's Cascade Lakes*.

DEEP CREEK (Crook Co.) A nice stream in the upper Crooked River drainage in Ochoco National Forest, about 45 miles east of Prineville. The stream is about 12 miles long and flows from the east into the North Fork of Crooked River about 4 miles east of Big Summit Prairie. Take Hwy. 26 east from Prineville about 16 miles to Forest Rd. 42, which follows Ochoco Creek to the Ochoco Guard Station, then swing SE to Big Summit Prairie, about 12 miles beyond the guard station. Three miles after leaving the prairie you will reach Deep Creek Campground, which is at the confluence of Deep Creek and Crooked River. Forest Rd. 42 continues east, closely following Deep Creek.

The stream is no longer stocked but supports native rainbow 6-10 inches.

DEER LAKE (Deschutes Co.) A very good early season brook trout and cutthroat lake in the Cultus Lake area SW of Bend. The lake is about one mile NW of Little Cultus Lake. Follow the directions to Little Cultus Lake, then turn north onto the road that skirts the north shore of Little Cultus. This road leads 2 miles to the Deer lake trailhead. Deer lake is about a quarter mile up the trail.

The lake covers 70 acres but is only 20 feet deep at most. It is stocked with cutthroat and brook trout 8-12 inches. Bait or cast lures are good in spring, and fly-fishing is good in fall. There are campsites at Big and Little Cultus. Supplies and accommodations are available at Cultus lake Resort.

DENNIS LAKE (Deschutes Co.) A real jewel of a brook trout lake, a scenic blue beauty one mile past Irish Mt. on the Pacific Crest Trail. Best route in is to pick up the PCT at Irish Lake. See Irish Lake for road directions. Head north for about 5 miles on the PCT. Dennis is about 1/4 mile west of the trail. There is no trail leading to the lake. The PCT reaches Blaze Lake about 1/2 mile past Irish Mt. A quarter mile beyond, it crosses a spring creek. From this point, Dennis Lake is 1/4 mile to the NW and a steep 400 feet above the trail. Carry the Irish Mt. topo map for this one.

Dennis covers 11 acres and is 42 feet deep. Any method will take trout. If you're fishing from shore, your best bet is to cast flies just outside the shoal area. Fly anglers won't have trouble with their backcasts here. With a rubber boat, bait fishing between 15 and 30 feet deep can be very effective. There are fair natural campsites nearby.

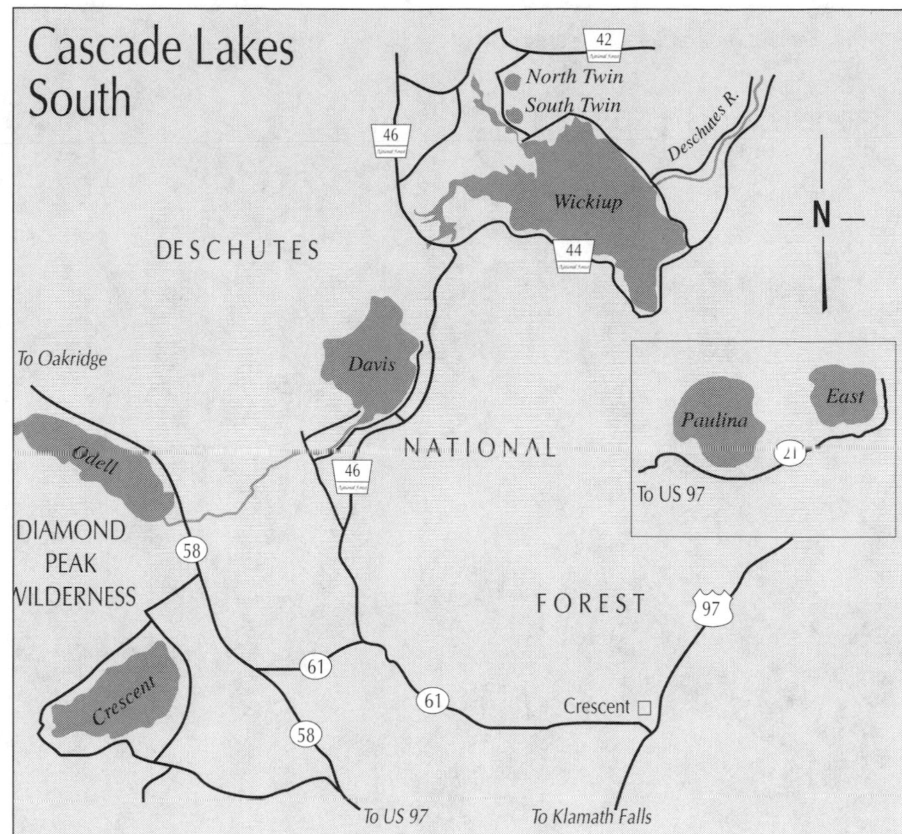

DESCHUTES POND No.1 One of the I-84 ponds adjacent to the Columbia River, located at hwy. mi. 99. It may contain any of the Columbia River warmwater species. An old paved road bisects this 3-acre pond, providing excellent vehicle access. It is south of Hwy. 30. See p. 206 for a map of Columbia River Warmwater Ponds.

DESCHUTES POND No. 2 One of the I-84 ponds adjacent to the Columbia River, located at hwy. mi. 98.5. It covers 5 acres and is south of Hwy. 30, with good off-road parking. It may contain any of the Columbia warmwater species. See p. 206 for a map of Columbia River Warmwater Ponds.

DESCHUTES POND EAST One of the I-84 ponds adjacent to the Columbia River. It is between hwy. mi. 99 and 99.8. It covers 10 acres between I-84 and Hwy. 30. Park along Hwy. 30, not along the freeway. The pond may contain any of the Columbia warmwater species. See p. 206 for a map of Columbia River Warmwater Ponds.

Many anglers catch-and-release all fish from the Deschutes.

DESCHUTES RIVER (mouth to Pelton Dam) One of America's most productive trout waters and a top producer of summer-run steelhead, managed primarily for wild fish. This 100-mile stretch of the river drops 1,233 feet, carving a canyon 700 to 2,200 feet deep out of volcanic rock. Brown palisades rise on either side of the wide stream, and brown hills roll to meet the horizon. The dry air, characteristic of the Cascade rain-shadow, is fragrant with sage, offering a happy alternative to western Oregon's wet-weather angling. Pungent junipers cluster in the draws. This is a land of cliff swallows, meadowlarks, hawks, snakes, and ranging cattle—a dominating landscape guaranteed to restore the perspective of world-weary anglers.

The Deschutes is wide and strong in this stretch, but it offers a variety of fishing environments. There are long slow runs, deep pools, spring creek-like weed beds, gravel bars, boulder pockets, and white water—including 12 major rapids and an impassable falls (Sherars). In the 42 river miles below Sherars Falls anglers can fish a chain of legendary steelhead holes and welcome runs of spring and fall chinook. Above, there is good shelter,

from ***Fishing In Oregon's Deschutes River***

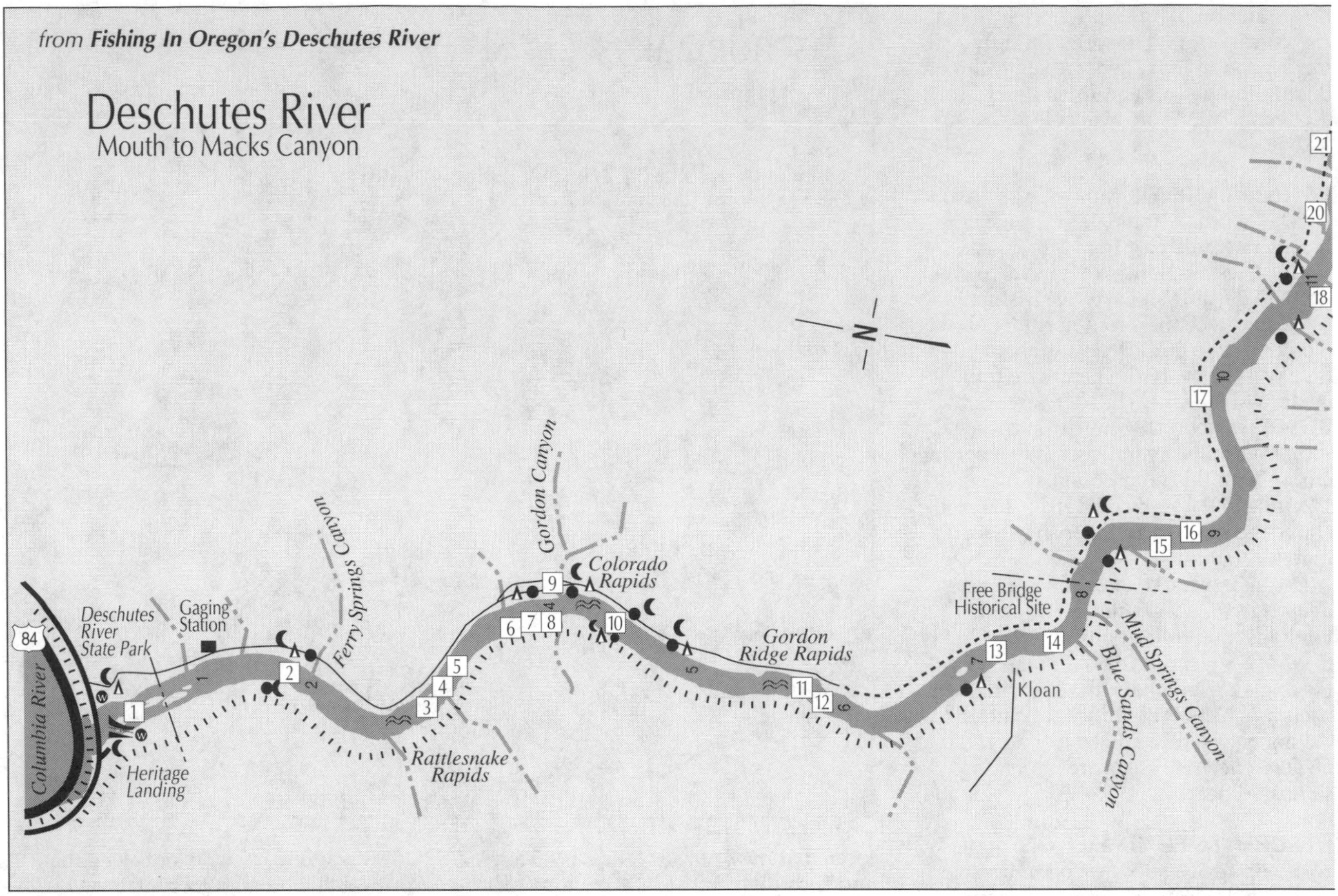

Deschutes River
Mouth to Macks Canyon

1 CABLE CROSSING
2 SAND HOLE
3 LAVA ROCK DRIFT
4 FENCE HOLE
5 TWIN ISLAND DRIFT
6 MERRILL HOLE
7 GRASSHOPPER HOLE
8 LEDGE HOLE
9 ZEKE'S RIFFLE
10 WAGON BLAST DRIFT
11 SHARP'S BAR
12 FIRST GREEN LIGHT HOLE
13 BATHTUB HOLE
14 TRAVELING HOLE
15 BEDSPRING HOLE
16 KORTEGE CORRAL DRIFT
17 NEWFOUND HOLE
18 SECOND GREENLIGHT HOLE
19 GRAVEYARD HOLE
20 AIRPORT DRIFT
21 EDDIE'S RIFFLE
22 TANK HOLE
23 COW DUNG HOLE
24 PARANOID HOLE
25 LOCKIT DRIFT
26 TIE CORRAL HOLE
27 DEAD COW HOLE
28 STEELIE FLATS
29 TWIN STUMPS HOLE
30 SHADE HOLE
31 BULL RUN RIFFLE
32 DOVE HOLE
33 ISLAND RIFFLE
34 NOOKIE ROCK
35 LOWER DIKE
36 DIKE
37 BRUSH HOLE

The Deschutes is popular with fly anglers.

feeding, and spawning ground for the native Deschutes rainbow trout, the redside, as well as additional rich steelheadter-ritory.

The Deschutes empties into the Lake Celilo impoundment of the Columbia River about 12 miles west of The Dalles, only a 2 hour drive from Portland. Deschutes River State Park, off I-84, affords access to angling at the mouth. From the west, take I-84 exit 97 at Celilo and follow Hwy. 206 east to the park. From the east, take I-84 exit 104 at Biggs. Follow Hwy. 97 south and Hwy. 206 west. A large developed boat ramp facility, Heritage Landing, is on the west bank of the river across from the park. Use of motors on the river above Heritage Landing is subject to a variety of restrictions. See Oregon Boating Regulations for current information (available from the Oregon State Marine Board).

There is no motor vehicle access from the mouth to the upper canyon, but anglers can follow the banks for 12 miles upstream through public property, thanks to the 1983 purchase of river frontage by the Oregon Wildlife Heritage Foundation, who gave it in trust to the people of Oregon following an enthusias-

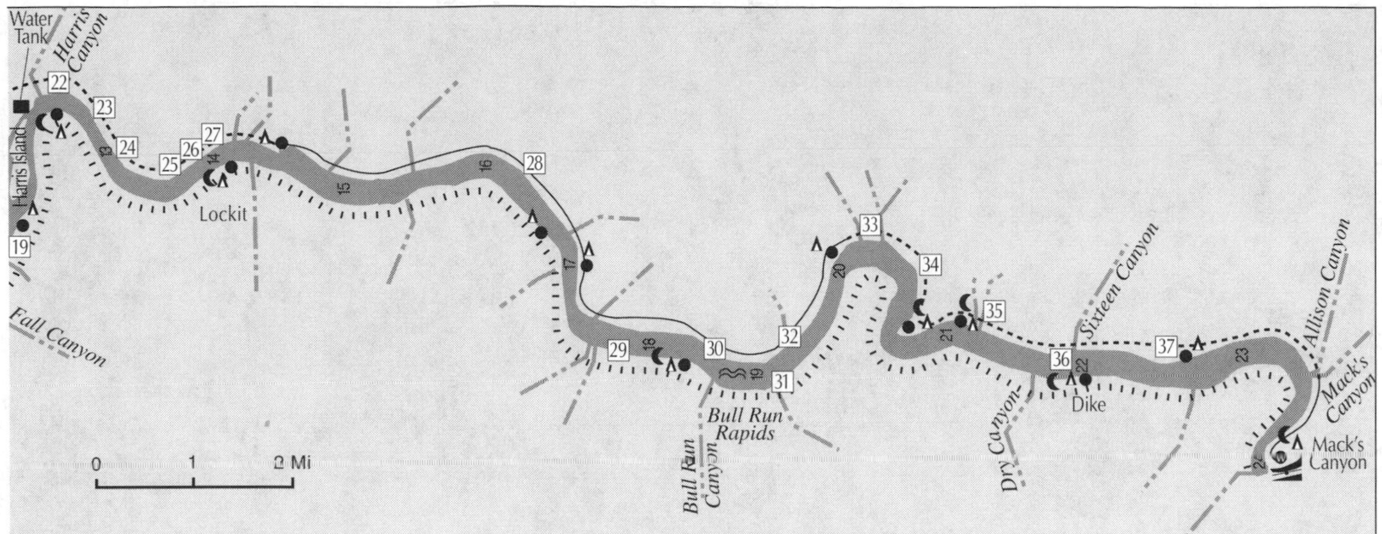

tic grass-roots campaign to save the Deschutes. The trust specifies continuance of the no motor vehicles policy in the lower canyon.

From Heritage Landing on the west bank, anglers can follow the trail upriver about 2 miles, or walk the railroad track. On the east bank, a trail suitable for hiking or mountain biking extends upstream 20 miles. Beyond that point the trail deteriorates too much for mountain bikes, but is negotiable for hikers all the way to Mack's Canyon at river mi. 24.

Drive-in access points on the east bank of the river are plentiful from Maupin downstream to Macks Canyon, and upstream to the Deschutes Club Gate. Additional east bank access is available at South Junction, Trout Creek, Mecca Flat, and Warm Springs. On the west bank, access is restricted to a dangerously rough road at Kloan, the Oak Spring Hatchery site off Hwy. 197, and Dry Creek Campground on Confederated Tribes Warm Springs Reservatin land.

From Sherars Falls at river mi. 44 to the mouth, the Deschutes is primarily steelhead water. In 1993, about 3,600 summer steelhead were hooked in this section. An additional 1,000 were hooked in the upper river. Of these, an estimated 60% were wild. All non-finclipped steelhead must be released unharmed. The Deschutes has been managed for the protection of wild steelhead since 1979. In 1993, the wild steelhead spawning above Sherars was estimated to be only 900 fish, the smallest return since the late 1970s. The wild run is currently supplemented by about 160,000 hatchery releases annually.

Steelhead begin moving into the Deschutes in mid-July. By September, they can be found throughout the river between the mouth and Pelton Dam. Steelhead continue to enter the river as late as December. In early season, when the Columbia water temperature is warm, additional steelhead (bound for home waters elsewhere in Oregon and in Idaho) slip into the lower Deschutes to cool off. Some wander as far up as Pelton Regulating Dam and may even stay to spawn in Deschutes tributaries. The Clearwater strain of steelhead can weigh up to 22 pounds. Most of these eventually drop back out of the Deschutes and continue moving up the Columbia system. Native Deschutes steelhead average 5-10 pounds. Steelheading at Maupin is generally prime mid-September through October. Good steelheading continues upstream through the end of the season (currently December 31). The average catch rate for this section is 3/4 fish per angler trip.

On the Deschutes, all rainbow trout over 20 inches are considered steelhead. To fish for steelhead, anglers must have a steelhead tag. Only finclipped steelhead may be kept. Except for a short reach from Buckhollow Creek upstream to Sherars Falls (a mere 0.9 miles, intended for use by salmon anglers), anglers must use artificial flies and lures with barbless hooks for both trout and steelhead.

A number of wet and dry flies have been developed especially for the Deschutes steelhead fishery, including Doug Stewart's black and orange Macks Canyon and its subtle variants (judged to be one of five top producers on the stream). Other classics are Don McClain's Deschutes Demon (yellow, orange and gold), his Deschutes Skunk, and the purple bodied Dr. Gillis. Randall Kaufmann's Freight Train and Coal Car (variations on the Skunk) are also popular. Most fly-caught steelhead are hooked on a tight, floating line on or just below the surface. Be prepared for a powerful hit.

Effective spinners and spoons for steelheading on the Deschutes should be large (sizes 3-5) and bright (silver or nickel). Even in summer, the Deschutes is deep and dark. Plugs in a variety of colors (depending on the light) are also effective.

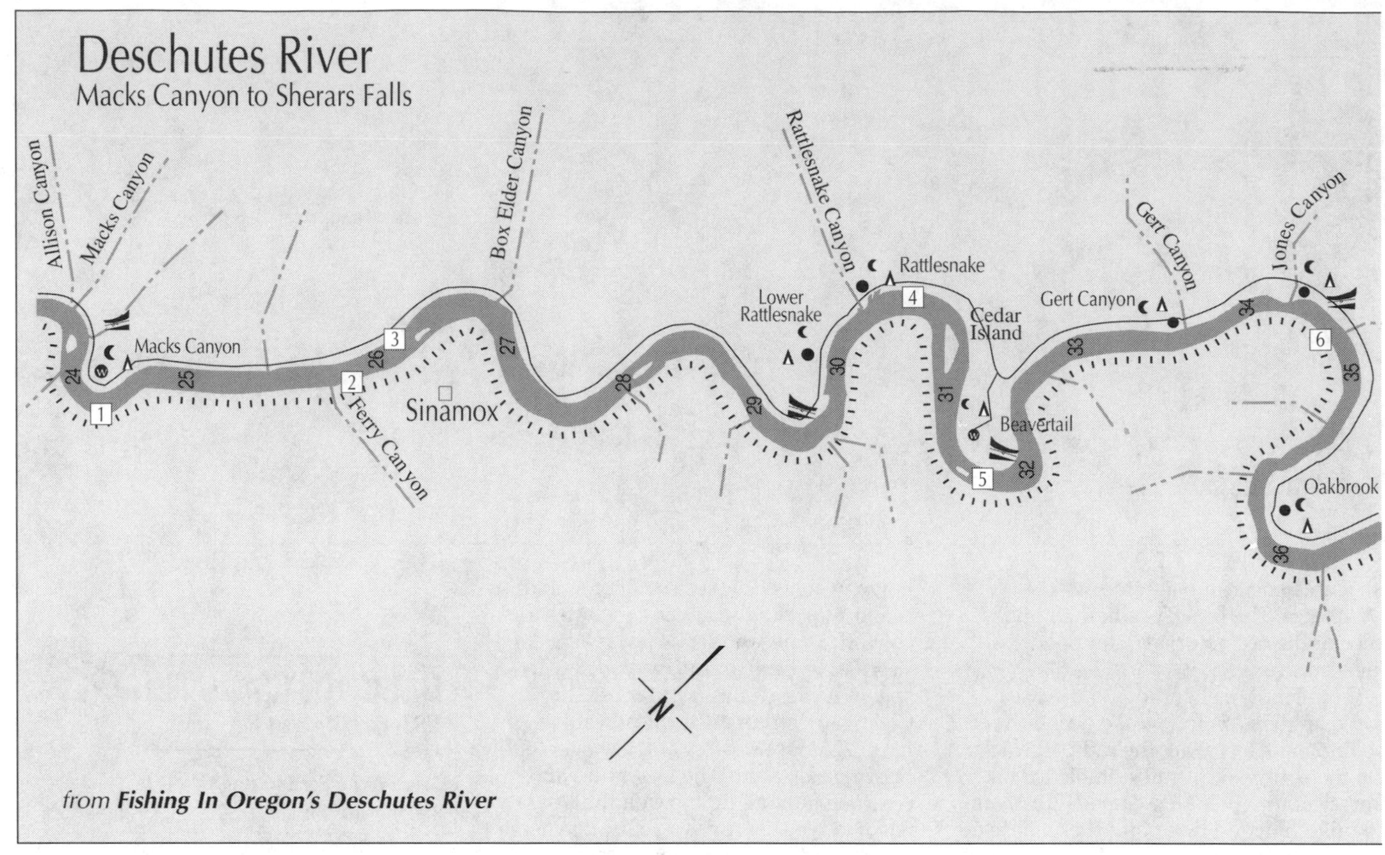

from ***Fishing In Oregon's Deschutes River***

The Deschutes trout fishery is outstanding. Year-round residence in this big, powerful river grows fish of superior strength. It is estimated that there are more than 1700 trout over 7 inches per mile in the river between Sherars Falls and Pelton Regulating Dam. These fish range 8-15 inches, and there are many larger. Hatchery-produced rainbow trout were last stocked in the Deschutes in 1978. A reduction in native trout following that stocking encouraged ODF&W to abandon the hatchery program and work, instead, to promote the native redside.At this time, only trout 10-13 inches may be taken. Check current regulations.

Much of the Deschutes is only accessible by boat.

Trout fishing is best above Sherars. Rainbow trout predominate in this section of the river, though there are a few bull trout and browns. All bull trout must be released unharmed. Whitefish are abundant throughout this stretch and provide good fishing in winter when trout are less active.

The Deschutes is open for year-round trout fishing from the mouth up to the Confederated Tribes Warm Springs boundary (at about river mi. 69). This open area includes a stretch of good bank-accessible trout water from Sherars Falls to 9 river miles above the Deschutes Club Gate. From the CTWS boundary upstream to Pelton Dam, trout season closes October 31.

Angling for spring and fall chinook is concentrated in the area from Sherars downstream, with most angling taking place in the area between the falls and Buckhollow Creek, where bait fishing is allowed. Salmon eggs are bait of choice.

Salmon runs on the Deschutes have been affected by both poor ocean conditions and drought. Since 1991, the river has been closed to fall chinook fishing to protect the dwindling number of upriver salmon. Only 700 upriver fall chinook reached their spawning grounds above Sherars Falls in 1992. In previous years, 2,500 to 4,000 made it to the upper river. The lower river fall chinook run is in good shape, however, with a population estimate of 7,000. In 1994, the river was

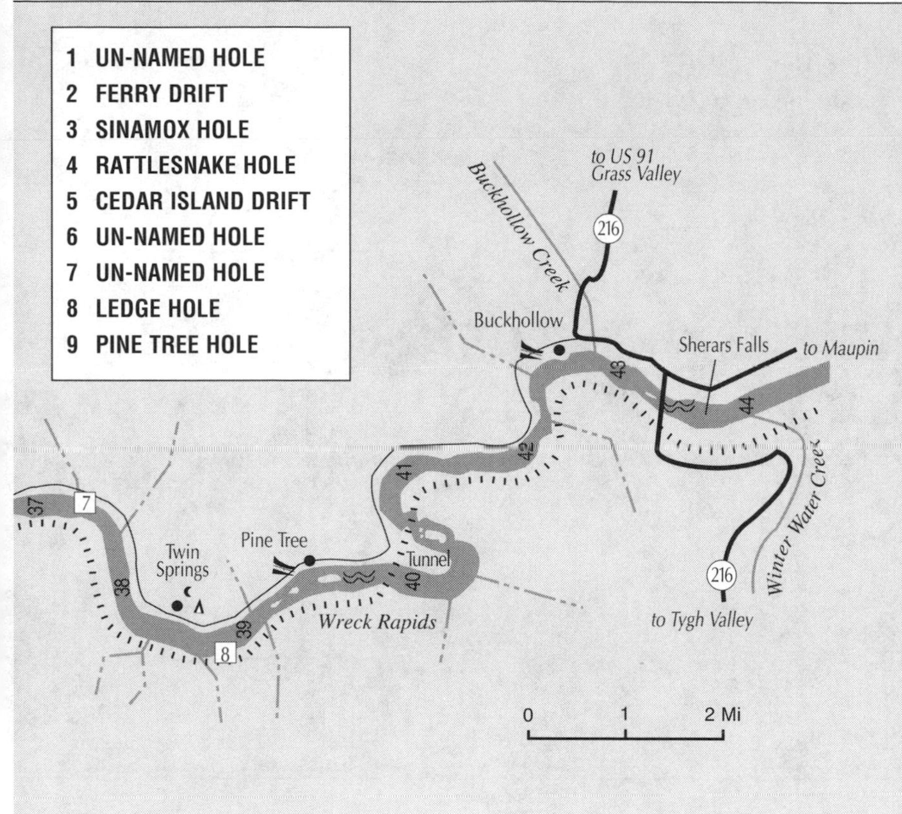

closed to spring chinook angling as well. The return of favorable ocean conditions will probably allow the spring chinook fishery to recover and re-open. The fall chinook population is composed entirely of wild fish, while the spring run has been augmented by a hatchery program since the construction of Pelton Dam.

The spring run begins in late March, peaking between mid-April and mid-May, and continuing to mid-June. The number of springers caught here in 1993 was 800. The most popular chinook fishery is at Sherars Falls. The season runs from the end of May to the end of July, when fall chinook begin passing through. The fall run extends to the end of October, but the fish begin to deteriorate about October 1. Most fall chinook fishing occurs from mid-August to September 30. The precarious-looking platforms constructed over Sherars Falls are limited to use by members of the Confederated Tribes of the Warm Springs Reservation.

Much of the Deschutes is accessible only by boat. Anglers drift to a likely spot and beach their craft before fishing. Angling from a floating device is prohibited. Among the popular one-day drifts are Warm Springs (river mi. 97) to Trout Creek (river mi. 87), Maupin (river mi. 51) to Sandy Beach just before Sherars Falls (river mi. 45), Pine Hollow (below Wreck Rapids at river mi. 57) to Beavertail Campground (river mi. 31), and Beavertail to Macks Canyon (river mi. 24). Longer trips include Macks Canyon to the mouth, and Trout Creek to Maupin. Immediately below Trout Creek, boaters should be prepared for a Class 3 rapids and additional heavy water. This stretch is very popular with whitewater rafters in summer. From Maupin to the mouth, boaters will encounter three Class 4 rapids and the impassable Sherars Falls. Do not attempt to boat the falls. The best take-out before the falls is at Sandy Beach. There is a raft take-out immediately above the falls, but it can be very crowded. Boaters are urged to camp at BLM sites, use the outhouses provided, and carry out all refuse.

Much good water can be reached by a combination of motor vehicle and easy hiking. From Sherars Falls to Macks Canyon, there are a number of developed access sites and campgrounds. In addition, in this stretch anglers can simply park along the road and walk over to the river through the sagebrush. The grade between road and river is not very steep. At Blue Hole (river mi. 48) there is a fishing platform over good trout and steelhead water. The platform can accommodate 15 wheelchairs.

At Maupin,near The Oasis Resort on the east bank, a gravel road accesses about 7 miles of river and leads to The Deschutes Club Locked Gate. The public is welcome to fish beyond the gate, but must leave all vehicles (including moun-

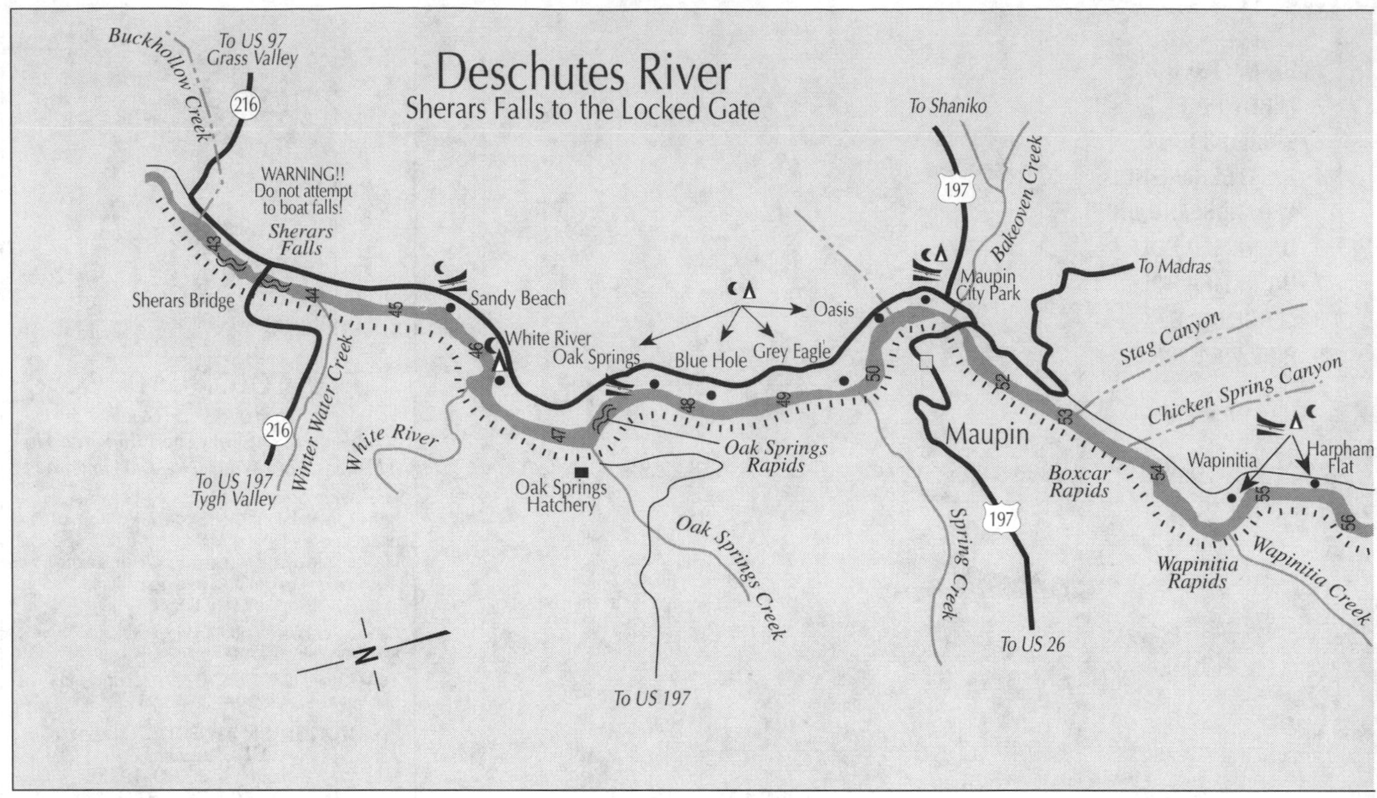

tain bikes) at the gate and proceed on foot. The 13-mile trail from the gate to North Junction is an old railroad bed which offers easy hiking. There are more than a half dozen primitive BLM campsites with outhouses along this stretch.

At North Junction, the Burlington Northern railroad track crosses from west bank to east bank. Some anglers continue upstream on foot along the railroad grade as far as South Junction (river mi. 84). Anglers should be aware that the railroad grade is private property, that the railroad does have the right to prosecute for trespassing, and that trains do not run on any set schedule. Keep alert for approaching trains and maintenance vehicles.

Between North and South Junction, the river's east bank includes a mix of BLM and private land. Respect "No Trespassing" signs. To reach South Junction by car, take Hwy. 197 south from Maupin to the junction with Hwy. 97 (Shaniko). A gravel road heads west to the river. The road down to South Junction is loose gravel and quite steep. There is a primitive BLM campground at South Junction and access to about 1.5 miles of good trout water.

Trout Creek is a popular access point with a large developed BLM campground and boat ramp. An old railroad bed trail follows the river from Trout Creek 10 miles upstream to Mecca Flat. The trail proceeds through some private land where BLM has an easement. There are outhouses at intervals along the path.

To reach Trout Creek by motor vehicle, follow Hwy. 97 to Lyle Gap, turning west toward Paxton at the first paved road south of Willowdale. Just north of Paxton, a gravel road leads to and through Gateway to Trout Creek, and follows the creek 3 miles to its confluence with the Deschutes.

On the west bank, anglers can fish for trout and steelhead upstream and down from the Oak Springs Hatchery. To reach the hatchery, take Hwy. 197 south from Tygh Valley, turning left onto the hatchery road about 2 miles south of the White River crossing. Be prepared for a spectacular drop down into the Deschutes canyon. The only other west bank access to the Deschutes in this stretch is at Dry Creek Campground, Confederated Tribes Warm Springs. (See below for information about this access.)

The richness of Deschutes insect life is legendary. Big stoneflies (both salmonflies and golden stoneflies) become active in May, emerging in late May and June and producing what some consider to be the best fly-fishing west of the Mississippi. Weighted stonefly nymph patterns are a staple for Deschutes anglers and will produce yearround. Caddis and cranefly hatches also occur during this time. Grasshopper, mayfly, and caddis are thick in August, with many big fish ignoring these morsels in maddening favor of minuscule midges.

Often, hatches of small mayflies occur simultaneously with caddis and stoneflies, and fish reluctant to go for imitations of these more visible insects may be feeding selectively on *Baetis* hors d'oeuvres. Evenings on the river often produce excellent spinner falls. Oregon fly tiers and anglers have long been studying ways to match and anticipate the river's hatches. The complex picture remains inscrutable, however, so wise anglers will come prepared with a range of insect, stage, and color imitations. And patience.

A word of warning to all Deschutes anglers: this is a big, swift, dangerous river, and wading it must be approached with proper respect. It can kill. Hip boots are not appropriate. If you wear rubber (as opposed to neoprene) waders, be sure to wear a wading belt. A wading staff and properly surfaced wading shoes are both prudent precautions.

Except for the drift from Mecca Flat to Trout Creek under most conditions, the Deschutes is not suitable for novice boaters. A boater pass system in effect throughout the river requires a daily use fee, but does not limit the number of boaters at this time. Passes may be purchased from the State Parks Department at 525 Trade St. SE, Salem 97310, from their regional office in Portland, and at tackle and supply stores along the river and in all metropolitan areas. The Deschutes fishery is affected by water discharges from Pelton Dam, which are variable in spring. Heavy discharge can put the fishery off for several days. To keep in touch with the dam discharge,

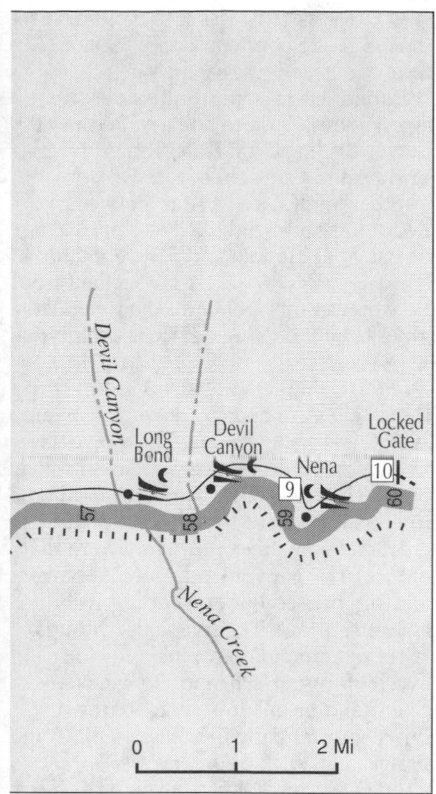

anglers can telephone PGE's 24-hr. information line (503) 464-7474.

Experienced Deschutes angling and river guide services are available through fly and tackle shops in all Oregon metropolitan areas, by contacting the Oregon Guides and Packers Association (see Appendix.), and in Maupin.

Supplies and services are available only in Warm Springs and Maupin. Overnight accommodations are limited but available in the Maupin area. Kaufmann's Streamborn of Portland maintains a house streamside in Maupin, available by advance reservation, which comes complete with food, guide, raft, local transportation, and a well-stocked fly-tying bench. C.J. Lodge in Maupin near the city park offers quality lodging and meals for guests.

The only campgrounds with drinking water in this stretch of the river are at Maupin City Park, Beavertail and Macks Canyon. All campers along the Deschutes are urged to respect the fragile desert environment, to camp lightly using wilderness (no trace) camping methods. Open fires are discouraged in this dry country at all times, and are prohibited between June 1 and October 1 due to fire danger. For environmental protection, there are outhouses up from the river bank at frequent intervals, even in areas accessible only by boat. Cattle with BLM grazing permits don't seem to bother with such niceties, unfortunately. This here's cow pie country, partner. If watching herds of large animals upsets your casting, you might prefer the stretch above Sherars Bridge. For more information, see *Fishing In Oregon's Deschutes River*.

DESCHUTES RIVER (Confederated Tribes Warm Springs Reservation) Confederated Tribes Warm Springs owns the entire Deschutes West bank from 16 miles south of Maupin to Lake Billy Chinook (and on up to Jefferson Creek on the Metolius River Arm). Daily and seasonal fishing permits are available for a small fee, allowing anglers to fish the CTWS Deschutes access at Dry Creek as well as other tribal waters. For information, contact the Dept. of Natural Resources, Box C, Warm Springs, OR 97761. Permits can be purchased in the community of Warm Springs at the Warm Springs Police Station, the Information Center, Rainbow Market, and Macy's Store.

To reach Dry Creek Campground at about river mi. 94, drive 3 miles north from Warm Springs on the paved road toward Kahneeta Hot Springs, then 2 miles east to Dry Creek Campground. When the road forks, keep to the right. The Deschutes is accessible from an unimproved road (closed to vehicle access) which follows the bank for about 6 miles downstream. There is no drinking water at the camp.

DESCHUTES RIVER (Pelton Dam to Bend) Heavily drawn upon for irrigation at times, but offering some opportunities for high quality trout fishing. This stretch of the river is currently open for year-round trout angling with barbless flies and lures. Irrigation withdrawals generally begin in April and continue until October. Temperatures in the reduced flow months can get as high as 80 degrees, forcing trout to migrate to cooler areas near Bend, below Lower Bridge, and wherever else springs offer relief. Best consistent fishing throughout this stretch is from October until April.

From Tumalo to Lake Billy Chinook (about 30 miles), the river flows through a narrow scenic gorge. Well back from the main roads and too shallow for boating due to withdrawals, it offers excellent angling for wild rainbow and brown trout. Bull trout are also in residence but must be released unharmed.

From Big Falls to the lake, the river cuts through BLM and National Forest land. There are access tracks into the

The Deschutes offers miles of good rainbow trout habitat.

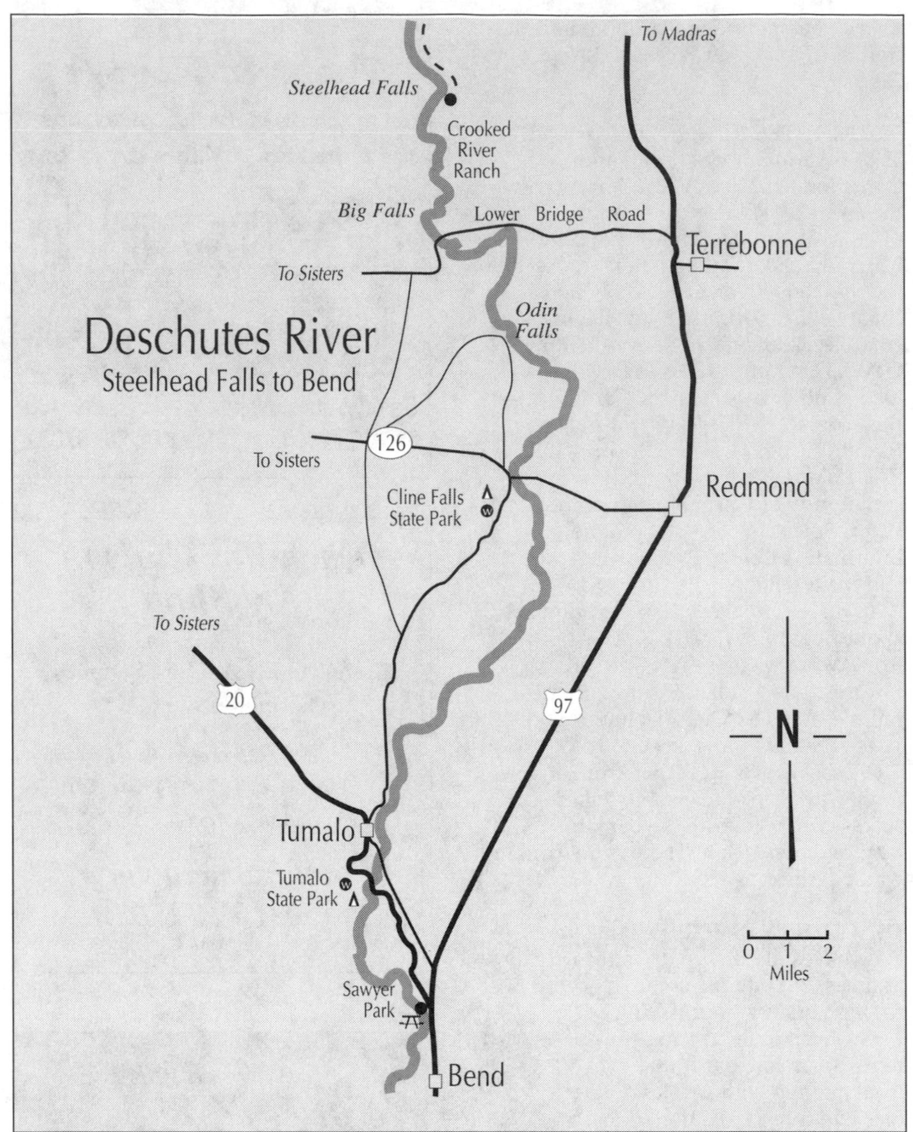

gorge and un-named trails, some of which show up on the USGS topographic map of the area, including a long hike down Squaw Creek northeast of Sisters. This remote stretch contains some of the upper river's best trout fishing.

Central Oregon

Steelhead Falls Trail, in the vicinity of Crooked River Ranch, offers hearty anglers access to about 12 miles of high quality gorge fishing. To reach it, turn west off Hwy. 97 (about 10 miles north of Redmond) onto Lower Bridge Rd. Follow signs for Crooked River Ranch—at present, a surreal landscape of desert scrub platted for development, complete with a labyrinth of hopefully named dirt roads. The best bet is to make your way to the development's fire station (don't be shy about asking directions from the occasional passer-by). At the station you can purchase a map of the development and solicit help in locating the trail at the end of River Rd. It's a steep hour's hike to the falls.

Other public river access points within the development include a fording possibility at the end of Folley Waters Rd., and a (currently barren) BLM recreation site at the end of Sundown Canyon Rd.

Upstream, the river flows through primarily private land. At this time, landowners are tolerant of anglers who stop in to ask permission to cross over to the gorge. Be courteous, and pack out all refuse to help preserve access.

Public access opportunities pick up again about 15 miles north of Redmond. Lower Bridge, Odin Falls, Tetherow Bridge, and Cline Falls State Park are popular angler access sites. Between Redmond and Bend, the Deschutes can be fished at Tumalo and Sawyer State Parks on Hwy. 97. There is excellent trout fly water in this section of the river. Angling from a floating device is prohibited.

DESCHUTES RIVER (Bend to Wickiup Reservoir) A rich, dark, powerful stream, 20-100 feet wide, characterized by deceptively smooth but powerful slicks broken by sharp rapids. The Deschutes is a big river as it emerges from Wickiup, but its character is distinctly different from that of the lower canyonland. Here its power is easily missed under its deceptively smooth surface. The river runs through fairly open ponderosa pinelands for much of this stretch, and the banks are often sand or tall grasses. It is drawn down substantially in winter to fill Crane Prairie and Wickiup reservoirs.

The Deschutes flows through the heart of the high desert community of Bend, which is at the edge of the Deschutes National Forest. Bend is the largest metropolitan area within the river's watershed. For 15 miles upstream from the city, the stream is easily fished from shore, and local anglers drive out the Mt. Bachelor road to try their luck on the evening rise.

To reach the river from Bend, take Hwy. 97 south. Secondary and forest roads access both sides of the stream at several locations. In the stretch between Lava Butte and the Lapine State Recreation Area the river flows through much private land, including Sunriver Resort.

Rainbow and brown trout predominate. The average fish is only 9 inches, but big browns are frequently taken. Anglers work the pockets and undercut banks of the meandering stream. Fishing this segment of Deschutes is restricted to barbless artificial flies and lures only. Fly-fishing is very popular here. Hatches take place throughout the year. An excellent hatch of yellow mayflies occurs in June. Wet flies seem to work best during the days, dry flies best in the evenings. Favorite dry fly patterns include stonefly, PMD, caddis, and mosquito imitations, with small patterns best in late summer. Most successful wet flies imitate the small trout relished by big browns. Whitefish are also plentiful and susceptible to all angling methods. Popular lures include Kwikfish in size ranges F-3 to F-7, silver and gold Rapallas, and crayfish-finish Rebels.

The trout bag limit in this stretch is currently limited to 5 trout per day, only 2 of which may be browns. Only one fish per day may be over 20 inches.

Angling from a floating device is permitted in this stretch. Bank and boat angling are both effective. The river is driftable starting about 1/4 mile below Wickiup Dam. There is some flow through private property, and permission should be obtained to bank fish there. There is a good 8-mile drift from below Wickiup to the Pringle Falls area. To reach Pringle Falls from Hwy. 97, turn west on County Rd. 43 just north of LaPine. Pringle Falls is not boatable, and the current gets very strong quickly as you near the falls. Keep a sharp watch for warning signs on the river.

One of the finest drifts on this section is the 17 miles from just below the log jam at Pringle Falls to Big River (a.k.a Colonel Patch) Bridge. Another nice drift is from Big River Bridge to the Spring River area. From there to Bend, much of the river is boatable, but it's advisable to check locally for trouble spots. In addition to Pringle, boaters should not attempt to boat Benham, Dillon, and Lava Island Falls. Know where you are putting in. These falls have taken the lives of ill-informed boaters. Guides for boating the upper river are available. Contact the Oregon Guides and Packers Association, or check locally in Bend, LaPine or at the area resorts.

Campgrounds are plentiful along the river beginning at Meadow Camp just 4 miles south of Bend. Other National Forest campgrounds are Lava Island, Slough Camp, and Benham Falls near the Lava Butte Geological Area, Session Camp near Spring River, Big River Bridge, LaPine State Recreation Area, Pringle Falls, Wyeth, Bull Bend, and Wampus. The Deschutes runs through Sunriver, a popular Oregon resort, about 12 miles south of Bend. This resort offers just about every recreational activity one could desire, and up-scale vacation homes and condominiums are usually available for short-term rental. There is an airstrip at the resort. For more information, see *Fishing In Oregon's Deschutes River*.

DESCHUTES RIVER (Crane Prairie Reservoir to Wickiup Reservoir) A beautiful wild brook trout stream and nursery for Wickiup's brown trout, flowing through flower-bedecked meadowland. To reach it from the east, follow County and Forest Rd. 42 west from Hwy. 97.

This lovely, meandering 3-mile section of the Deschutes offers excellent fly-fishing for brook trout to 5 lbs. Brown trout are also available at times. There is a wheelchair accessible fishing platform at the Forest Rd. 42 Bridge.

The Deschutes is a beautiful wild brook trout stream above Wickiup Reservoir.

Sheep Bridge Campground is located on the river's east bank. To reach it from the east, turn south off Forest Rd. 42, following signs for Twin Lakes Resort. At about 1/4 mile, when the main road makes a sharp left turn, continue straight to the camp. Supplies and overnight accommodations are available at Twin Lakes Resort on South Twin Lake.

DESCHUTES RIVER (Headwaters to Crane Prairie) Outlet of Little Lava Lake, which has no inlet streams, but is fed by springs whose source is snow-melt percolating into the porous lava underlying the region. From Little Lava the river flows south, first as a slow, clear slough, then as a sparkling meadow creek, entering Crane Prairie Reservoir after 8 miles.

Whitefish predominate in the slough waters from Lava Lake downstream about 2 miles. The meadow stretch below that, however, is a wonderful stream with firm, small resident rainbow and brook trout. This is a classic small stream, and fishing is rarely disappointing. The river is generally less than 10 feet across and can be waded at almost any point. Fly-fishing is the best method here, with dries almost always effective. Watch your backcast. The small pines along the shore eat flies.

The Cascade Lakes Hwy. parallels much of the stream. About 2 miles below the Deschutes Bridge Guard Station the road curves west, away from the river. Forest Rd. 40 crosses the river a mile or so below that point, and a mile above the outflow into Crane Prairie. Upstream from this bridge the river flows through a delightful setting of green meadow grass, waist-high lupine, and small pines, with Mt. Bachelor looking on.

Forest Service campgrounds are available at Little Lava Lake, Deschutes Bridge, and Cow Meadow, where the river enters Crane Prairie. Overnight accommodations and supplies are available at Twin Lakes Resort on nearby Wickiup Reservoir.

DEVILS LAKE (Deschutes Co.) A pretty little lake, especially nice for small fry, on Century Drive about 30 miles SW of Bend. It stretches along the south side of the road about one mile west of Sparks Lake.

Devils Lake is about 40 acres and only 9 feet at its deepest point. Brook trout reproduce naturally here, and catchable rainbow are stocked every couple of weeks during the season.

Fed primarily by a spring creek at its west end, the lake is remarkably clear. During most years, fish are available throughout the lake. If the water gets really low, they will concentrate in the deeper east end. Fly-fishing is good when there's a bit of wind to rough up the water, but all methods work. There is not a lot for trout to eat in Devils, so any offering looks good. Light gear is appropriate for these 8-11 inchers.

No motors are allowed, but a rubber raft would be nice. There is a trail from the campground to the east end of the lake. The road to the lake is usually blocked by snow until mid-June. There's a small campground at the lake. For more information, see *Fishing In Oregon's Cascade Lakes*.

DORIS LAKE (Deschutes Co.) A large hike-in lake in the Cascades west of Elk Lake, about 35 miles SW of Bend. Deep and cold, it provides only fair fishing for brook trout. From Forest Rd. 46, about 2

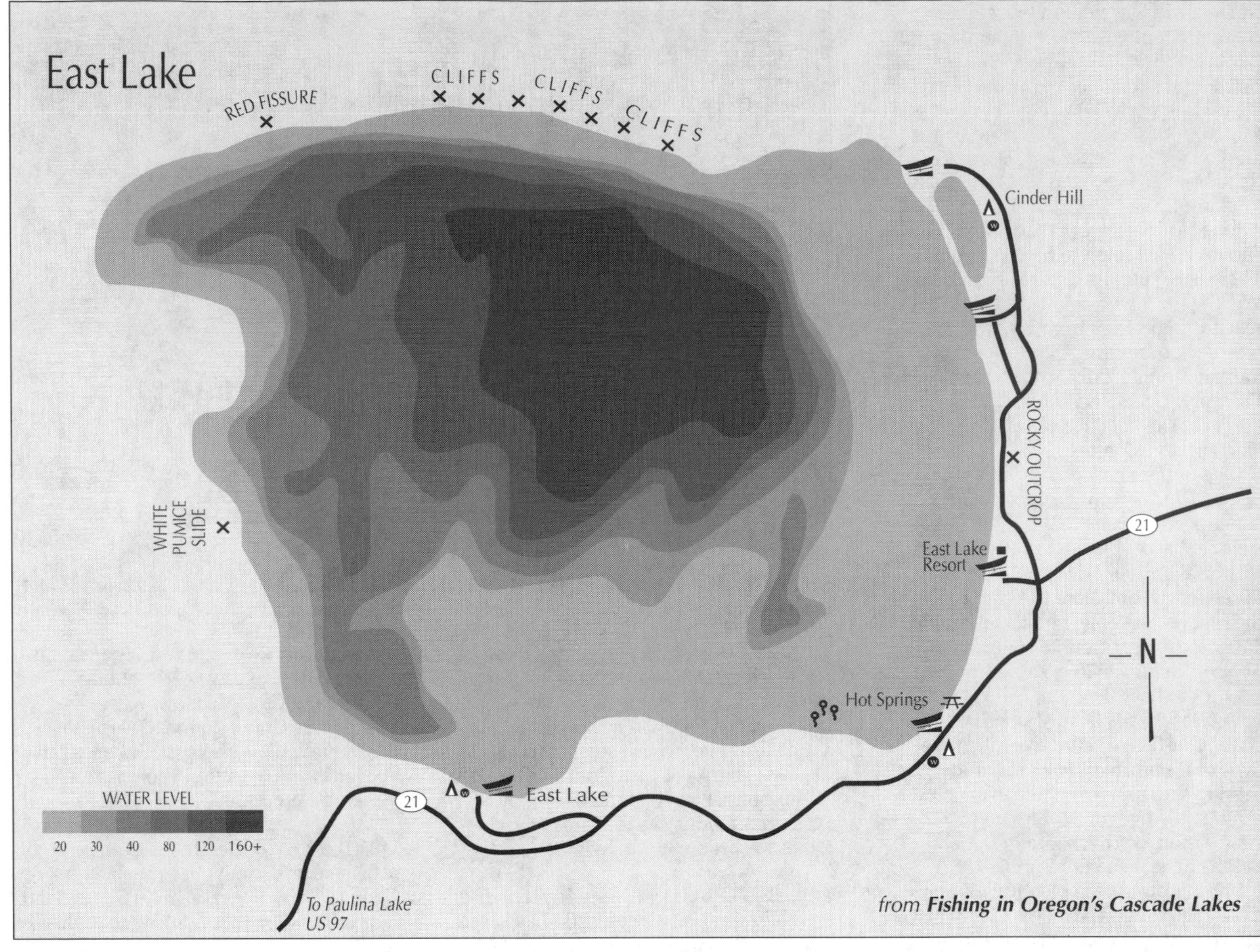

from **Fishing in Oregon's Cascade Lakes**

miles past the turn-off to Elk Lake Resort, watch for Six Lakes Trailhead 14 on the west side of the road. Follow Trail 14 about 3 miles west to Doris Lake, passing Blow Lake at about the half-way point.

Doris covers about 90 acres, and has a maximum depth over 70 ft. The lake is stocked annually with brook trout fingerlings which grow to 14 inches. Best method varies with the season, with bait popular early, and fly-fishing best in late fall. There are no improved campsites at the lake.

EAGLE CREEK (Columbia River) A very popular trout stream, with salmon and steelhead runs, located near Bonneville Dam about 43 miles east of Portland, entering the Columbia just above the dam. Eagle Creek flows 15 miles north from the slopes of Mt. Hood. It is not accessible by road except at the mouth and at the extreme headwaters. The upper stream is encircled by the forest road that runs from Larch Mountain to Wahtum Lake. A good trail follows the stream, and it is a popular hiking area.

A state salmon hatchery located on the creek just above its mouth provides an interesting spectacle during the fall run. Check current regulations for special closures related to salmon and steelhead angling. The stretch of lower creek from the railroad bridge to the mouth is within the Columbia River regulation zone.

A fair summer steelhead run shows up in the creek in July. Angling is closed below the hatchery rack August 15-Nov. 30. Fishing is only fair due to angler pressure. Non-finclipped steelhead must be released unharmed. Barbless hooks must be used December 1 through March 31. The upper stream has good angling for wild rainbow and cutthroat trout. A few brook trout are also taken in the upper reaches. Both bait and fly angling will take fish, although fly fishing is difficult. There is a large campground and recreation area near the mouth.

EAST LAKE A truly unique fishery—a prime trout lake in the maw of a dormant volcano in central Oregon, about 25 air miles SE of Bend. East Lake is one of two lakes within Newberry Crater in the Paulina Mountains of the Deschutes National Forest, recently designated a National Monument. East Lake is separated from its neighbor, Paulina Lake, by a high ridge. Both lakes produce trophy size brown trout. East also has a fine rainbow fishery and, as of 1992 and 1993, experimental stockings of landlocked coho and kokanee.

From Bend, drive south 20 miles on Hwy. 97 to the Newberry Crater turnoff. Turn east on paved Forest Rd. 21, and wind upward about 14 miles to Paulina Lake, then continue east another 3 miles to East Lake.

East is one of the most consistent large lakes in Oregon. It survived the early years of drought very well, but finally began to go down in 1992. It has not yet returned to normal fill. The lake offers slightly over 1,000 acres, with broad shoal areas and a maximum depth of 175 feet. This is high country, over 6,300 ft. in elevation, and it isn't unusual to find snow on the ground in June. It gets cold up here at night.

Rainbow trout make up 80% of the catch, ranging in size from 10-14 inches, though rainbow to 10 pounds have been caught. Rainbow size has decreased in recent years, for unknown reasons. Brook trout, once stocked regularly, were caught so infrequently that stocking has been discontinued, though a small population continues to reproduce naturally in the lake and may show up in the catch in early or late season. In the past, 4-pound brook trout were not uncommon. As for the browns, expert Jim Teeny developed his famous nymph while stalking monster browns in the shallows here. Browns over 20 pounds have been grudgingly dragged from the lake.

Kokanee were first stocked in the lake in 1993. Adults should be available in 1996. ODF&W biologists anticipate these will grow as well in East as they do in Paulina, which produced the state record kokanee. At East, anglers might look for kokanee in the depths to the north, particularly when the lake quiets down in late summer. Because East lake is shallower than Paulina, kokanee may be successfully still-fished in the shallows in spring. Trolling may also be effective in early season.

Landlocked coho were first stocked in 1992. In 1994, coho 18-20 inches were available, though they have not been caught in large numbers. Both coho and kokanee should be counted in the trout bag limit.

Still-fishing takes a lot of trout, but don't go too deep. In early season when the fish are close to the surface, a bobber rig is effective. The hot springs area in the southeast and the north side between the cliffs and Cinder Hill campground are good places to start in early season. Later it pays to go deeper. Bait anglers do best in early season.

Trollers generally work slowly around the shoreline of the lake, going deeper in the warm weather months. Chubs have been the primary natural forage in the past, though kokanee may begin to attract browns in years to come. Kwikfish-type lures and flasher-bait rigs are used, as well as dark colored woolly-worms and Teeny nymphs. S-l-o-w-l-y is the key here. Incidentally, there is a 10-mph speed limit in effect on the lake.

This is a great lake for fly-fishing. A rich insect population can turn on a rise at any moment, though evening is the usual time. The shorelines produce well. The southeast shoals get an influx of warm water from volcanic springs that might serve as a magnet to browns in early season. The east shoreline can be very good at evening, but slow during the day. Watch for feeding fish at the surface in the shoal areas along the southern shore.

Stalking big fish which cruise at dusk is an exciting and effective way to tie into a trophy trout. Try the north shore cliffs, east of the red fissure, along the west shore near the white pumice slide, and along the south shore. Try a Teeny nymph in sizes 4-6 and hold on tight. A partner on shore spotting from above will improve the odds of success. Polaroid glasses will make fish spotting much easier.

Two very attractive Forest Service campgrounds, East Lake and Hot Springs, are on the south shore within stands of ponderosa pine. A third, Cinder Hill, is on the NE shore. Each campground has a boat ramp. A resort on the east shore offers rustic accommodations, boat rentals, and supplies.

When the lake opens in spring, there is usually a lot of snow around the camps and, sometimes, ice on the lake, but ice-out fishing can be terrific. Bring plenty of cold weather gear.

Check the regulations for special bag limit, designed to encourage better carry-over, and bigger catches. For more information, see *Fishing In Oregon's Cascade Lakes*.

East Lake yields rainbow, browns, kokanee, and coho.

EIGHTMILE CREEK Much longer than its name, this stream flows east for about 30 miles from the east edge of Mt. Hood National Forest, crossed by Hwy. 197, before joining Fifteen Mile Creek to enter the Columbia near The Dalles. It is followed for most of its length by gravel and dirt roads.

Used quite a bit for irrigation, it doesn't provide much angling, but there is some fishing early in the season for wild rainbow trout. While roads follow the stream closely, there is a lot of private land. Best fishing is in the upper stream in early season, with worms, eggs or grasshoppers for bait. There are no campsites along the lower stream, but several in the upper headwaters in the forest, about 17 miles west of Dufur on Forest Rd. 44. The stream opens at the end of May.

ELK LAKE (Deschutes Co.) A scenic large lake in the Cascades west of Bend, in the heart of the popular Cascade Lakes recreational area. Brook trout and kokanee will occupy the fisherman, but sailing, wind surfing and swimming are a big part of the action here. The lake is just east of Century Drive (Hwy. 46), about 32 miles SW of Bend. It can also be reached from the south by forest roads branching off from Hwy. 97 to the east, and from Hwy. 58 to the south.

Elk Lake is in a picturesque setting, with the Three Sisters towering over the north end of the lake and Mt. Bachelor dominating the eastern horizon. It is about 1 1/2 miles long from north to south, and 1/2 mile wide, covering 250 acres. Most of it is over 25 ft. deep, with the southern half considerably shallower than the northern. There is a 65 ft. hole mid-way across the lake opposite Point campground and boat launch.

Fishing here is not the major activity, but it can certainly be good. Brook trout generally range 7-14 inches, but trout to 20 inches do show up. Early season offers the best catches, with June the prime month. After a long winter, these fish will take just about anything. Late fall evenings are a good time for taking large fish on a fly, and the weather is generally more dependable. These trout are primarily caught along the shoreline. Stick to water where you can see bottom. In this clear water, that means as deep as 20 feet. Caddis nymphs are the most abundant trout food. Fly anglers will find dark wet patterns a good bet anytime here. Crayfish are also plentiful, so crayfish imitations do well.

Elk has a well established population of kokanee which reproduces naturally. Success rate in 1988 was very high, though the fish are generally small since Elk is not a rich lake. Most kokanee are taken at the south end of the lake at the Kokanee Hole. This is an area about 100 feet in diameter which you can find by aligning your boat between a rockslide and the road culvert across from Point Campground. Most anglers take them by deep-trolling a lure tipped with corn at about the 50-ft. level. Jigging a one or two ounce lure is also effective. There is a 25 per day kokanee bag limit to encourage anglers to help keep the population under control.

There is a National Forest guard station at Elk, and several trails to prime high lake fishing areas begin here. See also Horse Lake, Mink Lake. Other big lakes accessible by motor vehicle line Century Drive, north and south. Hosmer Lake, with its unique catch-and-release fly fishery for Atlantic salmon, is just 3 miles by road from Elk Lake.

There are quite a few summer homes around the north and NE shore. A very nice public beach is at the southern tip of the lake and another is on the NW shore. Sailing has been popular here for decades, and windsurfing has really come on strong in recent years. On a fine summer weekend over a hundred sails will dot the lake. Power boats are allowed, but there is a 10-mph speed limit.

Elk Lake Resort on the western shore has rustic accommodations, boat rentals, some supplies, and a lunch counter that makes especially good milk shakes. This is the center of sailing activity. There is a boat launch at the resort and a public campground just south. Additional campgrounds are located at the southwest end of the lake off County Rd. 46, and at the southeast end off Forest Rd. 4625. All three campgrounds have boat ramps and drinking water.

In most years, the road to Elk Lake is snow-bound until late May. For more information,see *Fishing In Oregon's Cascade Lakes*.

FALL RIVER A beautiful spring fed stream restricted to fly-fishing, in the Deschutes National Forest SW of Bend. Clear and cold, it springs full-blown from the ground about 2 miles NW of Pringle Falls (on the Deschutes River) and winds its way NE 8 miles to join the Deschutes about 6 miles below the falls.

The north bank of the upper stream is followed closely by Forest Rd. 42 from the river's source to Fall River Hatchery. Forest Rd. 42 can be reached from Hwy. 97 by taking the Sunriver turn-off, or you may come in from the south from Pringle Falls by way of Forest Rd. 4360. The lower river offers easy hiking south from the hatchery, which is at about the midpoint of the river, or north from the Forest Rd. 4360 bridge which crosses Fall River one mile above its confluence with the Deschutes. In the lower 4 miles, the river flows through a lot of private property.

Fall River is not large, averaging 50-75 feet across, but it provides some interesting fly-fishing. Spring-fed, it is crystal clear and requires very light tackle. Rainbow, brook trout, and brown trout are present, and the state stocks aggressively with weekly releases of catchable rainbow and catchable brook trout throughout the season. Angling holds steady, as there is no water fluctuation. The average catch runs 7-12 inches. Best bet is the water below the hatchery in late June and July. Late afternoon and evening angling is the most productive.

The river closes at the end of September, from the falls to the Deschutes, to protect spawning brown trout.

There is a nice campground 1/2 mile below the river source, though it does not have drinking water. Drinking water is available at the hatchery. Additional campgrounds are nearby upstream and down on the Deschutes. Dexter's Fly Shop in LaPine is a good source for Fall River information and fly patterns. For more information, see *Fishing In Oregon's Cascade Lakes*.

FARRELL LAKE One of a pair of good hike-in brook trout lakes about one mile north of the road between Crescent and Summit Lakes. From Hwy. 58 at Crescent Lake Junction take Forest Rd. 60 around the NW shore of Crescent Lake to the Summit Lake turn-off, Forest Rd. 6010. This road begins at the west end of Crescent Lake about 1/4 mile south of Tandy Bay Campground. About 4 miles west, at the Meek Lake Trail turnout, head north (opposite Meek Lake) and hike 1/2 mile on Trail 43 to Farrell.

Farrell Lake is long and narrow, and lies just east of Snell Lake. Four acres and mostly shallow, its brook trout run 8-14 inches and average just under a pound. The lake is easy to fish from shore. There are good natural campsites at the west end of the lake.

FAWN LAKE A good hike-in brook trout lake just east of Diamond Peak Wilderness, about midway between Odell and Crescent Lakes. From the highway junction at Eugene, it's about 70 miles to the Odell-Crescent area. Trails lead to Fawn Lake from the east end of Odell Lake and from Crescent Lake Resort, which is 2 miles south of Hwy. 58. It's about a 3-mile hike from Odell by Trail 44, a little shorter from Crescent Lake.

At elevation 5,680 ft., the lake covers 43 acres, with a maximum depth of 27 feet. Brook trout average 12 inches and run to 16 inches. Bait angling is productive early in the year, and flies do best in summer and fall. There are natural campsites. The lake is usually accessible in late June, depending on snow pack.

FROG LAKE A small trout lake, heavily fished, just off Hwy. 26, 9 miles SE of Government Camp. The turn-off is well signed. The lake is east of the highway, with a road directly to it, though a short hike is required in spring before the snowdrifts clear. Fishing is for rainbow trout. The lake is heavily stocked with legal rainbow annually. All methods are used. Boats can be launched to fish this shallow 11-acre pond, but motors are prohibited. Recommended for small fry.

GIBSON LAKE (Confederated Tribes Warm Springs) A 6-acre brook trout lake 1/4 mile north of Breitenbush Lake by a trail that starts across from the Breitenbush Lake entry road. Maximum depth here is 14 feet. The lake is stocked semi-annually with brook trout. A permit is not required, and overnight camping is permitted.

GOVERNMENT COVE One of the I-84 ponds adjacent to the Columbia River. Government Cove is 90 acres, located at hwy. mi. 47, two miles east of Cascade Locks. Access is from I-84 at the Herman Creek Exit. As with all the ponds in this series, Government Cove may contain any of the species found in the Columbia, including largemouth and smallmouth bass, crappie, yellow perch, pumpkinseed sunfish, bullhead catfish, and even channel catfish. See Appendix for a map of Columbia River Ponds.

GREEN LAKES (Deschutes Co.) A series of three lovely glacial lakes in the Three Sisters Wilderness west of Bend. The lakes are nestled between South Sister and Broken Top Mountains, with South Sister dominating the skyline. They are most commonly reached by a 5-mile hike on a well marked trail north from North Century Drive (Hwy. 46). The trail begins at a turn-out across from Sparks Lake about 28 miles west of Bend. This trail has an elevation gain of 1,000 ft.

An easier, but less well known approach is possible from Crater Ditch Creek north of Todd Lake. It's still a 5-mile hike by well marked, scenic trail, but there is almost no elevation gain. Follow the signs to Todd Lake off Century Drive, but continue past Todd Lake on Forest Rd. 370 (a fair dirt road) about 3 miles to Forest Rd. 380, which branches north toward Broken Top and ends in 1 1/2 miles at the head of Trail 10. There's an impressive view of the blown away south face of Broken Top from the trailhead. Follow Trail 10 an easy 5 miles to Green Lakes.

Middle Green is the largest, covering 85 acres, and it has the best angling. Both wild brook trout and rainbow are available, and run to good size. The rainbow range 10-14 inches, the brook trout a shade smaller. North Green is the next largest, about 10 acres, just north of the main lake. South Green is the smallest at 8 acres, and is the first one you see from the trail. South is stocked with rainbow.

The setting here is breathtakingly beautiful, a high rocky saddle which is mostly unforested. Fly anglers will have no trouble with their backcast here. At elevation 6,500 ft., the snow rarely clears before mid-July. Pack sun screen. At this altitude you'll roast in no time. Good natural campsites are available.

GRINDSTONE LAKES Two privately owned desert lakes about 100 miles east of Prineville. The lakes grow rainbow to 12 pounds and are available to fly-fish for a price, which includes meals and accommodations. Contact Kaufmann's Streamborn, Tigard for additional information.

HAND LAKE A 4-acre trout lake in the Cache Lake Basin, Deschutes National Forest. See Island Lake, Link Lake for directions. From Hwy. 20 north of Sisters, take Forest Rd. 2068 west, then turn right on Forest Rd. 600 to Hand Lake. The lake is 16 ft. deep and is stocked by ground and air with cutthroat and brook trout.

HANKS LAKES (Deschutes Co.) A series of 3 good trout lakes one mile east of Irish and Taylor Lakes, a short hike from the road. The trailhead is on Forest Rd. 600 about 1 1/2 miles east of the Pacific Crest Trail crossing at Irish Lake. Forest Rd. 600 can be reached from the west by way of Waldo Lake, or from the east by way of Little Cultus Lake. Trail 15 leads north from the road about 1/3 mile to the west shore of Middle Hanks Lake. West Hanks is just to the west, and East Hanks is slightly SE, of Middle. The current Deschutes National Forest map shows the lakes and the trail, but fails to give their names. Middle Hanks is the first lake the trail encounters. The lakes are usually accessible by the end of June.

East Hanks is about 8 acres, and middle and west lakes are about 6 acres each. All the lakes contain rainbow trout. West and East also contain brook and cutthroat trout. Angling is comparable in all three lakes, with the west lake probably the best. All are good on bait or lures most of the time, and fly-fishing can be excellent. Fish here range 10-14 inches, with some larger.

In the area to the north are many lakes and potholes, some of which have been stocked, and there's good angling in several of them. There are campgrounds at Irish and Taylor Lakes. Mosquito repellent is essential in late spring when the fish may or may not be biting, but hordes of skeeters can be depended upon.

HARVEY LAKE (Confederated Tribes Warm Springs) A scenic, lightly fished hike-in brook and cutthroat trout lake occupying a narrow flat step between two very steep slopes, about 4 miles south of Olallie Lake. A former road from Warm Springs to the trailhead has been closed. The lake is now only accessible by trail from Breitenbush Campground. The trail begins at the south end of the camp near the inlet. It is a 3-mile hike to Harvey.

Harvey is at elevation 5,400 ft. and covers 27 acres. It is located in a cirque at the base of a 300 ft. talus slope, very similar to Dark Lake to the north, and rivals Blue Lake for beauty. The inlet stream tumbles down from Lake Hilda, 300 feet above. The outlet flow shoots over a 200 foot sheer cliff into Shitke Creek. It has a maximum depth of 40 feet with limited shoal area. The lake has some brook trout along with residual cutthroat trout from earlier stocking. A permit is required to fish this lake. No overnight camping is allowed due to fire danger.

Late fall evenings are a good time to fish for Elk Lake's big brook trout.

HAYSTACK RESERVOIR A fair size reservoir 9 miles south of Madras in Crooked River National Grassland, not especially attractive, but with plentiful bank angling opportunity and an unusually wide choice of fisheries for this area. It is used as a storage reservoir, so there can be considerable daily fluctuation in water level. It grows good size fish and supports excellent angling for kokanee, and fair fishing for largemouth bass, black crappie, brown bullhead, stocked rainbow, and the occasional brown trout. From Madras drive 8 miles south on Hwy. 97, turning east onto a county road about one mile south of the Culver turnoff. From there it's about 2 miles to Haystack.

Haystack is extremely productive for kokanee, growing fish 10-18 inches. Best catches are in spring and fall. Anglers have success both trolling and bank fishing. About 5,000 legal rainbow are stocked annually, with best fishing in spring and fall near the south shore. Crappie are small but plentiful, especially near the inlets. Largemouth bass have established themselves and are reproducing naturally.

In 1993 the reservoir was so heavily drawn-down that much of the fishery was lost. It will be restocked with 30,000 kokanee fingerlings annually, and it is anticipated that the fishery will rebound by 1995 or 1996.

Haystack is heavily used by water-skiers in summer. However, there is a 5 mph speed limit near the SE and SW shores which should help diminish conflicts between anglers and speed-boaters.

There is a primitive forest service campground on the east shore. The reservoir is open year-round, but is sometimes frozen over for short periods in winter (though not thick enough for ice fishing).

HERMAN CREEK A trout stream with small steelhead and chinook runs, entering the Columbia River about 2 miles east of Cascade Locks. It heads about 12 miles upstream in several small lakes in the Wahtum Lake area and is crossed by I-84 just above the mouth. The lower stretch of the creek from the railroad to the Columbia is under Columbia Zone angling regulations.

You must hike in if you want to fish this stream. A good trail begins at the Columbia Work Center, joining the Herman Creek Trail one mile up the hill. The Herman Creek Trail parallels the mainstem of the creek to the forks, then follows the east fork to the headwaters. Small wild cutthroat can be taken all along this stretch. It has some big holes where nice size trout are taken.

Herman Creek has a fall chinook run, and there is a hatchery near the mouth, just off I-84. The run usually makes the creek in late August. Angling is prohibited up to the hatchery dam from August 15 through November 30. There is a small summer steelhead run in the stream from June through October. Non-finclipped steelhead must be released

The East Fork Hood River has small runs of wild summer and winter steelhead.

unharmed. Barbless hooks are required from December 1 through March 31.

HICKS LAKE A small brook trout lake in Mt. Hood National Forest north of Wahtum Lake, about 25 miles SW of Hood River. Hicks Lake is 1/2 mile NW of Wahtum at the head of Herman Creek. Only about 2 acres and shallow, it has frequently winterkilled, and stocking has been discontinued.

HIDDEN LAKE (Deschutes Co.) A 13-acre lake, sometimes confused with Found Lake, way off the beaten path in the Deschutes National Forest east of Waldo Lake. The lake has a small population of little brook trout. It is on the western slope of Gerdine Butte, about 1 1/2 miles south of Charlton Lake.

HOOD RIVER A large stream with a very good steelhead run, flowing into the Columbia River at the town of Hood River in the Columbia Gorge, about 50 miles east of Portland. The river's source is the glaciers on the north and east slopes of Mt. Hood. The main forks of the river join near the community of Dee, about 14 miles upstream from the Columbia. The lower river provides most of the steelhead angling, and there is opportunity to hook a steelhead any month of the year.

Hood River supports both winter and summer steelhead runs. The total annual catch varies between 1,000 and 4,000 fish. The 1991-92 summer steelhead catch in the mainstem was estimated at 1,500 The winter steelhead catch was 353. Most steelhead angling takes place on the lower 3 miles of the river. Trout angling is fair in the lower river for both native and stocked fish. All non-finclipped steelhead and trout must be released unharmed.

Bank angling can be productive. There is some boat angling at the lower end near the mouth, mostly in the short stretch between I-84 and the Columbia. There is a boat ramp at a park on the river's east bank.

There are no camping areas on the lower river.

HOOD RIVER, EAST FORK A stocked rainbow trout stream, heading on the SE slopes of Mt. Hood and flowing over 20 miles to join the main river about 2 miles north of Dee. It also has small wild runs of summer and winter steelhead available for catch and release angling. The fork is closely followed by Hwy. 35, which is clear of snow in late spring. Prior to that, access is from Hwy. 30 at Hood River. Hwy. 281 follows the stream south from Dee, where it joins Hwy. 35 at Parkdale.

Legal rainbow trout are stocked annually from Parkdale upstream throughout the spring and summer. Fishing is usually good through the summer months. All non-finclipped trout must be released unharmed.

There are three campgrounds along the river in Mt. Hood National Forest—Polallie, Sherwood, and Robinhood.

HOOD RIVER, LAKE BRANCH A tributary of the West Fork of the Hood River, beginning as the outlet creek for Lost Lake on the NE slope of Mt. Hood. It is now used as a steelhead spawning sanctuary and is not open to angling except in the headwaters. The branch is followed closely by Forest Rd. 13 all the way to Lost Lake.

The open area is found above the Sawtooth Spur Rd. (Forest Rd. 700/1300). Angling above this point is for wild trout, and a fair number of cutthroat and rainbow are taken with some hard work. All non-finclipped trout must be released unharmed. There is a pleasant campground and resort at Lost Lake.

HOOD RIVER, WEST FORK The West Fork of Hood River joins the mainstem about 1 1/2 miles north of Dee. The stream heads near the east boundary of the Bull Run Reserve and flows NE for about 5 miles to the confluence. It offers fair angling for wild trout in the upper waters, and primarily catch and release steelheading below the Punchbowl. All non-finclipped steelhead must be released unharmed. The West Fork is a designated steelhead sanctuary, and is no longer stocked with hatchery trout. There are campgrounds at Lost Lake and about 5 miles west of the crest of Lolo Pass.

HOOD RIVER POND No.1 One of the I-84 ponds adjacent to the Columbia River. Located at hwy. mi. 66.3, this 4 acre pond is accessible to eastbound vehicles only, with parking in a limited unimproved area. It may contain any of the Columbia River species, including largemouth and smallmouth bass, crappie, yellow perch, pumpkinseed sunfish, bullhead catfish, and channel catfish. See p. 206 for a map of Columbia River Ponds from Cascade Locks to the Deschutes.

HOOD RIVER POND No. 2 One of the I-84 ponds adjacent to the Columbia River, located at hwy. mile 67. It covers 3 acres south of I-84, with limited unimproved parking for eastbound traffic only. It may contain any of the Columbia's warmwater species. See p. 206 for a map of Columbia River Ponds.

HOOD RIVER POND No. 3 A 3-acre pond south of I-84 adjacent to the Columbia River at hwy. mile 67. There is limited unimproved parking for eastbound traffic only. It may contain any of the Columbia River species, including largemouth and smallmouth bass, crappie, yellow perch, pumpkinseed sunfish, bullhead catfish, and channel catfish. See page 206 for a map of Columbia River Ponds.

HORSESHOE LAKE (Olallie Lake area) A pretty, 14-acre brook and rainbow trout lake between Olallie and Breitenbush lakes off Forest Rd. 4220. You can drive right to this scenic beauty. A spit of land juts into the lake from the west shore, giving the lake its characteristic shape. It's easy to fish from shore. There is a campground at the lake.

HOSMER LAKE One of the richest lakes in the Deschutes National Forest, one mile SE of Elk Lake on Century Drive, 34 road miles SW of Bend. It offers fishing for very large brook trout, and a catch-and-release fishery for landlocked Atlantic salmon. Angling is restricted to fly-fishing only with barbless flies.

The lake is composed of two large main pools connected by a long channel through which Hosmer's big fish glide. The pools are thick with submerged weeds, and water lilies hover at the surface. The channel is lined with bullrushes, but is weed free. Even when the bite is off, there is some satisfaction in boating the channel, where big fish are clearly visible at all times. A mid-day tour on the channel is like cruising an aquarium.

Hosmer's dumbbell shape offers many views to the boater. Red Crater (a forested cinder cone) looms over the main pool, Bachelor Butte provides a handsome backdrop to many of the campsites. The Three Sisters guard the back pool. In one cove the water slips into a lava field and disappears. Wildlife abounds, and osprey will put your best fishing efforts to shame. The early riser may slip through the fog and surprise otter, mink, or deer along the shore, while countless marsh birds grumble in the rushes.

To reach Hosmer Lake drive south from Bend on Century Drive. The turn-off to Hosmer is about 3 miles past the entrance to Elk Lake Resort and is well marked. The road reaches the lake in about one mile. Century Drive (County and Forest Rd. 46) can also be reached from the Willamette Valley by driving SE from Eugene on Hwy. 58 to the Davis Lake turnoff 3 miles past Crescent Lake Junction. Following the signs to Davis Lake will put you on Hwy. 46 heading north. Hosmer is 10 miles north of the Crane Prairie junction.

Hosmer is a large shallow lake, the channel connecting its two main pools extending north to south. The southern pool is the deeper of the two, yet its maximum depth is only 10 ft. It has two campgrounds on its western shore. The richly organic water limits visibility to about 6 ft. depth. Fish are found throughout this portion of the lake. Try the bullrushes along the western shore.

A winding channel almost a mile long leads to the northern pool. By anchoring, standing, and using polaroid glasses you can watch the movement of these fish and cast accordingly. A short channel branches off towards the northeast, ending at a floodgate which regulates the flow of water into a natural lava sink.

The northern (back) lake covers more area but is generally shallower. Here, a cold, clear, spring fed stream, Quinn Creek, joins Hosmer from the north. Several heather covered islands dot this portion of the lake. Fishing activity is concentrated along its southern and eastern shores.

The rich waters of Hosmer have long grown the largest brook trout in Oregon. For some time it has also been home to a good population of planted Atlantic salmon which average around 15 inches and go to over 20. Brook trout are periodically stocked here to maintain the fishery, and they reach very impressive size. These old hawgs (which can live to be 10-20 years old) are hard to fool.

The salmon are a catch-and-release fishery, and most anglers treat the occasional trout hooked here similarly. But the brook trout population is doing very well, and ODF&W urges anglers to catch and keep the brook trout (which are growing too numerous for the lake's size).

The original strain of Atlantic salmon stocked in Hosmer was surface oriented and took the fly eagerly. Unfortunately, they were also easy prey for ospreys. The current strain is more challenging for the birds, and for anglers as well.

Tackle is restricted to barbless flies only. Hosmer has good insect hatches in the spring, and leaches and water boatmen are a staple in the salmon's diet throughout the season. *Callibaetis*, midge, damselfly, and crayfish imitations are all worth trying.

Stalking fish in the channels is a favorite method, but slow trolling in the southern pool and the channels will often work when nothing else seems effective. Best fishing is late June through mid-July and again in fall.

There are two excellent forest campgrounds located on the southern pool, and there is a boat ramp at the southern tip. Only electric motors are permitted on the lake. This is a great lake for float tubes and canoes. Mallard Marsh Campground at the north end of the lake has a little canoe slip through the bull rushes. There is a 10-mph speed limit on the lake. For more information, see *Fishing In Oregon's Cascade Lakes*.

HUSTON LAKES Two bass and panfish lakes in the Powell Butte area about halfway between Redmond and Prineville in central Oregon. The lakes are on private land, and neither is currently open for public access.

INDIAN CREEK (Hood River Co.) A small stream which flows right through the town of Hood River. Used for agricultural drainage, it no longer supports aquatic life.

INDIAN FORD CREEK (Deschutes Co.) A small creek flowing about 11 miles through mostly private land into Squaw Creek just north of Sisters. The upper stretch is crossed by Hwy. 20 about 5 miles NW of Sisters. The stream flows to the east then south to Sisters. Its north bank is followed fairly closely by a forest road. The creek supports a few small wild rainbow averaging 6-10 inches. There is a nice campground on the upper end at the Hwy. 20 crossing 5 miles west of Sisters.

IRIS LAKE One of the I-84 ponds adjacent to the Columbia River, located at hwy. mi. 56.2. It covers 5 acres at the east end of Viento State Park. Take Exit 56. The lake may contain any of the Columbia's warmwater species. See page 206 for a map of Columbia River Ponds from Cascade Locks to the Deschutes.

IRISH LAKE A scenic trout lake near the summit of the Cascades that you can drive to if you're careful and have a high center vehicle. The access road is not quite a jeep trail, but not a lot better. Irish Lake is about mid-way between Waldo and Cultus Lakes, SW of Bend in Deschutes National Forest. The Pacific Crest Trail follows the western shore of the lake.

Irish can be approached from either the east or the west. Access from the east is usually available first. From Bend follow Century Drive (County and Forest Rd. 46) SW past Lava Lake to the Cultus Lake turn-off. Take Forest Rd. 4630 about 2 1/2 miles to Forest Rd. 600, passing the Cultus Resort turn-off and following signs for Little Cultus Lake. Irish Lake is 6 fairly rough miles west from this point. Drive slowly. From the east, Forest Rd. 20031 leads north from North Waldo Lake Campground towards Taylor Burn. It intersects Forest Rd. 600 one mile west of Irish Lake. This last mile is even worse than the stretch from little Cultus. Irish Lake is at 5,500 ft., and the snow lingers until late June most years. This usually blocks the western access.

Irish has 28 acres of clear water and is mostly shallow. The lake is a consistent producer of large brook trout, and is stocked with cutthroat trout from time to time. Brook trout predominate. Trout are typically 8-12 inches, but quite a few run to 16 inches or better. Bait angling or lures will work most of the time, but fly angling in the early morning and evening hours produce best results. Brook trout feed in the shoal areas after the sun goes down, and some evenings any fly will entice them. Fishing is best as soon after ice-out as you can get in.

Taylor Lake, just 100 yards south of Irish, is bigger but less productive. Other smaller fishable lakes can be reached by hiking the PCT north, or by taking Trail 15 (Deer Lake Trail) north from Forest Rd. 600 (1 1/2 miles east of the PCT crossing). This area is riddled with lakes and tarns, and hordes of mosquitoes breed in them, especially in early season. Bring repellent and consider head nets.

There is a rustic improved camping area at the lake (no drinking water). Motors are prohibited on the lake, and there is no boat ramp.

ISLAND LAKE (Jefferson Co.) An 8 acre lake just south of Suttle Lake in Deschutes National Forest west of Link Lake. See Link Lake for directions. Island is 18-ft. deep and contains cutthroat and brook trout.

ISLAND LAKE (Confederated Tribes Warm Springs) Island Lake is the fourth downstream lake in the Olallie-to-Trout Lake chain. The oval lake's name is derived from a one acre island located in the middle of it. It is accessible only by unimproved trail from either Olallie Lake east or Trout Lake west. From Trout Lake, it's about one mile to Island Lake. The first 1/4 mile of trail is a fairly steep uphill grind, but the remaining distance is more easily traveled. The trail from Olallie Lake begins at the SE end of the lake, and is most easily reached from Olallie Peninsula Campground.

Island covers about 26 acres at elevation 4650 ft. It is the shallowest lake of the chain, with a maximum depth of only 10 feet. Most of the lake is 3 feet deep or less. Brook trout are stocked here. The lake is difficult to fish without a raft or float tube. A permit is required to fish. No overnight camping is allowed due to fire danger.

JACK LAKE A small, easily reached but, probably fishless lake in the Deschutes National Forest west of the Metolius recreational area. Jack is 5 air miles NW of Hwy. 20 at Suttle Lake, about 14 miles west of Sisters. Only about 7 acres and quite shallow, it is no longer stocked due to frequent winterkills. There is a good campground at the lake.

JEAN LAKE A 6-acre rainbow trout lake 1/2 mile NW of Badger Lake on the SE slope of Mt. Hood. To reach Jean Lake, drive east from Government Camp on Hwy. 26, and take Hwy. 35 toward Hood River. Six miles from the intersection at Bennett Pass, take Forest Rd. 3550 SE about 3 miles to the Camp Windy Rd. 3530, which leads NE. Take this a little over one mile past Camp Windy to the Jean Lake Trail. The trail descends about 240 feet in 1/2 mile. These roads are high and rough. Don't expect to get in before late June.

Jean Lake is about 1/2 mile NW and 800 feet above Badger lake. It isn't heavily fished (after you drive the road you'll understand why) and provides very good angling for a small lake. Formerly stocked with brook trout, it now contains predominantly rainbow trout. Anglers usually find a good population of 8-9 inch fish, with some to 13 inches. There are no campsites at the lake, but there are facilities at Camp Windy.

JEFFERSON CREEK A small, pretty stream that heads on the SE slopes of Mt. Jefferson and flows into the Metolius River at Candle Creek Campground north of Sisters. Jefferson serves as a rearing stream for Metolius bull trout and is closed to angling.

JOHNNY LAKE A brook trout lake in the center of a triangle formed by Waldo Lake, Davis Lake, and Crane Prairie. From the intersection of Century Drive and Hwy. 42, take Forest Rd. 5897 heading west towards Waldo Lake. Follow this road about 3 miles, then take Forest Rd. 200 south for one mile. A trail leading south 1/2 mile to the lake begins where Forest Rd. 200 cuts sharply back to the east. Johnny covers about 20 acres and is fairly deep. There is a good campsite at the lake, but no improvements.

KERSHAW LAKE A 4-acre, lightly fished lake in the Irish Lake area, a good producer for those who find it. It is within a group of small lakes between Little Cultus Lake and Irish. Starting from the trail along the west shore of Middle Hanks Lake, hike north on the trail about 1/2 mile. See Hanks Lakes for road directions. The lake is east of the trail, and you will cross a depression with a small creek connecting a chain of ponds just before reaching it. Bring the Irish Mt. topo map with you. Total hike from the road is just under one mile.

The lake is 4 acres and 13 feet deep. It has a drop-off ledge along the east side. Try casting just over this ledge to bring up the biggest fish. Brook trout average 8-10 inches here. Mosquitoes are terrible in spring.

KINGSLEY RESERVOIR (a.k.a. Green Point Reservoir) One of the largest lakes in the Hood River area, this 60-acre impoundment offers fishing for stocked rainbow trout. It is about 11 miles by road SW of Hood River. Two roads lead west to the reservoir over 6 rough miles.

The rainbow run 6-13 inches, averaging 10 inches, and there is usually a good supply of catchables. Bait angling or trolling are the most popular methods. Fishing is good off the gently sloping dam face, and other bank fishing spots are available.

The campground at Kingsley is closed to use by trailers. Recommended for small fry.

KOLBERG LAKE One of the I-84 ponds adjacent to the Columbia River. Kolberg is at highway. mile 65.8, covering 5 acres directly across I-84 from the Kolberg Beach State Rest Area. Anglers should park at the rest area and walk across the highway. Kolberg may contain any of the Columbia River species, including largemouth and smallmouth bass, crappie, yellow perch, pumpkinseed sunfish, bullhead catfish, and channel catfish. See p. 206 for a map of Columbia River Ponds from Cascade Locks to the Deschutes.

LAKE CREEK (Jefferson Co.) A short creek flowing out of Suttle Lake and into the Metolius River just south of Camp Sherman. It is the only Metolius River tributary that is still open to angling, since it contains no brook trout. The stream is crossed near the lake several times and again near the mouth, but no roads follow it. There is some private land along the lower creek.

The creek behaves most peculiarly about a mile below Suttle Lake, dividing into three braids which parallel each other about a half mile apart. These are known as the North, Middle, and South Forks, with the middle carrying the most water. They rejoin about a mile up from the mouth. The South Fork flows through a private resort, Lake Creek Resort, located near the lower end. Another private resort, The Pines, includes 27 acres on the lower North Fork. This portion is stocked with rainbow by the owners of the resort and is open only to resort guests. Some of these rainbow run to 16 inches. The main creek has wild rainbow and browns, which slip in from Suttle Lake.

Lake Creek is usually worth a try on bait or fly. There are forest camps at Suttle Lake and along the Metolius River. Supplies are available at Camp Sherman.

LAURANCE LAKE A small irrigation reservoir on the Clear Creek Branch of the Middle Fork of Hood River. Motor boats are prohibited on the lake, which covers about 104 acres 19 miles south of the city of Hood River. From Parkdale School drive about 3 miles south to Forest Rd. 2810, Clear Creek Rd. This road swings west and reaches the reservoir in another 3 miles.

Laurance is stocked with catchable rainbow and contains a population of wild cutthroat. It also has a spawning population of bull trout, one of the last in the Hood River watershed. To protect them, all tributaries to the reservoir, and Clear Branch Creek below the reservoir, are closed to angling. Within Laurance itself, only finclipped trout may be kept.

Anglers are required to use artificial lures or flies with barbless hooks.

The reservoir opens the fourth Saturday in April. There is a very small campground on the lake with a paved boat ramp, and several unimproved campsites on the creek above the pool.

LAVA LAKE, BIG A scenic and excellent trout fishery in the Deschutes National Forest, 38 miles south of Bend on the Cascades Lakes Highway (County and Forest Rd. 46). The lake is about 20 miles beyond Mt. Bachelor. For early season access it is usually necessary to approach from the east. Drive south from Bend on Hwy. 97 to the Sunriver turn-off, County Rd. 42, which can be followed east to its eventual junction with the Lakes Highway, about 13 miles south of Lava Lake.

Big Lava is a beautiful lake with much of the character of Hosmer Lake to the north. Mt. Bachelor dominates the horizon. A wealth of wildlife adds to the enjoyment of its mountain setting. Although the lake is spring fed, the water is rich with organic material. This forms a food base that grows big fish quickly. Lava is about 1/2 mile square and 30 feet at its deepest point near the NE end. Bullrushes line much of the shoreline, and a good deal of shoal water can be effectively fly-fished.

Rainbow are the predominant catch, ranging 12-24 inches, averaging 12-15 with many 16-17 inchers taken. Brook trout currently run smaller, averaging 12 inches, but some 19 inchers are taken. Big Lava has grown trophy brook trout in past years, and there's good reason to suspect the current population will eventually include a good number of challenging old lunkers. (Brook trout can live and grow 20 years). Best fishing for brook trout is just after ice-out and again in fall, though the fall fish are in spawning condition, and catch and release is recommended (they don't taste their best at this time, and will serve us all better in the redd than in the pan.).

Bait-fishing is the most popular tactic, and PowerBait is the most popular bait used, replacing Velveeta™, for which Velveeta Point on the NE shore was named. Trolling picks up in July and August, with spinner-bait combinations effective. Spinners and small Kwikfish-type lures are both popular. In late summer and fall, fly-fishing can really pay off, both trolling bright streamers and fishing to the shoreline shelves. Grasshopper imitations are occasionally just what the fish are waiting for.

There is a Forest Service campground and boat ramp on the south shore, and another camp at nearby Little Lava Lake. A rustic resort on the lake has RV hookups, boat rentals, and supplies. There is a 10-mph speed limit on the lake. For more information, see *Fishing In Oregon's Cascade Lakes*.

LAVA LAKE, LITTLE A fair trout lake 1/4 mile SE of Big Lava Lake, headwaters of the Deschutes River. See Big Lava for road directions. Little Lava is 110 acres and offers angling for stocked rainbow and brook trout. Whitefish and (too many) chubs are also present.

Rainbow are stocked each year. They run 6-15 inches and make up most of the catch. Brook trout are stocked occasionally and grow to 12 inches or better. All methods of fishing are used, with trolling very popular and trolled flies effective. Most fish are caught near the shoreline.

There's a small attractive campground with boat ramp at the lake and more facilities at Big Lava. For more information, see Fishing In Oregon's Cascade Lakes.

LEMISH LAKE A very good hike-in lake 3 miles south of the west end of Cultus Lake SW of Bend. It's about a 1/2 mile hike south to the lake on the Lemish Lake Trail, which takes off about 3 miles west of the Little Cultus Lake Rd. junction. The lake is 1/2 mile due west of Lemish Butte, after which it is named. Lemish is the Klamath Indian word for thunder.

Some nice brook trout are taken in this 16-acre lake, with catches 8-16 inches. The lake is usually good in early season and again in late fall. There's good fly-fishing in evenings. The nearest campground is at Little Cultus.

LILY LAKE (Deschutes Co.) A nice hike-in trout lake just off the Pacific Crest Trail on the north side of Charlton Butte, 2 miles east of the northern end of Waldo Lake. Shortest approach is from the south, taking the PCT north from Charlton Lake a bit over one mile to Trail 19, which leads east a short way to the lake. Charlton Lake is on the east-west stretch of Forest Rd. 5897, the Waldo Lake Rd., one mile east of the North Waldo Lake Campground turn-off. Forest Rd. 5897 intersects the Cascade Lakes Highway one mile south of Crane Prairie.

This 15 acre lake is fairly rich and has good shoal areas and cover. The deeper water is over 40 feet. Lightly fished, it is a consistent producer, with all methods effective. Average catch is about 10 inches, with some to 15 inches. It is air stocked with fingerlings, as the lake is not conducive to spawning. Lily is usually not accessible until late June.

Laurance Lake is stocked with catchable rainbow.

LINDSEY POND One of the I-84 ponds adjacent to the Columbia River at hwy. mi. 54, covering 60 acres at the mouth of Lindsey Creek. Best parking and access is for westbound traffic at the truck weigh station. See p. 206 for a map of Columbia River Ponds.

LINE POND One of the I-84 ponds adjacent to the Columbia River at hwy. mile 68, just one acre at the Hood River/Wasco County line. It has limited unimproved parking for eastbound traffic only. See p. 206 for a map of Columbia River Ponds.

LINK LAKE A good trout lake 2 miles SW of Suttle Lake in the Deschutes National Forest. From the Corbett snow-park west of the Suttle Lake turn-off on Hwy. 20, drive west about 2 1/2 miles to Forest Rd. 2076, which leads south. Link is about 2 miles south and about 1/8 mile west of the road. A fire road, which may not be marked, leads to the lake.

Link covers 18 acres and reaches a depth of 20 feet maximum. It has been stocked with cutthroat, rainbow and brook trout. Brook trout predominate The fish run 8-16 inches, averaging 12 inches most years. There are several good campsites at the lake.

LITTLE CULTUS LAKE See Cultus Lake, Little.

LITTLE DESCHUTES RIVER A good brown trout stream which flows 91 miles from its headwaters near Miller Lake in Klamath County to its confluence with the Deschutes River about 15 miles south of Bend. The upper stream, south of Gilchrist, flows through Deschutes National Forest, but much of the lower river flows through private property. County roads cross and parallel much of the stream, however, and road easements provide public access.

The stream is crossed by Hwy. 58 about 15 miles SE of Odell Lake. From this point, forest roads follow the stream up to its headwaters. Other roads branching off highways 58 and 97 cross and follow the river to Bend.

The Little Deschutes is a meandering, slow-moving stream with deeply undercut banks and a sandy bottom. Big browns to 20 inches lurk in the undercuts, and stealth is advisable as you approach the bank. Casting from as far back as 15 ft. might be necessary, as browns can detect bank vibrations from their cavern hideaways. There are also some rainbow trout in the river, primarily in the faster water upstream from Lapine.

Little Deschutes Campground, the only camp on the stream, is about 15 miles east of Odell Lake.

LITTLE THREE CREEKS LAKE See Three Creeks Lake, Little.

LIONS POND A one-acre pond 1/4 mile east of Hwy. 97 at the south end of Redmond. It contains largemouth bass, bluegill, brown bullhead, and catchable rainbow trout. It is restricted to fishing by children 14 years or younger and by disabled anglers. A paved jetty at the pond is wheelchair accessible, as is the grassy west bank. The fishery is the project of the Redmond Fire Department.

LONE PINE POND One of the I-84 ponds adjacent to the Columbia River at hwy. mi. 86.6. It covers 5 acres north of the freeway and immediately west of Hwy. 197. Parking is difficult, and the east shore of the pond is privately owned. It may contain any of the Columbia's warmwater species. See p. 206 for a map of Columbia River Ponds.

LONG LAKE (Jefferson. Co.) A 16-acre trout lake in Deschutes National Forest on the Cascade slope east of the Santiam summit. Long Lake is the middle lake in a chain that begins with Square Lake and ends at Round Lake. The best hike in begins at Round Lake. Take Forest Rd. 12 one mile east of the Suttle Lake junction on Hwy. 20. This road leads a mile to Forest Rd. 1210, which goes to Round Lake. It is accessible in June in most years.

Long Lake is 1/3 mile long but quite narrow. It will yield trout almost any time, though the catch is generally small, averaging about 8 inches with some to 15 inches. All methods can be used, but bait and lures are best in early season. There is a small improved tent campground at Round Lake.

LONG POND One of the I-84 ponds adjacent to the Columbia River, located at hwy. mi. 94. It covers 27 acres between east and westbound freeway lanes. Best access is from Exit 97 at Celilo, then follow a gravel road west from Celilo Park. It may contain any of the Columbia's warmwater species. See p. 206 for a map of Columbia River Ponds.

LOST LAKE (Mt. Hood) A large, very scenic, and very popular lake on the NW slope of Mt. Hood. At 3100 ft., Lost Lake offers a picture postcard view of the mountain. Clear and deep, and almost 1/2 mile square, it contains three varieties of trout plus kokanee, but you must leave your boat motor behind. A prohibition against use of motors on the lake contributes to the tranquillity of the setting and does little harm, if any, to angler success.

Lost Lake must be approached from the east side of Mt. Hood. Take Hwy. 35 to the community of Dee, about 16 miles south of Hood River. From Portland, cross Mt. Hood on Hwy. 26 to reach Hwy. 35 at its southern end, or take I- 84 east through the Columbia Gorge to Hood River, and pick up Hwy. 35 at its northern end. From Dee, follow Forest Rd. 13 for 9 miles west to the lake. The route is well signed. The snow is usually clear in May. Check with Mt. Hood National Forest or Lost Lake Resort for early season road conditions.

Fishing is generally good in the summer and fall. The lake supports natural reproduction of rainbow, brown, and brook trout, and is heavily stocked with legal rainbow each year. Rainbow are the most frequent catch, averaging 10 inches and running to 16. The browns go to 18 inches.

The lake was last stocked with kokanee 15 years ago, and there is still a small naturally reproducing population. The kokanee are about the same size as the rainbow.

Trolling with flasher and worm is the most popular fishing method, though trolled flies work well on the edge of the shoal areas. Troll s-l-o-w-l-y for best results. Much of this lake is quite deep (to 200 feet) but there are good shoals in the western lobe of the lake across from the campground. Single eggs and worms are usually effective. Lures will take some of the larger fish, with small Kwikfish type lures, Hotshots, and flash-type artificial working well.

A pretty trail encircles the lake (about 3 miles). This is a pleasant place, and if you're lucky, you'll get to see otters shucking crayfish while you tempt the wily trout. Lost Lake Resort at the north end of the lake, has a boat ramp, boat rentals, paddleboats, cabins, and supplies. The resort also manages a large Forest Service campground along the eastern shore of the lake. There is a fee to park. Recommended for small fry.

LUCKY LAKE A pretty good hike-in lake for brook trout, one mile west of Lava Lake in Deschutes National Forest. Take the Cascade Lakes Hwy. south from Bend for about 40 miles to the Lava Lake turn-off, about 5 miles past Elk Lake. Lucky Lake Trail 148 heads on the west side of the highway about 1/4 mile past the turn-off. It's about a 1 1/2 mile hike to the lake. Lucky covers 30 acres and is over 50 feet deep. Brook trout run 8-16 inches. No motors are allowed, so don't pack in your outboard. There are fair natural campsites.

MAIDEN LAKE A small, deep hike-in brook trout lake on the south slopes of Maiden Peak, a familiar landmark in the Odell Lake-Davis Lake area. From Crescent Lake Junction 2 miles south of Odell Lake on Hwy. 58, drive south on Hwy. 58 about 3 miles to County Rd. 61, which branches off to the east and leads to Davis Lake. At the Davis Lake turn off (Forest Rd. 61), turn north and drive about 3 miles to Forest Rd. 4660, which leads NW. Follow signs to Maiden Lake Trail, about 5 miles from the turn. Trail 41 leads west about 3 miles to the lake. The trail continues west about 2 miles to the Pacific Crest Trail, just north of Rosary Lakes.

Only 6 acres but over 20 feet deep, Maiden Lake offers fair fishing for brook trout 6-10 inches. The lake is usually accessible in late June, though there is often still some snow.

MARKS CREEK A fair trout stream heading in the Ochoco National Forest and flowing into Ochoco Creek 7 miles above Ochoco Reservoir, about 17 miles east of Prineville by Hwy. 26. The creek is crossed by Hwy. 26 at the Ochoco confluence, then followed closely by the highway NE to its headwaters.

Marks Creek contains native redband trout 6-10 inches. Bait angling is the usual method, but lures and flies will also produce. The upper section is good late in the season. In some years this stream almost dries up. There is a Forest Service campground at Cougar and Ochoco Divide on the upper creek.

MARTIN LAKE A 4-acre hike-in rainbow trout lake, 2 miles south of Three Fingered Jack and a few miles north of Hwy. 20, east of the Santiam Pass summit. Take the Pacific Crest Trail north from Hwy. 20, 1/2 mile east of Hoodoo Ski Bowl, and hike a short distance to Square Lake Trail 65. About 3 miles on the trail gets you to Booth Lake. Continue 1/4 mile north on the trail, and head due west up a draw. Martin is about 1/3 mile west of the trail.

Martin is deep for its size and has rainbow 6-12 inches. It's a nice fly-fishing lake and a fairly consistent producer. Bait and lures can be effectively used. It is usually accessible in late June.

MATTHIEU LAKES These hike-in lakes are on the east edge of an impressive lava field south of McKenzie Pass near the Dee Wright Observatory. This lava looks like it spilled out yesterday, an enormous field of gray rubble stretching as far as the eye can see. Take the Pacific Crest Trail south from Hwy. 126 at the Observatory, and hike about 3 miles to the lower (north) lake. The upper (south) lake holds no fish.

North Matthieu Lake, about 6 acres and not very deep, is a steady producer of medium size rainbow. There is some spawning here, but the lake also gets airdrops of fingerlings.

McCLURES LAKE One of the I-84 ponds adjacent to the Columbia River at hwy. mi. 74. It covers 50 acres and is immediately east of Memaloose State Park and Rest Area. Best access is for westbound traffic, with parking available at the rest area. It may contain any of the Columbia's warmwater species. See Appendix for a map of Columbia River Ponds.

MEADOW LAKE A good trout lake in the Deschutes National Forest SW of Suttle Lake and south of Hwy. 20, on the west side of Cache Mountain. Follow the Suttle Lake road off Hwy. 20, then drive west about 2 1/2 miles to Forest Rd. 2076, which leads south. Meadow Lake is about 3 miles south and 1/4 mile west of the road. A very rough fire road leads to the lake. The Forest Service has considered closing the fire roads in the area, but the road is open to public use at this time.

Meadow Lake covers about 16 acres, a consistent producer of nice trout 10-16 inches. Brook trout and cutthroat are stocked. Fly-fishing is especially good, with best results late in the year. The lake is usually accessible in June, and early season angling is good. There are several nice natural campsites at the lake. Motors are prohibited.

The spring-fed Metolius maintains a constant temperature year-round.

MEEK LAKE A brook and cutthroat trout lake in Deschutes National Forest about mid-way between Crescent and Summit Lakes. From Crescent Lake Junction on Hwy. 58 SE of Oakridge, take Forest Rd. 60 around the western shore of Crescent Lake to Forest Rd. 6010, the Summit Lake Rd. Drive about 5 miles west, and watch for Meek Lake Trailhead on the south side of the road. The lake is just 1/2 mile off the road by Trail 43.

Rather deep for its 11 acres, it offers fair angling for brook trout and cutthroat. All methods can be effective, although bait angling is probably best. Fish to 14 inches have been taken here.

In late summer, try fly-fishing in Summit Creek, which the trail crosses. Larger brook trout sometimes wander in from the lake. The nearest campground is at Summit Lake. Meek is usually accessible in late June.

METOLIUS RIVER A beautiful spring fed stream in central Oregon, which gushes full blown from a fern carpeted hollow at the base of Black Butte, managed primarily for wild trout. Tackle restrictions and a catch-and-release fishery for these wild beauties throughout the mainstem have successfully restored the Metolius' reputation as world class trout water.

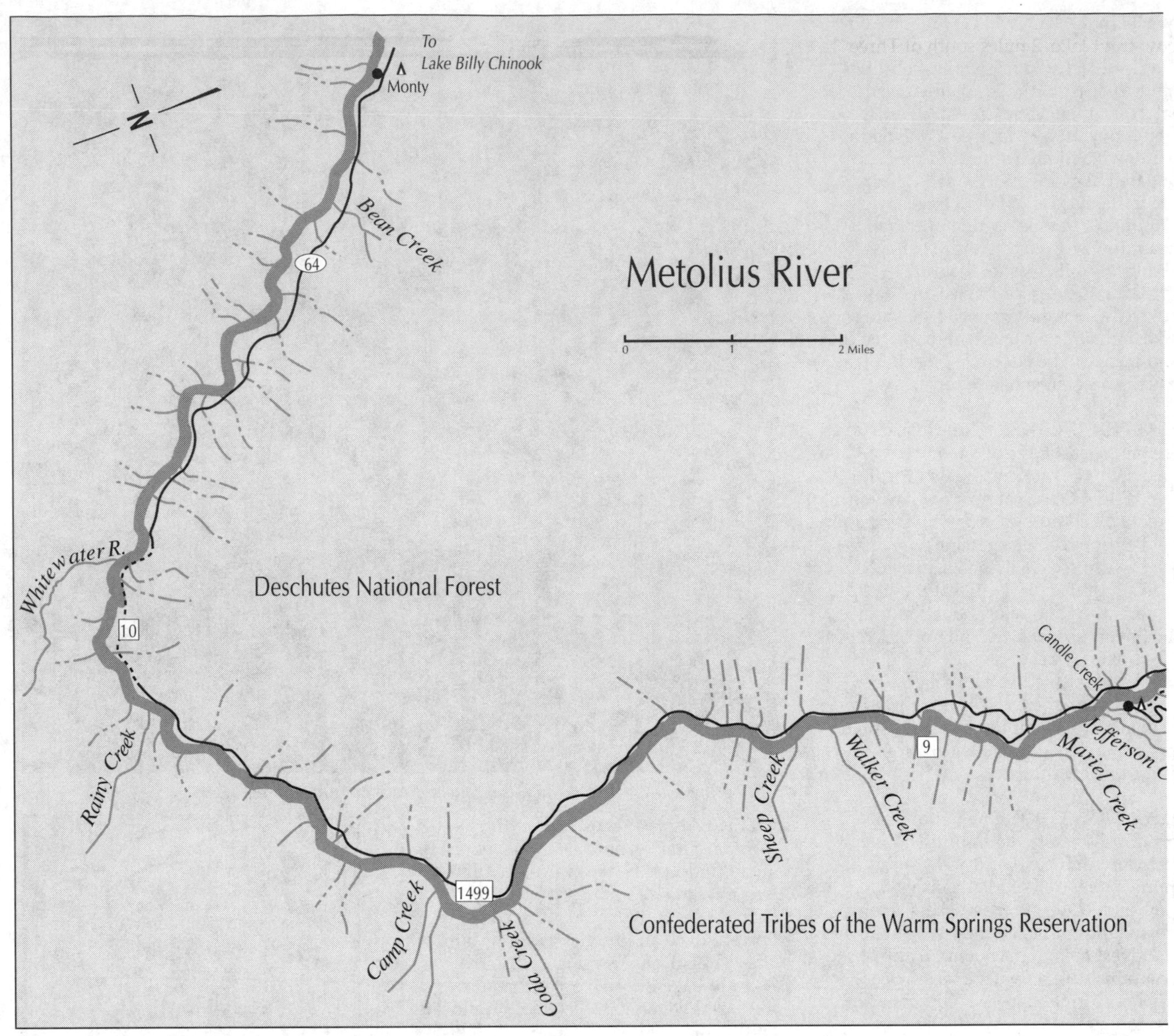

To get there, take Hwy. 20 NW from Sisters, or east from the Willamette Valley. Follow signs to Camp Sherman, a small resort community near the Metolius headwaters about 3 miles east of Suttle Lake. From Sisters, turn off Hwy. 20 at Forest Rd. 14. Skirt the west flank of Black Butte, reaching Camp Sherman in about 5 miles.

The Metolius flows about 9 miles through a handsome pine forest before entering a canyon, joining the Deschutes River in Lake Billy Chinook 20 miles further. Its source spring can be viewed from a paved stroll-in path about one mile south of Camp Sherman, just off Forest Rd. 14. The spring site is well marked.

Throughout the Metolius, all non-fin-clipped trout must be released unharmed. Above Bridge 99, the river is restricted to fly-fishing only with barbless hook. Below Bridge 99, both barbless flies and lures may be used. There is a small bait area associated with a deep hole near Bridge 99, which stretches from the bridge downstream about 1/2 mile to the ODF&W markers.

The Metolius maintains a constant temperature year around, shows no more than a few inches of fluctuation, and always runs clear. Insects hatch throughout the year, and the river is open for fly-fishing year-round above Bridge 99. All Metolius River tributaries, except Lake Creek, are closed to angling.

The Metolius supports wild rainbow, bull trout, browns, and brook trout, as well as whitefish and a spawning run of kokanee. Rainbow, reared in the Wizard Falls Hatchery on the river, are currently being stocked in small numbers from Allingham Bridge downstream. Stocking may be discontinued in the future.

Water clarity is only one of the challenges confronting anglers here. Matching the hatch is another. Though its water temperature remains constant, the river flows through a wide variety of mini-environments, each of which produces its own insect hatch on its own time schedule. The three general environments are from Lake Creek to Gorge Campground, Gorge to Bridge 99, and Bridge 99 to Lake Billy Chinook. But within each of these sections there is great variety. To check on the status of the major hatches, anglers might call or stop by The Fly Fisher's Place in Sisters. The general store at Camp Sherman may also be helpful.

Some of the best fly-fishing occurs in early May and early July, when anglers match the big green drake hatch, followed by the golden stonefly. Caddis and mayfly hatches occur throughout summer. A second hatch of smaller green drakes takes place in fall, along with hatches of smaller caddis and mayflies.

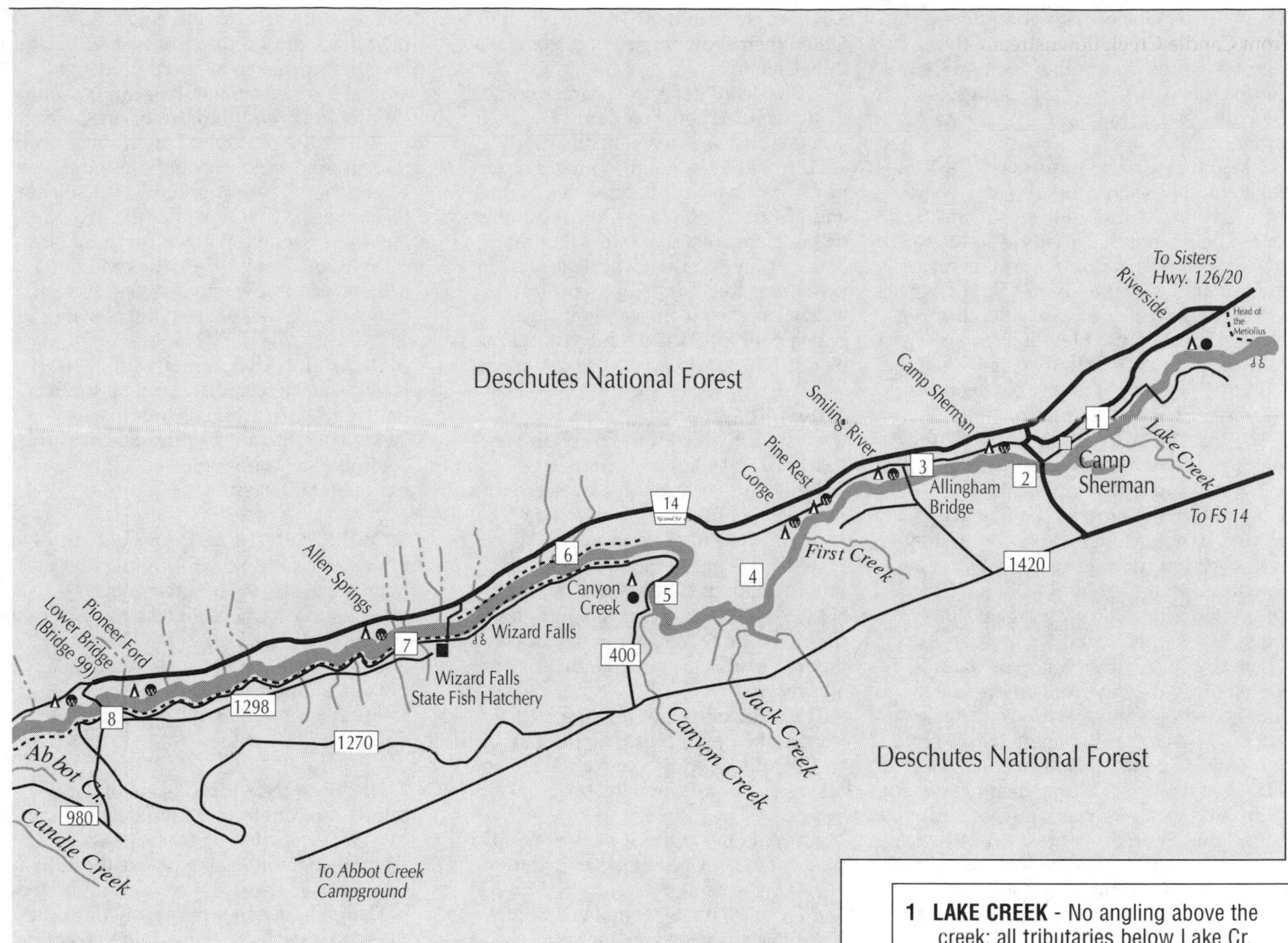

1 **LAKE CREEK** - No angling above the creek; all tributaries below Lake Cr. are closed to angling.

2 **CAMP SHERMAN BRIDGE** - Trout viewing area; no angling within 100 ft. of bridge.

3 **LAKE CREEK TO GORGE**- Easier wading for smaller hatchery trout.

4 **GORGE** - Tricky wading but some good bank casting for larger, wild trout; be wary of mid-stream holes.

5 **CANYON CR. CONFLUENCE** - Deep hole mid-stream known for large lurking trout.

6 **GORGE TRAIL** - East bank access to some of the river's larger, wild trout; mostly private land on east bank.

7 **BRIDGE 99** - Deep hole beneath bridge; bait fishing with barbless hook allowed for 1/2 mile downstream; see regulations for tackle restrictions upstream and down.

8 **WEST BANK TRAIL** - Nine mile access to fast water with occasional good fishing, best below hatchery.

9 **CONFEDERATED TRIBES WARM SPRINGS** - No public access to this bank below Candle Creek.

10 **TRAIL**- Two miles access to east bank; nice pools and tailouts.

Insect hatches continue throughout the winter, including small Baetis mayflies, small caddis, midges, and a tiny blue winged olive mayfly November through February. Nymphing produces most consistently, with stonefly nymphs, tied-down caddis, hares ear, and green drake patterns frequently used.

Because the use of lead or split shot is illegal on the Metolius, some anglers tie on a large stonefly to weight their line, then add one or two dropper nymphs, casting upstream and fishing the nymphs dead-drift close to the bottom in a drag-free presentation. Retrieving with short jerks can also be effective. Many anglers use a strike indicator to better detect the take. Small dry flies (size 16-18) will take fish when they are feeding on the surface.

The Metolius is primarily a bank fishery, with some wading possible. Insulated waders are essential, as the river is always very cold. Though the river appears fairly smooth in the campground area below Gorge Campground, whitewater and downed timber make it treacherous for boats of all kinds. Easiest wading is in the stretch between Lake Creek and Gorge Campground. Below Gorge, wading is trickier, since the river is powerful and rife with holes. Wading becomes very difficult in the Gorge itself, and in the canyon. However there are many good bank casting spots all along the river. Below Bridge 99, these spots are a well guarded secret by local anglers. You can look for pull-offs along the road, but trails down to the river are not obvious.

From its source, the Metolius flows due north, with Forest Rd. 14 following its eastern bank for about 9 miles to Bridge 99. There is some private property on the west bank in the Camp Sherman area, but beyond that the river flows through national forest, with only two small private land holdings, one below Gorge Campground, the other just above Pioneer Ford Campground. At Bridge 99, the pavement ends where the main road crosses the Metolius. Candle Creek Campground is on the west side of the river about 2 miles downstream from the bridge on a good gravel road.

Below Bridge 99 and Lower Bridge Campground, which is right below the bridge on the east side, a rough gravel road follows the river's east bank downstream. This road is best suited to 4-

wheel drive vehicles with good tires. From Candle Creek downstream, the Metolius forms the southern boundary of Confederated Tribes Warm Springs, and the west bank of the river is closed to public access.

The gravel road continues to follow the east bank till the river bends east, where the road ends. A trail follows streamside for the next 2 miles, providing access to many nice pools and rapids. At its east end, the trail is met by Forest Rd. 64, which leads west from Perry South Campground on the Metolius Arm of Lake Billy Chinook. Monty Campground is on the Metolius half-way between the east end of the trail and Perry.

The most popular angling area on the Metolius is from Lake Creek (2 miles below the source) to Bridge 99 (just before the river reaches CTWS land), about a 10 mile stretch. Stocked rainbow in this section run 9-12 inches. Wild rainbow reach 15 inches. Bull trout are found throughout the river, with bigger bulls in the deeper lower river.

The Gorge is within this area, a 2-mile stretch of river away from any roads. It offers good fishing for wild trout, since hatchery plants are not made in this section of the Metolius. You can fish a short section of the upper Gorge near Gorge Campground on the main paved road from Camp Sherman, Forest Rd. 14. Access downstream from Gorge Campground is limited by the private grounds of House on the Metolius, a private resort. Access to most of the Gorge, however, is available from a trail that follows the river's west bank. Lower Canyon Creek Campground is at the upper end of the trail, and Wizard Falls Hatchery on Forest Rd. 14 is at the lower end. There is also some trail access on the east side of the river in the Gorge area upstream from Wizard Falls.

Smaller wild rainbow can be taken in the waters above Gorge Campground, where the river is shallow and offers easy wading. Larger rainbow are more prevalent below Canyon Creek, where wading is more difficult. There are a number of deep holes in the river's mid-section where large trout sulk, including the Canyon Creek confluence and the water near Allen Springs Campground. Canyon Creek is on the west bank. To get there, take Forest Rd. 1217 about 1/4 mile west of Camp Sherman, then turn north on Forest Rd. 1420. Allen Springs is below Wizard Falls Hatchery off Forest Rd. 14.

Bull trout 5-20 pounds lurk beneath bank cover and submerged structures throughout the river. They may be enticed by sculpin, mouse imitations, and streamers. Brown trout are numerous in the Metolius but are not popularly fished. Brook trout are the least plentiful breed here, and are primarily taken in fall.

Kokanee come into the Metolius in the fall on their spawning run up from Lake Billy Chinook.

There are 10 developed campgrounds along the road between Camp Sherman and Candle Creek, each in an attractive setting of huge ponderosa pine. The fee-pay camps have drinking water. Supplies and gas are available in Camp Sherman, where there are also a number of motels and low key resorts. A short closure exists near the Camp Sherman store, where large trout are clearly visible, cruising for bread and other trifles tossed by tourists, but the area is clearly marked.

MILL CREEK (Wasco Co.) A fair-size trout stream which flows through the heart of The Dalles and enters the Columbia River through a culvert at the west edge of town. It is crossed by Hwy. 30 near its mouth. The creek heads at the eastern edge of Mt. Hood Forest and flows NE about 20 miles. It is followed and crossed by many paved and gravel roads. In The Dalles, it may be fished at the road crossings, but adjacent land is all private.

The creek offers fair angling for wild trout in the upper area. The Dept. of Fish and Wildlife stocks the stream with legal rainbow near the outskirts of The Dalles.

MILLER POND One of the I-84 ponds adjacent to the Columbia River at hwy. mi. 97.5. Covering 8 acres between I-84 and Hwy. 30, it may contain any of the Columbia's warmwater species. Best access is from Exit 97, then proceed east on Hwy. 30 for one mile. Parking on the freeway is prohibited. See p. 206 for a map of Columbia River Ponds.

MONON LAKE A large trout lake adjacent to Olallie Lake north of Mt. Jefferson. It is just south of Olallie, about 35 miles south of Hwy. 26. Take Forest Rd. 42 south from Hwy. 26 about 2 miles past the Clear Lake turn-off, and follow the signs to Olallie Lake. Monon is just beyond Olallie on the same road. It can also be reached from the south by about 28 miles of forest road from Detroit. It's usually late June before the north road is open, and the road from the south rarely opens before July.

Monon is over 90 acres. It reaches 40 ft. in the portion nearest Olallie Lake, but most of the lake is shallow. It is lightly fished in comparison with its popular neighbor.

Monon is stocked with Montana black spotted cutthroat, a breed which is supposedly easier to catch than rainbow (which were stocked previously) or the more challenging brook trout which were last stocked here in 1983 and are still present. The cutthroat are disappointingly small. The brook trout run 7-18 inches and are only occasionally taken. All methods work on the cutthroat, with bait angling the most consistent producer. Trolled lures or spinner-bait combinations should work, and flies can be effective.

Motors are prohibited on the lake, and there is no developed campground. There is a full service campground at Olallie on the peninsula that separates the two lakes, and there is one top notch campsite on a rocky point that juts into the center of Monon, accessible only by boat. Monon offers a good escape from the crowds.

MORAINE LAKE A pretty but fishless lake in a very scenic area on the south flank of South Sister in Three Sisters Wilderness. Stocking of this lake was discontinued a number of years ago due to frequent winterkill.

MOSIER POND EAST One of the I-84 ponds adjacent to the Columbia River at hwy. mi. 69. It covers 6 acres and is immediately east of Exit 69 between I-84 and Hwy. 30. Parking along the freeway is prohibited. The pond may contain any of the Columbia's warmwater species. See p. 206 for a map of Columbia River Ponds.

MOSIER POND WEST One of the I-84 ponds adjacent to the Columbia River at hwy. mi. 69. Covering 8 acres, it is bisected by the Union Pacific Railroad south of the freeway. There is limited unimproved parking for eastbound freeway traffic at the west end of the pond. It is also accessible from Hwy. 30 by way of I-84 Exit 69. The pond may contain any of the Columbia's warmwater species. See page 206 for a map of Columbia River Ponds from Cascade Locks to the Deschutes.

MUSKRAT LAKE An 8-acre hike-in trout lake in the Cultus Lake area SW of Bend. The lake is 1 1/2 miles NW of the west end of Big Cultus Lake and is reached by a 5-mile hike on the Winopee Lake Trail 16 from the east end of Big Cultus Lake. You can save 3 miles by boating across Big Cultus Lake to the campground at the west end of the lake and picking up the trail to Muskrat. See Cultus Lake for road directions.

Muskrat is a difficult lake to fish. The brook trout average 8 inches and run to about 15 inches. Fly angling can be good late in summer and fall. An old trapper's cabin survives in good repair. Please help preserve it. Natural campsites are available. It is usually accessible in late June. Mosquitoes can be devilish.

NAP-TE-PAH LAKE (Confederated Tribes Warm Springs) A 2-acre lake between Olallie and Monon lakes, reached by trail from Peninsula Campground at the south end of Olallie.

Maximum depth is 25 feet. Both this lake and a smaller neighbor, Mangriff Lake, are stocked with brook trout. A good float tube lake. Although located on CTWS land, no permit is required.

NORTH LAKE A 6-acre hike-in brook trout lake, 3 miles south of the Columbia Gorge in the NE corner of Mt. Hood National Forest. It can be reached by a strenuous hike up from the gorge on Trail 411, which heads at the Forest Service campground at Wyeth, 12 miles west of Hood River. The trail ascends 3,800 ft. in about 4 miles. For Sunday morning anglers who can't make the grade, as it were, the alternative is to approach the lake from the south. Trail 416 heads at Rainy Lake Campground and gets you there in 1 1/2 miles. (Had you worried there, eh?) See Rainy Lake for road information. North Lake is at 4,000 ft.

Fly anglers do well here, as the lake is only 8 ft. at its deepest point. Brook trout average 9 inches, but an occasional 16 incher is taken. The lake is stocked every other year. There are some fair natural campsites around the lake and a good improved camp at Rainy Lake. The road is usually snowbound until mid-June. Check with Mt. Hood Forest Service for early season conditions.

OCHOCO CREEK A good size stream near Prineville, flowing into Ochoco Reservoir from the east. It is followed closely by Hwy. 26 for 6 miles upstream from the reservoir, then by Forest Rd. 22 to it's source at Walton Lake, 14 miles to the NE. It is accessible for most of its length, but there is some private land in the lower stretch, and permission must be obtained.

The creek has wild rainbow trout and is stocked with catchable rainbow in the area around Prineville. Angling is usually good early in the season and again in the fall, with bait the most popular method. The trout range 6-12 inches, and the catch rate is good. There are two campgrounds on the upper creek, one at Ochoco Guard Station and the other at the source at Walton Lake.

OCHOCO RESERVOIR A large reservoir with good fishing for rainbow trout 5 miles east of Prineville. Ochoco covers over 1,000 acres and is a popular recreational area. To reach it, drive east from Prineville on Hwy. 26, which follows the north shore.

In the spring of 1994 Ochoco Dam was breached for repairs, and the reservoir's fishery was lost. The reservoir will be restocked upon completion of the work, and fishing is scheduled to resume in 1995. Snowpack in 1994-95 will affect the reservoir's return to full pool.

Under normal circumstances, the reservoir is stocked annually, and rainbow average 10-12 inches with some to 15 inches. Large fish are available some years, and limits are common. For several years following the re-stocking, the trout fishery should be better than average.

Ochoco is open year-round, and fish are caught in every season, with best catches in spring and fall. Bank angling and trolling are both popular, with most bank anglers working the north shore below the highway. Ice fishing is sometimes popular.

There is a good state park with camping facilities at about mid-point on the reservoir off Hwy. 26. Trailers are prohibited, but a modern trailer court is located across the highway from the park. Several resorts with rental boats, motors, and supplies are also on the highway.

ODELL CREEK The outlet stream from Odell Lake, flowing NE 6 miles from the SE tip of Odell into Davis Lake. Forest roads parallel it without coming too close for the first 4 miles. and a poor road follows the lower two miles. It is crossed by Forest Rd. 4660 2 miles above Davis.

The creek has a small population of wild rainbow and bull trout. The bull trout must be released unharmed. Kokanee move through from Odell to Davis, but few are caught in the creek. This is a good creek for whitefish in the fall, but not much of a trout stream. There is a handsome resort with lodge and cabins at the creek source at Odell Lake, and there are forest service campgrounds on each bank of the creek at the Davis Lake inlet.

ODELL LAKE One of the largest mountain lakes in Oregon, 5 miles long with over 3,300 surface acres, offering outstanding fishing for trophy size Mackinaw trout and some of the best kokanee fishing in the state. Odell also contains bull trout and a good population of rainbow. Angler success rate for all species is extremely high.

Odell stretches along the east side of Willamette Pass just south of Hwy. 58, distracting drivers with glimpses of sparkling water or churning whitecaps through the dark firs that surround it. Diamond Peak stands guard just 5 miles away on the western horizon. More than thirty creeks and a number of springs feed the lake, keeping its water level constant to within a foot throughout the year. Glacially scoured to over 280 ft. deep near the east end, Odell provides a rich and variable environment for its residents, all of which are self-sustaining.

Odell Lake is about 70 miles SE of Eugene by Hwy. 58, and 23 miles NW of the junction of hwys. 58 and 97. Hwy. 58 follows its NW shore for about 5 miles.

The lake was first stocked with Mackinaw trout (also known as lake trout), in 1902, and stocking continued through 1965. Mackinaw have been successfully propagating ever since. Lake trout commonly live to be over 20 years old and can exceed 40 pounds. A 30-year-old Mack was caught here in 1992. The state record Mackinaw came from Odell in 1984, weighing 40 pounds 8 ounces. A 32-pound 6-ounce Mackinaw was caught in 1992. Most run 10-20 pounds.

In the early years Mackinaw preyed primarily on Odell's whitefish and chubs, but in recent years they have enjoyed the growing population of tasty kokanee. One of the tricks anglers use to locate Mackinaw (which often hunt in groups) is to first find the kokanee. The bottom of Odell is a varied landscape, with many submerged buttes (or shoals), around which the kokanee cower and dart in schools. One theory is that Mackinaw hover just above the buttes, which are located east of Princess Creek boat ramp, east of the Hwy. 58 viewpoint, east of Chinquapin Point boat ramp, near the railroad slide on the south shore east of Serenity Bay, and off Burly Bluff near West Bay. Use a depth finder to locate these shoals (at 60-90 ft.), or ask the folks at Shelter Cove to point out landmarks that can line you up. They can also usually tell you where Mackinaw and kokanee have been schooling lately. Electronic depthfinders and fish finders are very useful at Odell.

The Luhr Jensen Nordic jig has been especially successful here. Most anglers use the No. 060 in silver and fluorescent green with a very sharp treble hook. They locate a likely spot, and lower the jig on an 8-pound line, raising it up several feet and letting it flutter down on a slack line. Strikes almost always occur when the lure in falling.

Trolling is effective for picking up single Mackinaw cruising through deeper water. Trollers work off the shoals rather than over them, using leaded line with sinkers or downriggers to get to 60-90 ft., trailing big Kwikfish-type lures or Rapallas. (White and blue lures are supposed to look very kokanee-like down in the depths.) As much as 90% of the catch is taken trolling Kwikfish of Flatfish. Average angler success rate for Mackinaw is about one Mackinaw per 2 anglers per day. Only one trout over 20 inches may be kept.

For better numbers and faster action, try for the kokanee. Kokanee are a delicious tasting landlocked sockeye salmon, first stocked in 1931. They are now a very large and self-sustaining population in Odell. Their average size is just 12 inches, but they are very abundant and 20 -inchers are occasionally caught. Because of their fine taste, abundance, and ease of

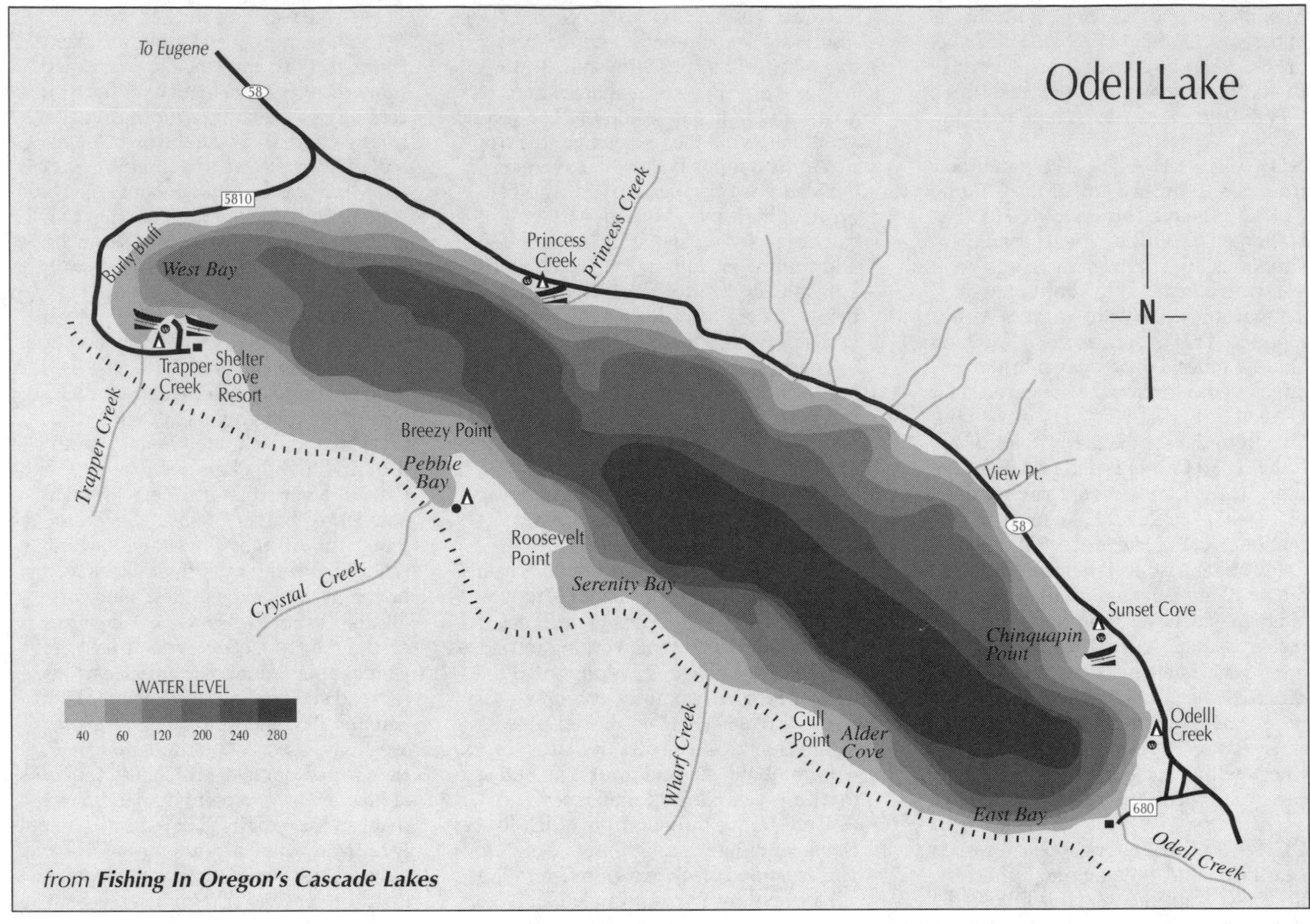

from **Fishing In Oregon's Cascade Lakes**

catch, most kokanee are sought by anglers as meat for the table rather than angling sport. Some anglers still-fish for them early in the season using shelled caddis fly larvae, single eggs, or worms. Most anglers troll, using a small flasher, 18-inch leader, and a small kokanee lure tipped with a piece of worm and a kernel of corn. Shelter Cove Resort makes a lure called Kokanee Glow that has proven to be effective. The Wedding Ring is also popular, as well as Super Duper in late season. If you're using heavy gear, you'll need a rubber snubber to absorb some of the shock of the initial hook-up. A downrigger will enable you to use lighter gear more suited to the kokanee's size.

Kokanee can provide good sport to anglers who use a downrigger (rather than heavy hardware) to get down to kokanee level, and light gear—a light, sensitive rod, light line (6 pound test monofilament, 4 pound leader), and light terminal tackle (a few fluorescent beads, a tiny spinner with the blade removed, a No. 6 hook, and a single kernel of white corn). The downrigger usually has to be manually released, since the kokanee bite is more subtle than most tension mechanisms can detect. Jigging is also effective and popular, especially using the Nordic in pink pearl or fluorescent green.

In early season, kokanee schools can generally be found within 8-20 ft. of the surface. But kokanee prefer water temperatures 50 degrees or colder, and as the lake warms in June they descend to about 50 ft., then to around 75 ft. in July, and down to 100 ft. in August. Towards fall, kokanee move closer to shore, seeking spawning inlets. You can observe kokanee spawning in Trapper Creek, at the Shelter Cove dock, and in Little Creek from mid-September to mid-November. During spawning, best fishing is mid-lake from 40 to 150 ft.

Electronic fish finders can locate where and at what depth the schools are holding, though looking for congregations of boats on the lake and asking other anglers what depth they're fishing is just as effective. Kokanee anglers tend to be generous with information, since there are plenty here for all. Best fishing is in early morning and late in the day, which suits Odell's temperament perfectly.

Odell Lake is aligned with a major mountain pass and, at elevation 4,788 ft., the wind can really whip through, churning up the water. When it does, you want to be safely ashore, perhaps sipping coffee beside the big stone fireplace at Odell Lodge on the east end of the lake, or cleaning fish and talking shop with the knowledgeable owners of Shelter Cove Resort on the west end. The weather can change quickly in spring and late fall, so keep a weather eye out. Typically, the lake is calm in the morning, and boating even by canoe can be quite pleasant. (There is, in fact, an annual canoe race on Odell). Afternoons, the wind can be counted on to pick up, a fact which sail boarders have taken note of in recent years. Most anglers pack it in afternoons, or move over to Odell Creek or nearby Crescent Creek. The lake generally calms again by early evening.

Other species available in Odell include bull trout and rainbow. Both reproduce naturally here and reach good size. Bull trout are usually taken incidentally by anglers fishing for Mackinaw. Bull trout average 12-14 inches and must be released unharmed. The rainbow typically range from 8-16 inches with many to 20 inches and better. They can be taken by all methods though trolling with lure or spinner/bait combinations is most common. Rainbow anglers work the shorelines from mid-June throughout the season, with best catches in fall.

There are excellent campgrounds at the east and west ends of the lake and along the north shoreline. Princess Creek, Trapper Creek, and Sunset Cove campgrounds have boat launches. Pebble Bay Campground is a small tent camp on the south shore, accessible only by boat.

There are two fine resorts on Odell, one at each end of the lake, each offering accommodations, supplies, tackle, boats and motors. The resorts have telephone service. The fireplace at Odell Lake Lodge is worth a visit, and you can get an excellent meal there. Shelter Cove Resort has attractive modern cabins (some of locally hewn logs) and a general store. For more information, see *Fishing In Oregon's Cascade Lakes*.

OLALLIE LAKE A large popular trout lake on the backbone of the Cascade Range north of Mt. Jefferson. Olallie is the largest of many interesting lakes in a portion of Mt. Hood National Forest known as the Olallie Lake Scenic Area. There are over a dozen fair to good lakes within a 3-mile radius. Olallie itself is at one end of a chain of 5 trout lakes that drain east into Confederated Tribes Warm Springs land. The others must be reached by hiking. See Trout, Island, Dark, Long.

The best routes to Olallie are from Hwy. 26 from the north, and from Detroit Reservoir from the west. From Portland the quickest route is by Hwy. 26. From Government Camp on Mt. Hood continue south on Hwy. 26 to Forest Rd. 42, which cuts off from the west side of the highway about 2 miles south of the Clear Lake turn-off. It's about 35 miles from the intersection to the lake, the last 12 miles or so unpaved but good when dry. At Warm Springs Meadow, pick up Forest Rd. 4220. The way is well signed. This area is snowbound into June most years.

From Salem south, the best route is by way of the Breitenbush River Rd. (Forest Rd. 46). From Detroit on the east side of Detroit Reservoir, drive east on Forest Rd. 46 past Breitenbush Campground and on up the North Breitenbush River. In the upper reaches of this river the road turns north sharply upslope. Just after passing beneath a power transmission line, Forest Rd. 4220 turns off to the east. It is signed for Breitenbush Lake. This road is the shorter but rougher way in to Olallie, which is 3 miles beyond Breitenbush Lake. The first 4 miles of road are the worst, but no problem if you take it slow and easy. Alternately, continue north on Forest Rd. 46 about 6 miles to Forest Rd. 4690. Follow 4690 east about 8 miles to Forest Rd. 4220, about 4 miles north of Olallie Lake.

From June through October you can expect good rainbow fishing at Olallie, along with a few nice brook trout that wander in from the higher lakes. Olallie is shallow but does have some deep spots. The lake is over a mile long and covers 240 surface acres. It is stocked with legal rainbow trout and with occasional brood fish. Trout average 10-14 inches, with a few to 20 inches. Slow trolling around the lake about 200 ft. from shore is effective. It'll be easy to bracket your trolling speed, since motors are prohibited on the lake. Popular lures used are Triple-Teasers, Flatfish, and flash baits and spinner-worm rigs. Fly-fishing can be good in the evenings on standard patterns. Bank anglers should look for spots close to shore where the bottom drops sharply into deeper water

The Pacific Crest Trail follows the northern tip of the lake, and other good trails lead west from the north end to a number of small trout lakes. See Red, Averill, Fish, Lower, Gifford. A trail east from the Peninsula Campground follows the creek that links the five lake chain. The downstream lakes are on CTWS property, and a permit is required to fish. Monon Lake, a good size lake just south of Olallie, is an easy stroll from Olallie's Peninsula Campground and contains small cutthroat and some brook trout.

Though motors are prohibited on Olallie, there is a boat ramp at Peninsula Camp. There are two other smaller campgrounds—Paul Dennis and Camp Ten. Paul Dennis is a boat or hike-in camp on the NE shore. There are also good campgrounds north and south of the lake on Forest Rd. 4220. A resort at the north end has cabins, boat rentals, food and tackle. At one time the Forest Service published an excellent map of the Olallie Lake Scenic Area. It may be out of print, but if you can find a copy, it's an excellent reference for the lakes and trails in the area.

OLDENBERG LAKE A 28-acre hike-in brook trout lake in Deschutes National Forest 3 miles south of Crescent Lake. From Crescent Lake Junction on Hwy. 58, take the Crescent Lake Rd. south about 7 miles to Oldenberg Lake Trailhead, 1/2 mile west of the entrance to Spring Campground. Its about a 3-mile hike to the lake past Bingham Lakes. The trail continues south to Windigo Pass.

The typical brook trout caught here is 8-10 inches, with some fish to 14 inches. Lures and bait will work during the day, with fly-fishing best in the evening, as is the rule on most high lakes. Good natural campsites are available, and there are campgrounds at Crescent Lake.

ONE-MILE LAKE One of the I-84 ponds adjacent to the Columbia River at hwy. mi. 90-91. It covers 9 acres and is between the east and westbound lanes on I-84. There is no parking for westbound traffic, and parking for eastbound traffic is unimproved and limited. It may contain any of the Columbia's warmwater species. See P. 206 for a map of Columbia River Ponds.

OTTERTAIL LAKE (a.k.a. Otter Lake) A 2-acre lake at the head of Green Point Creek, 1/2 mile east of Wahtum Lake on the opposite side of the ridge. Follow Forest Rd. 2810 from Punchbowl Falls, one mile north of Dee, to the lake. Ottertail supports a population of brook trout.

PAULINA CREEK Outlet stream for Paulina Lake in the Newberry Crater of Paulina Mt. SE of Bend. The creek can offer fair angling for migrants from Paulina Lake. It is not stocked.

The creek flows down the western slope of the mountain, and enters the Deschutes River about 6 miles south of Bend. Much of the lower creek flows through private lands. It is followed upstream from Prairie Campground by Trail 56.

Though the lower creek is used for irrigation purposes, it usually retains a flow. Its trout are fair size but scarce, a nice stream to fish on bait or flies. Prairie Campground is on Forest Rd. 2120 three miles east of Hwy. 97. McKay Crossing Campground is 2 miles further east.

PAULINA LAKE A big, very productive, very popular lake in the crater of a dormant volcano in the Paulina Mountains, an isolated roughly circular range east of the Cascades about 20 air miles SE of Bend. It shares this handsome setting in Newberry Crater with East Lake, from which it is separated by a high ridge. Paulina is at elevation 6,350 ft. and is about 1 1/2 times the size of East Lake. Newberry Crater has been designated a National Monument.

Paulina is managed for trophy browns and kokanee. Its kokanee are the egg source for kokanee fisheries throughout the Northwest. Both the state record brown and state record kokanee were taken from Paulina. Rainbow trout are also present, averaging under 12 inches. All gamefish in Paulina are stocked, as there are no tributaries suitable for spawning.

To reach Paulina, drive south from Bend on Hwy. 97 about 19 miles to County Rd. 21, which leads east about 12 miles up the slope of Paulina Mountain to the Crater and its lakes. For a better appreciation of the unique geology here, plan a stop at Lava Lands Visitor Center, a Forest Service interpretive center 8 miles south of Bend on Hwy. 97. You'll pass it on the way to Paulina. The Center is located atop a high, relatively recent cinder cone and presents a good overview of this interesting area.

Newberry is actually a double crater, for both Paulina and East have their own lava dome. Unlike East Lake, Paulina has very little shoal area. It is over 200 ft. deep almost throughout. Even its lava dome comes to within only 60 feet of the surface. The lake's only shoal areas are on the SW edge near the resort, and directly across from the resort at the black slide. The cream colored basalt crater walls are clearly visible around the perimeter, and these, combined with the great depth, color Paulina's waters an unusual turquoise.

Kokanee are doing quite well in Paulina and make a good contribution to the mid-summer catch. They can be found all over the lake, including the center. These fish run to 22 inches, which is large for the species. The state record kokanee was taken from Paulina, weighing 3 pounds 6 ounces.

Rainbow anglers work the shorelines at Paulina Lake.

Two subsequent record-breaking brown trout have come out of Paulina, the most recent in 1993 at 27 pounds 12 ounces. Browns do not reproduce naturally in Paulina, but they do live to be 18-20 years old. In addition to providing opportunity for trophy catches, the browns help curb the lake's chub population.

Rainbow trout fingerlings are planted annually and make up the majority of the catch. Most are 9-14 inches, though the lake has some lunkers over 5 pounds. Trolling and bait-fishing are a toss-up for popularity, with trolling probably taking the larger fish. Rainbow anglers work the shorelines, usually keeping within depths of 20 ft. or less. Popular trolling and still-fishing areas are off the rocky points on the mid-eastern shore and off the western shore between Green Slide and Paulina Resort. Trollers also work the area SE of Big Point (the rocky point near the main campground). There is good still-fishing in the little cove between Red Slide and the warm springs. Most of the fly action is over the moss beds near the warm springs and Black Slide in the NE, between Green Slide and Big Bay in the NW, and north of the Clay Banks in the SE.

There are two developed general-use campgrounds on the lake—Paulina Lake Campground at the NW end of the lake, and Little Crater Campground on the NW shore. Both have boat ramps. Little Crater offers the most privacy of the two. In addition, there are two hike-in or boat-in camps on the northeast and northwest shores. Newberry Group Camp, on the southeast shore, is available by advance reservation. Chief Paulina, across County Rd. 21 from Newberry Group Camp, is a horse camp with corrals and stock water.

There is a rustic log resort with attractive restaurant, cabins, boats, motors, and supplies at the west end of the lake. A few summer homes are located on the south shore. A 7-mile trail (foot traffic only) encircles the lake. Boaters should observe the 10-mph speed limit on the lake and keep a weather eye out, as Paulina gets rough in a blow, and storms can come up in a hurry. Winter holds on long up here, and the campgrounds are often blocked with snow at season's opening. The weather is usually pleasant by late June in most years, but bring warm clothes. For more information, see *Fishing In Oregon's Cascade Lakes.*

PINE HOLLOW RESERVOIR An irrigation reservoir which has turned into a fine fishery for trout, bass, catfish, and bluegill, located near Wamic south of The Dalles. From Hwy. 197 at Tygh Valley head 5 miles west to Wamic. The reservoir is one mile NW of Wamic by county road.

At high water the reservoir covers 240 acres. It's managed cooperatively by

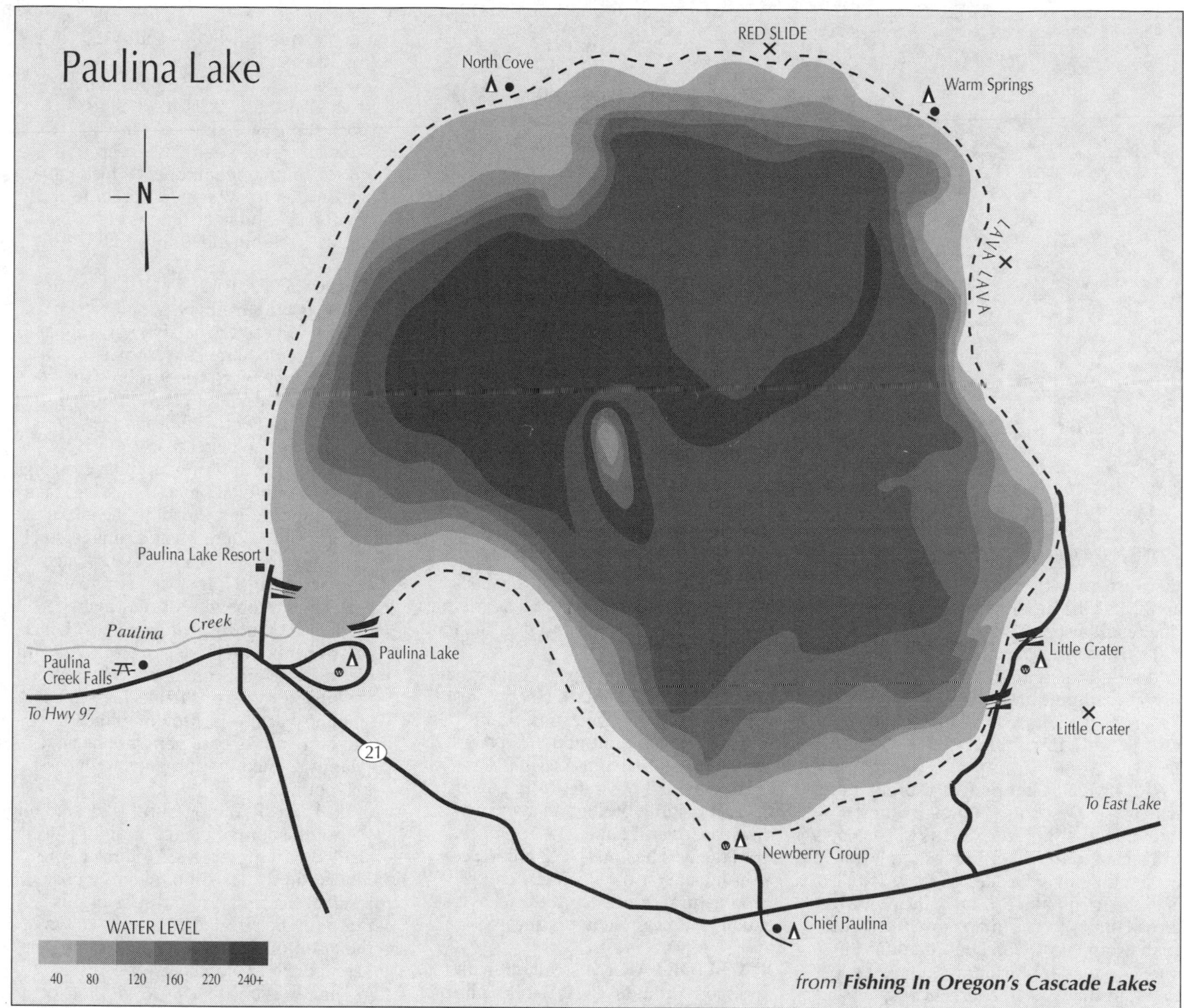

from **Fishing In Oregon's Cascade Lakes**

ODF&W and the irrigation company. By agreement, the reservoir will retain enough water to allow fish to hold over from year to year. It is drawn down considerably in late season, however, and isn't very pretty at that time. The state has bought a 10 ft. access above the high water line all around the lake. The public is entitled to use this easement, except for the area around Camp Morrow at the west end.

Pine hollow is stocked with catchable rainbow and fingerlings. A largemouth bass and brown bullhead fishery is developing as well. There are two public boat ramps on the reservoir and, at the NE end of the lake, a private campground with store, boat rentals and restaurant. Recommended for small fry.

PRINEVILLE RESERVOIR A large reservoir stocked with a variety of game fish, formed by a dam on the Crooked River 12 miles SE of Prineville. Hwy. 27 reaches the dam about 19 miles south of Prineville, and gravel roads up Bear Creek and Birch Canyon reach points on the south shore. These roads lead in from Hwy. 27, several miles south of the dam.

The reservoir was dramatically affected by the drought, losing most of its "class of '92" when the reservoir was drawn down to 13% of its storage capacity. The reservoir was re-stocked with 170,000 fingerlings in 1994. The warmwater fishery should re-establish itself by 1996-97.

Prineville Reservoir was created for flood control and irrigation, and varies considerably in water level during even a normal season. At maximum water the reservoir covers almost 5 square miles, at low water, under 3 square miles. Lake level varies about 30 feet most years, preventing successful spawning by many of the reservoir's warmwater fish.

Trout fishing is generally good throughout regular trout season. Lahontan cutthroat, held over from an abandoned stocking program, may still show up occasionally. When the ice is thick enough, ice fishing can be excellent here.

In addition to trout angling, the reservoir supports populations of brown bullhead, and largemouth and smallmouth bass. Bullhead angling takes off in spring when the water warms above 55 degrees, and slows down once it gets over 60 degrees. Catfishing picks up again in mid-September. The bullhead run 8-10 inches. Worms are the popular bait. Bass angling is good from May through September.

A boat is really handy here, though there are excellent bank fishing opportunities along the NE shore, where Prineville Reservoir State Park roads follow 3 miles of shoreline. The most popular bank angling spots are at Jasper Point, the State Park, and the dam. There are good boat ramps at the State Park and at Jasper Point. Another ramp is located about one mile south of the dam, and

A boat is handy at Prineville Reservoir, but there is good bank fishing on the NE shore.

there are ramps at the Crook County Park and Prineville Resort east of the state park. The resort also rents boats and motors.

There is a campground at the State Park (which accepts reservations) and a private campground run by Prineville Resort. Supplies are available at the resort and in Prineville.

RAFT LAKE A lightly fished brook trout lake in the Deschutes National Forest, one mile west of Little Cultus Lake. No trails lead to the lake. To reach it, head west a little over 2 miles on Forest Rd. 600, the Irish Lake Rd. Then head north cross-country a half mile. You'll need the Irish Mountain USGS quad map for this one. You may hit Strider or Lois Lake first, but they are smaller. Both have fish, incidentally.

Raft Lake is 10 acres and about 30 ft. deep. It has good shoal areas which provide fine fly-fishing in the evenings. It takes a raft or float tube to get out to the deep spots. There are brook trout 8-16 inches in good supply as well as a few good size cutthroat. There are some fair natural campsites at the lake. Mosquitoes are fierce in spring.

RAINY LAKE A 10-acre brook trout lake you can drive to in Mt. Hood Forest SW of Hood River. From the community of Dee, drive north about 2 miles toward Punchbowl Falls, and pick up Forest Rd. 2820, which twists and winds its way west about 10 miles to the lake's campground. Rainy is just a short walk north of the road. This road can be a bit rough in wet weather. The lake is usually accessible in June.

Rainy is a shallow lake, not over 10 feet deep, and provides good fly-fishing. Bait and lures can also be used. Brook trout run 6-15 inches. Rainy is fished heavily but produces well. There is a nice Forest Service campground near the road.

RED LAKE (Marion Co.) A good small rainbow trout lake in Mt. Hood Forest west of the Olallie Lake area. From Lower Lake Campground, head south on Trail 719 past Wall and Averill Lakes. Red Lake is about 3 1/2 miles from Lower Lake. It is south of the trail about 1/4 mile past Averill Lake. The approach from the west is only 1 1/2 miles. See Averill Lake for directions. There are good natural campsites at the lake. It's usually inaccessible until June.

RED SLIDE LAKE A small, difficult to find brook trout lake 1 1/2 miles north of Irish Lake, about 1/4 mile south of Brahma Lake, which is on the Pacific Crest Trail above Irish Lake. No trail leads to Red Slide. You might get lost for a while, as this is tricky terrain with potholes and lakes all about. Happily, many of them hold fish. Some that you may stumble across are Timmy, Brahma, Lady, Gleneden, and Pocket. Hiking due west will get you back on the trail anywhere in here. Bringing along the Irish Mt. USGS quad map will help some.

Red Slide covers only 2 acres but is deep. There aren't a lot of fish here, but the brook trout present reach good size. Mosquitoes in this area are fierce in early season.

REYNOLDS POND A 60-acre pond near Alfalfa, offering warmwater fishing. From Alfalfa, about 14 miles east of Bend, follow the Alfalfa-Market Rd. to the Johnson Market Rd., heading south to the landfill. The pond is about 1/2 mile past the landfill.

Reynolds contains largemouth bass and redear sunfish. It is about 100 yards from the parking area to the pond, so only light boats or float tubes are appropriate. Bank fishing is good, with the south shore accessing deeper water. To avoid snagging your hook, keep an eye out for submerged junipers which have been added to the pond to provide additional fish habitat. Fishing is best in spring. Recommended for small fry.

ROCK CREEK RESERVOIR A small reservoir with trout, bass, and brown bullhead in eastern Mt. Hood National Forest, about 10 miles west of Tygh Valley. From Tygh Valley, follow the paved road to Wamic, continuing west on this road for about 5 miles to the reservoir. It can also be reached from Hwy. 26 by cutting north from Wapinita, crossing the White River at Smock Crossing, then following the signs north to the lake.

Part of the White River drainage, Rock Creek Reservoir has about 100 surface acres when full. It is stocked annually with legal rainbow trout. The average catch is 9-13 inches, with some to 18 inches. All fishing methods are effective, with bait fishing most common. Trollers do well using Kwikfish, Triple-Teasers, or spinner-worm rigs. Brown bullhead and largemouth bass populations have steadily gained ground here, with bass to 5 pounds.

Rock Creek Campground is located on the south shore of the reservoir. It is well shaded with pine trees. Motors are prohibited on the lake, but there is a boat ramp at the campground. Use of this ramp can be affected by a draw down of the reservoir in late season. Most anglers here launch car-top boats.

The reservoir is shallow with lots of accessible shoreline. Recommended for small fry.

ROSARY LAKES A series of three hike-in trout lakes on the Pacific Crest Trail one mile north of Odell Lake. Lower Rosary Lake is 2 1/2 miles by trail from the PCT crossing of Hwy. 58 at Willamette Pass. The lower lake is 42 acres, the middle 9 acres, and the upper lake 8 acres.

The lower lake has rainbow, brook trout, and cutthroat averaging 8-12 inches with some to 16 inches or better. The other two have brook trout in the same size range, but less abundant. Lures or bait work well early in the season, but all three lakes are easily fished with a fly. In early season, come prepared for mosquitoes. The trail is snowbound into June most years.

ROUND LAKE (Jefferson Co.) A trout lake in the Santiam Pass area NW of Suttle Lake. Take Forest Rd. 12 north from Hwy. 20 one mile east of the Suttle Lake turn-off. Forest Rd. 1210, a loop road, leads to the lake. Ignore the first cross-road one mile from the highway, and continue a bit over one mile to the second intersection. From there it is about 4 miles to the lake.

Round is only 22 acres but is fairly deep and holds up well. Brook trout and rainbow are stocked, and a lot of trout are caught here averaging 8-12 inches, with a few to 18 inches. There is a small improved campground on the east side of the lake. The Forest Service grants a use permit to church groups for an area on the west side. Motors are prohibited on the lake.

SALISBURY SLOUGH A backwater of the Columbia River, off I-84 at hwy. mi. 76. It covers about 50 acres and can be accessed at Mayer State Park, where there is a concrete boat ramp and ample parking. Take Exit 76. The slough may contain any of the Columbia River species. See Appendix for a map of Columbia River Ponds.

SAND LAKE One of the I-84 ponds associated with the Columbia River, located at hwy. mi. 94. Just one acre, it is south of I-84, with limited unimproved parking for eastbound traffic. It may contain any of the Columbia's warmwater species. See p. 206 for a map of Columbia River Ponds.

SAND DUNE LAKE One of the I-84 ponds adjacent to the Columbia River at hwy. mile 92.3. This one-acre pond is between the east and westbound freeway lanes. There is no parking for westbound traffic, and only limited parking for eastbound. It may contain any of the Columbia's warmwater species. See p. 206 for a map of Columbia River Ponds.

SCOUT LAKE (Hood River Co.) A 3-acre lake in the Wahtum Lake area, just south of Wahtum on the same road. See Wahtum Lake for directions. Scout is stocked with brook trout. Fish caught range from 7-9 inches.

SCOUT LAKE (Jefferson Co.) A small lake 1/2 mile south of the west end of Suttle Lake. This lake is currently not stocked and is probably barren. A campground is located on the east shore.

SIMTUSTUS, LAKE (Confederated Tribes Warm Springs) A reservoir created by Pelton Dam, a power dam on the Deschutes River west of Madras. Most fishing here is for kokanee, but browns are taken as well as the occasional huge rainbow trout. This is the smaller of two major impoundments on the Deschutes. The second, Lake Billy Chinook, is just upriver.

To reach the reservoir's western shore, take the Pelton turn-off about 3 miles south of the community of Warm Springs. A paved road leads to Pelton Park, where PGE maintains a boat launch. West shore access is from Indian Park, a campground on CTWS land. Best bet here is to ask for directions at Warm Springs Information Center when you stop to pick up your fishing permit.

The dam backs up about 7 miles of river, all the way to Round Butte Dam. Angling is almost exclusively by boat, as there is no access to the canyon much above the dam. The lake is stocked with kokanee and brown trout. Angling is generally only fair, with most fishing in the upper part of the lake, although early and late in the season anglers have good luck throughout the reservoir.

Trolling is the most popular method, with bait angling the next choice. Rainbow trout average 10-12 inches, but some go larger—much larger. Trout weighing 25 pounds have been taken here. Not many anglers know about or go after these large fish, and anglers must use different tactics to attract them. Big fish want big lures, and stay fairly deep throughout most of the season. Here's a chance to see if that fish finder was worth what you gave that friendly fellow at the boat show.

Bull trout are infrequently taken on troll and bait, averaging 10-12 inches, with a very few 3-4 pounds. Lakes Simtustus and Billy Chinook have the only consumptive fisheries for bull trout in Oregon.

Lake Simtustus is on CTWS land, and a permit is required to fish it. A daily permit covers the whole family. Permits are available at the grocery store in Warm Springs, at Cove Palisades State Park, at the general store in Camp Sherman, at the sporting goods store and fly shop in Sisters, in stores at the rim of the canyon above Billy Chinook, and from other vendors in Warm Springs and Madras.

A 10 mph speed limit is in effect on all but the lower 3/4 mile of the reservoir. Landing boats on the western shore is prohibited, except at Indian Park. There are campgrounds and boat ramps at Pelton Park and Indian Park. Supplies are available at Pelton Park. Simtustus was named after a Warm Springs warrior who served as a US Army scout in the Piute wars of the 1860s and lived on the reservation till his death in 1926.

SISTERS MIRROR LAKE A very scenic lake in the Wickiup Plains area north of Elk Lake, south of the Three Sisters. The lake is no longer stocked due to frequent winterkills. There are good campsites all around the lake, and fishing in nearby lakes. See Denude, Burnt Top, Nash.

SNELL LAKE A nice 9-acre hike-in trout lake in the Deschutes National Forest between Crescent and Summit Lakes. Snell can be reached by trail 1/8 mile NW of Farrell Lake, less than one mile from the Summit Lake Rd. See Farrell for detailed road and trail directions.

Both cutthroat and brook trout are stocked, but brook trout dominate the catch. Brook trout average 10-12 inches, and fish up to 18 inches have been reported. Snell Lake is fairly shallow, and fly-fishing is good late in the year. Nearby Farrell Lake also contains trout.

SNOW CREEK A small, clear trout stream which joins the upper Deschutes River just above Cow Meadow on the north shore of Crane Prairie Reservoir. Snow Creek flows only about 5 miles from springs NE of the Deschutes Bridge Guard Station on the Cascade Lakes Hwy. It offers difficult fishing for rainbow and brook trout. Spring fed, it is very clear and cold, and light tackle is a must. The fish here will take a fly. No good trail follows the stream, and the banks are very brushy. The upper portion is crossed by Forest Rd. 4270 south of Deschutes Bridge. Forest Rd. 40 to Cow Meadow crosses the creek one mile above its mouth.

Snow Creek is open June 1 through August 31.

SNOWSHOE LAKES Three remote hike-in trout lakes roughly half-way between Big Cultus Lake and Mink Lake in Three Sisters Wilderness. The area is at least a 7-mile hike from the nearest road. The lakes are north of Winopee Lake on a trail that runs from the west end of Big Cultus Lake to Mink Lake. The trail is usually clear of snow by late June, but bring dry footwear, as the snow melt tends to pool along the Winopee Trail. Unless you are camped in the Mink Lake Basin, you will probably approach from Big Cultus.

First chore is to reach the western end of Big Cultus. Your choices are to hike around the north shore on a good trail, to hike north from road's end near Deer Lake, or to boat across to West Cultus Lake Campground. The latter will save about 3 miles of hiking. From the west end of Big Cultus Lake take Trail 16 north about 5 miles to Winopee Lake. Here the trail splits. Follow Trail 35, the eastern fork. Lower Snowshoe Lake is about 1/3 mile north of Winopee on the east side of the trail.

This fairly shallow lake is 18 acres, with a rocky ledge that runs along the west shore. Infrequently visited, it has some nice brook trout 8-12 inches, with some to 16 inches. All methods of angling can be effective, but this is a great fly-fishing situation.

Middle Snowshoe Lake, 1/4 mile west of the north end of Lower, is only 3 acres. It's stocked with rainbow trout. Continuing north on the trail 1/2 mile brings you to Upper Snowshoe Lake, the largest of the group, covering 30 acres. It is also the shallowest, with a maximum depth of only 8 ft., and will occasionally winterkill. Upper Snowshoe produces medium-size brook trout.

From Upper Snowshoe the trail continues north into the rich Mink Lake Basin, reaching Mink Lake in about 2 1/2 miles. There are many opportunities for anglers willing to explore with map and rod from Winopee north.

SPARKS LAKE A large fly-fishing only brook trout lake just off the Cascades Lakes Hwy. directly south of the Three Sisters. The lake is visible from the highway, about 28 miles SW of Bend and 3 miles beyond the Mt. Bachelor ski area. A spur road leads to the east shore of the lake.

Sparks Lake covers a lot of area, about 400 acres, and none of it is more than 10 feet deep. Its water is a rich nutrient broth that can produce plump trout. A narrow extension of the lake winds south about one mile from the campground into the lava field that created Sparks. The lake is deeper near the lava dam, and fish congregate here when the lake warms.

The natural lava dam that created Sparks has always leaked, and the lake has always dropped significantly by late summer. Sparks was particularly hard-hit by the years of drought. Some patchwork on the dam may have helped, but at this time its brook trout are running considerably smaller than usual. In good times, Sparks Lake brook trout average 8-13 inches, with some 16-17 inches. Fishing is best right after ice-out if you can fight your way in through the snow.

There is a boat ramp at the end of Forest Rd. 400, but during low water it is sometimes necessary to drag boats to deeper water. Motors are allowed for transportation on the lake, but fishing is prohibited while the motor is operating. This still allows trolling a fly while rowing or wind drifting. A canoe is probably best for exploring Sparks. Hiking the rocky shoreline is almost impossible due to rock walls and crevasses.

There is a day-use area with outhouse near the boat ramp, but camping is limited to natural sites off Forest Rd. 400 and a couple of sites at the NW corner of the lake. From the NW, a canoe can be slipped into Satan Creek and paddled to the lake when the water is high. The road to these campsites turns off the highway 1/2 mile east of Devils Lake. For more information, see *Fishing In Oregon's Cascade Lakes*.

SPOON LAKE (Confederated Tribes Warm Springs) A shallow 2-acre lake on the west side of the Skyline Rd. between Horseshoe and Breitenbush Lakes. A small population of brook trout is present but subject to winterkill. The lake is on CTWS land, but no permit is required to fish. Overnight camping is permitted. See Breitenbush Lake for road directions.

SQUARE LAKE A hike-in trout lake one mile NE of the Santiam Pass on Hwy. 20. Take the Pacific Crest Trail north 1/4 mile from its crossing of the highway 1/2 mile east of the entrance to Hoodoo Ski Bowl. Trail 65 takes off to the east and leads a bit over one mile to the lake.

Square lake is 55 acres and fairly deep. It's fished pretty hard, but continues to produce good catches. Cutthroat trout are stocked. Most fish are 8-11 inches, with some to 14 inches. A float tube would come in handy. Bait angling is good in spring, and lures and flies will also work. Following the trail along the outlet creek brings you to Long Lake, 1/2 mile to the east, where there is also good fishing. Good natural campsites are available.

SQUAW CREEK (Jefferson Co.) Heading on the eastern slopes of the Three Sisters and flowing through the town of Sisters into canyon country to the NE. It joins the Deschutes about 3 miles upriver from Lake Billy Chinook. Below Sisters, Squaw Creek flows through its own canyon. Unimproved roads drop down to it at Camp Polk and at several points to the north. These roads are shown on the Deschutes National Forest map.

Much of the creek goes dry during irrigation season, as water is removed from above. Except in early spring, there is little or no fishing in the upper creek. There is good early angling at the lower end.

STRIDER LAKE A seldom-fished, deep 3-acre lake above Little Cultus, just off the road to Taylor Burn. See directions to Little Cultus Lake. At Little Cultus Lake Campground, follow the primitive Irish and Taylor lakes road (Forest Rd. 600) west about 2 miles. Strider is about 3/4 mile past the Lemish Lake Trailhead, on the north side of the road. There is no trail to the lake, but it's a fairly easy 1/2 mile bushwhack north.

You will be rewarded with some very sporting rainbow trout. There are a few logs to cast from, and the fishing's generally good along the rock slide, but a raft or float tube would come in handy.

SUMMIT LAKE (Klamath Co.) A large alpine lake on the summit between the Willamette and Deschutes River watersheds. From Crescent Lake Junction on Hwy. 58, drive around the NW shore of Crescent Lake to Forest Rd. 6010, the Summit Lake Rd. This road leads west about 1/4 mile south of Tandy Bay Campground. Summit Lake is a bit over 5 miles by good dirt road. Diamond Peak stakes out the northern horizon, and Sawtooth Mountain the southern. This is a beautiful lake, surrounded by spruce and pine, but like Waldo Lake to the north, the fish come hard here. At an elevation of 5,553 ft., the lake is usually snowbound until late June.

Summit is about 500 acres but is not a rich lake, and fishing is only fair. Some anglers do well, but locating the fish here is a problem. Brook and rainbow trout are stocked, and a population of Mackinaw is self sustaining. The altitude and extremely clear water lead to slow growth of the stocked fish. Brook trout average about 10 inches, get up to 18 inches, and are plentiful if you can locate the schools. Trolling in different areas is the best way to do this. Not many large fish are seen. Most rainbow caught are 8-10 inches, but fish to 20 inches are present. Both rainbow and brook trout can be taken by fly-fishing in early morning and evening. Few anglers try for the Mackinaw, but they do show up occasionally on deep trolls. Summit Lake Mackinaw rarely exceed 8 pounds.

There's a good campground at the N W corner, and Summit makes a nice base camp for exploring other smaller lakes. See Windy Lakes, Suzanne, Darlene. The Pacific Crest Trail touches the SW corner of Summit and crosses the road 1/4 mile west of the camp. Bring lots of mosquito repellent.

SUTTLE LAKE A popular multi-use lake in the Deschutes National Forest just off Hwy. 20 NW of Sisters, featuring both kokanee and water-skiing. Follow Hwy. 20 (from Albany or Bend). The lake is just 7 miles east of the Santiam Pass summit.

Kokanee (landlocked salmon) are the main feature for anglers on this 240-acre lake. Late May and June are most produtive, but fish are taken throughout the season, with bait the favored method. Bait anglers fish perrywinkles or caddis fly larvae as one would a single egg. The kokanee are currently running to 14 inches, but are less abundant than in previous years.

There are a tremendous number of whitefish and a good reproducing population of browns. Browns to 16 inches and an occasional 4-5 pounder are taken on lures or bait. Lake Creek and nearby Blue and Scout lakes offer additional angling opportunities.

A good family lake, Suttle offers pleasant swimming and opportunities for recreational boating, with an area roped-off for water-skiing. Mosquitoes, for some reason, are a rarity here. Forest Rd. 2070 circles the lake, and there are four boat ramps on the south shore. Four USFS campgrounds are located at NE and SW ends of the lake and on the south shore. Equipment rentals, lodging, and supplies are available at a resort on the NE end and at Blue Lake Resort nearby.

SUZANNE LAKE One of a pair of good hike-in trout lakes above Crescent and Summit Lakes. The Trailhead is 1/2 mile west of the Spring Campground entrance road at Crescent. It's about a 3-mile hike to the junction with Trail 46. Hike about 1/2 mile east on 46 to reach Suzanne and her neighbor Darlene. From Summit Lake it's about a 5 mile hike on Trail 46, past Windy Lakes, to Suzanne. The trailhead is off the south side of Forest Rd. 6010.

Suzanne covers about 14 acres and is very deep. Rainbow average 12 inches, with an occasional 18 incher. Brook trout are also stocked, with catches to 16 inches. Fly-fishing is good at times other than mid-day.

TAYLOR LAKE (Deschutes Co.) The larger, but slightly less productive, of a pair of closely nestled Cascade summit lakes known as Irish and Taylor. These are scenic trout lakes that you can drive to if you're careful and have a high-center vehicle. The road in is not quite a jeep trail, but not a lot better. Irish and Taylor are about mid-way between Waldo and Cultus Lakes SW of Bend in the Deschutes National Forest. The Pacific Crest Trail follows the west shore. (See Irish Lake for complete directions.)

Brook trout predominate, though the lake is occasionally stocked with cutthroat. Fish average 9-12 inches, with a few to 16 inches. Taylor's trout usually run slightly smaller than those in Irish, but are generally easier to catch. There's good fly angling here, but be warned—the mosquitoes can be ferocious, especially in spring. Try fishing the ice-out or in early fall to avoid these pests. Motorboats

A natural lava dam created shallow Sparks Lake, restricted to fly-fishing only.

are prohibited on the lake, so plan to row or paddle if you want to troll. There are good primitive campsites here and at Irish, and the Pacific Crest Trail leads north to other high lakes. See Brahma, Red Slide.

The roads in are generally snowbound till late June or early July. Check with the Forest Service for road conditions.

TAYLOR LAKE (Wasco Co.) A popular and productive pond west of The Dalles. It is one of the I-84 ponds adjacent to the Columbia River, offering good angling for largemouth bass, redear sunfish, and crappie. Legal trout and fingerlings are stocked in early season. There is limited unimproved parking for westbound traffic, but best access for parking and boat launching is on Taylor Lake Rd. Take Exit 83 north, then go west on Frontage Rd. to the Taylor Lake Rd. Taylor covers 35 acres. See map p. 206.

There's no boat ramp, but it's easy to launch car-top boats. A hiking and bike trail with footbridge across the lake are planned to run from Lone Pine Pond (east of The Dalles) to the Columbia Gorge Interpretive Center. At this time there is a half-mile paved trail at Taylor. Recommended for small fry.

TEDDY LAKES North and South Teddy Lake are two good hike-in lakes, far enough away to take the pressure off but close enough (if you have a boat) for an easy day hike. The lakes are in the Cultus Lake area about 50 miles SW of Bend. The Cultus to Mink Lake Trail runs between the lakes about one mile north of the west end of Big Cultus. Start at Big Cultus Lake Campground, and follow Trail 16 along the north shore. At the west end of the lake the trail heads north, and South Teddy is one mile up on the west side of the trail. From the campground it's about 4 miles to the lake. Many anglers use a boat to get to the west end of Big Cultus, then hike the remaining mile.

South Teddy, at 17 acres and 10 ft. maximum depth, is smaller and shallower than North. It provides brook trout 7-18 inches with the average 11-12 inches. The north lake is 1/4 mile NE of South Teddy, and is twice as large and deep. It is stocked with rainbow which run to about 13 inches. Both lakes offer excellent fly-fishing, but bait and lures are also used. There are nice campsites at Big Cultus Lake.

THE DALLES POOL (a.k.a. Lake Celilo, Celilo Lake) See Celilo.

THREE CREEKS LAKE A 28-acre trout lake in the Deschutes National Forest on the north slope of the Cascades west of Bend. It's cupped in a depression in the mountains, at elevation 6,500 ft. and receives one of the heaviest snowfalls in the forest. To reach the lake, take Forest Rd. 16 about 15 miles south from Sisters about 15 miles to the lake. The road is paved to within 1/2 mile of lake, and the rest is rough. From Bend it's 24 miles by way of Tumalo Creek Rd. west, then Forest Rd. 4601, following the NW spur. The last 8 miles of this approach are rough. These roads usually open in mid-June or, in heavy snowpack years, around July 4.

The lake has rainbow trout and a sustaining population of brook trout. The trout run 8-15 inches. All fishing methods are used with success. There are two camping areas on the lake, and a third one mile north on Forest Rd. 16. A trail

South Twin is a fine lake for children.

leads west from Driftwood Campground, on the north shore of the lake, to Little Three Creeks Lake. This lake is about half the size of Big Three Creeks and has nice brook trout to 14 inches.

THREE CREEKS LAKE, LITTLE A wild brook trout lake just beyond Big Three Creeks Lake. About 14 acres and 10 feet deep, it can be reached by Trail 97 from Big Three Creeks. Its brook trout are self-sustaining and reach 14 inches. See Three Creeks Lake for directions.

TIMBER LAKE A hike-in lake in the Olallie Lake area north of Mt. Jefferson, about 100 miles from Portland. It is about one mile west of the south end of Olallie Lake. Take the trail west from the north end of Olallie, which meets the Pacific Crest Trail, and at 1/2 mile, head south on Trail 733 to Timber. The lake is less than 1/2 mile from the trail junction.

Timber is about 10 acres and fairly shallow. It's stocked by air every few years with brook and rainbow trout. The fish don't get large because of fairly heavy pressure, but fly-fishing in late summer and fall can net some nice fish. The setting's real pretty, and the hiking is easy. The road into Olallie Lake usually opens in late June. There are many other small hike-in lakes south and west.

TIMMY LAKE A tiny rainbow trout lake on the west side of the Pacific Crest Trail in the area north of the Irish-Taylor Lakes group. It's a bit over one mile NE of the north end of Irish Lake, and 1/3 mile south of Brahma Lake. See Brahma for trail directions. The lake is on the top of a knoll and is hard to spot.

Timmy is easy to fish from shore. Only 3 acres but fairly deep, it has produced some big fish in the past. You can expect eager medium size brook trout if you can find the lake. There are other good lakes close by. See Red Slide, Gleneden, Lady, Brahma. A maze of potholes in the area breed confusion and a wretched excess of mosquitoes in spring.

TODD LAKE A deep brook trout lake 2 miles due north of Bachelor Butte in Deschutes National Forest west of Bend. Take Hwy. 46 (Cascades Lakes Hwy.) about 2 miles past the Bachelor Ski Resort parking area to Forest Rd. 370, which joins from the north. At 1/2 mile, the Todd Lake Rd. heads east. This is blocked to motor vehicles, so you'll have to hike in the last quarter mile.

Todd is 45 acres and up to 60 ft. deep in places. It provides angling for brook trout to 15 inches. For a week or so after the ice melts fishing is hot, but during the rest of the year the fish are hard to catch. A trail encircles the lake. There is a small tent campground on the west shore, as well as a picnic area. Snow may linger here until late June or July.

TOOLEY LAKE One of the I-84 ponds adjacent to the Columbia River, located at hwy. mi. 79. It covers 30 acres south of the freeway, with limited unimproved parking at the west end of the lake for eastbound traffic only. Most of the north shore is privately owned. It may contain any of the Columbia's warmwater species. See p. 206 for a map of Columbia River Ponds.

TROUT LAKE (Confederated Tribes Warm Springs) The lowest of a chain of five good lakes which begins with Olallie Lake. It gets its name from a self-sustaining population of trout which has maintained a fishery in the lake without any additional stocking for more than 20 years. It is 6 1/2 miles NW from Warm Springs by way of Hwy. 26, then 18 miles west on a good gravel road.

Trout is at 4,600 feet and covers 23 acres, about 1/3 in shoal area. It is a pear-shaped lake with a maximum depth of 28 feet. A CTWS fishing permit is required. There is a campground here. The lake's outflow is the source of Mill Creek.

TUMALO CREEK A popular trout stream, about 20 miles long, which heads on the east slope of the Three Sisters west of Bend. It flows east and north to join the Deschutes River north of Bend. It is the municipal water supply for Bend. Several good roads follow the stream and cross it several times. Forest Rd. 4601 picks up the creek about 7 miles from the west end of Bend and parallels the stream for several miles to Tumalo Falls Campground. Here trails follow the major tributaries of the creek west.

The creek has a fair population of small wild trout averaging 7-9 inches, and it is stocked every other year. Bait, lures, or flies can all be used. The creek is a nice close-in recreation area for Bend residents. Shevlin City Park is located on the creek 3 miles NW of town.

TUNNEL LAKE One of the I-84 ponds adjacent to the Columbia River, located at hwy. mi. 72.6. Just one acre, it is immediately west of Memaloose State Park between I-84 and the railroad. Best access is for westbound traffic. It may contain any of the Columbia's warmwater species. See P. 206 for a map of Columbia River Ponds.

TWIN LAKE, NORTH (Deschutes Co.) A good size trout lake one mile north of Wickiup Reservoir in the Deschutes Forest SW of Bend. South Twin, similar in character and productivity, is one mile south. North Twin is a little over 45 miles from Bend by way of the Cascade Lakes Hwy. 46. For directions, see South Twin.

North Twin is about 130 acres and 60 feet deep. It is stocked heavily with rainbow, and the catch averages 10 inches, with some larger. Bait angling and trolling are both good, and fly-fishing is excellent at times. Best fishing is in the shallows except when the water warms. There is a good campground with boat ramp on the north shore of the lake. A short trail at the south end leads to North Twin. Motorboats are prohibited. For more information, see *Fishing In Oregon's Cascade Lakes*.

TWIN LAKE, SOUTH (Deschutes Co.) A delightful family lake, offering very good fishing, swimming, and other activities and attractions (not the least of which is Wickiup Reservoir just 1/2 mile north. South Twin is about 40 miles SW of Bend. Many people fishing Wickiup camp here. From Bend you can drive to the lake by the Cascades Lakes Hwy., taking the Wickiup turn-off (County Rd. 42) east. The Twin Lakes turn-off is one mile past the Deschutes crossing.

Alternately, you may drive south from Bend on Hwy. 97. Take the Sunriver turn-off, which is the east end of County Rd. 42, and follow it to the Twin Lakes turn-off, following signs to Crane Prairie or Wickiup Reservoir. From the Willamette Valley, drive SE from Eugene on Hwy. 58 to the Davis Lake turn-off, 3 miles past Crescent Lake Junction. Follow Davis Lake signs to the south end of the Cascades Lakes Hwy., and drive past Davis to the Wickiup turn-off, County Rd. 42.

South Twin is about 120 acres and reaches a depth of 55 feet. Stocked with both fingerling and legal rainbow in the spring, it has been providing outstanding fishing in recent years. The catch average is 9-10 inches, and trout to 15 inches are taken.

The lake lends itself to all methods of angling. Bait fishing is popular, but doesn't seem to produce any better than other methods. Many anglers fish too deep, below the oxygen layer, so stay shallow (under 30 ft feet). A trail encircles the lake and accesses very good water.

If fishing on South Twin is slack, an arm of Wickiup Reservoir is only 200 yards west. There is a good Forest Service campground, West South Twin, on this arm directly across from Twin Lakes Resort. The resort keeps boats here for use on Wickiup.

Twin Lakes Resort, on the west shore, has extensive facilities, including a variety of accommodations, an RV park with full hook-ups, restaurant, convenience store, laundry, and showers. It also has motor boat, canoe, and paddle boat rentals. South Twin Campground offers pleasant sites north of the resort. There is a short trail to North Twin that starts at the campground. Recommended for small fry. For more information, see *Fishing In Oregon's Cascade Lakes.*

TWIN LAKES (Wasco Co.) Two good hike-in brook trout lakes 6 miles south of Government Camp on the south slope of Mt. Hood, reached by way of the Pacific Crest Trail. The lower lake covers 12 acres, and the upper or north lake about 10 acres. Follow Hwy. 26 four miles south from its junction with Hwy. 35 to the crossing of the Pacific Crest Trail 1/2 mile north of Frog Lake (Watch for a road sign). The lower lake is an easy mile hike east and north on the PCT. The upper lake is 1/2 mile further north.

These lakes are stocked with fingerling brook trout every other year. They are fairly deep (lower, 40 feet; upper, 50 feet) and usually have some holdover fish of good size. The lakes see a lot of angling pressure. There is a campground at lower Twin and one at Frog Lake south of the trailhead.

UPPER LAKE An easy to reach hike-in brook trout lake in the Olallie Lake area, about 100 miles from Portland. See Olallie Lake for road directions. Take the Pacific Crest Trail west about 1 1/2 miles from the north end of Olallie Lake.

Upper is stocked by air with brook trout fingerlings every few years. The lake covers 8 acres and is of moderate depth. It's a good fly-fishing spot for brook trout 6-12 inches. There are fair natural campsites at the lake.

VIENTO LAKE One of the I-84 ponds adjacent to the Columbia River, at hwy. mi. 56. It covers 4 acres at the mouth of Viento Creek, with good access from Viento State Park at Exit 56. It may contain any of the Columbia's warmwater species. See p. 206 for a map of Columbia River Ponds.

VIEW LAKE Offering a good view of the large and small lakes within the eastern half of the Olallie Lake area. This 10 acre lake is one of many which are a short hiking distance from the Skyline Rd. at Olallie Lake. See Olallie Lake for road directions. To reach View, take the cut-off trail to the Pacific Crest Trail from the north end of Olallie (about 1/2 mile) and go south past Timber Lake for another 1/2 mile, or head due west from the Skyline Rd. at about the middle of Monon Lake, for a half mile uphill bushwhack.

View is stocked every other year by air with brook trout fingerlings. Covering 7 acres, it offers good fishing for trout 8-12 inches, but no large fish. Fly-fishing is good, but bait and lure are also effective.

WAHTUM LAKE Next to Lost Lake, the largest lake in the northern Mt. Hood area. Some nice fish are taken out of it each year. It is 6 miles north of Lost Lake, about 25 miles from Hood River. From the community of Dee SW of Hood River, drive 3 miles west to Forest Rd. 13, the Lost Lake Rd. At about 10 miles, take Forest Rd. 1310 to the right and follow it about 6 miles to Wahtum Lake Campground. The lake is to the west, at the bottom of a quarter mile trail which descends about 200 ft. from road level.

Wahtum covers 57 acres and is exceptionally clear and deep. Mid-lake, the bottom is 180 ft. below, and the depth and clarity give the lake a deep blue hue. It sits in a depression and is often sheltered from the wind. In the morning calm a fly line seems to hang suspended in air as it floats on the lake surface.

Wahtum is more easily fished from a boat than from shore. A canoe can be (has been) lugged down to the lake, but it's a chore on steep switch-back terrain. A float tube would be easier. Fishing is best in the 10-30 ft. shoal areas. Brook trout average 10 inches, with a few to 15. Once in a while the lake will turn up a real lunker.

There are several nice natural campsites here, and huckleberries in season. Bring your rain gear and warm clothes when you come. Maybe it's just the luck of the draw, but Wahtum seems to have its own private cloud. If the weather is crummy anywhere within 200 miles, it'll be cold and crummy at Wahtum. For other fishing lakes nearby, see Hicks and Scout.

WALTON LAKE Very popular with Prineville locals, a 25-acre lake in an attractive pine forest setting town. Walton was created by damming a spring creek in the headwaters of Ochoco Creek, a contribution of Isaac Walton League members in the Prineville area. Take Hwy. 26 about 15 miles east of Prineville. At the junction, take Hwy. 23 toward Ochoco Ranger Station. Just past the station, turn left on Hwy. 22. Follow signs to the lake.

Walton is at elevation 5,150 ft. and is 25 ft. deep maximum. It is stocked with legal rainbow annually, and catches 8-10 inches are taken on bait and lure. A few reach 16 inches. Best fishing is in May and June.

Canoes or float tubes are great here. Only electric motors are allowed. A trail encircles the lake. Facilities include a wheelchair accessible platform with paved path and a large campground.

WARM SPRINGS RIVER (Warm Springs Indian Reservation) The Warm Springs River is open to fishing only in the vicinity of Kah-Nee-Ta Resort. To reach it, drive north from Warm Springs about 10 miles. The way is well signed. The open area is between Kah-Nee-Tah Village Bridge and the marker at the east end of the golf course. A paved road follows the northern bank of the fishing area.

The river is well stocked with rainbow trout. Anglers are prohibited from using

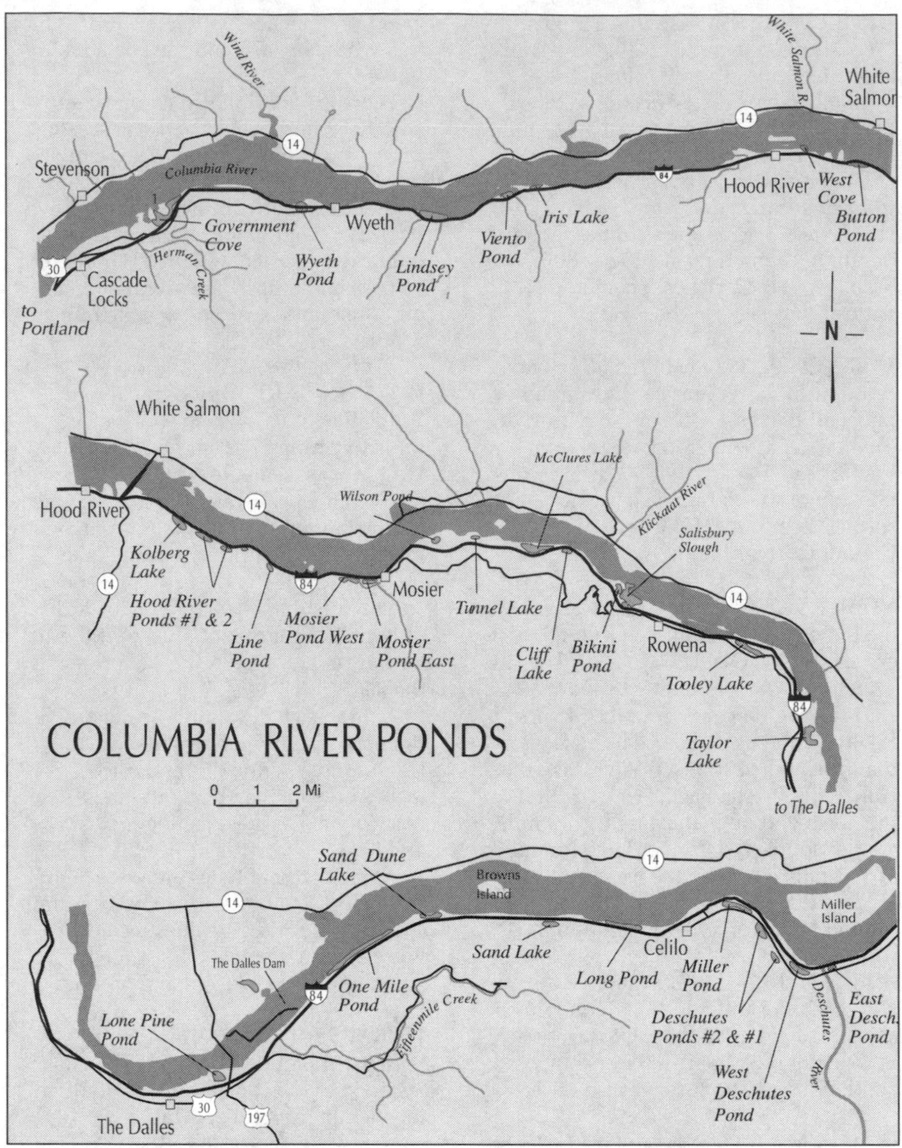

cluster eggs, spinners, wobblers, or any attractor blade or device. A tribal permit specifically for this area is required.

WARREN LAKE A 5-acre brook trout lake at the head of Warren Creek, which flows north 3 miles into the Columbia River, 9 miles west of the town of Hood River. The lake is 1/4 mile from the end of a primitive road SE of Mt. Defiance. You might want to walk the last mile of road. To reach the trailhead, follow the directions to Bear Lake, but take Forest Rd. 2821 when it forks NE off Forest Rd. 2820. The road forks after 2 miles. Take the left (west) fork. (Here is where you should begin to consider the capabilities of your vehicle). About 3/4 mile beyond, the road makes a T intersection with the Mt. Defiance Rd. Turn right, away from Mt. Defiance. About 1/3 mile ahead the road ends at a trail crossing. The trail west leads to Warren Lake.

WASCO LAKE A good brook trout and cutthroat lake below the Pacific Crest Trail 2 miles NE of Three Fingered Jack in Mt. Jefferson Wilderness. The most direct approach to the lake is 1 1/2 miles by Trail 65, which heads at Jack Lake. The trail passes along the west shore of the lake 1/2 mile before joining the Pacific Crest Trail just north of Minto Pass. See Jack Lake for road directions.

Wasco is at elevation 5,150 ft. and covers 20 acres. The lake is over 20 ft. deep, and all methods will take fish. A hike up to the PCT and back south 1/2 mile will take you to Catlin and Koko lakes, two small brook trout lakes that are lightly fished.

WEST COVE One of the I-84 ponds adjacent to the Columbia River, located at hwy. mi. 62.3. It covers 10 acres at the west end of the Hood River Industrial Park and is accessible from Exit 63. It may contain any of the Columbia's warmwater species. See Appendix for a map of Columbia River Ponds.

WHITE RIVER A good size tributary of the Deschutes, flowing almost 50 miles from its glacial origin on Mt. Hood's south face to its confluence with the Deschutes north of Maupin.

To reach it from Portland, follow Hwy. 26 to Mt. Hood, then Hwy. 35, which crosses the upper end of the river. Forest Rd. 48 heads south from Hwy. 35 just beyond the crossing and parallels the river's Iron Creek tributary, reaching the river itself at Barlow Crossing Campground. The primitive Old Barlow Rd. also accesses the river at Barlow Crossing. Forest Rd. 3530 follows the stream's west bank for about 4 miles from Barlow Crossing past White River Station Campground. Other campgrounds on and near the stream include Keeps Mill, Forest Creek, Grindstone, and Devil's Half Acre Meadow.

East of Mt. Hood National Forest, the river cuts a deep canyon. Anglers can reach the canyon in the Smock Prairie area. Take Hwy. 216 to a north-bound county road about mid-way between Wapinita and Pine Grove. The canyon is about 2 1/2 miles past the Oak Grove School. This road crosses the river and continues north to Wamic. Hwy. 197 crosses the river east of Tygh Valley, and there is pretty good early season fishing in the flatland stretch from there to the series of three falls about 3 miles above the Deschutes confluence. Rainbow average 7-11 inches.

Below the first falls, angling is restricted to the use of artificial flies or lures with barbless hooks. Trout above 20 inches are considered to be steelhead, and all non-finclipped steelhead must be released unharmed.

WICKIUP RESERVOIR One of Oregon's largest and most productive artificial impoundments, created by a dam on the upper Deschutes River in Deschutes National Forest, about 40 miles SW of Bend. Wickiup is a fertile lake with large self-sustaining populations of brown trout and kokanee. Coho salmon and rainbow trout are stocked annually. Wickiup is most successfully fished by anglers who have dedicated their weekends and vacations to learning how the fish respond to discreet changes in water level, temperature, and light.

To reach Wickiup from Bend, take Hwy. 97 south to County Rd. 43, just north of LaPine. Turn south onto Forest Rd. 4380 about 2 1/4 miles beyond Pringle Falls. This road follows all but the west shore of the lake. Paved forest roads connect the reservoir to all the major lakes in the area, including Odell, Crescent, and Davis lakes to the south.

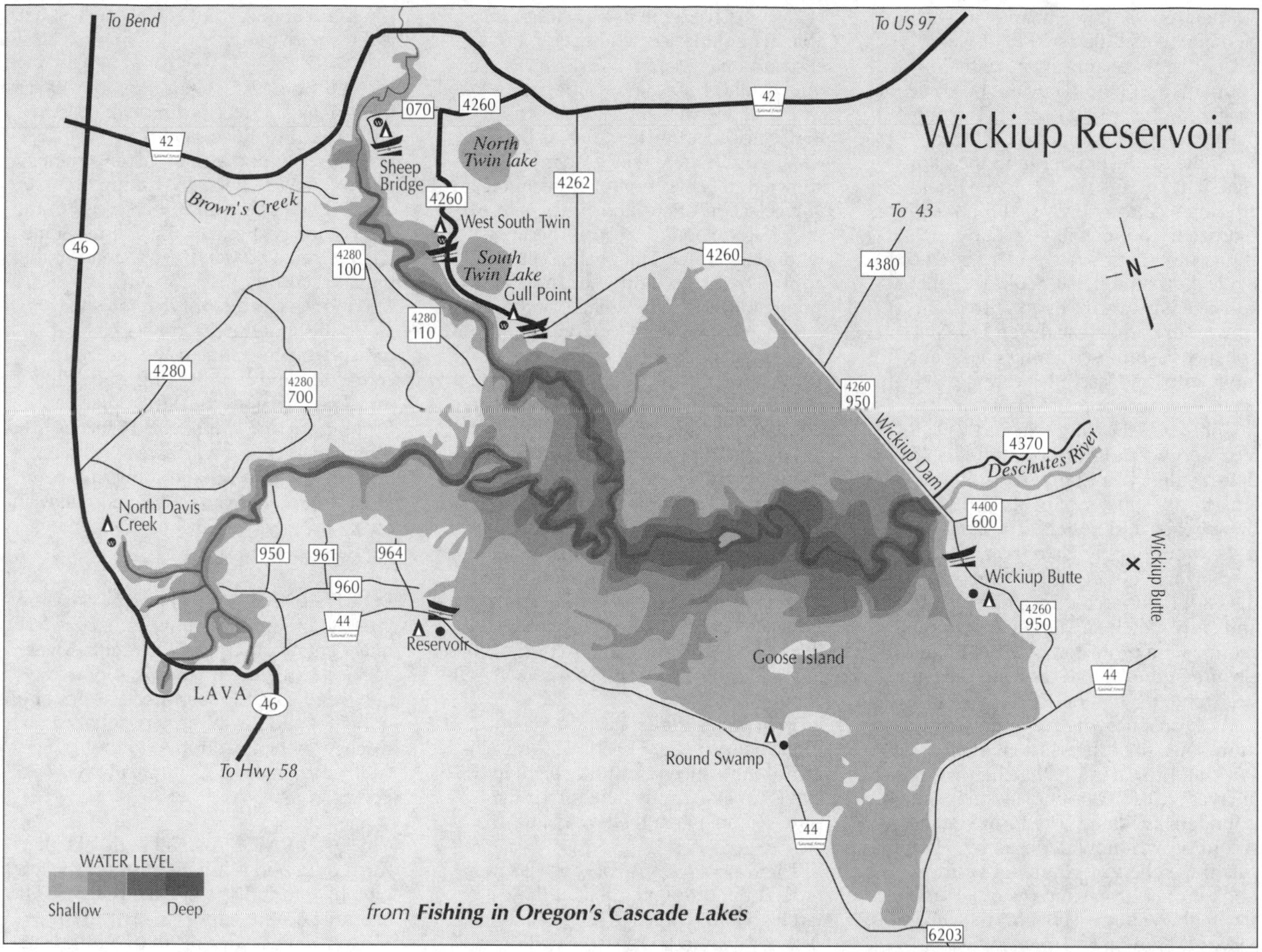

Wickiup Reservoir

*from **Fishing in Oregon's Cascade Lakes***

Wickiup covers nearly 10,000 acres when full. It is primarily an irrigation reservoir, and it is heavily drawn-down throughout the summer even in years of normal precipitation. Much of the reservoir is under 20 ft. deep, but the old Deschutes channel carves an arc in the lake bed from the Deschutes arm in the north to the southern end of the dam in the east. The river had cut a steep rocky channel, and this now provides a cool deep water refuge for fish in late summer. The water in this channel is over 60 ft. deep in places, with much irregular structure. A shallower channel leads east from the Davis Creek arm. Deepest water in the reservoir is at the intersection of a line drawn out from the Deschutes and Davis channels. Wickiup is significantly affected by drought. Heavy draw-downs destroy many juvenile coho and kokanee, but the brown trout seem able to cope.

Wickiup is very large and difficult to fish. Its fishery changes as the water level changes even during a normal season. At high water, fish are generally widely scattered. As draw-down occurs, they move into the channels. In spring the water

Most of Wickiup Reservoir is less than 20 feet deep.

temperature is uniform, and catches can be made in as little as 10 ft. of water.

Coho and kokanee provide the most popular sport here. They are taken beginning with the spring opener. Throughout the summer, bait anglers and trollers work the main channels and the dam area. Bait anglers seem to fare better, offering a concoction called the Wickiup sandwich—a pinch of crawdad tail, a chunk of nightcrawler, and a kernel of white corn on a size 8 hook. Trollers use kokanee hardware tipped with nightcrawler or corn. Near the end of August, kokanee assume spawning colors and move into the Deschutes channel, which is closed to angling.

Coho are schooling fish and tend to feed in concert. If the splashing itself doesn't alert you to the performance, look for the cluster of boats and follow the whoops and hollers. The coho fishery lasts through early October, with fish feeding actively in the channels and in the Gull Point area through September and early October. Salmon spawning grounds are protected by a September 1 closure of the Deschutes from the Gull Pt. boat ramp up to Crane Prairie Dam.

Wickiup's browns are imposing, if less numerous, than the salmon. The typical Wickiup brown is 10-20 inches, weighing an average of 2-3 pounds, with 9 and 10 pounders available. The former state record brown (now deposed by a Paulina catch) weighed 24 pounds, 14 ounces. Look for big browns in the old channels where the water is cool and the current serves up the meal. Trollers work at about 15 ft. depth, trolling shallower as the weather cools. They troll quickly, attempting to imitate the natural forage (chubs, whitefish, and kokanee). Anglers also cast to the edges of drop-offs and along channel ledges.

Browns are nocturnal feeders. As evening approaches, they venture into the shallows where they are available for fly-fishing. Fly anglers also work the points and ledges. Early morning and dusk are said to be the best times to catch the big trout, whose many years in the lake increase their savvy as well as their girth. Fish before and after the sun hits the water. Cloudy days can also be good.

In September browns begin to gather along the Deschutes channel and off Gull Point, feeding enthusiastically prior to their late (November or December) spawning. In addition to whatever insects are available, they gorge on crayfish and on Wickiup's hearty population of chubs and whitefish. Gold or bronze-finish minnow imitations (Rapalla, Rebel, Bomber) do a good chub imitation. Kwikfish and large streamers are also popular. Crayfish (whole or tails only) are hard to beat.

Tasty native whitefish are also available in quantity in the reservoir and shouldn't be ignored. Averaging 2 pounds and running to 4, they are good eating, especially smoked. Look for them in the clear cold water (such as the Davis Creek Arm, where they gather prior to spawning). Schools may also congregate in creek coves, flats, and riffles where they feed on aquatic insects. Because they favor clear water, whitefish must be approached with light line. They have small mouths, so use small bait (natural insect larvae on small egg hooks) or imitations (small dark patterns sizes 14 to 18). A light, flexible rod will allow you to play the fish to a satisfactory conclusion without breaking the line.

Wickiup is primarily a boat fishery, though early season anglers do well at the dam and along the channel. There are good boat ramps at Gull Point and North Wickiup campgrounds at the mouth of the Deschutes Arm, at West South Twin Campground on the lower Deschutes Arm, and at Reservoir Campground on the SW shore. Boats can also be launched at Wickiup Butte Campground on the SE shore.

Twin Lakes Resort keeps a fleet of rental boats on the Deschutes Arm. There is a 10-mph speed limit there and in the Davis Creek Arm. Watch out for the pumice flats when the lake is low. It's easy to get stuck.

There are a number of campgrounds around the reservoir. Most of these are left high and dry when the reservoir is drawn down in late season. Gull Point and West South Twin are full-service Forest Service campgrounds with access to water throughout the season. Supplies, gas, a restaurant and accommodations are available at Twin Lakes Resort on the Deschutes Arm at the north end of the reservoir. For more information, see *Fishing In Oregon's Cascade Lakes*.

WILSON POND One of the I-84 ponds adjacent to the Columbia River, located at hwy. mi. 71.4. Privately owned, it covers 5 acres between I-84 and the Union Pacific Railroad. Access is from Hwy. 30 with landowner permission only. See P. 206 for a map of Columbia River Ponds.

WINDY LAKES A group of 4 hike-in lakes not far from the Pacific Crest Trail SE of Summit Lake. The trail begins on the road about 1/2 mile south of Tandy Bay Picnic Area on Crescent Lake. It's a fairly steep hike in.

The Windys haven't been very productive, perhaps due to their location at 6,000 ft. They are currently all stocked with brook trout. South Windy has cutthroat, too, but they haven't shown well in the catch. The lakes range from 5-16 acres and are close together. The best bet is the south lake.

WINOPEE LAKE A fairly remote 40-acre hike-in lake between Mink Lake Basin and Big Cultus Lake. Winopee is a fair producer of good size brook and rainbow and offers very good fly-fishing. It is about 8 miles by trail from the end of the road at the east end of Big Cultus. Some anglers run a boat to the west end of the big lake, cutting the hike in half.

Winopee has a lot of marshy shoals along the shoreline. A rubber or float tube boat comes in handy. (Old Paint comes in handy for lugging a boat this far.) The lake goes to 30 ft. in places. Brook trout and rainbow 8-14 inches (both stocked and wild) are available. You can get through the snow in June in most years. There are other good lakes in the vicinity. See Snowshoe. Mosquitoes are fierce here in spring.

WYETH LAKE An I-84 pond adjacent to the Columbia River at hwy. mi. 50.6. It may contain any of the Columbia River species. Covering 6 acres, it is located between I-84 and the railroad and is one of the few ponds in the series that can be reached by boat from the Columbia. See p. 206 for a map of Columbia River Ponds.

YAPOAH LAKE A small high lake that turns out good rainbow trout for the few who hike to it. Yapoah Lake is at 5,800 ft., one mile east of Yapoah Crater in the McKenzie Pass area north of North Sister. To reach the lake you can take an unusual hike on the Pacific Crest Trail, heading south from the Dee Wright Observatory's lunar-like lava flow area. Hike a little over 2 miles south to the Matthieu Lakes, then take Trail 95 (Scott Trail) east one mile. From that point the lake is a 1/4 mile bushwhack due south. The trail in begins high, so there's not a lot of climbing. Bring your USGS Three Sisters Quad map.

Rainbow stocked here run to 12 inches. The lake covers 10 acres and is 25 ft. deep. This is fairly open country, and the lake is easy to fish from shore. It's in a scenic area, worth the hike for the view of North Sister.

SOUTHEAST ZONE

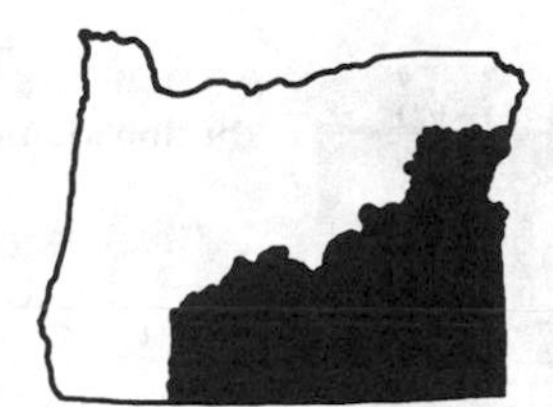

The Southeast Zone is all waters of the Snake River system above Hells Canyon Dam (including impoundments and tributaries); the Silvies River drainage in Grant County; all waters in Malheur and Lake counties; all waters in Harney County except So. Fork John Day drainage; and all waters of Klamath Basin in Klamath County.

The Southeast Zone includes more than a third of all land in Oregon, but only a tenth of the state's population. The reason for the disparity is the lack of abundant water. But western anglers know that nothing grows fish like a desert climate, and what water there is in Southeast Oregon proves the point.

Trout in the 18-20 inch class are usually available in a dozen desert reservoirs, including Ana, Chickahominy, Holbrook, Malheur, Priday, Thompson Valley, and Thief Valley. Even when drought drains one of these reservoirs dry, a single good growing season can bring the fishery back to trophy size. Mann, Miller, and Upper Klamath (all natural lakes) also yield big trout, as do the zone's major rivers—Ana, Burnt, Klamath, Malheur, Sprague, and Williamson.

Other Southeast waters are equally productive for bass and panfish. Brownlee, Oxbow, Gerber and Hells Canyon reservoirs provide outstanding catches of crappie, as does Hart Lake in some years. Smallmouth bass are abundant in Brownlee, Owyhee, and Warm Spring reservoirs and in Owyhee River. Dog Lake and Willow Valley Reservoir produce fine catches of good-size largemouth bass, and Ana Reservoir produced the state record hybrid bass.

Some lakes and streams in the region are notable not so much for the size of their fish, but for their offer of a pleasant refuge from the region's fierce summer weather. Big Creek, the Blitzen River, Dairy Creek, Delintment Lake, the upper Malheur, and Wood River are such oases.

A portion of the southern Eagle Cap Wilderness, with its glacial lakes and mountain streams, is also within this zone, as are the waters of Gearhart Mt., Mountain Lake, and Sky Lakes wilderness areas. Freemont, Winema, and portions of the Ochoco, Malheur, and Wallowa-Whitman national forests are encompassed by this zone. The Malheur National Wildlife Refuge, Steens Mountain, Hart Mountain National Antelope Refuge, the Alvord Desert, and Warner Valley Lakes are among the region's scenic treasures.

US highways 97 and 395 provide primary north-south access to the region. Highways 20 and 140 are the major east-west routes. Most secondary roads are unpaved. The only towns of any size in this vast area are Klamath Falls, Lakeview, Burns, and Ontario. Most other communities in the Southeast offer little more than a gas station, post office, general store, and maybe a cafe. (Some offer all of the above under a single name.)

Travelers in this area should be prepared with spare water and gas, and would do well to be as self-sufficient as possible. This is a land of wide open spaces, wild windy places, and big fish.

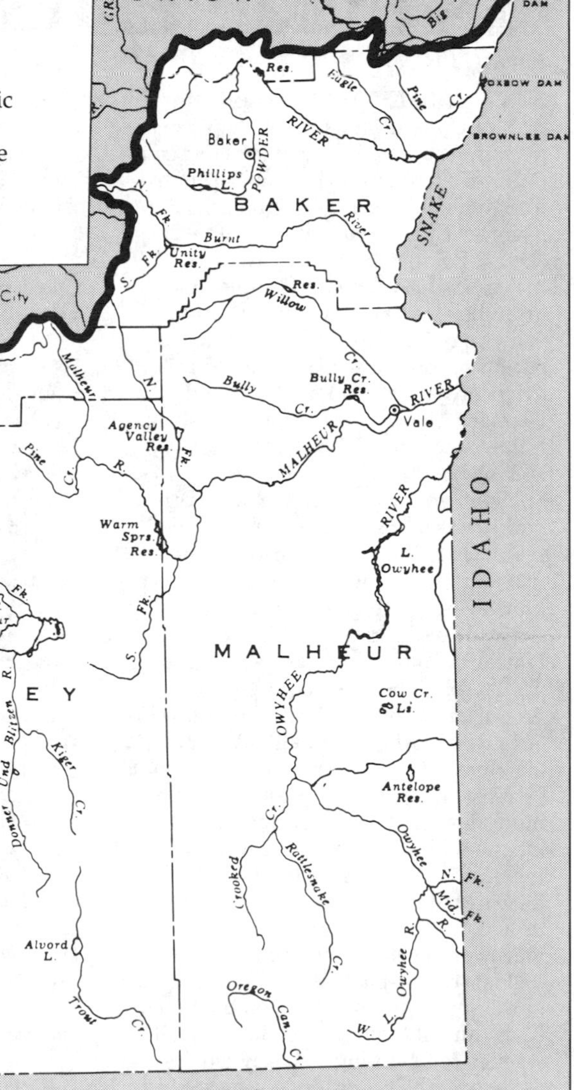

Anthony Lake is fished for stocked rainbow trout.

AGENCY LAKE The large northern pool of Upper Klamath Lake, separated from the main body by a narrow natural channel, offering excellent opportunities for large rainbow and brown trout. From Klamath Falls take Hwy. 97 north to Modoc Point, then the old Hwy. 162 NW to Agency Lake, about a 23-mile drive. From Bend, follow Hwy. 97 south to Chiloquin, then take the Klamath Agency cut-off south of town, about a 115-mile drive. Hwy. A secondary road south of Klamath Agency crosses the narrows and follows the Wood River tributary. Hwy. 162 follows Agency's east shore.

Like Upper Klamath, Agency is primarily a trout fishery, with even larger rainbow and occasional browns. The big fish migrate through Agency's main tributaries, Wood River and Sevenmile Creek. In early spring, anglers troll slowly near the mouths of these streams at the north end of the lake and in the narrows. As the lake warms in June, they troll closer to the Wood River mouth. Angling usually slows by July. Large lures seem to be most successful, with bait paying off more slowly. Rainbow average 18-20 inches, with some 15-pounders taken in the north. Fishing is traditionally best in the early morning. Large perch and brown bullhead are also available, primarily at the north end of the lake.

Boats can be launched at Henzel Park in the south, at Petric Park on the Wood River, and at the resort on the NE shore. Agency can get rough, so stay close to the shore. The lake is open year around for panfish, with no limits on bullhead and perch.

ALTNOW LAKE A privately owned 8-acre bass and panfish pond in Harney County with largemouth bass and bluegill. It is located NE of Drewsey, just off Hwy. 20 about 47 miles east of Burns.

The pond is behind the ranch house, and visitors are requested to stop in at the house before fishing. If no one is home, head on down the road to Cottonwood Reservoir instead. There is a user fee, which was instituted due to occurrences of vandalism and excessive littering. Anglers are urged to respect the owner's generosity and help keep this lake available for all. Small boats can be launched here. Camping at the lake is prohibited.

ANA RESERVOIR A 60-acre reservoir north of Summer Lake, offering year-round, ice-free fishing for hybrid bass and stocked legal trout. The lake is in a popular waterfowl hunting area. It is about 2 miles east of Hwy. 31, 5 miles north of the community of Summer Lake.

Ana is stocked annually with rainbow trout, legal size since anything smaller just feeds the huge chub population. These in turn fatten the big hybrid bass, a sterile cross between white and striped bass. Bait, lures, and flies are all effective, though bait anglers have some problem with chubs taking their offerings. Anglers may keep one bass per day, 16 inches and over. Hybrids to 13 pounds have been taken, including the state record catch in 1992.

Ana continues to be unaffected by drought, as it is fed by underground streams whose flows remain constant. Their temperature remains constant as well, 58 degrees, which keeps the reservoir ice free for winter fishing. There is no structure to speak of in the lake. The fish just cruise around. Boats can be launched from the beach, but most fish are caught from the bank. Camping is allowed, though facilities are primitive.

ANA RIVER A short but excellent trout stream, popular with fly anglers. It flows south from Ana Reservoir into Summer Lake Marsh. Hwy. 31 parallels the river and provides primary access to it, though some hiking is required. It is approached near the marsh by a road east from the community of Summer Lake and, at the reservoir, by the Ana Reservoir Rd. north of town. Floating the 5 miles in float-tube or raft can be pleasant and productive. Take out at the county road crossing.

The river maintains a stable, clear, cool flow and a constant 50-60 degree water temperature that produces insect hatches throughout the season. Planted rainbow fingerlings rear in the stream, averaging 8-12 inches, with 16-18 inch fish common and some to 5 pounds. Small dry fly patterns work best, though streamers imitating chubs may take the larger fish. There is a state park picnic area at Summer Lake, with camping available at the reservoir, at natural sites along the river, and at the River Ranch Campground at Summer Lake Wildlife Area.

ANDERSON LAKE See Warner Valley Lakes.

ANNIE CREEK A spring-fed trout stream heading in Crater Lake National Park, tributary to the Wood River. Hwy. 62 follows the creek closely from its headwaters about 5 road miles south of the lake, to its confluence with the Wood just north of Fort Klamath. Fort Klamath is near the junction of highways 62 and 232, about 40 miles north of Klamath Falls.

Annie Creek is about 14 miles long and offers good angling for wild rainbow, brown, and brook trout, especially in the lower end. It is not stocked. Fly angling is good in the evenings. The stream has a high pumice content and retains a milky color throughout the year. There is a good campground at its head, off Hwy. 62, with the Pacific Crest Trail passing just to the west of camp.

State licenses are not required to fish in the national park. Fishing permits may be obtained at park headquarters on the south rim.

ANTELOPE CREEK A remote Lahontan cutthroat stream. It is closed to all fishing to protect the Lahontan, which are listed as a threatened species. It's estimated that the Lahontan population throughout the basin dropped 90 percent during the 1987-92 drought.

ANTELOPE RESERVOIR A stark but scenic irrigation reservoir off Hwy. 95 east of Burns Junction near the state line. It is no longer stocked or recommended for recreation due to the presence of mercury in the water. Antelope was last stocked in 1989 and went dry in 1992. There are a few campsites on the northwest shore, plentiful waterfowl, and an occasional rise near the dam.

ANTHONY LAKE High in the Elkhorn Mountains of Wallowa-Whitman National Forest NW of Baker. This 19-acre lake is one of many located about 20 miles east of the town of North Powder, which is on Hwy. 30 between LaGrande and Baker. A good paved road heads west from North Powder, connecting with Hwy. 411, which becomes Forest Rd. 73 and leads to the lake. Hwy. 411 can also be picked up in Haines. Other good forest roads lead in from Ukiah (off Hwy. 395 between Pendleton and John Day). Anthony Lake is the site of a popular ski resort.

Fishing is good for stocked rainbow to 14 inches from early summer through fall. There are also wild brook trout to 10 inches. Fly-fishing can be productive, but most anglers troll or cast bait. The lake is 30 feet at its deepest point. There is a boat ramp, but motors are prohibited.

There is a large campground at the lake, and there are camps at tiny Mud Lake and at Grande Ronde Lake to the north. Other lakes in the area include hike-ins Van Patten, Black, Crawfish. There is a resort at Anthony with accommodations, supplies, and boat rentals. At elevation 7,100 ft., ice-out is generally around July 4.

ARRITOLA RESERVOIR A 200-acre reservoir on the Jaca Ranch 20 miles south of Jordan Valley. It has contained largemouth bass, bluegill, and bullhead, but the lake went dry in 1992. It may have been restocked. Check in at the ranch before approaching the reservoir. If no one is home, go elsewhere to fish.

ASPEN LAKE A 500-acre marsh area west of Klamath Falls, with rumored catches of brown bullhead. To get there, take Lake of the Woods Rt. 140 north from Klamath Falls about 16 miles, turning south onto Aspen Lake Rd. one mile past Rock Creek Ranch. There are no campgrounds in the vicinity.

AUGUR CREEK A small, wild trout stream, tributary of Thomas Creek and of Goose Lake. It is now closed to protect Goose Lake redband trout, most of which were lost when the lake went dry in 1992. In past years it was fished for wild brook trout to 10 inches, and for redband. It is a spawning stream for redband.

BACA LAKE A 300-acre irrigation reservoir for the Malheur Wildlife Refuge north of French Glen. It is closed to angling.

BALM CREEK RESERVOIR A good size reservoir near the head of Balm Creek, a tributary of the lower Powder River NE of Baker. It contains rainbow trout and smallmouth bass. Follow Hwy. 203 about 25 miles north to Medical Springs, then take Forest Rd. 70 east about 10 miles to the reservoir. Forest Rd. 7040 approaches from Hwy. 86 to the south. The turn-off to the reservoir is about 22 miles east of Baker.

The reservoir covers about 110 acres when full. In 1992 it was drawn way down, and the smallmouth bass fishery (illegally stocked) was eliminated. Since then smallmouth have been (illegally) restocked, as well as catchable rainbow trout and fingerlings. Trout to 13 inches were available within a season of restocking, however Balm Creek is at high elevation, and growth rate can be a little slower than at other Eastern Oregon reservoirs. Anglers may anticipate some carry-over rainbow to 15 inches. Bait is the most popular method.

Motors may be used to get around, but cannot be operated while fishing. Fishing usually holds up well into mid-summer when the water level drops. There are no improved campsites at the lake, but there is space for trailers. There are two campgrounds on Forest Rd. 67 north and east of the reservoir. Follow Forest Rd. 475 north to the junction with 67.

BEAR CREEK (Harney Co.) An eastern Oregon trout stream entering the upper Silvies near the community of Seneca on Hwy. 395 between John Day and Burns. About 25 miles long, it is followed east from Hwy. 395 (about 26 miles south of John Day) by Forest Rd. 16. Forest roads 1530 and 1640 access the waters upstream from Parish Cabin.

Lightly fished, the creek produces an average catch for this country. Bait-angling is the usual method, but flies will work. May, June, and July are the best months, but fish can be taken later. Parish Cabin Campground is located streamside, about 11 miles east of Seneca.

BEAR CREEK (Lake Co.) A small tributary of the Chewaucan River in the Winema National Forest, joining the main stream near the community of Paisley. You'll find Paisley on Hwy. 31 (Bend to Lakeview) south of Summer Lake. To reach the creek's confluence with the Chewaucan, follow the Chewaucan River Rd. (Forest Rd. 330) south about 6 miles from town. A northbound gravel road just west of town (Forest Rd. 331) crosses the upper stream, as does Forest Rd. 348.

The creek flows about 9 miles and offers good rainbow fishing in late spring and early summer. Its trout run small but are numerous, as the creek is lightly fished. Bait is usually best.

BECKERS POND A small lake within the city limits of Ontario, stocked with bluegill, channel catfish, and largemouth bass. It doesn't have many channel cats, but its bluegill and bass populations are thriving. The shoreline is developed, but anglers can reach the pond through the city park.

BENDIRE CREEK A little-known, lightly fished trout stream, tributary to Beulah Reservoir, which flows into the reservoir's NE arm. See Beulah Reservoir for directions from Burns and Vale. Flowing about 12 miles from spring-fed headwaters north of Bendire Mountain, its lower waters are primarily within the Butler Ranch, though it is crossed several times by roads. Ask permission to fish on ranch property.

Wild trout make up most of the catch, averaging 9-12 inches, with a few to 16 inches. Bait is most frequently used. Beulah Reservoir has the only improved campground in the area.

BERT LAKE A small off-trail brook trout lake, in the southern Sky Lakes Wilderness of Winema National Forest. Bert is about 1/4 mile north of Trail 3712 to Island Lake. To reach the area, follow Rt. 140 NW from Klamath Falls toward Lake of the Woods. Get out your Winema National Forest map. The trail to Island Lake heads into the wilderness off Forest Rd. 3659 in the Big Meadows area. Bert is about 1/2 mile from the trailhead, off to the right about 1/4 mile.

Covering only 2 acres, it usually has good numbers of brook trout 10-11 inches. Though the lake is accessible in late June, fishing is best in fall. In addition to Cold Springs Campground, there are nice campsites at Island Lake, one mile west of Bert.

BEULAH RESERVOIR (Agency Valley Res.) A large irrigation reservoir on the North Fork Malheur which is severely drawn down in dry years. From Juntura, on Hwy. 20 mid-way between Burns and Vale, a gravel road leads north about 15 miles to the reservoir. Juntura is about half-way between Burns and Vale. Roads also lead in from Drewsey on the west, and from Hwy. 26 at Ironside to the north.

After three dry years, the reservoir filled in 1993. It covers 2,000 acres when full and is stocked with rainbow fingerlings which grow to good size. Whitefish and bull trout are also present, though bull trout must be released without removal from the water.

Bait is usually most effective for taking the larger fish, when they're available. Ice fishing is popular after a decent growing season. Open all year, the lake makes a convenient base camp for deer hunters. There is a hot spring near the NE arm just west of Bendire Creek between the lake and the road.

There are generally quite a few campers and trailers here. There's no drinking water, but there are outhouses just above the dam. Supplies and gas are available at Juntura, Burns, or Vale.

BIG ALVORD CREEK A remote Lahontan cutthroat stream. It is closed to all fishing to protect the Lahontan, which are listed as a threatened species. It's estimated that the Lahontan population throughout the basin dropped 90 percent during the 1987-92 drought.

BIG CREEK (Grant Co.) A beautiful wild trout stream in the Logan Valley of Malheur National Forest, tributary to the Middle Fork Malheur River, with headwaters in the Strawberry Mountains. From John Day, follow Hwy. 395 south 9 miles to Seneca (about 45 miles north of Burns). Turn east on Forest Rd. 16. Big Creek Campground is 18 miles east on Forest Rd. 16, only 2 miles from the creek's mouth. About one mile east beyond the campground turn-off, Forest Rd. 1648 leads further upstream and ends at the head of Trail 377, which follows Big Creek to its headwaters.

Big Creek flows through an open meadow valley with fingers of forest reaching down to the stream. The creek is no longer stocked but offers good fishing for wild rainbow, brook trout, and whitefish. The trout run small (7-10 inches) but are plentiful, due to light pressure. Bull trout are also present and must be released without removal from the water.

In 1990 the east side of Big Creek burned from the campground to the wilderness boundary. The US Forest service re-planted grass and some trees, and the creek is running clear. In addition to Big Creek Campground, there are other Forest Service camps on Forest Rd. 14 to the east. When camping along the creek, camp well back from fragile streamside vegetation and use no-trace camping methods.

Catfish are available throughout Brownlee Reservoir.

BLACK LAKE A small brook trout lake above Anthony Lake in Wallowa-Whitman National Forest. The trail to Black heads east from Anthony Lake Campground. It reaches the lake in less than one mile.

BLITZEN RIVER See Donner And Blitzen River.

BLUE JOINT LAKE See Warner Valley Lakes.

BLUE LAKE (Lake Co.) A large, deep rainbow lake in the Gearhart Mt. Wilderness of Fremont National Forest. It's the only lake in the wilderness, though spring-fed creeks are plentiful. The wilderness covers 18,709 acres and is accessed by the 12-mile Gearhart Trail 100, with trailheads at the north-central and southeast boundaries.

Blue Lake is near the northern border at elevation 7,031 ft. It's a 2-mile hike to the lake from the northern trailhead, with a 600 ft. elevation gain. The 10-mile hike to the lake from the SE trailhead involves a 760 ft. climb over 3 miles, followed by a spectacular ridge walk among the volcanic spires of Gearhart Mountain, with views of the area's many meadows, the distant Cascades, and Steens Mountain.

From Lakeview, follow Rt. 140 west to Quartz Mt. Pass, turning north onto Forest Rd. 3660, which leads to the SE trailhead. To reach the northern trailhead, cut north off Rt. 140 about 4 miles west of Lakeview onto County Rd. 2-16. Turn west onto 2-16A, which follows Thomas Creek into Freemont Forest, becoming Forest Rd. 28. Turn west onto Forest Rd. 3428 at Dairy Pt. Campground and, at the next junction, head north on Forest Rd. 3372 along the Sprague River. A primitive track leads south to the trailhead about 8 miles from the junction.

Blue Lake covers 20 acres. It is annually stocked with rainbow fingerlings that can reach 16 inches in their short growing season. Bait fishing is most common, and success rate is high, but fly-fishing is good later in the season, mornings and evenings.

Trails into the Wilderness are generally clear by mid-June and stay clear until November. There are campsites at the lake. Camp well back from fragile lakeside vegetation, and use no-trace camping methods.

BOSENBERG CREEK A short tributary of the Middle Malheur River offering fair trout angling. It flows near Big Creek in the Malheur National Forest south of Strawberry Mountain Wilderness. From John Day follow Hwy. 395 south, turning east onto County Rd. 65 (following Canyon Cr.) which becomes Forest Rd. 15 beyond Wickiup Campground. Beyond Parish Cabin Campground, turn left onto Forest Rd. 16, which crosses the creek at Kimberling Cabin just east of the turnoff to Big Creek Campground. Forest roads north of the cabin follow the creek to its headwaters.

Bosenberg is not stocked, and its wild trout, mostly brook trout, run to 12 inches, averaging 9-10 inches. Bait fishing is good in May and June.

BOYLE (J.C.) RESERVOIR (a.k.a. Topsy Reservoir) A 450-acre impoundment on the Klamath River, used to store water for power generation. Fluctuation is heavy, as much as 3 ft. daily. Nevertheless, it is fished from boat and bank.

Boyle contains largemouth bass, black and white crappie, brown bullhead, and yellow perch. The bass population is modest, and the catch average is 2 pounds, though some 6-pounders have been taken. The reservoir is lightly fished, and bank anglers seem to stick close to the boat ramps and picnic areas.

There is a boat ramp and parking area on the east shore where Hwy. 66 crosses the maintenance bridge. On the west side of the bridge is a picnic area. Topsy Campground and Boat Ramp are on the south shore of the reservoir, south of Hwy. 66 on Topsy Rd. A fishing pier at Topsy Campground accesses good perch and crappie water and is wheelchair accessible.

BRIDGE CREEK (Harney Co.) A fair trout stream flowing off the west slope of Steens Mt. into the Blitzen River in the southern Malheur Wildlife Refuge NE of Frenchglen. Frenchglen is at the south end of the Blitzen valley and is reached by Hwy. 205 about 55 miles south of Hwy. 20 from Burns. To reach the creek, drive toward Page Springs Campground from Frenchglen. Just after crossing the Blitzen River, take a dirt road that leads north. The creek flows out of a low canyon about 3 miles down this road, which leads through mosquito infested marshlands, home to many aquatic birds.

Bridge Creek has native redband trout that average 10 inches. Occasionally much larger fish are taken, probably spawners from Baca Lake. Most anglers bait fish here, but flies or lures will work. Page Springs BLM Campground is located nearby. The mosquitoes seem to stay pretty much in the marshland.

BRIDGE CREEK (Lake Co.) A shallow stream flowing about 20 miles from the northern edge of Fremont National Forest into Paulina Marsh, just north of the community of Silver Lake. The stream is crossed by Hwy. 31 NW of town, and by County Rd. 650-N beyond the forest service landing strip SW of town. Dirt roads south from 650-N access the upper waters.

Rainbow trout predominate in the lower stretch, brook trout in the upper, with the upper waters most productive. Trout go to 10 inches. Best time to fish is spring and early summer. Bait is most effective, but flies dropped off the vegetation along the pools often find takers.

BROWNLEE RESERVOIR At 14,000 acres, the largest inland fishery in Oregon. In recent years its abundant catfish and 14-inch crappie have attracted more than 200,000 anglers annually. Brownlee is formed by Brownlee Dam, the uppermost dam on the Snake River. The dam also backs up the Powder River near Richland and the Burnt River near Huntington. Most angling is in these arms and at the upper end of the reservoir near Weiser, Idaho. In addition to crappie and catfish, Brownlee offers angling for smallmouth and largemouth bass and for rainbow trout.

To reach the lower reservoir from Oregon, take Hwy. 86 north from Richland, through Halfway, to Oxbow Reservoir. At Copperfield Campground, turn right and head south along Oxbow to Brownlee Dam. The road crosses the reservoir at the dam and continues south to Woodhead Park in Idaho.

To reach the Powder River Arm from Baker, take Hwy. 86 to Richland. About 1/2 mile east of town, when Hwy. 86 veers left and uphill toward Halfway, continue straight toward Hewitt Park, which is on Brownlee's Powder River Arm.

To reach the main reservoir from Richland, turn south on First St., a gravel road which is signed for Huntington. After crossing the Powder River, continue east on the Snake River Rd., which meets the main reservoir at Swede's Landing. The Snake River Rd. continues south to Spring Recreation Area, then crosses the Burnt River Arm and follows it upstream to Huntington.

To reach Farewell Bend State park (the upper reservoir) from Baker, take Hwy. 84 south to the Huntington Exit (Hwy. 30). Continue through Huntington. The road to the park is well signed.

Crappie can be found in Brownlee's shallows during spring spawning.

Crappie is king throughout Brownlee. White and black crappie range in size from 9 to 12 inches. In 1989-90, more than 2 million crappie were taken from Brownlee, and while such harvesting has kept the population under control, it has not diminished the fishery.

Crappie are most aggressive in late spring during their spawning season. Look for them in 5-6 ft. of water over small gravel beds that are interspersed with rocks. A moderately sloping bank is often a good indicator of nearby gravel beds. At this time of year they will attack almost anything, including a bare hook. Tube baits in sizes 1-2 inch or curly-tail grubs on 1/32 to 1/16 ounce jig heads are popular. Cast and retrieve parallel to the bank, using a short hopping retrieve along the bottom.

Even during spawning season, crappie can be found in both deep and shallow water. By mid-June, most spawning activity is concluded and the crappie leave the shallows. Big schools of crappie may be found suspended off the larger points. Look for them at 12 to 30 ft., though in low light (or when the surface is wind-rippled) they may move to within 5 ft. of the surface.

Catfish are also available throughout the reservoir, but fishing for them is especially popular at the upper end. There are 7 species of available, including channel cats that run 16-18 inches, and flatheads that approach 40 pounds. (The current record breaker is a 41-pound flathead caught in the Snake River itself.) Dead minnows, cut bait, or nightcrawlers work well. In June, anglers seem to be able to catch the cats on anything, using every method. Peak catches are made from April 1 through July. Anglers frequently launch at dusk, anchor, and fish through the night.

Smallmouth bass are present in numbers throughout the reservoir, with fishing best in the western arms at the upper end of the lake. There are also a few largemouth bass. Sturgeon are present in dwindling numbers. Regulations allow anglers to catch and release them, but because the mortality rate of hooked and released sturgeon is high, anglers are encouraged not to target this fishery. Rainbow trout are stocked as soon as possible after ice-off. Though rainbow average 10-14 inches, trout to 3 pounds have been taken here in recent years.

Brownlee is big and can get rough. Most anglers keep to the shallows and around the islands. Winds in the canyon can reach 30-70 mph when a front comes through. Call the ODF&W district office at Ontario for weather information and reservoir levels.

Reservoir levels can affect boat launching. Draw-downs particularly affect the upper ramps. Fluctuation may be driven by power generation at any time of year, or by salmon needs in spring. Spring draw-downs have been used to help flush Snake River spring and summer chinook seaward from mid-May to mid-June. Some boat ramps in the upper reservoir may be unusable during draw-downs. However boaters should have no problem launching at Hewitt Park (on the Powder River Arm) and at Spring Park (near Huntington). When levels are below 2,060 ft. boaters should keep to the main channels to avoid hitting rocks and sand spits.

There are no commercial facilities on Brownlee, and public facilities are limit-

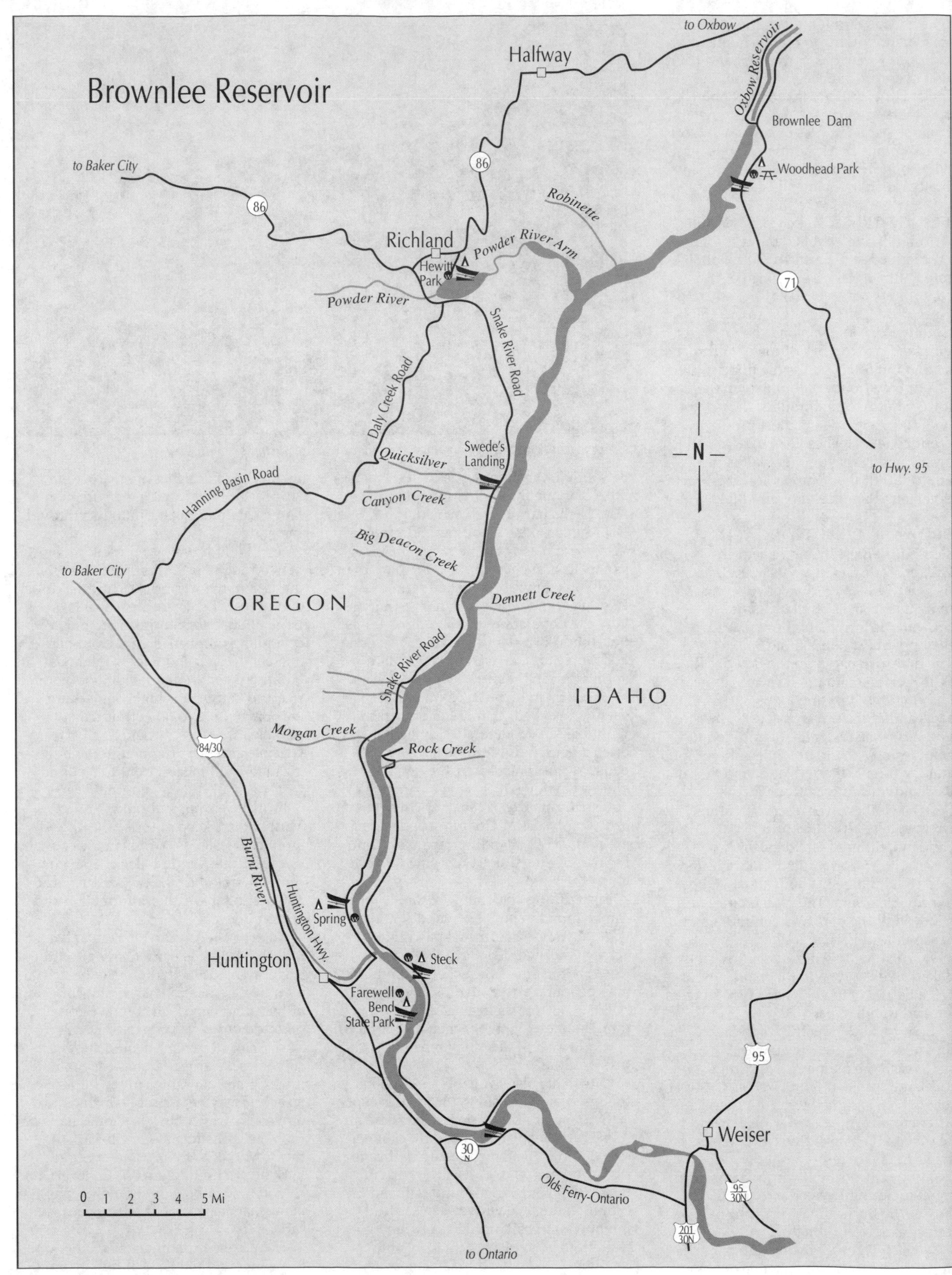
Brownlee Reservoir
to Oxbow
Halfway
Oxbow Reservoir
Brownlee Dam
Woodhead Park
to Baker City
86
86
Robinette
Richland
Powder River Arm
Hewitt Park
71
Powder River
Snake River Road
Daly Creek Road
Quicksilver
Swede's Landing
N
to Hwy. 95
Hanning Basin Road
Canyon Creek
Big Deacon Creek
to Baker City
Dennett Creek
OREGON
Snake River Road
IDAHO
84/30
Morgan Creek
Rock Creek
Burnt River
Huntington Hwy.
Spring
Huntington
Steck
Farewell Bend State Park
95
Weiser
30 N
Olds Ferry-Ontario
95 30N
201 30N
0 1 2 3 4 5 Mi
to Ontario

ed. Woodhead Park in Idaho is the only facility on the lower reservoir. It includes a boat ramp, campground, picnic area, and drinking water. There's good crappie fishing from the bank at Brownlee Dam.

Hewitt Park on the Powder River Arm offers a boat ramp, campground, picnic area, drinking water, and fish cleaning station. Good catches (primarily crappie) are made from the shore and docks. Boaters on the Powder River Arm may notice a scattering of what appear to be floating cabins. These floats were cabled in place before the reservoir was filled. They are privately owned, but many are open to public use as overnight shelters. Look for signs reading: "You're welcome to use it, but please leave it as you found it." Respect "No Trespassing" signs.

Spring Recreation Area on the lower reservoir north of Huntington includes a boat ramp, campground, and drinking water. Farewell Bend State Park south of Huntington, offers these and other amenities, including electrical hook-ups for RVs, showers, a picnic area, fish-cleaning station, swimming beach, and good bank fishing for catfish and bass.

Boaters can also put-in at a ramp on the Olds Ferry-Ontario Rd. Small boats and canoes can slide into the reservoir along Hwy. 201 (where the highway follows the reservoir toward Weiser, and the banks are flat). This area is known locally as "The Slides."

There are no public facilities on the Burnt River Arm, but you can park along the Snake River Road south of Huntington and fish from the rocks or from the culverts near the mouth.

Brownlee is fished year-round. Ice-fishing is popular at the upper end. In 1992-93 the ice was 10 inches thick.

An Oregon license is required to fish the Powder River Arm. Elsewhere on the reservoir, either Oregon or Idaho licenses are valid. Idaho anglers should remember that Oregon law allows only one rod per angler.

In 1994, the Idaho Department of Health and Welfare warned that mercury levels in fish taken from Brownlee Reservoir might pose a health hazard if eaten in sufficient quantities. Though tests revealed mercury levels below those considered to be hazardous by the Federal Food and Drug Administration (under 1 part per million in 30 percent of the fish tested), prudent anglers may choose to limit consumption. For further information contact the Idaho Department of Health and Welfare in Boise.

BUCK CREEK A good eastern Oregon stream, about 20 miles long, heading in the Yamsay Mt. area and flowing into Paulina Marsh near the town of Silver Lake. From LaPine on Hwy. 97, drive about 43 miles SE on Hwy. 31. The creek is crossed by Hwy. 31 two miles west of Silver Lake. One mile closer to Silver Lake, County Rd. 660 follows the creek west. It leads to Forest Service and logging roads that access the creek's headwaters.

The upper creek has some nice water. It's small, but supports a good population of little brook trout. Redband trout are found in the lower reaches, but most of the land there is private. There are no improved camps, but lots of nice natural campsites.

BULLY CREEK RESERVOIR An irrigation reservoir that generally supports bass and panfish, located about 8 miles west of Vale. Vale is about 12 miles west of Ontario by way of Hwy. 20. From Vale, drive west on Hwy. 20 about 8 miles, then take a road leading north at Hope School which reaches the reservoir in about 7 miles. The road continues along the northern shore of the reservoir then west up Bully Creek.

White crappie, yellow perch, and largemouth and smallmouth bass offer a self-sustaining fishery. Even following winterkills and severe draw-downs, Bully Creek eventually re-populates. Crappie fishing is best near the upper end where the lake is shallower. There is a nice county park with camping and boat ramps about one mile above the dam. There are two undeveloped hot springs near the upper end of the reservoir. One is near the road at the upper end of the pool, and the second, O'Neal Hot Spring, is one mile further west along the road.

Little more than a depression in the sagebrush, Bully Creek Reservoir is dedicated to irrigation and has no minimum pool requirement. It was drawn dry in three successive years (1990-92) and winterkilled in the spring of 1993.

BUMPHEAD RESERVOIR A 100-acre irrigation impoundment in Klamath County, east of Klamath Falls near the California line. It is located 10 miles NE of Langell Valley, which is 18 miles south of Bonanza and 3 miles north of Willow Valley Reservoir. The reservoir was drawn dry in 1992 and 1994. It will be restocked with crappie and largemouth bass when the water supply stabilizes and should offer good fishing within 2-3 years thereafter.

BURNT CREEK A short trout stream about 5 air miles, (but many more road miles) SE of Lakeview. From Lakeview drive north on Hwy. 395 about 5 miles to the intersection of Rt. 140. Take 140 east about 7 miles to Forest Rd. 391, which leads a bit over 3 miles to the creek then parallels it south. It can be fished for wild redband trout to 12 inches.

BURNT RIVER Outlet of Unity Reservoir, featuring large trout and smallmouth bass. The river flows east 77 miles, joining the Snake just east of Huntington on I-84. It is followed east by paved county roads from the reservoir downstream 30 miles to Bridgeport. This stretch is cross-ditched for irrigation purposes. From Bridgeport to Durkee on I-84, the river flows through the Burnt River Canyon and is followed by a gravel road. At Durkee the river turns south and is followed by I-84 to Huntington. There are lots of rough fish in this section. Much of the river flows across private lands, so get permission prior to crossing fences. From Huntington downstream the river is backed up by Brownlee Dam (the Burnt River Arm of Brownlee Reservoir). It is closely followed by the Snake River Road. Anglers park along the road and fish from the bank.

Trout angling just below Unity Reservoir Dam can be excellent at times. Some large trout are scattered through the lower river. Smallmouth bass and crappie are available near the mouth in the Huntington area.

Farewell Bend State Park on Brownlee south of Huntington, and Unity Lake State Park north of Unity, offer developed camping facilities. Other campgrounds are available in the national forest along the South Fork 8 miles south of Unity.

BURNT RIVER, SOUTH FORK One of the finest trout streams in the area, heading on the east slope of the Blue Mts. SW of Baker, a major tributary of Unity Reservoir. The South Fork is only about 12 miles long and is followed by gravel Forest Rd. 6005 to its headwaters. It's crossed by Hwy. 26 about 3 miles above the reservoir. Several roads lead from Unity to the upper South Fork, which flows within Wallowa-Whitman National Forest.

The spring-fed upper stream offers good trout fishing in spring and summer, as do several of its tributaries, including Elk and Last Chance creeks. It maintains a good flow within the forest throughout the season.

The South Fork has a good population of wild trout and is stocked with rainbow catchables. Bait-fishing is the most popular method. Four campgrounds are available on Forest Rd. 6005 within a 3-mile stretch, beginning about 8 miles SW of Unity.

BURNT RIVER, NORTH FORK A 25-mile long trout stream, major tributary of Unity Reservoir, located in the southern Wallowa-Whitman Forest. County Rd. 507 leads NW about 2 miles east of Unity Dam and picks up the North Fork about 2 miles above the reservoir. Dirt roads follow the creek downstream from this

A tour boat will deposit anglers on Crater Lake's Wizard Island for a day's fishing.

crossing to the reservoir. County Rd. 503 follows the river along its best reach, above Whitney.

The North Fork has a good supply of wild trout in spring. Above Whitney Valley, the river is of high quality and maintains a good flow throughout much of the summer. Below Whitney, water is withdrawn for irrigation, and the stream can get low and warm in summer. Rainbow are typically 6-10 inches.

The nearest campground is at Unity Reservoir State Park.

CACHED LAKE A tiny but productive trout lake off the trail to Eagle Lake, in the Eagle Cap Wilderness of Wallowa-Whitman National Forest. Only 2 acres, it supports a lot of small brook trout. From the end of Forest Rd. 7755, follow the Eagle Creek Trail 1922 north 5.7 miles towards Eagle Lake, gaining 1,649 ft. elevation. One mile south of Eagle Lake, turn east on Trail 1931 for a fairly easy (600 ft. elevation gain) mile to Cached Lake. Snow may block access until July.

To reach this area from Baker or LaGrande, follow Hwy. 203 east. From Baker, follow Forest Rd. 67 NE to the trailhead. From LaGrande, follow Forest Rd. 77. Both are all-weather roads. Trout season is determined by trail conditions, with best fishing in August and September. Camp well back from fragile lakeside vegetation when in the wilderness, using no-trace camping methods. There are campgrounds on Forest Rd. 77.

CALAMITY CREEK A small trout stream in the upper Malheur system. It enters the Malheur south of Van, which is on County Rd. 306 east of Silvies. To reach the upper waters, follow County Rd. 309, a primitive track, west from Van. The creek heads in the Malheur National Forest near Calamity Butte. It has a population of wild trout (up to 10 inches) that don't get to see a lot of anglers. Rock Springs Campground is off Forest Rd. 17 about 10 miles west of Van.

CAMAS CREEK A fair trout stream in the Lakeview area. It heads in the Fremont National Forest about 6 miles east of Lakeview and flows east about 15 miles into Deep Creek. From Lakeview head north 4 1/2 miles on Hwy. 395, turning east onto Warner Canyon Rd. 140. At the junction of Forest Rd. 391 about 7 miles east, the highway hits the creek near its head and follows it east. Several other roads cross it at points where it leaves the main road. It can be reached from Warner Valley by going west from Adel.

In wet years Camas Creek can be good after the spring run-off, and holds up through early summer. Fishing picks up again in fall. The creek is no longer stocked but supports good numbers of wild rainbow. Most fish caught will be around 12 inches, but a few go to 16 inches. Beaver ponds along the creek are worth exploring for larger wild rainbows. Bait angling is most popular, but flies take fish in late afternoon and evening. Spinners and small lures work well in the larger holes.

Camas has been low and warm in recent years, suffering from the drought and from heavily grazed riparian vegetation.

CAMP CREEK (Grant Co.) A fairly good trout stream, about 14 miles long, entering the Silvies River between Seneca and Silvies near Hwy. 395. Silvies is on Hwy. 395 about 32 miles north of Burns. The creek flows out of Malheur National Forest to the west and joins the Silvies River about 3 miles north of Silvies. Forest Rd. 37, which leaves the highway 4 miles north of Silvies, follows the creek about 6 miles, and Forest Rd. 370 continues to the headwaters.

Camp Creek has a fair number of native rainbow trout 9-12 inches. Most angling takes place in May and June on bait or flies.

CAMPBELL LAKE A fair high mountain rainbow lake in Fremont National Forest, 34 air miles NW of Lakeview, about halfway between hwys. 140 and 31. The lake, a little over 20 acres, is reached by fairly good graded roads. From Paisley on Hwy. 31 it's about 23 miles by forest roads, primarily Forest Rd. 331. From Bly on Rt. 140 it's about 35 miles by Forest Rd. 348 NE to 331. Other forest roads come in from Lakeview and the Sycan Marsh area to the NW. Campbell is one mile east of Dead Horse Lake. The time period in which the lake is accessible is fairly short, from July through October. The US Forest Service locks the road gate in spring and doesn't open it until the road is passable. Check with the ranger stations at Bly, Lakeview, or Paisley.

Campbell is tied with Dead Horse lake for best catch rate in the district for stocked brook trout, but there is little carry-over. This is a good fly-fishing lake, but lures or bait also work. Troll slowly with a lot of line. Small boats with trailers can be launched, but motors are prohibited. There is a good camp here. Dead Horse Lake is one mile west.

CAMPBELL LAKE, UPPER See Warner Valley Lakes.

CAMPBELL LAKE, LOWER See Warner Valley Lakes.

CAMPBELL RESERVOIR A 200-acre reservoir 8 miles NE of Bly which has contained largemouth bass. The reservoir is mostly on private land, though there is some public access across BLM property. It has gone dry a number of times in recent years, and the status of the fishery is unknown.

CHERRY CREEK A nice trout stream west of Upper Klamath Lake. When Rt. 140 turns west toward Lake of the Woods, continue north on Forest Rd. 3459 about 4 miles, then west on Forest Rd. 3450. Trail 3708 at road's end follows Cherry Creek for several miles toward its headwaters, then leads to Horseshoe Lake in the Sky Lakes Basin.

Cherry Creek offers very good angling for wild brook trout and doesn't get a lot of pressure. Though not a large stream, it's worth the effort. Sneak tactics may be necessary since these trout tend to be spookier than most.

CHEWAUCAN RIVER The largest and one of the best trout streams in Fremont National Forest. About 50 miles long, it flows NW from the mountains SW of Lakeview, past the town of Paisley, and into the Chewaucan Marsh. The lower end near Paisley is crossed by Hwy. 31. From Lakeview, drive north on Hwy. 395 then turn NW onto Hwy. 31 at Valley Falls. The stream is followed south from Paisley by Forest Rd. 330, a good graded road. The upper stream and tributaries are followed and crossed by forest roads branching from Forest Rd. 351, which is reached by 330. From Bly, on Rt. 140, follow Forest Rd. 348 to Paisley.

The river is well stocked with legal rainbow in all the upper areas, and they make up most of the catch. There has been some attempt to improve fish habitat here. Cut junipers were wired in along the banks in places to stop bank erosion, reduce siltation, and provide cover. Work around the clumps.

The stream is large enough for all types of fishing. Drifted worms are always a sure bet, but wet and dry fly anglers can do well. There are catfish in the extreme lower stream. Check locally for more information.

There is a good campground at Marster's Spring, about 8 miles south of Paisley. Other campgrounds are available in the headwater area.

CHICKAHOMINY RESERVOIR A desert reservoir near Burns, managed especially for anglers by the Oregon Department of Fish and Wildlife, known for growing big rainbow trout. It can usually be counted on for catches 16-20 inches (up to 5 pounds). ODF&W owns most, but not all, the water rights to Chickahominy. It went dry in three years in a row, completely dry in 1992, and was chemically treated to get rid of a bullhead infestation. It was re-stocked in 1993, and by spring of '94 they were catching 20-inch trout.

The 530-acre reservoir is just north of Hwy. 20 about 32 miles west of Burns, 100 miles from Bend.

Chickahominy is stocked with up to 80,000 rainbow fingerlings each spring. In good years, the fingerlings grow about 2 inches per month during the summer. Anglers use all methods to fish here. There's a boat ramp, and many anglers troll or cast bait. It's an excellent float-tube lake, and fly anglers take advantage of the mobility to fish for the big trout that cruise near the weed beds. The reservoir has good hatches of dragonflies and damselflies.

It should be noted that Chickahominy sits among the sagebrush, its banks and the landscape for miles around entirely devoid of trees. The wind can really pick up here in a hurry, and the summers are very hot. Fishing is best in spring.

BLM maintains a primitive campground at the reservoir, with pit toilets, drinking water, a fish cleaning station, and a few shaded picnic tables. Camp anywhere in the parking lot or sagebrush. A fee charged to camp is used to maintain and upgrade the campsite.

CLOVER LAKE A small, lightly fished brook trout lake in the southern Mountain Lakes Wilderness in Winema National Forest. It's a 2-mile hike by trail north from the end of the Buck Peak Lookout Rd. Buck Peak is about 12 miles SW of Lake of the Woods Resort.

The lake is in a basin of potholes at the head of Clover Creek. It's only a couple of acres, but offers good angling for brook trout to 12 inches. Clover is stocked with fingerlings by air. Fairly shallow, it's an easy lake to fly-fish. Some of the other small lakes in this area just might offer surprises.

COMO LAKE A very nice lake in the Mountain Lake Wilderness of the southern Winema National Forest. There are three main trails into the basin. From Rt. 140, about 7 miles east of Lake of the Woods, take the Varney Creek Rd. (Forest Rd. 3610) south about 1 1/2 miles, turning left onto Forest Rd. 3637 and right on Forest Rd. 3664. Varney Creek Trailhead 3718 is at the end of the road. It's about a 4 mile hike to Como Lake.

The lake is 7 acres and quite deep. It's stocked with brook and rainbow trout averaging 10-14 inches, with a few larger. Bait is best in spring, and all methods can be effective in fall. For other good lakes in the area see Harriette, Echo, South Pass.

COTTONWOOD CREEK (Lake Co.) A redband trout stream NW of Lakeview, tributary to Goose Lake. All Goose Lake tributaries are closed to fishing to allow natural regeneration of the system's redband trout population. Goose Lake redband suffered severe losses in fall of 1992 when the lake went dry.

COTTONWOOD CREEK (Malheur Co.) A fair, lightly fished trout stream near Westfall, about 56 miles west of Ontario. Follow Hwy. 20 to Harper Junction, then go north to Westfall and the confluence of Cottonwood and Bully -reeks. A graded gravel road heading SW from town follows a good portion of the stream. The creek is also accessible north of Drewsey (on Hwy. 20). A road follows the stream above and below Cottonwood Creek Reservoir.

Bully Creek does not offer any fishing, but Cottonwood has wild trout and a pretty good catch rate due to little angling pressure. Trout average 9-10 inches and run to 12 inches. Bait or flies are effective. There is no camping along the stream.

COTTONWOOD CREEK RESERVOIR (Harney Co.) An impoundment north of Drewsey in Harney County which offers only fair trout angling. Drewsey is reached by paved road north from Hwy. 20, about 47 miles east of Burns. A gravel road leads north from town to the reservoir. Watch for a sign. The reservoir covers about 120 acres.

Cottonwood is stocked with 5,000 rainbow fingerlings annually. They don't grow very large, and the reservoir may be re-directed to warmwater fisheries in the future.

COTTONWOOD MEADOWS LAKE (Lake Co.) In the Fremont National Forest, about 22 miles NW of Lakeview, created by the Forest Service and the Dept. of Fish and Wildlife. From Lakeview, take Rt. 140 about 20 miles west to Forest Rd. 3870. Follow 3870 about 6 miles NW to the lake. Do not confuse it with Cottonwood Reservoir, a much larger impoundment near Lakeview on lower Cottonwood Creek.

The Meadows Lake is a nice body of water that holds up well during dry years. It offers about 42 acres of good fishing. Rainbow fingerling are stocked each year, and the catch rate is high. The rainbow average 9-12 inches with a lot to 15 inches. Brook trout run larger, with most 14-16 inches. All methods work, but there's always a slack period in late summer because of algae. Late fall produces good fly fishing.

There are two campgrounds on the lake. Motor boats are prohibited. The road in is usually open by May.

COTTONWOOD RESERVOIR (Lake Co.) A 900-acre reservoir on lower Cottonwood Creek, 8 miles downstream from Cottonwood Meadows Lake. The reservoir is part of the Goose Lake system. All Goose Lake tributaries are closed to fishing to allow natural regeneration of the system's redband trout population. Goose Lake redband suffered severe losses in fall of 1992 when the lake went dry.

COW LAKES Two large panfish lakes near the Idaho border south of Ontario, only the upper of which provides angling. Roads approach the lakes from Hwy. 95, just south of Sheaville, or from Jordan Valley. The access road is gravel.

Covering almost 1,000 acres, the upper lake maintains a population of brown bullhead and white crappie. There is a

BLM campground and boat ramp, but no drinking water. Fishing's best at the west end near the lava bed.

CRACKER CREEK A short tributary of the Powder River, entering the mainstream at Sumpter about 30 miles west of Baker. It offers angling for stocked and wild rainbow and wild brook trout. Bull trout are also present and must be released unharmed. From Baker, take Hwy. 7 south and west along the Powder River, following the river to Sumpter. A gravel forest road follows Cracker Creek north about 4 miles, and dirt roads follow its forks.

Fishing in the main creek and its forks is quite good after the spring thaw and holds up well into summer. Stocked annually with rainbow trout, it also has lots of wild fish, though they seldom run over 10 inches. The nearest campground is at McCully Forks, west of Sumpter.

CRATER LAKE (Baker Co.) A good brook trout lake high in the SE corner of Eagle Cap Wilderness in the Wallowa Mountains. Crater Lake is at the head of Kettle Creek, a tributary of the upper East Fork of Eagle Creek, and you'll work hard to get to it. Best route to the lake is from the south from Baker or Halfway. Snow may block access until July. From Baker take Hwy. 203 north to Medical Springs and pick up Forest Rd. 67, which leads to Eagle Creek, meeting it at Tamarack Campground. From here, follow the creek downstream on Forest Rd. 77.

You have your choice of two trails, one a steep but somewhat shorter punishment, and the other a bit longer but not quite as steep. For the eager hiker, Trail 1945 will get you there quickest. Turn up the East Fork of Eagle Creek on Forest Rd. 7740, and follow it about 5 miles north to its end at Kettle Creek Campground. Trail 1945 grinds east following Little Kettle Creek for about 6.6 miles to the lake, switch-backing most of the way and gaining 3,000 ft. in elevation—a killer.

The better route in is by Trail 1946. About 6 miles beyond the East Fork junction on Forest Rd. 77, take Forest Rd. 7732 NW to its end. Trail 1946 leads NE towards Pine Lake and eventually Crater Lake. This hike is 7.7 miles long, but it's over an interesting ridge route. Total elevation gain is still at least 3,000 feet.

Crater Lake covers 12 acres and is only 10 feet at its deepest point. The lake is cupped on a high saddle between Red Mountain and Krag Peak at an elevation of 7,500 feet. It produces good catches of brook trout 8-13 inches. This is a good place to give your fly rod a workout. The scenery is grand and the fish are willing.

CRATER LAKE (Klamath Co.) This is a great scenic attraction, but it doesn't grow large fish and attracts few anglers. Filling a somnolent volcano, Crater Lake is the showpiece of Crater Lake National Park. The lake is reached by Hwy. 62 from Medford, and by Hwy. 97 from Klamath Falls or Bend. The park shows up on every map.

The lake is about 5 miles in diameter and 2,000 ft. deep. It is no longer stocked, though in the past it was stocked with rainbow trout and kokanee. Anglers are welcome to fish the lake from Cleetwood Cove (at the end of the single trail into the crater) or from Wizard Island. The tour boat that leaves from Cleetwood will drop anglers off at the island and pick them up later in the day. Camping is prohibited on the island. A state fishing license is not required, and there is no catch limit.

Cleetwood Cove is on the SW shore below park headquarters. You can check there for an update on regulations and fishing conditions. This is high country, and the snow lingers well into June.

There are two campgrounds in the park, as well as primitive sites in the back-country. The day lodge at the rim has a restaurant and some supplies. Accommodations include Mazama Village Cabins and the restored Crater Lodge, which is scheduled to open in spring, 1995.

CRATER LAKE (Harney Co.) A 2-acre lake in Malheur Wildlife Refuge that has contained largemouth bass and white crappie. The lake periodically winterkills and has not been restocked.

CROOKED CREEK (Klamath Co.) A short tributary of lower Wood River flowing south of Fort Klamath. Only about 5 miles long, it has some fair angling for rainbow, browns and brook trout. The creek is closely followed north by Hwy. 62 from the junction of the Chiloquin road and Hwy. 97.

A state hatchery is located on Crooked Creek about 2 miles north of Klamath Indian Agency. The creek is closed on the hatchery grounds. In good water years, fishing can be good in spring and early summer. Mosquitoes are a problem in spring. Much of this creek is on private land, so ask permission to fish.

CROOKED CREEK (Lake Co.) A fair trout stream, easily reached, located between Lakeview and Valley Falls. It flows into the lower Chewaucan River just north of Valley Falls. The creek is followed south by Hwy. 395 and is accessible from the west by Hwy. 31. The upper creek is only 10 miles north of Lakeview.

In good water years fishing is good for a short time in spring and early summer. The creek is quite small, and bait-fishing produces best. Chandler State Park is on the creek about 5 miles south of Valley Falls.

CRUMP LAKE A large shallow lake at the south end of Warner Valley, due south of Hart Mountain. To reach it, take the gravel road north from Adel to Plush. You'll hit the west shore of the lake in about 7 miles. When full, it has 3,200 surface acres.

In drought years, Crump is one of the last lakes in the valley to go dry. It did so in 1992. At this time, warmwater fish are present in low numbers. Within 2-3 years after it refills and stabilizes, Crump will again offer good fishing for bullhead catfish in spring, black and white crappie to 12 inches, and the occasional largemouth bass.

Supplies are available at Adel. This is remote country, so check your gas gauge.

CULVER LAKE An 8-acre brook trout lake in southern Eagle Cap Wilderness, about 6 trail miles from Boulder Park, elevation gain about 2,050 ft. From Baker, follow Hwy. 203 then Forest Rd. 67 to Boulder Park, about 45 miles. Take Eagle Creek Trail 1922 into the wilderness, then follow 1921 and 1921A to Culver. Other lakes in the basin include Bear and Lookingglass. Trails are generally accessible by July 4, and fishing is good through September.

DAIRY CREEK (Lake Co.) A nice creek in Fremont National Forest NW of Lakeview. It flows through a lodgepole pine forest and is a cool refuge from the valley heat. It heads on the east slope of Gearhart Mt. in the Gearhart Mt. Wilderness Area, and flows east into the upper Chewaucan River. It enters the river about 18 miles south of Paisley, forming a major western fork of the river. A network of forest roads follow and cross the creek. A Fremont Forest map will come in handy. One good route to the upper stream from Lakeview is to take Rt. 140 west 3 miles to a paved road leading north (County Rd. 2-16). About 8 miles north it becomes Forest Rd. 28, which follows Thomas Creek to its headwaters and eventually reaches Dairy Point Campground. Dairy Point is on the creek.

Dairy Creek is stocked each spring with rainbow trout. Wild rainbow and a few brook trout are also present. Average size is 9-10 inches, with some to 12 inches or better. Bait angling is the preferred method, but there's a lot of nice fly water. Happy Camp is about 2 miles further upstream on Forest Rd. 047.

DEAD HORSE LAKE A pretty good trout lake in Fremont National Forest just north of Dead Horse Rim. The lake is about 45 miles NW of Lakeview on a fairly good road. From Paisley on Hwy. 31, the lake is about 23 miles by forest roads, primarily Forest Rd. 331. From Bly, on Rt. 140, it's about 35 miles. Take Forest Rd. 348 NE from Bly to Forest Rd. 331. Other forest roads come in from the Sycan Marsh area to the NW. Follow the signs. Dead Horse Lake is accessible for only a short period, from July through October. The Forest Service locks the gate in spring and doesn't open it until the road is passable. Check with the Ranger Stations at Bly, Lakeview, or Paisley.

About 20 acres, Dead Horse is stocked with legal size rainbow trout and brook trout fingerlings. Trolling is popular as well as still-fishing with bait, but any method will produce fish. The success rate is pretty high, but few large fish are caught. Rainbow and brook trout average 10 inches.

Boats can be launched and effectively used, but motors are prohibited. There is a small campground at the lake, and hike-in or boat-in camping units are available along the shoreline for a more solitary experience.

DEE LAKE One of the hike-in lakes in the Island Lake area of Rogue River National Forest, about 10 miles north of Lake of the Woods. From Lake of the Woods on Rt. 140, drive about 5 miles east, then turn north on Forest Rd. 3561 to the Big Meadows spur road (Forest Rd. 3659). This leads west a bit over one mile to a hairpin turn north, on which you will find the Lost Creek Trailhead. Follow Trail 3712 west about 3 1/2 miles to Island Lake. Dee Lake is just west of Island Lake.

Dee is not heavily fished and has some nice brook trout. The average size is 10 inches, with some fish to 18 inches taken occasionally. The lake is 14 acres and fairly shallow, stocked by air. It's an excellent fly-fishing lake, with best results in August and September. It's usually accessible by late June. There are good campsites at Island Lake to the east. Others of the Island Lake group are also worth fishing. See Red, Pear, Camp.

DEEP CREEK (Lake Co.) A very good eastern Oregon trout stream SE of Lakeview, flowing into Warner Valley near Adel. The creek heads near the California state line SE of Lakeview in the Fremont National Forest. The upper water is reached by Forest Rd. 391, which runs south from Rt. 140 north of Lakeview. The creek flows out of the forest into Big Valley, and the Sage Hen Creek Rd. picks it up for about one mile as it leaves the valley. Deep Creek then plunges into a canyon and has no road access until it reaches Rt. 140 about 5 miles west of Adel. The highway follows it closely into Adel.

Deep Creek fishing is very good in late spring and summer. The creek is no longer stocked but has wild trout to 15 inches. There is excellent fly-fishing water in the stretch west of Adel along the highway after the water clears, usually around the beginning of July. Special regulations are in effect from the USGS Gauge upstream to the BLM boundary at Big Valley (the gauge is where Rt. 140 leaves the creek upstream from Adel). Only 2 trout per day may be kept in this stretch.

Willow Creek and Deep Creek Campgrounds are located on Forest Rd. 391 in the headwaters.

DEEP LAKE (Klamath Co.) A fairly good hike-in brook trout lake in the Sky Lakes Wilderness, Winema National Forest. A popular route into the area begins at Cold Springs Campground on Forest Rd. 3651. To reach the campground from Klamath Falls, follow Rt. 140 north along the lake. Rt. 140 makes a sharp turn west toward Lake of the Woods (just before Pelican Guard Station). About 3 1/2 miles further, turn right onto Forest Rd. 3651. Cold Springs is at the end of the road (about 9 miles from the highway).

From the campground, Trail 3709 leads north to Heavenly Twin Lake. At the junction with Trail 3762, take the right fork to Trapper Lake. From there Trail 3734 leads past Donna Lake to Deep Lake. The hike to Deep is about 6 miles. Other approaches are possible. Take along a USGS topographic quad map or the Sky Lakes Wilderness map.

Deep Lake is lightly fished and has large numbers of brook trout averaging 9 inches. The lake is 4 acres and is not too deep. It's an easy lake to fish, best in late summer and fall. All methods will take fish, with spinner-and-bait or wet flies very effective. Other lakes in the area include Trapper, Donna, Sonya, Marguerette. The Pacific Crest Trail passes about 1/2 mile to the west.

DEER LAKE (Klamath Co.) A small brook trout lake at the SW end of the Sky Lakes area of the Winema National Forest. A popular route into the basin begins at Cold Springs Campground on Forest Rd. 3651. See Deep Lake for directions to the campground. From Cold Springs, hike a little less than one mile on Trail 3710 to the junction with Trail 3762. The left fork leads to Deer Lake. It's about 6 miles to the lake. Continuing 1/2 mile on this trail brings you to the Pacific Crest Trail.

Deer Lake is a fairly shallow 5-acre lake that is stocked by air with brook trout fingerlings. The fish average about 11 inches with few big ones. Fly-fishing is usually good here in late summer and fall.

DELINTMENT LAKE A popular 50-acre trout lake in Ochoco National Forest NW of Burns, featuring large rainbow. The lake and its surrounding ponderosa pine forest are a welcome oasis in the eastern Oregon landscape. From Burns, travel south on Hwy. 20 to Hines, then NW on Forest Rd. 47 to its junction with Forest Rd. 41, about 15 miles from Burns. Forest Rd. 41 reaches the lake in about 35 miles. Additional roads access the lake. Refer to the forest map.

Delintment usually offers good angling for large rainbow. Fingerlings are added annually to replace those lost during the winter. The lake is deep and rich, and fish grow well. Efforts have been made to keep the water level high enough to allow more big fish to survive. Trout average 10-14 inches, with some 3-4 pounds. There's a good shoreline for bank casting.

The campground is large and attractive, with many flat grassy sites tucked discretely among the tall pines. There is a boat ramp and a 5-mph speed limit.

DENIO CREEK A remote Lahontan cutthroat stream. It is closed to all fishing to protect the Lahontan, which are listed as a threatened species. It's estimated that the Lahontan population throughout the basin dropped 90 percent during the 1987-92 drought.

DEVIL LAKE (Klamath Co.) An irrigation reservoir with bass and panfish 7 miles SE of Bly. From Bly, drive south on Rt. 140, then turn south on Fishhole Creek Rd. Devil is on the west side of the road.

The reservoir normally covers about 100 acres. It was once stocked with trout, but they've all but disappeared and there are no plans to re-stock. Fishing is for brown bullhead to 14 inches, yellow perch, and largemouth bass. Boats are allowed, but there is no ramp. Fishing is generally best in fall. There is no campground nearby.

DOG LAKE A large lake in Fremont National Forest about 25 miles SW of Lakeview. From Lakeview, head west on Rt. 140 about 9 miles. Turn right on County Rd. 1-13. At about 4 miles. turn right on County Rd. 1-11. At the forest boundary, the road becomes Forest Rd. 4017. It leads to the south end of Drews Reservoir and reaches Dog Lake in another 5 miles.

About 500 acres, Dog Lake provides fair fishing for perch, brown bullhead, black crappie, white crappie, blue gill, and largemouth bass. Experienced anglers can take trophy-size bass, but few small bass are present. There are 2 campgrounds, Cinder Hill and Dog Lake. Dog Lake Campground has a boat ramp.

DONNA LAKE A small brook trout lake in the northern end of the Sky Lakes Wilderness of the Winema National Forest. A popular route into the basin begins at Cold Springs Campground. See Deep Lake for road directions. From Cold Springs follow either Trail 3710 or 3709 north to Heavenly Twin Lake, then continue north on trail 3762 to Trapper Lake. From there Trail 3734 leads to Donna Lake. Donna is just east of the trail, slightly north of Trapper and Margurette Lakes. Other approaches are possible. Bring a topographic map (Sky Lakes Wilderness or USGS).

Only 2 acres and 9 ft. deep, Donna doesn't provide very large fish. Brook trout range 8-14 inches. The lake is stocked every other year. There are good natural campsites, and fishing at larger lakes to the south.

DONNER UND BLITZEN RIVER (a.k.a. Blitzen) A good trout stream in its upper waters, flowing 40 miles off Steens Mt., through Malheur Wildlife Refuge, and into Malheur Lake. Hwy. 205 (Burns to Frenchglen) follows a portion of the lower stream, as do secondary roads within the wildlife refuge. Within the refuge, however, from Bridge Creek downstream, the river is closed to angling. This is of little concern since there are almost no trout below Bridge Creek due to heavy irrigation ditching.

The river offers fairly good angling for native redband trout. It is approached by a maze of primitive mountain roads and by the Steens Mountain Loop Rd. The Loop Rd. heads east from Hwy. 205 about 4 miles north of Roaring Springs Ranch, crossing the river in about 13 miles at Blitzen Crossing just below the Indian Creek confluence. There is no longer a campground at the crossing. Poor dirt roads lead north between the crossing and Roaring Springs to access points at Tombstone and Burnt Car. The other end of the Loop Rd. is at Page Springs Campground just south of Frenchglen. The Loop Rd. is generally snowbound until mid-June.

Donner und Blitzen used to be stocked below the dam at Page Springs Campground east of Frenchglen. This dam isolated the fish population of the upper stream, which is 100 percent wild redband trout. The redband is a desert-adapted fish that can withstand water temperature extremes fatal to other trout, silted bedding gravel, and extremely alkaline waters.

During spring run-off the river becomes extremely turbid, and in heavy snowpack years it may not clear until mid-July or later. Spring angling requires bait, but wet and dry flies work well in summer and fall in the upper stretch. Trout average 10-12 inches, with fish 20 inches and larger sometimes taken.

Though remote for most anglers, the Blitzen can be fished in conjunction with other waters in the area. See Fish Lake and Krumbo Reservoir. Or it can be enjoyed as one activity in an exploration of this fascinating corner of the state. In addition to a lush assemblage of wildlife on the refuge, there is the historic Frenchglen Hotel, ghost towns, lava tube caves, hot springs, and other geologic phenomena (from the curious Diamond Craters to the majestic fault-block Steens Mountain itself). Mosquitoes, by the way, are a curse along the stream into July, particularly near the marshlands of the refuge. Donner und Blitzen is German for thunder and lightning. The river was named in 1864 by army troops who crossed it during a thunder storm. Storms in the high Steens (wind, rain, and snow), are legendary and often come up suddenly.

In addition to the campground at Page Springs, there are camps at Fish Lake and Jackman Park on the upper Steens slope. The Frenchglen Hotel (part of the National Park system) offers home-style food and lodging. Supplies and gasoline are also available in Frenchglen. Bunks and cooking facilities are available for a modest fee at Malheur Field Station, which is on the Refuge about 32 miles south of Burns, half-way to Frenchglen. Facilities include mobile homes, dorms with kitchens, and dorms without kitchens. Reservations must be made in advance. Dinners are also available at the Field Station by advance reservation. The station is open year-round, with limited lodging in winter.

DRAKE CREEK A good small creek east of Lakeview, tributary to Deep Creek, which flows into the Warner lakes near Adel. From Lakeview, follow Hwy. 395 north. Turn east (right) onto Rt. 140 and follow it to Adel. Drake flows into Deep Creek from the north about 6 miles west of Adel. The creek heads on the east slopes of Drake Peak to the NW, but flows through mostly private property, limiting fishing to the mouth.

Drake Creek is not stocked, and native trout aren't large, averaging about 10 inches with an occasional 14 incher.

DREWS CREEK A fair early season trout stream, crossed by Rt. 140 about 23 miles west of Lakeview. It is dammed to form Drews Reservoir then drains into Goose Lake. All Goose Lake tributaries are closed to fishing to allow natural regeneration of the system's redband trout population. Goose Lake redband suffered severe losses in fall of 1992 when the lake went dry.

DREWS RESERVOIR A large reservoir, lightly fished by local anglers, located about 18 miles west of Lakeview on Rt. 140. The reservoir is encircled by gravel and dirt roads.

When full, Drews covers about 4,500 acres, but it is used for irrigation and in some years gets very low. It contains a lot of rough fish, but there are fair numbers of white crappie 6-10 inches, brown bullhead to 12 inches, and some nice yellow perch to 13 inches. Though no longer stocked, channel catfish were introduced in 1978 and still make it into the catch. An occasional large rainbow is also taken. There is a boat ramp at the south end of the reservoir.

DUNAWAY POND A one-acre borrow pit on the east side of the highway south of Nyssa, containing bluegill, largemouth bass, and brown bullhead. From Nyssa (heading toward Owyhee Junction on Hwy. 201), when the road makes a sharp 90 degree turn, veer left onto a gravel road, passing under a viaduct. This road leads to the pond.

DUNCAN RESERVOIR A small impoundment about 2 miles SW of Silver Lake which has produced nice size trout. From the town of Silver Lake, 40 miles east of LaPine, it's about 6 miles by good gravel road SE to the reservoir.

Duncan covers about 33 acres. In the late 1970s it put out some fine large rainbows, but by the end of the decade a flourishing population of chubs was crowding them out. In 1980 ODF&W used Rotenone to get rid of the chubs and re-stocked with rainbow fingerlings. Currently the lake is still clear of rough fish and raising nice trout. Bait, lures, and flies all take fish here.

Duncan Creek is open year-round to give anglers the opportunity to take trout that leave the reservoir in the spring water release. The creek dries up completely in summer. There are some camping facilities at the reservoir.

DUTCH FLAT LAKE A small wild brook trout lake in the southern Wallowa-Whitman National Forest west of North Powder. The easiest approach is by way of Trail 1611 above Anthony Lake.

EAGLE CREEK (Baker Co.) A beautiful stream, once premier chinook water, a tributary of the lower Powder River. It drains a number of the southeastern lakes of Eagle Cap Wilderness and enters the Powder River Arm of the Snake River's Brownlee Reservoir near Richland. Wilderness trails follow its upper waters, and good roads access the lower stream. It supports a population of wild rainbow and is heavily stocked. Angling is good from June to September for trout to 12 inches.

Hwy. 86 crosses Eagle Creek at Richland, and the paved northbound road to Newbridge follows the creek into the Wallowa-Whitman National Forest, becoming Forest Rd. 7735. From Eagle Forks Campground (the confluence of Little Eagle Creek with the mainstem 7 miles north of Newbridge) Trail 1878 follows the mainstem upstream about 5 miles.

To reach the upper creek from Eagle Forks Campground, follow Forest Rd. 7735 up Little Eagle Creek. Pass up the first spur on the left (which reaches Eagle Creek but is rough). Continue to the next fork, and turn left onto Forest Rd. 77, Eagle Creek Rd. This road reaches Eagle Creek at the upper end of Trail 1878.

To reach the upper stream, from Hwy. 86 about 20 miles east of Baker, turn left (north) on County Rd. 852. After about 3.5 miles, turn left (north) onto County Rd. 891 (Collins Rd.), then right onto Forest Rd. 7015 (Empire Gulch Rd.), which crosses Eagle Creek shortly after a hairpin turn. Continue north along the creek to road's end. Trail 1922 heads up the creek to Eagle Lake.

One of the prettiest streams in the Wilderness, Eagle Creek has high quality water which flows through scenic canyon and meadow land.

In addition to Eagle Forks Campground on the lower stream, there are two campgrounds on Forest Rd. 77 beside the upper creek, Tamarack and Two Color.

ECHO LAKE (Eagle Creek Watershed) A brook trout lake at the head of Eagle Creek's West Fork, in the southern Eagle Cap Wilderness, Wallowa-Whitman National Forest. From Catherine Creek State Park on Hwy. 203 (between LaGrande and Baker) continue south on Hwy. 203, then turn left (east) on Forest Rd. 77 (the Eagle Creek Rd.). Trailhead 1934 is on the left about 13 miles from the turn-off. Keep a copy of the forest map open for reference as you negotiate the forest roads. There are many spurs that could mislead you.

Trail 1934 gains 1,500 feet elevation before reaching Echo in 5 miles. The trail continues north 1.6 miles to Traverse Lake and connects with other wilderness trails, including an arduous 12.7 mile connection to the lake group at the head of the main Eagle Creek Trail. Echo covers 28 acres and has a maximum depth of 19 feet. At 7,100 ft. it is one of the lower lakes in the wilderness. It has an abundant population of small eastern brook trout which take a fly enthusiastically in August and September.

Donner und Blitzen offers fairly good desert angling for redband trout.

ECHO LAKE (Mountain Lakes Wilderness) A small, fairly good hike-in brook trout lake in the Mountain Lakes Wilderness of Winema National Forest, east of Lake of the Woods.

From Rt. 140, about 7 miles east of Lake of the Woods, take the Varney Creek Rd. (Forest Rd. 3610) south about 1 1/2 miles. Turn left onto Forest Rd. 3637 and right on Forest Rd. 3664. Varney Creek Trailhead 3718 is at the end of the road. Follow Trail 3718 about 4 miles, then take the left fork, Trail 3127, which reaches Harriette Lake in about 1 1/2 miles. Follow the trail around to Harriette's north shore. Echo is left of the trail.

Echo is only about 5 acres and is lightly fished for brook trout 7-2 inches, and a few that run larger. Some good size lunkers are reported from time to time. Flies or spinner/bait combinations work well. There are fair campsites along the trail near Harriette Lake. Most of the other small lakes in this area are too shallow to support fish.

ELDER CREEK A small trout stream south of Paisley, flowing into the upper Chewaucan River. Paisley is about 130 miles SE of Bend by way of highways 97 and 31. The creek enters the river about 18 miles south of Paisley. It contains native redband and some brook trout, with few over 8 inches. Several campgrounds are located a few miles south of the creek, west of Dairy Creek Guard Station.

ELIZABETH LAKE A small brook trout lake in the southern Sky Lakes area of Sky Lakes Wilderness, Winema National Forest. A popular hike in begins at Cold Springs Campground. See Deep Lake for road directions. From Cold Springs, take Trail 3710 about 3 miles to Elizabeth Lake, which is 1/4 mile north of Natasha Lake.

Elizabeth is just 5 acres and lightly fished, but it's a steady producer of brook trout to 11 inches. Quite shallow, it is best suited to fly-angling. Fishing is best in early spring and in fall.

EMIGRANT CREEK A better than average trout stream flowing 30 miles in the southern portion of Ochoco National Forest near the Malheur Forest boundary. It enters the Silvies River 20 miles NW of Burns.

From Hines, head NW on County Rd. 127 (Hines Logging Rd.). This road crosses Emigrant Creek just before the road enters Malheur National Forest. Just before the crossing, turn left (west) on Forest Rd. 43, which follows Emigrant upstream past Falls and Emigrant campgrounds. At about 15 miles, Forest Rd. 4360 branches to the right (north) and follows the creek to its headwaters. Near its confluence with the Silvies, Emigrant flows through a patchwork of BLM and private ranchland. Primitive roads follow the lower stream, but be careful not to trespass.

Fishing is good in late spring and summer, with a catch rate considerably better than that of other streams in the area. Stocked annually with legal rainbow, there are also natives up to 15 inches. Average size is 10 inches. Bait is a sure bet, but fly-fishing is effective.

FISH LAKE (Harney Co.) A remote but popular lake high on the west slope of Steens Mt. Deer hunters like to camp here in fall. The lake is on the Steens Mt. Loop Rd., which is usually snowbound at its upper elevations until July. Take Hwy.

205 from Burns south through the Malheur Wildlife Refuge to the tiny community of Frenchglen, a 55-mile trip. To reach the Loop Rd., drive east from Frenchglen towards Page Springs Campground, turning north immediately after crossing Donner Und Blitzen River. Steens Loop Rd. is blocked by a gate until the snow has cleared. It climbs the mountain for 15 or so rough miles to Fish Lake.

The lake is tucked within a sparse aspen grove near the rim of Steens Mt, at 7,200 ft. Winter hangs on hard here, and there are snow banks and cold nights into early July. The lake is stocked annually with legal rainbow trout, and you might hook a brook trout from previous stockings. The lake is only about 20 acres, but lots of fish are caught. The rainbow are typically 8-10 inches, and brook trout reach 3 pounds. Fly-fishing can be excellent, especially in the fall.

Be sure to continue the extra 4-5 miles to the rim for a spectacular view of the Steens escarpment and the desert below. There are a number of nice BLM campsites around the lake. Occasionally a strong, steady wind comes up here, and there is little to break it. Storms in the high Steens (wind, rain, and snow), are legendary and often come up suddenly. A second campground, at Jackman Park (a natural meadow), is located a mile further east on the Loop Rd., and Page Springs Campground is at the base of the mountain near Frenchglen.

Fish Lake is ideal for a rubber raft , float tube, or canoe. Motors are prohibited on the lake. Supplies and limited accommodations are available in Frenchglen.

FLAGSTAFF LAKE See Warner Valley Lakes.

FORT CREEK A short tributary of Wood River, south of Fort Klamath, crossed by Hwy. 62 about 2 miles south of town near Fort Klamath Park and Museum. It's a very clear, spring-fed creek, accessible by road for most of its 3 mile length. A dirt road takes off just north of Klamath Junction and follows the headwaters of the creek to the east.

Fort Creek has some good size brook and rainbow trout in its upper waters. The lower stream has good-size brown trout, but flows through land owned by Fort Creek Resort (for use by guests only).

FOURMILE LAKE A large lake on the east edge of Winema National Forest, 9 miles west of Klamath Lake. It supports brook trout, rainbow, and kokanee. The lake is on the divide between the Rogue and Klamath basins, high in the Cascade range. To reach it, take Forest Rd. 3661 north from Rt. 140 at Lake of the Woods Visitor Center. See Lake Of The Woods for complete directions.

Fourmile has 740 surface acres and a maximum depth of 170 ft. At 5,744 ft. elevation the winters are long and the growing season short. Nevertheless, kokanee are doing almost too well here, with a large self-sustaining population holding the size range to 6-10 inches. Kokanee are taken by trolling with large spinners trailing a small baited hook, and by still fishing with eggs on the bottom. They can also be taken on small wet flies and nymphs on sinking lines.

Naturally reproducing brook trout reach 15 inches here and are present in good numbers. Trolling and flies take these speckled trout. Best time to go for the larger ones is in September and October. Stocked rainbow trout reach 18 inches. Best rainbow fishing is in spring and fall.

The lake is open all year but doesn't get much play in winter. There is no boat ramp, but you can launch from the beach at the campground. Fourmile gets awfully rough at mid-day, so be careful when boating. A Forest Service campground, recently enlarged, is located at the southern tip of the lake. Trails leading to nearby small lakes begin near the campground. See Badger, Long, Squaw.

FRANCIS LAKE (Klamath Co.) A small brook trout lake north of the Pelican Butte Lookout about 4 miles NW of Point Comfort on the west shore of upper Klamath Lake. You'll have to bushwhack in to this lake, which is one mile north and 1,500 ft. below the lookout. You won't have a lot of company. From Hwy. 140 (Lake of the Woods Rd.), follow Forest Rd. 33651 toward Cold Springs Campground. Just before the campground, cut west on the Lookout Rd. The lookout is at 8,000 ft. and provides a great view of the country. From the lookout, backtrack about 1 1/2 miles by road, and trek north around the butte at constant elevation. You'll reach the lake in 1 1/2 miles. Francis is within a draw that runs NE from the butte. Don't confuse it with Gladys Lake 1/4 mile NW.

Francis is 3.5 acres and is stocked periodically with brook trout. The typical fish here runs 8-10 inches. Gladys and the other small lakes nearby have no fish.

GERBER RESERVOIR A large reservoir in south central Oregon between Lakeview and Klamath Falls, fished for bass, panfish, and trout. A state record white crappie came out of Gerber Reservoir at 4-pounds 12-ounces (now topped by a 5-pounder from the Tualatin).

To get there from Klamath Falls, take Rt. 140 east 19 miles to Dairy, then County Rd. 70 SE about 17 miles to Bonanza and Lorella. Head NE about 8 miles to the reservoir. From Lakeview, take Rt. 140 west to Bly, and follow forest rds. 375 and 381 south 10 miles to the lake.

Gerber covers over 3,800 acres when full, but the water level fluctuates even in normal years. In 1991 and 1992 it nearly went dry. In 1993 and 1994 it was only half full. All fish populations are currently depressed, but there is still a good nucleus population which will replenish the reservoir once it fills. Trout will not be stocked until that time, but some holdover trout are present. Gerber's rainbow grow to 18-20 inches.

The reservoir produces fair size bass, but most anglers are after crappie and perch. The crappie run 7-14 inches, and perch about the same, though the average perch will be smaller. A lot of nice brown bullhead are also available. Gerber has been popular for ice fishing.

The BLM provides 2 campgrounds with boat ramps, one at the dam and another about 2 miles north.

GOOSE LAKE A very large lake on the Oregon-California border about 8 miles south of Lakeview. Prior to the drought it covered about 46 square miles. Over the years it has gradually been lowered by water withdrawals. In 1992 it went completely dry. All its trout (native redbands) were lost. Oregon and California have jointly agreed not to re-stock the lake, but rather to let redbands from Goose Lake tributaries re-populate the lake naturally as the water level allows.

HAINES POND A one-acre pond 1/4 mile north of Haines. It contains largemouth bass.

HARRIETTE LAKE The largest lake in the Mountain Lakes Wilderness of SE Winema National Forest. It's in a very scenic area, surrounded by tall peaks, with small lakes and potholes close by. From Rt. 140, about 7 miles east of Lake of the Woods, take the Varney Creek Rd. (Forest Rd. 3610) south about 1 1/2 miles. Turn left onto Forest Rd. 3637 and right on Forest Rd. 3664. Varney Creek Trailhead 3718 is at the end of the road. Follow Trail 3718 about 4 miles, then take the left fork, Trail 3127, which reaches Harriette Lake in about 1 1/2 miles.

The lake is at 6,750 ft., covers 70 acres, and is 63 ft. deep. It is heavily visited and heavily fished. Good catches of brook trout and rainbow are made, with the average about 10 inches. A few larger fish to 15 inches show up from time to time. Any method can be effective, with bait-angling from the west shore most popular. Best angling occurs in spring and fall.

Other fishable lakes in the area include Echo, Como, South Pass.

HART LAKE (Lake Co.) A large lake in Warner Valley north and downstream from Crump Lake. The rugged face of Hart Mt. rises 3,000 feet above the lake to the east. Hart Lake is due east of the tiny town of Plush on Rt. 140, 18 miles north of Adel. Adel is 31 miles east of Lakeview. Dirt roads lead north and east from Plush over a dike along the north edge of the lake. A jeep road runs along the east shore and eventually leads back to Rt. 140. The SW shore is reached by a jeep road that first follows the north shore of Crump Lake. This road leaves the Plush Rd. about 9 miles north of Adel.

Hart Lake covers 10,000 acres in wet years, but can go dry. See Warner Valley Lakes for additional information.

Hart is primarily fished for catfish and crappie. The cats are numerous and of good size. Average weight is one pound, but some tip the scale at 2-3 pounds. A favorite area in the spring is the narrows near the inlet from Crump Lake.

Fishing for white crappie is popular off the SE shore, with peak activity in July. Sometimes this lake really turns on for crappie, with thousands taken on jigs in a few days. The crappie run to 14 inches, averaging 8-10 inches. There's not much in the way of trout fishing, although a few large rainbow are caught. Largemouth bass have been stocked but aren't thriving. The Warner Sucker, a fish unique to the Warner Valley, is protected.

This is remote country, so check your rig, gas and supplies before you head out.

HEART LAKE (Eagle Cap Wilderness) A small lake in the southern Eagle Cap Wilderness, part of the upper Eagle Creek drainage. From Catherine Creek State Park on Hwy. 203 (between LaGrande and Baker) continue south on Hwy. 203, then turn left (east) on Forest Rd. 77 (Eagle Creek Rd.). Keep a copy of the forest map open for reference as you negotiate this road. There are many spurs that could mislead you. Follow signs toward Tamarack Campground, which is on Forest Rd. 7755. Eagle Creek Trail 1922 is at the end of Forest Rd. 7755.

Follow the Eagle Creek Trail about 2 1/2 miles. Trail 1937 to Heart Lake is on the left. This trail is steep, climbing over 1,500 feet in just 1 1/2 miles.

Heart Lake is at the head of Bench Canyon south of the main trail at 7,300 ft. It is 3 acres and supports rainbow trout to 15 inches, although the average size is about 9 inches. It provides good bait and fly-fishing in August and September.

HEART LAKE (Lake Co.) A 25-acre rainbow lake in Fremont National Forest about 28 miles west of Lakeview. Follow Rt. 140 to Quartz Mt. Pass. Turn south on Forest Rd. 3715. Heart Lake is about 9 miles from the junction. A primitive road on the right circles through a small lake basin that includes Spatterdock Lake, Tule Pond, and Heart Lake, the southernmost lake on the circle.

Rainbow to 10 inches are available. Bait is best in early season, with flies effective in summer and fall. The nearest campground is at Lofton Reservoir across the road from the Heart Springs turn-off.

HEAVENLY TWIN LAKES Two nice lakes in the Sky Lakes Area near the border between Rogue and Winema national forests. A popular route into the area begins at Cold Springs Campground on Forest Rd. 3651. To reach the campground from Klamath Falls, follow Rt. 140 north along the lake. Rt. 140 makes a sharp turn west toward Lake of the Woods (just before Pelican Guard Station). About 3 1/2 miles further, turn right onto Forest Rd. 3651. Cold Springs is at the end of the road (about 9 miles from the highway).

Follow Trail 3709 into the lake basin. The trail crosses a small ridge between the two lakes. Trails are usually accessible in late June, with good fishing then and in late summer and fall.

The larger of the two lakes covers about 25 acres and is fairly shallow, a good fly-fishing lake. Heavily fished, it is an excellent producer of rainbow and brook trout averaging 10 inches, but fish over 5 pounds have been taken. A rubber boat or float tube would allow you to troll lures for the big ones. The smaller lake covers about 7 acres and is deeper, providing mostly brook trout to 12 inches with occasional larger fish. There are good campsites around the lakes near the trail and at Isherwood Lake just east of Big Twin. Camp well back from fragile lakeside vegetation, and use no-trace camping methods. The season here is limited only by the weather.

HELLS CANYON RESERVOIR The lowest reservoir on the Snake River, 21 miles of harnessed flow between Oxbow

Hart Lake is one of a string of lakes in Warner Valley which offer fishing for catfish and crappie.

Dam at Copperfield, Oregon, and Hells Canyon Dam at the southern boundary of Hells Canyon Wilderness. Below Hells Canyon Dam, the river runs free through its magnificent gorge, accessed only by trails and intrepid river runners.

To reach the reservoir from Baker, follow Hwy. 86 to Copperfield. From Weiser, Idaho, take I-95 north to Hwy. 71. The highway crosses the reservoir at Brownlee Dam and follows the west shore of Oxbow to Copperfield. There is a boat ramp about one mile downstream from Copperfield Park. A gravel road then a dirt track follow the Oregon shore for about 8 miles. Trail 1890 continues downstream another 7 miles.

At Copperfield, a paved road crosses the reservoir and follows the Idaho shore down to Hells Canyon Dam. There is a boat launch on the Idaho shore at Hells Canyon Park, about 5 miles downstream from Oxbow Dam. At Hells Canyon Dam, the east side road crosses the reservoir to the Oregon shore, leading to Hells Canyon Creek Campground and Boat Ramp. This ramp is used to float Hells Canyon.

Hells Canyon Reservoir supports catfish, smallmouth bass, bluegill, and crappie. Channel cats average 10-14 inches and run to 20 inches. Anglers use bait, fishing from both bank and boats. Smallmouth bass are taken on lures and spinners. Bluegill and crappie are caught on jigs or cut bait. There are a small number of large old sturgeon present (stranded survivors of the dams). Hooked sturgeon must be released without removing them from the water.

There are campgrounds on the reservoir at Copperfield Park on the Oregon shore, and at Hells Canyon Park in Idaho. There are also several hike-in or boat-in camps on the Oregon shore between road's end and Hells Canyon Dam.

HIDDEN LAKE (Union Co.) A brook trout lake high in the Eagle Cap Wilderness. The outlet from the lake flows into the East Fork of Eagle Creek. The lake is about 1 1/2 miles NE of Eagle Lake on the opposite side of a ridge. Best approach is from the south by East Fork Trail 1910.

From Catherine Creek State Park on Hwy. 203 (between LaGrande and Baker) continue south on Hwy. 203, then turn left (east) on Forest Rd. 77 (Eagle Creek Rd.). Keep a copy of the forest map open for reference as you negotiate this road. There are many spurs that could mislead you. About 6 miles beyond Tamarack Campground, turn left (north) onto Forest Rd. 7745 (East Eagle Rd.). Trailhead 1910 is at road's end. About 5 1/2 miles in, follow Trail 1915 to the left. It reaches Moon Lake then Hidden Lake in about a mile.

Hidden Lake has lots of brook trout and produces well. Best fishing is August through September.

HIGGINS RESERVOIR A 100-acre impoundment on Camp Creek NE of Unity. An unimproved road less than one mile east of town heads north off Hwy. 26 toward the reservoir, a 5-mile drive.

Higgins has been stocked with rainbow trout, and there are frequent catches 14-15 inches, with 20 inch fish available. Trolling and bait fishing with eggs or worms are most productive. The reservoir is no longer open year-round. There's a state park with picnic facilities and campground at Unity Reservoir on Hwy. 7.

HIGH LAKE (Grant Co.) A 10-acre brook trout lake, highest in the Strawberry Mt. Wilderness of Malheur National Forest. It's nestled in a pretty alpine cirque just above timberline. Spring fed and not too deep, it provides a good fly-fishing lake, especially in fall.

The shortest route to the lake is from the south. At Seneca (on Hwy. 395 north of Burns) turn east onto Forest Rd. 16, and drive east about 13 miles to the intersection of Forest Rd. 1640. Drive north on 1640 to the end of the road. Trail 385 leads to the lake in about 1 1/2 miles, losing about 600 ft. of elevation in the process. If you are coming on Hwy. 395 from John Day, take County Rd. 65 (Forest Rd. 15) east about 9 miles. Turn left onto Forest Rd. 16 just beyond Parish Cabin Campground, and left again onto Forest Rd. 1640 in about 2 miles.

Alternately, you may hike in from the north by way of Strawberry and Slide Lake. Trail 385 leads from Slide Lake to High Lake, following a scenic route near timberline. Access in early spring may be impossible due to snowbound roads. This is a wilderness area. Leave all vehicles at the trailhead.

HIGHWAY 203 POND A 10-acre pond north of Baker at the junction of Hwy. 203 and I-84. It contains largemouth bass.

HOLBROOK RESERVOIR A very productive 40-acre reservoir on Fishhole Creek 2 miles downstream from Lofton Reservoir. Holbrook is south of Rt. 140 at Quartz Mt. Pass, about 28 miles west of Lakeview. The reservoir is managed for public fishing through a cooperative agreement between a private landowner, ODF&W, and the US Forest Service.

Holbrook was treated for its rough fish scourge in 1991, went dry in 1992, and was re-stocked in 1993. By fall of 1994 it was expected to be yielding trout to 18 inches. There is a boat ramp, and good catches are made from boat and bank. Most of the land surrounding the reservoir is privately owned. Camping on the private property is prohibited.

HOME CREEK A short wild redband trout stream, originating on Steens Mt. and flowing 9 miles east into the Catlow Valley. The creek crosses Hwy. 205 about 21 mile south of French Glen near Home Creek Ranch (about 7 miles south of the change from pavement to gravel). It flows mostly through BLM land, but the stretch near the highway flows through private property. BLM land touches the highway about 1/10 mile north of the crossing (mid-way through the kinked section). Dirt roads cross the upper creek in at least two places. You'd better have a BLM map in hand to find your way in the headwaters.

Home Creek is best fished in spring and early summer. Rainbow to 14 inches are available, though the population has been somewhat depressed by the drought.

HONEY CREEK A good trout stream which heads on Abert Rim in Fremont National Forest. Its headwaters can be reached from Forest Rd. 3615 or Forest Rd. 3720 before the creek flows into a canyon then down through private ranchland (which is closed to public access due to past vandalism). The lowest waters enter a small canyon that begins on the ranch, and through which the creek flows toward Plush. Plush is in Warner Valley on Rt. 140 east of Lakeview.

Best fishing on Honey is in the lower stretch, for wild redband and brook trout. However, we have been advised that lower Honey Creek Canyon is particularly rattlesnake infested. (It's so bad that most people never go back twice, even though the fishing is tremendous!) Our source assures us that this isn't a rumor propagated by the local folks to keep outsiders away from a good thing.

INDIAN CREEK A remote Lahontan cutthroat stream. It is closed to all fishing to protect the Lahontan, which are listed as a threatened species. It's estimated that the Lahontan population throughout the basin dropped 90 percent during the 1987-92 drought.

ISHERWOOD LAKE A very good 18-acre hike-in lake in the Sky Lakes group of Sky Lakes Wilderness, Winema National Forest. It's a 3 1/2 mile hike north by trail 3710 from Cold Springs Campground. See Heavenly Twin for directions. Near the north end of the largest Heavenly Twin, the Isherwood Trail branches west. Isherwood is on the west side of the trail.

The lake supports brook trout and rainbow 12-14 inches. All methods may be used successfully, but fly-fishing early and late in the day is especially productive. Mosquitoes, March Brown, Caddis or almost any standard pattern will do. Campsites are currently limited due to efforts to rehabilitate the lakeshore following years of heavy use. Camp well back from fragile lakeside vegetation, and use no-trace camping methods.

ISLAND LAKE (Klamath Co.) The largest lake in the Island Lake group of Sky Lakes Wilderness, Winema National Forest. From Lake of the Woods on Rt. 140, drive about 5 miles east, then turn north on Forest Rd. 3561 to the Big Meadows spur road (Forest Rd. 3659). This leads west a bit over one mile to a hairpin turn. Trailhead 3712 is at the apex or the turn. Follow Trail 3712 west about 3 1/2 miles to Island Lake. The lake can also be reached by longer trails from Fourmile Lake and the Blue Lake area on the Rogue side.

At elevation 5,906 ft., Island covers 40 acres but is only 17 feet deep at its deepest point near the northern end. Fishing from shore is easy and, more often than not, excellent.

The lake is stocked with brook trout and has natural reproduction. The average fish is 11 inches, with some to 18 inches. Fly-fishing is the preferred method here, but bait and trolling will also produce. Try tossing a fly into the shoal areas of the island around evening. Campsites are limited due to lakeshore rehabilitation efforts. Camp well back from fragile lakeside vegetation, and use no-trace camping methods.

JENNY CREEK A good trout stream heading south of Howard Prairie between the Rogue and Klamath drainages, 16 miles east of Ashland. Rainbow 8-10 inches make themselves at home throughout the creek, and brook trout are present in the lower stream.

The creek flows south, crossing Hwy. 66 at Pinehurst, and skirts the eastern border of the Siskiyou Mountains, finally reaching Iron Gate Reservoir on the Klamath River about 3 miles south of the California line. A fair stretch of the upper river is followed by the Jenny Creek Rd. south from the southern tip of Howard Prairie. Moon Prairie Rd. follows the creek from about one mile to the east from the end of Jenny Creek Rd. to Hwy. 66.

Jenny Creek has been the subject of large scale habitat enhancement programs. It provides good angling in early spring and again in the fall. Bait-fishing is most popular, but lures and flies work well. There are no improved campgrounds along the creek, but Tub Springs Wayside, about 4 miles west of the crossing on Hwy. 66, has a nice picnic area.

JONES LAKE See Warner Valley Lakes.

KILLAMACUE LAKE A small high lake in the Elkhorn Range of southern Wallowa-Whitman National Forest west of Haines. The lake contains small Mackinaw and brook trout and is not very productive. To reach it from Haines, take Hwy. 411 west to Rock Creek, continuing west past Rock Creek Power Station into the forest. The road becomes an unimproved track (Forest Rd. 5520) and follows the North Fork Rock Creek. About 2 miles from the paved road, Trail 1617 leads NW to Killamacue, following Killamacue Creek to the lake.

KLAMATH LAKE See Upper Klamath Lake.

KLAMATH RIVER In Oregon, a very productive trout stream, flowing only 38 miles within the state before crossing the border into California. Steelhead and salmon runs into Oregon were eliminated by California's Copco Dam in 1917. Within California the Klamath flows an additional 200 miles, entering the Pacific Ocean at the community of Klamath.

The Klamath River is the outlet of enormous Upper Klamath Lake, but flows freely only 18 miles within Oregon borders. The other 22 miles are captured by dams. That the river continues to produce good numbers of large, powerful rainbow, is a testament to the vitality of the Klamath—and to its lost potential.

The Klamath River once began at Upper Klamath Lake. A dam at Keno, 17 miles downstream, created Lake Ewauna, a pool that backs up to within a mile of Klamath Lake. The most productive stretch of Oregon's Klamath today is the flow between Keno Dam and J.C. Boyle Reservoir, only 6 miles. Highway 66 parallels this stretch on the south. Park on the highway shoulder and hike down at any point that looks accessible. A number of trails drop into the canyon. This is Weyerhauser land, but the public has unrestricted access to the river. The river pours through a relatively steep canyon and features a series of runs and deep holes with intermittant shallow riffles over a bedrock base. You can also enter the canyon at Keno Dam. This stretch is not boatable.

The average fish here is 14 inches, with many to 20 inches, weighing 2-4 pounds. This is heavy water. Fly anglers use big weighted nymphs on sinking or sink tip lines. Spin casters favor Rooster Tails, and bait casters use a heavily weighted worm rig. Check in at the Keno store for additional information and directions.

There is a special closure on this reach from mid-June until the beginning of October, related to the effects of rising water temperature on the trout. As the water climbs toward 70 degrees and the river fills with algae, the fish acquire an unpalatable taste. Trout also lose much of their strength when the water warms, and would suffer high mortality if catch and release were practiced.

At J.C. Boyle, Hwy. 66 crosses the reservoir and the river bends southward. The Klamath River Rd. closely follows its west bank to Boyle Powerhouse. In this 5-mile stretch, from J.C. Boyle to Boyle

Power House the river is cool and stable, though its flow is much reduced by diversion into a sluice that carries water to the generating station. The river runs its clearest here, and trout are abundant. Resident trout in this reach are only 8-12 inches, but larger fish move through. The flow is augmented by spring outflows from the reservoirs. The riverbed is much the same as in the Keno stretch. Best fishing is from the end of May until mid-June. From J.C. Boyle Reservoir to the Oregon border, angling is restricted to catch and release with barbless flies and lures throughout the year.

Below the powerhouse the river regains its size, and so do the fish, averaging 12-15 inches. In 1994, the 11-mile reach from J.C. Boyle Dam to the Oregon border won federal designation as a wild and scenic river. A portion of this reach is locally known as the Frain Ranch, named for Martin Frain who settled the valley in the late 1800's. The few remaining buildings and the original Frain orchard have been named an Oregon Historical landmark.

Fishing in this section is characterized by very unstable water conditions resulting from Boyle Power Plant. The water usually drops in late evening and rises at 7 or 8 a.m. Once the river rises and stabilizes, good fishing generally resumes. The fish here are larger than those in the Boyle section, but smaller than the Keno trout. Peak fishing in this stretch is from the end of May until mid-June. In early spring and summer stonefly nymphs are generally most effective. Try Polly Rosborough's Golden Stone and Dark Stone Bucktail, or the yellow Bucktail Caddis.

The east bank of the Frain reach is accessed by the Topsy road, which heads south from Hwy. 66 just east of Spencer Bridge. The road is passable only in dry weather. At other times of the year, the east bank can only be accessed by a road leading in from Copco Reservoir in California.

Public facilities on the Klamath in Oregon are very limited. Rafts can be launched below Boyle Power Plant. The only developed campground is Topsy, on J.C. Boyle Reservoir. There are two additional primitive BLM camps. One is midway through the Frain reach off Klamath River Rd. The other is at the end of the popular whitewater stretch on the east bank just over the California border.

KRUMBO RESERVOIR A reservoir on lower Krumbo Creek in the Malheur Wildlife Refuge with a good largemouth bass population and stocked rainbow trout. To reach it, drive south from Burns on Hwy. 205 toward Frenchglen. About 20 miles south of the Malheur Refuge Headquarters turn-off, a road leads east 4 miles to the reservoir.

Krumbo covers about 150 acres and is capable of growing fair fish. Best fishing is in spring. Over-population by roach has been a recurring problem. The reservoir was last treated in 1988 and was restocked. The creek above the reservoir has a fair population of wild trout. For other fisheries in the vicinity, see Donner Und Blitzen River, Fish Lake.

Camping is prohibited at the reservoir. The nearest campground is Page Springs, a pleasant BLM Campground on the Blitzen east of Frenchglen. Accommodations are available at the historic Frenchglen Hotel, which is included in the state park system. Good family style meals, and the most pleasant screened front porch for a hundred miles are available there. Don't neglect a visit to the handsome Refuge Headquarters.

LAKE CREEK (Grant Co.) A fair wild trout stream flowing south out of Strawberry Mt. Wilderness into the Malheur River. The creek begins as the outlet of High Lake, 7,400 ft. above sea level. It supports redband and brook trout to 11 inches, averaging 9-10 inches. Bull trout may also be present and must be released without removal from the water.

At Seneca (on Hwy. 395 north of Burns) turn east onto Forest Rd. 16, which crosses Lake Creek at the intersection of Forest Rd. 924. Watch for a sign to Lake Creek Organization Camp. At the end of Forest Rd. 924, Trail 378 follows Lake Creek to its source, about 4 miles. Lake Creek and Big Creek enter the Malheur River together about 2 miles downstream of the Forest Rd. 16 crossing.

LAKE OF THE WOODS (Klamath Co.) A large, popular lake on Rt. 140 near the summit of the Cascade range west of Klamath Lake. It offers good angling and varied recreational opportunities. The lake is a very popular spot with summer boaters and offers good fishing for kokanee, rainbow, brown trout, largemouth bass, and brown bullhead catfish.

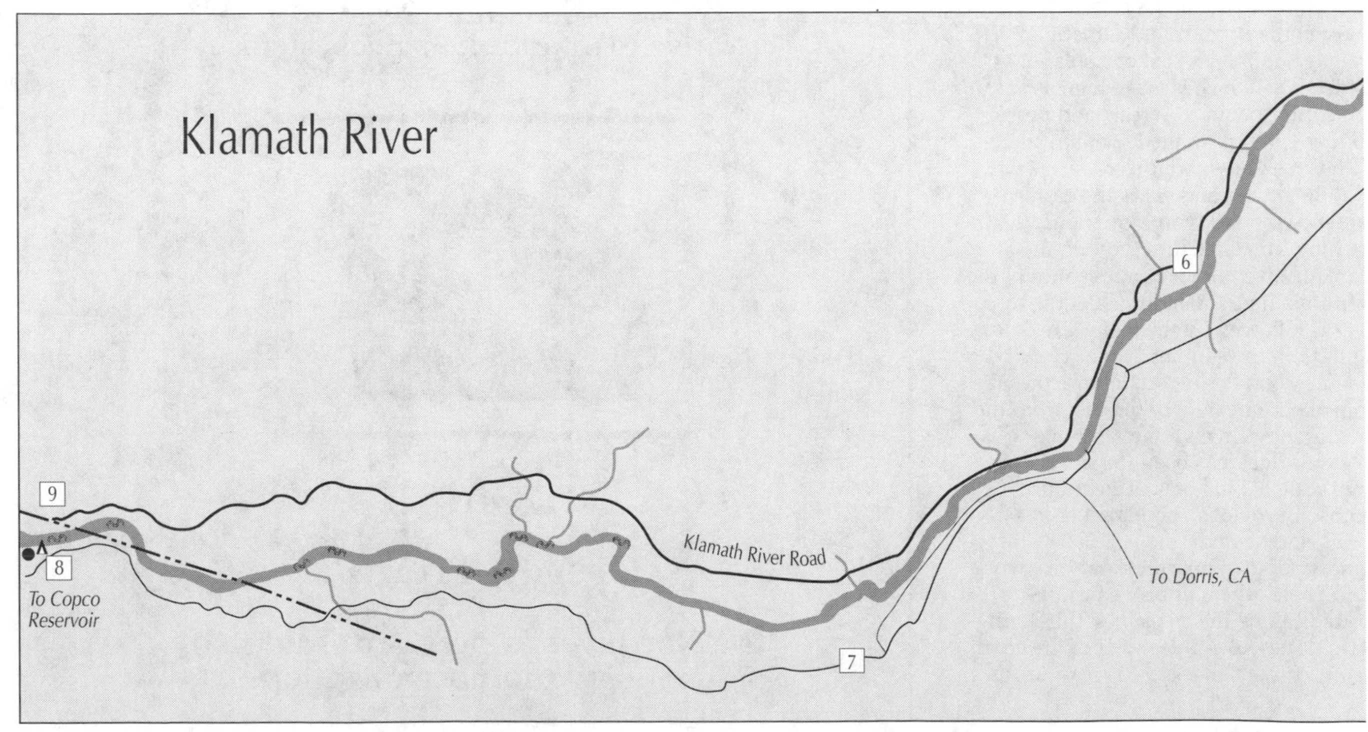

Direct routes access the lake from east, south, and west. From Medford, follow Rt. 140 east. From Klamath Falls, follow 140 west. From Ashland, follow signs to the airport then turn north just beyond the runway onto Dead Indian Memorial Rd., which becomes Forest Rd. 363 after entering the Rogue River National Forest. Lake of the Woods is about 35 miles from both Ashland and Klamath Falls, about 45 miles from Medford. It covers 1,113 acres and is circled by roads. There are a number of homes on its shore.

Lake of the Woods has never been very productive, though it has substantial shoal area, primarily at the north and south ends. The east shore has gravel beaches that are used by kokanee as spawning beds. The west shore is steep and rocky. Brown bullhead are abundant and average 8-13 inches. They make up over half the population in the lake, and anglers are urged to catch and keep as many as possible. There is no limit on bullhead.

Kokanee offer the best fishery in the lake. They are stocked at the rate of 25,000 annually and grow to 9-10 inches. The catch rate is low, though the fish are present in good numbers, and the lake isn't deep—only 50 ft. maximum.

Legal trout are stocked annually, and some holdovers grow to good size. An 11-pound rainbow was recently caught. Most are 9-14 inches. Hatchery brood fish are added to the lake as available. Brown trout are also present and grow to trophy size (up to 6 pounds).

Fishing is best early in the morning and late evening, when the water-skiers are otherwise occupied. There are campgrounds with boat ramps at the north end and near Rainbow Bay on the east. A large resort at the north end offers accommodations, supplies, food, and boat rentals.

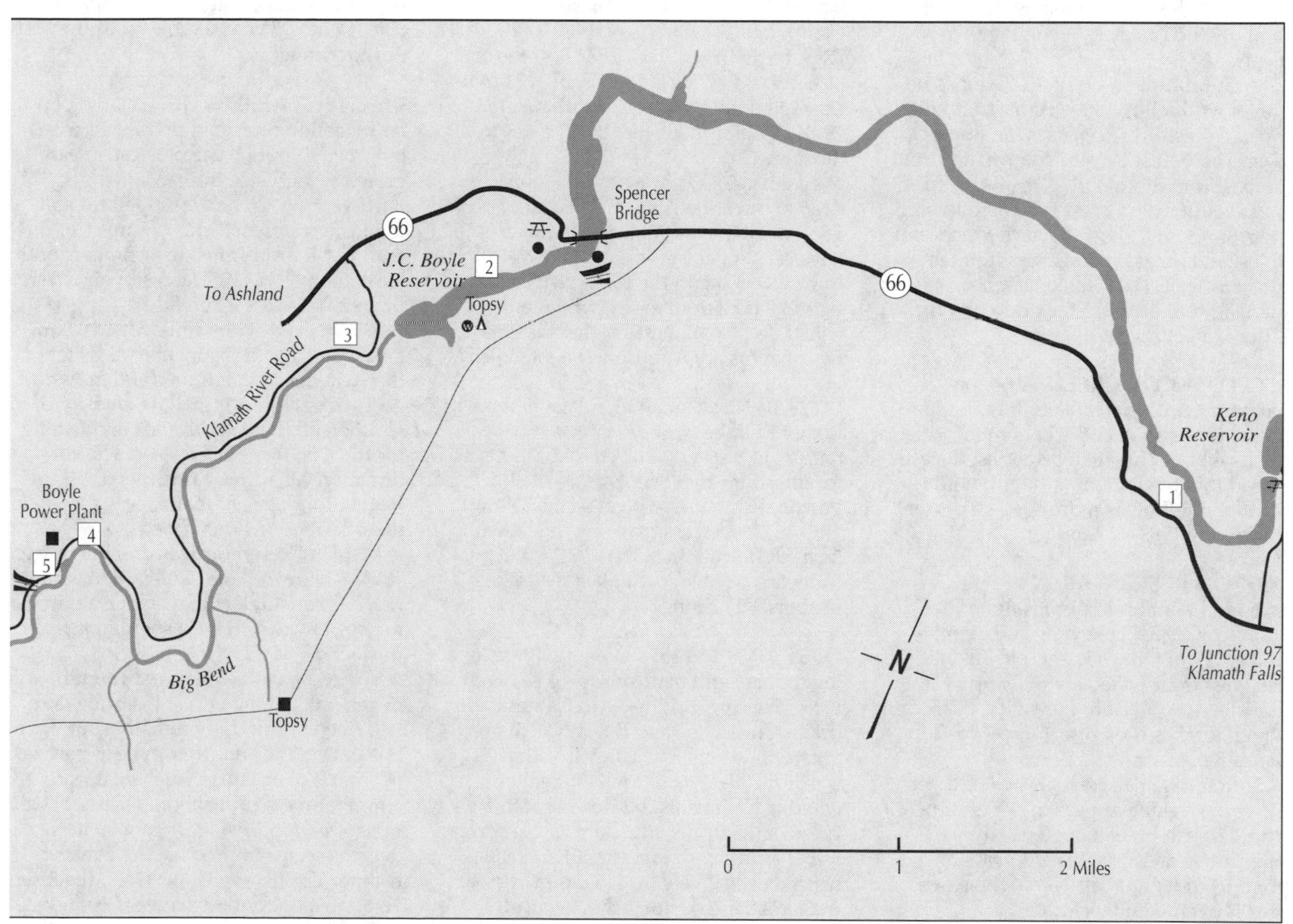

1 KENO REACH - Flows through private timber company land with unrestricted public access; park on Hwy. 66 shoulder & hike into (steep) canyon to fish very productive pocket water for rainbow to 6 lb; not boatable.

2 J.C. BOYLE RESERVOIR

3 J.C. BOYLE DAM TO POWERHOUSE - Park on shoulder and hike down (100-300 ft.) to river for smaller, but abundant, rainbows; artificial flies & barbless hooks; open year around, but catch & release June 15-Sept. 30.

4 BOYLE POWER PLANT - Heavily regulated flows, usually lower in afternoons. Call 1-800-547-1501 for c.f.s. schedule (best fishing during low flows); hike down to river for larger trout; public access throughout.

5 BLM ACCESS - Upper end of whitewater rafting section.

6 BLM CAMPGROUND - Primitive.

7 TOPSY ROAD - Hike & fish the south bank; Topsy Rd. is useable only in dry weather; otherwise, access from Doris, CA.

8 BLM CAMPGROUND - Primitive; rafters' take-out.

9 HOOVER RANCH - End of the road for north bank access in Oregon.

LITTLE ALVORD CREEK A remote Lahontan cutthroat stream. It is closed to all fishing to protect the Lahontan, which are listed as a threatened species. It's estimated that the Lahontan population throughout the basin dropped 90 percent during the 1987-92 drought.

LITTLE MALHEUR RIVER A good trout stream, tributary to the North Fork of the Malheur River. The Little Malheur joins the North Fork about 5 miles NW of Beulah Reservoir north of Juntura. It runs generally north-south, draining the south slope of the Blue Mts. Much of the creek is shown on the Malheur National Forest map, as it runs near or in the east edge of the forest. It offers fair fishing for wild rainbow to 11 inches, averaging 9-10 inches.

From Juntura on Hwy. 20, 23 miles of gravel road follow the river north to the forest. Forest Rd. 16 crosses the upper river, and Forest Rd. 457 follows it north 2 miles from that point. A primitive road leads south from Forest Rd. 16, following the river from a short distance for several miles, and other tracks access it in the forest as well. Trail 366, which heads at Elk Flat, follows Elk Creek down to the Little Malheur's headwaters.

LITTLE McCOY CREEK A remote Lahontan cutthroat stream. It is closed to all fishing to protect the Lahontan, which are listed as a threatened species. It's estimated that the Lahontan population throughout the basin dropped 90 percent during the 1987-92 drought.

LOFTON RESERVOIR A 40-acre impoundment on upper Fishhole Creek, 30 miles west of Lakeview and about 5 miles NW of Drews Reservoir. Take Rt. 140 west from Lakeview to Quartz Mt. Turn left (south) onto Forest Rd. 3715, which reaches the Lofton access road in about 5 miles.

Lofton has been treated several times for chubs, which appear to be re-introduced afresh by bait anglers. At this point there are probably 2-3 years of good trout fishing left before the reservoir is overtaken by chubs.

Lofton Dam maintains a reasonable water level throughout the year. Rainbow fingerlings are stocked, providing good angling for 8-12 inch fish, with some 16 inchers available. It's easy to fish from shore, but a rowboat, raft, or float tube could be useful. Most anglers use bait, but flies and lures can be equally productive. In late summer flies have the edge, as weed growth makes bait-angling difficult. There is a US Forest Service campground at the reservoir. Several other small lakes in this area that show up on the Freemont National Forest map might be worth investigating (Pete's Puddle, Spatterdock, Heart).

LOOKINGGLASS LAKE A nice glacial cirque lake just within the southern border of Eagle Cap Wilderness, Wallowa-Whitman National Forest. This is one of the easier lakes to hike to in this physically challenging wilderness. It is reached by a spur off the Eagle Lake Trail 1922.

From Catherine Creek State Park on Hwy. 203 (between LaGrande and Baker) continue south on Hwy. 203, then turn left (east) on Forest Rd. 77 (Eagle Creek Rd.). Keep a copy of the forest map open for reference as you negotiate this road. There are many spurs that could mislead you. Follow signs toward Two Color Campground, which is on Forest Rd. 7755. Eagle Creek Trail 1922 is at the end of Forest Rd. 7755. Follow Trail 1922 four easy miles, then cut back south on Trail 1921, climbing 1,300 feet in 2.2 miles to the lake.

Lookingglass is 31 acres and 45-ft. deep at elevation 7,500 ft. In addition to good numbers of brook trout, it may have carry-over Mackinaw (lake trout), from a stocking in the early 1970s. Bait or flies will take trout easily, while lures fished deep work best for the Mackinaw. Best months are August and September.

LOST LAKE A small high lake in the Elkhorn Range west of Haines. It contains wild brook trout. See Red Mt. Lake for directions to North Fork North Powder River Rd. At road's end, follow Trail 1632 west less than one mile, then turn left (north) onto Trail 1621, which leads first to Meadow Lake then to Lost in about 1 1/2 miles.

LOST RIVER A slow stream with fishing for bass and panfish east of Klamath Falls. The river originates in California. It drains Clear Lake and flows NW in a great arc through the Langell Valley, Bonanza, Olene, and Merrill, finally re-entering California and flowing into Tule Lake. In the upper stretch from California to Bonanza the stream is split and channelized extensively for irrigation. Rt. 140 parallels the river for a short way at Olene, and county roads follow it for most of the distance from Bonanza downstream. Klamath County has provided a public parking area and bank fishing access. There is public access for boat and bank anglers south of Olene on Crystal Springs Rd.

Lost River offers fishing for brown bullhead, crappie, perch, and bass. The bass range 2-7 pounds. Sacramento perch are common in addition to yellow perch, pumpkinseed sunfish, and crappie. The state record black crappie, at 4 pounds, was caught here in 1978. A few trout show in the catch but are not common.

Spring is probably the best time to fish, but good catches are made year-round. There are no campsites along the stream.

LUCKY RESERVOIR A 6-acre desert reservoir on BLM land SW of Adel. Take Rt. 140 west from Adel 3 miles then turn south, fording Deep Creek and following the powerline road 4 1/2 miles to the reservoir. You'll go through four gates. Please leave them as you find them. The creek isn't fordable until the spring runoff has dropped, usually in June.

The reservoir is stocked with rainbow, which grow to 18 inches, but the water is quite turbid throughout the summer and fishing is usually very slow. Bait is the normal method, although fly anglers take fish at times. The reservoir holds up well during droughts.

MALHEUR RESERVOIR A large popular irrigation reservoir, privately owned but open to public use. It is capable of growing good size trout. Malheur is north of Hwy. 26 between Ontario and John Day, approached by 15 miles of dirt road north from Ironside or Brogan, both located on Hwy. 26. The reservoir covers up to 2,000 acres when full.

It is stocked with rainbow and Mann Lake cutthroat, a distinct breed which thrive in desert conditions and grow to good size. The cutthroat are envisioned as a potential trophy fishery, and fishing for them is catch and release. The cutthroat are all adipose finclipped. Regulations specify that *fincipped* trout must be released unharmed.

Malheur Reservoir was drained in late 1994 to allow repairs. Given Malheur's rich habitat, anglers may anticipate finding cutthroat to 16 inches within a year of re-stocking.

The reservoir is open year-round, but in general, fishing is best in spring and fall. Keep in mind, though, that spring in this part of the country can be as early as February, or as late of July. Ideal water temperature is probably the better determinant of good fishing. From 50 to 60 degrees seems to produce the liveliest fishing. The fishery slows when the reservoir warms about 60 degrees (usually from late June through the end of August.

There are two boat ramps on the north shore. The improved ramp is in the NW corner, with bank fishing possible nearby. A more primitive launch is mid-way down the reservoir.

Camping is limited to a few spots near the improved ramp. Don't expect amenities like trees. This here is sagebrush country. Respect "No Trespassing" signs, clean up after yourself, and be cautious during fire season. Abuse of the reservoir by visiting anglers could lead to its closure.

MALHEUR RIVER A remote but very productive river that flows through a mix of national forest, BLM range, and private ranchland. It includes three distinct reaches, the Upper, Middle, and Lower river.

The Upper Malheur, fished primarily for large wild redband trout, is a fine Oregon trout stream. It flows 60 miles from its headwater tributaries in Logan Valley to its impoundment as Warm Springs Reservoir near Juntura, east of Burns. Included within this stretch are both a warmwater ranchland reach near the reservoir and a 10-mile wild and scenic segment in Malheur National Forest. The Malheur is designated wild and scenic from the confluence of its headwaters to its first intersection with private property near Hog Flat. The river begins as the confluence of Big and Lake creeks, which are formed in Strawberry Mt. Wilderness. They are joined by Summit and Bosenberg creeks in Logan Valley.

To access the upper river and its tributaries (See Lake Creek, Big Creek, Bosenberg Creek), follow Hwy. 395 to Seneca (about 24 miles south of John Day, 45 miles north of Burns). Follow Forest Rd. 16 east about 18 miles to the Big Creek area. Forest roads south of the main route approach and cross the river. The Malheur River National Scenic Trail follows the river from Malheur Ford Camp in Dollar Basin downstream about 6 miles to Hog Flat. To reach the upper trailhead from Big Creek Campground on Forest Rd. 16, follow Forest Rd. 16 east less than one mile, then turn right on Forest Rd. 1647. The trailhead is about 3 miles down this road.

Gravel roads follow the river between the communities of Drewsey and Van. To reach this area from Burns, follow Hwy. 20 east to the northbound graded gravel road just beyond the community of Buchanan. Take the right fork at Pine Creek School. This road follows the river south to Drewsey. Beyond Drewsey, the river flows into Warm Springs Reservoir.

The upper Malheur was last stocked with rainbow trout in 1992. These were always outshone by the native redband, and in 1992 ODF&W discontinued its stocking program. The upper Malheur is now managed for wild fish. Redband trout in the upper river reach 16-18 inches. Brook trout, white fish, and bull trout are also present. Bull trout must be released unharmed.

Smallmouth bass are present in fair numbers from the reservoir upstream about 12 miles. The smallmouth fishery has tapered off since the early 1980s when the river was running high. BLM and private property are well mixed in this stretch. Ask permission when in doubt as to land ownership, or walk upstream from the reservoir. Public land borders both sides of the river for about 3 miles upstream from Warm Springs. Best fishing for both trout and smallmouth is in spring, after the runoff recedes.

The middle reach of the Malheur River grows redband trout to 20 inches.

The Middle reach of the Malheur flows from Warm Springs Reservoir to Namorf Dam, offering 56 miles of productive trout water. This is an accessible stretch that is capable of providing excellent angling for trout to 20 inches. Hwy. 20 follows it closely from Juntura (about an hour east of Burns) to Namorf (which controls the flow to Bully Creek Reservoir). Much of the river flows through public BLM land, but there are some posted areas. Watch for signs.

This stretch of the river is occasionally plagued with rough fish. In recent years, hard winters have been keeping the rough fish in check. Beulah Reservoir trout migrate into this section, supplementing the available stock.

Fall offers the best angling in this reach, but spring can also be good. During irrigation season the water runs high and murky, though drifted bait can still take large fish. There are no camping opportunities along the middle reach.

The Lower reach of the Malheur is a 70-mile flow from Namorf Dam to the Snake River confluence. Affected by heavy irrigation withdrawals, the lower Malheur has limited public access to its primarily warmwater fisheries. Access with landowner permission only. Carp, catfish, and smallmouth bass are present.

A note on the river's name, French for unfortunate river: According to Lewis MacArthur, the river was so named by a Hudson's Bay trader in 1826, whose cache of furs and trade goods, hidden near the river, was discovered and stolen by natives.

MALHEUR RIVER, NORTH FORK A productive branch of the middle reach of the Malheur, heading in the Blue Mountains of Malheur National Forest and joining the mainstem at Juntura. It flows 41 miles south before its impoundment as Beulah Reservoir, and about another 18 miles below the reservoir to its confluence with the mainstem Malheur. The reach from Beulah Reservoir to the headwaters is designated wild and scenic.

Redband trout, whitefish, and bull trout are present in the river above Beulah. Bull trout must be released unharmed. To reach the upper stream from Prairie City on Hwy. 26 (east of John Day), turn south onto County Rd. 62. At about 8 miles, turn left on Forest Rd. 13, which approaches the North Fork and follows its west bank downstream to Short Creek Ranger Station. At Short Creek, Forest Rd. 16 comes in from the east and continues following the North Fork's west bank to Elk Creek Campground. Just south of Elk Creek, turn left on Forest Rd. 1675 to reach North Fork Malheur Campground. Trailhead 381 is about a mile further south. This trail follows the North Fork downstream to its intersection with private land. Forest Road 1675 leaves the river at the upper trailhead, but returns to the stream at Crane Crossing.

From Crane Crossing downstream, the North Fork flows through a canyon and is almost inaccessible. Trail 381 follows it 7 miles downstream from Crane Crossing. (Trail 381A, which intersects Trail 381 at Crane Crossing, is an old military road which follows Crane Creek through handsome old growth timber. Crane Prairie meadow, about 5 miles up this trail, is especially nice in spring.)

Two additional points of access to the North Fork canyon are Bear Creek and the Little Malheur. See the Malheur National Forest map for directions.

The lower river, below Beulah, is accessed by a graded gravel road that follows the river from Juntura, on Hwy. 20, north to the reservoir.

Below Beulah, the North Fork is stocked heavily with rainbow trout each spring. Angler success rate is very high in comparison with other streams in the area. Trout run 9-13 inches, with a few to 20 inches. The lower river flows through private ranchland with public access at BLM's Chukar Park and just below the reservoir dam. To reach the river below the dam, you can use the gravel road behind the gatekeeper's house. Check in at the house out of courtesy.

MALHEUR RIVER, SOUTH FORK A short stem of the Malheur, with headwaters in Virginia Valley east of Malheur Lake, flowing east to the Malheur Cave area and north to Juntura, where it joins the North Fork and mainstem. Hwy. 78 follows a section of the upper stream about 10 miles SE of Princeton, an hour's drive from Burns. An eastbound cut-off at Crane approaches the river's mid-section. The lower stream flows through a deep canyon to Juntura, but it's accessible in a few spots. Most of the land along the river is private property. Check in at the nearest ranch for permission to fish.

The South Fork is not stocked. Angling is only fair, with fishing best the first month or two in spring. There are no camping opportunities along the stream.

MANN LAKE One of the premiere trout fisheries in this corner of the state. After years of overflow following the heavy precipitation of the 1980s, the lake was almost reduced to its "normal" size following the 90s drought, though it is still above its historical average high water mark. It offers very good angling for big Mann Lake cutthroat, a strain especially adapted to life in the lake's high elevation alkaline waters. A similar desert strain, Lahontan, once grew to 40 pounds in Nevada's Pyramid Lake.

Mann sprawls at the summit of a gentle saddle in the rain shadow east of Steens Mt. Fishing is restricted to barbless flies and lures. This is a wild and wonderful place if you love open spaces and the vast scale of a desert. Keep an eye to the slopes of Steens Mt. and you are very likely to see antelope during your stay here.

Mann Lake is due east of Frenchglen, but there is no direct route from there. You'll have to drive around the mountain. It's about 100 road miles to Mann Lake from Burns. From the north, take Hwy. 78 SE from Burns, crossing over Steens Mt. east of New Princeton, and turning south at Folly Farm onto the east side Steens road to Fields. The lake is just west of the road, about 25 miles south of Folly Farm. Tencent Lake and Juniper Lake are sometimes mistaken for Mann Lake, but both are much closer to Folly Farm. Juniper Lake has also been stocked and in wet years shows good results.

Mann Lake averages about 275 acres. The lake is fairly rich and quite shallow, with an average depth of 8 ft. and a maximum depth of only 15 ft. Reeds encircle the shore, and aquatic vegetation flourishes. The water is often somewhat turbid due to gale force winds, which are not uncommon. The lake clears 24 hrs. after a blow. There is no forage fish in Mann, but a rich and varied population of aquatic insects thrive here, and trout grow quickly grazing upon them. Algal blooms tend to give the fish an off flavor by mid-summer.

The lake has been managed as a brood supply for high desert cutthroat trout, with eggs taken bi-annually, raised to fingerlings in hatcheries, and used to continue this fishery and stock other high desert waters. Special regulations are in effect to preserve both the quality of the fishing and a steady supply of eggs for these unique native trout. The stock preserved here is officially recognized as Mann Lake cutthroat, and (along with Lahontan) are among the largest and most predacious trout native to western North America.

Most trout landed here are in excess of 12 inches, with fish up to 20 inches. Fishing is restricted to the use of artificial flies or lures with barbless hooks, and any fish under 16 inches must be released unharmed. Fishing in the tributary streams is prohibited. Fly anglers can do very well here, despite the poor water clarity. By July there are swarms of dragon and damsel flies hatching, and big nymphs will bring in the fish if retrieved in short jerks through the shallows on a sinking or sink tip line. Fishing drops off in August due to water temperatures in the 1970s, but picks up again in fall.

The lake is on BLM land, and the area on the west side is used as an unimproved campground. There is no drinking water here. A raft or canoe can be used but isn't necessary.

The lake is at the top of a low pass, and the wind can really howl through occasionally, which makes fishing either unpleasant or impossible. When it gets like that, drive north toward Fields to Alvord Hot Springs, on the left side of the road around the midpoint of the Alvord Desert. Supplies and the best burgers for fifty miles around are at Fields. This is exceptionally remote country, so top off your gas and water tanks prior to heading out.

MARGURETTE LAKE A good hike-in brook trout lake, about 15 acres, located in the Sky Lakes group of Sky Lakes Wilderness, Winema National Forest. From Rt. 140 at Pelican Guard Station, north of Lake of the Woods, continue north about 10 miles, past Crystal Springs Roadside Rest, turning west on Forest Rd. 3450. At the end of the road, Trail 3708 follows Cherry Creek into the lake basin. At the trail junction about 4 miles in, turn right onto Trail 3762 past Trapper Lake to Margurette, which is 1/8 mile NW of Trapper. The trail loops west around the north end of Trapper and leads to Margurette.

You'll find good fishing in Margurette for medium size brook and rainbow trout. Most fish run 8-11 inches, with a few larger. Any method will take fish, except in mid-summer when they are finicky. A good trick to try is casting a large-blade spinner with a worm trailing, retrieve very slowly a yard at a time, and let it settle. This usually wakes them up. Campsites are limited here, as elsewhere in the basin, due to shoreline rehabilitation efforts. Camp well back from fragile lakeside vegetation, and use no-trace camping methods. For other good fishing opportunities nearby see Donna, Deep, Trapper.

McCOY CREEK (Grant Co.) A tributary of Lake Creek, which feeds the upper Malheur. It flows out of Logan Valley along with Bosenberg and Big creeks. McCoy can be fished for wild rainbow and brook trout. Bull trout may also be present but must be released unharmed. McCoy is bordered by private land throughout most of its run. It can be fished from Forest Rd. 16 using the road right of way as access, and from Forest Rd. 1648 which crosses the creek above Murray Campground.

Camping is available on Lake and Big creeks.

McCOY CREEK A tributary of the Blitzen River, flowing NW off Steens Mt. It joins the Blitzen on Malheur Wildlife Refuge about 14 miles south of the southern border of Malheur Lake. The creek enters the refuge through Diamond Valley, and several miles have been channelized for irrigation.

To reach it, take Hwy. 205 south from Burns toward Frenchglen. The turn-off to Diamond is about 16 miles south of the Refuge Headquarters turn-off. The road reaches the creek about 5 miles to the east. Dirt roads south of the Diamond area follow the creek east for many miles.

McCoy is about 25 miles long and has some good size trout, but it is lightly fished due of its remoteness. Much of the stream flows through private property, and permission to fish is hard to get. The trout reach 15 inches.

MILLER CREEK A small but good trout stream, outlet of Miller Lake, west of Hwy. 97 at Chemult. The creek is followed west from Hwy. 97 by the Miller Lake Rd. (Forest Rd. 9771), which intersects the highway 6 miles south of Chemult. The entire creek is only 10 miles long. It ends in beaver marsh and percolates into the ground, as do most of the creeks in this area. The upper 4 miles flow within Winema National Forest.

The stream is not stocked, but brown and rainbow trout are well established. The nearest campground is at Miller Lake.

MILLER LAKE One of the best brown trout fisheries in the state, a deep, clear lake of over 600 acres between Chemult on Hwy. 97, and Diamond Lake. It is reached by 14 miles of good road north of Chemult.

Rainbow and brown trout are stocked annually. The browns have been thriving. Fish for them on a slow troll with a long line, or in the evening when they move into the shallows. Flies, big streamers, Rapallas, and crawdad lures are all effective. Kokanee are over-abundant, and their average size has declined to 6-9 inches.

A nice campground with boat ramp and picnic facilities is located on the NW shore at Digit Point. Be prepared for mosquitoes. Supplies are available at Chemult.

MOON RESERVOIR A 619-acre desert reservoir SE of Riley 25 miles SW of Burns. It was treated for rough fish in 1987, went dry in 1993, and was restocked with largemouth bass and black and white crappie. It should provide good fishing in a couple of years.

MOSQUITO CREEK A remote Lahontan cutthroat stream. It is closed to all fishing to protect the Lahontan, which are listed as a threatened species. It's estimated that the Lahontan population throughout the basin dropped 90 percent during the 1987-92 drought.

MUD LAKE RESERVOIR (Lake Co.) A 170-acre desert reservoir NE of Adel. Take Rt. 140 about 12 miles east of Adel, and turn onto a dirt road heading north. The reservoir is about 10 miles north, and you'd best get a county or BLM map before setting out for it.

The reservoir has been stocked with rainbow, and most are in the 8-14 inch range. The fish are of excellent quality but slow biters in this muddy water. Bait is best here. The reservoir is undeveloped, and there are no camping facilities or shade trees.

MURRAY RESERVOIR A rainbow trout lake just off Hwy. 26 in western Baker County SE of Unity. From Baker, follow hwys. 7 then 26 south about 9 miles beyond the community of Unity. The 45-acre lake is on the north side of Hwy. 26.

Legal rainbow are stocked annually, and bank angling is good for trout 10-12 inches. Most anglers use bait. The reservoir is on private property but is open to public use. Be a courteous guest to protect future access. Angling from a floating device is prohibited. Recommended for small fry, but be careful near the dam.

MYRTLE CREEK (Harney Co.) A small stream flowing into the Silvies River north of Burns. The creek is within Malheur National Forest and joins the Silvies about 25 miles north of Burns, about 12 miles west of Hwy. 395. To reach it take Hwy. 395 north from Burns about 18 miles to Forest Rd. 31, which cuts west from the highway one mile north of Idlewild Campground. Forest Rd. 31 hits the creek about 12 miles NW, crossing it 7 miles above the Silvies. Forest roads follow it closely to its headwaters. Downstream, Trail 308 follows the creek almost to the Silvies River, providing the only access.

Myrtle produces a lot of small native redband trout. They are caught in spring and summer, averaging 10 inches. Bait-fishing is popular. Campground are located north and south of the intersection of Forest Rd. 31 and Hwy. 395.

NATASHA LAKE An exceptionally pure 6-acre hike-in lake in the southern Dwarf Lakes area of the Sky Lakes group, Sky Lakes Wilderness. See Deep Lake for road directions to the trailhead at Cold Springs Campground. Trails 3709 and 3710 lead from Cold Springs to the basin. Trail 3709 is less steep. Pass between the Heavenly Twins, then turn north onto Trail 3729. Lake Natasha is on the west side of the trail.

The lake is known for its outstanding water quality. It is no longer stocked, though 6-9 inch brook trout may still be available. There are good campsites off the trail to the east, at Heavenly Twins and Isherwood, though camping throughout the basin is currently limited due to rehabilitation efforts along the shorelines. Camp well back from fragile lakeside vegetation, and use no-trace camping methods.

NORTH PINE CREEK A rainbow trout stream, tributary to Pine Creek of the Snake River system, flowing mostly within Hells Canyon National Recreation Area of Wallowa-Whitman National Forest. It can be reached from Baker by taking Hwy. 86 east 51 miles to Halfway. Continue about 9 miles past Halfway to the mouth of North Pine Creek. The mouth is mid-way between the town of Copperfield, where Pine Creek enters the Snake River, and Halfway. From the south, take Idaho Hwy. 11 north from Robinette, crossing the Snake at Brownlee Dam, and continue north to Copperfield. A paved road, Forest Rd. 39, follows the creek north to its headwaters.

North Pine offers 16 miles of water with good road access. Fishing is fair for stocked and native rainbow to 12 inches. Bait is best, but spinner and bait will take fish in murky water. North Pine Campground is 5 miles up from the mouth, and Lakefork Campground is 3 miles further upstream. A good trail leads west from the latter, following Lake Fork, a tributary of North Pine that offers good fishing as well.

NORTH POWDER RIVER A rainbow trout stream, flowing west from the Blue Mountains, entering the Powder River just east of the town of North Powder at the junction of highways 84 and 237. North Powder is 20 miles north of Baker. The main stream is followed by paved road for about 7 miles SW from North Powder. Forest roads access its North Fork and Anthony Fork headwaters north of Anthony Lake. See the Wallowa-Whitman National Forest map, south half, for details.

The stream and its tributaries offer fairly good angling for native rainbow in late spring and summer. Bull trout are also present, but must be released unharmed. The nearest campgrounds are in the Anthony Lake area, with an unimproved camp at Rocky Ford, where the stream flows from the south toward the main road.

OBENCHAIN RESERVOIR A 40-acre reservoir 10 miles NE of Bly on Rt. 140. From Bly, follow Forest Rd. 34 toward Campbell Reservoir, turning left at the road junction before Dutchman Flat. Obenchain is less than 4 miles NW of the junction.

Privately owned but open to public use, Obenchain contains a dense population of small largemouth bass. The fishery has suffered during the drought but can be expected to rebound once rains resume and the water level stabilizes. It offers good active fishing for the family. Camping is permitted.

OWYHEE RESERVOIR A long, narrow reservoir near the Idaho line, which supports bass and panfish. The reservoir was formed by an irrigation dam on the Owyhee river about 25 miles SW of Nyssa, 40 miles from Ontario. Green and turbid, it fills a deep, scenic canyon with a pool about 40 miles long that has over 300 miles of shoreline. This canyon cuts through colorful volcanic rocks—a raw,

Good numbers of rainbow trout are caught in Oxbow Reservoir.

wild place that can be reached, for the most part, only by boat.

In spring of 1994, the Oregon Health Division issued a warning that fish in Owyhee Reservoir contain a level of methyl mercury that exceeds federal safety guidelines. Children 6 and under, pregnant women, nursing women, and women who hope to become pregnant should *eat no fish* caught in the reservoir. Half-pound per day servings, no more than 3 pounds per year, are judged to be safe for most other people—but prudent folks should probably consider Owyhee a catch-and-release fishery. The mercury is thought to be the result of naturally occurring mercury in the soil being leached into the reservoir as a result of mining and other soil disturbing activities.

A well-signed road 4 miles west of the town of Owyhee follows the river south to the dam and Lake Owyhee State Park, on the east shore near the dam. Other unimproved roads enter from Vale, Adrian and other towns along the Snake River near the border. Other access points are at the end of the Dry Creek Rd. on the west side of the lake about 10 miles up from the dam, and at Leslie Gulch, coming in from the Succor Creek Rd. on the east side of the lake. The Leslie Gulch road is well known for its dramatic naturally sculpted rock formations. These and other unimproved roads are shown on the Vale District BLM map.

Owyhee Reservoir State Airport, a dirt strip (1840 ft. x 30. ft) which shows on the sectional, is located at Pelican Point, over 20 miles south of the dam. This strip sees a surprising amount of use. Pilots should low-pass the runway to check for ruts before landing.

Owyhee's largemouth bass have attracted a lot of anglers in the past. Catches averaged 1-2 pounds, but reached 5 pounds. Bass anglers here traditionally use both sinking and surface plugs, but almost any method can be effective at times. Bombers, Sonics, plastic worms, and black eels are the most popular lures.

Black crappie, which have run 7-9 inches and weigh 5-8 ounces, are present in abundance. They are taken on bait, spinner, jigs, flies or almost anything. The water in the center is deep, so most anglers work the shorelines. The area around Leslie Gulch has provided channel cats to 15 lbs. Smallmouth and cat fishing is best at the head of the reservoir. Rainbow trout are not stocked, but some drift in from elsewhere in the basin. Big rainbow occasionally show up in the catch. Water fluctuation during the drought has been hard on all the fisheries.

Lake Owyhee Resort, about 5 miles east of the dam, offers house boats and motorboats for rent, supplies, accommodations, restaurant, and trailer parking. A State Park between resort and dam has 4 boat ramps, picnic facilities, and toilets. BLM campgrounds are located below the dam and toward the upper end at Leslie Gulch. Cherry Creek State Recreation Area also has a campground. All the recreation sites above have boat ramps. There is a hot spring near the south end of the reservoir on the south shore just west of the narrows, north of Red Rock Spring.

OWYHEE RIVER A very productive stream divided into two distinct reaches, above and below Owyhee Reservoir. The upper reach flows 186.5 miles within Oregon from headwaters in the Owyhee Mts. of northern Nevada, through the remote and rugged canyonland of Idaho and southeast Oregon. The Owyhee joins the Snake River just south of Nyssa on the Oregon shore, across the river from Nampa, Idaho. Below Owyhee Reservoir (a 42-mile impoundment described above) the river is approached and closely followed by gravel roads all the way to the Snake.

The upper river is extremely remote, and much of it flows through deep canyons. It is crossed by Hwy. 95 at the community of Rome (about 135 miles SW of Ontario, Oregon), and is approached by unimproved roads in the backcountry (check Malheur County maps). A popular access point is Three Forks, approached by 36 miles of gravel road from Hwy. 95. Turn south off the highway about 17 miles east of Rome.

Smallmouth bass and channel catfish are available in the upper canyon, which is best fished by float trip, and best floated with experienced Owyhee guides. Float trips usually take 3-5 days. The 60-mile stretch of canyon from Rome to the reservoir is rated advanced intermediate, with a Class IV rapids and several Class IIIs. Prime floating takes place during spring runoff from April to June. About 2,000 people make the trip yearly, encountering some of the nation's most difficult white water and some of its most breathtaking canyonland scenery. The river is designated "wild and scenic" from the Oregon State Line to the reservoir, with a brief private stretch near Rome. Permits to raft are not required, but users are asked to register with the BLM.

The lower Owyhee is very productive for large rainbow and brown trout. The river flows through public land for its first 10 miles below the reservoir. Lake Owyhee Rd. follows the river to Snively Hot Springs, where the hot flow is captured in rock pools. (The springs themselves are on private property.) From the dam to Snively the river is stocked with 40,000 rainbow annually, and with brown trout every other year. Rainbow to 8 pounds and browns to 5 pounds are available. There is a campground at Snively.

Below Snively the river is heavily drawn down for irrigation, and there is little public access. Bass, crappie, and catfish from the Snake are present.

Owyhee water runs murky year around, with best visibility in early fall. The entire upper river was treated for rough fish in 1970 and re-stocked with rainbow trout, smallmouth bass, and channel catfish. Angling has been very good for bass and channel catfish, but few trout are taken above the dam. Best catfishing is in the lower 50 miles from Rome to the reservoir.

OXBOW RESERVOIR A 12-mile impoundment of the Snake River between Oxbow and Brownlee dams, offering bass, channel cats, and stocked rainbow. From Baker take Hwy. 86 east 70 miles to the community of Copperfield, at the huge bend in the Snake from which the dam gets its name. A paved road follows the reservoir closely from Oxbow upstream to Brownlee.

Quite a few channel cats are taken in the heavy water near the dam. Rainbow 10-12 inches are caught in good numbers in spring. The smallmouth fishery is best in summer.

Boats may be launched at McCormick Park on the Idaho shore at the south end of the reservoir, just below Brownlee Dam. The Idaho Power Company maintains a campground there with good trailer sites. There is also a campground at Copperfield Park just below Oxbow Dam.

PELICAN LAKE See Warner Valley Lakes.

PHILLIPS RESERVOIR A large reservoir which has grown trout to 15 inches. Crappie, channel catfish, and yellow perch have been illegally introduced and may mark the demise of the large trout fishery. The reservoir is on the upper Powder River about 5 miles east of Sumpter, SE of Baker. It was created by Mason Dam, built in 1967. From Baker, head south on Hwy. 7 to Salisbury, then about 9 miles east toward Sumpter. The reservoir usually covers about 2,400 acres. It got very low during the drought, but as it has a minimum pool, the fishery was not lost. It filled in 1993.

Trout angling at Phillips has traditionally been very good, with the average catch 10-15 inches. Trolling or still fishing near the dam is often effective. The lake is open all year, and ice fishing is very popular. Winter efforts are generally well rewarded.

There are two campgrounds on the lake, one at the dam and the second at Union Creek, about 2 miles west of the dam. Both are easily reached from the highway, and each has a boat ramp. Supplies are available at Baker or Sumpter.

PIKE CREEK A remote Lahontan cutthroat stream. It is closed to all fishing to protect the Lahontan, which are listed as a threatened species. It's estimated that the Lahontan population throughout the basin dropped 90 percent during the 1987-92 drought.

PINE CREEK (Baker Co.) A good stream, though isolated and used for irrigation below Halfway. It enters the Snake River below Oxbow Dam. The stream heads in the SE corner of Eagle Cap Wilderness, flowing SE 15 miles to the town of Halfway, then swings east to the Snake. The stretch from Halfway to the Snake River at Copperfield is closely followed by Hwy. 86. Halfway is 51 miles east of Baker on Hwy. 86. A gravel road follows the creek upstream from Halfway to the headwaters, about 11 miles. Cornucopia, a semi-abandoned mining town, is located near the end of this road. Most of Pine Creek runs across private lands, so access is a problem.

The stream is well stocked with rainbow trout, and fair catches of wild fish are made. The fish aren't large, to 12 inches or so. Best trout water is upstream from Halfway. Bait or flies will take fish in spring and summer. There are no camping opportunities on the creek, but McBride Campground is only 4 miles west of Carson, mid-way between Halfway and Cornucopia.

PINE LAKES (Baker Co.) Two small, fairly deep brook trout lakes in the southern Eagle Cap Wilderness, Wallowa-Whitman National Forest. The lakes are about 3 air miles NW of Cornucopia, which is 10 miles NW of Halfway by County Rd. 413. Drive as far north on 413 as you can, and you'll reach the Pine Creek Trailhead. Follow Trail 1880 along Pine Creek all the way to the lake, about 7 miles of steady uphill hiking, elevation gain about 2,400 ft.

The lakes are side by side and quite deep. Upper Pine is the larger, 14 acres with a depth of 70 feet. Lower is only 3 acres, but is 35 feet deep. Each has a good supply of brook trout. Bait, flies, and lures all work. These fish aren't fussy. Average size is 10 inches.

POISON CREEK An 18-mile trout stream originating in Malheur National Forest, followed by Hwy. 395 for about 7 miles north from Burns. The upper waters are accessed by westbound forest roads in the vicinity of Joaquin Miller and Idlewild campgrounds. It offers fair angling for wild trout in spring, with bait most effective. The stream is fairly sluggish and gets low in summer.

POWDER RIVER A long tributary of the Snake River, heading near Sumpter and winding over 140 miles to the Snake near Richland, which is on Hwy. 86 south of Halfway. The lower 10 miles below Richland make up the Powder River Arm of the Snake's Brownlee Reservoir. Highway 86 follows the next 25 miles, and county roads provide access up to the crossing of Hwy. 203 at river mile 58 NE of Baker. From Hwy. 203 up to Thief Valley Reservoir, the river is designated Scenic. Access is difficult. The landowner on the Union County side does allow access right below the dam. (The road into the dam may be closed.) Watch out for rattlesnakes. Hwy. 30 parallels the river from North Powder to Baker, with many roads leading east to cross or follow the River. From Baker to Phillips Reservoir, the river is followed by Hwy. 7.

The Powder provides a diversity of angling. In the lower 10 miles from Richland to the Snake, bass, channel cats, crappie and perch predominate. Trolling, casting lures from shore, or bait fishing from boat or bank take fish throughout the season. The upper river is stocked heavily with rainbow, and a few natives are also caught. Best angling is in the tailwaters of Mason Dam (Phillips Reservoir) and Thief Valley Dam. Below Thief Valley Dam, trout reach 20 inches, with most 10-14 inches. The fish run considerably smaller elsewhere in the system, with average around 10 inches.

Above Phillips Reservoir the river has been devastated by gold mining. Hewitt County Park, 2 miles east of Richland, provides boating access to the lower river. Camping is available at Thief Valley and Phillips reservoirs.

PRIDAY RESERVOIR A very productive fishery for large trout. It covers has about 100 surface acres, located in Warner Valley about 57 miles NE of Lakeview. From I-395 follow Warner Canyon Rd. 140 east to Adel, then turn north toward

Warmwater fish thrive in Phillips Reservoir.

Hart Lake and the community of Plush. The reservoir is on the west side of the road about 12 miles beyond Adel.

The reservoir was poisoned in 1992 and was re-stocked in the fall of 1992. By spring of 1994 it had trout 18-20 inches. It's hard to catch them, though, in the reservoir's generally turbid water. The catch rate is slow even with bait.

PUCK LAKES Two fair fishing lakes on the east slope of the Cascades, off by themselves between the Sky Lakes Area to the south and the Seven Lakes Basin to the north. The Pucks are accessible by trail from either lake group. For direct access from the east, follow Upper Klamath Lake's westside road, County Rd. 531, to Forest Rd. 3484, 2 miles north of Crystal Springs Campground. Follow 3484 to the end. Trail 3707 (Nannie Creek Trail) reaches the lakes in less than 6 miles.

The larger southern Puck has about 25 acres, and the north lake has 10 acres. Fishing is fair for brook trout averaging 10 inches. There are no improved campsites. The lakes are usually accessible in June or earlier and are open as long as trail and weather conditions permit.

RATTLESNAKE CREEK A small desert stream east of Burns, with wild rainbow to 10 inches. It flows about 12 miles from headwaters in Malheur National Forest. From Burns follow Hwy. 20 east about 13 miles, turning north at the cut-off to Harney. A graded gravel road follows the stream from just north of Harney (near the Ft. Harney site) to its headwaters.

Late spring and early summer are the best times to fish. Worms, grasshoppers, and wet flies do well. Trout average 8 inches and smaller. There is a possibility that these trout may be a pure strain, untouched by stocking programs of the past. If so, they may eventually be protected from harvest.

RED LAKE (Klamath Co.) A shallow lake in the Island Lake group of the Sky Lakes Wilderness, Winema National Forest, about one mile north of Island Lake. Due to frequent winterkill, it will no longer be stocked, though fish may wander in from Island Lake.

RED MT. LAKE A small lake below Red Mt. in the Elkhorn Range west of Haines. It supports wild brook trout. To reach it, head west from Haines, turning north at Muddy Creek School. About one mile from the school, a road heads west toward Bulger Flat and the North Fk. North Powder River beyond it. Follow the North Fk. North Powder River Rd. (Forest Rd. 7301) into the forest. The trail to Red Mt. Lake is about 3 1/2 miles into the forest on the south side of the road. The lake is about one mile up the trail.

REYNOLDS POND A 5-acre reservoir SE of Alfalfa, containing largemouth bass and pumpkinseed sunfish.

ROCK CREEK LAKE A hike-in trout lake on the Elkhorn Ridge NW of Baker, in Wallowa-Whitman National Forest. The lake is the source of Rock Creek, which flows NE to the Powder River through Haines. The trailhead is reached from Haines, on Hwy. 30, by driving west for 10 miles on gravel and dirt roads toward the community of Rock Creek. It's about a 3-mile hike SE from road's end, following Trail 1626. Another trail, somewhat shorter, approaches from the east from Pine Creek Reservoir west of Wingville.

Rock Creek Lake is at elevation 7,600 ft. Although only 35 acres, the lake is over 100 ft. deep. It has a good population of fat little brook trout and skinny Mackinaw. The Mackinaw run to 20 inches but are not plentiful. You'll have to go deep for them, except right after ice-off. The lake may be stocked with rainbow in the future.

A lot of perch are caught in the lower Powder River.

ROUND VALLEY RESERVOIR 150-acre impoundment 15 miles east of Lovella, just south of Gerber Reservoir. It dried up during the drought and will not be re-stocked until it fills and stabilizes. At that time, it will be stocked with bass and sunfish. The reservoir is on BLM land and is open to public access.

SAWMILL CREEK A short tributary of Silver Creek, 29 miles east of Burns, with fair early season fishing for wild trout. Only about 10 miles long, it flows into Silver Creek about 12 miles north of Riley. From just west of Riley, on Hwy. 20, follow the Silver Creek Rd. north about 20 miles. Sawmill comes in from the NW and is followed and crossed by Forest Rd. 45 in Malheur National Forest. The stream has a fair population of small wild rainbow averaging 6-8 inches.

SEVENMILE CREEK An excellent fly stream, major tributary of Agency Lake, with headwaters in the Cascades SW of Crater Lake National Park. Despite its name, it is about 18 miles long. From Sevenmile Forest Station on Klamath Lake's Westside Road, paved Forest Rd. 3334 follows about 8 miles of the stream to Sevenmile Marsh. To reach this section from Hwy. 62, turn west onto Nicholson Rd. at Fort Klamath. The lower creek flows into Agency Lake, with an unboatable water level dam at the mouth of the creek.

Most of the lower stream is a canal, and is not fished. Above the canal, fishing is good for rainbow and brown trout. Brook trout are further upstream. Ask permission before fishing in areas where cattle are grazing.

SHERLOCK GULCH RESERVOIR A good little desert reservoir on BLM land NW of Plush. It has 10 surface acres. To reach it, turn north onto the Sunstone Rd. from Hogback Rd., which runs between Plush and Hwy. 395. The reservoir is about 4 miles NW of the Sunstone Area. Get local directions before seeking this one out.

Sherlock is stocked annually with rainbow fingerlings and grows trout 8-18 inches. The water is always turbid, making bait the most popular method here. Fly-fishing is occasionally productive. Winter ice-fishing can be good.

SID LUCE (SID'S) RESERVOIR A natural lake converted to irrigation reservoir in Warner Valley east of Lakeview. Its excellent rainbow population is lightly fished due to long, difficult access over rough roads. Though only 15 air miles from Lakeview, the drive is over 75 miles one way.

From Lakeview, follow Rt. 140 east to Adel. Turn north following the road toward Hart Lake and the community of Plush. Just north of Plush, head west toward the Fitzgerald Ranch. The road from Plush to Fitzgerald's is suitable for pick-up trucks. The road through the Fitzgerald property (which is open to public use) is very rough and turns into a power line access road shortly after the ranch buildings. If there have been recent rains, this road is impassable to all but off-road vehicles. There are 6 gates on the ranch road. Be sure to leave each as you found it. There are 2 creeks to ford after leaving the ranch, first Snyder (one mile past the ranch) then Colvin (shortly before Sid's).

The 50-acre lake sits in a bowl between Honey and Colvin creeks. It's rich with trout food (similar to Mann Lake in this respect), and stocked rainbow fingerlings show rapid growth, averaging 10-14 inches, nice and fat. Crawdads will eat fish left on stringers in the water, or can be trapped and eaten themselves. Most anglers use bait and fish from the shore, but a float tube would come in handy. Camping is prohibited. Be advised, too, that Sid's is at the beginning of snake country. Rattlesnakes are abundant.

SILVER CREEK (Harney Co.) A long stream NW of Burns, with trout in its upper waters. It heads in southern Ochoco National Forest a few miles north of Delintment Lake. The creek winds south through forest and high desert, finally emptying into Harney Lake. Hwy. 20 crosses the creek about 28 miles west of Burns near Riley. A paved road leads north from Riley, becoming Forest Rd. 45 upon entering the Ochoco Forest. This road leads to Delintment Lake, and crosses and parallels Silver Creek near the lake. (It first parallels Sawmill Creek, which also has fish.)

Most fishing takes place in the upper creek, north of Delintment and near Allison Ranger Station. Rainbow trout provide good catches in late spring until the water gets low and warm. The fish, mostly caught on bait, are 8-11 inches. The creek's upper basin burned in 1990, increasing sediment into the stream and raising the water's temperature. It is probable that the trout population is at a low level at this time.

There are three forest campgrounds near the stream in the vicinity of Delintment Lake. Buck Spring Campground is just west of Forest Rd. 45 near Sawmill Creek, SW of Delintment.

SILVER CREEK (Lake Co.) A good trout stream, flowing north from Fremont National Forest west of Hager Mountain, into Paulina Marsh near the community of Silver Lake. The stream is about 16 miles long. It is crossed near its mouth by Hwy. 31, and is followed by graded roads and logging roads to its headwaters. Forest Rd. 288 from Silver Lake takes reaches the upper stream.

Very low winter flows below Thompson Reservoir practically eliminate any wild population there. The West Fork (above Silver Creek Diversion Reservoir) is lightly stocked and contains a good population of small native rainbow (6-10 inches). Best fishing is in June and July.

There is a campground at Silver Creek Marsh on Forest Rd. 288 south of Thompson Reservoir, and two campgrounds at the reservoir.

SILVER CREEK DIVERSION RESERVOIR (Lake Co.) A 30-acre lake that rears big drop-out trout from the Silver Creek system. From the community of Silver Lake on Hwy. 31, drive south about 4 miles on County Rd. 4-12 toward Thompson Reservoir. The land at the north end is privately owned, but the SE arms are surrounded by BLM land, and you can fish from shore. Average fish taken exceed 14 inches.

SILVIES RIVER A 95-mile flow from headwaters in the southern Blue Mountains of Malheur National Forest south of John Day, to Malheur Lake south of Burns. Trout fishing is best in the upper waters from Seneca downstream about 20 miles to the confluence with Trout Creek.

Hwy. 395 follows the stream closely through most of this stretch. The catch rate is high, but the fish run small, 8-11 inches. Bait-fishing is most popular, but other methods will produce. About 8 miles south of the community of Trout Creek (16 miles north of Burns), Forest Rd. 31 heads NW towards Myrtle Park Meadows and the ice caves, crossing the Silvies at its Stancliffe Creek confluence. This confluence area has long been stocked with smallmouth bass, and they appear to be doing well.

The Silvies flows through Burns from the NW. A road heading due north beyond the city limits crosses and follows the river, deteriorating to ungraded gravel but sticking with the stream all the way to its confluence with Myrtle Creek. The Five-Mile Dam area, 5 miles NW of Burns, affords some good fishing. The lower 20 miles from Burns to Malheur Lake has no trout.

SKULL CREEK The first of two Catlow Valley streams crossed by the highway heading north from Fields towards Burns. It is bordered by private land near the road, but its headwaters are on public land. It may be fished for wild redband trout. The second stream of the pair is Threemile Creek.

SLIDE LAKE (Lake Co.) A 3-acre lake in an interesting geological area of Fremont National Forest, about 12 miles west of Paisley. Follow Hwy. 31 north from Paisley, then turn south on Forest Rd. 29 at the south end of Summer Lake. The road to Slide Lake cuts west after about 4 miles. Follow signs to Slide Mt. Geologic Area. It's about 8 miles to the lake. The road is not maintained for low clearance vehicles.

Slide Lake is stocked annually with rainbow fingerlings, but they don't last long. The real interest here is the opportunity to view volcanic geology and resulting earth movement. Slide Mt., once a large dome-shaped volcano, has been scarred by a giant prehistoric slide. The slide can be seen from Hwy. 31 on the way in. Withers Lake, a 5 acre lake about 2 miles to the east, also supports fish. Best access is a mile bushwhack up Withers Creek from Forest Rd. 3360.

SNAKE RIVER (Southeast Zone) This portion of the river is actually the more riverine portion of Brownlee Reservoir. Still influenced by the dam, it runs from the Idaho border about 20 miles south of Nyssa to Brownlee Dam. On the Oregon side, Hwy. 201 and county roads parallel the river from Adrian north to Ontario and the bridge at Weiser, Idaho. I-84 follows the river from Ontario north to Huntington, with county road exits leading east to the river. A county road closely follows the river for about 40 miles from Huntington north.

Most popular angling in this area is for channel catfish, although smallmouth bass are taken in growing numbers. Most of the cats are in the 2-pound range, but fish over 5 pounds are not unusual. Crappie are also available. This is primarily a bait show, with the best spots near the mouths of tributary streams. Local tackle shops can direct you to the current hot spots.

Boats can be launched at Nyssa, Ontario, Payette, Patch Island (south of Weiser), and Oasis (north of Ontario). For additional information, see Brownlee Reservoir.

SOUTH PASS LAKE A good hike-in lake, excellent on flies, most productive of all the lakes in Mountain Lakes Wilderness. It is on the eastern edge of the wilderness and may be approached from the west (Lake of the Woods, 9 miles), north (Varney Creek Camp, 7 miles), or south (Clover Creek Rd., 7

Best trout fishing on the Sprague is in late spring and early summer.

miles). From Harriette Lake on the main basin-circling trail, it's a steep 2-mile hike to South Pass Lake on an unmaintained track.

Covering 7 acres, the lake is quite shallow. It is stocked bi-annually with brook and rainbow trout. Fish average 8-10 inches with a few larger, and the lake has been known to grow some lunkers. Fly-fishing is good here, with fall and early spring best.

The entire basin has suffered from heavy use in recent years, and many good campsites are closed due to efforts to rehabilitate lakeside vegetation. Camp well back from the lake and use no-trace camping methods. The lake is open as long as weather permits.

SPALDING RESERVOIR One of the most productive reservoirs in SE Oregon, surrounded by BLM land 85 miles east of Lakeview. Turn north from Rt. 140 about 20 miles east of Adel, onto a dirt road that skirts the eastern edge of Guano Valley. The reservoir is 19 miles from the highway. This is remote country. Be prepared.

Covering 20 acres most years, Spalding occasionally goes completely dry, as it did in 1988 and 1992. It refilled in 1993 and has been re-stocked. Spalding grows fish quickly. By 1995, trout could easily reach 20 inches. While its water is turbid, it is less so than other reservoirs in the county. Flies and lures can be very effective.

SPENCER CREEK A very good trout stream, tributary of the Klamath River. It flows 18 miles from spring-fed headwaters south of Lake of the Woods into J.C. Boyle Reservoir on the Klamath west of Klamath Falls. The main creek and its tributaries are followed north by good graded roads from Keno on Hwy. 66.

Spencer Creek is managed as a wild trout stream. Fair numbers of large rainbow come into the creek from the Klamath River. The fishing is good on both bait and flies. The larger trout are usually taken early in season on lures or spinner/bait combinations. A late opening on the stream protects spawning fish.

SPRAGUE RIVER A long, good trout stream with some bass, flowing into the Williamson River at Chiloquin about 30 miles north of Klamath Falls. Managed for wild trout, the Sprague flows over 100 miles from east to west. Its central reach offers good fishing for largemouth bass.

The Sprague heads on the west slope of Gearhart Mt. and the rimlands to the south, about 30 miles west of Lakeview. Two major forks and Fishhole Creek combine near the town of Bly to form the main stream. Rt. 140 (Lakeview to Klamath Falls) follows the upper half of the river west from Quartz Mt. Pass to the town of Beatty at river mi. 70 on the mainstem.

The north fork provides excellent fly-fishing for rainbow, brook, and brown trout in its upper reaches near Sandhill Crossing. The south fork has abundant small brook trout. There are some nice browns in the lower stretches of this fork also. Fremont National Forest roads leading north and west from Bly and north from Quartz Mt. Pass provide access to these upper waters. Better bring a map.

Largemouth bass are available in the Sprague River Valley reach where the river meanders between the towns of Sprague River and Beatty. Bass fishing is best in mid-summer. A secondary road runs east from Hwy. 858 just north of the highway's crossing of the river at the town of Sprague River. This secondary road follows the north bank to a point north of Beatty.

Five miles west of Beatty, Hwy. 858 cuts NW from Rt. 140 and follows the river all the way to Chiloquin. Chiloquin is on Hwy. 97, about 30 miles north of Klamath Falls. Access to much of the lower stream is prohibited by landowners, but some grant permission to fish.

The lower Sprague has many rainbow to 3 pounds or better, and good-size browns take a fly nicely. Large streamers and bucktails can do the trick. Bait and lures are also effective. Best trout fishing is in late spring and early summer. The final mile of river below Chiloquin Dam is restricted to artificial lures or flies.

Sprague River Picnic Area, 5 miles east of Bly, is a nice lunch spot, but camping is prohibited. Several forest campgrounds are on or near the upper forks, including Sandhill Crossing, Lee Thomas, and Campbell Lake. S'Ocholis Campground is on the river 12 miles east of Chiloquin, along Hwy. 858.

SPRING CREEK (Klamath Co.) A very short tributary of the Williamson River, offering good spring and summer angling. Only 2 miles long, it flows into the Williamson at Collier State Park, accessible from Hwy. 97 about 4 miles north of Chiloquin. It's primarily a put-and-take fishery with most angling pressure from Crater Lake tourists.

Spring is stocked with 16,000 fish annually near the headwaters and in the area above Collier. In addition to these, some sizeable rainbow and brown trout wander into the stream from the Williamson.

Collier State Park is a very attractive full service park beside the river, with trailer hook-ups, tent sites, and showers as well as a picnic area. Mosquitoes are ferocious in spring and summer but die down in late summer and fall. Spring is an ideal canoeing stream. You can carry a canoe in from the rest area at the north end and canoe up to the head, or drive to the day-use area at the upper end and drift down to Collier. It's about 1 1/2 miles (2 hrs.) of leisurely drifting in an idyllic forest setting. For other good fishing in the area, see Sprague, Williamson.

SQUAW LAKE (Lake Co.) A 10-acre natural desert lake about 5 miles from Hwy. 31 north of Picture Rock Pass between

Summer and Silver Lakes. The road to Squaw heads east from the highway about 4 miles north of the community of Summer Lake. Squaw Lake is very turbid and receives little use by anglers. It is stocked periodically with rainbow fingerlings. The typical fish caught here is in the 8-10 inch range. Bait is the most effective method.

STONE CORRAL LAKE See Warner Lakes.

SUMMIT LAKE A small mountain lake in the Elkhorn Range west of Haines. It supports wild brook trout. See Red Mt. Lake for directions. The trail to Summit is a little more than one mile beyond the Red. Mt. Lake Trailhead, on the south side of the road. The hike to summit is about one mile.

SWAMP LAKE See Warner Valley Lakes.

SYCAN RIVER A fair tributary of the Sprague River, flowing through Fremont National Forest north of Beatty. It heads on the west slope of Winter Ridge and flows NW about 20 miles into Sycan Marsh. Leaving the marsh, it flows about 30 miles south to the Sprague at Beatty. In this stretch it forms the border between Fremont and Winema National Forests. It is only lightly fished, probably due to its remoteness and rugged access roads. But the upper river offers very good fly-fishing for small wild brook trout in a very pretty setting.

The Sycan is managed as a wild trout stream and has reproducing populations of brown, rainbow, and brook trout. Rainbow are found throughout the stream, but brook trout are mostly in the upper river above the marsh, and the browns are strictly in the waters below the marsh. Bull trout may be found in Long Creek, a tributary of the upper river, but must be released unharmed.

The Sycan enters the marsh at its SE corner. Upstream from this point, the river is reached and crossed by many forest roads. Use the Fremont National Forest map to locate road access and crossings.

Above the marsh, most fish are 6-10 inches, but larger fish exceeding 20 inches are occasionally landed. Some of the finest fly-fishing in the area is on the upper Sycan River and its tributaries.

Below the marsh, a maze of rough forest and county roads provide access to the river. Follow County Rd. 1193 north from Beatty. At the first junction, Forest Rd. 347 (to the left) leads to the river and crosses it below Teddy Powers Meadow, a popular take-out for drifters from the marsh. If you continue north instead of left onto Forest Rd. 347, you will reach Sycan Ford, a rough crossing. A Fremont Forest map will come in handy. Most of the lower 12 miles of river is on private land, and you will need permission to fish.

The waters below the marsh have suffered from overgrazing and excessive water withdrawals for irrigation. Designation as a Federal Scenic River might protect the Sycan from further degradation. Most of the fishing in this stretch is concentrated between Torrent Spring (2 miles above Sycan Ford) and the mouth. Early season angling can be quite good for rainbow 10-18 inches and for good size browns. The browns are probably spawners from the Sprague River. By summer the stream flow has dropped to the point where water temperatures make fishing unproductive.

There are quite a few good campsites along the stream in the upper area. Campgrounds to the south are available at Lee Thomas Meadow and the Sandhill Crossing of the North Fork of the Sprague.

TAFT MILLER RESERVOIR A large irrigation reservoir in the desert country east of Hart Mt. National Antelope Refuge. The reservoir is about 85 miles south of Burns and 85 miles east of Lakeview. It normally covers about 350 acres but went almost dry in 1992 and may not be restocked due to issues relating to the wild fish policy in the Rock Creek system. Wild trout from the creek may take up residence in the reservoir.

Camping is available near Frenchglen and on the Hart Mt. Refuge, both about 25 miles from the reservoir.

THOMAS CREEK (Lake Co.) A tributary of the Goose Lake, closed to fishing. All Goose Lake tributaries are closed to allow natural regeneration of the system's redband trout population. Goose Lake redband suffered severe losses in fall of 1992 when the lake went dry.

THOMPSON VALLEY RESERVOIR A large impoundment capable of providing very good angling for large trout, about 12 air miles SW of Silver Lake in northern Lake County. The reservoir is in the headwaters of the upper east fork of Silver Creek in Fremont National Forest. It is about 14 miles south of the town of Silver Lake, which is on Hwy. 31. Several roads lead south from the highway near the town. Look for signs to the reservoir.

The reservoir was drawn down to its lowest pool ever in 1992. Re-stocked in 1993, its yearling population showed good growth by summer 1994.

Thompson Valley reaches 2,500 surface acres when full. With a maximum depth of only 30 ft. and lots of sunshine, trout food is abundant. The current stocking program uses Eagle Lake rainbow and Lahontan cutthroat, both well adapted to desert lake conditions. The rainbow usually reach 12-24 inches and about 5 pounds maximum. The cutthroat are smaller, about 3 pounds, ranging 8-18 inches. An illegal introduction of smallmouth bass is expanding, but it's too early to tell how the trout will be affected.

With fish this big, fly-fishing the shallows can provide real thrills. Trolling with spinner and worm is productive, as is still-fishing with worms, cheese or eggs.

Thompson is open all year, and lots of anglers fish through the ice during winter season. If the snow's too deep, you may have to hike a short way. Winter anglers stick to bait fished just off the bottom.

There are two US Forest Service campgrounds on the reservoir, each with a boat ramp.

THREE MILE CREEK (Klamath Co.) A small native trout stream, heading near Puck Lakes in the Cascades west of Fort Klamath. The lower end is crossed by the Westside Upper Klamath Lake Highway about 10 miles out of Fort Klamath. A road heads part way up the stream, and a trail follows the rest of the way. There are about 5 miles of productive water with lots of rock-hard brook trout, not big, but tasty and full of scrap. Bull trout are also present in the headwaters but must be released unharmed. Three Mile offers a good chance for a mess of pan-size natives and not much company. There is no camping along the stream.

THREEMILE CREEK (Harney Co.) The second of a pair of Catlow Valley streams crossed by the highway heading north from Fields toward Burns. The lower portion of the stream runs through private land, but the headwaters are on public land and may be fished for wild redband trout. The first of the streams encountered is Skull Creek.

THIEF VALLEY RESERVOIR A beautiful desert reservoir on the Powder River. It is about 15 miles north of Baker, about 5 miles east of I-84. It can be reached from the road between Telocaset and Medical Springs. Telocaset is on Hwy. 237 eight miles south of Union and 7 miles NE of the North Powder Exit on I-84, south of La Grande.

The reservoir goes completely dry periodically, as it did in 1992. It was restocked with trout fingerlings in 1993. Trout grow very well in the reservoir when there isn't a lot of competition, so anglers can anticipate especially good fishing for nice size trout through 1996. Trout to 20 inches should be available, with plenty of others at the high end of the 10-14 inch range. After that, rough fish will probably begin to get the upper hand again and trout size diminish accordingly.

Crappie, bullhead, and quite a few largemouth bass drift into the reservoir from the Powder River. Brown bullhead 9-12 inches are also generally abundant. Bait-fishing from the bank is popular, with the dam a favorite spot.

The reservoir is open for angling year-round. Ice fishing is popular, and the success rate is high. The county maintains a small park with boat ramp on the reservoir.

TRAVERSE LAKE A nice brook trout lake in the SW Eagle Cap Wilderness. It is at the head of the West Fork of Eagle Creek, one mile above Echo Lake on the same trail. See Echo Lake (Eagle Creek Watershed) for directions.

Brook trout are numerous and of good size. Fly-fishing is excellent in August and September, and bait will produce fish at any time. This lake doesn't get much pressure.

TROUT CREEK About as remote as any you can drive to in Oregon. Located in the far southeast, the creek heads high in the Trout Creek Mts. near the Nevada border and flows north into the desert country SE of the Steens Mts. About 30 miles long, it is so remote it is hardly ever fished. Small, unique Alvord cutthroat inhabit its bracing upper waters.

Only the upper waters are available for fishing. The lower stream is all in private ownership. You'll want a good map before heading in here. The BLM Steens Mt. map covers the area well. Four-wheel drive or at least a high center vehicle is strongly recommended, along with a good stock of supplies. Inquire at the State Patrol office in Burns for road conditions prior to attempting this.

A graded road leads east toward Whitehorse Ranch from the Fields to Denio Rd., about mid-way between them and one mile north of Tum Tum Lake. This road reaches a gap formed by lower Trout Creek about 6 miles to the east, and follows the lower waters about 8 miles. Unfortunately, the creek flows across private land here.

To reach the upper waters, take the Whitehorse Rd. 5 miles east of Fields to the Denio Rd., and turn south on a graded road which loops on to Denio. A bit over one mile later, turn SE onto a road which will meet Oreanna Creek in about 3 miles. Stay on this road and follow it SE and up about 13 rough miles to a ford through Trout Creek. The road follows the creek for a mile or so. You'll have to hike for further access. You can continue on this road and loop north and back down to Whitehorse Ranch.

Trout Creek offers fair fishing for rainbow trout on bait or flies in the lower waters if you can get permission to fish. There's not a lot of water in the upper creek, and the trout above are generally under 8 inches and darkly speckled. There are natural campsites in the aspen groves and plenty of wide open spaces.

TWENTYMILE CREEK A pretty good desert trout stream, flowing east and north from springs near the California line into Warner Valley, about 7 miles south of Adel. Adel is on Rt. 140 about 30 miles east of Hwy. 395. Twentymile is followed by a gravel road that leads south from Adel to California. The upper stream is accessed by graded roads running NW from this road toward Big Valley and Big Lake, then on to Rt. 140.

Between the Big Lake Rd. and the Adel-to-California Rd., the stream flows into a canyon. Most of the fishing for native rainbow takes place here. Angling is good in spring and summer for trout to 15 inches, but the average is 9-10 inches. Bait or wet flies are best.

TWIN LAKES (Baker Co.) Two little rainbow trout lakes below Elkhorn peak in the Elkhorn Range NW of Baker. The trail to the lake is at the end of the Lake Cr. Rd. (Forest Rd. 030) which heads north from Deer Creek Campground. Trail 1633 reaches the lakes in about 2 miles.

UNITY RESERVOIR A large popular reservoir on the upper Burnt River south of Baker, 3 miles north of the town of Unity. It offers good angling for rainbow trout, smallmouth bass, and crappie. Just west of Unity, Hwy. 7 runs north to the reservoir.

Over 2,000 acres when full, Unity provides good catches of rainbow to 16 inches, with the typical fish 9-12 inches. Trolling and bait-fishing are both popular, but bait anglers fare better early in the season. There is lots of angling pressure here, but good success. A State Park south of the dam has welcome shade trees and a campground with boat ramps.

UPPER KLAMATH LAKE Often the largest lake in Oregon (vying with Malheur in wet years), shallow and extremely productive, featuring big native rainbow trout. Covering about 64,000 acres, Upper Klamath is connected by a natural strait to 8,200 acre Agency Lake. Its primary tributary is the rich Williamson River system, and from it flows the Klamath River. From its southern tip within the town of Klamath Falls, the lake stretches north almost 25 miles.

I-97 provides direct access from Bend and from Redding, California and follows a good portion of the east lakeshore. Rt. 140, a direct route from the Medford area, follows the more popular west lakeshore from Pelican Bay to Klamath Falls. There are no bridges or opportunities to cross the 20 mile spa of water and wetland between Klamath Falls and the northernmost reach of Agency Lake. Motorists on Hwy. 97 should continue on to Chiloquin, then take Hwy. 62 to Ft. Klamath. Secondary roads east from Rt.

1 **MALONE SPRINGS** - unimproved launch accesses Crystal and Recreation creeks (channels meander through marsh); fish in late summer for big rainbow seeking cool water; good fly fishing; motor up or down.

2 **ROCKY PT**. - paved public ramp, dock, facilities for handicapped anglers; adjacent resort offers boat rentals, moorage, gas, and restaurant.

3 **HARRIMAN SPRINGS** - pay to launch; access to Harriman Creek and Pelican Bay.

4 **PELICAN CUT PUBLIC ACCESS** - popular with duck hunters; overgrown road along canal accesses Pelican Bay.

5 **ODESSA CREEK** - gravel ramp accesses Odessa and Short creeks and Klamath Lake; spring water provides good fishing year 'round.

6 **EAGLE RIDGE/SHOALWATER BAY**- concrete county ramp accesses spring troll fishery in Shoalwater Bay & along Eagle Ridge; bank angling out to point in spring.

7 **HOWARD BAY** (Wocus Bay) - paved ramp with ample parking accesses spring troll fishery in Howard Bay, Squaw Pt., Eagle Ridge.

8 **SKILLET HANDLE** - troll the Handle in spring.

9 **PELICAN MARINA**- supplies, repairs, moorage.

10 **HAGELSTEIN PARK**- boat ramp; best for boats under 16 ft.; narow channel under RR not passable at low water;accesses spring troll fishery; park along highway and fish the springs.

11 **WILIAMSON RIVER RESORT** - pay to launch; accesses mouth of Williamson fishery in spring and early summer, lower Williamson throughout summer.

12 **HENZEL PARK** - concrete public ramp accesses spring and early summer troll fishery.

13 **NEPTUNE RESORT** - pay to launch; rv camping factlities.

14 **PETRIC PARK**- good boat ramp; motor down to mouth of Wood River; fish Agency Lake

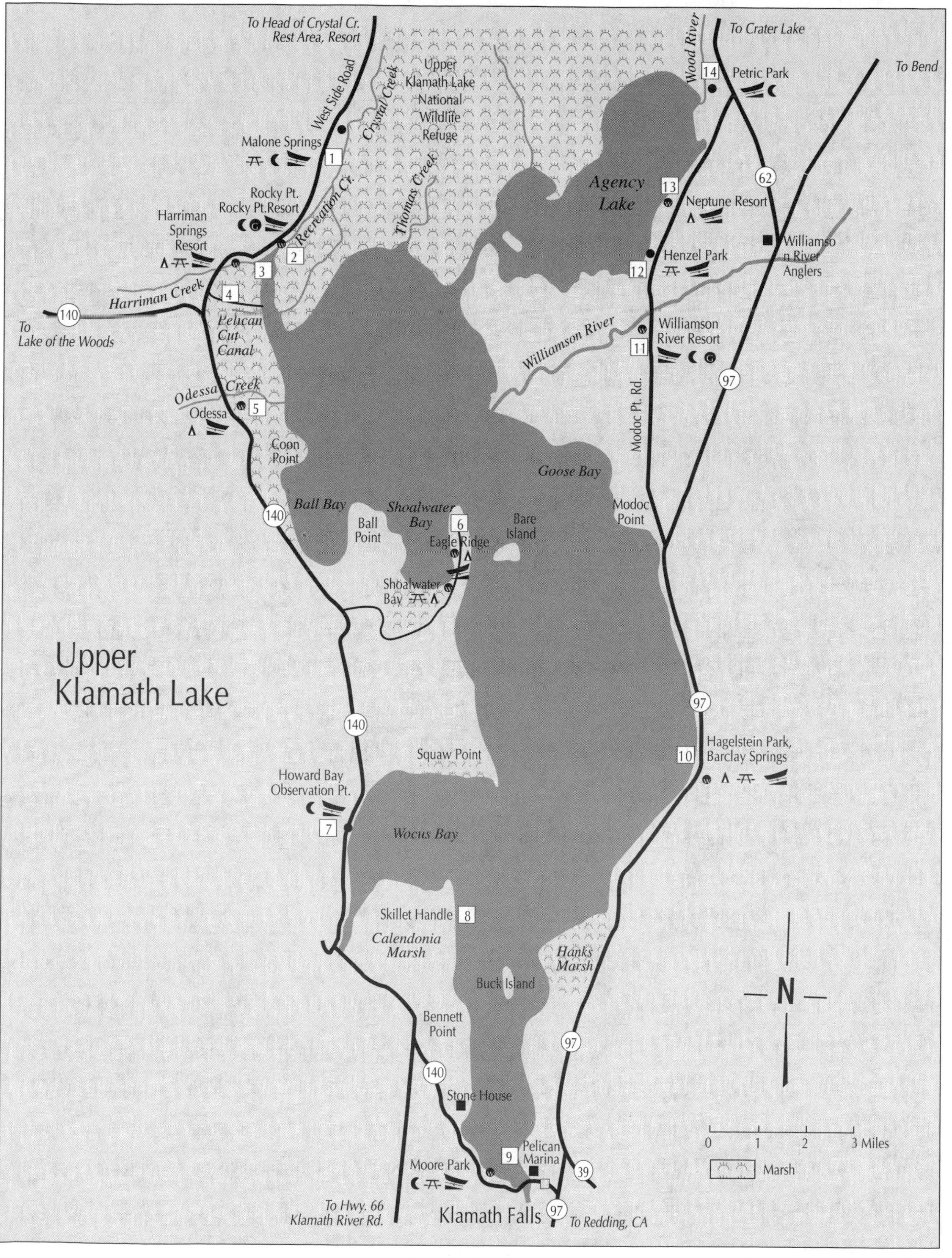
Upper Klamath Lake
To Head of Crystal Cr. Rest Area, Resort
West Side Road
Crystal Creek
Upper Klamath Lake National Wildlife Refuge
Thomas Creek
Wood River
To Crater Lake
14 Petric Park
To Bend
Malone Springs
1
Rocky Pt. Rocky Pt.Resort
Recreation Cr.
2
Harriman Springs Resort
3
4
Harriman Creek
140
To Lake of the Woods
Pelican Cut Canal
Odessa Creek
Odessa
5
Coon Point
Agency Lake
13 Neptune Resort
62
Williamson River Anglers
12 Henzel Park
Williamson River
Williamson River Resort
11
97
Modoc Pt. Rd.
Goose Bay
Modoc Point
Ball Bay
Ball Point
Shoalwater Bay
6
Eagle Ridge
Bare Island
Shoalwater Bay
140
97
140
10 Hagelstein Park, Barclay Springs
Squaw Point
Howard Bay Observation Pt.
7
Wocus Bay
Skillet Handle 8
Calendonia Marsh
Hanks Marsh
Buck Island
Bennett Point
97
140
Stone House
N
0 1 2 3 Miles
Marsh
Moore Park
9 Pelican Marina
39
To Hwy. 66 Klamath River Rd.
Klamath Falls
97
To Redding, CA

140 access boat ramps and popular fishing areas on the west shore, including Pelican Bay, Odessa Creek, Ball Bay, Shoalwater Bay, and Howard Bay.

Of Klamath Lake's 100 square miles, all but 2 percent is less than 25 ft. deep. This shallow water is high in nutrients and provides a food-rich environment that grows fish quickly. Large rainbow, over 20 inches, are the main attraction in Upper Klamath, with the *average* catch a whopping 18 inches. Studies have shown that rainbow trout in this lake reach 20 inches in only 3 years, and by 5 years have reached a length of 26 inches. A few 17-20 pound rainbow are occasionally taken. The lake's trout population is entirely dependent on natural reproduction, since past fish stocking programs have failed. Hatchery trout proved to be susceptible to a disease organism present in the lake.

By mid-summer the main lake becomes too warm for trout, and the fish move into spring-fed pockets and toward the mouths of tributaries, including the Pelican Bay area and Recreation Creek. Most fishing during the heat of the summer is catch and release, since annual summer algae blooms on the lake tend to give fish an off taste.

Bank angling is popular in winter, spring, and fall in Klamath Falls at Moore Park, Pelican Marina, and the Link River outlet. Anglers also fish along Howard (Wocus) Bay, in the SW and near springs on the east shore, just north of Hagelstein County Park off Hwy. 97. In early spring, a boat fishery develops near Eagle Ridge and in Howard (Wocus) and Shoalwater bays. In late April the northern lake opens and there are active troll fisheries out of Rocky Point and Harriman resorts, at the Recreation Creek inlet of Pelican Bay, and in the narrows between Upper Klamath and Agency lakes. In late summer fish gather in the Fourmile Creek inlet of Pelican Bay, which is cooled by springs, and at the mouths of cooler tributaries.

Klamath Lake has a large native chub population (Tui and blue), and bait fishing with chub chunks is popular and legal. Fathead minnows are also present in abundance, as are sculpins and lampreys. All fish bait must be dead. (Note that fish bait, alive or dead, is illegal in all other Oregon waters.) Bait is available at local shops. Trollers use large flasher-type lures or Flatfish and the standard spinner/bait set-up. The Andy Reeker No. 4 has been a standard lure here for years, and Rapallas are popular. Trolling with dead minnows behind a flasher is effective and legal here.

Other fish available in Upper Klamath include brown bullhead, yellow perch, and sturgeon. Largemouth bass have been introduced but have not thrived. Mullet (Lost River suckers) are a protected species and if caught, must be released unharmed.

Boat anglers are generally cautious and keep close to shore. Klamath Lake is mighty big and can kick up in even moderate wind. There is a public boat launch at Moore Park in Klamath Falls at the south end of the lake. Westshore ramps are off Rt. 140 at Howard Bay Observation Pt., Shoalwater Bay Campground, and Odessa Creek Campground. Three additional westside ramps allow boats to launch into tributary streams and drift down to Upper Klamath. They are at Harriman Springs Resort on Harriman Creek, Rocky Pt. Resort on Recreation Creek, and Malone Springs on Crystal Creek.

The only public boat ramp on the east shore is at Hagelstein Park. Boats can also be launched on the Williamson River at Williamson River Resort, and on Agency Lake at Henzel Park, Neptune Resort, and Petric Park. There is a 10 mph speed limit in the channels and resort areas.

Supplies, lodging, and boat rentals are available near the prime fisheries around the lake. Williamson, Wood, Sprague, and Klamath Rivers offer outstanding angling alternatives in the immediate area. Lake of the Woods, Fourmile Lake, and Mountain Lakes Wilderness offer additional angling, camping, and hiking opportunities nearby.

UPPER MIDWAY RESERVOIR A 40-acre reservoir on BLM land about 18 miles east of Lorella. The reservoir went dry in '92 and '93. It will be re-stocked with bass and forage fish when the reservoir refills and stabilizes. Camping is permitted at the reservoir.

VAN PATTEN LAKE A hike-in rainbow and brook trout lake in the Anthony Lake area west of Haines on Hwy. 411. From Haines, head west on Hwy. 411, which becomes Forest Rd. 73. Two miles east of Anthony Lake Guard Station, Trail 1634 leads to Van Patten Lake.

The lake covers 23 acres and generally offers excellent angling for rainbow that occasionally reach 12 inches. Fishing is good from late spring through fall. All methods can be used to take fish. The lake is stocked with fingerlings bi-annually. Supplies and accommodations are available at Anthony Lake Resort . There are campgrounds at Anthony Lake and at Grande Ronde Lake.

VEE LAKE A nice little 13-acre lake in Fremont National Forest that was created by a small dam to provide fish and goose habitat. The lake is in the North Warner Mts. NE of Lakeview. Drive east from Lakeview on Rt. 140 about 15 miles to the North Warner Road (Forest Rd. 3615), and follow this north about 25 miles to the lake.

Vee is shallow and weedy with lots of natural food to grow trout quickly. It is stocked annually, and most catches are 12-16 inches. Bait, lures and flies all produce well. Boats without motors are allowed on the lake. Several forest service campgrounds are nearby.

WARM SPRING RESERVOIR A large reservoir that grows good smallmouth bass and catfish as well as trout. It is SW of Juntura, a town on Hwy. 20 between Burns and Vale. The reservoir is 20 miles south of Juntura. Another road leads there from Crane on Hwy. 78.

Warm Springs covers 4,500 acres when full, but is used for irrigation and gets pretty low in the fall even in wet years. It went dry in '90, '91, and '92. It filled in 1993 and was re-stocked with rainbow fry. The reservoir grows trout well, so anglers may anticipate 20 inchers in 1995-96. Best fishing for trout is in spring and fall. Smallmouth bass, which survived the drought intact, run to 4 pounds and take small lures, spinners and small rubber worms with enthusiasm. Streamers with a lot of color work, too.

This is one of the few lakes in the state with channel catfish. A fair number are caught, with some to 24 inches. Brown bullhead are taken in larger numbers, but run only to 14 inches, with most just under a pound. There are no improvements at the reservoir. In dry years, it's hard to put a boat in late in the season, but bank fishing at the dam will produce.

WARNER VALLEY LAKES Eleven highly alkaline but life-supporting lakes in an eerie setting of desert vastness. They form a north-south chain across the floor of Warner Valley west of Hart Mountain. From north to south they are Blue Joint, Stone Corral, Lower Campbell, Upper Campbell, Flagstaff, Swamp, Jones, Anderson, Hart, Crump, and Pelican. All are interconnected during high water, and contain crappie, brown bullhead, and a few largemouth bass.

The most dramatic approach is to drop down into the valley from Hart Mt. From Burns, take Hwy. 205 south, turning east toward Hart about 6 miles south of Frenchglen. Hart Mt. Antelope Refuge Headquarters is 51 miles from the road junction. Take time to visit the headquarters, which has a small museum and informative literature related to this incredible landscape and its wildlife. There is also a rustic hot spring south of the headquarters which can be refreshing after the long drive through the desert, though one can't float and take in the view, since the pools are walled (less for modesty's sake than to thwart the wind).

Head down the west slope of Hart Mt. for a stunning vista of Warner Valley.

The first lake that comes into view is Big Upper Campbell, which has been known to cover 4 square miles. Its depth ranges from 10 ft. to less than 4 ft. All the Warner Lakes have been dry at one time or another. During high water their populations intermingle. The lakes were originally stocked in 1971-72 and have been self-sustaining since that time. Five years of good water lead to outstanding crappie catches in 1987, especially in Lower and Upper Campbell, with fish 16-18 inches and up to 2 1/2 pounds taken.

During the drought of 1988-92, all the lakes went dry (north to south), but many of the fish survived in a 20 mile slough. In '93 these washed back into the basin, from which point nature will take its course.

The lakes are quite alkaline, and aquatic weed growth is heavy in mid-summer. Most angling takes place from the roadside. Frequent high winds across the lakes discourage boating, but fishing is quite good from the roads. This is a wonderful area for aquatic bird watching. See also Hart Lake, Crump Lake.

WEST SUNSTONE RESERVOIR A small sometime desert reservoir 2 miles east of Sherlock Gulch Reservoir. For directions see Sherlock Gulch Reservoir. The reservoir covers 8 acres when full, but in recent years it has failed to hold water. If it refills and stabilizes, it will be re-stocked with rainbow trout. In the past, the catch generally ran from 8-16 inches. Turbid water made bait the preferred method.

WHITEHORSE CREEK A Lahontan trout stream. Closed to all fishing.

WILLIAMSON RIVER (Lower) A long, meandering river, major tributary of Upper Klamath Lake, with a national reputation for fine fly water and large rainbow. It was one of the first rivers in Oregon to be selected for wild trout management. The Williamson wanders over 70 miles from the Yamsay Mt. area of Winema National Forest, flowing west through Klamath Marsh, then south into Upper Klamath Lake, entering from the NE. Its headwaters are in National Forest, but after only 1/4 mile it enters private ranchland. Throughout the river, access is limited by extensive private landholdings.

Above Klamath Marsh the Williamson offers spring-fed water, native rainbow, and brook trout 8-15 inches. More than half the property through which it flows is privately owned and closed to public access. The other half is Winema National Forest Land, and accessible, but not obviously so.

The river below Kirk Canyon Falls provides exceptional angling for large native rainbow. Much of the credit for the preservation of this wonderful fishery must go to the efforts of a local fly-fishing club which countered a trend of declining fishing that occurred in the late 1950s and early '60s. Their efforts, and those of the Dept. of Fish and Wildlife, have preserved a true trophy trout fishery.

The Williamson's large rainbow grow to size in the incredibly productive waters of Klamath Lake, where 3-year-old fish normally reach 20 inches or better. The cycle of migration is poorly understood, but probably tied to both spawning and avoidance of warm lake temperatures in summer. Large fish are in the Williamson in good numbers from late June through fall. By late August many of these fish have moved into the upper stretches all the way up to the falls.

Eighteen-inch rainbows are ho-hum here, and fish that go well over 10 pounds have shocked many an angler. Available in smaller numbers are good size browns, particularly below the mouth of Spring Creek. The Williamson remains high through June, with big-fish fishing best in August and September. Fishing remains good for resident trout through October.

To reach the upper river from Chiloquin, follow the Sprague River Rd. (County Rd. 858) east to Braymill, then turn left on the Williamson River Rd. (County Rd. 600), which crosses the Williamson near the Yamsi Ranch. Head of the River Campground is just north of the crossing on Forest Rd. 4648. Within 1/4 mile of the head springs, the river enters the Yamsi Ranch and is accessible only to the ranch owners and invited or paying guests. Within that quarter mile, anglers will find brook trout, and there may be a few rainbow. The springs themselves are a fine sight, gushing out of a hillside. The pool downstream from the springs is on private property.

The river flows north 27 miles to the marsh, followed up to a mile distant by Forest Rd. 4648 through a mix of private and Winema forest land. Within the forest it is approached from the west by the occasional rough road. You'll need a close reading of the Winema Forest map and an adventurous spirit to make your way, but there's worthwhile fishing in this stretch for the hearty angler.

The reach below the marsh is 38 miles long and is quite different in character from the upper river, though similarly frustrating in terms of public access. Most of the lower river flows through private property, so check locally for permission to fish when property ownership is in doubt.

First good fishing below the marsh is below the falls near the end of Kirk Canyon. County roads follow both sides of the canyon, which is about 200 ft. deep but accessible. Look for pull-outs and the occasional campsite, indicating rough trails to the river. The best approach is from the vicinity of Wiliamson River Campground. To reach the campground from Hwy. 97 north of Chiloquin, turn right on Forest Rd. 9730. The road ends about one mile beyond the campground, and a trail follows the river upstream about a mile, past some nice long pools where large rainbow hold in late summer and fall.

A road forking right at the end of Forest Rd. 9730 follows the River's east bank downstream 1 1/2 miles through national forest. Canoes and drift boats can be launched here for a nice float through Collier Memorial State Park. The mouth of Spring Creek at Collier is a popular and productive spot. There are minor rapids below the park. Angling from a floating device is prohibited from Chiloquin upstream.

At Chiloquin, a community just off Hwy. 97, there is about 1/2 mile of public access to the NW bank. The river is wadeable, and boats can be launched for a drift down to the Hwy. 97 crossing. Just below Chiloquin, 11 miles above the mouth, the cooler spring fed waters of the upper river are joined by the warmer waters of the Sprague River at a point known as Blue Hole. This mixing generally results in water temperatures in the lower river that are ideal for trout. A boat can be put in at Blue Hole to float the river below the Sprague confluence. This is flat water, and a canoe is sufficient.

The next access downstream is at the Hwy. 97 crossing. There is a boatable rapids at the crossing. Most anglers take-out at The Rapids Cafe just above, or at Water Wheel RV park just below the rapids. There is a modest fee to use either pull-out. Anglers can also pay to fish the bank at Water Wheel.

The lowest public access to the river is at Williamson River Resort on Modoc Pt. Rd. The river is slack and lake-like at this point, but anglers launch to fish the slack water, or motor down to Upper Klamath. Fishing from a boat is permitted below Chiloquin, but not while the motor is running (in other words, no trolling).

All anglers must use barbless hooks throughout the river, and artificial flies and lures everywhere except the reach from Kirk Bridge upstream to Silver Lake Road at the head of Klamath Marsh. From Chiloquin Bridge up to Kirk Bridge, trout are catch and release from August 1 through October 31. In addition to trout, the Williamson hosts a population of Lost River suckers, locally called mullet, which are a protected species and must be released unharmed.

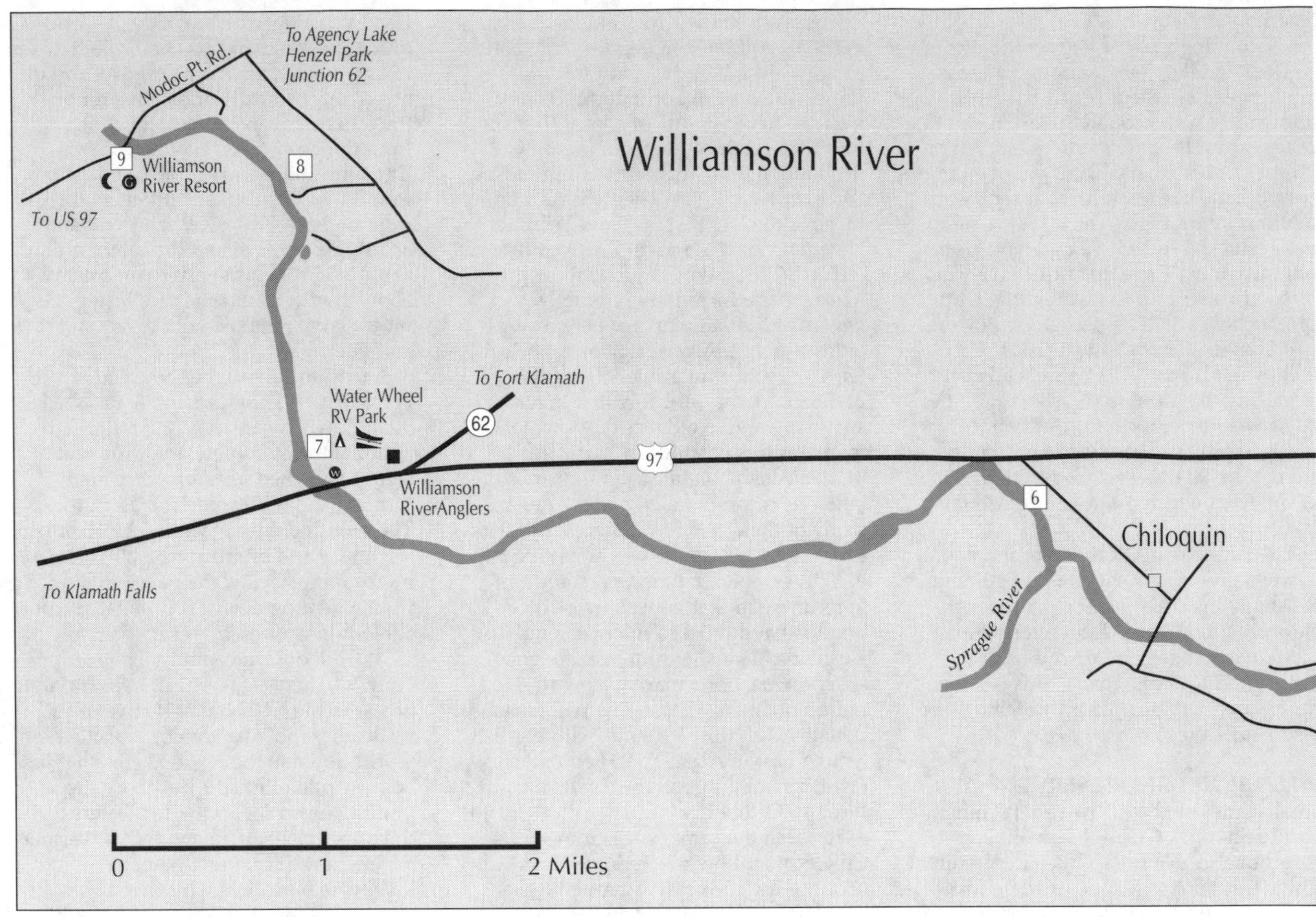

Large flies and streamers are most popular. Try black and white patterns such as the maribou leech and muddler, or a bucktail coachman. There are good mayfly and caddis hatches in June and July, and large October caddis are present in fall. Williamson River Anglers at the junction of hwys. 97 and 62 is a good source of local information and supplies.

In addition to a couple of RV parks off Hwy. 97, camping is available at Williamson River Campground east of 97, Collier State Park north of Chiloquin, and Kimball State Park at the source of Wood River 3 miles north of Ft. Klamath. There's a nice picnic area on the Wood River at Ft. Klamath.

Accommodations in the area offer pretty slim pickings—a couple of very expensive fishing resorts, and a couple of roadside motels. There is a good cafe in Fort Klamath, a truck stop near Chiloquin, and a cafe with great pies on Hwy. 97 near its crossing of the river. More plentiful supplies and accommodations are available in Klamath Falls, 20 miles or so to the south.

WILLOW CREEK (Malheur Co., East Face Steens) A remote Lahontan cutthroat stream. It is closed to all fishing to protect the Lahontan, which are listed as a threatened species. It's estimated that the Lahontan population throughout the basin dropped 90 percent during the 1987-92 drought.

WILLOW CREEK (Malheur Co., Trout Creek. Mts.) A remote Lahontan cutthroat stream which runs out into the desert at White Horse Ranch and dries up. It is closed to all fishing to protect the Lahontan, which are listed as a threatened species. It's estimated that the Lahontan population throughout the basin dropped 90 percent during the 1987-92 drought.

WILLOW CREEK (Malheur Co., Vale area) A long stream in extreme eastern Oregon, flowing into the lower Malheur River at the town of Vale. Only the upper reaches are good for trout angling. Below Malheur Reservoir the creek is heavily infested with rough fish.

The upper creek flows into Malheur Reservoir about 15 miles NW of Brogan and has a good population of native trout. It is followed by dirt roads above the reservoir and crossed by Hwy. 26 near Ironside. Secondary roads follow Willow Creek south from Ironside.

Willow is not stocked but has a large number of resident rainbow as well as trout that move up out of Malheur Reservoir. Most of the catch runs 9-10 inches, but some fish to 15 inches are landed. Anglers don't put much pressure on this creek. Bait is the most common method, but flies or small lures can also produce well. There is no camping along the stream.

WILLOW VALLEY RESERVOIR A 500-acre irrigation reservoir 50 miles east of Klamath Falls, featuring fine bass fishing. Located right above the California line, it's a long drive for most people in the state, but if you're a bass bug, you'll want to take a look at these good size largemouth. From Klamath Falls follow Rt. 140 to Dairy, then turn right on County Rd. 70 to Bonanza, continuing SE on the Langell Valley Rd. through Lorella and south toward California. As you near the border, watch for the sign to the reservoir, which is east of State Line Rd. The reservoir is on BLM land about 5 miles from the turn-off.

Willow Valley harbors good populations of bass, white crappie, a few brown bullhead and bluegill.

WOOD RIVER A spring-fed, crystal-clear, productive little stream in the Fort Klamath area north of Agency Lake,

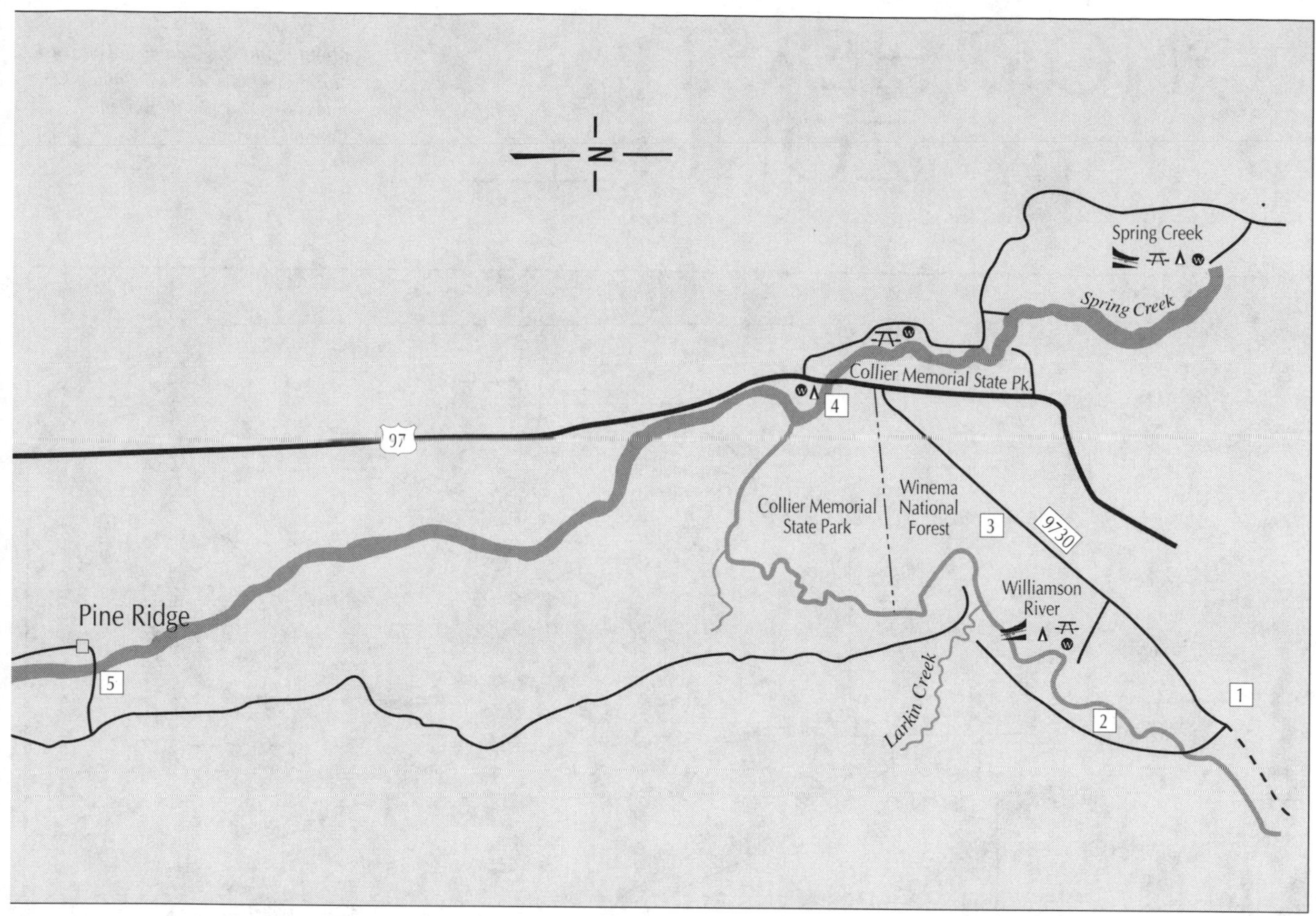

1 CLOSED ROAD - Park and hike road upstream about a mile; long pools offer good rainbow holding water in late summer and fall.

2 EAST BANK ACCESS - At dead end, access to 1.5 miles of east bank through State Park and Forest Service land.

3 PRIMITIVE FOREST ROADS - Off Forest Rd. 9730 reach river and can be used for launching drift boats and canoes; no angling is allowed from a floating device.

4 COLLIER STATE PARK - Bank access to west side only; river here is slow flowing and deep with minor rapid below park; mouth of Spring Creek is a popular spot.

5 PINE RIDGE - Private (expensive) fee-pay access to excellent water; old mill site provides good holes & cover.; inquire at Williamson River Anglers at Hwy. 97 rapids.

6 CHIILOQUIN - Access to .5 miles of NW bank; wadeable, but beware of holes; wading staff recommended; boat slide; drift to rapids at Hwy. 97 crossing about 4 miles; novice drift boat water; canoes ok, but skill required.

7 WATER WHEEL- Commercial RV park; modest fee to launch or take-out; shuttle service available at Williamson River Anglers on west bank; popular float tube drift from here to beginning of slack water.

8 SLACK WATER - Beginning of slack water.

9 WILLIAMSON RIVER RESORT- modest fee to launch; fish slack water; run 5 miles to Upper Klamath Lake.

about 35 miles from Klamath Falls. Hwy. 62 crosses the river at Ft. Klamath. Much of the lower stream flows through grazing land, so ask permission to fish.

This is a delightful spring creek, generally under 30 feet wide and not too deep. It runs through lush meadowland and has undercut banks, log jams, and occasional deep pools. Perfect fly water. No longer stocked, it has a fair population of wild rainbow that reach 4-5 pounds, as well as some large browns of similar size. There are also some brook trout. The stream flow is consistent throughout the year.

Good boating water is available below Kimball State Park. Boats can be launched and taken out at the Ft. Klamath Picnic Area, Loosley Rd. crossing, and Weed Rd. crossing. The river is best suited to canoe, raft, or a small driftboat. The float from Kimball to the Forest Service picnic area near Ft. Klamath, or to Hwy. 62 makes a pleasant day's drift. Anglers also put in at Weed Rd. and drift to Petric Park.

Jackson F. Kimball State Park is located at the source spring of the river above the intersection of highways 232 and 62. It has a dirt put-in suitable for raft or canoe. Boats must be hand carried to the water's edge. There is a small tent campground at Kimball. Ft. Klamath Picnic Area has a dock that is wheelchair accessible. Mosquitoes can be thick in summer.

YELLOWJACKET LAKE A 35-acre impoundment on upper Yellowjacket Creek in Malheur National Forest south of the Blue Mountains, about 40 miles NW of Burns. To get there, turn west off Hwy. 20 just south of the Hines Mill (south of Burns), and follow Forest Rd. 47, watching for a road sign. The lake covers about 35 acres and supports good size rainbow. It's stocked with rainbow each year. Most anglers fish from shore, but small boats can be used. There is an improved campground at the lake.

NORTHEAST ZONE

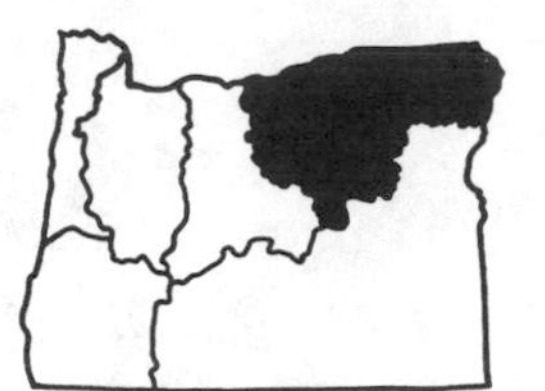

The Northeast Zone is all waters draining into the Columbia River east of the Deschutes River, including the Snake River system up to Hells Canyon Dam.

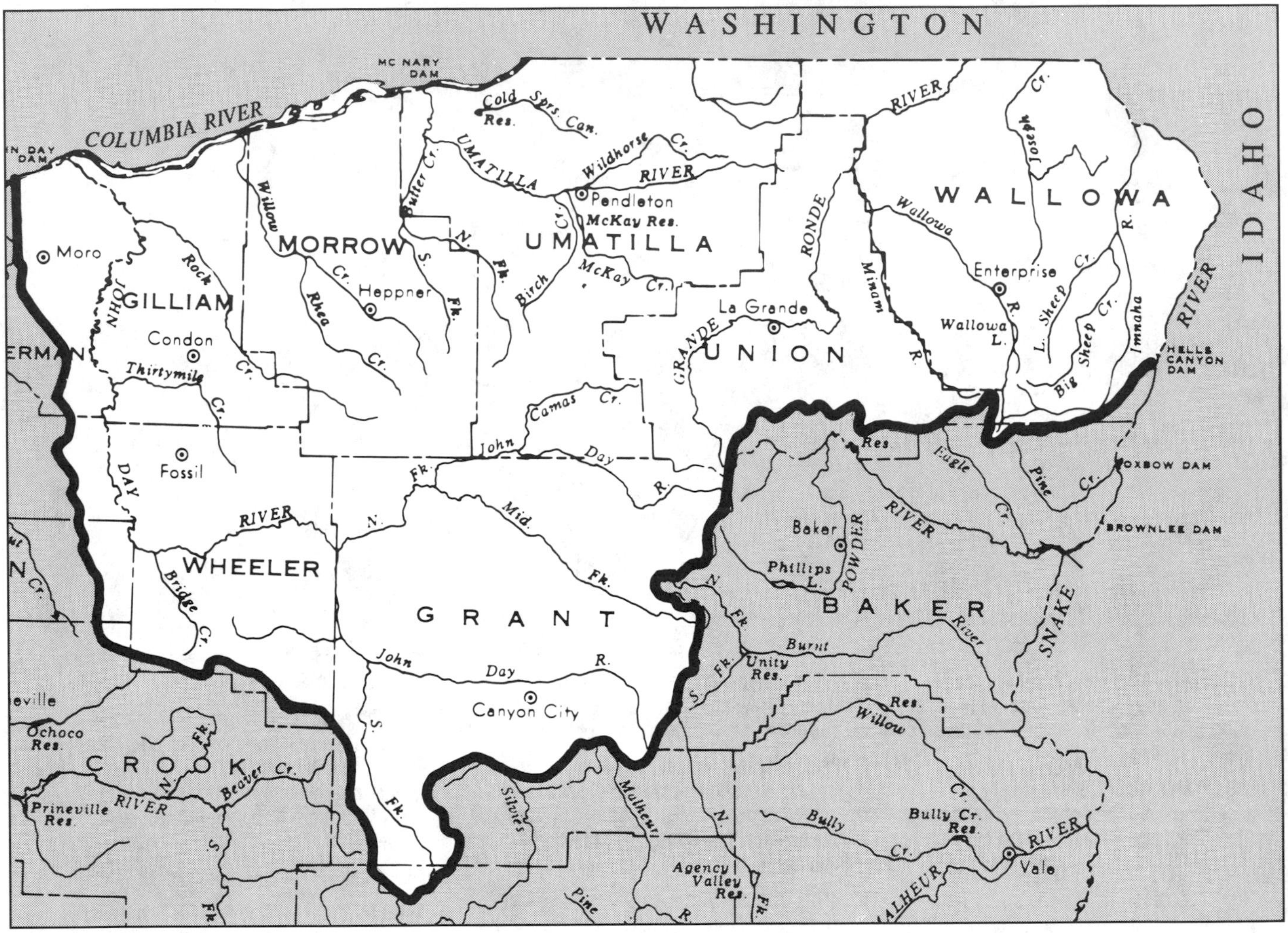

To most Oregon anglers, the Northeast Zone is defined as "far away." It is nearly 200 miles from Portland to Pendleton, another 44 miles to LaGrande, and miles more by secondary roads around the great and scattered uprisings of Wallowa and Blue mountains to reach the premiere fisheries of this region. Yet anglers come, attracted by the very fact of distance from home, work, and concentrations of other anglers.

They come to hike and fish the nearly 50 trout lakes of the Eagle Cap Wilderness and to enjoy the grandeur of Wallowa Lake, with its imposing glacial moraine and backdrop of granite peaks. They come for the thrill of rafting and fishing remote stretches of wild and scenic John Day, Grand Ronde, and Snake rivers, and for the pleasure of wading the lovely Wenaha, Wallowa and Imnaha rivers in autumn.

The Northeast Zone also offers opportunities to fish for summer steelhead in the Grand Ronde, Imnaha, John Day, Snake, Wallowa, and Umatilla rivers. Smallmouth bass fishing is excellent in portions of the Snake and Grand Ronde, in the big Columbia River reservoirs (Lake Umatilla and Lake Wallula), and in Cold Springs Reservoir. Lake Umatilla also offers a walleye fishery of growing national prominence.

The Northeast Zone includes the entire Umatilla National Forest, and portions of the Wallowa-Whitman, Ochoco and Malheur forests. It encompasses five wilderness areas: Bridge Creek, Eagle Cap, Hells Canyon, Strawberry Mt., and Wenaha-Tucanon.

I-84 cuts diagonally across the zone (between Wallowa and Blue mountain ranges), along which are located the major communities of Pendleton, LaGrande, and Baker. Paved secondary roads lead to the small communities that serve as gateways to the major fisheries. Most other roads in the zone are unpaved.

Well-maintained trails access most back-country lakes and streams. Trails in the Wallowas are noted for their steepness. Pack trains are popular and are available through guide services in Joseph, Enterprise, and LaGrande.

Campgrounds are plentiful in the national forests. Wallowa Lake State Park offers a full-service camping facilty with many amenities. There are motels in all the major communities, with visitor conveniences especially concentrated in the vicinity of Wallowa Lake east of Joseph.

Fishable Lakes of Eagle Cap Wilderness

B= brook trout, R= rainbow, M= Mackinaw, G= rumors of golden trout

Aneroid Lake R,B
Bear Lake (Eagle) B
Bear Lake (Bear Cr.) B
Billy Jones Lake R
Blue Lake B
Catched Two Lake B
Cheval Lake B
Chimney Lake B
Crater Lake B
Crescent Lake B
Culver Lake B
Diamond Lake B
Douglas Lake B
Eagle Lake B
Echo Lake (Eagle Cr.) B
Echo Lake (Hurricane Cr.)
Frances Lake R,B,C
Frazier Lake B
Glacier Lake R,B
Green Lake B
Hazel Lake B
Heart Lake R
Hidden Lake B
Hobo Lake R,G
Horseshoe Lake B
Ice Lake B
John Henry Lake B
Lee Lake B
Legore Lake B
Lily Lake B
Long Lake R,B
Lookingglass Lake B,M
Maxwell Lake B
Minam Lake B
Mirror Lake R,B
Moccasin Lake B
Pine Lakes B
Pocket Lake R
Prospect Lake R
Razz Lake B,G
Roger Lake B
Steamboat Lake B
Swamp Lake B,G
Tombstone Lake B
TraverseLake B
Unit Lake R,B
Wild Sheep Lake B
Wood Lake B,G

ANEROID LAKE Often one of the more crowded lakes in Eagle Cap Wilderness. Aneroid is cradled among high peaks at 7,520 ft., six miles by good trail from the southern end of Wallowa Lake. Elevation gain is 2,320 ft. Trail 1804 heads south from Wallowa Lake State Park. Snow may block access until July. It has a privately owned camp with cabins on it shores.

Covering 39 acres, the lake supports populations of brook and rainbow trout to 14 in., averaging 10 in. Fly-fishing is good in August and September. There are good campsites at the lake. Camp well back from the water to preserve fragile vegetation, and use no-trace camping methods.

BARTH QUARRY POND A lightly fished half-acre pond, but worth a visit. Take Exit 193 off I-84. Head north 50 yards, turn east onto Whitmore Rd. 1.6 miles, then north on Nolan Market Rd. 0.3 mile. Park on the shoulder of the gravel road.

The pond supports crappie and largemouth bass to 3 pounds. L-shaped, the pond abuts a rock cliff on one edge and is brushy on another, but the brush is not impassable. A float tube would be very helpful. Best fishing is up against the brush and just off the rock cliff.

BATES POND An 8-acre former mill pond about 30 miles NE of John Day, just west of Bates. It is privately owned and its spillway and dam have been declared unsafe. It is closed to public use.

BIBBY RESERVOIR A 16 acre impoundment 5 miles west of Kent on Buckhollow Creek. It contains largemouth bass.

BIG SHEEP CREEK A tributary of the Imnaha River, lightly fished and supporting excellent populations of wild rainbow and bull trout. All bull trout must be released unharmed. The creek flows 25 miles to its confluence at the town of Imnaha, 32 miles east of Enterprise or Joseph on Hwy. 82. A primitive road follows the lower 12 miles, but all but the first 1.5 miles is private and closed to public use. Obtain permission from the owner before continuing. There is a 2 mile trail at road's end. To reach the headwaters from the west you'll need a map. Wallowa-Whitman National Forest map, north half, shows the network of gravel and dirt tracks that take off from Little Sheep Rd. east of Joseph.

Trout average 9-12 inches. Bait and flies are both productive, with angling best from August until October. There are no campgrounds in the vicinity.

BILLY JONES LAKE A 6-acre hike-in lake above the tree-line near the top of Hurricane Divide in Wallowa-Whitman National Forest. Anglers will find small rainbow and cutthroat. From Joseph, take the Hurricane Creek Rd. south to Hurricane Creek Campground. Follow Hurricane Creek Trail 1807 south about 7 miles to Trail 1824, a steep 3-mile switchback to Echo Lake. Billy Jones can be reached by hiking south up-ridge one mile from Echo Lake. There is no trail, and snow may block access until July. You'll need good knees if you're hiking back down with a loaded pack.

The lake supported a population of fine rainbow to 14 inches until someone took it upon themselves to introduce cutthroat. The cutthroat are thriving, and the rainbow are decreasing in number and size. Anglers can anticipate good cutthroat fishing until overpopulation and stunting kick in.

Worms or eggs will work well in summer, with flies best in September. Try black ant, red ant, mosquito, and similar patterns. Angling season is determined by snowpack. The trail is generally open July through September.

BIRCH CREEK A tributary of the lower Umatilla River which joins the river at Pendleton. About 30 miles long, it heads in the Pine Grove area south of Pilot Rock. It is followed closely by Hwy. 395 and by secondary roads from Pendleton to Pilot Rock. Most access is through private property. Ask permission to fish. South of Pilot Rock the creek is followed by paved and gravel roads up both the east and west forks. Fishing for wild rainbow is fair to good in early season. There are no campgrounds in the area. The creek has steelhead runs but is closed to steelhead and salmon angling.

BLUE LAKE (Wallowa Co.) A deep 30-acre hike-in brook trout lake, headwaters of the Minam River, in Wallowa-Whitman National Forest. From the community of Lostine east of Enterprise, follow the Lostine River Rd. to the end. The trail to Blue heads south from Two Pan Campground. Follow the Lostine River

Trail 1670 about 5.7 miles to Minam Lake. Blue Lake is 0.9 mile south of Minam's southern tip. Take the right fork at the trail junction. Snow may block access until July.

Blue Lake derives its rich color from its 62 ft. depth. It supports a large population of fair size brook trout, which take flies and bait. Trout season is determined by snowpack. August and September are generally the best angling months.

BOARDMAN POND No.2 A 1/4 acre pond on Umatilla National Wildlife Refuge south of I-84. Turn right at the Boardman Exit. When the road deadends, work your way over to the pond. It has excellent bluegill, and reportedly contains crappie and walleye. Pond No.1 is closed.

BRIDGE CREEK A scenic stream both near its source and confluence, tributary of the John Day, offering fair trout angling. It flows through a variety of interesting eastern Oregon terrain, including a forest wilderness (Bridge Creek Wilderness, created in 1984), and the Painted Hills of the John Day Formation, a geologic study area.

Bridge Creek originates in springs near Mt. Pisgah in the Ochoco Mountains just south of Mitchell. Mitchell is on Hwy. 26 48 miles NE of Prineville. There is an undeveloped campground (Carroll Camp, Ochoco National Forest) at the head of the creek near Pisgah Springs. The main attraction of the wilderness is North Point, a 600 ft. cliff overlooking central Oregon and the Cascade peaks. The wilderness itself, through which Bridge Creek flows 4 miles, is a mix of fir, larch, lodgepole, and ponderosa pine, with clearings of sagebrush, grass, and mountain mahogany typical of Oregon's high desert plateau.

To reach Pisgah Springs from Mitchell, follow County Rd. 8 south from Mitchell. It becomes Forest Rd. 22. At the first crossroads, turn right onto Forest Rd. 2630 (Scotts Campground and Allen Cr. Reservoir are to the left). At the next crossroads, the left fork climbs Mt. Pisgah. Follow the right fork, and turn right again onto Forest Rd. 430, which leads to the springs.

To access the Painted Hills reach of Bridge Creek, from hwy. 26 about 4 miles west of Mitchell, turn north onto Bridge Creek Rd., which follows the creek through the Painted Hills toward its confluence with the John Day near Burnt Ranch. The Painted Hills are handsome red and yellow layered volcanic formations that contain a wealth of fossils and are widely studied for the geologic story they tell—of volcanic eruptions, oceanic inundation, and climatic changes in this area over the past 75 million years.

Bridge Creek provides fair trout angling in May and June after the spring run-off. Other than Carroll Camp in the headwaters, there is no camping streamside. There is a State Picnic Area on Bridge Creek Rd. about 10 miles NW of Mitchell at the beginning of the Painted Hills, a very pretty spot. This reach of the Creek has been treated to intensive habitat improvement projects. In-stream structure has been added, and riparian vegetation is on the rebound. Better trout fishing should follow.

BULL PRAIRIE RESERVOIR Good trout water within easy reach, offering year-round angling. It's located about 35 miles south of Heppner, about 15 miles north of Spray, in the Umatilla National Forest. From Heppner, drive south on Hwy. 207 to Forest Rd. 2039, which leads 2 1/2 miles east to the reservoir.

The 27-acre reservoir was built cooperatively by the Forest Service and ODF&W in 1961. Fishing has been good for rainbow and brook trout 8-13 inches. Trout to 16 inches are occasionally caught.

There is a campground with boat ramp on the lake. Motors are prohibited. Ice fishing is popular, but snow depth can make it a snowmobile or ski trek to get in. Check with ODF&W in John Day for an update on the ice and the snowpack. Remember that holes cut in the ice must be 12 inches or smaller in diameter by regulation. Recommended for small fry.

BUTTE CREEK (Wheeler Co.) A tributary of the lower John Day River, entering the river near the county line between Gilliam and Wheeler counties. The creek, 27 miles long, heads SE of Fossil at Butte Creek Summit on Hwy. 19. The upper waters of the creek are crossed and followed by Hwy. 218 in the vicinity of Fossil. The lower creek is approached by a private gravel road leading NW from Fossil. Get permission to use this road. The road roughens after about 3 miles. After another 2 or 3 miles it can hardly be called a road.

Irrigation withdrawals from the creek lower it considerably in summer. In early spring it's too high for good fishing due to run-off. But in late spring and early summer Butte offers good angling for wild rainbow. Bait-fishing with worms, eggs or grasshoppers is the most common method. There are several state picnic areas on Hwy. 19 north and south of Fossil, but no campgrounds.

CANYON CREEK (Grant Co.) A popular 27-mile long trout stream, tributary to the upper John Day River, which joins the river at the city of John Day. The creek is closely followed by roads throughout most of its length. Hwy. 395 follows it south from the town of John Day about 11 miles. Forest Rd. 15 continues along the creek for another 8 miles, and Forest Rd. 1520 picks up the final 3 miles to Canyon Meadows Reservoir. The few miles of stream above the reservoir are followed by a logging road on the slope to the north.

The reach from Canyon City to the intersection of Hwy. 395 and Forest Rd. 15 is stocked with legal rainbow in late May. There's good angling for wild trout in the headwaters above the reservoir. Bait fishing is best until water drops in late spring.

Starr Campground is on Hwy. 395, 3 miles south of its intersection with Forest Rd. 15. Wickiup Campground is on Forest Rd. 15 about 8 miles upstream from the highway intersection, and there is a campground at Canyon Meadows Reservoir.

CANYON CREEK MEADOWS RESERVOIR A 25-acre impoundment of upper Canyon Creek in Malheur National Forest. For directions, see Canyon Creek. The reservoir is stocked with rainbow and has wild brook trout and cutthroat. Angling is good in spring and late fall. The dam leaks, and the pool drops to low levels during July, August, and September.

All fish run to good size, and winter fishing through the ice can be very good when the snowpack isn't too heavy. The canyon can really pile on the snow. There is a campground with tent sites, drinking water, and a boat ramp.

CARPENTER POND A private, one-acre pond near John Day, closed to public access.

CARTER SLOUGH A 2-acre pond NW of Cove, offering mediocre fishing for largemouth bass, crappie, bluegill, and brown bullhead.

CATCHED TWO LAKE A 14-acre lake in Eagle Cap Wilderness offering good angling for smaller brook trout. To reach it, follow Trail 1670 about one mile from Two Pan Campground on the Lostine. At about one mile, Trail 1679 forks to the right and leads to Catched Two in about a mile.

The lake is in a very small basin with a little meadow. Tributary streams enter from the NW. There are no suitable campsites.

CATHERINE CREEK A good trout and steelhead stream, flowing into the upper Grande Ronde River north of Union. It heads on the SW slope of the Wallowa mountains and flows about 32 miles below its forks. It is closely followed by gravel roads SE from Union for about 10 miles. Forest Rd. 7785 follows the North

Fork, and Forest Rd. 600 follows the South Fork.

The creek is open to steelhead angling from the upper Hwy. 203 bridge (above Catherine Creek State Park) downstream. A lot of effort has gone into rebuilding the Catherine Creek run, with good results in 1990-91 and 1991-92. Subsequent runs have been increasingly depressed. The 1993-94 run hit an all time low.

Access to good steelhead water is limited. Anglers fish at Catherine Creek State Park, at the park in Union, along the highway, and at bridge crossings in the lower river. There's a popular hole near the Sewage Treatment facility downstream from Union, which allows public access to the creek. All non-finclipped steelhead must be released unharmed.

Catherine is lightly stocked with rainbow trout from the State Park downstream. About 5 miles upstream from the park, the stream flows through Wallowa-Whitman National Forest. This reach, including the forks, serves as spring chinook spawning grounds and supports small wild rainbow. Anglers are urged not to harass the chinook. The upper mainstem and forks are patrolled by State Police in summer, and if illegal salmon fishing becomes a problem, the upper creek will be closed to all angling.

There is a campground at Catherine Creek State Park 8 miles SE of Union, and another about 5 miles up the North Fork Rd.

CATHERINE CREEK SLOUGH A privately owned 10-acre fishery east of LaGrande, offering mediocre catches of largemouth bass, brown bullhead, crappie, yellow perch, bluegill, and smallmouth bass.

CHESNIMNUS CREEK A wild steelhead and rainbow trout stream, flowing 25 miles through a remote section of NE Wallowa-Whitman National Forest west of Joseph. It serves as an index stream for the Joseph Creek system and is closed to steelhead angling but open for rainbow. Coming in from the west, Chesnimnus joins Joseph Creek near its confluence with Crow Creek, about 15 miles above Joseph Creek Canyon.

From Enterprise, follow Hwy. 3 north 13 miles, then turn east on Forest Rd. 46, which follows Elk Cr. Turn right onto Forest Rd. 4625, to pick up Chesnimnus. About 3 miles past Vigne Campground, Forest Rd. 4690 (on the right) picks up the stream and follows it to its forks near Thomason Meadow Guard Station.

Best angling for rainbow is in early spring and late fall. Trout average 8-12 inches. Larger fish are available in the canyon in early summer. The canyon is not deep and is quite accessible.

CHEVAL LAKE A 10-acre brook trout lake in Eagle Cap Wilderness, accessed from the Lostine River Trail. To reach the trailhead, follow the Lostine River Rd. south from the community of Lostine on Hwy. 82. At road's end (about 18 miles), follow Lostine Trail 1670 for 2.8 miles, then take the Elkhorn Creek Trail 1656 five miles to its junction with Trail 1681. Follow this trail south and west to the lake, 2.3 miles. Elevation gain is 3,095 ft. over 10.1 miles. Snow may block access until July.

Trout run to 12 inches, though most are smaller. Angling is best in August and September. You'll want a fly rod or your spinner outfit here.

Trout grow to good size in Canyon Cr. Medows Reservoir.

CHIMNEY LAKE A very good 30-acre lake with a spectacular chimney formation at one end. The lake is cupped beneath Lookout Mountain in northern Eagle Cap Wilderness. From Hwy. 82, follow the Lostine River Rd. south about 16 miles to Lillyville Horse Camp. Follow Bowman Creek Trail 1651 west 3.6 miles, climbing a steep saddle, then follow Trail 1659 about one mile to Chimney Lake. Snow may block access until mid-July most years, and the first week in August occasionally.

Small brook trout are plentiful and bite eagerly at anything. There's an island in the middle of the lake that seems to attract the fish, but you'll need a float tube to reach it. There are good campsites here, and Chimney Lake makes a nice base camp for exploring other lakes in the area. See Hobo, Wood. Camp well back from fragile lakeside vegetation and follow no-trace camping guidelines.

COLD SPRINGS RESERVOIR An excellent warmwater fishery about 4 miles east of Hermiston, in Cold Springs Wildlife Refuge. It usually fluctuates from about 1,500 acres in spring to less than 500 at the end of irrigation season. Best access is from Hermiston. Head east from town, then north to the Refuge.

In 1994-95 the reservoir will be drained to allow work on its dam. It will be refilled from the Columbia River. The reservoir offers warmwater fish a rich environment with excellent submerged structure. Recovery of the fishery is anticipated by 1996.

At that time, the reservoir should once again offer excellent fishing for large white crappie, largemouth bass, and brown bullhead. Bluegill and smallmouth bass (which were illegally introduced in the years prior to drainage) should no longer be present.

Crappie at Cold Springs are typically caught on jigs by anglers wading deep and jigging in the bushes. Anglers in the know suspect that the next state record crappie may come out of Cold Springs. Bait-fishing is popular near the inlet. The reservoir has proven itself capable of growing 5-pound bass and bullhead to 18 inches. Fish the inlet canal for bullhead in summer.

A boat or float tube is necessary to get at the best fishing. The south and east banks are brushy and inaccessible at high pool. There are two boat ramps, on the south and southeast shores. At low water, only the south ramp is available. Boating is restricted to electric motors. There's no camping allowed at the reservoir, which is closed during waterfowl season. The entire reservoir is open to fishing from March 1 to September 30. From October 1 till the end of February, fishing is permitted only from the dam face and along the inlet canal. At that time of year, the catch is primarily bullheads.

Cold Springs Wildlife Refuge welcomes more than a dozen species of waterfowl and is home to 13 species of hawks and eagles as well as mule deer, coyote, bobcat, and ring-necked pheasant.

CONFORTH PONDS (Confederated Tribes of Umatilla) A series of ponds north and south of Hwy. 730 offering fishing for largemouth bass. Other warmwater species may have been illegally introduced by local anglers. Park on the road shoulder. A tribal permit is required. Call (503) 276-4104 for regulations and license information. Recommended for small fry.

CRAWFISH LAKE A 15-acre brook trout lake near the Grant-Baker County Line, a short hike from the road. It is reached from the Baker County side by a 20-mile drive west from the town of North Powder, which is on Hwy. 30 south of La Grande. Follow the signs for Anthony Lake Ski Area. From the ski area, continue west on Forest Rd. 73 about 3 miles to the trailhead, which is on the east side of the road. The lake is a mile hike in.

Brook trout are very plentiful, too plentiful. Take your limit. The fish are stunted from over-population. There is no minimum keeper size. Campgrounds are available near Anthony Lake.

CRESCENT LAKE (Wallowa Co.) A small but very productive lake in the basin SW of Wallowa Lake. From Joseph drive around Wallowa Lake to the end of Hwy. 82, one mile south beyond the lake. Hike up the Wallowa River on Trail 1820 for about 6 miles to the intersection of Trail 1821, which leads west and climbs into the lake basin. In 3 miles you'll reach Horseshoe Lake, and the climbing is over. Douglas Lake is 1 1/2 miles beyond, and Crescent is just north of it across the trail. Total hike is about 10 1/2 miles, elevation gain 2,600 ft.

The basin can also be reached from the upper Lostine River by a hike of about the same distance up the East Fork Lostine River. From the end of the Lostine Rd., hike upstream along the East Fork Trail 1662. It's 6 1/2 miles to the west end of the Lake Basin at Mirror Lake. Snow may block access until July.

Crescent covers 24 acres and is about 20 feet deep. It puts out good catches of brook trout and holds up well through the season, with fish 7-13 inches and some to 15 inches. Larger fish may be taken by float tube at dusk. Flies and lures are the preferred methods. There are several good campsites around the lake. Other lakes nearby provide good fishing as well.

CUTSFORTH PONDS Two small trout ponds in an attractive forest setting in Umatilla National Forest along Willow Creek SE of Heppner. The ponds are in Cutsforth Park about 20 miles south of the Heppner-Ukiah Road. They cover about 1/2 acre and are connected by a channel. The ponds are stocked with legal trout in late spring, and fishing holds up all season. There is a dock with wheelchair accessible ramp. Camping is permitted. Recommended for small fry.

DEER CREEK (Baker Co.) A small wild rainbow trout stream, tributary to the upper Powder River west of Baker. It flows about 8 miles from the north into Phillips Reservoir. Hwy. 7 crosses the stream at Mowich Park, a picnic area. Forest Rd. 6550, west of Mowich Park, leads to Deer Creek Campground, and forest rds. 6540 and 220 follow the creek to its head. Deer Creek offers good angling for wild rainbow 8-9 inches and up to 12 inches. All methods can be used here from late spring through summer.

DESOLATION CREEK A nice trout stream, tributary to the North Fork of the John Day, entering the river near Dale on Hwy. 395. This is about 15 miles south of Ukiah. The creek flows about 40 miles, counting the upper forks.

Forest Rd. 10 follows the creek from Dale upstream over 20 miles to the creek fork, then follows the North Fork to its headwaters, continuing several more miles to Olive Lake. From Dale, an unimproved road also follows the east bank of the lower creek closely for about 6 miles before joining Forest Rd. 10. The South Fork has no direct access. Forest Rd. 45 approaches the upper creek area from Susanville.

Desolation Creek has wild trout and is stocked each year. Most trout caught are 8-11 inches. The creek is fished fairly heavily in late spring and summer, and good catches are made using all methods. Heavy run-off slows the fishing early in the spring.

Tollbridge Campground is located near the mouth of Desolation Cr., and there are camping facilities at Olive Lake. A ranger station at Ukiah can provide additional information.

DIAMOND LAKE (Eagle Cap Wilderness) A remote brook trout lake just north of Tombstone Lake, near the southern border of Eagle Cap Wilderness. The lake is about 20 acres, and its outlet flows into Elk Creek, a small tributary of the upper Minam River. From any direction, it can only be reached by a considerable hike.

Best approach is by Trail 1944, the Middle Fork Trail, which can be reached from Forest Rd. 7787. From Hwy. 203 south of Union take Forest Rd. 77 east about 3 miles to the Catherine Creek turn-off. Follow Forest Rd. 7785 about one mile up the creek to the Buck Creek Rd. (Forest Rd. 7787) and head up Buck Creek about 4 miles to the trailhead, which is on a hairpin turn. Hike north 1/2 mile on Trail 1944A to the main trail, then head east up-slope. The trail follows the middle fork to its head and crosses a saddle north of Burger Butte, about 4 miles from the trail junction. It's another 3 miles, downhill, to Diamond Lake, and Tombstone Lake is just .4 miles further along. Total elevation gain is about 1,500 ft.

At elevation 6,900 ft., Diamond Lake is 11 acres and has a maximum depth of 24 feet. Angling is usually good for brook trout to 12 inches. August and September are the best months. Flies and lures are equally effective. There's fishing in nearby Tombstone Lake as well. Snow may block access until July.

DODD POND A small privately owned pond east of Hermiston and McNary Dam. It is closed to public access.

DOLLARHIDE POND A one-acre pond at Mitchell, off Hwy. 26, between

You don't have to be a mountain goat to make it up to Eagle Lake.

Prineville and John Day. It is closed to public access.

DOUGLAS LAKE A 44-acre brook trout lake in the popular lake basin at the headwaters of the West Fork Wallowa River. Douglas is about half-way between Eagle Cap and Matterhorn mountains. From Joseph drive around Wallowa Lake to the end of Hwy. 82, one mile south beyond the lake. Hike up the Wallowa River on Trail 1820 for about 6 miles to the intersection of Trail 1821, which leads west and climbs into the lake basin. In 3 miles you'll reach Horseshoe Lake, and the climbing is over. Douglas Lake is 1 1/2 miles beyond, and Crescent is just north of it. Total hike is about 10 1/2 miles, and the elevation gain is 2,600 ft. Snow may block access until July. These trails get chewed up by the pack horses, so be prepared for a bit of mud.

The basin can also be reached by a hike of about the same distance up the East Lostine River. From the end of the Lostine Rd., 18 miles south of the town of Lostine, hike upstream along the East Fork on Trail 1662 to the west end of the basin at Mirror Lake (6 1/2 miles). Horses and packers are available at Joseph. You'll want to make reservations for guided trips. Supplies and tackle are available in Enterprise and Joseph.

Fishing for brook trout can be very good in August and September. The lake covers about 44 acres and has a maximum depth of 80 ft. Trout run to 10 inches and are plentiful. Flies and lures are best. This is a good dry fly lake in late July. Other nearby lakes offer good angling. See Crescent, Moccasin, Mirror, Unit, Horseshoe.

DUCK LAKE A low elevation, hike-in trout lake, about 20 acres, above the Imnaha River in Hells Canyon National Recreation Area. It sees little angler pressure.

From Joseph, head east 8 miles on the road to Imnaha, then go south about 30 miles on the graded gravel road that becomes Forest Rd. 39. Turn west on (dirt) Forest Rd. 3960 across from Ollokot Campground. Trail 1875 heads south from Indian Crossing Horse Camp, about 8 miles from Ollokot. The trail passes the lake and continues to the southern wilderness trailhead on Forest Rd. 66. To access the lake from the Baker area to the south, follow Hwy. 86 east to Forest Rd. 39. Turn west on Forest Rd. 66 to its junction with Forest Rd. 3960. The trail heads north from the junction. It's a 2-mile hike from either trailhead.

Duck Lake is stocked every other year with rainbow trout which grow to an average 10 inches and may reach 13 inches. The lake is open all year and, at elevation 5,366 ft. (lowest of all natural lakes in Wallowa-Whitman National Forest) Duck Lake provides an early opportunity for hike-in angling.

The Grand Ronde is a medium-size river, even after it is augmented by the Wenaha at Troy.

EAGLE LAKE A deep lake at the head of Eagle Creek in the Eagle Cap Wilderness of Wallowa-Whitman National Forest, featuring Mackinaw as well as rainbow trout. It's a 7-mile hike up the main Eagle Creek Trail 1922 from the end of the Eagle Creek Rd., with an elevation gain of 2,609 ft. See Eagle Creek for directions to the trailhead.

The rainbow reach 12 inches and respond well to flies. The lake trout go to 16 inches and are best taken with deep lures or spinner and bait. Eagle Lake is 90 ft. deep and covers 37 acres. At elevation 7,400 ft., the lake is generally only accessible from July through September.

ECHO LAKE (Eagle Cap Wilderness) A small brook trout lake high in the Hurricane Creek watershed of Eagle Cap Wilderness, just a ridge to the east of the upper Lostine River. From Joseph, take the Hurricane Creek Rd. south to Hurricane Creek Campground. Follow Hurricane Creek Trail 1807 south about 7 miles to Trail 7775, a steep 3-mile switchback to Echo Lake. Snow may block access until July.

Echo is at elevation 8,320 ft. near the top of Hurricane Divide. It is the source of Granite Creek. Lightly fished, its brook trout have overpopulated the lake and are under 8 inches. Keep your limit.

The lake is only 7 acres, but almost 50 feet deep. Fishing is fair from late July through September. Bait, lures, or flies can all be effective. Billy Jones Lake, a 1/2 mile bushwhack south-southeast, also contains trout. Keep an eye out for bighorn sheep and mountain goats.

FISH LAKE (Baker Co.) An 86-acre drive-in brook trout and rainbow lake just south of Eagle Cap Wilderness in the Wallowa-Whitman National Forest. From Halfway on Hwy. 86, drive due north on Forest Rd. 66 a long 36 miles to the lake. Early in the summer, call the Forest Service at Pine Creek Ranger Station SE of Halfway to check on the road. Fish Lake is at elevation 6,640 ft. and is usually accessible only from July through September.

The lake has a maximum depth of 50 ft. Trout are plentiful here, but on the small side. Brook trout outnumber rainbow 2 to 1, and you'll be lucky to find many over 12 inches. Rainbow fingerlings are stocked every other year, and brook trout reproduce naturally. There's a guard station at the lake and a good campground with boat ramp. Several interesting trails head at the campground, including those heading east into the Hell's Canyon Recreation Area.

FRANCES LAKE (Wallowa Co.) One of the more productive lakes in the Eagle Cap Wilderness. Large and scenic, it is cupped on a bench of the Hurricane Divide east of the Lostine River. The old trail to Francis reached the lake in just 4 miles, with an elevation gain of about 1,000 ft. per mile. A new trail is 9 miles with lots of switchbacks. The trailhead is 3 miles south of Lostine Guard Station.

Richer than most lakes at this elevation, Frances covers 30 acres and is 21 ft. deep. It supports brook trout, which average 10-12 inches and occasionally reach 15 inches, and west slope cutthroat. The cutthroat are stocked every three years, since they won't reproduce without an inlet stream. All methods will take fish. Fly-fishing is good in September.

Frances is very scenic, with opportunities to see bighorn sheep and mountain goats.

FRAZIER LAKE (Wallowa Co.) A fairly shallow lake in the headwaters of the West Fork Wallowa River, within Eagle Cap Wilderness. From Joseph drive around Wallowa Lake to the end of Hwy. 82, one mile south beyond the lake. Hike up the Wallowa River on Trail 1820 for about 10 miles to Frazier Lake. This is an easy trail with a total elevation gain of about 1,800 ft., much of it spread out along the first 8 miles. The last 2 miles are fairly steep. These trails get chewed up by pack horses, so be prepared for a bit of mud. Little Frazier Lake is above Frazier but holds no fish.

Frazier covers about 16 acres and offers good fishing for brook trout 7-10 inches and larger. Glacier and Prospect lakes to the west also offer good fishing. Horses and guides are available at Joseph.

GLACIER LAKE A scenic, deep lake high in Eagle Cap Wilderness at the head of the West Wallowa River. Glacier Lake is cradled in a cirque on the east slope of Eagle Cap, which towers above it.

From Joseph on Hwy. 82, take the road to the south end of Wallowa Lake, where Trail 1820 begins. It's a 12-mile hike up the West Wallowa River to the lake. You can also hike in from the north following the East Fork of the Lostine River. Horses and guides are available at Lostine and Joseph.

Glacier is at elevation 8,200 ft. in a beautiful alpine setting. The lake is crystal clear. Fishing for brook trout can be excellent in August and September. The trout run 7-15 inches, averaging 10 inches. All methods can be used effectively. Be prepared for sudden snow squalls in late September, though fishing can be best in September and early October. For other fishable lakes in the area, see Prospect, Frazier. Supplies and tackle are available in Enterprise and Joseph.

GRAND RONDE LAKE A heavily used trout lake in the Anthony Lakes area of the Elkhorn Mountains, within the southern Wallowa-Whitman National Forest. The lake outlet flows north into the Grand Ronde River. The spur road leading to Grand Ronde is on the right about 1/2 mile beyond the Anthony Lakes turn off.

This 10-acre lake has both rainbow and brook trout and is stocked with rainbow annually. Fishing is good almost anytime after the lake becomes accessible, usually in late June. Maximum depth is 20 ft. There is a campground on the lake and other good campgrounds at Anthony Lakes.

GRAND RONDE RIVER (Below La Grande) One of Oregon's "Wild and Scenic" rivers, flowing over 200 miles from the Blue Mountains SW of La Grande and running NE through Union and Wallowa counties, crossing into Washington and entering the Snake River. The lower 35 miles are in Washington.

The "Wild" section is between Rondowa and Wildcat Creek. Below Wildcat, the Oregon segment of the river is dedicated "Recreation," and offers both quality fishing and easy access.

Historically, the Grand Ronde hosted sizable runs of native salmon and steelhead, all of which were decimated by the usual combination of dams and agricultural and forestry practices. Efforts to restore these runs through hatchery plants, habitat restoration, and angling regulations have begun to show modest success, though the salmon run is still below harvestable level.

Returns of summer-run hatchery reared steelhead have been generally good since 1986, and the lower river is open for steelhead angling from the mouth to Beaver Creek above LaGrande. Grand Ronde steelhead enter the Columbia from July through mid-September, make their way up the Snake, and enter the Grand Ronde throughout the fall, winter, and (sometimes) even as late as spring. The 1991-92 season offered spectacular returns with an estimated 5,173 fish landed. The sport catch in 1992-93 was 1,287 and the downward trend continued in 1993-94 here as elsewhere in Oregon.

Immediately below La Grande, the Grand Ronde traces a meandering course through agricultural and marshlands. Hwy. 82 follows the river from La Grande to Elgin, and county roads follow at some distance from there to Palmer Junction.

From Palmer Junction to Wildcat Creek, the river flows through forested canyons that can only be accessed by riverboats. This stretch is suitable for both rafts and drift boats and is popular with whitewater enthusiasts. It is managed by the BLM, which requires floaters to use low-impact camping methods. These include packing out human waste (most folks bring a porta-potty) and discouraging open fires. Campfires are permitted in fire pans only, and campers are asked to pack out campfire ashes.

After its run through the canyon, the river emerges at Wildcat Creek and flows through a mix of State, BLM, private forest, and ranch land. Avoid posted property, and ask for permission to cross unposted private land to insure your welcome and protect future access.

At Wildcat Creek the river is met by the Wildcat Creek Rd. and by County Rd. 500 (Powwatka Road) from Wallowa . County Rd. 500 follows the river's north bank downstream to the community of Troy and into Washington. A gravel road out of Troy accesses the south bank downstream for about 3 miles.

It's about 9 river miles from Wildcat to Troy, another 6 to the State Line, and 10 more to the Hwy. 129 crossing in Washington where all roads leave the river. Many anglers carry both Oregon and Washington licenses so they can forget about boundaries and just follow the fish.

At Troy, the Grand Ronde is augmented by the Wenaha, but it is still just a medium-size river. Boats are discouraged in this reach during steelheading season, as they can hardly avoid disturbing water that is being fished by bank or wading anglers. Most anglers drive to a favorite reach, park at the road side, and walk down to the river. Look for car pullouts along the road.

Those who do wish to boat this stretch can put in at Wildcat or Mud Creek, and pull out 8 or 9 river miles later at Troy. The Troy boat access is a gravel bar on the south bank next to the school. The nearest official take-out below Troy is a long day's drift to the Hwy. 129 crossing in Washington.

Steelhead season throughout the river is currently September 1 to April 15, but the run usually holds off until October, with peak catches generally mid-October through November (or whenever rain and cold drive anglers from the stream). In very warm years, steelheading can be good throughout the winter. By March, water conditions for successful fishing have usually deteriorated due to spring run-off, though fish are generally present throughout the month.

Rainbow trout are plentiful throughout this portion of the river, occasionally exceeding 15 in., with the average catch 10-12 in. All trout are wild and must be released without removal from the water, though some steelhead smolts (adipose clipped) take up residence and may show up in catch.

Smallmouth bass are present in the vicinity of Troy from about mid-June through mid-September. Fish for them in slower water near the shorelines and in deeper, rocky holding water.

From Rondowa (the confluence of the Wallowa River) to the State Line, the Grand Ronde is regulated for fishing with barbless hooks only for all species. Only adipose clipped trout and steelhead may be taken. The wild steelhead population is quite small, but a good 40% of all resident trout are wild. Regulations require the release of all wild trout and steelhead without removing them from the water.

Panfish are present primarily in the river's valley reach, from La Grande to Elgin. Bass, crappie, catfish, perch, and bluegill are taken in good numbers in the stretch between Cove and Elgin.

Primitive campsites are available at Wildcat Creek and downstream from Troy on north and south banks. There is also a commercial RV camp at Troy.

GRAND RONDE RIVER (Above La Grande) Two distinctive river environments, the stretch below Starkey Creek, and that which flows through national forest above the Starkey confluence. The lower portion includes a flow along the edge of LaGrande, marking the city's northern boundary. Hwy. 244 follows the stream for 23 river miles west from La Grande. Paved Forest Rd. 51 continues upstream another 12 miles, and Forest Rd. 5125 continues upstream to the river's upper tributaries in the meadows.

The upper Grand Ronde originates in alpine meadows, but as it flows beyond the forest toward LaGrande, its streambed deteriorates, the legacy of years of logging in which the river was used as a giant flume. Today, in the stretch that parallels Hwy. 244, there is no natural structure to provide year-round habitat for trout, no pools where salmon and steelhead can escape the summer heat. In summer the water superheats, driving the fish upstream.

To see the river as nature intended, head for the mountains. Angling in the upper river is good in late spring, summer, and fall for wild rainbow. All wild trout must be released unharmed. Most fish run 8-12 inches, with a few larger. This reach of the water is lightly stocked below River Campground at river mile 191. There's lots of good fly water in this stretch.

There are three campgrounds on Forest Rd. 51 in the upper river. Camping facilities are also available at Hilgard State Park just west of LaGrande. Red Bridge State Park, on Hwy. 244 west of Hilgard is for day-use only.

GREEN LAKE (Wallowa Co.) A solitary brook trout lake high in the North Minam River drainage, within Eagle Cap Wilderness. Green Lake sits pretty much by itself, 2 miles south of (and about 1,800 feet above) the North Minam. There really is no easy way to get to the lake, although a good trail leads in.

The easiest hike is probably up the Minam River from Red's Horse Ranch, but you have to fly or pack into the ranch. Most backpackers approach from the lakes east of the river. The Bowman Trail 1651 leads west from the Lostine Rd. about 2 1/2 miles south of Lostine Guard Station. Take Trail 1651 past John Henry Lake and down into North Minam Meadows, then ascend the steep Green Lake Trail (1666) to the lake. The total hike is over 12 miles, with many steep, long pitches. Naturally, you won't suffer from a lot of company once you get there.

The lake is at elevation 7,000 ft. in a glacial cirque on the north side of Hazel Mt. It covers about 15 acres. There are rumors of abundant brook trout to 16 inches. Flies and lures can both be effective. August and September are the best times to be up here. If the walk sounds daunting, horses and guides are available at Lostine.

HAT ROCK POND A six-acre pond stocked with legal trout and containing largemouth and smallmouth bass. The pond is at Hat Rock State Park, which provides every facility a state park can offer. Free Fishing Day activities for area youngsters take place here. The park is 98 miles east of Umatilla on Hwy. 730. Recommended for small fry. Wheelchair accessible.

HOBO LAKE A small lake with rumors of golden trout, high on the east side of Lookout Mt., west of the Lostine River within Eagle Cap Wilderness. Head south 15 miles from Lostine on Hwy. 82 to the Bowman Creek Trail 1651, about 2.5 miles south of Lostine Guard Station. Climb east on this trail for 3.6 miles to the junction of Trail 1659, which you follow north 1.2 miles to the short spur trail

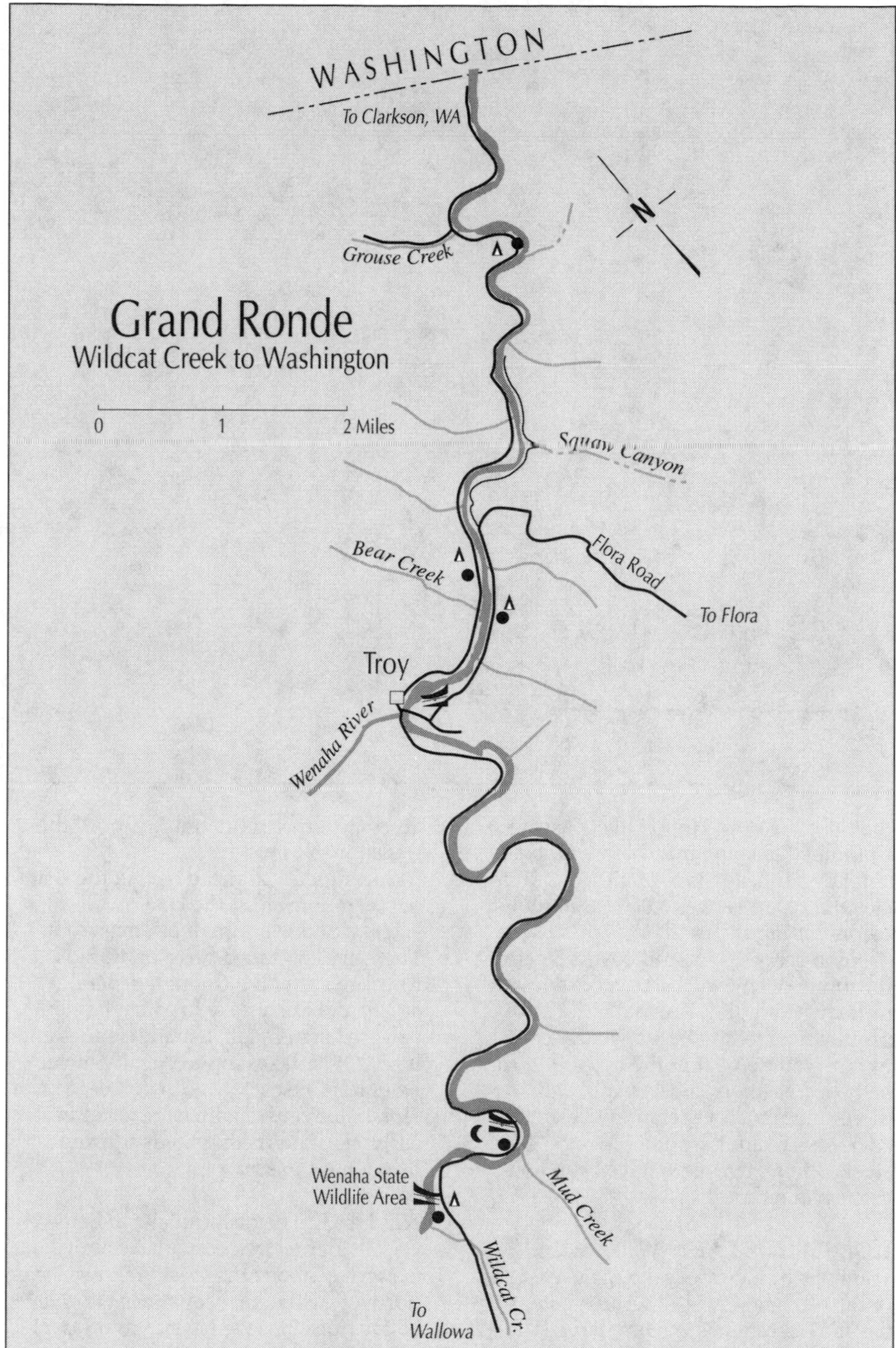

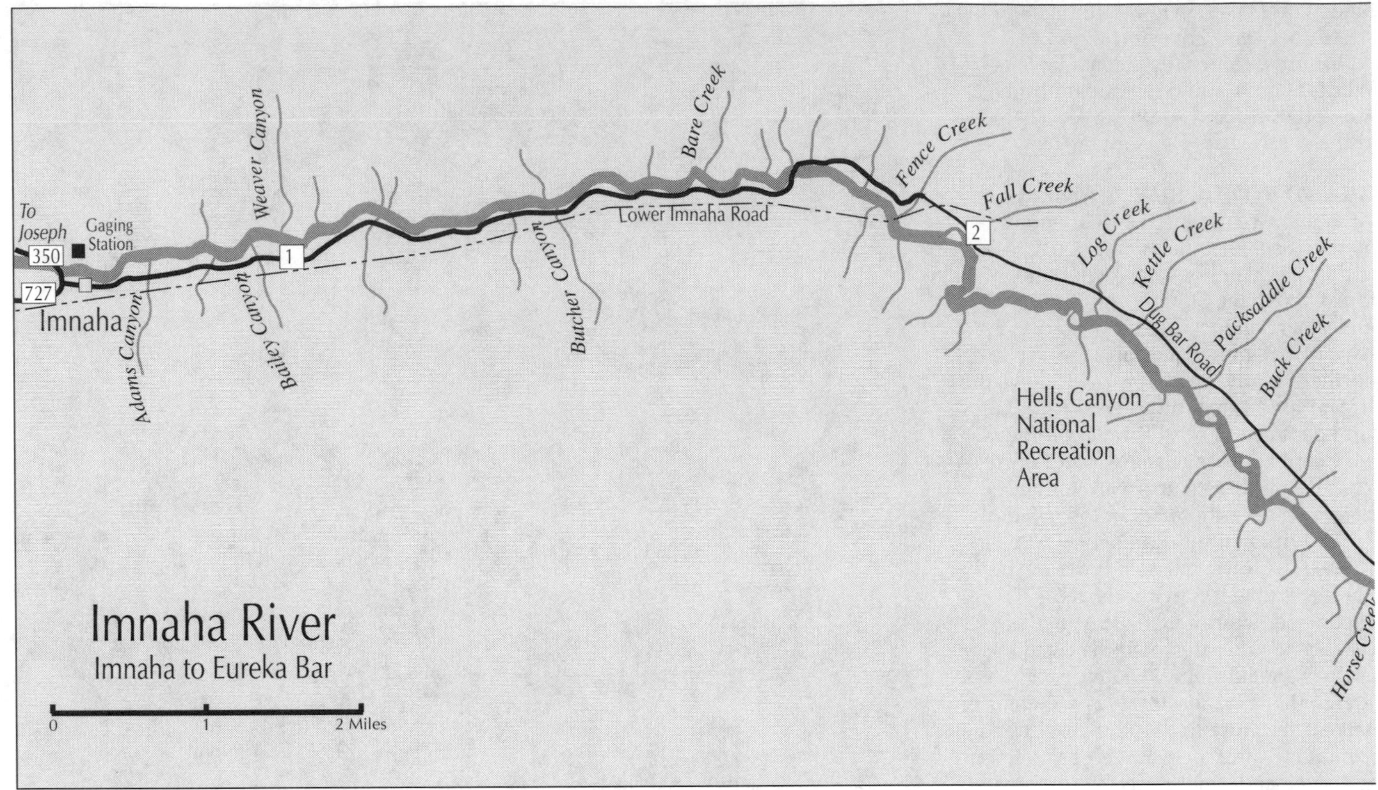

that leads west to Hobo Lake, passing Chimney Lake one mile before Hobo. Total trail mileage is 5.4 miles, and total elevation gain is over 3,000 ft., so fuel up before hitting the trail.

Hobo is at 8,320 ft and covers 8 acres. It is quite deep for its size, stocked with rainbow trout. Bait is usually the most productive method, but a wet fly or nymph can do well in the late fall. It can be fished easily from the bank, and there's not much vegetation to catch a back-cast. Golden trout were once stocked here, but there have been no catches in recent years.

HORSESHOE LAKE (Wallowa Co.) A gorgeous brook trout lake at the east end of the of Eagle Cap Wilderness lake basin. Horseshoe is the first large lake approached by the trail from the east. From Joseph, drive south around Wallowa Lake to the end of Hwy. 82, one mile south beyond the lake. Hike up the Wallowa River on Trail 1820 for about 6 miles to the intersection of Trail 1821, which leads west and climbs into the basin. In 3 miles you'll reach Horseshoe Lake, and the climbing is over. Douglas Lake is 1 1/2 miles beyond, and Crescent Lake is just to the north. The total hike is about 9 miles, with an elevation gain of 2,400 ft.

You can also approach from the north along the East Fork Lostine River, Trail 1662. It's 6 1/2 miles from the end of the Lostine River Rd. to the west end of the basin at Mirror Lake. Snow may block access to either route until July. All these trails can get muddy.

Surrounded by meadows, in the shadow of granite cliffs, the lake covers 40 acres with maximum depth over 70 ft. There are good reed beds. and Brook trout are abundant (though generally small) and fairly easy to catch. Larger fish are taken in fall, usually on flies and lures. Other lakes in the vicinity include Douglas, Crescent, Moccasin, Lee, Mirror. Horseshoe can usually be reached in early July, and fishing holds up well throughout the season.

ICE LAKE The deepest lake in Eagle Cap Wilderness. Spectacularly alpine, Ice is perched above the West Wallowa River north of a ridge that separates the river valley from the lake basin. From Joseph, drive around Wallowa Lake to the end of Hwy. 82, one mile south of the lake. Hike up the Wallowa River on Trail 1820 for 2.8 miles to the intersection of Trail 1808, which climbs west. Grit your teeth and switch back up-slope for 5.1 miles to the lake. Total elevation gain for this stretch is 2,300 ft., but the trail is well laid out.

Ice Lake is nestled on the east side of Matterhorn Mt. at elevation 7,900 ft. Its basin, possibly created by volcanic action, is over 190 feet deep, and its setting is breathtaking. Ice covers about 46 acres and has lots of fishable shoreline.

The lake is extremely cold but supports brook trout 7-11 inches. Bait is best in July, and lures and flies work best by September. Four tributaries enter from the west in a small meadow area, and another from the SE. There are a couple of primitive campsites. Camp well back from fragile lakeside vegetation and use no-trace camping methods. Packers and guides are available in Joseph.

IMNAHA RIVER A beautiful high gradient stream pouring out of the Wallowas, offering an enticing mix of cascades, riffles, glides, and short pools. Designated Wild and Scenic throughout most of his run, it is tributary to the Snake, hosting a good population of wild rainbow trout, a recently restored run of steelhead, and a small number of chinook. As with most waters in the northeast zone, fishing here is best in the fall.

The Imnaha flows 75 miles from its headwaters in Eagle Cap Wilderness to its confluence with the Snake River at Eureka Bar, about 22 miles north of the town of Imnaha. From Hwy. 82 at Joseph, it is 32 miles to the Imnaha by way of the paved Little Sheep Creek Rd. From there, a dirt road follows the river upstream for about 45 miles and downstream to within 5 miles of the Snake. A trail continues from Cow Creek Bridge to Eureka Bar.

Most access to the lower river is in private hands from the town of Imnaha to Fall Creek, though permission to approach the river may be given to courteous anglers who knock at the door. From Fall Creek to Horse Creek, Dug Bar Road follows the river a steep 1,000 ft. or more above the stream. At Horse Creek, the road returns to the river and follows it to the bridge.

There is excellent fishing throughout this stretch and along the trail. Trail 1713 winds through a narrow canyon in which observant hikers may spot big horn sheep and golden eagles. (Keep a weather eye out for poison oak and rattlesnakes as well.)

the 1987-1988 season. An estimated 1,500 fish have been caught since that time, with close to 600 fish taken in a single season (1991-92).

The river is currently open for steelhead up to Big Sheep Creek (at the town of Imnaha). Fish are hooked throughout this stretch in the spring, with most fall fishing in the lower 5 miles. Steelhead show up at the mouth in mid-September and hold there until the water cools, about mid-October. Best early fall fishing is often in the Snake itself just below the Imnaha confluence. Popular steelhead flies include the Silver Hilton, Black Wooly Bugger, Purple Peril, Freight Train, and Muddler Minnow.

1 **IMNAHA TO FENCE CREEK** - Private land; access with permission of landowner; most landowners live on premises.

2 **FENCE CREEK TO HORSE CREEK** - private land; road 1000 ft. above river; access with landowner permission

3 **HORSE CREEK TO COW CREEK** - unpaved road along river through public-private mix; USFS land well signed; good fishing in holes and pockets from late June; smallmouth plentiful July-Aug.

4 **COW CREEK TO EUREKA BAR** - Well maintained trail closely follows river 4 miles to Eureka Bar; moderate gradient. Watch for poison ivy.

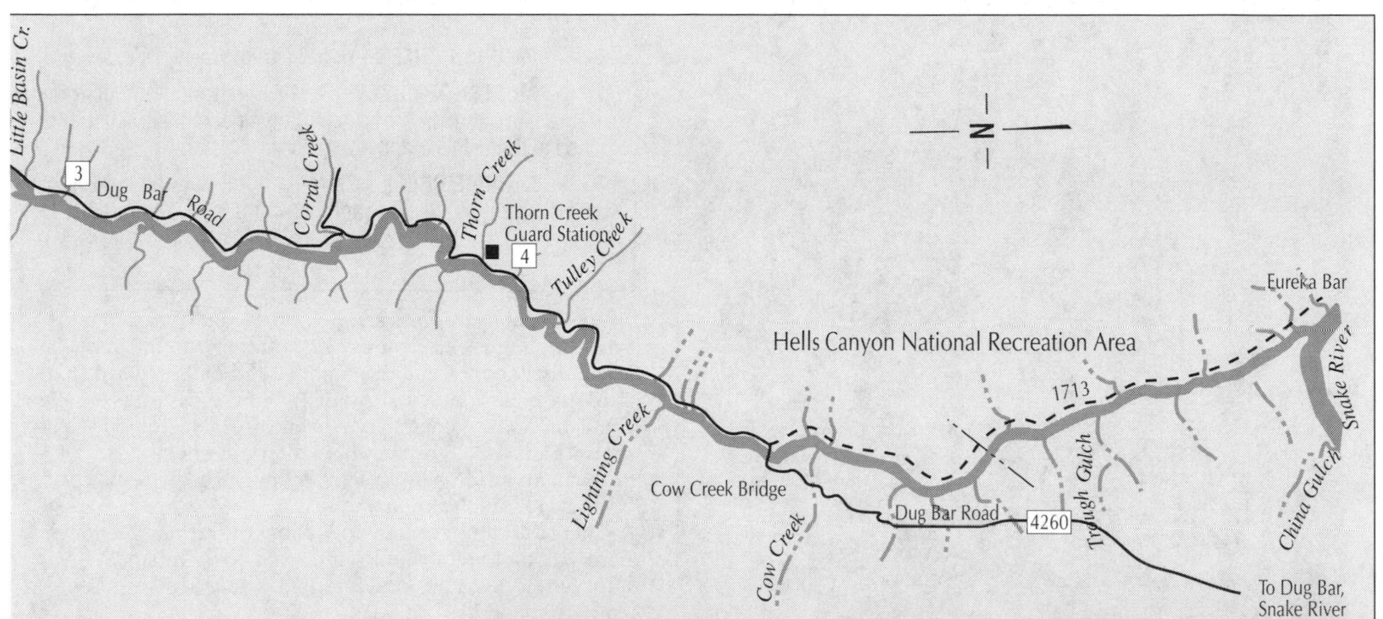

Above Big Sheep Creek the Imnaha is open for wild trout and plentiful whitefish of good size. The river flows through private land up to the Palette Ranch, where the US Forest Service owns a 5-mile easement. Watch for signs that say "Begin Public Fishing Access." There are pull-outs along the road. This stretch is deeper than most Imnaha reaches and is best fished from the bank with spinner and bait, or fly-fished with a nymph. Above Palette, public access continues along the Imnaha River Road up to Indian Crossing campground, and along Trail 1816 to the headwaters. Best fishing is below the forks (7 miles above Indian Crossing).

Like other tributaries of the Snake River System, the Imnaha once hosted sizable runs of chinook salmon and steelhead. These native runs were all but destroyed by the imposition of hydroelectric dams. Efforts to restore the runs through hatchery plants have met with some success. The first harvest of reintroduced steelhead was permitted in

A streamside trail follows a fine fly-fishing stretch of the beautiful Imnaha.

1 **NORTH FORK CONFLUENCE** - Gravel parking area with access to gravel bar boat launch; good bank angling for steelhead (late winter-early spring) and smallmouth (spring-summer).

2 **BALOGNA CREEK ACCESS** - BLM access; gravel bar boat launch with good bank angling for steelhead and smallmouth.

3 **MILE POST 99** - BLM access; watch for paved turnout; primarily used as launch and pull-out by steelhead anglers; some bank fishing.

4 **ODOT GRAVEL STORAG**E - Boat launch and pull-out for steelhead & bass anglers.

5 **SPRAY**- Sand launch immediately above county road bridge; private property, but no permission needed at this time; be courteous and pack out your litter to protect continued public access

6 **PARRISH CREEK** - Upper end of Scenic Waterway.

7 **MULESHOE CREEK** - BLM campground and boat ramp; some bank angling for bass and channel catfish; launch for bass and steelhead anglers.

8 **SERVICE CREEK** - Gravel bar pull-out and launch for popular drift to Twickenham; bank angling for bass and steelhead.

The Imnaha supports a large population of native rainbow. Angling is excellent during summer and fall above and below the town of Imnaha. Spinner and bait are used (particularly grasshoppers in August), but the river has excellent fly water and is generally wadeable. Golden stoneflies hatch around July, with grasshopper imitations effective in August, and caddis in September and early October. The river is closed to salmon angling.

There are campgrounds in Wallowa-Whitman National Forest along the Imnaha River Road above Imnaha. Supplies, tackle, and local information are available in Enterprise and La Grande.

JOHN DAY ARM OF LAKE UMATILLA See Umatilla, Lake (John Day Arm).

JOHN DAY RIVER (Below Kimberly) One of Oregon's premiere summer steelhead rivers, also offering world class angling for smallmouth bass. The John Day is one of the longest undammed rivers in the lower 48 states. It enters the Columbia River about half-way between Biggs Junction and Blalock on I-84, about 25 miles east of The Dalles. It is crossed by the highway just above its mouth. The John Day Dam on the Columbia backs the Columbia 9 miles into the lower John Day Canyon, forming a productive pool that can only be approached from the Columbia due to an impassable falls.

The river flows 185 river miles between the mouth and Kimberly, a community on Route 19. At Kimberly, the John Day is augmented by its major tributary, the North Fork. The stretch between Kimberly and Service Creek is both productive and accessible. Route 19 follows the river's north bank from the Hwy. 26 junction near picture Gorge to Service Creek, through a checkerboard of public land and private holdings, some of which are open to public use. Anglers need to ask permission to fish from private land and are urged to be courteous guests.

Below Service Creek, the river flows through a colorful lava rock canyonland. Designated Scenic Waterway, much of it is accessible only by boat. ODF&W manages this portion of the river for quality bass fishing (bass over 12 inches). Rafting is an exciting and practical way to fish it. For a day's drift, anglers can put in at Service Creek (river mile 157, at the junction of routes 19 and 207) and drift 12 river miles to Twickenham (river mile 145). A popular longer drift is from Twickenham to Clarno Rapids (river mile 110 off Hwy. 218 west of Fossil Beds National Monument). Another good day's drift is from Cottonwood Bridge (river mile 40, at the crossing of Hwy. 206) to the mouth of Rock Cr. (river mile 22, east of Wasco).

Whitewater rafting is very popular from Service Creek to Cottonwood Bridge. More than 400 rafts have been seen on the river in a single day. This stretch includes four Class III rapids (Russo, Homestead, Burnt, and Basalt) and one Class IV (Clarno). At highest spring flow (not recommended for boating), Clarno can involve a 30 ft. freefall drop. The recommended flow for boating the river is 2,000 to 6,000 cubic feet per second. Minimum flow for rafts is 1,500 cfs. Minimum flow for canoes and other small craft is 500 cfs. For updated flow conditions, call the National Weather Service (503) 261-9246.

Bank access improves again near Clarno Rapids. There is BLM access from just below Clarno to 1/2 mile above Butte Creek, about 12 river miles. Fished for both smallmouth and steelhead, this is a classic stretch of John Day water, shallow riffles alternating with deep pools. An unimproved road that follows the river's east bank is closed to public use.

About 15 river miles from the mouth, gravel roads from Wasco to the west, and Rock Creek to the east, reach the river at Scotts Ford. A gravel road leading west from Mikkalo follows Hays Creek down into the canyon and parallels the river from river mile 30 to river mile 27. Much of this land is private, though there are a few parcels owned by BLM. Ask permission to fish at the nearest ranch if you're in doubt as to ownership.

The arrival of steelhead to the John Day fluctuates from year to year. In some years, they may enter in late August and spawn the following May. In other years, they may be present from December or January until March or April. In general, fishing is good in this stretch from September through March. Early activity is best below Clarno Rapids. The estimated annual steelhead catch for the entire John Day mainstem has been as high as 8,600 (in 1987-88). In the past several years, run sizes (and reported catches) have been substantially reduced by poor conditions. At this time, both wild and hatchery steelhead may be kept throughout the river, except in the John Day Arm of Lake Umatilla.

The John Day River has a popular fishery for smallmouth bass near Kimberly.

Smallmouth bass were first stocked in the John Day in the early 1970s at Service Creek and later at Picture Gorge. From Kimberly to the mouth, the river provides ideal smallmouth habitat, and the fishery has thrived. Smallmouth are fished from March through the end of October. In early spring, they can be found in the deeper pools. During spawning season they head for the backwaters and linger along the rimrock ledges. After spawning, they can be found throughout this portion of the river, feeding and holding.

Tumwater Falls, about 10 miles from the mouth, marks the beginning of the John Day Arm of Lake Umatilla. Approachable only from the mouth, this portion of the river contains crappie, brown bullhead, channel catfish and smallmouth bass, as well as steelhead. Non-finclipped steelhead must be released unharmed. See Umatilla, Lake (John Day Arm) for further information.

The John Day runs through a patchwork of private and BLM lands. Watch for signs, and check with nearby landowners when in doubt as to ownership. While on or moving through private land, be a courteous visitor. There is a BLM campground at Muleshoe Creek, and camping is permitted elsewhere on BLM land. There is also a campground at Sheldon State Park about 10 miles north of Service Creek, and in Ochoco National Forest to the south.

JOHN DAY RIVER (Above Kimberly) A 100-mile flow out of the Strawberry Mountain Wilderness, fished for wild trout and wild summer steelhead in the upper reaches, and for smallmouth bass closer to Kimberly. Its passage through national forest is brief. Good roads parallel the river downstream, but much of this reach flows through the private ranchlands of the John Day Valley.

From Kimberly upstream, the river is followed by Hwy. 19 to Dayville, by Hwy. 26 to Prairie City, and by county rds. 61 and 14 to its headwaters. In the last 15 miles, the roads turn to dirt and gravel.

For many years, the ranchland portion of this stretch has been inhospitable to trout and steelhead. Barren of sufficient streamside vegetation, the river grows warm in summer, and rough fish (which prey on trout and steelhead fingerlings) have been a problem. Recently, considerable effort has been devoted to riparian recovery, with good results.

The river is not stocked, but wild rainbow are available, especially in the headwaters. Steelhead reach this stretch in November and December. The river is closed to steelhead angling above Indian Creek.

Clyde Holliday State Park east of Mt. Vernon provides camping facilities and access to good steelhead water. Though the park is officially closed in winter, and camping is prohibited then, anglers may park and walk in to fish. Trout Farm Campground is near the headwaters, about 16 miles south of Prairie City on County Rd. 62, the road to Drewsey.

JOHN DAY RIVER, MIDDLE FORK A major tributary of the John Day, joining the North Fork of the John Day 15 river miles west of the community of Ritter. The Middle Fork flows through Ritter, which is about 10 air miles SW of Dale. It offers steelhead and trout angling and has good road access for all but its lower 9 miles. The Middle Fork is 75 miles long, and heads near Hwy. 26 east of Prairie City. More riffle than pool throughout most of its run, the Middle Fork has a narrow flood plain and flows through a shallow rimrock canyon below its headwaters. The head of the Middle Fork, in the Bates area, is a meandering meadow stream at about 4,800 ft.

The lower 9 river miles have no road access. Paved and gravel roads follow the river closely from a few miles below Ritter, to its headwaters above Austin Junction on Hwy. 26 east of Prairie City. The river is crossed by Hwy. 395 about 7 miles east of Ritter, 12 miles south of Dale, and 15 miles north of Long Creek. A good road, County Rd. 20, follows the stream from Hwy. 395 SE past Susanville, and all the way to Austin Junction, where it joins Hwy. 26. Landowners have been generous along the Middle Fork, but anglers are urged to ask permission to fish, and to be courteous guests.

Rainbow trout provide the primary fishery in this stretch. Fingerlings are stocked every third year and reach 9-14 inches. They are taken in good numbers from June through late fall. Fly-fishing can be good in summer and fall, with bait best early. Above Hwy. 395, angling is restricted to a single point hook no larger than 1/4 inch. Lures are prohibited.

Hwy. 395 is the legal deadline for steelhead angling on the Middle Fork. The annual steelhead catch varies from 100-500. Most of these are taken in March.

Middle Fork Campground is at river mile 60, about 6 miles north of Hwy. 26. Dixie Campground is about 6 miles SW of the upper river on Hwy. 26, about 12 miles east of Prairie City.

JOHN DAY RIVER, NORTH FORK A large tributary of the John Day River, joining the mainstem at Kimberly on Hwy. 19. Rich in good habitat and food resources, the North Fork has historically been a natural rearing stream for steelhead. Steelhead fishing is permitted in the lower river. Resident rainbow are scarce, and only a small segment of the stream is stocked. Bull trout are present in the upper stream, though angling for them is restricted to catch and release.

The North Fork is about 113 miles long, heading in the Elkhorn Mountains 20 miles west of Baker. The upper waters of this fork flow through Umatilla National Forest. This is a big river with a strong flow, yet more riffle than pool throughout most of its run. The best pools are below the confluence of the Middle Fork (at about river mile 17).

The North Fork has an adequate flow for river boats, and there is some boat angling. Boaters put in at the mouth of Wall Creek and drift to Monument, about 6 miles, or from Monument to Kimberly, about 15 miles.

Much of the river is accessible from nearby roads, though private property may present a problem below Dale. Upstream from Kimberly, a paved road follows the northern bank 15 river miles to Monument. A gravel road continues upstream from Monument as far as river mile 28 at Birch Creek. The next 11 miles, to Potamus Creek, are roadless. A gravel road follows the river downstream from Dale to Potamus Creek. Dale is on Hwy. 395 south of Ukiah at about the midpoint of the river. Desolation and Camas Creek, both good size tributaries, join the North Fork at Dale.

The North Fork above Dale is followed by paved and gravel forest rds. 55 and 5506 for about 11 miles. Above that, Trail 5506 follows the stream through a steep forested canyon to its headwaters in the North Fork John Day Wilderness. The river flows at a moderate gradient over a boulder strewn bed. This is primarily chinook spawning grounds and juvenile steelhead rearing area. Few resident rainbow are present. Anglers are encouraged not to fish for the young steelhead. Bull trout may be found in the deeper pools, but must be released unharmed.

Legal rainbow are stocked annually from the mouth of Desolation Creek (at Dale) upstream about 5 miles to Texas Bar Creek. Nearby Camas Creek also provides opportunity to fish for stocked legal rainbow.

There is fair steelhead angling in the lower river from the mouth up to the Hwy. 395 Bridge at Dale, the steelheading deadline. Annual catches have varied greatly, but an average of 300 steelhead are landed each year. Steelhead may appear in the North Fork as early as October, but steelheading usually begins in November and continues until mid-April. In most years the river maintains an adequate flow, but it can get very low and clear during winter cold spells, even freezing over. In fact, ice chunks in the river can be a problem to winter anglers.

There is no improved camping on the river below Dale, although you can set up camp anywhere on BLM land. Ukiah Dale State Park offers camping facilities on Hwy. 395, about 8 miles north of Dale. There are four campgrounds on the river in Umatilla National Forest upstream from Dale. Tollbridge Campground is just one mile east of Dale. Trough Creek is about 4 miles further east on Forest Rd. 55. Two primitive camps, Gold Dredge and Oriental Creek, are further upstream on Forest Rd. 5506.

JOHN DAY RIVER, SOUTH FORK A large tributary of the upper John Day River, entering the main stream from the south at Dayville on Hwy. 26, about 30 miles west of John Day. The South Fork heads in the Snow Mountain area south of Izee and flows about 60 miles through high desert country. It has fair road access along its entire length. You can pick up this road at its intersection with Hwy. 26 at Dayville, or by taking the Post-Paulina Hwy. east from Prineville and continuing east 29 miles to the upper river, just north of Izee. (This tiny community took its name from a ranch brand, I Z).

The South Fork has some wild trout and is stocked with rainbow. Bait-fishing is the preferred method. There is a lot of private property along the river, but public access is available on Murderer's Creek Wildlife Management lands which are scattered along the stream. Take a look at the riparian restoration along the South Fork within Murderer's Creek, and ask yourself why more of our streams can't look like this. Nearest campgrounds are in the national forest to east and west.

JOHN HENRY LAKE A shallow, rich lake in the central Eagle Cap Wilderness. It is approached by Trail 1651 which heads about 1 1/2 miles north of Shady Campground on the Lostine River Rd. Only 13 ft. deep at maximum, John Henry may winterkill some years, but generally supports a good population of brook trout to 9 inches.

The lakes sits in a basin that contains several small meadows interspersed with alpine timber. A float tube would be useful, but there is a talus slope on the SW shore that offers access to the deepest portion of the lake. There are several campsites nearby. Camp well back from fragile lakeside vegetation, and use no-trace camping methods.

JOSEPH CREEK Formed by the confluence of Chesnimnus, Crow, and Elk creeks about 25 miles north of Enterprise. It flows through a big, deep, picturesque canyon north of Joseph Creek Ranch, offering good early and late season angling for wild rainbow. About 23 miles north of Enterprise, Hwy. 3 offers a view of the canyon from the west rim, but access to the creek is from the east.

From Enterprise, follow Hwy. 3 north about 15 miles, turning east on Forest Rd. 46, which leads to the head of Joseph Creek near the M. Davis Ranch. A road follows the creek downstream to Joseph Creek Ranch.

There is a public trail along the creek which offers good angling opportunities.

The trailhead is on Table Mt. and involves a steep 4-mile hike. To reach it, continue north on Forest Rd. 46 to Coyote Campground, turning west on Forest Rd. 4650 to Table Mt. The trail may also be reached from Joseph Creek Ranch, but permission is required. Joseph Creek enters the Grande Ronde near its confluence with the Snake River in Washington.

Best trout fishing is in late season. Smallmouth bass are available in summer and fall below the mouth of Swamp Creek. Joseph also has a wild steelhead run, but is closed to steelhead angling.

JUBILEE LAKE A 97-acre impoundment which provides good angling for rainbow trout in an area where lakes are scarce. Jubilee is about 60 miles NE of Pendleton in Umatilla National Forest. It is at the head of Mottet Creek, about 12 miles north of Tollgate, which is on Hwy. 204. Take Forest Rd. 64 north from Tollgate directly to the lake. Jubilee reaches a depth of 55 ft. Its rainbow are small but numerous.

The Forest Service maintains a large campground here with boat ramp. Motors are prohibited on the lake.

KINNEY LAKE A 20-acre catfish and rainbow trout lake in the upper Wallowa Valley 5 miles due east of Wallowa Lake. From Joseph on Hwy. 82, drive about 5 miles east on paved road S393, the Little Sheep Creek Rd. Turn south onto a gravel road and drive 1 1/2 miles to Pleasant Center. A dirt road leads east to the lake, one mile from Pleasant Center School.

Kinney offers good fishing for brown bullhead and stocked rainbow trout. The rainbow are plentiful and average 9-13 inches. Bait fishing is most popular here, but fly anglers do well.

This is a private lake to which the public has been granted recreational access. Be a courteous guest. Trashing incidents have been a problem and may eventually lead to closure. Camping, boating, and float tubes are prohibited.

LANGDON LAKE A fair size lake on Hwy. 204 about half-way between Elgin and Weston at the community of Tollgate. It is privately owned and operated as part of a resort, with angling for patrons only.

LEE LAKE A deep lake in Eagle Cap Wilderness which supports a large naturally reproducing population of small brook trout. To reach Lee, follow Trail 1820 from the power generator south of Wallowa Lake to Trail 1821, which branches west at about 6 miles. The trail reaches Lee in another 4 miles.

Covering about 9 acres, Lee reaches a depth of 80 ft. and offers anglers very little shoal area. A float tube would be helpful The outlet in the NE corner, used by spawning brook trout, could be productive in fall. Rimrock surrounds the lake, and there are no natural campsites. Nearest good camping is at Horseshoe or Douglas.

LEGORE LAKE One of the highest lakes in Oregon, 30 ft. deep and only 2 acres, located in Eagle Cap Wilderness. Access is poor and fishing is marginal at best for small brook trout. Best approach is from the north through Murray Saddle. There are no trails to the lake. The nearest trail ends at the head of Scotch Creek.

LITTLE SHEEP CREEK A nice little wild rainbow trout stream with good road access, heading about 10 miles SE of Joseph and flowing NE to join Big Sheep Creek at the town of Imnaha. From Joseph, a paved road heads east about 8 miles to meet Forest Rd. 39 and the creek. The paved forest road follows the creek south to its headwaters. The county road continues north along the creek to Imnaha. Most of the upper waters and some of the lower flow within the Wallowa-Whitman National Forest.

Best catches are made in late summer. Campgrounds are available at Wallowa Lake State Park and at Lick Creek Campground south of the creek on Forest Rd. 39.

LEE LAKE One of the better lakes in the NE lake basin of Eagle Cap Wilderness above the west fork of the Wallowa River. It's about 10 miles by trail to the lake, which is 1/3 mile west of Horseshoe Lake. See Horseshoe Lake for directions.

Lee Lake is only 9 acres, but is 80 ft. deep. It provides excellent angling for brook trout averaging 8 inches. Any method will take fish here, though bait seems to be best in the early season. The lake offers good fishing from July through September, and later if the weather holds. There are no campsites at the lake.

LITTLE STRAWBERRY LAKE See Strawberry Lake, Little.

LONG CREEK A tributary of the Middle Fork of the John Day River, about 30 miles long, entering the Middle Fork near Ritter. It heads north of Magone Lake about half-way between the communities of Long Creek and John Day. Hwy. 395 crosses it about 15 miles above its mouth, just north of the town of Long Creek. The creek is inaccessible downstream from the highway, flowing across private, roadless ranchland. Good gravel roads parallel the upper creek SE into Malheur National Forest.

Long supports a fair population of wild rainbow and is lightly fished. There's a forest service campground at Magone Lake. Several unimproved campsites can be found along the stream.

LONG LAKE (Wallowa Co.) A fair size lake in the headwaters of the North Fork of the Minam River. From the town of Lostine on Hwy. 82 drive south to the end of the road. Take the Lostine River Trail 1670 2.8 miles to the junction of the Elkhorn Trail 1656, which continues SW. Follow 1656 about 5 miles to a trail junction above Swamp Lake. Follow the trail down to Swamp Lake, and take Trail 1669, which follows the outlet stream about one mile NW to Long Lake. Its a 10-mile hike on moderately steep trails.

Long Lake is 25 acres, stocked with brook trout 6-12 inches. Fishing is best in August and September. There's also good fishing in Swamp and Steamboat lakes one mile due east of Swamp.

LOSTINE RIVER A pretty trout stream heading at Minam Lake, high in the Eagle Cap Wilderness of Wallowa-Whitman National Forest. Crystalline and idyllic within the wilderness, tranquilly majestic in the valley below with its mountainous backdrop, the Lostine flows 31 miles north to join the Wallowa River 2 miles east of the town of Wallowa on Hwy. 82, about 45 miles east of La Grande. The stream is followed 24 miles south by Forest Rd. 8210. The upper river is followed to its source by Trail 1670. Its major tributary, the East Fork, is followed by Trail 1662. Both trails head at Two Pan Campground at the end of the Lostine River Rd. The Lostine Rd. is the jump-off point for several key trails into the Wallowas.

Lostine provides poor angling for small wild trout in its upper reaches. It is no longer stocked. The average trout 7-11 inches, with a few larger. Bait is most commonly employed, but fly-fishing is good in late fall. The Lostine is not open for salmon and steelhead.

There are five forest campgrounds along the Lostine River Rd. from the forest boundary south to road's end. These are heavily used by horse packers—dusty, noisy, crowded with vehicles, and unsuitable for long stays. Don't expect solitude down below. There are many attractive natural campsites along the upper stream, however. Camp well back from fragile streamside vegetation, and follow no-trace camping guidelines

MACK POND See R.D. Mack Pond.

MAGONE LAKE A popular trout lake in Malheur National Forest, about 10 air miles due north of the town of John Day. The lake can be reached by several routes. About 9 miles east of John Day County Rd. 18 leaves Hwy. 26 and runs NE to the lake. From Hwy. 395 near Mt.

Vernon, Forest Rd. 36 winds about 10 miles to the lake.

Covering 50 acres at elevation 4,900 ft., the lake is very rich and quite deep, about 100 ft. It is heavily fished for nice size rainbow and brook trout. Fish up to 16 inches are taken. The north end of the lake has good shoal areas where flies will take large fish in the fall.

Magone is open all year. Ice fishing is popular and yields good catches when snowpack allows. Check with ODF&W in John Day or with the Malheur National Forest Ranger Station. There is a campground at the lake. Boats can be launched, but fishing from a motor propelled craft with the motor running is prohibited. There is a 10-mph speed limit on the lake.

MAXWELL LAKE A pleasant brook trout lake in Eagle Cap Wilderness, approached by trail up the Lostine River. Follow Trail 1674 about 3 miles from the Shady Campground trailhead. The trail is very steep and not suitable for horses.

Covering 16 acres and 50 ft. deep, Maxwell has some good shallows for bank fishing. Deepest water is in the NE. Tributary inlets enter from the west. Brook trout reproduce naturally in the outlet stream and in subsurface springs in the northern portion of the lake. There are a few natural campsites at the lake. Be sure to camp well back from fragile lakeside vegetation and use no-trace camping methods.

McKAY CREEK (Umatilla Co.) The outlet stream of McKay Reservoir, a tributary of the Umatilla River. Hwy. 395 leads to the area from Pendleton, and several secondary roads follow the creek from the reservoir and the Pilot Rock area. Only about 5 miles of creek above the reservoir are outside the Umatilla Reservation. For angling on reservation lands, check with the agency at Mission.

There is very little angling in the creek below the reservoir because of water fluctuation. The upper creek has nice riffles and pools and offers good fishing for wild rainbow. Fish also move into the creek from the reservoir. Fishing is best in early summer.

Unlike most streams in this district, McKay Creek opens with the early trout opener at the end of April. There are no camping areas nearby.

McKAY RESERVOIR (pronounced McEye) A large reservoir, the heart of McKay Creek National Wildlife Refuge, managed primarily for irrigation and waterfowl. It generally provides excellent crappie fishing and plentiful perch. Success of the largemouth bass in McKay is limited by severe water withdrawals. The reservoir is about 4 miles due south of Pendleton, just to the east of Hwy. 395. A good gravel road cuts in from the highway and follows the west shore of the reservoir.

When full, McKay covers about 1,300 acres, but it's not unusual for this lake to be drawn down to 250 acres in the fall. Bass redds, always vulnerable in the reservoir's shallows, have been particularly hard hit during the drought years. As the bass population has declined, yellow perch have overpopulated. Anglers are urged to fish the perch heavily. There is no perch bag limit. Until the bass population rebounds, bass fishing is limited to 3 per day with a minimum length of 15 inches.

Fishing continues to be excellent for black crappie 6-10 inches, with some to 12 inches. Brown bullhead, and channel catfish are also available. The unofficial state record channel cat was caught here in 1980, weighing 36 pounds 8 ounces.

The entire reservoir is open for public use March 1 to September 30. The southern half remains open throughout the State Waterfowl Season but is closed to fishing.

The reservoir is open for day use only. Camping is prohibited. Of its two boat ramps, the south ramp is usable only at full pool.

McCORMACH SLOUGH A 2-mile stretch of Columbia backwater just west of Irrigon on the Umatilla National Wildlife Refuge. It offers limited fishing for smallmouth bass and crappie. Dikes have been built to create three separate ponds

From I-84, take Hwy. 730 Exit. Turn left on Patterson Ferry Rd. Trails to the slough are well-signed at every parking lot. Other trails are provided for wildlife viewing. There is a huge mule deer herd on the refuge, as well as a large population of blue herons, several species of ducks, curlews and pelicans. Park at the north end of the slough.

The ponds are rich, with good submerged structure to provide habitat. However they are very shallow. Recent stockings seem to have been quickly fished out. The west pond may be full of carp. The others may contain largemouth bass and black and white crappie.

There are two boat ramps, but motors are prohibited. A canoe or float tube would be handy, but there is good bank access.

McNARY CHANNEL PONDS Six ponds and connecting channels, covering about 25 acres below McNary Dam on the Columbia River off I-84. They contain largemouth bass, channel catfish, bluegill, and stocked trout.

A combination of backroads and bike paths make the ponds accessible for youngsters riding bikes out from Umatilla or Hermiston. Fishing is good in early spring and summer. To reach the ponds, continue west beyond the fish viewing window at the dam.

The pond area is pleasantly shaded with cottonwoods and willows. Free Fishing Day events take place here every June, sponsored by the Ladies Angle Society. Recommended for small fry. Wheelchair accessible.

MEACHAM CREEK A 30-mile tributary of the Umatilla River with good angling, accessible to strong hikers. It heads near Meacham, SE of Pendleton, and winds through canyons to the east and south. Meacham joins the Umatilla at Gibbon, about 26 miles upstream from Pendleton.

The creek is quite inaccessible. Forest roads leave the Meacham area to the east and stay high on the ridge above the creek. A Union Pacific railroad line follows the creek from Meacham downstream, and anglers can walk the railroad right-of-way to access the creek. It offers good fishing for wild trout. The lower 5 miles flow within the Umatilla Indian Reservation, and tribal permits are required.

MEACHAM LAKE A private 12-acre lake in the Blue Mountains, one mile SW of Meacham. The area around it has been developed, and there is no longer public access.

MEADOW CREEK A 24-mile long trout stream entering the upper Grand Ronde River about 10 miles west of Hilgard, a community on I-84 about 8 miles west of La Grande. Hwy. 244 follows the lower stream from the Grande Ronde confluence to Starkey, 6 miles upstream. The upper stream flows within Wallowa-Whitman National Forest, and the portion followed by roads is a designated study area, currently closed to angling. This stretch is followed by forest rds. 2120 and 21. The upper 6 miles of the creek, above Smith Creek, are open for angling and may be accessed by Trail 1855.

Meadow offers good angling for wild rainbow in the lower creek late in spring and again in fall. The trout run 7-11 inches, with a few larger. The stream closure is from the forest boundary just above Bear Creek to the end of the road at Smith Creek. Nearest camping is at Camas Campground on Hwy. 224, about 12 miles south of Starkey.

MESSNER POND No. 2 A rich pond, with nice size largemouth bass and white crappie. Covering about 12 acres, it is one mile east of Boardman north of I-84. To reach the pond from I-84, take the Port of Morrow Exit (No. 165) and drive due north.

Messner is fished primarily for bass and crappie, but since a culvert connects it to the Columbia, it might hold anything, including a lot of carp. Efforts to screen out the carp have been unsuccessful.

MILL CREEK (Umatilla Co.) A beautiful pristine trout stream in extreme northeast Oregon with headwaters in Washington. It flows through Oregon for about 7 miles before doubling back to Washington, where it enters the Walla Walla River about 10 miles east of Milton Freewater. Mill Creek is just north of the North Walla Walla River. A portion of its flow in Oregon is closed to angling, as it is the source of drinking water for the city of Walla Walla.

Fishing in Mill is for wild trout in fast water, with lots of brush to hang you up. But the creek does have a lot of good riffle areas. It abounds with rainbow and bull trout. Bull trout must be released unharmed.

MINAM LAKE A fair size brook trout lake in Eagle Cap Wilderness at the head of the Lostine River. While near the head of the Minam River, it does not drain into that watershed. From the community of Lostine, east of Enterprise, follow the Lostine River Rd. about 18 miles to its end. Follow the Lostine River Trail 1670 upstream from Two Pan Campground 5.7 miles to Minam Lake. Total elevation gain is about 2,000 feet, but it's spread out along the entire hike, making this one of the easier trails in the Eagle Cap. Snow may block access until July.

The lake is at elevation 7,400 ft. and covers 33 acres. Maximum depth is 30 ft. Fishing for brook trout is terrific from late July through September, with all methods taking fish that average 9-12 inches, with some to 14 inches. Blue Lake, one mile beyond Minam, also offers good fishing.

MINAM RIVER A major tributary of the Grand Ronde River, heading at Blue Lake, high in Eagle Cap Wilderness, and flowing NNW 50 miles to join the Wallowa River at the town of Minam. Designated a Scenic Waterway, the Minam has limited road access throughout its length. It is a favorite of rafters and hikers.

The town of Minam is 15 miles east of Elgin, 12 miles west of Wallowa on Hwy. 82. The lower 9 river miles from the mouth to Meads Flat are followed by roads south from Minam. Secondary roads upstream of the Flat are a mile or more from the river and have been closed. Trail access is excellent. Trail 1673 follows the river all the way from Meads Flat to Blue Lake, a distance of over 40 miles. See the Wallowa-Whitman National Forest map for details.

Red's Wallowa Horse Ranch offers unique access at about the midpoint of the river, just outside the wilderness boundary at the notch above Jim White Ridge. Red's has an airstrip deep in the canyon, and private flyers can literally drop right in. If you don't fly, you can charter a flight at Enterprise Municipal Airport. If you do pilot your own craft, stop at Enterprise anyway for a briefing on the approach, and plan your flight for early morning. Red's only other access is by an 8-mile pack or hike from Horse Meadow on Forest Rd. 62.

Angling on the Minam is good in late summer and fall. The stream is not stocked but has a good native population, with rainbow 8-15 inches and a few brook and bull trout as well. Bait, flies, or lures will all take fish. As you might expect, the best fishing is away from the roads. Fishing gets underway as soon as the run-off drops, usually in June. Fishing on the lower river slows by August, but picks up again in September.

The river is closed to salmon and steelhead fishing. There are no drive-in campgrounds along the river. Packers can camp on Bear Creek or on the lower Lostine before heading into the Wilderness. Natural campsites are available in the forest. Supplies, tackle, and local information are available at Enterprise.

MIRROR LAKE (Wallowa Co.) A scenic trout lake only one mile north of Eagle Cap, highest peak in the Wallowas at 9,595 ft. Mirror is at the west end of the NE lake basin within the Wilderness. The most direct route to it is from the north by way of the East Fork of the Lostine River. From the end of the Lostine Rd., 18 miles south of the town of Lostine, hike upstream along the East Fork on Trail 1662, 6 1/2 miles to the lake. Total elevation gain is 2,000 ft. You can also hike in from Wallowa Lake, following trails 1820 and 1810 into the eastern basin, crossing west to Mirror. This route covers about 14 miles.

Mirror Lake is 26 acres with a maximum depth of 77 ft. Brook trout average 10 inches and range from 6-13 inches. Other lakes in the basin to the NE provide good angling as well. You can usually get in by July, but fishing is best in August and September. There are quite a few good campsites. Camp well back from fragile lakeside vegetation, and follow no-trace camping guidelines.

MOCCASIN LAKE A fair size brook trout lake in the NE lake basin of Eagle Cap Wilderness. The hike in can be made from either Wallowa Lake or Two Pan Campground on the Lostine River. The distance is almost identical. See Mirror Lake for directions. Moccasin is just NE of Mirror. Total trip is about 11 miles, with elevation gain 2,400 ft.

Moccasin doesn't have very large fish, but there are lots of them. These brook trout run to 10 inches, and they can be taken easily on bait, lures or flies. Spinner and bait combinations retrieved very slowly will take the largest fish. Other lakes in the basin provide good angling as well. See Mirror, Douglas, Unit, Lilly, Crescent. There's one improved campsite at this centrally located lake, and several other good sites nearby. Camp well back from fragile lake-side vegetation and follow no-trace camping guidelines.

MORGAN LAKE A 60-acre trout and crappie lake, just 5 miles SW of LaGrande. A gravel and dirt road leads from I-84 to the lake. The lake is stocked annually with rainbow and occasionally with brook trout. The catch rate is very good for rainbow trout 9-12 inches, and brook trout to 15 inches. Crappie to 10 inches are also taken. Fishing is best in early summer. Bait is the most popular method.

There is a campground at the lake and a day-use area. Recommended for small fry. Wheelchair accessible.

OLIVE LAKE A good trout and kokanee lake of 160 acres near the headwaters of Desolation Creek in Umatilla National Forest, about 30 miles west of Baker. This lake is worth the trip when it's hot. Gravel and dirt roads approach it from several directions. Forest Rd. 10 leads west about 11 miles from Granite to the lake. Granite can be reached by State Rd. 220 from Hwy. 7 south of Baker. From Dale, on Hwy. 395, go SE on Forest Rd. 10 up Desolation Creek to the lake. It can also be reached from Susanville to the south.

Olive sits at a cool 6,200 ft. elevation. It's over 100 ft. deep and offers good catches of rainbow to 15 inches. Brook trout of the same size make up about half the catch. An occasional cutthroat is also taken. Trolling and bait fishing are both popular methods here.

Olive also has lots of kokanee, with some to 12 inches, but most a little smaller. Best method for taking kokanee is trolling with spinners trailing a small baited hook. Kokanee tend to school, so when you get a strike, stay in the same area. Fall is a good time for both rainbow and kokanee, with flies taking the larger rainbow. The lake is also full of crayfish. Throw out a trap near the boat ramp while you're fishing, and hors d'oeuvres are practically guaranteed.

There's a campground and boat ramp at the lake.

PENLAND LAKE A remote but accessible (and extremely productive) drive-in trout lake about 25 miles SE of Heppner. It was built by local private interests but is open to the public. From Heppner, follow County Rd. 678 (the Blue Mountain Scenic Byway) east and south into Umatilla National Forest. About 1.5 miles beyond Cutsforth County Park, turn right onto Forest Rd. 21. At 2.5 miles turn left onto Forest Rd. 2105, which leads to the lake.

There are thousands of trout in this lake, which is open year-round. Fishing is great mornings and evenings. Penland covers 67 acres and is fairly shallow. It can winterkill, but legal trout are stocked after severe winters, and the trout put on weight fast. Trout have been known to grow quite large here.

Good catches are made from the bank, and by wading, but trolling in a row boat or canoe is best. Try trolling a dry fly. The lake is too weedy for float tubes. Motors are prohibited on the lake.

An attractive campground set among the big trees offers secluded campsites. Recommended for small fry.

PILCHER CREEK RESERVOIR A 140-acre reservoir north of the community of North Powder, offering fishing for rainbow trout and crappie. From Hwy. 84 at North Powder, follow signs toward Anthony Lakes. At about 3 miles, the road to Anthony Lakes makes a sharp left turn. Continue straight (west) another 3 miles to a cut-off on the right (County Rd. 4330, Tucker Flat Rd.) which leads to Pilcher.

Pilcher went dry during the drought, but is stocked annually with rainbow fingerlings. It has grown nice size crappie as well, though the crappie may not have survived. There is a boat ramp and a campground set among pine trees.

POCKET LAKE A small brook trout lake in Eagle Cap Wilderness, perched in a glacial cirque 700 ft. above Moccasin Lake. It is 1 1/2 miles SE and 700 ft. above Moccasin. See Moccasin Lake for directions. Follow Lake Creek, the outlet of Moccasin Lake, about 1/2 mile to a tributary which enters from the south, then bushwhack up this creek to Pocket Lake.

Though only 9 acres, Pocket is very deep for its size. There's not a lot of traffic up here, and the lake produces well for small to medium size brook trout.

POWER CITY PONDS In Power City Wildlife Area, 4 miles north of Hermiston. The ponds contain largemouth bass and brown bullhead catfish.

PRAIRIE CREEK (Wallowa Co.) A small stream that grows large trout near Enterprise. About 18 miles long, it heads a couple of miles east of Wallowa Lake and flows NW, joining the Wallowa River at Enterprise. Gravel roads leading east and south from Hwy. 82, between Enterprise and Joseph, follow and cross the stream.

The creek is no longer stocked, but has a fair wild trout population. Nutrient enriched as it passes through agricultural lands, Prairie grows rainbow and brook trout to 18 inches. It is fed by springs and maintains a moderate temperature year-round. Bait is the best method early in the year, and flies are good in late summer and fall.

The creek flows almost entirely through private agricultural lands. Ask permission to access the creek and be a courteous guest.

PROSPECT LAKE A good, small rainbow lake at the very head of the West Wallowa River in Eagle Cap Wilderness. It sits below a ridge that separates it from Glacier Lake, 1/2 mile south. There is no trail to the lake. Hike to Little Frazier Lake (See Frazier Lake) and follow the inlet stream up to Prospect Lake, 1/2 mile NW. It's about a 12-mile trip in all.

Prospect is at 8,380 ft., so be prepared for cold nights and the possibility of snow showers in September. The lake has been known to have some nice rainbow trout for a small lake, possibly because of its great depth. Though only 14 acres, the lake is over 100 ft. deep. Average size is 10-12 inches, with some fish to 20 inches taken in August and September.

RAZZ LAKE A small but interesting brook trout lake high in Eagle Cap Wilderness just to the north of the popular lake basin south of Wallowa Lake. Razz is about one mile north of Horseshoe Lake at 8,100 ft., about 900 ft. above Horseshoe. See Horseshoe Lake for trail directions. Follow Horseshoe's inlet stream upslope one mile to the lake. Change your pacemaker batteries before starting out.

The lake is about 14 acres and 26 ft. deep. The brook trout here are 7-10 inches. Fishing is good in August and September.

R.D. MACK POND A one-acre pond close to the Grand Ronde River near Island City. The pond is behind the gravel operation off Hwy. 82. To reach it, follow Hunter Lane to the first street on the left. The pond is stocked annually with fingerling and legal rainbow. Recommended for small fry.

RHEA CREEK A good wild trout stream about 35 miles long, flowing into Willow Creek, 2 miles east of Ione about 15 miles north of Heppner. Most of its flow is through private property, so ask permission before you fish. Ione is on Hwy. 74, which intersects I-84 east of Arlington. The creek is followed upstream by 20 miles of paved and gravel roads from Ione to the crossing of Hwy. 207 at Ruggs, 10 miles SW of Heppner. From there, gravel roads follow the creek to its headwaters.

ROCK CREEK (Gilliam Co.) A 40-mile tributary of the lower John Day River, with wild rainbow in its upper stretches. It enters the John Day about 15 miles above the mouth, just above the bridge on the road from Wasco to Rock Creek. It is followed east by a gravel road (the Arlington-Condon Rd.) from Rock Creek to Olex , and crossed again further south by several gravel roads and Hwy. 206, the Condon-Heppner Rd.

There is a lot of irrigation withdrawal from the creek, and trout fishing is confined primarily to the upper areas, where there's a fair wild rainbow population. There are a lot of rough fish in the lower end.

ROGER LAKE A small shallow lake near Aneroid Lake in Eagle Cap Wilderness. Though only 4 ft. deep, warm springs keep the lake from freezing solid and allow a healthy brook trout population to thrive. Though the fish are not large, they are well formed and plentiful. See Aneroid for trail directions. Roger is 1/4 mile east of Aneroid and is visible from the trail.

ROULETTE POND A former gravel pit north of Elgin, stocked annually with legal rainbow. Not very scenic, but it's a reliable place to take beginners who need practice in learning how to set a hook. Recommended for small fry.

ROWE CREEK RESERVOIR A 30-acre impoundment south of Hwy. 19 about 17 miles south of Fossil. From Hwy. 19 about 10 miles SE of Fossil, turn south onto the gravel road going SW to Twickenham. The turn is just west of Sheldon Wayside.

Although a private lake, the public has gained access through an agreement made between its owner and ODF&W. A 50 ft. strip around the shore is reserved for anglers. Be sure to close the gate behind you.

Rowe is stocked with legal rainbow trout and fished very hard by the local folks. The rainbow range 8-11 inches. The reservoir has gotten pretty low in recent years, but fishing generally holds up well through spring. The reservoir is open to fishing all year. Motors on the lake, open fires, and camping are prohibited.

SEARCY POND (a.k.a. Kinzua Reservoir) A rainbow fishery near the old Kinzua Mill site east of Fossil. It is stocked annually with legal rainbow.

SERVICE CREEK A small creek, tributary to the lower John Day River. It enters the John Day at the community of Service Creek at the junction of highways 19 and 207, between Fossil and Mitchell. It is followed closely by Hwy. 19 north from Service Creek to Sheldon Wayside. The creek is only 9 miles long and is little more than a trickle in summer. It supports trout, but seldom attracts anglers.

SLIDE LAKE (Grant Co.) A small lake high in the Strawberry Mt. Wilderness south of Prairie City. The wilderness is a handsome alternative to the arid John Day Valley over which it towers, with its snowy peaks and cool coniferous forest. Follow Main St. (County Rd. 60) south from Prairie City to Malheur National Forest. Forest Rd. 6001 continues to the trailhead at Strawberry Camp. The upper road is usually poor in early spring. Trail 375 leads south into the wilderness, meeting Trail 372 about 1/2 mile in. Take this trail about 2 miles to the east, and swing south on Trail 385 to the lake. It's a 4.3 mile hike, steep enough to discourage traffic.

Slide Lake is 13 acres and only 8 feet at its deepest point. It fills a glacial cirque at 7,200 ft. but has plenty of aquatic vegetation and grows nice trout. It's not stocked, but has a good self-sustaining population of brook trout. Fly-fishing is enjoyable here late in fall, but bring your long johns if you plan to stay for the evening rise. Just south of Slide Lake is Upper or Little Slide Lake, a 3-acre lake that holds a lot of brook trout. It's a bit deeper than the lower lake. Both can usually be reached in June.

SNAKE RIVER (Northeast Zone) Perhaps Oregon's wildest Wild and Scenic River, offering some of the best fishing in the state—when you can get to it. The section from the Oregon/Washington border upstream to the Hell's Canyon Dam is the heart of Hells Canyon Wilderness. Access is the tough part, as this portion of the river runs through spectacular Hells Canyon, an awesome gorge over 6,000 ft. deep in places.

In recent years, civilization has begun to encroach on the canyon. Commercial rafting and jet boat operations have flourished. There are many more visitors, and the Forest Service has responded by creating additional facilities to serve them. But access is still limited.

From the west , this portion of the river is only approached by road at Hells Canyon Dam and Dug Bar. From the east, roads reach the river at Pittsburg Landing, Wolf Creek and Dry Creek. Dug Bar is at the confluence of the Imnaha and is reached from Joseph by going east on the Sheep Creek Rd. to the community of Imnaha, then following the river road downstream. Hells Canyon Dam is reached by taking Hwy. 86 from Halfway to Copperfield, crossing to Idaho, and following the river downstream on the Idaho side to the bridge. The boat ramp and campground are on the Oregon side. There are no trails upstream or down from the dam area.

The facility at Pittsburgh Landing in Idaho has recently been enlarged to include a new ramp and R.V. hook-ups. There are also boat-in only facilities at Cache Creek about 9 miles downstream from the dam, and at Kirkwood, near the mid-point of this reach. The Kirkwood facility includes an historic ranch and museum.

Commercial rafting and jet boat operations will take you the whole length of this wild river. Boaters who want to go it alone should be aware that the river above Kirkwood is suitable for experts only.

The best map for hiking the area is the Hells Canyon National Recreation map, available at the visitor center in Enterprise and from vendors throughout Oregon and Idaho. There are a number of trails into the canyon. Among those most popular with anglers are the Battle Creek Trail and the Dug Bar Trail. The Battle Creek Trail heads off the Hells Canyon Rim Rd. and reaches the river about 4 miles downstream from the dam. The Dug Bar Trail begins at river level at the end of Dug Bar Rd. several miles upstream from the mouth of the Imnaha. The road is gravel and is passable for passenger cars at low speeds, though higher clearance vehicles may weather the potholes better. The trail follows the river's west bench, sometimes at river level, sometimes high above, all the way to Saddle Creek. The trail is well-maintained. There is also a trail down Saddle Creek which heads on Forest Rd. 4230 off the Imnaha River Rd. A number of other trails begin on spur roads leading east from the Imnaha River Rd.

Smallmouth bass to 3 pounds and better are plentiful. Best smallmouth fishing is late spring to early fall. Rainbow trout are numerous and range 8-20 inches. Tributary mouths are always good places to look for trout, but you can find them anywhere in the canyon. Trout over 20 inches are considered steelhead.

Steelhead angling has been improving over the past few years as a result of an intense program of hatchery plants, mitigation programs to offset losses caused by dams, and angling restrictions system. Barbless hooks are required throughout the river, and non-finclipped steelhead must be released unharmed. Most steelhead are caught by trolling hotshots or casting lures. Best fishing is November to February. Returns have been excellent in recent years. In 1991-92, the total estimated catch was 1,714. In 1992-93, 1,992 steelhead were reported for the first half of the season alone.

Channel catfish are a popular fishery in the Snake. The bigger the bait, the bigger the fish. Channel cats to 20 pounds have been taken from this stretch. Sturgeon in the 8-9 ft. class are also in the river, but anglers are urged not to target them. All sturgeon must be released without removal from the water.

Jet boats are available for hire in Lewiston, ID and Clarkston, WA. Guides and outfitters are available in Oxbow, Enterprise, and Joseph, as well as other areas of the state. Write the Oregon Guides and Packers Association, PO Box 3797, Portland Or. 97208, for a complete listing of professional guides.

STEAMBOAT LAKE A fair size lake in the headwaters of the North Fork of the Minam River. See Long Lake for directions to Swamp Lake. From Swamp Lake, follow the trail that leads across the saddle to the east, dropping down to Steamboat. It's a 10-mile hike, and the trails aren't too steep.

Steamboat is 30 acres and just over 100 ft. deep. It has a good population of eastern brook trout, but the fish don't get large. Most are 7-10 inches with a few larger caught in the late fall. Bait and flies are both productive methods here. Long Lake is just one mile west and can be reached by a trail leading down from Swamp Lake.

STRAWBERRY LAKE The largest lake in the Strawberry Mt. Wilderness, reached by a real pretty one-mile hike. The Strawberry Mountains, compact and distinct from other Oregon ranges, rise stately and cool above the arid John Day Valley. Their slopes are covered in dense conifer forest, meadows are carpeted with wildflowers in June, the forest floor with wild strawberries in July. Strawberry Lake is one of several glacially created lakes in the wilderness, with a scenic backdrop of snowy crests. It was formed during glacial retreat when steep valley walls collapsed, blocking Strawberry Creek. See also Little Strawberry, Slide.

County Rd. 60 leads south from Prairie City into Malheur National Forest, and Forest Rd. 6001 continues to the trailhead at Strawberry Camp. The upper road is usually poor in early spring. Trail 375 leads south into the wilderness area and skirts the eastern border of Strawberry Lake in just one mile. The trail continues south past Strawberry Falls, a 40 ft. cascade, and on to Little Strawberry Lake.

Strawberry is at 6,320 ft. and covers 31 acres, with a maximum depth of 40 ft. The lake offers good angling for naturally reproducing rainbow and stocked brook trout. Both tend to grow nice and plump and run to 16 inches. Fly-fishing is best in the southern half of the lake. There are some good deep holes in the center and at the north end. A float tube would be helpful. Fishing is best in early spring and again in late fall. These fish seem to sulk during the middle of the summer.

There is a camping area just north of the lake between Strawberry and Little Strawberry. Camp well back from fragile lakeside vegetation, and use no-trace camping techniques.

STRAWBERRY LAKE, LITTLE A small high lake 1/2 mile south of Strawberry Lake in Strawberry Mt. Wilderness. See Strawberry Lake for directions. Trail 375 leads south into the wilderness, skirts the eastern border of Strawberry Lake, and climbs 1.1 miles to Strawberry Falls. Here a side trail leads east 0.6 mile to Little Strawberry Lake, cupped in a glacial cirque.

Little Strawberry is at elevation 6,960 ft. with a handsome craggy backdrop. It covers 4 acres and is 10 ft. deep. It contains large numbers of brook trout, small but easy to catch. There is a camping area to the north between Little Strawberry and Big Strawberry Lakes.

SWAMP LAKE Fairly shallow and more productive than most in Eagle Cap, offering rainbow trout and rumors of golden trout. It is west of the head of the Lostine River, above and south of Steamboat and Long Lakes. See Long Lake for directions. It's a 9-mile hike on moderately steep trails.

Swamp covers about 43 acres and is 23 ft. deep. This is one of the few lakes in Oregon that was stocked with golden trout, a beautiful fish native to the high Sierras of California, last stocked in the 1960s. The last known catch of a golden in Oregon was at Swamp Lake five years ago.

Fishing is generally excellent in August and September on flies or lures. Still-fishing with worms or eggs will take fish almost anytime. The rainbow average 8-12 inches with a few to 15 inches. Both Long Lake and Steamboat Lake are less than one mile away and offer good fishing.

TATONE POND A one-acre trout pond off Tower Rd. From I-84, take Exit 159 (Tower Rd.). Head north about 50 yards, then turn east on a dirt road and go about 1/4 mile to the parking area. Cross a fence, a railroad track, and another fence. Then walk north about 1/8 mile.

Tatone is stocked annually with legal rainbow. It can be fished year-round but is best in spring. It is very deep in spots. A float tube could be useful.

THIRTY-MILE CREEK A wild rainbow creek, tributary of the lower John Day River, it is actually 39 miles long. It enters the John Day at river mile 84, about halfway between Hwy. 206 and 218. Trout angling is confined to the upper portions of the creek, where there are quite a few trout. The upper creek is reached from Kinzua just east of Hwy. 19 and south of Fossil.

UMATILLA LAKE (John Day Pool) One of four pools in Oregon's chain of Columbia River reservoirs, with a fine population of smallmouth bass and a national reputation for trophy walleye. Of the growing number of walleye fisheries in the state, Lake Umatilla offers the biggest fish and best structure. The state record walleye was pulled out of Lake Umatilla in 1990 weighing 19 pounds 15.3 ounces.

Walleye are year-round residents of the lake. They are found throughout the pool, though most walleye fishing takes place from Arlington upriver to Umatilla. In general, the walleye seem to concentrate upstream in spring, then move downriver throughout the summer to spawn on submerged gravel bars. Anglers use depthfinders to locate popular walleye structures such as submerged islands, rock piles, rocky points, and ledges. Walleye also prowl the isolated flats, which can be identified without sonar by referring to NOAA charts. Most walleye are caught at 20-30 ft. depths.

Walleye are sluggish in spring when the water is cold. As the water begins to warm in June, walleye become aggressive hunters, prowling the flats close to the bottom or hovering in ambush near rocky structures.

When walleye are most active (in the week or so before spawning), power trolling can be effective. Anglers troll at 20-30 feet, using large plugs that imitate their natural forage (shad, squawfish smolts, sculpin, and the occasional salmon, steelhead, or trout smolt). Hood River lure manufacturer Luhr Jensen has developed some plugs especially for Oregon's new walleye fishery, including the Power Dive Minnow and Hot Lips Express, which feature hydrodynamic bills that keep the plugs at the appropriate level. They are trolled on 150 to 200 feet of line, allowing the walleye room to move back into the trolling lane after the boat's sound and shadow have passed. Best trolling is along the stepped cliffs and ledges that line the river, and over the flats.

In addition to the large plugs (up to 8 inches), anglers troll bottom walkers, jig blade baits such as Ripple Tail or Silver Buddy, and fish night crawlers and minnows.

The walleye fishery accelerates throughout the summer and can be good into November when autumn is mild. Night fishing by full-moon is especially popular from August on. This is a boat fishery. Bank anglers have had little success. Average catch ranges 3-13 pounds, with 17 pounders not uncommon.

Lake Umatilla also offers excellent smallmouth bass angling. The first smallmouth open tournament on the lake took place in 1988, sponsored by the Blue Mt. Bass Club of Pendleton. Tournament catches have reportedly been on a par with the best in the country. Most smallmouth are caught in the mid-pool area from Fulton Canyon to above Irrigon. Using plugs and jigs, anglers start taking fish in May and continue throughout the fall. Smallmouth to 6 pounds have been taken, and 3 pounders are not uncommon. A growing number of smallmouth anglers are practicing catch and release.

The sturgeon population in the Columbia above the dams is low, and anglers should anticipate fluctuating regulations over the next few years. In fall of 1994, the sturgeon fishery in this portion of the river was closed due to fear of over-fishing.

Salmon and steelhead angling is concentrated at the upper end of the pool around McNary Dam and at the mouths of the tributaries (especially the John Day and Umatilla rivers). Steelhead are usually available September through January.

A shad run is fished primarily in the vicinity of Umatilla from April to June. Crappie fishing is popular in fall, particularly in the boat basins, where there's good fishing from the docks.

There are public boat ramps at the mouth of the John Day River, Blalock Canyon, Arlington, Threemile Canyon (between Arlington and Boardman), Boardman, Patterson Ferry, Irrigon, and Umatilla.

The Blalock Canyon ramp is a good gravel ramp between I-84 and the railroad tracks. Launch into the backwater between the tracks and highway, then motor under the railroad bridge. Blalock is a popular access for a smallmouth bass fishery around the nearby rip-rap.

Arlington, Boardman, and Umatilla facilities includes concrete ramps, docks, and enclosed boat basins. There is also a beach at the Boardman marina. The Threemile facility is rough and unimproved. Patterson Ferry is unimproved but easy on a vehicle and seldom used. To reach it from Hwy. 730, follow Patterson Ferry Rd. (near McCormach Slough) north onto the grounds of the Umatilla Hatchery. A second smaller marina in Umatilla is located on the Umatilla River upstream from the Hwy. 730 bridge at Umatilla Park.

Bank access throughout the lake is limited due to the proximity of I-84 and the Union Pacific railroad tracks. Best bank access is at the boat basins, except for Blalock and Patterson Ferry. There is also good bank access for crappie, smallmouth bass, and brown bullhead at Umatilla Park near the mouth of the Umatilla River.

Camping and RV facilities are available at Boardman and Umatilla marinas. There is also a developed boat-in campground on the John Day Arm of the lake. Supplies are available in Boardman, Umatilla, Irrigon, and Arlington.

UMATILLA LAKE, JOHN DAY ARM Cut off from access above by a major falls, accessible only by boat from Lake Umatilla, the last 9 miles of the John Day offer fine fishing in a stunning environment—a narrow canyon with sheer rock walls, and the added attraction (for some) of a full service boat-in campground complete with running water, picnic tables, grassy lawn, and two boat docks. It can get crowded in here, but fishing is excellent for summer steelhead, very good for smallmouth bass, good for channel catfish and brown bullhead, and fair for crappie.

Steelheaders fish the upper 2 miles, where their quarry congregate at the base of Tumwater Falls. Bass and panfish angling takes place throughout.

UMATILLA RIVER A good steelhead, salmon, and trout stream. The Umatilla enters the Columbia River about 3 miles below McNary Dam at the town of Umatilla. It heads in the northern Blue Mts. and flows west past Pendleton and Hermiston. From Pendleton to the Columbia the stream is easily reached by a paved road that follows it from Rieth to Echo, both of which are on I-84. East of Pendleton, paved and gravel roads follow the stream for another 30 miles, mostly through Umatilla Indian Reservation lands.

Summer steelhead are fished from September through mid-April in the water below the deadline at the Hwy. 11 Bridge in Pendleton. Bait-fishing with eggs or nightcrawlers produce most of the fish. The estimated catch from the 1991-92 run was more than 600 fish, but subsequent runs and catch rates have been considerably smaller. Non-finclipped steelhead must be released unharmed.

Coho adults and jacks and fall chinook jacks are available for harvest September 1 through November 30. These fish were re-introduced beginning in 1981 following extinction of the native runs 70 years ago. The runs have fluctuated between 500 and 4,300 for coho. Fall chinook returns have been poor to fair, and only jacks may be harvested at this time.

Spring chinook appear usually in late May or early June and may be fished in some years. The spring chinook run, also being re-built following extinction, has fluctuated between 500 and 2,200. Call the Pendleton office of ODF&W for information about openings.

Fall chinook jacks and coho are fished downstream from Stanfield Dam at river mile 32. Spring chinook have generally been fished upstream from Stanfield Dam to the forks. Fishing for steelhead and salmon is prohibited within Confederated Tribes of Umatilla boundaries. All non-finclipped steelhead must be released unharmed.

The Umatilla has a good population of wild rainbow and a fair population of bull trout. Good catches of rainbow are made in the Bingham Springs area upstream from Pendleton. Tribal Permits are required to fish on reservation land and may be purchased at Mission. Bull trout must be released unharmed. There is some concern that the river might be closed if the angling public does not cooperate in the protection of the bulls. Signs posted at popular trout angling access points should help anglers differentiate the species.

There are many irrigation diversion dams on the river which are unsafe to boat. The major dams are Stanfield at river mile 32, Cold Springs at river mile 28, Westland at river mile 27, and Threemile at river mile 4. Elsewhere, do a good job of scouting before you venture down the river.

Boats may be launched at Yocum (river mile 37), Barnhart (river mile 42), Reith (river mile 48.5, and the Prowler Plant gravel bar (river mile 51). Additional facilities are scheduled for construction in 1994-95 at river mile 52.5 (Babe Ruth Boat Ramp) and at river mile 55 at the mouth of Wildhorse Creek.

Bank access at Echo State Park (river mile 26.5) includes about 100 yards of rip-rap on the east bank. Bank access at Steelhead Park (river mile 9) is a brushy 200 yards on the east bank. From just below Threemile Dam to the mouth, anglers can fish along the Umatilla River Rd. Look for pull-outs along the road. Anglers also fish the river within Pendleton, including the dike on the south bank. There are a number of good steelhead holes within the town.

UMATILLA RIVER, SOUTH FORK A rather short stream, tributary to the upper Umatilla River, which it joins about 32 miles east of Pendleton upriver from Bingham Springs. Forest Rd. 32 (Umatilla National Forest) follows the lower 3 miles of the fork. Trail 3076 continues up the fork an additional 2 miles. Forest Rd. 3128 follows the upper waters along a ridge about one mile west of the

The south end of Wallowa Lake is a jumping off place for trails into Eagle Cap Wilderness.

river and could serve as a jump-off for the bushwhacking enthusiast.

The Fork provides good trout angling for wild trout. Bull trout and rainbow are found in its upper waters. Bull trout must be released unharmed.

Umatilla Forks Campground is about 3 miles above Bingham Springs. There are two additional camps (Elk and South Fork) 3 miles south.

UNIT LAKE A 15-acre lake in the popular lake basin about 10 trail miles south of Wallowa Lake. It is 1/2 mile NE of Horseshoe Lake by trail. See Horseshoe Lake for directions. Unit has brook trout to 11 inches and rainbow to 14 inches. Brook trout predominate.

WALLA WALLA RIVER A fair steelhead stream just south and east of Milton Freewater in the northeast corner of the state. The river heads in Oregon and flows NW into Washington, meeting the Columbia River a few miles above the Oregon border. About 12 miles of the river flow through Oregon up to the forks, which are about 5 miles SE of Milton Freewater.

The river flows right through Milton Freewater, and is open for steelhead up to the forks. However, there is little public access to the river. Ask permission to access the river through the orchards. Marie Dorian County Park, about 4 miles upstream from Walla Walla, accesses good steelhead water.

A few trout are picked up in the mainstem, but most angling for them takes place on the upper forks. There is no camping in the area.

WALLA WALLA RIVER, NORTH FORK A tributary of the Walla Walla joining it about 5 miles east of Milton Freewater. The stream is about 20 miles long, but a road only follows it up about 8 miles through private property, which is closed to public access. Forest Trail 3222 follows the river to its headwaters, offering the only public angling opportunity. You can reach the trail from Forest Rd. 65 about 4 miles below Deduck Campground off Tiger Canyon Rd., or from the end of a dirt road which follows the lower fork above Milton Freewater. Check the Umatilla National Forest map.

The fork below the forest is heavily used for irrigation, and water gets very low in summer and fall. The North Fork contains bull trout and rainbow. Bull trout must be released unharmed. Best fishing for the rainbow is in early season. Camping is available at Deduck Campground.

WALLA WALLA RIVER, SOUTH FORK A large tributary of the Walla Walla River joining the North Fork about 5 miles east of the city of Milton Freewater. The South Fork is about 30 miles long, although roads only follow it upstream about 12 miles. It heads 3 miles south of the upper corner of the state and arcs south through Umatilla National Forest, emerging SE of Milton Freewater. In the forest it can be fished from Trail 3225, which begins at Bear Creek Guard Station and follows the river to its head near Deduck Campground.

The South Fork carries more water than the North Fork, and angling holds up well into summer. Trout fishing is good from opening through August. Wild bull trout and rainbow are present in the upper waters. Bull trout must be released unharmed. Camping is available at Deduck Campground. A Umatilla National Forest map will be useful.

WALLOWA LAKE The largest natural lake in northeast Oregon, just south of Joseph at the foot of the Wallowa Mts. The lake was formed by the terminal moraine of a glacier that carved out the Wallowa River Valley. The moraine forms an immense natural dam on the Wallowa River and towers over 400 ft. above the surface of this 1,600-acre lake. To reach the lake drive to Joseph, south of Enterprise on Hwy. 82, and continue south to the lake. This highway follows the lake's eastern shore to its southern tip.

Wallowa is a clear, deep lake, with ideal conditions for kokanee and Mackinaw. Kokanee (landlocked sockeye salmon) are actually native to Wallowa but have been supplemented. The kokanee average 9-10 inches, but there are some 15-20 inches. Large numbers of fish are present, and angling is excellent, with best catches in May, June, and the first part of July. Up to 30,000 are caught annually.

Mackinaw are no longer stocked in the lake, and few are left. They are caught by deep trolling with spinners and lures, or combinations along a shelf at about 250 ft. The lake is 300 ft. at its deepest point.

Rainbow trout are stocked annually and average 9 inches, with a few reaching 16 inches or larger. A 20-pound rainbow was caught in 1993. Rainbow are taken both by trolling and still-fishing with bait. Fishing around the edges in the fall often produces nice catches. There are also some nice fish in the river below the dam.

To protect spawning fish, all angling in the tributaries of the lake (up to the falls on the West Fork and the PP&L intake on the East Fork) is prohibited from September 1 through October 31.

Wallowa lake is a popular multi-use recreational lake, but users segregate themselves pretty well. Most kokanee fishing takes place at the NW end of the lake. Most trout anglers fish the southern shoreline. Water-skiers pretty much stick to the NE end.

Boats are available for rent at the State Park on the south end of the lake. Private boats can be launched there and at the county ramp at the north end. There is a full-service campground at the State Park and many private resorts in the vicinity. The south end of Wallowa Lake is a popular jumping-off place for trails intothe Eagle Cap Wilderness. Horses and guides are available in Joseph.

WALLOWA RIVER A popular and accessible trout and steelhead stream, tributary to the Grand Ronde River. The Wallowa flows 80 miles from headwaters in the central lake basin of Eagle Cap Wilderness to its confluence with the Grande Ronde about 16 miles downstream from Elgin. The river feeds Wallowa Lake, skirts the eastern edges of Joseph and Enterprise, and absorbs Lostine and Minam rivers on its journey north and west. Hwy. 82 follows the river from Wallowa Lake to the Minam confluence. Trails 1820 and 1804 follow the West and East forks from South Park Picnic Area at Wallowa Lake into Eagle Cap.

From the town of Wallowa down to Minam, the river offers especially good fly-fishing water. Fairly fast, with a medium size flow, this stretch is characterized by riffles and glides, a liberal distribution of large boulders, a few deep holes, and many excellent wading opportunities. Best public access is from Rock Creek downstream. Permission to access the river through private land can be obtained through guide services for a fee. For information, contact the Wallowa Outdoor Store in Enterprise.

Steelhead are generally in the river from mid-February into April. The Wallowa's steelhead fishery is composed almost entirely of hatchery plants, the original runs of both steelhead and salmon having been destroyed by Columbia River dams. Since the steelhead sport season re-opened in 1986, close to 9,000 fish have been caught, with up to 4,000 fish taken in a single season. The hatchery is on Deer Creek, and returning fish holding in Big Canyon near the hatchery offer a popular spring fishery.

Trout angling throughout the river is excellent from late spring through late fall, with best river conditions generally in September and October. In addition to hatchery rainbow, the river hosts a population of wild rainbow and brook trout. Bull trout are also present but are a protected species and must be released without removal from the water. The average trout runs 8-14 inches, with some wild

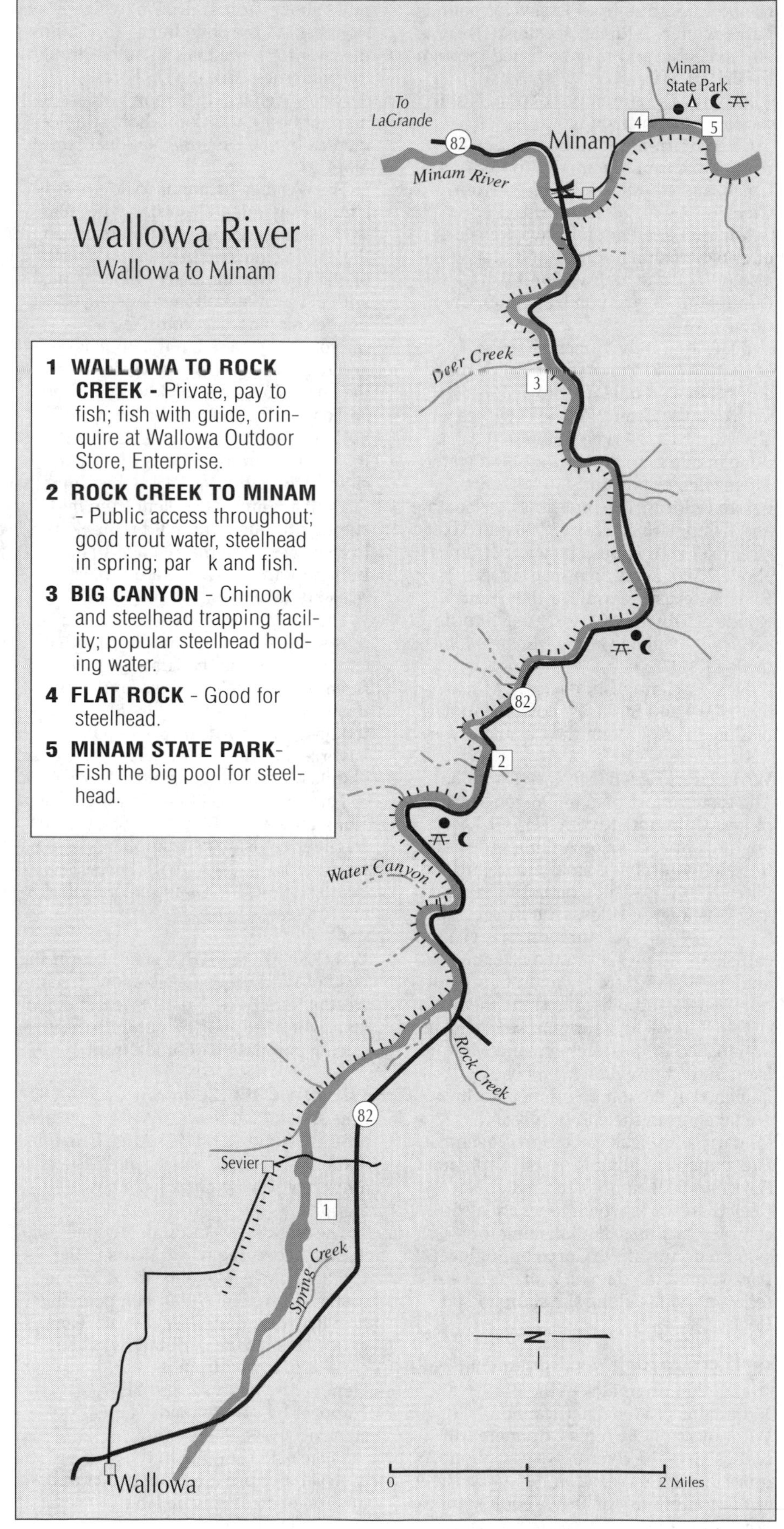

rainbow and bull trout to several pounds. Large whitefish (delicious smoked) are also available and may be fished through the end of March.

The river's salmon population is still too low for sportfishing.

Check current regulations for tackle restrictions from the mouth to Rock Creek, and from Rock Creek to Trout Creek (just west of Enterprise).

Minam State Park and two waysides offer bank fishing opportunities. Anglers also pull off the highway and fish throughout the canyon from Rock Creek downstream.

Boats are rarely launched above Minam. A boat ramp at Minam commits anglers to a 43-mile float to Wildcat Creek on the Grand Ronde, a trip generally requiring 2-4 days (though it can be done in one long day during high water). There is no opportunity to take-out before Wildcat. The best flows for boating and fishing are between 1,500 and 3,000 cfs. Small craft should be wary of flows above 2,500. For a flow reading, call River Forecast Central for the Grand Ronde at Troy at (503) 261-9246 Shuttle service is available at the Minam Motel (503) 437-4475.

Nearest campgrounds are at Minam State Park and in the Wallowa-Whitman National Forest along the Lostine River.

WALLULA, LAKE (McNary Dam Pool) The easternmost pool in Oregon's string of four Columbia River reservoirs. Most angling effort in Lake Wallula is devoted to smallmouth bass. Smallmouth are taken near the islands on both Oregon and Washington sides, with catches up to 6 pounds. Walleye, sturgeon, and channel catfish are all present in the lake, but anglers here are still trying to figure out how, when, and where to catch them.

Fall chinook and summer steelhead are both fished immediately behind McNary Dam at the buoy line, from boats launched at the dam. Summer steelhead are taken from the end of July into January, with peak catches in November. Fall chinook angling is best in September. A second boat ramp is located at Hat Rock State Park, where there are also camping facilities. Bank fishing for salmon occurs at the Corps of Engineers park behind the dam as well as at a scattering of points along the shore to Hat Rock.

WENAHA RIVER A beautiful wild trout stream that originates in the Blue Mountains of Wenaha-Tucannon Wilderness in Oregon's extreme northeast corner. The river flows east about 35 miles and enters the Grande Ronde River at the community of Troy, about 30 miles north of Wallowa. There are no roads near the stream, except for the lower few miles above Troy. Trail 3106, which heads right behind the Shilo Inn at Troy, follows the river for more than 30 miles through the wilderness. See the US Forest Service's Wenaha-Tucannon Wilderness map for best trail information, supplemented by the Umatilla National Forest map.

The Wenaha-Tucannon Wilderness is a huge canyonland, especially popular with horse packers and hunters. It has the nation's highest population density of elk. The Wenaha River valley is lined with old growth cottonwoods, fir, and ponderosa pine. The south facing canyons are covered in the bunchgrass and sage typical of eastern Oregon, while the north slopes are thick with conifers and sumac that burns a brilliant red in autumn. The name Wenaha is Nez Perce for ha (domain) of Wenak, a Nez Perce chief (as Imnaha was ha of Chief Imna).

Trout angling is excellent from midsummer through fall. Wild rainbow run to 15 inches, with the average 10 inches. Bull trout are also present but must be released unharmed.

The Wenaha is open for catch and release steelheading from the mouth of Crooked Creek to the Grand Ronde confluence. Crooked Creek is about 6 miles upstream from Troy. Barbless hooks are required, and fly-fishing is popular. Favorite steelhead patterns including the Skunk, Macks Canyon, and Silver Hilton.

There are no developed campgrounds along the stream. Camp well back from fragile streamside vegetation, and use no-trace methods. Check with Forest Service guard stations for a camping permit during fire season.

WILD SHEEP LAKE A small lake at the head of Wild Sheep Creek about 3/4 mile west of Blue Lake. No trails lead to the lake, which supports a naturally reproducing population of brook trout.

WILLOW CREEK (Morrow Co.) An 80-mile stream that flows NW from the area around Arbuckle Mt. Ski Area, Umatilla National Forest, SE of Heppner. There is a reservoir on the creek just above Heppner.

The creek flows through Heppner on its way across the wheat fields to the Columbia, which it joins about 11 miles east of Arlington. Within Heppner, it is heavily stocked with legal trout. There's good access at the park in town. The creek is followed from its mouth to Heppner by Hwy. 74, and SE from Heppner by county road. There is no stocking above the reservoir.

There's no camping in the area and quite a bit of private property. Ask permission to cross private land. Recommended for small fry.

WILLOW CREEK RESERVOIR (Morrow Co.) An impoundment on Willow Creek, just south of Heppner in Morrow County, which grows big trout. It has a maximum pool of 110 acres. A gravel road leads SE from Heppner along the creek to the reservoir.

The reservoir is stocked with legal rainbow trout, since anything smaller is quickly devoured by the lake's illegally planted and flourishing warmwater residents. Smallmouth bass, largemouth bass, crappie, and pumpkinseed sunfish are all available.

This is a big deep reservoir with good bank access and an angling area where water-skiing is prohibited. The Army Corps of Engineers has provided excellent boat ramps, docks, and campground facilities.

WOLF CREEK RESERVOIR A 230-acre irrigation reservoir south of North Powder, with angling for rainbow trout. From North Powder, follow Wolf Creek Rd. about 4 1/2 miles west to the reservoir. The reservoir went dry during the drought, but is stocked annually with rainbow, which grow to 12 inches. There is a county picnic area and boat ramp. The reservoir is drawn down considerably in fall.

WOOD LAKE (Wallowa Co.) A very good lake in the northern Eagle Cap Wilderness, happily not on the way to anything. The trail isn't suitable for horses, either, which means it's a good hike-in lake. It is west of the Lostine River and doesn't see much traffic.

Wood sits in a real nice meadow about one mile north of Hobo Lake. From Lostine on Hwy. 82, head south to the Bowman Creek Trail 1651, about 2.5 miles south of Lostine Guard Station. Climb east on this trail for 3.6 miles to the junction of Trail 1659, which leads north past Chimney Lake and Hobo Lake, reaching Wood Lake 1 1/2 miles beyond Hobo. The total hike is just over 6 miles, with elevation gain over 3,000 ft.

Wood Lake contains brook trout and was once stocked with golden trout, though none have been caught in recent years. The brook trout run 6-10 inches. Lures are best early in the season. Fly-fishing is good in late summer and fall.

APPENDIX

FOR FURTHER INFORMATION

Bureau of Land Management (BLM)
Oregon State Office
1515 SW Fifth Ave.
Portland, OR 97201
(503) 280-7001

Eugene	(503) 683-6600
Hines	(503) 573-5241
Klamath Falls	(503) 883-6916
Lakeview	(503) 947-2177
Medford	(503) 770-2200
North Bend	(503) 756-0100
Prineville	(503) 447-4115
Roseburg	(503) 440-4930
Salem	(503) 375-5646
Tillamook	(503) 842-7546
Vale	(503) 473-3144

Oregon Department of Fish and Wildlife (ODF&W)
State Headquarters
2501 SW First St.
Portland, OR 97207

Information Desk	(503) 229-5403
Recorded Information (24-hr.)	(503) 229-5222
NW Region	
Corvallis	(503) 757-4186
Newport	(503) 867-4741
Salem	(503) 378-6925
Florence	(503) 997-7366
Springfield	(503) 726-3515
SW Region	
Roseburg	(503) 440-3353
Charleston	(503) 888-5515
Gold Beach	(503) 247-7605
Central Point	(503) 826-8774
Central Region	
Bend	(503) 388-6363
The Dalles	(503) 296-4628
Klamath Falls	(503) 883-5732
Prineville	(503) 447-5111
NE Region	
La Grande	(503) 963-2138
John Day	(503) 575-1167
Pendleton	(503) 276-2344
Enterprise	(503) 426-3279
Columbia Region	
Clackamas	(503) 657-2000
Seaside	(503) 738-7066
Tillamook	(503) 842-2741
Marine Region	
Newport	(503) 867-4741
Astoria	(503) 325-2462

US Forest Service
333 SW First St.
Portland, OR 97208
(503) 326-3644

Deschutes Nat'l Forest	(503) 388-2715
Bend RD	(503) 388-5664
Crescent RD	(503) 433-2234
Fort Rock RD	(503) 388-5674
Sisters RD	(503) 549-2111
Fremont National Forest	(503) 947-2151
Bly	(503) 353-2427
Lakeview	(503) 947-3334
Paisley	(503) 943-3114
Silver Lake	(503) 576-2107
Malheur National Forest	(503) 575-1731
Bear Valley	(503) 575-2110
Burns	(503) 573-7292
Long Creek	(503) 575-2110
Prairie City	(503) 820-3311
Mt. Hood Nat'l Forest	(503) 666-0771
Barlow	(503) 467-2291
Bear Springs	(503) 328-6211
Clackamas	(503) 834-2275
Columbia Gorge	(503) 695-2276
Estacada	(503) 630-6861
Hood River	(503) 352-6002
ZigZag	(503) 666-0704
Ochoco National Forest	(503) 447-6247
Big Summit	(503) 447-9645
Paulina	(503) 477-3713
Prineville	(503) 447-6247
Snow Mountain	(503) 573-7292
Rogue River Nat'l Forest	(503) 776-3600
Applegate	(503) 899-1812
Ashland	(503) 482-3333
Butte Falls	(503) 865-3581
Prospect	(503) 560-3623
Siskiyou National Forest	(503) 471-6516
Chetco	(503) 469-2196
Galice	(503) 476-3830
Gold Beach	(503) 247-6651
Illinois Valley	(503) 592-2166
Powers	(503) 439-3011
Siuslaw National Forest	(503) 750-7000
Alsea	(503) 487-5811
Hebo	(503) 392-3161
Mapleton	(503) 268-4473
Waldport	(503) 563-3211
Umatilla National Forest	(503) 276-3716
Heppner	(503) 676-9187
N. Fk. John Day	(503) 427-3231
Pomeroy	(509) 843-1891
Walla Walla	(509) 522-6290
Umpqua National Forest	(503) 672-6601
Cottage Grove	(503) 942-5591
Diamond Lake	(503)498-2531
N. Umpqua	(503) 496-3532
Tiller	(503) 825-3201
Wallowa-Whitman National Forest	(503) 523-6391
Baker	(503) 523-4476
Eagle Cap	(503) 426-4978
LaGrande	(503) 963-7186
Pine	(503) 742-7511
Unity	(503) 446-3351
Wallowa Valley	(503) 426-4978
Willamette Nat'l Forest	(503) 465-6521
Blue River	(503) 822-3317
Detroit	(503) 854-3366
Lowell	(503) 937-2129
McKenzie	(503) 822-3381
Oakridge	(503) 782-2291
Rigdon	(503) 782-2283
Sweet Home	(503) 367-5168
Winema National Forest	(503) 883-6714
Chemult	(503) 365-2229
Chiloquin	(503) 783-4001
Klamath	(503) 883-6824
Crater Lake Nat'l Park	(503) 594-2211

Other Useful Telephone Numbers

National Weather Service
(503) 261-9246
Oregon Guides & Packers
(503) 683-9552
Oregon State Parks and Recreation Dept.
(503) 378-6305
Campground Information
(503) 238-7488
Oregon State Marine Board
(503) 3788-8587
PGE Fish Line
(503) 464-7474
Snake River Information
(509) 758-0616
Willamette Falls Fish Report
(503) 657-2059

UNOFFICIAL OREGON GAMEFISH RECORDS

September, 1994

Species	Weight	Location	Date	Angler
Bass				
Largemouth	11 lb. 9.6 oz.	Butte Falls farm pond	4/15/94	Randy Spaur
Smallmouth	7 lb. 4.5 oz.	Hagg Lake	9/2/94	Raymond Currie
Hybrid Striped	15 lb. 4 oz.	Ana Reservoir	1/26/94	Mike Sabin
Bullhead				
Yellow	3 lb. 6 oz.	Brownlee Reservoir	6/10/86	Loretta Fitzgerald
Brown	2 lb. 4 oz.	Eckman Lake	6/10/82	Joshua Spulnik
Catfish				
Channel	36 lb. 8 oz.	McKay Reservoir	9/17/80	Boone Haddock
Flathead	42 lb.	Snake R.	6/27/94	Joshua Kralicek
White	15lb.	Tualatin R.	4/22/89	Wayne Welch
Crappie				
Black	4 lb.	Lost R.	5/01/78	Billy R. Biggs
White	4 lb, 12 oz.	Gerber Reservoir.	5/22/67	John Duckett
Salmon				
Chinook	83 lb.	Umpqua R.	1910	Ernie St. Claire
(dressed)	62 lb.	Nestucca R.	10/70	Craig Hansen
Chum	19 lb.	Kilchis R.	11/11/83	Richard Weber
Coho	25 lb. 5 oz.	Siltcoos Lake	11/05/66	Ed Marti
Kokanee	4 lb. 2 oz.	Paulina Lake	6/17/90	Howard Morgan
Shad	5 lb. 13 oz.	Columbia R.	5/31/94	Patricia Young
Striped Bass	64 lb. 8 oz.	Umpqua R.	7/13/73	Beryl Bliss
Sturgeon	(none - regulations limit catch size)			
Sunfish				
Bluegill	2 lb. 5.5 oz.	Farm Pond, Prineville	5/12/81	Wayne Elmore
Green	11 oz.	Umpqua	4/25/91	John L. Baker
Red-ear	1 lb. 15.5 oz.	Reynolds Pond	8/1/92	Terence Bice
Warmouth	1 lb 14.5 oz.	Columbia R.	12/27/75	Jess Nowell
Pumpkin seed	5.1 oz.	Lake Oswego	6/12/88	Jeffrey Crump
Trout				
Brook	9 lb. 6 oz.	Deschutes R. (below Little Lava Lake)	6/21/80	Burt Westbrook
Brown	27 lb. 12 oz.	Paulina Lake	5/21/93	Guy Carl
Bull	23 lb. 2 oz.	Lake Billy Chinook	3/25/89	Don Yow
Searun cutthroat	6 lb. 4 oz.	Siltcoos Lake	8/20/84	Kay Schmidt
Inland (introduced)	9 lb. 8 oz.	N. Fork Malheur R.	4/09/86	Phillip Grove
Golden	7 lb. 10 oz.	Eagle Cap Wilderness	7/16/87	Douglas White
Mackinaw	40 lb. 8 oz.	Odell Lake	9/84	Ken Erickson
Rainbow	28 lb.	Rogue R.	5/19/82	Mike McGonagle
Steelhead	35 lb. 8 oz.	Columbia R.	9/19/70	Berdell Todd
Walleye	19 lb. 15.3 oz.	John Day Pool	2/20/90	Arnold R. Berg
Whitefish	4 lb. 14 oz.	Crane Prairie Reservoir	7/21/94	Roger A. Massey
Yellow Perch	2 lb. 2 oz.	Brownsmead Slough	6/05/71	Ernie Affolter III

If you think you have caught a record-breaking fish:

- Photograph a side view of the fish to accompany your record catch application.
- Weigh your catch as quickly as possible on a state certified scale (e.g. supermarket meat dept.).
- Identify two witnesses you can later ask to sign your application; one of them must be the person weighing the fish.
- Obtain and complete an application, including signatures of witnesses. Coldwater record applications are available at each district ODF&W office, or from ODF&W, Information and Education Dept., P.O. Box 59, Portland, OR 97207. Warmwater record applications are available from The Oregon Bass and Panfish Club, Contest Manager, P.O. Box 1021, Portland, OR 97207.

To be eligible, a fish must have been caught legally, in Oregon, by hook and line.

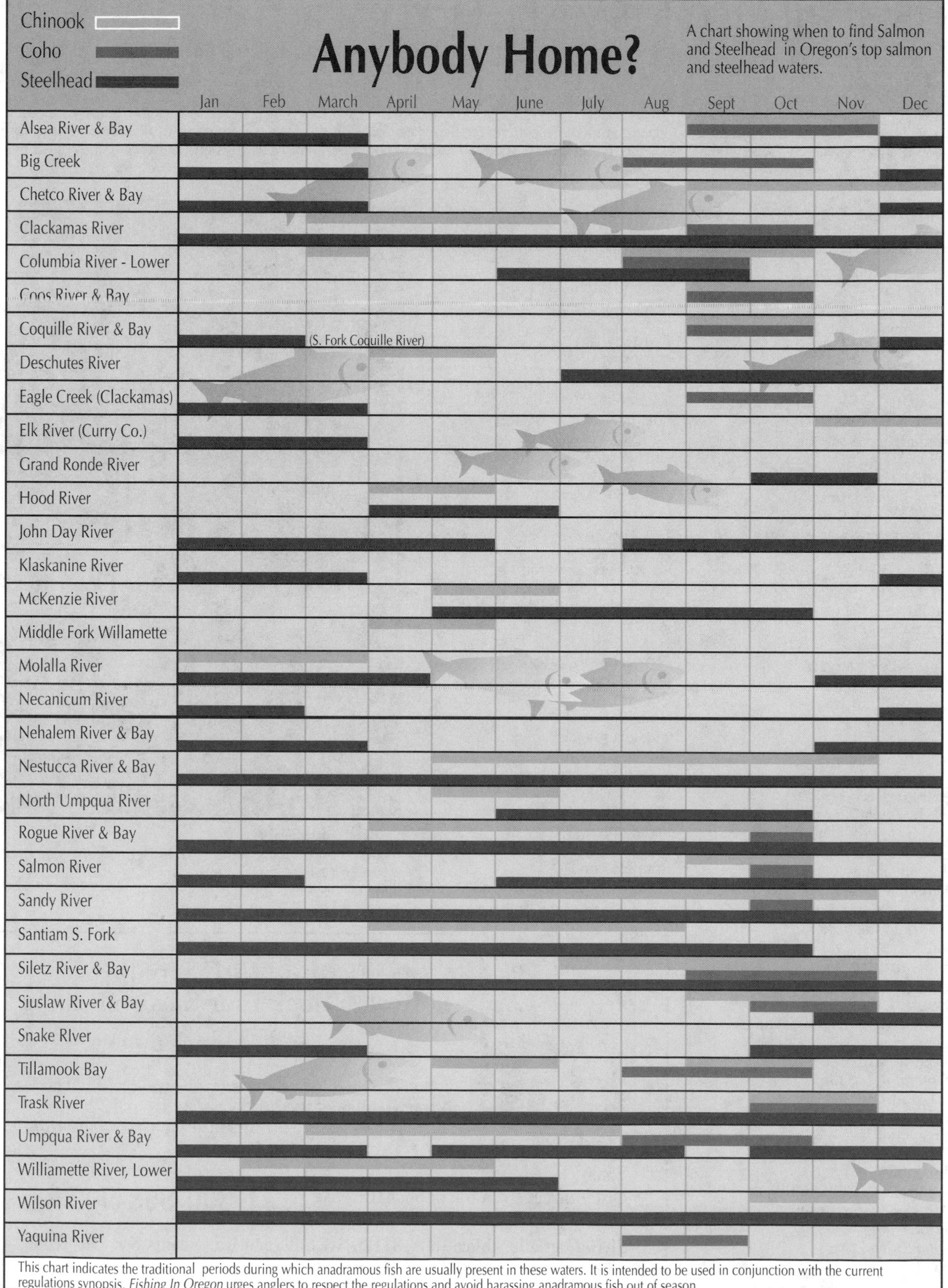

This chart indicates the traditional periods during which anadramous fish are usually present in these waters. It is intended to be used in conjunction with the current regulations synopsis. *Fishing In Oregon* urges anglers to respect the regulations and avoid harassing anadramous fish out of season.

FISHERIES FOR SMALL FRY

These waters are especially suitable for young anglers. Selection was based on some or all of the following criteria: ease of access, liklihood of angler succcess, safety (shallow depth, gentle gradient), availability of complementary facilities and features (camping, comfort, alternative activities).

Northwest Zone
Alder Lake
Alsea Bay
Big Creek Reservoir
Carter Lake
Clatskanie Slough
Coffenbury Lake
Crescent Lake (Tillamook Co.)
Cullaby Lake
Dune Lake
Elbow Lake
Siltcoos Lake
Triangle Lake

Southwest Zone
Canyonville Pond
Cooper Creek Reservoir
Denman Management Area Ponds
Dutch Herman
Eel Lake
Emigrant Lake
Empire Lakes
Expo Ponds
Galesville Reservoir
Herbert Log Pond
Howard Prairie Lake
Libby Pond
Loon Lake
Millicoma River, West Fork - interpretive center
Plat I Reservoir
Powers Pond
Selmac Lake
Squaw Lakes
Tenmile Lakes
Umpqua River (shad fishery, Scottsburg Park to the forks)

Willamette
Adair Pond
Benson Lake (Lane Co.)
Brown-Minto Island Complex
Delta Ponds
Detroit Lake
Dorena Reservoir
E.E. Wilson Pond
Foster Reservoir
Freeway Ponds
Johnson Creek
Junction City Pond
Little North Santiam River
Mt. Hood Community College Ponds
Pine Ridge Lake
Roslyn Lake
Spirit Lake
St. Louis Ponds
Tenas Lakes
Trillium Lake
Walter Wirth Lake
Willamina Pond

Central
Cody Ponds
Devils Lake (Deschutes Co.)
Frog Lake
Kingsley Reservoir (a.k.a. Green Point Reservoir)
Lions Pond
Lost Lake (Mt. Hood)
Ochoco Creek
Pine Hollow Reservoir
Reynolds Pond
Rock Creek Reservoir
Taylor Lake (Wasco Co.)
Twin Lake, South (Deschutes Co.)
Walton Lake

Northeast Zone
Bull Prairie Reservoir
Conforth Ponds
Umatilla)
Cutsforth Ponds
Hat Rock Pond
McNary Channel Ponds
Morgan Lake
Pilcher Creek Reservoir
Penland Lake
R.D. Mack Pond
Roulette Pond
Willow Creek (Morrow Co.)

Southeast Zone
Becker Pond
Murray Reservoir
Obenchain Reservoir

WHEELCHAIR ACCESSIBLE FISHERIES

Northwest
Big Creek Reservoirs
Coffenbury Lake
Hebo Lake
Nehalem River, North Fork- at hatchery
Siltcoos Lake - Westlake fishing pier
Siuslaw Bay -Rock Dock
Siuslaw River - at Lake Creek confluence
Tillamook Bay - Garibaldi Coast Guard Pier
Vernonia Lake

Southwest Zone
Chetco Bay - jetty
Cooper Creek Reservoir
Eel Lake
Empire Lakes
Loon Lake
Rogue River - Dodge Bridge
Tenmile Lakes
Applegate Reservoir
Chetco River

Willamette
Benson Lake (Multnomah Co.)
Blue Lake (Multnomah Co.)
Clackamas River - Fish Creek, Indian Henry, Two Rivers
Detroit Lake
Dexter Reservoir - south bank below dam
E.E. Wilson Pond
Hagg Lake - near Elk Point Picnic Area
Junction City Pond
Leaburg Lake
Lost Creek - Lost Cr. Campground (Clackamas Co.)
Lost Lake
McKenzie River - Hendrick's Bridge Wayside
Mill Creek - Stewart Grenfell Park
Olallie Lake - Peninsula CG
Roaring River (Linn Co.) - pier near hatchery
Rock Creek
Roslyn Lake
Sandy River - Dabney State Park, Oxbow State Park Santiam River, South Fork - Yukwah and Fern View campgrounds
St. Louis Pond No. 3
Timothy Lake
Trail Bridge Reservoir
Trillium Lake
Vernonia Lake
Walter Wirth Lake
Willamette River - Meldrum Bar, Alton Baker Park, Armitage State Park
Willamina Creek - Blackwell Park
Willamina Pond
Wilsonville Pond
Woodburn Pond

Central Zone
Antelope Flat Reservoir
Deschutes River (Crane Prairie Reservoir To Wickiup Reservoir) at Forest Rd. 42 Bridge
Deschutes River (Pelton Dam To The Mouth) - Blue Hole Campgound
Lions Pond
Walton Lake

Northeast Zone
Brownlee Reservoir - Hewitt Park
Bull Prairie Reservoir
Camas Creek - Camas Creek State Park
Cold Springs Reservoir
Cutsforth Ponds
Hat Rock Pond
John Day Arm of Lake Umatilla
McCormach Slough
McNary Channel Ponds
Morgan Lake
Penland Lake
Phillips Reservoir
Pilcher Creek
Thief Valley Reservoir
Umatilla River - at the forks on the east bank, just south of Hwy. 730
Unity Reservoir
Lake Wallula - docks behind McNary Dam

Southeast Zone
Alkali Lake Reservoir
Becker's Pond
Boyle Reservoir- Topsy Campground
Campbell Reservoir
Dead Horse Lake
Klamath Lake - Moore park, just above the dam
Loften Reservoir
Malheur Reservoir
Wood River - Fort Klamath Picnic Area

OREGON WATERS RESTRICTED TO ARTIFICIAL FLIES AND LURES

Waters with asterisk (*) are fly-fishing only

Northwest Zone

Lily Lake	
Salmonberry River	Mainstem and tributaries
Siletz River *	North Fork (during trout season)
Youngs River	Above Youngs River Falls

Southwest Zone

Illinois River	Mainstem up to Pomeroy Dam
North Umpqua*	Rock Creek to Soda Springs Dam
North Umpqua*	Tributaries from Rock Creek to Soda Springs Dam (except Steamboat Creek)
Rogue River*	Gold Ray impoundment upstream to ODF&W markers below Cole Rivers Hatchery, Sept. 1-October 31
Rogue River*	Between Cole Rivers Hatchery diversion dam and Lost Creek Dam
Shuttpelz Lake	

Willamette Zone

Clackamas River	Mainstem and tributaries above North Fork Dam not listed in regulation synopsis
Clackamas River	Oak Grove Fork and tributaries from USFS Bridge on Hwy. 57 to Timothy Lake Dam
Gold Lake*	
Lost Lake *	Santiam Pass
McKenzie River	River mouth to Hayden Bridge
McKenzie River	Paradise Campground to Trail Bridge Dam
Round Lake	Marion County
Salmon River*	(Sandy System) Forest Bridge 2618 up to Final Falls
Willamette River	Hwy. 99 Bridge (Harrisburg) to McKenzie River
Willamette River	Middle Fork: Lookout Point Reservoir to Hills Creek Dam
Willamette River	North Fork: mouth to railroad bridge at Westfir
Willamette River*	North Fork: above railroad bridge at Westfir

Central Zone

Crooked River	Bowman Dam down to Lake Billy Chinook, except during trout season.
Crooked River	South Fork
Davis Lake*	Entire lake plus Odell Creek Channel to ODFW markers at Davis Lake Campgrounds
Deschutes River	Mouth (I-84 Bridge) up to Pelton Regulating Dam, except for bait area associated with Sherars Falls
Deschutes River	Lake Billy Chinook to North Canal Dam in Bend
Fall River*	
Hood River*	West Fork: above Dry Run Bridge
Hosmer Lake*	
Laurence Lake	
Metolius River*	Mainstem above Hwy. 99 Bridge
Metolius River	Mainstem from Hwy. 99 Bridge to Lake Billy Chinook
Sparks Lake*	Lake and tributaries up to Cascade Lakes Hwy.
White River	Up to first falls
Willow Creek	Within National Grasslands

Southeast Zone

Blitzen River	Mainstem, canals and tributaries above and south of Steens Mt. North Loop Road
Guano Creek	
Klamath River	Keno Dam to JC Boyle Reservoir
Klamath River	Boyle Dam to Oregon/California border
Mann Lake	
Rock Creek	Lake Co.
Sprague River	Below Chiloquin Dam
Williamson River	Modoc Point Road up to Kirk Bridge and Silver Lake Road to headwaters
Wood River	

The above listing is current as of 1994. Check the regulations synopsis for additions or amendments in subsequent years.

DIRECTORY OF OREGON FLY SHOPS

Call or visit the following fly shops for information about the waters listed in italics

Blue Heron Fly
109 Hargis Lane, Idleyld, OR 97447
(503)496-0448
North Umpqua

Caddis Fly
168 W. 6th Ave., Eugene, OR 97401
(503) 342-7005
McKenzie, Willamette, Middle Fork Willamette, North Fork Willamette, So. Santiam

Countrysport
1201 SW Morrison Ave., Portland, OR 97205 (503) 221-4545
Clackamas, Deschutes, John Day, McKenzie, Nehalem, Sandy

Creekside Fly
345 High St. SE, Salem, OR 97301
(503) 395-2565
North Santiam, South Santiam

Deschutes Canyon Fly
PO Box 334, Hwy. 197, Maupin, OR 97037
(503) 395-2565
Deschutes

Dexter's Fly
52582 Hwy. 97, LaPine, OR 97739
(503) 536-9038
Crane Prairie, Davis, East, Fall, Hosmer, Paulina, Upper Deschutes, high Cascdes hike-in lakes

Dublin House
251 West 7th Ave., Yachats, OR 97498
(503) 547-3200
Yachats, Alsea, Beaver Cr., mid-coast surf

The Fly Box
1293 SE Third St., Bend, OR 97702
(503) 388-3330
Deschutes, Crooked, private lakes

The Fly Fishing Shop
PO Box 368, Hwy. 26, Welches, OR 97067
(503) 622 4607
Sandy, Salmon, lower Deschutes

Flyfisher's Place
PO Box 1179, Main St., Sisters, OR 97759
(503) 549-3474
Crooked, Deschutes, Fall, Metolius

Gorge Fly Shop
416 Oak St.
Hood River, OR 97031
(503) 386-6977
Deschutes, Hood River, Mt. Hood high lakes

Grand Ronde Angler
103 First St., LaGrande, OR 97850
(503) 9633-7878
Powder, Wallowa R., Imnaha, John Day, Catherine Cr.

Homewaters Fly
444 W. Third Ave., Eugene, OR 97401
(503) 342-6691
McKenzie, North Fork.Willamette, Gold Lake

Kaufmann's Streamborn
8861 SW Commercial, Tigard, OR 97223
(503) 639-6400
Deschutes, Sandy, Clackamas, Lewis, NW coastal streams, private lakes

NW Flyfishing Outfitters
17302 NE Halsey,St., Gresham, OR 97230
(503) 252-1529
Deschutes, Clackamas, Sandy, Salmon

The Patient Angler
55 NW Wall, Bldg. B, Bend, OR 97701
(503) 389-6208
Crane Prairie, Deschutes, Hosmer

The Scarlet Ibis
905 NW Kings Blvd., Corvallis, OR 97330
(503) 754-1544
McKenzie, North and South Santiam, Willamette

Wallowa Outdoors
110 South River Rd., Enterprise, OR 97828 (503) 426-3493
Wallowa R., Grand Ronde, Imnaha, Snake

Valley Fly Fishers
153 Alice Ave. So.
Salem, OR 97302
(503) 375-3721
Willamette, No. Santiam

DIRECTORY OF ADVERTISERS

WARMWATER FISHERIES

Northwest Zone

Beaver Creek
(Columbia Co.)
Beaver Slough Complex
Big Creek Reservoirs
Blind Slough
Bradbury Slough
Brownsmead Slough
Buck Lake
Burkes Lake
Cape Meares Lake
Cemetery Lake
Clatskanie Slough
Clear Lake (Clatsop Co.)
Clear Lake (Lane Co.)
Cleawox Lake
Collard Lake
Crabapple Lake
Crescent Lake
(Tillamook Co.)
Cullaby Lake
Deer Island Slough
Devils Lake (Lincoln Co.)
Eckman Lake
Goat Island Slough
Hult Reservoir
Lost Lake
Lytle Lake
Magruder Slough
Maple Creek
Marie Lake
Mayger Slough
Mercer Lake
Munsel Lake
Neacoxie Lake
Ocean Lake
Olalla Reservoir
Prescott Slough
Rilea Slough
Rinearson Slough
Sandy Island Slough
Santosh Slough
Shag Lake
Siltcoos Lake
Siuslaw Bay
Slusher Lake
Smith Lake (Clatsop Co.)
Spring Lake
Sunset Lake
Sutton Lake
Tahkenitch Lake
Tillamook Bay
Triangle Lake
Vernonia Lake
West Lake
Westport Slough
Wilson River

Southwest Zone

Agate Reservoir
Applegate Reservoir
Babyfoot Lake
Beale Lake
Ben Irving Reservoir
Bradley Lake
Burma Pond
Butterfield Lake
Cooper Creek Reservoir
Coos Bay
Coos River
Coos River, South Fork
Coquille River
Cow Creek
Davidson Lake
Denman Management
Area Ponds
Dutch Herman
Eel Lake
Emigrant Lake
Empire Lakes
Expo Ponds
Floras Lake
Fords Mill Pond
Garrison Lake
Galesville Reservoir
Gold Ray Forebay
Hall Lake
Hoover Ponds
Horsfall Lake
Howard Prairie Lake
Hyatt Reservoir
Jordan Lake
Lake Marie
Little Hyatt Lake
Loon Lake
Lost Creek Reservoir
Medco Pond
Plat I Reservoir
Powers Pond
Saunders Lake
Selmac Lake
Skookum Pond
Smith River, Mainstem
Snag Lake
Squaw Lakes
Tenmile Lakes
Triangle Lake
Trumis & Bybee Ponds
Umpqua River Estuary
Winchester Bay
Umpqua River
Umpqua River, South
Willow Creek Reservoir

Willamette Zone

Adair Pond
Benson Lake
(Multnomah Co.)
Beth Lake
Bethany Lake
Blue Lake (Multnomah Co.
Near Troutdale)
Bluegill Lake
Bond Butte Pond
Brown-Minto Island
Complex
Bybee Lake
Canby Pond
Cleary Pond
Colorado Lake
Columbia Slough
Cottage Grove Ponds
Cottage Grove Reservoir
Creswell Ponds
Cunningham Lake
Cunningham Slough
Delta Park Ponds
Delta Ponds
Dorena Reservoir
Dorman Pond
Fairview Lake
Fern Ridge Reservoir
Foster Reservoir
Freeway Ponds
Gilbert River
Goose Lake
Government Island Lake
Green Peter Reservoir
Grossman Pond
Hagg Lake
Haldeman Pond
Hills Creek Reservoir
Horseshoe Lake
(St. Paul Area)
Jefferson Junction
Borrow Pit
Johnson Creek
Junction City Pond
Kirk Pond
Lambert Slough
Long Tom River
Lookout Point Reservoir
McKay Creek
McNary Lakes
McNulty Creek
Mercer Reservoir
Mill Creek (Marion Co.)
Milton Creek
Mirror Pond
Mission Creek Reservoir
Mission Lake
Muddy Creek (Benton Co.)
Muddy Creek
(Sandy River)
Multnomah Channel
Oswego Creek
Pete's Slough
Pope Lake
Pudding River
Rooster Rock Slough
Santiam River, South Fork
Santosh Slough
Skookum Lake
(Marion Co.)
Smith Lake
(Multnomah Co.)
St. Louis Ponds
St. Paul Ponds
Sturgeon Lake
Thomas Creek
Tualatin River
Walling Pond
Walter Wirth Lake
Walterville Pond
Waverly Lake
Willamette River
Willamina Pond
Wilsonville Pond
Withee Lake
Woodburn Pond
Yamhill River

Columbia Zone

Bonneville Pool
Columbia sloughs
Lake Celilo
Lake Umatilla
Lake Wallula

Central Zone

Big Houston Lake
Bikini Pond
Billy Chinook Reservoir
Celilo Lake
Cody Ponds
Crane Prairie Reservoir
Davis Lake (Deschutes Co.)
Deschutes Pond East
Deschutes Pond No. 2
Deschutes Pond No.1
Government Cove
Haystack Reservoir
Hood River Pond No. 1
Hood River Pond No. 2
Hood River Pond No. 3
Huston Lakes
Iris Lake
Kolberg Lake
Lions Pond
Lone Pine Pond
Long Pond
McClures Lake
Miller Pond
Mosier Pond East
Mosier Pond West
One-Mile Lake
Pine Hollow Reservoir
Prineville Reservoir
Reynolds Pond
Rock Creek Reservoir
Sand Dune Lake
Sand Lake
Taylor Lake (Wasco Co.)
The Dalles Pool
Tooley Lake
Tunnel Lake
Viento Lake
West Cove

Northeast Zone

Barth Quarry Pond
Bibby Reservoir
Boardman Pond No.2
Carter Slough
Catherine Creek Slough
Cold Springs Reservoir
Conforth Ponds
Grand Ronde River
Hat Rock Pond
John Day River
John Day Pool
Joseph Creek
McKay Creek
McKay Reservoir
McKormach Slough
McNary Channel Ponds
McNary Dam Pool
Messner Pond No. 2
Morgan Lake
Pilcher Creek Reservoir
Power City Ponds
Snake River
Umatilla, Lake
Wallula, Lake
Willow Creek Reservoir

Southeast Zone

Altnow Lake
Ana Reservoir
Arritola Reservoir
Balm Creek Reservoir
Becker's Pond
Boyle (J.C.) Reservoir
Brownlee Reservoir
Bully Creek Reservoir
Bumphead Reservoir
Burnt River
Campbell Reservoir
Cottonwood Creek
Reservoir
Cow Lakes
Crater Lake
Crump Lake
Devil Lake
Dog Lake
Drews Reservoir
Dunaway Pond
Gerber Reservoir
Haines Pond
Hart Lake
Hells Canyon Reservoir
Highway 203 Pond
Krumbo Reservoir
Lake Of The Woods
Lost River
Malheur River
Moon Reservoir
Obenchain Reservoir
Oxbow Reservoir
Phillips Reservoir
Powder River
Reynolds Pond
Round Valley Reservoir
Silvies River
Snake River
Sprague River
Thompson Valley Reservoir
Thief Valley Reservoir
Unity Reservoir
Upper Midway Reservoir
Upper Spring Reservoir
Warm Spring Reservoir
Warner Valley Lakes
Willow Valley Reservoir

INDEX